By Mark Porter and Paul Land

"I have found out there ain't no surer way to find out whether you like people or hate them than to travel with them."
Mark Twain (Tom Sawyer Abroad)

Every effort has been made to ensure that the information in this guide is correct and up to date at time of going to print. Baytree Publishing Ltd, however, accepts no liability for any loss incurred as a result

LAOIS COUNTY LIBRARY
3 0010 00895013 4

Laois County Li...
Leabharlann ... Laoise
Acc. No. 07/14435
Class No. 914.04
Inv. No. 9534

56/6 Timberbush
Edinburgh
EH6 6QH
Tel: 0131 553 6093
Tel: 01835 862 745
info@baytreepress.com
www.baytreepress.com

Print Management by Polska Book.
Printed by Interak Printing House.

Wholesale and distribution: Gardners Books, Eastbourne.
www.gardners.com

ISBN: 0-9544827-6-X

No part of this publication can be reproduced in any form without prior consent of the publisher.

Copyright Baytree Press 2005.

Three cheers for the humble supporter

FOREWORD

by Roy Laidlaw
Ex British & Irish Lions
Scotland and Jed-Forest

It is often forgotten when the rugby circus comes to town that it is the humble supporter who makes the modern, multi-million pound game possible. It is you who pay for the Red Arrows, the fireworks and the razzmatazz, the wage packets and lifestyle of the professional game. Whether you are travelling to the ground or watching it all on television, without your support none of this would be possible. Never forget it.

So I am delighted to see a simple service being offered here by Grand Tour: where the hell to find a good pub and have a good time. At the end of the day, that's what it is really all about. In an era in which the game has become serious business, it is important to get back to grassroots level, where the real future of rugby lies.

Supporters play a huge part in a team's success. I'll never forget the vocal support at Cardiff Arms Park back in 1982, when our fans out-sang the Welsh and we ran in five tries. It was Jim Telfer's 47th cap and he had never won away before. It was the dawn of a new era. And I'll never forget the chants of 'Easy, easy...' as we ploughed England under at Murrayfield in 1986. They lined the streets outside our hotel and we drank with them at the Café Royal. There was never a game in which the fans did not play a big part.

In those days we rubbed shoulders with the supporters and were on first-name terms with many of them. We'd drink with them and see them in the streets. Local sides were exactly that: local sides, and they attracted local supporters in their thousands. Many of us would be back at work on the Monday morning after a big match, working with the very people who cheered us on at the weekend.

Whilst professionalism has undoubtedly worked in many countries, Scotland is being left behind and it saddens me deeply to see this. Really talented players are going to the professional sides while local teams are forced to import players who are passing through and who put little back into our rugby communities. Consequently, the crowds have shrunk and important grass roots ties are in danger of being severed every season. But there is good cheer elsewhere, Ireland and Wales being cases in point.

Whatever can be done to boost the numbers attending games is very important and I like the idea of a guide which points the way to having a good time. You, the supporters, are the torch bearers of the old, amateur game. Social sides may be on the decline and the days when you went out for a friendly match followed by a few pints may be distant memories. But it is vital for the future of rugby that we continue to appeal to you, the supporters.

CONTENTS

CONTENTS

Symbols:
Hotels: s = single room; d = double; t = twin; tpl = triple
Paris Metro: Ⓜ
Triple Restaurants: prices listed are for 3 courses without drinks.

SIX NATIONS NEEDS

THE idea for Grand Tour was inspired by a group of hapless Frenchmen roaming the streets of Edinburgh after their side's massacre of Scotland in 2004. It was a dismal east coast winter's day, a cold wind whipping showers across a darkening sky. Paul Land and I had been having a pint at the Diggers pub, half way between the ground and the Old Town, when one of them came over and asked directions to the nearest Pizza Hut. Why Pizza Hut? I asked. "Apart from breakfast it is the only edible food over here," he replied.

I explained that Edinburgh, in terms of restaurants and bars, was a really happening place. You could eat here better than in most of Paris, I ventured. Eventually I pointed him in the direction of one of the city's many new Scottish restaurants and a great service was duly rendered. I felt like the Good Samaritan.

When we got to the Bow Bar, as much in search of shelter as refreshment, the seed for the book was sown. I had just written a couple of similar guides to cycle routes and walks. Why not rugby?

Supporters are the lifeblood of the game, and always have been. But with the stampede into professionalism and the increasingly odd times and dates for games, life is much easier for the armchair supporter than for those who trail to distant cities for a Sunday kick-off during a February blizzard. Those who make the trip deserve every support they can get and in these increasingly commercialised times, the individual – paying opera prices for tickets – often seem forgotten in the hurly-burly of corporate packaging.

This information has been compiled over the past 18 months by a food writer, a rugby fanatic and a travel writer, taking in recommendations from top rugby journalists, whose other mission is to find the best places to disburse their expenses. The team trawled the length and breadth of Paris, Rome, London, Cardiff, Dublin and Edinburgh to collate the evidence. And the end result? Simple, we hope (but that is for you to judge): to help guide you round six of Europe's finest cities whilst following the world's greatest rugby tournament.

If you required the quality of up-to-date information gathered between these two covers you would have to buy at least half a dozen books: for the UK alone, you would need a Michelin Red Guide; a Good Food Guide; a Good Pub Guide; Time Out, the List; Blue Guides, and various other essential pathfinders. Whilst they are all excellent in their different ways, and well worth collecting, that's an awful lot to stuff in the pocket of your Barbour.

Grand Tour, therefore, is not just

Feel-good role of a

By Feidlim MacLoughlin

"As someone who has travelled extensively as a businessman and as a supporter I am delighted to pen a few words for Grand Tour. Detailed research into pubs (and hotels and everything tucked between these two covers) is just what the faithful follower needs. The supporter is the kernel of all sport – not just rugby. The older eminences (not quite the silly old farts as Will Carling once described them) who ran the world of rugby for a century were absolutely necessary in their time and, to them, it was like the crack of doom when professionalism arrived. For these were the very men who had staked the clubs and made it possible for the game to develop into what it is now, ironic though some may find this.

"When TV and mass media demanded that match times be changed and games be played (harrumph!) on a Sunday, the alickadoos chuntered into their ale. But gradually things are coming round to the 21st century. The fact that 15,000 fans – young and old alike – went to New Zealand for the

. JUST ONE GUIDE

a rugby book. It is meant to straddle travel as well as sport. As an all-purpose guide to the six cities, Grand Tour should be just as useful outside match weekends for the business community or the weekend traveller.

It has also been designed with partners in mind. There are shopping sections, plus general and cultural information designed to appeal to those with little or no interest in watching 30 blokes hurtling around a mud patch to the deafening applause/approbation of 80,000 fans.

All six cities are exciting and changing places so it is our intention to update regularly. Of the capitals, Cardiff has undoubtedly changed the most in recent years. Gone is the grime of coal and shipping days. Old Tiger Bay has been transformed as much as the City of London was after the Great Fire in 1666. Edinburgh, meanwhile, has moved away from its narrow, inward looking and nepotic past into a truly cosmopolitan 21st century city. London never sits still and Dublin is positively jumping. Only Rome and Paris stand like still points in a turning world – their architecture and heritage marking many of the milestones of western civilisation. But the scene in the clubs and bars, restaurants and swish hotels certainly keeps pace with these changing times.

Mark Porter

- *The author was once an underpowered hooker operating in the lower circles of junior rugby in England and France. He is now a travel writer and contributing editor to Waitrose Food Illustrated and has written about rugby for Scotland on Sunday and the Sunday Times for the past five seasons. His 15 years as a roving hack in 'Fleet St' helped give him a sound working knowledge of many of Europe's top restaurants at the expense of various proprietors and shareholders.*
- *Co-author Paul Land was, in his day, a fine full-back. His energetic odyssey around far-flung restaurants and bars, plus an encyclopaedic knowledge of the game, proved invaluable in putting this together. Paul lives in Paris, is a self-confessed rugby anorak and has played for a number of French clubs.*
- *Special thanks to Dave Coyle, whose general technical expertise, organisational skills and patience made this whole thing happen.*
- *And last, but definitely not least, Lewis Stuart, once on the production desk at the Scotsman, ex-prop forward and renowned rugby writer, who was our chief sub-editor. He has possibly forgotten more about rugby than most experts will ever know. And he understands computers.*

about the true fan

Lions tour proves that there is some forgiveness in the camp. And that new ways are, at last, triumphing over the old.

"As someone who was involved as a player and administrator in the Jurassic era and who is now involved on the professional side of the IRFU, I can predict that there are further changes coming. The professional game has forced issues and put many more demands on the game, as witnessed in Scotland, where there is cureently a big shake-up in progress. In short, it is getting more and more like football. Though the game has yet to fully acclimatise to the rigours of professionalism, I have every confidence it will make this transition – just so long as the fans stick with it and keep the turnstiles clicking and the tellies tuned in."

- ***Feidlim MacLoughlin played for the Barbarians, was capped for Ireland, captained Northern FC 74-76. President of Northern 90-91. He was also President of the Irish Exiles 95-02 and is on the IRFU committee. His brother Ray also played a bit.***

England rugby

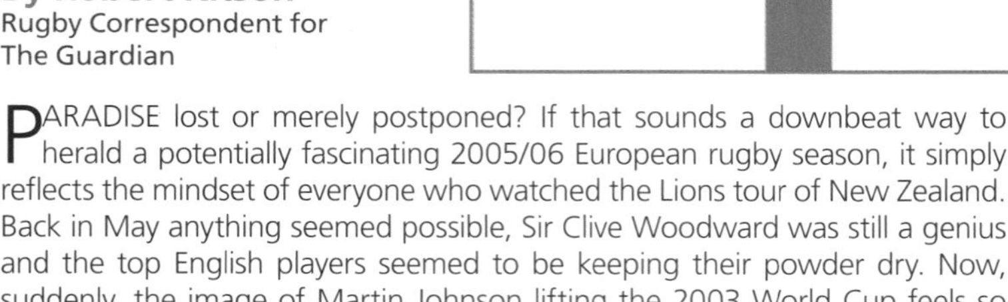

Rose ready to rise again

By Robert Kitson
Rugby Correspondent for The Guardian

PARADISE lost or merely postponed? If that sounds a downbeat way to herald a potentially fascinating 2005/06 European rugby season, it simply reflects the mindset of everyone who watched the Lions tour of New Zealand. Back in May anything seemed possible, Sir Clive Woodward was still a genius and the top English players seemed to be keeping their powder dry. Now, suddenly, the image of Martin Johnson lifting the 2003 World Cup feels so long ago it should be dipped in sepia.

This is not to say that English clubs or the national side should abandon all hope as they embark on a season of urgent self-discovery. On the other hand, it is seven years since pre-campaign expectations have had to be dampened down to such an extent. If an English club wins the Heineken Cup this season, for example, it will be against all the odds. If England finish higher than third in the Six Nations championship, behind France and Wales, they will not have done badly. Anyone wanting to put money on England to retain the World Cup in 2007 at this precise moment is placing patriotic optimism before financial prudence.

The revised challenge, therefore, is for players, coaches, administrators and spin doctors to absorb the lessons of the Lions and move on as swiftly as possible. In no particular order, the England coach Andy Robinson must kick-start the stalled Twickenham chariot, Jonny Wilkinson must put his fitness problems behind him, Premiership players must narrow the gap in basic skill levels which became so glaringly apparent in New Zealand and something tangible should be done to reduce the schedule demands on leading players. Sweep any of the above under the carpet and the Webb Ellis trophy will be heading elsewhere in 2007.

So, let's start with Robinson's options. Succeeding Woodward was always going to be a thankless task but not even Robinson guessed quite how tough it would be. From the moment he appointed Wilkinson as captain - the Newcastle fly-half never pulled on the white jersey, let alone the armband - it was as if someone, somewhere was sticking pins in a voodoo doll. Either he was too loyal to off-form World Cup stalwarts or promoted youth too soon, leading to criticism from Newcastle over the handling of their precocious centre Mathew Tait.

To avoid a deeply uncomfortable autumn – England face Australia, New Zealand and Samoa at Twickenham – Robinson has to be surer-footed this time. If the management team wish to set the tone, the first priority should be to advise Wilkinson he is not required at Test level until the New Year. By then the fly-half should have worked his way back to full match fitness at Newcastle and will not be plunged cold into the maelstrom of international rugby as he was on the Lions tour. Charlie Hodgson, who ironically launched the domestic season by sprinting clear of Wilkinson to score a decisive try for Sale against the Falcons at Edgeley Park, would equally have three matches to demonstrate once again that he is a maturing force.

There is also the question, or conundrum, of Andy Farrell. Signed from Wigan by Saracens in a joint deal with the Rugby Football Union, it will inevitably take time for Farrell to bed down in an unfamiliar sport. If he is winning matches for Saracens by Christmas it will, frankly, not reflect too highly on the opposition; from Robinson's perspective, nevertheless, Farrell is already 30 and does not have time on his side. He is strong enough and mentally tough enough to be a valuable squad member at Saracens but the million-dollar question is whether he will ever be the stand-out union Test back-rower England crave.

Better, while Farrell learns his trade, to discover how many of the younger brigade possess what it takes. The 2003 World Cup campaign effectively began at least two years out from the actual event; there is no time to waste, therefore, to discover if the next generation are ready to step into the stud-marks of Johnson, Lawrence Dallaglio, Jason Leonard et al. There are some fine fringe players out there, not least the Wasps' flanker Tom Rees, Gloucester's athletic No8 James Forrester, the mercurial James Simpson-Daniel and the eye-catching Wasps centre Ayoola Erinle. A good start to the domestic season could see some, or all, of them making rapid strides into the public consciousness.

Rugby, though, remains a team game and it is easier to shine if your club are turning it on. Hence why this autumn is so ripe with possibilities for players untainted by the Lions' failure. At Wasps, for example, they were convinced Woodward should have picked more from England's champion club and, with Ian McGeechan taking over the head coaching role from Warren Gatland, they have every incentive to maintain the lofty standards they have already set at home and abroad.

The Guinness Premiership end-of-season play-offs have

England: Rose ready to rise (cont)

been slightly amended, the top four progressing to two semi-finals to determine the grand finalists, Wasps have the same view they always do; they will aim to play dynamic, resourceful rugby, confident their superior fitness and ability to rise to the occasion will pay dividends later in the season. It will be a surprise if they, Leicester and Sale are among the leading domestic quartet next May but the other one is less easy to spot. Perhaps Leeds, back in Europe this year, will come through on the home front as well.

As far as the Heineken Cup is concerned, however, nothing less than top-quality rugby will do. To beat the French sides they have to mix power with pace and seek space rather than contact, when necessary. There is now general recognition, expressed most recently by the former England backs coach Brian Ashton and Wasps' Josh Lewsey, that English rugby has concentrated too much on bashing through brick walls and not enough on the handling and visionary skills. It will be fascinating to see which clubs grasp this crucial nettle, particularly in a season when a disciplinary crackdown has been announced. A gratuitous punch or cynical use of the elbow could earn the perpetrator a ban of between three and six months.

The English clubs will need all the sang-froid they can muster to prevent another French takeover of Europe's elite competition, but the autumn's most eagerly-awaited club fixture will be Toulouse's visit to Wasps on October 30. The result of that game will go a long way towards determining what realistic hopes the English clubs have of breaking the French stranglehold. Leicester, for their part, are in a pool with two French sides, Stade Francais and Clermont Auvergne, who will clearly pose difficulties. The Tigers should also have a clearer idea of their fate by the end of October when they will have met both French opponents but there will be no margin for error for Pat Howard and his squad in the absence of Johnson and the also-retired Neil Back.

The other English contenders in the Heineken Cup are Bath, Sale, Saracens and Leeds, few of whom can claim to be in straightforward pools. Sale must do battle with Munster, Newport-Gwent and Castres while Saracens have been paired with Biarritz and Ulster and Bath must get the better of Leinster and Bourgoin. On paper, Sale look best equipped if their key men stay fit. Even if they reach the knock-out stages, however, it is hard to see the Sharks rolling out the artillery to stop the likes of Toulouse, even with Frenchman Philippe Saint-Andre in charge.

Saracens, who have much firmer foundations up front these days, have the personnel but not yet the confidence to trust their backs at all times. The same, occasionally, is true of Leeds Tykes but these are interesting times in Yorkshire. Their pool is promising: Cardiff, Perpignan and Calvisano may all find it tough at Headingley. The All Black scrum-half Justin Marshall has arrived, winger David Doherty is another probable star of the future and their centre pairing of Andre Snyman and Chris Bell don't fear anyone.

For every rugby lover, however, the key reference points in the coming months will be the All Blacks tour and a Six Nations championship of beguiling possibilities. Will New Zealand under Graham Henry become the first side in history to win a Lions series, a Tri-Nations crown and achieve a coveted grand slam on tour in Europe in the same calendar year? Will they be able to reproduce their best rugby on the softer pitches of the northern hemisphere or will the Lions, in the guise of their individual countries, bite back with a vengeance? And can England, or anyone else, prevent Wales repeating last season's spectacular Grand Slam? It will not be a season for faint hearts.

RIVER VILLAGE

THE thing to remember about this sprawling and daunting metropolis is that it is really no more than a series of interconnected villages and communities. If you bear this in mind, the place becomes much more approachable. Whether you are in Highgate, Southwark, Barnes or Clapham there is a communal focus. Often this is based around the wonderful pubs and bars of the city's constituent parts.

The Twickenham corner of south west London is one of the finest: nearby are Teddington, Kew and Richmond, with their rich historical links: the great gardens of Kew; the riverside village of Teddington, the very quintessence of olde England with its pubs and charm; and the grand but intimate setting of Richmond, with all its ancient royal connections.

But you'll find these places a little packed on match day so we have thrown open the rest of town for your choice, offering a big range of accommodation, all manner of pubs and clubs plus a pretty comprehensive list of London's best restaurants – area by area. As you will see in our transport section, it is not too hard to reach the overgrown cabbage patch, where in 1907 the national ground was planted in a cheaply purchased allotment.

If you are here for a weekend or even several days, it is probably worth pitching camp somewhere close to the main attractions of the centre. There are no fewer than four World Heritage Sites (Westminster Abbey, the Palace of Westminster, St Margaret's church and the Tower of London), 30,000 shops and at least as many bars and restaurants.

The City itself is a quiet retreat, and across the water, Southwark is a newly chic bastion of weekend calm. All along the south bank of the Thames there is a vibrant feel: new restaurants, small hotels and comfortable lodgings are to be found within a stone's throw of train and bus links.

Indeed, London has never been better blessed with restaurants and bars and whilst many of the hotels are far from cheap, there's a huge choice. We can recommend budget options close to the heart of Mayfair, the London Eye, Regents Park or even in the swish streets of Chelsea.

Because London is so vast, an event such as a big match makes little difference to hotel prices unlike in the smaller cities of Cardiff, Dublin and Edinburgh, so you should still be able to secure a good deal if you remember to book sufficiently in advance.

FIND YOUR WAY AROUND

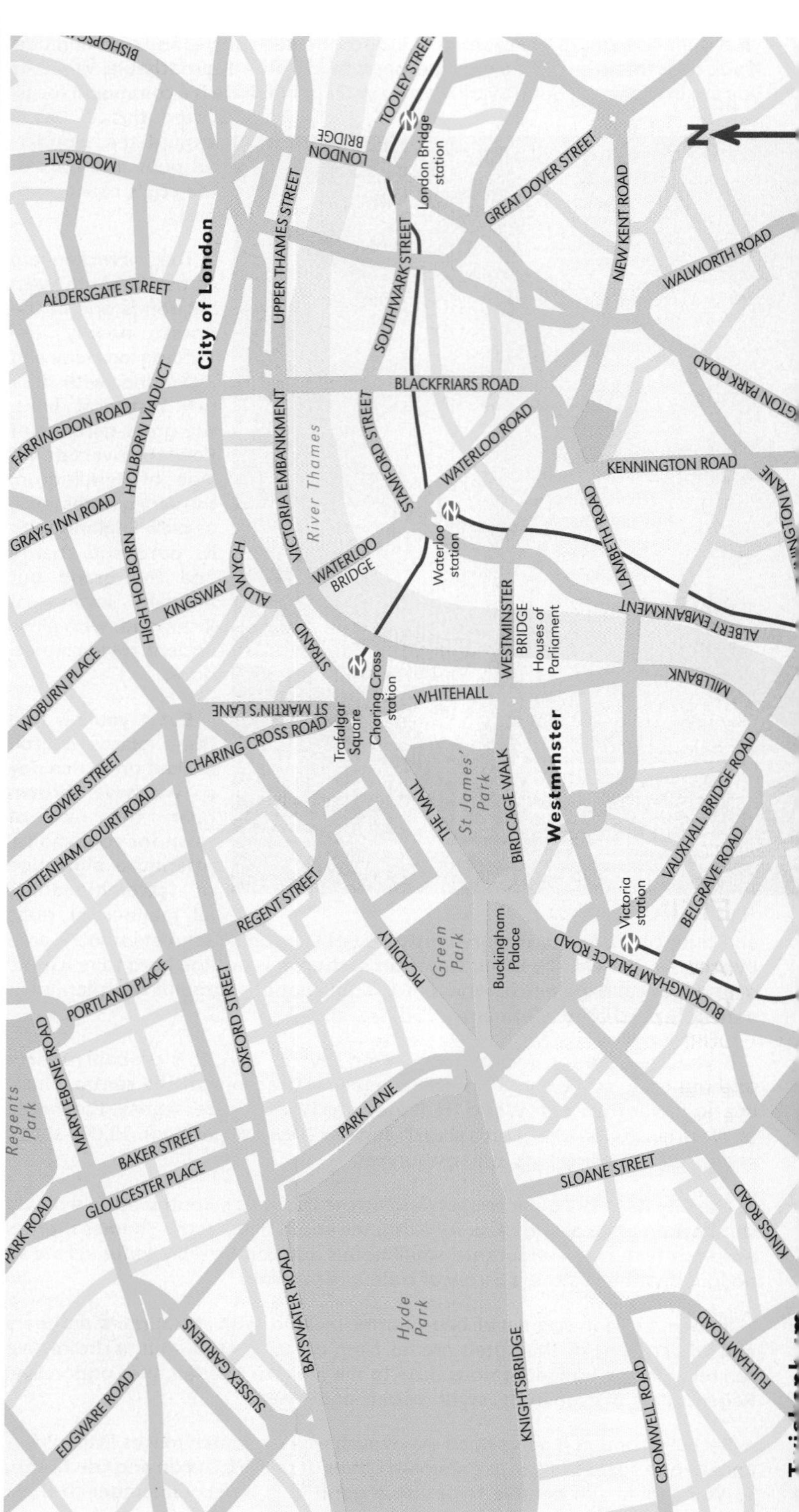

TRAVEL

AIR

London is supported by five airports (London Heathrow, London Gatwick, London Stanstead, London Luton, and London City). You can travel from Heathrow and Gatwick directly to England's international stadium at Twickenham but have to go through the city centre to get there from any of the other three. All five connect to central London by train, coach and taxi. The London Underground runs to Heathrow.

Twickenham is 11 miles from London Heathrow, expect to pay in the region of £20 for a taxi dircect to the ground. It is 30 miles from London Gatwick, expect to pay around £50 for a taxi.

Heathrow Airport

Heathrow is one of the world's busiest and most sophisticated airports, handling more international passengers than any other. Ninety airlines serve 183 destinations from its four terminals. A fifth terminal is currently under construction. Each terminal has competitive currency exchange facilities, information counters and accommodation desks.

CONTACTS

ADDRESS	Heathrow Airport, 1st Floor Heathrow Point West, 234 Bath Road, Haynes, Middlesex, UB3 5LP
TELEPHONE	0870 0000 123
FAX	020 8745 4290
INTERNET	www.baa.co.uk

GETTING INTO TOWN

TRAIN

COST	£26 return
JOURNEY TIME	15 min each way to Paddington

The **Heathrow Express** covers the 20-mile trip between Paddington station and the airport. Journey time compares favourably with the Underground. It calls at both the stations serving the airport, one for Terminal 1-3 and the other for Terminal 4. Reduced fares are available if you book ahead. Travelcards are not valid on the Heathrow Express.

For information and tickets phone 0845 600 1515.

LONDON UNDERGROUND

COST	£3.80 single to central London
JOURNEY TIME	50 min to Piccadilly Circus

The Piccadilly Line connects to central London and the rest of the Underground system. It is the cheapest way to travel but it takes a lot longer and is less comfortable than the Heathrow Express. There are trains every few minutes from approximately **0500** (**0550 Sundays**) to **2345** (**2250 Sundays**).

Air: Heathrow (cont)

There are two Underground stations at Heathrow Airport, one serves Terminals 1-3 and the other serves Terminal 4.
London Underground's Heathrow Terminal 4 station is closed until September 2006 to allow for construction of the Piccadilly line extension to the new Terminal 5. Customers for Heathrow Terminal 4 need to change at Hatton Cross Underground station to a dedicated bus shuttle, extending journey times by 15 minutes. Any passengers who may have difficulty using the stairs at Hatton Cross should travel to Heathrow Terminals 1, 2 & 3 and use the free Heathrow Express Service to reach Terminal 4, allowing an extra 30 minutes for this journey.

For more information visit the **Transport for London** website (www.tfl.gov.uk) or call 020 7222 1234.

COACH

COST	**£10 single/ £15 return**
JOURNEY TIME	**40 min to Victoria Coach Station (approx, depending on traffic)**

National Express runs frequent coach services between Heathrow's central bus station and Victoria Coach Station. Some services stop en route in Hammersmith or Earl's Court. Services from Heathrow start at around **0530** and run until **2130**. Coaches from Victoria leave from around **0715** until **2330**. When travelling by coach it is advisable to check details of the service and consider booking in advance, particularly at weekends or peak times. Allow plenty of time in case of road delays. For more information visit go online or telephone 0870 580 8080.

SERVICE BUS

Between **00.00** and **05.30**, the **N9** runs every 30 minutes to central London (Trafalgar Square). Journey time is approximately 65 minutes. For details, visit the **Transport for London** website (www.tfl.gov.uk) or call 020 7222 1234.

TAXI

COST	**£40 approx (tipping discretionary, possible surcharges)**

There are usually black cabs queuing for customers. The cost of the cab is metered and displayed inside the cab. Surcharges, such as evening and weekend journeys, are also shown here. Tipping, about 10% of the fare, is optional.
Each of Heathrow's terminals has an approved taxi desk.

Terminal 1:	020 8745 7487
Terminal 2:	020 8745 5408
Terminal 3:	020 8745 4655
Terminal 4:	020 8745 7302

DISABLED TRAVELLERS

The Heathrow Express has a range of features to make travelling easy for everyone. Trains have dedicated areas for passengers using wheelchairs and a free service by **Skycaps** provides assistance to passengers with special needs at Heathrow airport. Exiting at Paddington is also straightforward.
All National Express passengers who qualify as disabled are automatically entitled to receive a discount of up to 50%. The company also has a Code of Practice and a disabled persons' travel helpline: 012 1423 8479

Disabled travellers should be aware that a significant number of Underground stations are not equipped with lifts. Similarly, there is considerable variation with bus services; only the newer additions to the fleet are equipped for wheelchairs. You should plan your journey. Go to the Transport for London website (www.tfl.gov.uk) or call the information line on 020 7222 1234.

Gatwick Airport

Gatwick is the busiest single runway airport in the world, the second largest in the UK and the sixth busiest in the world. This two-terminal airport will be handling around 40 million passengers a year by 2010/2011; currently handles 30 million on behalf of 85 airlines flying to 209 destinations.

CONTACTS

ADDRESS	Gatwick Airport, West Sussex , RH6 ONP
TELEPHONE	0870 000 2468
INTERNET	www.baa.co.uk

GETTING INTO TOWN

EXPRESS TRAIN

COST	£12 single/ £23.50 return
JOURNEY TIME	30 min each way to Victoria Station

The Gatwick Express is the quickest way into central London. Trains leave Gatwick Airport from **0435** to **0135**. The station is in the South Terminal and linked to other areas by escalators and lifts. At peak times trains run every 15 minutes (from **0605** to **2005**) and roughly every 30 minutes off-peak.
British Airways and **American Airlines** passengers can check in at Victoria station. For more information and tickets go online or telephone 0845 850 15 30.

SERVICE TRAINS

COST	£8 - £9.80 single
JOURNEY TIME	40 min-plus to a number of stations

Thameslink runs to London Bridge, Blackfriars and King's Cross stations. Trains leave approximately every 30 minutes. The journey to London Bridge takes 40 minutes. For details or booking go online or telephone 08457 48 49 50.
South Central Trains runs to Victoria, leaving every 15 minutes during the day and every hour between 0100 and 0400. The journey time is 45 min. Serves both terminals but takes a longer than the Express. Additional info and tickets are available from the website or by phone: 08457 48 49 50.

COACH

COST	£6.20 single/ £11.40 return
JOURNEY TIME	1hr 30min to Victoria Coach Station (approx, depending on traffic)

National Express runs a service departing approximately hourly. Some services stop at Hooley, Wallington, Mitcham Junction, Mitcham London Rd, Streatham, Stockwell and Pimlico.
Details are available online or by calling 08705 80 80 80.

TAXI

COST	£70 approx (tipping discretionary, possible surcharges)

There are usually cabs queuing for customers at the airport. Find out from the driver beforehand how much your journey will cost. Only use a black cab or reputable mini-cab and never use unauthorised drivers who offer their services at airports or stations.
The official Gatwick taxi concession is **Checker Cars**, 0800 747 737.

Air: Gatwick (cont)

DISABLED TRAVELLERS

The Gatwick Express has a range of features to make travelling easy, including dedicated areas for passengers with wheelchairs. For info and assistance telephone 0845 850 15 30. **South Central** train staff can help you on your journey. To arrange this service telephone 0845 123 7770 at least 24 hours before you travel. **Thameslink** passengers should call 0845 330 3648.
All **National Express** passengers who qualify as disabled are automatically entitled to a discount of up to 50%. The company also has a Code of Practice and a disabled persons' travel helpline: 012 1423 8479.

London City Airport

Six miles from the City and two miles from Canary Wharf, London City Airport is the most convenient hub. Easily accessible by taxi, bus and Tube/Dockland Light Railway (DLR), the airport provides a direct and fast link with more than 20 European cities. The single terminal incorporates shops, information and taxi desks, a bureau de change and left-luggage facility.

CONTACTS

ADDRESS	London City Airport, The Royal Docks, E16 2PX
TELEPHONE	020 7646 0088
FAX	020 7511 1040
INTERNET	www.londoncityairport.com
E-MAIL	info@londoncityairport.com

GETTING INTO TOWN

TRAIN

No direct link. Shuttlebus between the airport to Canning Town and Canary Wharf stations. Jubilee Line or Dockalands Light Railway to the city centre.

BLUE AIRPORT SHUTTLEBUS

COST	£6 single
JOURNEY TIME	25 min to Liverppool Street

The Blue Airport Shuttlebus operates between Liverpool Street station and the airport. It runs every 10/15 min during the week and every 25 min at weekends. Services go via Canary Wharf. Times: **0655 - 2120** Mon-Fri, **0645 - 1315** on Sat and **1155 – 2120** on Sun.
Contact: 020 7646 0088

GREEN AIRPORT SHUTTLEBUS

COST	£2 single
JOURNEY TIME	5 min to Canning Town Station

The Canning Town station link From there catch the Jubilee Line. Buses depart every 10 min from **0600** (**1005 on Sun**) until **2220** (**1315 on Sat**).
Contact: 020 7646 0088

TAXI

COST	£20 approx (tipping discretionary, possible surcharges)

There are usually Black cabs queuing for customers. The cost of the cab is metered and displayed inside the cab. Only use a reputable mini-cab and try to avoid using unauthorised drivers who offer their services at airports or stations.

DISABLED TRAVELLERS
The Docklands Light Railway was the UK's first fully-accessible railway for wheelchair users. There are lifts, escalators and/or ramps on every station platform of the DLR and all platforms are level with the trains for step-free access. There is also a designated wheelchair/pram bay on every train. **The Airport Shuttlebuses** are wheelchair accessible.

RELATED LINKS

Transport for London	www.tfl.gov.uk

London Luton Airport

Many of the flights to Luton are provided by low-cost airlines. Luton Airport is 35 miles (56km) north-west of London.

CONTACTS

ADDRESS	London Luton Airport, Navigation House, Airport Way, Luton, Beds LU2 9LY
TELEPHONE	01582 405100
FAX	01582 395035
INTERNET	www.london-luton.co.uk
E-MAIL	marketing@ltn.aero

GETTING INTO TOWN
TRAIN

COST	£10.70 single
JOURNEY TIME	30-40min to King's Cross

Thameslink operates regular services to stations including King's Cross, Farringdon, London Bridge and Blackfriars in central London, and beyond to Brighton. Trains leave from approximately 7am to 10pm Mon-Fri and 9am to 10pm on Sunday. A regular shuttle bus links the airport to Luton Airport Parkway station in around eight minutes. Contact: 0845 748 4950

COACH

COST	£9 single/ £12.50 return
JOURNEY TIME	1hr 10min (approx)

Greenline 757 goes to Victoria Coach Station with stops at Brent Cross, Finchley Road Station, Baker Street and Marble Arch. Services run from 0300 until 0000 daily from three times an hour. Contact: 0870 608 7261.

TAXI
There are usually cabs queuing for customers. Enquire with the driver beforehand how much your journey will cost

DISABLED TRAVELLERS
Thameslink passengers with wheelchairs are advised to call at least 24 hours in advance to make arrangements for travel. 0845 330 3648.
Greenline Coaches are unable to accommodate wheelchairs.

RELATED LINKS

Greenline	www.greenline.co.uk
Thameslink	www.thameslink.co.uk

London Stansted Airport

Stansted is 35 miles (56km) to the north-east of London. It lies between London and Cambridge and is reached from the M11 at Junction 8, which is about 20 minutes from the M11 junction with the M25 London Orbital Motorway, junction 27. The airport is signposted on both motorways. Journey time into central London is around 70 minutes. Stansted is home to many of the UK's low-cost airlines, serving mostly European and Mediterranean destinations.16 million passengers use Stansted every year to connect with 30 different airlines

CONTACTS

ADDRESS	London Stansted Airport Ltd, Enterprise House, Stansted Airport, Essex, CM24 1QW
TELEPHONE	01279 662705
FAX	01279 662932
INTERNET	www.baa.co.uk
E-MAIL	janet-morris@baa.co.uk

GETTING INTO TOWN

TRAIN

COST	£14.50 single/ £24 return
JOURNEY TIME	45 min to Liverpool Street

Stansted Express is the quickest way. Trains run from **0600** to **2359**. Every 15 minutes at peak times (from **0800** to **1700** Mon-Fri) and every 30 minutes off-peak. Trains also stop at Tottenham Hale where there is an underground link.
Contact: 0845 748 4950

Stansted Express	www.stanstedexpress.co.uk

COACH

COST	£10 single/ £15 return
JOURNEY TIME	1hr 40 min to Victoria Coach Station (appox, depending on traffic)

National Express operates a 24 hour-service to Victoria Coach Station which stops at Golder's Green, Finchley Road Underground station, St John's Wood, Marylebone, Baker Street, Marble Arch and Hyde Park Corner. This service runs at intervals of up to an hour.
Contact: 08705 808080

TAXI

COST	£70-£80 approx (tipping discretionary, possible surcharges)

The cost of the cab is metered and displayed inside the cab. Extra charges, such as evening and weekend journeys are also shown here. Only use black cab or reputable mini-cab and never use unauthorised drivers who offer their services.
The official Stansted taxi concession is **Checker Cars** 012 7966 2444.

DISABLED TRAVELLERS

The Stansted Express is equipped with for disabled passengers with specially designed seating areas and toilet facilities. 0845 8500 150 for details.

Air Travel Web Links

Aer Lingus	0845 084 4444	www.aerlingus.com
Aeroflot	020 7355 2233	www.aeroflot.com
Air Canada	0870 524 7226	www.aircanada.com
Air France	0845 084 5111	www.airfrance.com
Air New Zealand	020 8741 2299	www.airnz.com
Alitalia	0870 544 8259	www.alitalia.com
American Airlines	0845 778 9789	www.aa.com
British Airways	0845 773 3377	www.british-airways.com
British European	0870 567 6676	www.flybe.com
British Midland	0870 607 0555	www.flybmi.com
Cathay Pacific Airways	020 7747 8888	www.cathaypacific.com
Continental Airlines	0800 776 464	www.continental.com
Delta Air Lines	0800 414 767	www.delta.com
EasyJet	0870 600 0000	www.easyjet.com
El Al Israel Airlines	020 7957 4100	www.elal.com
Iberia	0845 601 2854	www.iberia.com
Icelandair	020 7874 1000	www.icelandair.com
Icelandexpress	0870 850 0737	www.icelandexpress.com
KLM UK	0870 507 4074	www.klm.com
Lufthansa Airlines	0845 773 7747	www.lufthansa.com
Monarch Scheduled	0870 040 5040	www.flymonarch.com
Qantas Airways	0845 774 7767	www.qantas.com
Ryanair	0870 156 9569	www.ryanair.com
Scandinavian Airlines (SAS)	0845 607 2772	www.sas.se
Singapore Airlines	0870 608 8886	www.singaporeair.com
SN Brussels Airlines	0870 735 2345	www.flysn.com
South African Airways	020 7312 5000	www.flysaa.com
TAP Air Portugal	0845 601 0932	www.tap.pt
Thai Airways International	0870 606 0911	www.thaiair.com
Turkish Airlines	020 7766 9300	www.turkishairlines.com
United Airlines	0845 844 4777	www.ual.com
Virgin Atlantic	01293 747747	www.virgin-atlantic.com

It's always a good idea to shop around and compare prices with buying direct from the airline. The following are some of the best online travel shops.

eBookers	www.ebookers.com
Opodo	www.opodo.com
Expedia	www.expedia.co.uk
Cheapflights	www.cheapflights.co.uk
Lastminute.com	www.lastminute.com
Travelocity	www.travelocity.co.uk

RAIL

Eurostar

Eurostar is a quick and easy way to travel between the UK and the Continent via the Channel Tunnel. Paris to London takes 2 hours 35 minutes; Brussels is 2 hours and 20 minutes away. Some services stop at Ashford (Kent), Calais Fret-hun, Disneyland Paris, Lille and Avignon. Winter, services run to the ski resorts of Moutiers and Bourg St Maurice in the Alps.
Eurostar Plus is run in association with the high-speed rail services in France (TGV) and Belgium (Thalys). It provides connections within France and Belgium as well as links to Germany, the Netherlands, and Italy.

TICKETS

Ticket prices vary to meet all budgets. Book ahead to get the cheapest fares – from £70 adult return. Discounts for children (aged 2-12), young people (under 26), and over 60s. All prices are market-based to undercut competing modes of transport. For telephone reservations and information call 08705 186 186. A £5 booking fee applies to all telephone bookings

All **Eurostar** trains are wheelchair accessible. It's a good idea to telephone in advance as there is a maximum of two wheelchairs per train. 08705 186 186.

UK rail links

London is the hub of the UK's rail network, with frequent services to all corners of the country from the city's nine centrally-located mainline railway stations.
Rail services in the UK are run by a set of private operators.

London Waterloo, for trains to and from the south coast and south-west of England and Eurostar.	020 7401 8444
London Paddington, for trains to and from the west and south-west of England and South Wales, including Bath, Bristol, Penzance and Cardiff.	020 7262 0344
London Charing Cross. Charing Cross for the South-East of London and into Kent.	020 7401 8444
London Victoria provides services to Gatwick, Brighton and rest of Sussex. Over 110 million people pass through Victoria every year.	020 7963 0957
London Bridge, on the Kent and South East London routes into Charing Cross and Cannon Street. The remainder of the station is the terminus for routes from Sussex and South London.	08457 48 49 50
London Fenchurch Street accommodates the trains of the London Tilbury and Southend Railway, as well as those of the London and Blackwall Railway.	08457 48 49 50
London Liverpool Street carried 123 million passengers each year.	020 7247 4297
Kings Cross/St Pancras. Kings Cross is the London terminus of the East Coast main line for services to Leeds, York, Newcastle, Edinburgh and beyond into Scotland. The station was opened in 1852 and the station roof, the largest at the time, was supposedly modelled on the Russian Czar's riding school. Midland Mainline services to the East Midlands including Nottingham, Derby and Leicester.	020 7837 4334
London Euston is the main gateway to the west Midlands and West Coast, serving Birmingham, Manchester and stations to Glasgow.	020 7387 1499

TICKETS

Booking in advance secures a seat and can also save you money. There are discount schemes available for young people, family groups and over 60s. **The BritRail Pass** gives you the freedom to travel on all National Rail services for a set period of time. Book online or telephone National Rail enquiries 08457 48 49 50.

USING TRAINS WITH A DISABILITY

There is variation in wheelchair accessibility for trains and stations. It's a good idea to check before travelling to ensure a hassle-free journey. Telephone National Rail enquiries on 08457 48 49 50.

Suburban trains

Several rail companies operate passenger trains in London, including the **Silverlink** (or North London) line 0845 601 4867 and the **Thameslink** 0845 748 4950. Silverlink includes services from the southwest of London with North Woolwich in the southeast via Kew, West Hampstead, Camden Road, Highbury & Islington and Stratford stations. Thameslink goes from Elephant & Castle and London Bridge in the south through the City to King's Cross and as far north as Luton. **South Eastern Trains** 0845 748 4950 depart from the major train stations and run southbound services to Greenwich, Brixton, and Lewisham. **South West Trains** 0845 748 4950 run services to Richmond and Hampton Court. Most lines connect with the Underground system, and Travelcards are accepted.

The Twickenham rugby ground is reached most easily by rail, with the nearest station only a few minutes walk away from the stadium. The Twickenham station is serviced by South West Trains, which run from Waterloo Station. The rail service links with the District Line of the London Underground at Richmond station, which is two rail stops, or about 30 minutes walk, from the stadium. There is also a rail-coach link to Heathrow Airport via Feltham station, another two stops down the line.

Most of the large mainline London stations have left-luggage facilities available, although due to the perceived threat from terrorists, baggage lockers have been phased out. **Excess Baggage** 0800 783 1085 has services costing £4 per bag per 24 hours or part thereof. The service operates at Paddington, Euston, Waterloo, King's Cross, Liverpool Street, and Charing Cross stations.

RELATED LINKS

National Rail	www.nationalrail.co.uk
BritRail	www.britrail.net
Disabled Persons Railcard	www.disabledpersons-railcard.co.uk
Excess Baggage	www.excessbaggage.co.uk
Silverlink Trains	www.silverlink-trains.com
Thameslink	www.thameslink.co.uk
South West Trains	www.southwesttrains.co.uk

London Underground

The 'Tube' as **London Underground** is known to Londoners, is normally the quickest and easiest way of getting round the capital.

London travel information centres sell tickets and provide free maps to the network. There are centres at all Heathrow terminals and at the **Britain & London Visitor Centre** on Lower Regent Street. For general information on the Tube, buses, the DLR or trains within London ring 020 7222 1234 or visit the **London Underground** website (www.thetube.com) or the **London Transport** website (www.tfl.gov.uk/tube). For news of how services are running, call **Travelcheck** on 020 7222 1200.

Rail: Underground (cont)

NETWORK

Greater London is served by 12 Tube lines, along with the independent (though linked) and privately owned **DLR** and an interconnected rail network. The first Tube train operates at around **5am Monday to Saturday** and around **7.30am Sunday**; the last train leaves between **11.30pm** and **12.30am** depending on the day, the station and the line.

Remember that any train heading from left to right on the map is designated as eastbound, and any train heading from top to bottom is southbound – no matter how many squiggles and turns it makes.

FARES

The Underground divides London into six concentric zones. If you're caught on the Underground without a valid ticket (and that includes crossing into a zone that your ticket doesn't cover) you're liable for an on-the-spot fine of £10.

ONE WAY ADULT TICKETS (JANUARY 2005)

Zone 1	**£2 (carnet £1.50)**
Zone 2 (to Z1)	**£2.30**
Zone 3 (to Z1)	**£2.80**
Zone 4 (to Z1)	**£2.80**
Zone 5 (to Z1)	**£3.80**
Zone 6 (to Z1)	**£3.80**

TRAVEL PASSES AND DISCOUNT FARES

If you're travelling several times in one day or through a couple of zones, you should consider a Travelpass or some other discounted fare. Valid all day, a Travelcard offers the cheapest way of getting about London.

TRAVELLING WITH A DISABILITY

Access to most underground stations is via numerous steps. The system can become extremely crowded at peak times and, therefore, difficult for those with mobility problems.

Jubilee Line trains are wheelchair accessible from all the new stations between Westminster and Stratford – stations can be reached via lift. You are advised to check the operation of lifts by calling 020 7308 2800 (during office hours) or 020 7222 1234 (evenings and weekends).

RELATED LINKS

Tourists Guide to the Tube	www.tfl.gov.uk/tube/tourists
Transport for London	www.tfl.gov.uk

Docklands Light Railway

The independent, driverless **Docklands Light Railway** (DLR) 020 7363 9700 links the City at Bank and Tower Gateway at Tower Hill with Beckton and Stratford to the east and north east and the Docklands (as far as Island Gardens at the southern end of the Isle of Dogs), Greenwich and Lewisham to the south. The DLR runs from **0530** to **0030** Monday to Friday, from **0600** to **0030** Saturday and from **0730** to **2330** Sunday. Tickets must be purchased before boarding a train and fares are the same as those on the tube though there is a host of daily, weekly, monthly and annual passes valid uniquely on the DLR. For news of how services are running, call Travelcheck on 020 7222 1200.

USING DOCKLANDS LIGHT RAILWAY WITH A DISABILITY

There are lifts, escalators and/or ramps on every station platform of the DLR and all platforms are level with the trains for step free access. There is also a designated wheelchair bay on every train.

COACH

Victoria Coach Station is London's principal coach gateway. It is run by Transport for London and is the base of National Express and Eurolines services as well as a selection of smaller coach operators. National Express is the UK's largest coach carrier and operates from all over the country. It runs both express services from many major towns and cities as well as connecting services for smaller towns and villages. 08705 80 80 80.

RELATED LINKS

Victoria Coach Station	www.tfl.gov.uk/vcs
National Express Coaches	www.gobycoach.com
Eurolines	www.eurolines.com
Coach Tourism Council	www.coachtourismcouncil.co.uk
Green Line	www.greenline.co.uk

CAR

Driving in London

When driving into central London then it is essential to remember to pay the Congestion Charge which covers central London from Kennington and Bermondsey in the South to Kings Cross/ St Pancras in the North and Hyde Park in the west to Shoreditch and Spitalfields in the east.

For a comprehensive map of areas covered by the Congestion Charge then please contact Transport for London website (www.tfl.gov.uk) or call the information line on 020 7222 1234.

The Congestion Charge operates between **0700-1830** Monday to Friday (public holidays excluded) and is £8 per car per day. Evenings and weekends are free. The Congestion Charge can be paid online (www.cclondon.com), in selected shops and petrol stations, by post, by sms from your mobile phone or by phone on 020 7649 9122.

Parking in London can be extremely difficult and is particularly restricted between **0830** and **1830** Monday to Friday and from **0830** to **1330** on **Saturdays**. Many of London's roads operate 'Pay & Display' schemes, which can prove expensive for extended stays.

In addition, there are car parking companies operating in London with properties throughout the city. Two of the larger ones are **Masterpark** and **National Car Parks** (NCP). Masterpark is a service provided by the City of Westminster and there are 18 sites situated throughout central London. NCP runs around 100 car parks in London.

LOCAL CAR PARKING

The Box Office has a limited number of labels for parking in Rosebine Avenue (just off A316). Please call the **Twickeham Box Office** for further details contact: 028 892 2000

DRIVING TO TWICKENHAM

Twickenham Rugby Stadium is situated close to the M3, M4 and M25 motorways, and is signposed clearly from all three. When close to the ground, come off the A36 Chertsey Road, then turn left onto the B361 Whitton Road, or cross straight into Rugby Road.

Car: Driving in London (cont)

RELATED LINKS

Driver and Vehicle Licensing Agency	www.dvla.gov.uk
Masterpark	www.masterpark.org.uk
NCP Parking	www.ncp.co.uk
Transport for London	www.tfl.gov.uk
Congestion Charging	www.cclondon.com

Eurotunnel

Eurotunnel provides high-speed car, coach and freight services between the UK and the Continent via the Channel Tunnel between Coquelles (Calais) and Folkestone. Folkestone has good access to the motorway network and London. The approximate channel crossing time is 35 minutes.

Return fares start at £100 per car.

Ferry

The quickest ferry crossing is between Calais and Dover; which takes between 70 and 90 minutes. Ferries are operated by **Sea France** and **P&O** and run regularly throughout the day and night. **Hoverspeed** also operates quick services between Dover and Calais and Newhaven and Dieppe, although this service does not run in winter.

Longer routes from France and Spain are operated by **P&O** and **Brittany Ferries** from Portsmouth, Poole and Plymouth, crossings take between 6 and 24 hours.

The fastest routes for ferry crossings from Ireland to mainland Britain are Dublin-Holyhead and Dun Laoghaire-Holyhead. On both routes, high speed vessels operate alongside normal ferry services. The services are operated by **Irish Ferries** and **Stena Line** and journey times are approximately 2 hours on the high speed vessels and 3 hours on the traditional ferries.

Services to Holland and Denmark operate out of Harwich by **DFDS Seaways** to Cuxhaven and Esbjerg, and journeys take approximately nineteen hours.

London is easily reached by road from the major ports. For foot passengers, there are frequent train services into London's Victoria Station from Dover, Folkestone, Ramsgate and Newhaven. Harwich services terminate at Liverpool Street station. For timetables and fares by train from other UK ports visit www.thetrainline.com.

RELATED LINKS

Brittany Ferries	www.brittany-ferries.com
HoverSpeed Seacat	www.hoverspeed.com
Eurotunnel	www.eurotunnel.com
Eurostar	www.eurostar.com
SeaFrance	www.seafrance.co.uk
P&O Ferries	www.poferries.com
Stena Line	www.stenaline.com
Irish Ferries	www.irishferries.ie
DFDS Seaways	www.dfdsseaways.com
TheTrainLine	www.thetrainline.com

BUS

Buses are a quick and convenient way to travel around London, providing plenty of sightseeing opportunities en route. London has over 17,000 bus stops. Privatised in 1994, London's bus services are under the **Transport for London** umbrella.

INFORMATION

There are 28 local guides available free of charge to areas as far-flung as Harrow, Romford and Hounslow. Known as Journey Planners, they encorporate all forms of public transport for the specified area, including bus routes. Most visitors, however, will find the **Central London Bus Guide** sufficient, which is essentially a map and is available from travel information centres. If you can't get to a centre, ring 020 7371 0247 to have one sent or write to **London Buses (CDL), Freepost Lon7503, London SE16 4BR**. For general information on London buses call 020 7222 1234 (24 hrs). For more information on how services are running, phone **Travelcheck** on 020 7222 1200.

TAXI

BLACK CABS

The black London taxicab is as much a London feature as the red bus. Taxis are formidably expensive but come into their own at night, though prices are even higher. Cabs are available for hire when the yellow sign above the windscreen is lit; just stick your arm out to signal one.

Fares are metered, with a minimum charge of £2.20, and increments of 20p for each 219m (after the first 438m). There are no additional charges for extra passengers or luggage. You can tip taxi drivers up to 10% but most people round up to the nearest pound.

Hailing a taxi in popular nightlife areas of London such as Soho late at night (and especially after pub closing time at 11pm) can be tricky. If you do find yourself in any of those areas, signal all taxis – even those with their lights off. Many drivers are very choosy about their fares at this time of night.

MINICABS

Minicabs are now fully licensed and are cheaper, freelance competitors of black cabs. Minicabs cannot legally be hailed on the street – they must be hired by phone or directly from one of the minicab offices (every high street has at least one – look out for a flashing orange light). Licensed minicabs carry their licenses in their car and are also displayed in the operator's office.

Unlicensed minicabs are illegal. You may be approached by unlicensed minicab drivers seeking fares; it's advisable to avoid this as there have been a number allegations of assault made against unlicensed cab drivers.

Minicabs don't have meters, so it's essential to fix a price before you start (it is therefore not usual to tip minicab drivers). Make sure you bargain hard, as most drivers start higher than the fare they're prepared to accept.

Ask a local for the name of a reputable minicab company, or phone a large 24- hour operator. Alternatively, check if the operator is licensed by calling Transport for London 020 7222 1234.

WOMEN

Women travelling alone at night can choose **Ladycabs** 020 7254 3501, which has women drivers.

RIVERBOAT

With the drive to make more use of London's often overlooked 'liquid artery', companies running shuttle boats on the river have been sprouting up in recent years.

There is good news for Travelcard holders: you get one-third off all fares listed below. Private boat operators crowd the piers and will often tout for customers – you'll find them around Embankment, Westminster and even down as far as Richmond.

For something more romantic, there is no shortage of dinner cruises, offering dancing, music and fine food against a backdrop of the city at night. Prices start at £16.50 per person.

EASTWARD ALONG THE THAMES

Bateaux London - Catamaran Cruisers: Links Embankment, Tower and Greenwich Piers for £5.70 to £9 (adult) and £3.50 to £5.50 (child) return depending on the stage and season. The River Pass allows one day's unlimited use of the service. Schedules vary according to season, with six or seven daily departures in winter.

River Pass	Adult £10.50-£11.50
	Child £5.50-£6.50
Hours	Every 30 min 1000-1400.
Contact:	020 7987 1185 or 020 7925 2215

Circular Cruise: Runs from Westminster Pier as far as St Katharine's Pier in Wapping. Vessels call at London Bridge City Pier and, on weekends in the summer season, at Festival Pier on the South Bank. Fares are cheaper between just two stages (e.g. Westminster Pier to/from London Bridge City Pier costs £4.30 adult/ £2.20 child/ £3.20 student & senior/ £11 family).

Hours:	Every 30-40 min 1100-1900 Apr-Sep
	1100, 1220, 1340 & 1500 Oct-May.
Prices:	Adult £6
	Child (5-15) £3
	Student & Senior £5
	Family £15.80
Contact	020 7936 2033

City Cruises: Most boats are wheelchair-friendly with wheelchair-accessible toilets and refreshment facilities. Breakfast, lunch, tea and dinner services are available but must be pre-booked. Cruises with a multi-language commentary facility depart every 40-45 minutes all year (except 25 December) between Westminster, Waterloo (London Eye), Tower and Greenwich from 10am until 4.30pm with additional cruises between Westminster, Waterloo and Tower in summer and evening cruises between Westminster, Waterloo and Tower in June, July and August

Prices	Adult £6.50 -£6.80 single, £6.80-£8.60 return
	Children (5-16) half price, other concessions
All-day hop-on/ hop-off	£9 adults £22 family .
Contact:	020 77 400 400

Thames Clippers: Commuter service that operates a weekday service with frequent sailings. There is also good service at weekends. Stops include Greenwich, Mast House Terrace (Isle of Dogs), Greenland Pier (Surrey Quays), Canary Wharf, St Katharine Docks, London Bridge, Bankside (Tate Modern), Blackfriars and Savoy Pier (Embankment).

New to the service is the River Roamer Ticket offering families 'hop-on/ hop-off' travel to some of London's most exciting attractions including Tate Britain, London Eye, the London Aquarium, the Globe Theatre, Tate Modern, London Dungeons, HMS Belfast and Tower of London.

Hours	0620-2025 (0925-1805 weekends)
Prices	Adult single from £2.50
	Child single from £1.25
	33% discount available with Travelcard;
The Riverline	0870 781 5049

WESTMINSTER TO GREENWICH

Thames Passenger Boat Service: These cruise boats leave Westminster Pier for Greenwich, passing the Globe Theatre, stopping at the Tower of London and continuing under Tower Bridge and past the docks. The last boats return from Greenwich at about **1700** (**1800** in summer).

Hours	every 30 min **1000-1600/ 1700** peak season.
Prices	Adult: one way £6.50, return £8
	Child: one way £3.25, return £4
	Senior: one way £5.25, return £6.50
	Family: one way £17.50, return £21.5
Contact	020 7930 4097

WESTWARD ALONG THE THAMES

These boats go upriver from Westminster Pier, an enjoyable excursion although it takes much longer and is not (perhaps) as interesting as the trip east The main destinations are the Royal Botanic Gardens at Kew and Hampton Court Palace. It's possible to get off the boats at Richmond in July and August. No boats run in this direction from the end of October until the end of March. Boats to the Royal Botanic Gardens at Kew sail from Westminster Pier via Putney up to five times a day from 1015 to 1400 from late March to September with limited services in October. Boats to Hampton Court leave Westminster Pier at 1030, 1115 and noon April to September/October.

Westminster Passenger Service Association 020 7930 4721; Royal Botanic Gardens one way adult/child/senior £7/3/6, return £11/5/9, journey time 1hrs; Hampton Court one way adult/child/senior £10/4/8, return £14/7/11. Journey time 3 hrs.

RELATED LINKS

Bateaux London	www.bateauxlondon.com
City Cruises	www.citycruises.com
Crown River Cruises	www.crownriver.com
Thames Clippers	www.thamesclippers.com
Thames River Boats	www.wpsa.co.uk
Westminster Pier	www.westminsterpier.co.uk

VITAL STATISTICS

Population: 7,465,000

Phone Code: country code 44, area code: 020

Time zone: GMT (GMT + 1 from last Sunday in March to Saturday before last Sunday in October).

Electricity: 220 volts AC, 50Hz; square three-pin plugs are standard.

Average January temp: 5°C (41°F).

Tipping: A tip of around 10% is customary in restaurants. Round up for taxis. Tipping in bars is rare.

Airport Transfers: See transport section.

Getting around: See transport section. London is a vast sprawl of communities and has a very complex and effective transport infrastructure.

Shopping: Most shops are open from 9am – 6pm with late night shopping widely available. Sunday opening from 10am – 4pm. (see p??? for further details).

Getting there: See transport section

Getting to the ground:
By road: Twickenham Stadium in on the northern side of the A316, heading into London from the south west Exit M25 at Junction 12 onto the M3 and then A316. Stay on the A316 until the roundabout. The Stoop (the Harlequins' rugby ground) will appear on your right. Turn left at the next roundabout and the entrance (gate L) is on the left.

By rail: The Stadium is about 10 minutes walk from Twickenham train station. Frequent train services to Twickenham are from London Waterloo, Clapham Junction, Windsor and Reading.

By London Underground and bus: Bus services operate from close to Hounslow East (Piccadilly Line). Nearest Underground station is Richmond (District Line). Richmond about 30 minutes walk from the Stadium. There is also an overland train service to Twickenham station.

HOSPITALS

Guy's Hospital,	St Thomas Street. London. SE1 9RT. 020 7188 7188
Hammersmith Hospital,	Du Cane Rd., W12 ONS. 020 8743 2030
Royal Free Hospital,	Pond Street, NW3 1DU. 020 7794 0500
Saint Bartholomew's Hospital,	West Smithfield, EC1 A7BE 020 7377 7000
The Royal London Hospital,	Whitechapel Road, E1 1BB. 020 7377 7000
Street Thomas's Hospital,	Lambeth Palace Rd, SE1 7EH. 020 7188 7188

Middlesex Hospital,	Mortimer Street, London, W1 T3AA. 020 7636 8333
The Harley Street Clinic,	Weymouth St, London, W1G 8BJ. 020 7935 7700
London Bridge Hospital,	Tooley St, City of London, SE1 2PR. 020 7407 3100
Chelsea & Westminster Hospital,	Fulham Rd, SW10 9NH. 020 8746 8000
Italian Hospital Fund,	Wilton Rd, SW1V 1DE. 020 7233 6675
West Middlesex University Hospital,	Twickenham Rd, Isleworth, TW7 6AF 020 8560 2121
The Royal Marsden Hospital,	Downs Rd, Sutton, SM2 5PT. 020 8642 6011

USEFUL CONTACTS

Twickenham Stadium:	020 8892 2000
British Tourist Authority (BTA):	www.visitbritain.com (followed by / and the initials for your country)
BTA, Paris:	Maison-de-la-Grande-Bretagne, 19 Rue des Mathurins, 75009 Paris (1) 4451 5620
BTA, Australia:	Level 16, Gateway, 1 Macquarie Place, Sydney, NSZ 2000. (2) 9377 4400
BTA, Canada:	5915 Airport Rd, Suite 120, Mississauga, Ontario, L4V 1T1 (905) 405 1835
BTA, Italy:	Corso Magenta 32, 20123 Milano. (02) 7201 0078
BTA, Dublin:	18/19 College Green, Dublin 2. (1) 670 8000
BTA, Japan:	Akasaka Twin Tower 1F, 2-17-22, Minato-Ku, Tokyo. (3) 5562 2548
BTA, Netherlands:	Aurora Gebouw (5e) Stadhouderskade 2, 1054 ES Amersterdam. (20) 689 0002.
BTA, New Zealand:	17th floor, 151 Queen St, Auckland 1. (9) 303 1446
BTA, South Africa:	Lancaster Gate, Hyde Park Lane, Hyde Park, Johannesburg 2196 or PO Box 41896, Craighall 2024. (11) 325 0343
BTA, USA:	7th Floor, 551 Fifth Avenue, New York, NY 10176-0799 2120 986 2200

PLACES OF INTEREST
FOR HISTORY

Tower of London

Tower of London: Royal riverside residence

Home to the Crown Jewels. Built almost a millennium ago and expanded upon over the intervening centuries, the Tower of London has protected, housed, imprisoned and been, for many, the last sight they saw on Earth. It has been the seat of British government and the living quarters of monarchs. It has housed lions, bears, and (to this day) flightless ravens; not to mention notorious traitors and framed members of court, lords and ministers, clergymen and knights.

Westminster Abbey

Since 1066, Westminster Abbey has been the setting for every coronation as well as numerous other important royal occasions. The present structure is an architectural masterpiece built between the 13th to 16th centuries and contains the shrine of St Edward the Confessor, the tombs of kings and queens, and countless memorials to the famous and the great. Today it is still a church dedicated to regular worship and to the celebration of great events in the life of the nation. It is neither a cathedral nor a parish church, Westminster Abbey is a "Royal Peculiar" under the jurisdiction of a Dean and Chapter, and subject only to the Sovereign.

Houses of Parliament

The present Houses of Parliament were built after a fire in 1834, when all except Westminster Hall was destroyed. Until the blaze, the orginal Palace of Westminster, as the building is also known, had stood on the site since the time of Edward the Confessor. The present building was designed specifically to house the two chambers of parliament and was laid out in its famously Gothic style by Sir Charles Barry. It was completed in the 1840's. The clock tower housing the bell of Big Ben, is probably London's best known icon.

Hampton Court Palace

The oldest Tudor palace in England with many attractions including the Tudor kitchens, tennis courts, maze and State Apartments and King's Apartments. The real tennis court and the banqueting house are open during the summer months. Attractions include a unique garden restoration, King William's Privy Garden of 1702, and the private apartments of the Georges, last occupied in 1737 but which have now been refurbished.

CONTEMPORARY FUN

London Eye

Possibly London's most popular tourist attraction, it was built to mark the millennium. The Eye stands 135 metres high on the South Bank between Waterloo and Westminster Bridges, right opposite Big Ben and the Houses of Parliament and provides stunning views over central London and beyond. It's £12.50 a trip.

Docklands

Awesome example of modern architecture, where offices and shops meld into a giant mall - a great hub and hive of communal activity.

ART & CULTURE

St Paul's Cathedral

Sir Christopher Wren's masterpiece constructed out of the ashes of the Great Fire of 1666. Somerset House & the Courtauld Gallery. Massive and elegant construction on the Embankment, a stroll away from St Paul's.

St Paul's Cathedral: Rose from the ashes of Great Fire of London

National Gallery

Houses the national collection of Western European painting, more than 2,300 pictures dating from 1250 to 1900. The collection includes all the major European schools of painting and masterpieces by many great artists. The National Gallery, Trafalgar Square, WC2 N5DN.

British Museum

Great Russell St, near Holborn and Tottenham Court tubes. Founded in 1753, the British Museum contains world-famous collections of antiquities from Egypt, Western Asia, Greece and Rome, as well as Prehistoric, Romano-British, Medieval, Renaissance, Modern and Oriental collections, Prints and Drawings, Coins, Medals and Banknotes. Perhaps most famously, it is home to the Elgin marbles, still the subject of controversy because of Greek demands for their return.

SHOPPING

With more than 40,000 shops and 83 major street markets to choose from, the sheer variety on offer is hard to imagine. The city that gave the world the miniskirt, punk and Alexander McQueen continues to bubble over with excellent fashions, from in-the-know East End boutiques to the world-famous Selfridges. Different areas have their own specialities. Jewellery lovers will find nirvana in Clerkenwell, and record collectors will discover second-hand heaven in Hanway Street and Notting Hill. So get the credit card out and start spending.

ANTIQUES

Atlantic Antiques Centres Ltd

One of London's most famous and best loved antiques villages. Over 100 specialist dealers offering antiques and collectables from all periods for all budgets. Recently redecorated, with air conditioning. **Atlantic Antiques Centres Ltd, Chenil House 181-183 King's Road, London, SW3 5EB.**

Phone	020 7969 1500
Email:	antique@dial.pipex.com
Internet:	www.collectors-items.org.uk/Atlantic_Antiques_Centres_Chelsea.htm

The Mall

In the heart of Camden Passage and a regular haunt for interior designers and collectors alike, is the focus of Islington's thriving antiques community. This former tram station, and fine example of Victorian industrial architecture, houses more than 35 specialist dealers in porcelain, silver, Art Deco, Art Noveau, clocks, glass, Oriental antiques, paintings, brass, antique English and Continental furniture, jewellery and collectables. Across the road is Gateway Antiques Arcade, providing a total of more than 70 specialist antiques shops and stalls.
The Mall On Upper Street, 359 Upper Street London, N1 N10PD.

Phone	020 7351 5353

Greenwich Market

Famous for its stalls selling antiques, there's also bric-a-brac and books. Opening Times: Open all year, Thu, Fri, **0630-1700**, Sat, Sun, **0930-1730**. Closed Mon-Wed. Rail: Greenwich Directions: general **Greenwich Market, Greenwich High Road London SE10.**

Phone	07515 7153

Silver service: All sorts of fasctinating antiques are on sale in London's many markets

BOOKSHOPS

The big ones are on or around Oxford Street and Charing Cross Rd.

Borders

Borders is the upcoming bookshop, now with coffee shop included and even open mics for budding poets. This is your chance – the audience is captive – at least for the first couplet.

Borders, 203 Oxford Street, W1D 2LE.

Phone:	0800 195 9809

Borders Books & Music, Market Pl Kingston upon Thames, KT11JT.

Phone:	020 8974 9444

Borders Books Music Café, 120 Charing Cross Road, WC2H 0JR.

Phone:	020 7379 8877

Foyles

This favourite old institution now houses a brilliant jazz, with everything from traditional to avant-garde. An extensive collection of re-presses and originals.

Foyles, 113-119 Charing Cross Rd, WC2 H0EB.

Phone:	020 7437 5660
Email	customerservices@foyles.co.uk
Internet	www.foyles.co.uk

Heywood Hill

London's finest small bookshop and favourite haunt of the literati. Subject of a recent book by John Saumarez Smith. They will track down almost anything and post it on. Next door to Geo. Trumper, the world's most famous barber shop.

Heywood Hill, 10 Curzon St, W1J 5HH.

Phone:	020 7629 0647

Stanford Edward Ltd

The capital's leading travel book shop. Maps of everything. Truly encyclopaedic.

Stanford Edward Ltd, 12-14 Long Acre, WC2 E9LP.

Phone:	020 7836 1321

Waterstone's

Europe's largest bookstore complete with gallery, restaurant and even a bar with great London views. Combine this with a visit to Heywood Hill (see above) in Curzon St, Mayfair, and you will experience two extremes of London bookshop.

Waterstone's, 203-206 Piccadilly, W1J 9LE.

Phone:	020 7851 2400

DEPARTMENT STORES

Fortnum & Mason

Established in 1707 and holder of three Royal Warrants with five floors of luxury, Fortnum & Mason is legendary. The genteel ground floor, as well as the three restaurants, offer the very best in British regional foods. Afternoon Tea available from 3pm - 5pm daily. The world's best corner shop, as the swanky residents of nearby Albany apartments like to say.

Fortnum & Mason Plc, 181 Piccadilly, W1A 1ER.

Phone:	020 7734 8040
Email	info@fortnumandmason.co.uk
Internet	www.fortnumandmason.co.uk

Shopping: Department stores (cont)

Harrods

One of the world's most famous department stores, established in 1849 as a humble grocery store employing two assistants. Today, it offers everything from food to fashion, furniture to sportswear plus 20 in-store restaurants serving every kind of cuisine imaginable, from pizza to sushi. Services range from piano tuning to saddle fitting. Must-see sights include the Food Halls, the Egyptian Hall and the Pet Department. At night the store is illuminated by 11,500 light bulbs. Have a look at the Dodi-Diana shrine.

Harrods, 87-135 Brompton Road, Knightsbridge, SW1 X7XL.

Phone:	020 7730 1234
Internet	www.harrods.com

Selfridges

Selfridges is another of the world's finest department stores and dominates the west end of Oxford Street, as the picture shows. The shop runs to six floors that between them offer a staggering ten acres of shopping space, eleven places to eat, two exhibition halls and countless other services. From high fashion to hi-fi, wardrobe co-ordination to wedding lists, it's every shop you'll ever need within a single building.

Selfridges & Co, 400 Oxford Street, W1A 1AB.

Phone	0870 8377 377
Email	contactservices @selfridges.co.uk
Internet	www.selfridges.com

John Lewis

The store for sensible shoppers, which boasts the catchphrase "never knowingly undersold". It's great for finding life's little essentials, with a brilliant homes, kitchen and china department in the basement, plus fabrics buttons and crafts on the ground floor to nursery furniture and school uniforms of every conceivable shape and style. Whether you want towels, lights, electrical goods or masking tape John Lewis has it all. Opening times: Monday, Tuesday, Wednesday: 9.30am to 7pm. Thursday: 9.30am to 8pm. Friday, Saturday: 9.30am to 7pm.Sunday: 12noon to 6pm.

John Lewis, Oxford Street, W1 A1EX.

Phone	020 7629 7711
Email	jl_oxford_street@johnlewis.co.uk
Internet	www.johnlewis.co.uk

Liberty

Liberty's alluring window displays hint at the wealth of treasures to be found in the Regent Street store - Liberty print gifts and toys, ethnic jewellery, modern and antique furniture, oriental carpets and wares.

Liberty, 210-220 Regent Street, W1R 6AH.

Phone	020 7734 1234
Email	customerservices@liberty.co.uk
Internet	www.liberty.co.uk

Peter Jones

Recently re-launched after a five-year renovation, this much-loved department store on Sloane Square has been transformed into eight floors of shopping heaven. Peter Jones has always offered 'the best in everyday essentials and luxuries for modern living.' Now, as well as choosing from irresistible fashion and homeware, you can enjoy expert pampering in the beauty treatment rooms - or relax in the Top Floor restaurant, with its spectacular views over London. known for its well-informed services and spacious interior, Peter Jones is the place to come for shopping in style and comfort. **Peter Jones, Sloane Square, SW1 W8EL.**

Phone	020 7730 3434
Email	peter-jones@johnlewis.co.uk
Internet	www.peterjones.co.uk

FASHION

Designer Warehouse

The Designer Warehouse Sales hold five men's and five women's wear sales a year offering over 100 designer collections all reduced up to 80% off the original price. There are also two Nicole Farhi sales and one Ghost sale per year. For dates and further information, visit their website. **Designer Warehouse Sales, 45 Balfe Street Kings Cross, London, N1 9EF.**

Phone	020 7704 1064
Email	info@designerwarehousesales.com
Internet	www.designerwarehousesales.com

Seven Dials

Seven Dials is a leading destination for visitors in search of a shopping experience. There are many fashionable boutiques, cafes, gastro bars and designer houses. The area is a fashionable and exciting destination. Buying cutting edge designer clothes, hip vintage selections, the latest trainers or drinking in a fashionable bar; the area offers a unique experience. What sets this corner apart from other shopping areas is its location on the doorstep of Covent Garden. It is also steeped in history. Seven streets lead from the Dial; Main shopping streets are Earlham St, Monmouth and Shorts Gardens. Neal Street does not run directly from the Dial but also has many great boutiques and shops. Thomas Neal, a property speculator created the design of seven streets running off in 1690. Neal's Yard is named after him and today is home to an array of new age shops plus homeopathic remedy stores. **Seven Dials, Covent Garden London, WC2.**

Phone	020 7693 6963
Internet	www.sevendials.co.uk

Blackout II

When a place is this popular amongst cutting edge celebs and models, you know you're onto a winner. Stocking loads of vintage designer gear from whatever decade you choose, you can't fail to find/hire something your nostalgic heart desires. **Blackout II, 51 Endell St London WC2H9AJ.**

Phone	020 7240 5006

Burberry

Posh clothing for the outdoor types. Popular with Americans and, latterly, young thugs. Stylish, nonetheless.

Burberry Ltd, 21-23 New Bond St London, W1 S2RE.

Phone	020 7839 5222

Oxfam

For people who don't have time to rummage through rails of polyester slacks. Oxfam Originals cuts out the dodgy knitwear, and gets straight to retro sixties and seventies gear. Cool clothes you'll want to wear (but probably not to the office). **Oxfam, 26 Ganton St London, W1F7QZ.**

Phone	020 7437 7338

COSMETICS

Cosmetics a la carte

Cosmetics a la carte have pioneered custom beauty with skin tone matching and one-off colour creation. The make-up artists in the studio encourage customers to try before they buy in an easy atmosphere of shared tips and techniques.
Cosmetics a La Carte, 19b Motcom Street London, SW1 X8LB.

Phone	020 7235 0596
Email	cosmetics@cosmeticsalacarte.com
Internet	www.cosmeticsalacarte.com

Pout

You are encouraged to make use of the fabulous array of testers and the staff are easygoing. Great for gifts and hunting out unusual brands.
Pout, 28 Shelton St, WC2H 9JE.

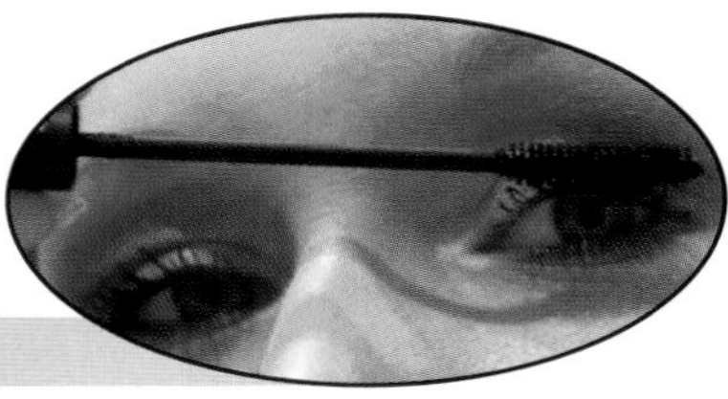

Phone	020 7557 9950

Refinery Ltd

A spa for men only - massages, facials and hairdressing. It's a natural progression from shampoo and conditioner instead of Wright's Coal Tar Soap. Perfectly above board pampering station.
Refinery Ltd, 60 Brook St, W1K 5DU.

Phone	020 7409 2001

MARKETS

Covent Garden Market

Covent Garden Market in the heart of London offers top quality shopping. Arts and crafts, street entertainment, a range of restaurants and cafes in an historic and entertaining setting.
Covent Garden Market, 41 The Market Covent Garden, WC2 E8RF.

Phone	020 7836 9136
Email	info@coventgardenmarket.co.uk
Inernet	www.coventgardenmarket.co.uk

Greenwich Market

Greenwich Market known for its designer makers and small cottage industries, many items cannot be found anywhere else. Enjoy the vibrant atmosphere, take in some classical music performed by students from nearby Trinity College of Music, and enjoy the continental food court whilst browsing more than 120 stalls.
Greenwich Market, College Approach London, SE10 9HZ.

Phone	020 8293 3110
Email	john.burton@urban-space.co.uk
Inernet	www.greenwichmarket.net

Brick Lane

New clothes, second hand goods. **Brick Lane Market, Brick Lane, London, E1.**

Phone:	020 7364 1717

Columbia Road Market

London's principal flower market selling plants, flowers, garden fittings and equipment. **Columbia Road Market, Columbia Road, E2 7RG.**

Petticoat Lane Market

Operating since the 1750s, Petticoat Lane market has more than a thousand stalls, specialising in clothes and household goods.
Petticoat Lane Market, between Middlesex and Goulston Streets, E1.

Phone	020 7364 1717

Portobello Road Market

Easily accessible from Notting Hill Gate, Ladbroke Grove and Westbourne Park tube stations and by bus routes servicing Ladbroke Grove and Notting Hill Gate. Main market days are Friday and Saturday with a smaller market running Monday to Thursday. An exciting day out for all the family. Opening Times: Open all year, Mon-Wed **0900-1900**, Thurs **0900-1300**, Fri-Sat **0900-1900**. Market open Good Friday but closed on other Bank Holidays. Ladbroke Grove: exit into Thorpe Close, then Lancaster Rd (east side). Westbourne Park: turn right out of station, 1st right into Tavistock Rd to junction with Portobello Rd. **Portobello Road Market and Golborne Road Market, Portobello Rd, W11 1AN.**

Phone	020 7727 7684

Camden Lock Market

Set next to Regents Canal, Camden Lock is one of London's top visitor attractions with it's unique shopping experience and cosmopolitan atmosphere. Open seven days a week (10.00am - 6.00pm, and 364 days of the year, closed Christmas Day), it offers an extensive range of high quality goods ranging from arts, crafts and clothes to accessories, food and furnishings. Just about anything you could conceivably want can be found somewhere among all the the craft workshops, stalls, shops, cafes restaurants and bars. The nearest tube stations are Camden Town and Chalk Farm (Northern Line).
Camden Lock Market, Camden Lock Place Chalk Farm Road, NW1 8AF.

Phone	020 7284 2084
Email	lock@norcam.demon.co.uk
Internet	www.camdenlockmarket.com

SHOPPING MALLS

West One Shopping Centre

West One Shopping Centre is in Oxford Street, the heart of the West Endand is open seven days a week. Situated above Bond Street underground station and has a variety of fashion, health and beauty and food outlets. There are a variety of cafes. Great for that last-minute purchase or a late quick snack.
West One Shopping Centre, 75 Davies Street, W1K 5JN.

Phone	020 7493 4820
Ineternet	www.westoneshopping.com

COMPUTERS

Head for Tottenham Court Road. Everything is here, from a large Apple shop to smaller outlets. Make sure you get a guarantee should you buy from one of the fast talking souks.

Shopping: (cont)

SHOPPING DISTRICTS

Canary Wharf

More than 200 shops, bars, cafes and restaurants can be found at **Canary Wharf** in the three shopping malls, as well as riverside locations. Stores cater for every need, ranging as they do from supermarkets and high street favourites through to independent boutiques and designer shops. Amongst the many names on show are Waitrose Food & Home, Reebok Sports Club London - the largest health club in Europe - and Marks & Spencer Food. Ladies fashion is well represented with a wide range of shops including Top Shop, Karen Millen, Whistles and Next with Thomas Pink, Cecil Gee, TM Lewin and Hackett amongst those catering for the gentlemen. Jubilee Place, the newest mall on the estate, opened in September 2003 and features Molton Brown, Choice, Reiss and Fiorelli stores among its wide and impressive range. **Canary Wharf, One Canada Square Canary Wharf, E14 5AB.**

Phone	020 7418 2000
Internet	www.mycanarywharf.com

Carnaby Streets

Cosmopolitan West Soho mixes designer fashion with cafe society and boasts health clubs, pubs, specialist shops and a street market. Made its name as a centre for fashion, which is reflected in the fact that there are more than 80 clothes shops in the complex. Everything is within easy walking distance of Oxford Circus, Tottenham Court Road and Piccadilly Circus Underground stations, has plenty of bus links with the rest of the city and, unusually for London, is even well served with nearby car parking.

Carnaby Streets, 46A Carnaby Street London, W1F 9PS.

Phone	020 7287 9601
Internet	www.carnaby.co.uk

The Old Truman Brewery's

The Old Truman Brewery's retail village is home to some of the most exciting outlets in London. Along its pedestrianised lanes cafes sit alongside hairdressers, fashion boutiques, organic delis and vintage scooter shops. In the evenings Londoners descend upon the Old Truman Brewery's popular nightspots for some of the coolest nights out. Between the Vibe Bar, live music venue 93 Feet East, Café 1001, and the Big Chill Bar & Restaurant, there is something to suit everyone's tastes. The Old Truman Brewery is also home to Sunday (Up)Market, London's newest weekly indoor market for fashion, lifestyle, accessories, home-wares, art, food, drink and much more. A unique ambience that cannot be compared with anything else in London.

Old Truman Brewery, 91 Brick Lane London, E1 6QL.

Phone	020 7770 6100
Email	events@trumanbrewery.com
Internet	www.trumanbrewery.com

Hamleys

Established in 1760 as a toy emporium which has over the years built an international reputation for the innovative and imaginative toys. **Hamleys of London Limited, 188-196 Regent St, London W1B 5BT and Heathrow Airport.**

Phone	020 8897 1524
Email	marketing@hamleys.co.uk
Internet	www.hamleys.co.uk

EAT, DRINK & SLEEP

CENTRAL LONDON

(Soho, Westminster, Knightsbridge, Marylebone, Covent Garden & Fitzrovia)

BARS

The name Fitzrovia was coined by the artists and writers, such as Dylan Thomas and George Orwell, who frequented the Fitzroy Tavern in Charlotte Street between World War I and II. The dignified Fitzroy Square was named after Henry Fitzroy, the son of Charles II, and later Earl of Euston. It is basically the area around the Post Office Tower which hovers above the West End like a futuristic mosque.

TRADITIONAL PUBS

Bear & Staff, 11 Bear St, Soho, WC2H 7AX.
Near to Charing Cross underground, heading towards the bright lights of Soho, Adnams, Draught Bass, Fuller's, Greene King plus guests.

Buckingham Arms, 62 Petty France, Westminster, SW1H 9EU.
18th century hostelry with a large saloon and a special drinking corridor for where the staff of toffs could drink out of sight of their masters.

Carpenters Arms, 12 Seymour Place, Marylebone, W1H 7NE.
Sports pub offering a wide range of beers. Good spot to watch the game. Fuller's beers.

Cask & Glass, 39 Palace St, Victoria, SW1E 5HN.
Smallest pub in the Westminster area. Model planes above bar and dates back to 1862. Shepherd Neame beers.

Coach & Horses, 29 Greek St, Soho, W1D 5DH.
Famous for having London's 'rudest landlord' (Norman Balon, who has just retired, was in charge for longer than the average customer's liver holds out) this pub is an institution, a monument to Bohemian behaviour. Private Eye hosts its lunches here and the late Jeffrey Bernard's frequent bouts of 'unwellness' coincided with visits. If you were to ask them to turn the racing over for the rugby, you'd be told to fuck off. Be warned. Fullers, Marstons, Tetleys, not always in that order.

Dog & Duck, 18 Bateman St, Soho, W1D 3AF.
Oldest pub in Soho, dating back to 1777 when this area was a bog, and passing huntsmen made the cry 'So Ho'. According to CAMRA's Good Beer Guide, it is Madonna's favourite London hostelry.

Duke of Wellington, 94A Crawford St, Marylebone, 1H 2HQ.
Lots of memorabilia of the Duke, including a cheque written in 1828. Adnams and Wells beers.

Duke of Wellington, 63 Eaton Terrace, Belgravia, SW1W 8TR.
Close to Victoria coach station this place is owned by the Shepherd Neame brewery. Built in 1826 it is basically a locals' pub.

Endurance, 90 Berwick St, Soho, W1F 0QB.
Stylish and spacious once you get inside. Good food.

Bars: Central London (cont)

Fox & Hounds, 29 Passmore St, Belgravia, SW1W 8HR.
Young's beers. Refurbished but retains character.

Harp, 47 Chandos Place, Covent Garden, WC2N 4HS.
You'll see a harp depicted in leading on the front window. Handy for theatres, not to mention Fuller's and Harveys.

Hope, 15 Tottenham St, West End, W1T 2AJ.
Just behind the Tottenham Court Road (Goodge St tube) this is a basic back street boozer serving Adnams, Fullers, Taylor Landlord.

Jugged Hare, 172 Vauxhall Bridge Rd, Victoria, SW1V 1DX.
Fuller's Ale & Pie pub in a converted bank on the busy Vauxhall Bridge Road.

Nag's Head, 53 Kinnerton St, Belgravia, SW1X 8ED.
Lovely mews pub on two levels serving Adnam beers from Southwold in Suffolk.

One Tun, Goodge St, West End, W1T 4ND.
Now owned by Young's brewery there's a pool table at this popular locals' pub.

Pillars of Hercules, 7 Greek St, W1D 4DJ.
Referred to by Charles Dickens in A Tale Of Two Cities, there has been a Pillars of Hercules on this site since 1733. It is a busy and fun place with several beers to choose from.

Star Tavern, 6 Belgrave Mews West, Belgravia, SW1X 8HT.
Another mews pub just off Belgrave Square (just a stone's throw from Harrods). Delightful spot full of character.

Ship, 116 Wardour St, Soho, W1F 0TT (closed Sunday).
Popular with those who like loud music. Fuller's pub. Hip and fun.

Wargrave Arms, 40-42 Brendon St, Marylebone, W1H 5HE.
Good place to watch the game if you are ticketless. There's music on a Friday and chess is popular. Food available. Young's brewery.

Westminster Arms, 9 Storey's Gate, Westminster, SW1P 3AT.
Bang next door to the concrete QEII conference centre, bells are often to be heard interrupting conversation. These are the division bells for voting at the nearby Houses of Parliament.

TRENDY BARS

On Anon, London Pavilion Piccadilly Circus, W1V 9LA.
The most versatile and flexible choice for any celebration. Eight distinct areas, each with its own design, style and personality; Onanon offers a choice of bars and music until 3am. The lounge, loft lodge, raffles, studio bar, study, and club offer cool contemporary and sophisticated surroundings for your party with stunning views over Piccadilly Circus.

Phone	020 7287 8008
Email	info@onanon.co.uk
Internet	www.latenightlondon.co.uk

Oxygen, 18 Irving Street Leicester Square, WC2H 7AZ.
Oxygen is open seven nights a week blending a fusion of tunes that you know with ones that you'd forgotten. Three floors of classic and cutting edge sounds. Open to 3am and the only licensed retailer of pure oxygen in London.

Phone	020 7930 0907
Email	info@oxygenbar.co.uk
Internet	www.latenightlondon.co.uk

The Loop, 19 Dering St London, W1S 1AH.
Don't be deceived by the deceptively small bar on the ground floor because underneath lies a venue with the most happening tunes and a lively crowd. The middle floor is occupied by a lounge/chill-out area. 1am on Thu, Fri and Sat.

Phone	020 7493 1003

Ruby Blue, 1 Leicester Place, Leicester Square, WC2H 7BP.
The beautiful Ruby Blue combines subtle pastel furnishings; an airy interior and contemporary art with well thought out lighting, Ruby Blue offers a wide range of dishes that will suit all but the most difficult to please. Booth seating encourages a cosy atmosphere. The club's full drinks list is shared by the restaurant. Happy Hour from 5 to 7pm. No under 18's allowed.

Sugar Reef, 42 Great Windmill St , W1D 7NB.
This is an exclusive haunt and the patrons are expected to pay for that privilege, inside you'll find a good atmosphere combined with the occasional B-List celebrity. The drink and cocktail list is extensive if not extortionate.

Phone	020 7851 0800

Sway , 61-65 Great Queen St London, WC2B 5BZ.
Another smart bar with prices to match although there is a great happy hour. Late opening times provide the opportunity to drink as much as you can hold. Bar food is varied from tapas to more traditional main courses.

Phone	020 7404 6114

Aint Nothin But Blues Bar, 20 Kingly St London, W1B 5PZ.
Specialises in original blues, with live performers every night. The atmosphere is relaxed and friendly. Musicians and music-lovers alike come and enjoy a few drinks.

Phone	020 7287 0514

Bar Gansa, 2 Inverness St London, NW1 7HJ.
An out and out Spanish bar where the impression given is that as much pride is taken in authenticity as appearance. Extensive list of Spanish red wines and great tapas menu.

Phone	020 7267 8909

Bartok, 78-79 Chalk Farm Road London, NW1 8AR.
A classical music bar is far from the norm these days, however for those who care for Schubert with their sherry are bound to enjoy the relaxed ambience and genteel surroundings. One to look out for if you fancy something a little less run of the mill.

Phone	020 7916 0595

Boardwalk Soho,18 Greek St London, W1V 5LF.
One of the least pretentious establishments in this locale, more suited to hardcore drinkers than those wishing to spend a night amongst wheelers and dealers. Lively atmosphere and a sure fire hit if you want to drink and be merry rather than spend and be broke.

Phone	020 7287 2051

Cheers, 72 Regent St London, W1B 5RJ.
Themed bar along the same lines as the one featured in the hit US comedy. Populated by lost looking tourists who are taking shelter from all the manic activity of Regent Street. Hit-and-miss location that is more of tourist trap than a genuine bar.

Phone	020 7494 3322

The Couch, 97-99 Dean St London, W1D 3TE.
The Couch Bar offers a varied menu of International dishes at affordable prices. As the name suggests they offer comfortable surroundings whether you are looking for lunch, dinner or simply a drink.

Phone	020 7287 0150

Trendy bars Central London (cont)

Digress, 10 Beak St, W1F 9RA.

Digress fits the bill for a trouble-free drinking session. Often quieter than the rest of its Soho neighbours, so more suited to those who are not in the mood for a full throttle evening. Food served all night.

Phone	020 7437 0239

Freedom Brewing Co, 41 Earlham St, WC2H 9LD.

A change of name and owner for this Covent Garden cellar bar. Still a microbrewery and still has the brewing apparatus visible behind glass walls.

Phone	020 7240 0606

The French House, 49 Dean St London, W1D 5BG.

A cornerstone of theatreland for actors. Good selection of lager and ales, but they only do half pints. Francis Bacon, Brendan Behan and General De Gaulle were here and Dylan Thomas reputedly lost the manuscript for Under Milkwood. A fine place

Phone	020 7437 2477

Fuel, 21 The Market/Covent Garden London, WC2E 8RD.

In the centre of the piazza, a labyrinth of cubbyholes and caves. Cosy early evening tends to be more couples than anyone else. Fills up later with young professionals out for fun. Relaxed door policy and great cocktails, an upbeat atmosphere and late licence.

Phone	020 7836 2137

The Roundhouse, 1 Garrick St, WC2E 9BF.

A favourite meeting place in Covent Garden (it's easy to find) this pub provides a pretty decent service given the circumstances - ie hordes of tourists. Not one to linger in, but handy.

Phone	020 7836 9838

The Warwick, 1-2 Warwick St, W1B 5LR.

A little late opening bar, from Wednesday to Saturday when the dark, downstairs bar is open, things are carefree and unpretentious. You'll need to pay admission after 10pm on Fri and Sat but upstairs has large windows, and good views of the local street life.

Phone	020 7734 4409

The Soho Lounge, 69 Dean St, W1D 3SE.

This very intimate lounge bar and night club is a new entry to the Soho scene. Staff will accommodate your catering needs, from canapés or platters to sushi to traditional dining. Cocktails are unique and very good. The bar staff are friendly and experienced.

Phone	020 7734 1231

Moon Under Water, 28 Leicester Sq, WC2 H7LE.

One of the smaller Wetherspoons, which is surprising, given the location. As ever (for a Wetherspoons pub), cheap booze and food, without the distractions of music, pool and TV. However, its claustrophobic interior (low ceilings), means it is very, very noisy. The service is prompt and attentive and it's easy for your out-of-town mates to find - you could do far worse in the immediate vicinity.

Phone	020 7839 2837

Tiger Tiger, 29 Haymarket, SW1 Y4SP.

The rooms, bars and restaurant of Tiger Tiger combine laid back lunches, vibrant early evening drinking and sexy,. chic late nights. Focused on guest lists, booth bookings and free event hire, a unique experience either as a midweek hangout or weekend destination. Set over several floors, the contemporary restaurant, laid-back lounge, funky Kaz Bar and upbeat club each have their own style, decor and soundtrack. Open from midday until late, with a goor reputation.

Phone	020 7930 1885
Email	info@tigertiger.co.uk

CLUBS

Soho, Westminster, Knightsbridge, Marylebone, Covent Garden & Fitzrovia

Astoria, 157 Charing Cross Road, WC2H 0EN.
The big names play and the medium names watch. Catch the stars on their way to stadium success and mingle with an excited B-list of punters.

Phone	020 8963 0940

Zoo Bar, 13-17 Bear Street, WC2H 7A8.
Formulaic and dull populated by confused drunk tourists and teenagers keen on anywhere they can gain admission, good deals on pitchers and predictable selection of lagers.

Phone	020 7839 4188

Attica, 24 Kingly St, W1B 5QP.
Has fallen from grace in recent times but ok if you're willing to pay through the nose. Nothing to distinguish it from other similarly pretentious estalishments.

Phone	020 7287 5882

Bar Rumba, 36 Shaftsbury Ave, W1D 7EP.
A small club in the heart of Soho with a loyal following. Best known for Monday's THIS! (That's How It Is), where DJ Gilles Peterson and colleagues Ben Wilcox and Raw Deal push the envelope with an eclectic mix of drum 'n' bass, jazz, hip hop and global beats. There is a dress code - no jeans or trainers on a Saturday.

Phone	020 7287 2715

The Borderline, Orange Yard, Manette Street, W1D 4JB.
A small venue with a huge reputation. The likes of Oasis, Pearl Jam, REM, Crowded House, Ryan Adams, Blur, Pulp, Suede, Dawn of the Replicants and Texas have all performed here.

Phone	020 7734 2095

The Gardening Club, 4 The Piazza, WC2E 8HB.
Things here are pretty much as they should be. The two venues join force for club nights throughout the week, there's still a bit of live music in the Rock Garden on Sundays. Food is desperately average and the clientele definitely don't hail from these parts. Still, if you don't take yourself too seriously, there's plenty to amuse.

Phone	020 7497 3153/4

Sound, 10 Wardour Street, W1D 6QF.
Home of the Pepsi chart, this is a bar, club and restaurant which does well despite the Leicester Square location. Fun, loud, youthful and exuberant. There's a large dance floor, a happy hour and with some really well executed club nights.

Phone	020 7287 1010

Cafe de Paris, 3-4 Coventry Street, W1 D6BL.
A flow of young things with cash to flash and reputations to taint fills these lavish surroundings. If you don't want to pay a small fortune for a table/dinner you'll have to get onto the dance floor where personal space is an outdated concept.

Phone	020 7734 7700

Propaganda Bar, 201 Wardour St, W1F 8ZH.
Opened a while back in the wake of Reggie Reggie's Soul Café, Propaganda has proved itself to be a hell of a lot more than just the new kid on the Soho block. With a massive capacity, late licence, slick design, random indoor garden and an excellent mix of club nights, the most recent addition being Leeds northern soul night. Move on Up, this place rocks.

Phone	0207 434 3820

Twelve Bar Club, 23 Denmark Place, WC2H 8NL.
Still an excellent place for aspiring acts to cut their teeth. An intimate little venture where music, mainly acoustic, comes first. Hear some of London's finest artists.

Phone	020 7916 6989

RESTAURANTS

Soho, Westminster, Knightsbridge, Marylebone, Covent Garden & Fitzrovia

Benihana, 37 Sackville Street, Marylebone, W1.

Japanese Benihana specialises in the fine art of Teppanyaki cookery. Red-capped chefs dazzle with juggling and knife skills as they cook a variety of succulent meat, crisp vegetables and fresh seafood at the diner's teppan table.

Phone	020 7494 2525

Chowki, 2-3 Denman St, W1D 7HA.

This place defies the laws of finance: it's a chi-chi setting just yards from Piccadilly Circus; it serves first class food from all over the Indian sub-continent; it has a short but good wine list; it's comfortable and even fashionable. And yet it is cheap. How can this be? The answer is its turnover. Despite appearing cosy and small, it seats 120 upstairs and down, and averages three sittings a day. A typical meal might comprise lamb mince samosas with liver and spices, from Delhi; Prawn patties crumbed and golden fried with a hint of mint and pepper, from Bombay; and Tilapia fillet marinated in turmeric, red chilli and garlic, gram flour batter fried and served with mint chutney from Madras. ITV Restaurant of the Year award winner.

Basic price	£15
Phone	020 7439 1330
Internet	www.chowki.com

Christopher's, 18 Wellington St, Covent Garden, WC2E 7DD.

Very Upper East Side: cool, sophisticated and glamorous. The Bloody Marys are enough to conquer a hangover of heroic proportions. Some say it's the best New England outside Boston. Try smoked tomato soup, then blackened salmon and jambalaya. Banana tart tatin with rum and raisin ice cream is a triumph.

Basic price	£45
Phone	020 7976 5522
Internet	www.christophersgrill.com

Citrus Restaurant, Piccadilly, W1J 7BX.

Next to the Sheraton Park Lane Hotel in Piccadilly, this good all-round Mediterranean restaurant commands views Green Park. Flavours of France, Italy, Greece, Spain and Morocco. Popular with Mayfair residents, despite its modest prices. 60 seats run by Andrew Bennett, an experienced 5-star hotel chef. Try the starter of scallops stuffed with foie gras and broccoli, followed by poached (corn fed) chicken, ricotta gnocchi and girolles mushrooms and finish with Rhubarb, saffron and honey tart with cardamom infused cream to get a typical flavour.

Basic price	£25
Phone	020 7499 6321
Email	izania.downie@starwoodhotels.com
Internet	www.sheraton.com/parklane

Deca, 23 Conduit St, Fitzrovia, W1S 2XS. £20 plus.

Deca is part of the great Nico Ladenis empire. The Michelin 3-star chef may have retired, but his patronage lives on. His two daughters run the show (plus Incognico in Shaftesbury Avenue). Set in a converted period Mayfair building, the dining room and the service are formal but the interior is modern. The food is formal French. Roast pepper stuffed with feta and foie gras, duck breast with honey and peppercorns, or beef fillet with mustard and tarragon sauce. Options available for pud: lemon tart with raspberry coulis, prune and Armagnac ice cream plus a reckless chocolate mousse. The wines are terrific, as are the prices.

Phone	020 7493 7070

L'Escargot, 48 Greek St, Soho, W1D 4EF.

There are two-restaurants-in-one at this venerable culinary institution, now run by Marco Pierre White and his business partner. L'Escargot has survived many distinguished ownerships and has been for a long time one of the better French establishments in town. Now the Picasso Room, upstairs, specialises in more formal (and expensive) dining, while the Ground Floor restaurant runs a stylish brasserie. Genuine Picasso and Matisse offerings. Both score highly in the Good Food Guide and both are under the skilled eye of rising star Jeff Galvin. There are too many dishes to begin listing. Well worth 'le detour', as Michelin would say.

Basic price	£50
Phone	020 7439 7474

Galileo's Ristorante Bar Italiano, 71 Haymarket, Soho, SW1Y 4RW.
A trendy restaurant bar in Haymarket, serving great Italian food with an extensive Italian aperitif menu. Reopened last year, with a new bar area where you can eat, drink, discuss life and business over an extensive list of classic Italian cocktails, campari based. The bar area is smart and very bright with a mixed crowd of local office workers and theatregoers. The restaurant menu is simply good food and unpretentious, and the wine offer is available by the glass.

Basic price	£25
Phone	020 7839 3939
Internet	www.metroreStreetcom

The Gay Hussar, 2 Greek Street, Soho, W1D 4NB.
The Gay Hussar is a London institution, famous as an old Labour party hangout and popular with the older generation of West End thespian. It also serves some very good and robust Hungarian cooking in a warm and cosy atmosphere. There are intimate dining rooms upstairs, and the service is old-fashioned and courteous. Smoked goose breast; fish dumplings; poached pike perch; beef goulash soup.

Basic price	£30
Phone	020 7437 0973

Getti, 42 Marylebone High Street, Fitzrovia, W1.
Getti is set on two floors and has the right ambience for all occasions. Cosy alcoves make it perfect for intimate romantic evenings or for important business lunches.

Basic price	£30
Phone	020 7486 3753

The Langley, 5 Langley Street, Covent Garden, WC2H 9JA.
Enjoy the classic retro styling of The Langley, comfort food, classic cocktails and funky tunes provide the backdrop to a unique experience in Covent Garden until 1am. The private rooms and booths of The Langley offer a comfortable and popular hideaway for late night drinks in stunning surroundings.

Basic price	£25
Phone	020 7836 5005

Restaurants: Central London (cont)

Locanda Locatelli 30 Portman Square, Fitzrovia, W1.
Locanda Locatelli offers a menu typical of Chef Giorgio Locatelli's style – simple sophistication and subtlety. Fresh pasta features on the menu and dishes are determined by seasonal produce.

Phone	020 7486 5800

The Loop, 19 Dering Street, Hanover Square, Mayfair, W1R 9AA.
Spread over 3 floors and offering a sexier environment than your average bar, a livelier environment than most restaurants and a relaxed upbeat but unpretentious club, playing a wide range of pop classics with commercial dance. The restaurant features dishes such as grilled goat's cheese potato rusti, cod and dill fish cakes and pan fried fillet steak. Larger groups can benefit from a set menu at £22.95 before enjoying the bars until late.

Cost	£22.95 set menu for groups
Phone	020 7493 1003
Email	info@theloopbar.co.uk
Internet	www.latenightlondon.co.uk

Maggiore's, 33 King Street, Covent Garden, WC2E 8JD.
Well known for its award-winning 1,500-choice wine list. Food inspired by country inns of Provence and Tuscany and Maggiore's offers a romantic and cosy spot. Winter log fires, summer courtyard. Try slow-cooked pork belly with carrot puree and glazed salsify, or braised fillet of turbot in red wine with fondue of leeks and Parisienne potatoes.

Basic price	£20
Phone	020 7379 9696
Internet	www.maggiores.uk.com

Motion, Hungerford House, Victoria Embankment, WC2N 6PA.
Set over two floors, Motion blends contemporary slick styling with deep and comfortable furniture to create a unique and funky environment for over 21s. Open late every night with contemporary blend of current pop, dance classics and upbeat funky tunes; Motion is set to offer a fun and stylish experience for any occasion.

Phone	020 7389 9933
Email	manager@motion-bar.co.uk
Internet	www.latenightlondon.co.uk

Maharani, 77 Berwick St, Soho, W1F 8TH.
Venerable Indian institution on the doorstep of Berwick Street's famous market, it will not win any interior design awards, but its curries are carefully put together and diverse. Try the jalpari kabab (halibut fish rolls stuffed with king prawns, matured in creamed yoghurt, with saffron and coriander) and paneer mirch masala (fresh cottage cheese tossed with lots of garlic, chillies, peppers, mint and onion).

Basic price	£15
Phone	020 7437 8568

Palm Court, Sheraton Park Lane Hotel, Piccadilly, W1J 7BX.
The Palm Court is at the heart of the hotel. In addition to traditional afternoon English Tea this is a prime Mayfair spot 'to see and be seen'. Offers an enticing menu selection, fine champagne, cognac, caviar, cigars and lively music.

Phone	020 7290 7170
Email	izania.downie@starwoodhotels.com
Inernet	www.sheraton.com/parklane

Poons, 4 Leicester St, Soho, WC2H 7BL.
Chinese landmark, this cavernous restaurant has specialised in cheap but cheerful food for a long time. Service is perfunctory but efficient and fast. Fish dishes well executed though recent reports have suggested a lack of consistency.

Phone	020 7437 1528

La Porte des Indes, 32 Bryanston Street, Fitzrovia, W1.
French/Indian La Porte des Indes is a restaurant resplendent with palm trees, exotic flowers and antiques, serving Indian cuisine 'with a difference' and French Creole specialities from Panicherry.

Phone	020 7224 0055

The Providores, 109 Marylebone High St, Fitzrovia, W1.
World Tapas. The Providores has two dining areas provide totally different dining experiences with food presided over by Peter Gordon (ex Sugar Club chef) and Anna Hansen. The Tapa room is an all-day café/wine bar while the Providores is a first floor dining area.

Phone	020 7935 6175

Ruby Blue, 1 Leicester Place, Leicester Square, London WC2H 7BP.
Ruby Blue aims to offer an interesting eating experience, combining it's new funky design with bold décor and a relaxed atmosphere. Its ambitious goal is to offer fun and informality in an efficient environment, but that's for you to judge. With a Happy Hour from 5pm till 7pm their mission is to provide a one-stop-shop.

Basic price	£25
Phone	020 7287 8050
Internet	www.rubybluebar.com

Savoy Grill, The Savoy, Strand, WC2R 0EU.
Since reopening in May 2003 after a stunning refurbishment, the Savoy Grill is thriving. The famous and beloved banquettes have been dressed in bold stripes, the silver-leaf ceiling adds a touch of drama and the rich wood panelling has been restored to its original cognac shades. Although the décor is breathtaking, the food continues to take centre stage. Under the guiding hand of Marcus Wareing, one of the country's premier chefs, is modern European.

Basic price	£50
Phone	020 7592 1600
Internet	www.fairmont.com/savoy

Red Fort, 77 Dean St, W1D 3SH.
One of the West End's great Indian eateries, the Fort has been around for years and serves up consistently reliable dishes from across the subcontinent. Anglo shades - seared Scottish salmon and Orkney lamb with attitude. Expensive.

Phone	020 7437 2525

Stanleys, 6 Little Portland Square, W1.
Stanleys restaurant and lively bar specialises in handmade sausages and a fantastic range of draught and bitter beers. Excellent value in London's West End.

Phone	020 7462 0099

Sugar Reef, 42-44 Great Windmill Street, Piccadilly Circus, W1D 7NB.
Sugar Reef offers great food, classic cocktails and late night dancing all set to a funky soundtrack. Designed to be accessible by all and enjoyed by most, the Happy Hour from 5 to 7pm cuts the cost of wines and cocktails.

Phone	020 7851 0800
Email	info@sugarreef.net

Sway, 61-65 Great Queen Street, Covent Garden, WC2H 5BZ.
Bars, stylish restaurant and funky club all rolled into one, this is a place for eating, drinking, dancing or all three. The restaurant features dishes such as garlic sautéed tiger prawns, chilli crusted lamb cutlets and baked leek and parmesan tartlet. Groups can can take the set menu at £25.95.

Phone	020 7404 6114
Email	info@swaybar.co.uk
Internet	www.latenightlondon.co.uk

Restaurants: Central London (cont)

YMing, 35-36 Greek Street, Soho, W1D 5DL.
Genuine cooking from the northern provinces of China, away from the tourist traps of Chinatown, the other side of Shaftesbury Avenue. Crab with salt and pepper is golden, juicy bricks of crab scattered with salt and pepper and garlic to make a sweet and piquant dish, or the double braised pork hot pot: a rich broth of wintry veg with strips of slow cooked meat so soft there's no need to chew. 'Village duck', come with lily flowers and shiitake mushrooms in a fermented bean curd sauce, and a fine spicy-sour stir-fry of Chinese cabbage.

Phone	020 7734 2721
Email	info@yminglondon.com
Internet	www.yminglondon.com

Lindsay House, 21 Romilly Street, W1.
British/Irish Lindsay House is headed by award winning chef, Richard Corrigan, and is a quirky Soho success story. The modern British cooking recalls his Irish roots and fits perfectly into the vibrant West End dining scene.

Phone	020 7439 0450

Delhi, Brasserie 44 Frith Street, W1.
Indian Delhi Brasserie is renowned for high standards of food and service, this Indian restaurant is ideally situated in Soho for pre and post-theatre dinners.

Phone	020 7437 8261

Masala Zone, 9 Marshall Street, W1.
Masala Zone serves real Indian food at excellent prices. It is a new, casual dining experience specialising in authentic Indian street food.

Phone	020 7287 9966

HOTELS

Soho, Westminster, Belgravia, Marylebone, Covent Garden & Fitzrovia

LUXURY

Berkeley, Wilton Place, SW1X 7RL.
214 rooms. £433 s. £492 t/d. £3,642 top suite. Breakfast extra. Knightsbridge. Ideal for shops in Knightsbridge and Sloane Street Boasts Gordon Ramsay's Boxwood Café and Marcus Wareing's Pétrus restaurant. The Blue Bar is one of London's hottest spots for cocktails.

Phone	020 7235 6000
Email	info@the-berkeley.co.uk
Internet	www.the-berkeley.co.uk

City Inn, Westminster, John Islip Street, SW1P 4PX.
460 rooms. £163 s. £193 d/t. Westminster.
City Inn is one of central London's newest and largest hotel. Views of the Houses of Parliament, the London Eye and the city's easterly skyline.

Phone	020 7630 1000
Email	westminster@cityinn.com
Internet	www.cityinn.com

Claridge's, Brook Street, Mayfair, W1A 2JQ.
203 rooms. From £200 s/d/t. Epitome of grand English style following its restoration by English Heritage. Now hailed as the Art Deco jewel of Mayfair. The omnipresent star chef Gordon Ramsay oversees the restaurant.

Phone	020 7629 8860
Email	info@claridges.co.uk
Internet	www.claridges.co.uk

Connaught Hotel, Carlos Place, W1K 2AL.
95 rooms. £329 s. £464 d/t. Top suite £1,530.
Surrounded by antique shops, churches and a quiet public garden, plus two of London's loveliest squares, Grosvenor and Berkeley, the Connaught is near Bond Street and the West End stores. Restaurant is one of London's best

Phone	020 7499 7070
Email	info@the-connaught.co.uk
Internet	www.the-connaught.co.uk

Chesterfield Mayfair, 35 Charles St, W1J 5EB.
110 rooms. £265 s. £350 d/t. £620 suite. Breakfast extra. Green Park.
In the heart of Mayfair, a short stroll to Bond Street, Regent Street and Oxford Street.

Phone	020 7491 2622
Email	bookch@rchmail.com
Internet	www.chesterfieldmayfair.com

Dolphin Square Hotel, Dolphin Sq, Pimlico, SW1V 3LX.
148 rooms. £205 single. 3-bed suite sleeping 6, £450.
Set in 3 acres of glorious private gardens in the heart of London, the Dolphin is bordered by the River Thames and the busy back lanes of Westminster. An all-suite Hotel, each suite has a kitchen and most have a separate sitting rooms. The range of health and fitness facilities is unrivalled; the air-conditioned gym is suitable for all types and levels of exercise. It is fully equipped with a comprehensive range of free weights and the latest cardio vascular & resistance equipment. Allium, the hotel's fine dining restaurant, offers contemporary European cooking from the kitchen of Chef Owner, the legendary Anton Edelmann. Alternatively the brasserie, overlooking the hotel swimming pool, serves breakfast, lunch and dinner in a relaxed, informal atmosphere.

Phone	020 7834 3800
Email	reservations@dolphinsquarehotel.co.uk
Internet	www.dolphinsquarehotel.co.uk

Dorchester, Park Lane, W1K 1QA.
250 rooms from £275 s, £375 d/t. Hyde Park Corner.
Built in 1931, London's Dorchester hotel was designed as the perfect grand hotel; ultra-modern in its convenience, traditional in its atmosphere and service. Relaunched in 2003 following a multi million pound refurbishment.

Phone	020 7629 8888
Email	reservations@ dorchesterhotel.com
Internet	www.dorchesterhotel.com

Dorset Sq, 39-40 Dorset Sq, Marylebone, NW1 6QN.
37 rooms. From £125 s. £175 double £195 twin. (prices exclude VAT & breakfast).
Maybe a touch expensive but it is full of character and lies in a quiet square on the site of the original Lords cricket ground. Michelin describes this hotel as a 'country house in the city.'

Phone	020 7723 7874
Email	reservations@ dorsetsquare.co.uk
Internet	www.dorsetsquare.co.uk

Durrants, 26-32 George St, Marylebone, W1H 5BJ.
88 rooms. From £155 d/t. Single room £115. Bond St, Baker Street Smart and reasonable family run hotel – has been with the Millers since 1921. Very British, has changed little since it first opened in 1790 (though the creature comforts have come on somewhat).

Phone	020 7935 8131
Email	enquries@durrantshotel.co.uk
Internet	www.durrantshotel.co.uk

ENGLAND

Hotels: Central London (cont)

Grosvenor House, 90 Park Lane, W1K 7TN.
378 rooms. From £235 s/d/t. Hyde Park Corner.
Overlooks Hyde Park and is full of Edwardian style and charm. Boasts a swimming pool and Europe's largest ballroom. Afternoon tea, cocktail bar etc. Lots going on.

Phone	020 7499 6363
Internet	www.marriott.co.uk

Halkin, Halkin St, SW1X 7DJ.
41 rooms. £376 s/d/t. £405 king size. £465 deluxe. Junior suite £600. Conservatory suite £820. Double bedroom suite £1300. Hyde Park Corner.
This establishment is ultra-contemporary and very stylish. Another place for celebrity spotting, though this may be tricky as even the staff are kitted out in Armani.

Phone	020 7333 1000
Email	res@halkin.como.bz
Internet	www.halkin.como.bz

Hampshire, Leicester Square, Soho, WC2H 7LH.
119 rooms. From £209 s/d/t – normal rack rate £432. Leicester Sq.
Relaxing retreat in the frenetic midst of Soho. Formidably expensive unless you can negotiate a deal for yourself. Trouser presses included – and throwaway slippers, if you want to splash out the price on a Superior Room.

Phone	020 7839 9399
Email	reshamp@radisson.com
Internet	www.radissonedwardian.com

Hazlitt's, 6 Frith St, Soho, W1D 3JA.
22 rooms. From £199 s/d/t. Leicester Square.
Former home of William Hazlitt, the essayist. You can stay in the Earl of St Albans' bedroom. A beautifully restored and stylish Queen Anne period piece.

Phone	020 7434 1771
Email	reservations@hazlitts.co.uk
Internet	www.hazlittshotel.com

Kingsway Hall, 66 Great Queen St, WC2B 5BX.
170 rooms. From £200 s/d/t
In the heart of Covent Garden, and minutes away from Holborn and Covent Garden underground stations. Also close to the City and the Eurostar Terminal at Waterloo.

Phone	020 7309 0909
Email	enquiries@kingswayhall.co.uk
Internet	www.kingswayhall.co.uk

Lowndes Hotel, 21 Lowndes St, SW1 X9ES.
78 rooms. From £200 s, £315 d/t. Junior suite: £435. Executive suite: £585.
In the heart of Belgravia offering afternoon tea, fine food and all the facilities of its sister hotel, the Carlton Tower, across the road (spa, fully equipped gym, swimming pool etc). Knightsbridge Station.

Phone	020 7823 1234
Email	contact@lowndeshotel.com
Internet	www.lowndeshotel.com

Le Meridien Piccadilly, 21 Piccadilly, W1J 0BH.
266 rooms. From £135 s/d/t. Five star international comfort in the heart of the West End and near the financial district. Rooms have everything you could possibly need.

Phone	0870 400 8400
Email	impiccres@lemeridien-hotels.com
Internet	www.lemeridien-piccadilly.com

Metropolitan, 19 Old Park Lane, W1K 1LB.
From £275 d/t - £2,450. The Metropolitan is contemporary in style and attracts a fashionable market. Nobu, the Japanese restaurant and the chic Met Bar, are on site.

Phone	020 7447 1000
Email	res@metropolitan.co.uk
Internet	www.metropolitan.co.uk

Millennium Hotel, 39-44 Grosvenor Sq, W1K 2HP.
From £229 single. £323 d/t. Green Park. Offers traditional British hospitality with unobtrusive yet friendly service. Conveniently situated for the historic sites, London theatreland and prime shopping areas.

Phone	020 7629 9400
Email	reservations.mayfair@mill-cop.com
Internet	www.millenniumhotels.com/mayfair

One Aldwych, 1 Aldwych, WC2B 4RH.
From £250 s/d/t.
Temple, Charing Cross.
Contemporary hotel in a great location in Covent Garden, two lively restaurants and a swimming pool. Sauna, steam room, beauty/therapy treatments etc.

Phone	020 7300 1000
Email	sales@onealdwych.com
Internet	www.onealdwych.com

Park Lane Hotel, Piccadilly, W1J 7BX
S/d/t from £150. Piccadilly.
Exceptional location: stroll across Green Park to Buckingham Palace, or round to Bond Street or Knightsbridge. Fine Art Deco building and backdrop to many films.

Phone	020 7499 6321
Email	reservations.theparklane@sheraton.com
Internet	www.sheraton.com/parklane

Renaissance Chancery Court, 252 High Holborn, WC1V 7EN.
S/d/t from £180 to £1,500. Holborn, Chancery Lane. One of the top five business hotels in the world, according to Conde Nast Traveller, and just a short stroll from the West, Theatreland and Covent Garden. Perfect base. All the usual perquisites.

Phone	020 7829 9888
Email	sales.chancerycourt@renaissancehotels.com
Internet	www.renaissancechancerycourt.com

Hotels: Central London (cont)

Ritz Hotel, Piccadilly, W1J 9BR.
133 rooms. From £400 s/d/t.
The imposing façade of this world-famous establishment resembles a French chateau. Returned to private British ownership in 1995, the Ritz has now, eight years later and at a cost of more than £40 million, been restored with no detail left untouched.

Phone	020 7493 8181
Email	enquire@theritzlondon.com
Internet	www.theritzlondon.com

Royal Horseguards, 2 Whitehall Court, SW1A 2EJ.
276 rooms. From £110 to £253. Charing Cross.
Good deals available at this venerable and imposing edifice right in the heart of the Establishment. Overlooks the Thames and is not far from Downing Street. Grade I listed with charming dining area.

Phone	0870 333 9122
Email	royalhorseguards@thistle.co.uk
Internet	www.thistlehotels.com/ royalhorseguards

St James's Club and Hotel, 7 Park Place, SW1A 1LP.
56 rooms. £195s. £245 d/t. Room only. £350-£950 suites.
Green Park tube. In the heart of London's vibrant clubland, the hotel was founded in 1857 by Lord Granville after he was involved in a diplomatic incident at the nearby Travellers Club. Nothing untoward has happened since.

Phone	020 7629 7688
Email	mail@stjamescluband hotel.co.uk
Internet	www.stjamescluband-hotel.co.uk

St Martins Lane, 45 St Martin's Lane, WC2N 4HX.
200 rooms, 4 suites. From £250 s/d/t.
At the hub of Covent Garden, West End theatres and Trafalgar Square, a dramatic and daring reinvention of the urban resort. Ultra contemporary design by Philippe Starck. Asia Cuba, its in-house, bar stocks 350 rums. And if that's not enough...

Phone	020 7300 5500
Email	sml@morganshotel group.com
Internet	www.morganshotel-group.com

Savoy, Strand, WC2R 0EU.
From £220 for s/d/t. Charing Cross.
In the heart of Theatreland, the hotel is ideally situated for the leisure visitor with a host of first-class restaurants, shops and entertainment venues on its doorstep. The Michelin-starred Savoy Grill, with Chef Patron Marcus Wareing, is one of London's best known fine-dining establishments. The hotel's other restaurant is first class, as well. The iconic American Bar remains a firm favourite for champagne and cocktails.

Phone	020 7836 4343
Email	savoy@fairmont.com
Internet	www.fairmont.com/savoy

Sofitel Street James, 6 Waterloo Place, SW1Y 4AN.
186 rooms. From £180. Rack rate £380. Piccadilly Circus.
Buckingham Palace and Trafalgar Square are near this 5-star hotel and Piccadilly and Theatreland only two minutes' walk away. The Eurostar terminal at Waterloo is also nearby. The Brasserie Roux is run by Albert Roux of Le Gavroche fame.

Phone	020 7747 2200
Email	h3144-re@accor-hotels.com
Internet	www.sofitelstjames.com

Soho Hotel, 4 Richmond Mews, Soho, W1D 3DH.
85 rooms. Oxford Circus. £290 s (VAT). £294 d/t. £350 deluxe doubles. Suites: £411 – £3,000.
Soho's first deluxe hotel. Honesty bar and personal trainer on hand. Very trendy. Expect to meet 'celebrities'.

Phone	020 7559 3000
Email	reservations@sohohotel.com
Internet	www.sohohotel.com

Swissotel London, The Howard, Temple Place, WC2R 0EU.
148 rooms. From £150 s/d/t. Temple.
Splendid location opposite Temple Underground – a quiet corner of a bustling part of town. The Howard, as it was always known, has long been a favourite bolt hole for those with discreet affairs at heart. Cool, elegant and handsome with splendid views of the Thames. Look out for weekend bargains.

Phone	020 7836 3555
Email	reservations.london@swissotel.com
Internet	www.london.swissotel.com

Trafalgar, 2 Spring Gardens, SW1A 2TS.
129 rooms from £163. Piccadilly Circus.
The Trafalgar Hilton was the group's first 'style' hotel. Each room has five star amenities. It is London's first Bourbon Bar, with over 80 American whiskies and looks across Trafalgar Square (both of them).

Phone	020 7870 2900
Email	sal_the-trafalgar@hilton.com
Internet	www.hilton.co.uk/trafalgar

22 Jermyn St, St James's, SW1Y 6HL.
5 rooms, 13 suites. From £180 s/d/t. From £265 suites. St James's.
Smart town house in bespoke shirt-making area. It may lack a restaurant and bar but the treatment is five star and the rooms are very stylishly done. Spa and health facilities.

Phone	020 7734 2353
Email	office@22jermyn.com
Internet	www.22jermyn.com

Waldorf Hilton, Aldwych, WC2B 4DD.
303 rooms, from £340 s/d/t.
Embankment, Temple or Charing Cross.
Synonymous with style and elegance, a classical, five-star hotel offering excellent service in one of London's best locations. Everything is state of the art.

Phone	0870 400 8484
Email	amanda.scott@hilton.com
Internet	www.hilton.com

MODERATELY PRICED

Academy, 17-21 Gower St, WC1E 6HG.
Boutique. 49 rooms. Single: £135. D/t: £160 to £220. Breakfast £10.95 to £15.
Five terraced Georgian town houses have been linked up to create a boutique hotel in Bloomsbury, on the edge of the West End.

Phone	020 7631 4115
Email	resacademy@theetoncollection.com
Internet	www.theetoncollection.com

ENGLAND

Hotels: Central London (cont)

Blooms Town House Hotel, 6-7 Montague St, WC1B 5BP.
26 rooms. From £135. Russell Sq.
An elegant Georgian townhouse hotel set in the heart of literary Bloomsbury, close to many tourist attractions, Theatreland and Oxford Street.

Phone	020 7323 1717
Email	blooms@mermaid.co.uk
Internet	www.bloomshotel.com

Bonnington in Bloomsbury, 92 Southampton Row, Bloomsbury, WC1 4BH.
247 rooms. Single rooms from £90. £104 d/t. Russell Sq, Holborn.
A superior 3 star hotel with 4 star contemporary wing. Only 10 mins from the West End while its close proximity to both underground and main-line stations makes it ideal for both the leisure and business traveller.

Phone	020 7242 2828
Email	sales@bonnington.com
Internet	www.bonnington.com

Cavendish, 81 Jermyn St, St James's, SW1Y 6JF.
230 rooms. From £100. Standard rate £245. St James's Park.
A modern and uncluttered hotel sited opposite Fortnum & Mason. Since it is 15 floors high, it is worth visting if only because the top storeys command superb views of the London skyline.

Phone	020 7930 2111
Email	cavendish.reservations@devere-hotels.com
Internet	www.cavendish-london.co.uk

Express by Holiday Inn, 106-110 Belgrave Rd, SW1V 2BJ.
52 rooms. From £90 s/d/t. Victoria.
Modernised Georgian terraced houses close to the station. Comfortably done out with all the basics, and more.

Phone	020 7630 8888
Email	info@hiexpressvictoria.co.uk
Internet	www.hiexpress.co.uk

Hart House, 51 Gloucester Place, Marylebone, W1U 8JF.
37 rooms. From £90 s, £68 d/t. £120 tpl. £150 fam. Marble Arch.
Yet another fine, family-run historic building with a rich history. Michelin, whose links are very French, says that the building was once occupied by French aristocrats escaping arrest and the guillotine following the revolution in 1789. Close to Oxford Street.

Phone	020 7935 2288
Email	reservations@harthouse.co.uk
Internet	www.harthouse.co.uk

St George, 49 Gloucester Place, Marylebone, W1U 8JE.
19 rooms. From £85 s, £100 d/t. Baker Street, Marble Arch.
A Grade II listed town house only a short walk from both Oxford Street and Baker Street. Recently awarded the sparkling diamond award for housekeeping by the RAC and the silver service award for its hospitality by the European Travel Commission. Good value and good service.

Phone	020 7486 8586
Email	reservations@stgeorge-hotel.net
Internet	www.stgeorge-hotel.net

Showtime: Almost all of the central London hotels are within a short walk of the city's vibrant theatre section with shows ranging from the long-running Moustrap to more recent hits such as The Lion King at the Lyceum.

Tophams Belgravia, 28 Ebury St, SW1W 0LU.
35 rooms. From £105 s. £120 d/t. Sloane Square.
The essence of an English country house in the heart of Belgravia.

Phone	020 7730 8147
Email	tophams@zolahotels.com
Internet	www.zolahotels.com

Winchester, 17 Belgrave Rd, SW1V 1RB.
18 rooms. £85 s/d/t. Victoria.
Well run privately owned retreat at bargain price given the location.

Phone	020 7828 2972
Email	winchesterhotel17@hotmail.com
Internet	www.winchester-hotel.net

BUDGET ACCOMMODATION

Marble Arch Inn, 49 Upper Berkeley St, Marylebone, W1H 5QR.
29 rooms from £70 d/t, £70 tpl, £100-£110 family rooms for 5 & 6. Satellite TV, showers, telephones, hairdryers – basic list of refinements.

Phone	020 7723 7888
Email	sales@marblearch-inn.co.uk
Internet	www.marblearch-inn.co.uk

Sidney Hotel, 68-76 Belgrave Rd, Victoria, SW1V 2BP.
81 rooms, from £70 s/d/t. £120 for family 5 beds.
Victoria Georgian house popular with repeat tourists from home and abroad.

Phone	020 7834 2738
Email	reservations@sidneyhotel.com
Internet	www.sidneyhotel.com

Stanley House Hotel, 19-21 Belgrave Rd, Pimlico, SW1V 1RB.
44 rooms, from £35.00 s, £55 d/t, family 4 bed: £90.
Close to Victoria in the midst of elegant Pimlico. Clean, spacious and functional.

Phone	020 7834 5042
Email	cmahotel@aol.com

Victor Hotel, 51 Belgrave Rd, Victoria, SW1V 2BB.
20 rooms, £50 s, £60 d/t. Victoria, Pimlico.
A small, but clean and well-run modern Bed &Breakfast to be found close to Victoria.

Email	sales@victorhotel.co.uk
Inernet	www.victorhotel.co.uk

WEST LONDON

Knightsbridge, South Kensington, Chelsea, Fulham, Chiswick & Hammersmith

BARS

(Arranged by District)

Chelsea

Chelsea Ram, 32 Burnaby St, SW10 0PL.
Good, down to earth local pub in a very flash part of town. Refreshing.

Crown, 153 Dovehouse St, SW3 6LB.
This has been a proper alehouse since it opened more than 150 years ago. It continued to serve real ale during the 'keg' revolution and is still a decent pub now. Near South Kensington tube.

Surprise, 6 Christchurch Terrace, SW3 4AJ.
You can watch the game, play bar billiards or sit in an old-fashioned snug supping some of the best Adnams and Fullers the capital has to offer.

Kensington & South Kensington...

Anglesea Arms, 15 Selwood Terrace, SW7 3QG.
Not to be mistaken for the gastro-haven near Hammersmith. Truly great Georgian pub serving very well looked-after beer. It also has a restaurant.

The Australian, 29 Milner St, SW3 2QD.
A decent, quiet backwater, you can watch the game here over a pint of good beer.

The Beauchamp, 43 Beauchamp Place, SW3 1NX.
Quiet pub – there's no music and it's refreshingly unsophisticated. A straightforward boozer in an area not renowned for such things.

Churchill Arms, 119 Kensington Chruch St, W8 7LN.
Heading towards Notting Hill Gate. Full of sporting mementoes – everything from hurling to rugby. Good quality food and drink. Medium sized screen.

Kensington Arms, 41 Abingdon Rd, W8 6AH.
Three large screens make this little pub match friendly.

Uxbridge Arms, 13 Uxbridge St, W8 7TQ.
Another place to watch the game, surrounded by warm wood panelling in an old-fashioned London pub serving a great pint of Brakspear or Fuller's.

Paddington

Archery Tavern, 4 Bathurst St, W2 2SD.
Just off the Bayswater Road, the Tavern is popular with tourists. It is also keen on sports – especially darts – the telly will be on for the big match. Good beers, too.

Mad Bishop & Bear, First Floor, The Lawn, Paddington Station, W2 1HF.
Good place to recover from the horrors of travel. Has little connection with mad bishops though there is a fictional bear from Peru who once showed up here. You can get a good breakfast, if travelling early.

Prince Edward, 73 Princes Square, W2 4NY.
Big and Grade II listed, with some fine ales and thoroughly professional service.

Rob Roy, 8 Sale Place, W2 1PH.
Good television pub, fine for match days so long as it's not England v Scotland and you happen to be English.

Chiswick

Bell & Crown, 72 Strand on The Green, W4 3PF.
Riverside pub serving good food. Great location.

George & Devonshire, Burlington Lane, W4 2QE.
Fuller's flagship pub, right next to the brewery at the Hogarth roundabout. Proper old fashioned bar and lounge.

Hammersmith

Andover Arms, 57 Aldensley Rd, W6 0DL.
One of the best places to drink in the area, it also serves good Thai food. Cosy and friendly serving Fuller's beer.

Brook Green Hotel, 170 Shepherd's Bush Rd, W6 7NB.
Does large-screen TV, serves Young's beer and is also a reasonably priced 14-bed-room hotel. Could be a one-stop-shop (see hotel listings). 020 7603 2516

Chancellors, 25 Crisp Rd, W6 9RL.
Opposite Riverside Studios this is a friendly little pub governed by an attentive landlady. Proper local for a proper pint.

Cross Keys, 53 Black Lion Lane, W6 9BG.
Near Stamford Brook tube on the district line, this is another pub where you can watch the game in complete confidence that you will be in good hands, company and drinking good beer (Fuller's).

Dove, 19 Upper Mall, W6 9TA.
17th century gem of a pub on the river with a terrace looking over the Thames. There are four different bars and an eating area. However be warned – it is so nice it is often packed.

Plough & Harrow, 120-124 King St, W6 0QU.
Wetherspoons. Does breakfast. Lots of choice beers.

TRENDY BARS AND CLUBS

Knightsbridge, South Kensington, Chelsea, Fulham, Chiswick & Hammersmith

Ad Lib, 246 Fulham Rd, SW10 9NA.
This part of town is known as Chelsea Beach because of its Mediterranean feel – in the summer, there is lots of bared flesh and glamour on show. Ad Lib is about the smartest place along the seafront, winning the Evening Standard Bar of the Year in 2004. Proper food and drink before this place morphs into a dance place at night, with top DJs spinning the decks.

Phone	020 7376 7775

Jerusalem, 33-34 Rathbone Place, Marylebone, W1T 1JN.
A split personality bar-restaurant which, during the daylight hours is a perfectly normal and good brasserie. Then the DJs start to strut their stuff and the music takes over from the char-grilled antelope burgers. But the Krug continues to flow – a young and funky place to be seen.

Phone	020 7255 1120

Lunasa, 575 Kings Rd, SW6 2EB.
We quote Itchy, the excellent 'style' guide:
"One of the best bars in the area. Classy types downing vodkas at unprecedented rates and then mingling over a bottle of Stella. The atmosphere at Lunasa is always buzzing, the bar staff phenomenally attractive and the décor stylish. In fact, we can't think of a single bad thing to say about the place. Not one. Honestly, you'd think it was owned by the reviewer's best mate from primary school or something."
We trust that it is not the case.

Phone	020 7371 7664

Trendy bars: West London (cont)

Motion, Hungerford House, Victoria Embankment, WC2N 6PA.
Set over two floors, Motion offers a funky environment. Open late every night with contemporary blend of current pop, dance classics and upbeat tunes.

Phone	020 7389 9933
Email	manager@motion-bar.co.uk
Internet	www.latenightlondon.co.uk

Blue Bar, The Berkeley Hotel, Wilton Place, Knightsbridge, SW1X 8RL.
A frequent haunt of the famous, The Blue Bar is within the Berkeley Hotel and serves a wide range of cocktails and boasts that it has more than 50 different types of malt whisky. An intimate venue which holds up to 50 guests.

Phone	0871 332 2978

Met Bar, Metropolitan Hotel, Old Park Lane, W1K 1LB.
Exciting venue with a hot reputation in the heart of London's Park Lane. Private members and hotel guests gather to take advantage of the innovative drinks menu and to listen to the funky music playing until the early hours.

Phone	020 7447 1000
Email	info.lon@metropolitan.como.bz

Rumi Bar, 531 Kings Road, Chelsea, SW10 0TZ.
Smack in the heart of groovy King's Rd, this is a cocktail bar that gradually metamorphoses as the evening progresses into a dance venue as the beat gradually turns up. Local glitterati add lustre to the scene.

Phone	020 7823 3362
Email	www.rumibar.com

151 Club, 151 Kings Rd, Chelsea, SW3 5TX.
"There is hardly a couple north of the river whose first, tentative kiss did not take place on the dancefloor of this dive," says Leonora, an habitue. Nice, polite regulars – doesn't encourage pretension. Poll position in the Good Snog Guide.

Phone	020 7351 6826

Deco, 294 Fulham Road, Fulham, SW10 9EW.
Clientele can be noisy – you know the sort. But the bar is cool enough to absorb quite a lot of braying. Deco has quite a bit going for it – there's good beer, a wide-ranging wine list, the food is not bad at all and the cocktails are inspired. One of Fulham's best.

Phone	020 7351 0044

Novello's, 47 Parson's Green Lane, SW6 4HH.
Not quite the epicentre of coolness, Novello's has someone called Lou Jordan doing Elvis impressions every Saturday and regulars include people who might be over 25 – even 'middle class mums' according to Laura Walton, a social commentator. One of Fulham's top pubs, also goes in for big screen sporting events.

Phone	020 7736 2713

Hammersmith Palais, 242 Shepherds Bush Road, W6 7NL.
The Palais is not just a venue – it is a heritage. Immortalised in Rock 'n Roll lyrics, revered throughout the world, it has been a creative entertainment Mecca since it opened in 1918. Spiritual home of Rock 'n Roll, venue for award ceremonies and even corporate functions, the Palais is a multi-tasker.

Phone	020 7341 5300
Internet	www.hammersmithpalais.com

Cuba, 11 Kensington High Street, W8 5NP.
It can get hot amongst the Mojito-swilling, cigar chomping dance-dudes and Castro-wannabes, sporting their rub-off Cuban flags in this loud and cheerful joint. Genuinely great fun. We're not taking the mickey.

Phone	020 7938 4137

RESTAURANTS

Knightsbridge, South Kensington, Chelsea, Fulham, Chiswick & Hammersmith

Anglesea Arms, 35 Wingate Rd, Near Hammersmith, W6 0UR.

Near Ravenscourt Park tube. Very popular gastropub that caters for the well-spoken denizens of W6. A pleasant little place when quiet, it can get a bit wild at feeding time. Although furnished in the archetypal gastropub uniform of stripped floors and wooden chairs, this is still a more comfortable place to drink in than most of the dives on the nearby Goldhawk Road. Word of warning - if you are here to eat rather than just drink, it's first come first served, so you may have to wait an age for a table. Pigeon and duck foie gras alongside pork pie and piccalilli, piperade and Swiss chard. Electic. Get in early.

Phone	020 8749 1291

Aubergine, 11 Park Walk, Fulham, SW10 0AJ.

Aubergine's chef/patron, William Drabble, has gained wide recognition, including a Michelin Star, for producing excellent Modern French cuisine, complemented by an outstanding wine list. This is the restaurant from which Gordon Ramsay launched himself with such, how shall we say, inimitable style? You can go for the straightforward 3-course dinner (£55) or the 7-course tasting menu (£72). French in style.

Basic price	from £55
Phone	020 7352 3449

The Atlas, 16 Seagrave Rd, SW6 1RX.

Gastropub popular with trendy West Bromptonians, a wealthy species from west of Chelsea. There's an attractive courtyard and though the food is good, it is still a proper pub with excellent real ale (London Pride, Adnams Broadside Deuchars IPA). A large TV for big games. Outside area means things don't get too cramped.

Phone	020 7385 9129

The Belvedere, off Abbotsbury Rd, Holland Park, W8 6LU.

Run by the one-time 3-star Michelin enfant-terrible, Marco Pierre White, this is formal, starched linen, French service in a quiet corner of posh, leafy London. Variously described as 'outstanding', 'sumptuous' and, in the case of the crème Caroline soup, 'flawlessly silky', the Belvedere serves up such classics as veal cutlet with morel jus, fondant potatoes and roast carrots, with great aplomb.

Basic price	£30
Phone	020 7602 1238
Internet	www.whitestarling.org.uk

Blue Elephant, 4-6 Fulham Broadway, SW6 1AA.

Jungle setting. Dr Livingstone would not have presumed to dine here without his corporate Amex. Trees and fecundity abound, carp swimming in small pools and a gold-gilt bar, beyond the fronds. Silly or surreal, either way it's a Thai-style experience and the food is good enough to warrant a mention in the Good Food Guide. Whatever you think, this bustling old haunt is certainly no white elephant. Distinctive curries and succulent, subtle starters.

Basic Price	£32
Phone	020 7385 6595
Internet	www.blueelephant.com

Restaurants: West London (cont)

Blue Lagoon, 286 Kensington High St, Kensington, W14 8NZ.
You can't get more old school Thai than this: silks on the walls, ornate figurines, running water, and festooned with orchids and greenery. The executive chef here used to work for the Thai royal family. Ingredients, they say, are flown in fresh daily from Thailand. The full gamut of classical dishes is a part of the Lagoon's repertoire. Set menus make life easy for those who find choice a tricky business.

Phone	020 7603 1231

Brasserie St Quentin, 243 Brompton Rd, Chelsea SW3 2EP.
Brasserie St Quentin was one of London's very first brasseries, offering cuisine Bourgeoise, sourcing produce from suppliers and farmers around the country. Morecambe Bay shrimps, meat from the Marquess of Salisbury's estate, Castle Brae fillet of beef. Directly opposite the Brompton Oratory, not far from Harrods, the hallmark of St Quentin is simple classic dishes from the best affordable ingredients. Grilled calf liver accompanied by olive oil mash, French beans and sage sauce is a good, simple example of a main course. A typical starter might be roast Lough Neagh eel with horseradish cream and mache salad.

Basic price	£25
Phone	020 7589 8005
Internet	www.brasseriestquentin.co.uk

Chez Kristof, 111 Hammersmith Grove, Hammersmith, W6 0NQ.
Great cocktails and good wine list. Owned by Jan Woroniecki, who made his name with such Polish establishments as Baltic (see South London) and Wodka (see below), but has created a thoroughly French establishment in Hammersmith. What about jellied pig's head and veal trotters? Roast pigeon with puy lentils?

Basic price	£25
Phone	020 8741 1177
Internet	www.balticrestaurant.co.uk

Chutney Mary, 535 King's Rd, Chelsea SW10 0SZ.
Not to be confused with Typhoid Mary, a cook who killed by unwittingly passing on more than chutney. This is altogether more upmarket – possibly London's most expensive curry house, and seen by many as the best. Fine setting for a good Euro-Indian experience, picking up some fine dishes from all over the sub-continent, from Goa and further south up to the Punjad and Himalaya.

Basic price	£35
Phone	020 7351 3113
Internet	www.realindianfood.com

Cotto, 44 Blythe Rd, Earl's Court W14 0HA.
Tucked away behind the Olympia Exhibition Centre, Cotto serves modern European food with a touch of the Med and the Orient. A local favourite, as well as a big hit with the critics. Stunning artwork on a whitewashed background. What to eat? Roast saddle of rabbit with Parma ham (Italy), braised neck of lamb with onion and boulangere sauce (France), steamed sea bass with pak choi, soy and ginger (further east), red mullet with pequillo peppers, lentils & salsa verde (Spain), braised hare and roast saddle with spatzle & cabbage with crab apple puree (Austria).

Basic price	£20-plus
Phone	020 7602 9333

Daphnes, 112 Draycott Avenue, Chelsea SW3 3AE.
Full of posh young ladies and Etonians behaving as if they were on a weekend shooting party in the country. Has been popular with the in-set for a decade and keeps its ratings up by putting a lot of effort into the grub. Italian cooking. Look out for the roast suckling pig and the casa buitoni Eton mess pudding.

Basic price	£35-£40
Phone	020 7589 4257

El Andalousse, 32 Fulham Palace Rd, Fulham, SW6 9PH.
Traditional Moroccan restaurant/bar which pulls in a young and vibrant crowd, down in deepest Hammersmith. Revuelto de verduras (mixed peppers and vegetables sauteed with tomatoes sauce and cheese), a wide variety of couscous and tagines, plus chorizos in tomato sauce with butter. Ideal for sharing.

Phone	020 8563 7176

Gordon Ramsay, 68-69 Royal Hospital Rd, Chelsea SW3 4HP.
At time of going to press, GR was Britain's pre-eminent chef, scoring 100% in the Good Food Guide and commanding 3 Michelin stars. Ramsay is a TV celebrity running a huge culinary empire. One wonders how on earth he manages to find time to do any cooking. Langoustines with pork belly is one singled out for special praise, the delicacy of the shellfish combining with the tender fattiness of the pork; tortellini of lobster with a vinaigrette of crustace and herb veloute or roasted tranche of foie gras with caramelised endives, carrot puree and Sauternes jus. One could continue with the greatest pleasure. And the drawback? You'll probably need to book before you have even read this review.

Basic price	£65-80
Phone	020 7352 4441/3334
Internet	www.gordonramsay.com

Kensington Place, 201-209 Kensington Church St, W8 7LX.
Excellent and bustling modern European cuisine with Rowley Leigh in charge of the kitchen. Bold glass fronted and still pulling in the crowds nearly 20 years after it cut the mustard. Seasonal cooking with typical dishes including grilled scallops with pea puree or grilled sea trout with samphire and peppered hollandaise. Puddings and desserts an absolute triumph. One reviewer managed seven whilst lunching with a newspaper executive from a nearby newspaper.

Basic price	£32
Phone	020 7727 3184
Internet	www.egami.co.uk

Lou Pescadou, 241 Old Brompton Rd, SW5 9HP.
Strong rugby ties. The basement bar is full of memorabilia and pictures of teams of old. It is also a famous seafood restaurant, an outpost of France Maritime on the Old Brompton Road. Lunch for around £10 and excellent value for money. Try monkfish with mustard sauce, poached halibut or Dover sole meuniere. Good French service in a place that positively summons up the Davy dark – portholes, blue frontage; all that's missing are oilskins for the waiters and a ship-to-shore phone line.

Basic price	£16
Phone	020 7370 1057

Memories Of India, 18 Gloucester Rd, Chelsea, SW7 4RB.
Informal and relaxed, with a conservatory dining room at the back. Harks back to colonial days, with such dishes as officers' chops. Also has all the other usual suspects (old favourites such as chicken tikka massala, jalfrezi etc), plus more exotic offerings such as lamb cooked in a honey and soya sauce, or lemon sole dipped in a blend of spices with mango extract, garlic and red chilli.

Phone	020 7581 3734

Petrus, The Berkeley, Wilton Place, Knightsbridge, SW1X 7RL.
One of the capital's very best fine dining experiences. That it only has one Michelin star is a mystery to many. Marcus Wareing is executive chef here and at the Savoy Grill (see below). Very swish surroundings – burgundy leather seats in a richly dark dining room. Wareing has worked with some of the world's top chefs, including Gordon Ramsay, with whom he is in partnership. The tasting menu takes care of an entire evening and hits all the right notes on the culinary register. Take a look at the website.

Basic price	£60-£70
Phone	020 7235 1200
Internet	www.marcuswareing.com

Restaurants: West London (cont)

Sabai Thai, 270-272 King St, W6 0SP.

Imported fittings from the Orient and a classic Thai menu. The genuine article. Green curry comes highly recommended. All the usual suspects (prawns in pastry with sweet chilli sauce, tod mun pla, and peek kai yad sai, stuffed chicken wings in red wine sauce) amongst the starters. Vegetarian friendly.

Phone	020 8748 7363

Racine, 239 Brompton Rd, Knightsbridge, SW3 2EP.

Winner of Time Out best new restaurant when it launched in 2003, Racine is a Parisian bistro down to the last chunk of lapin a la moutarde. Specialises in cuisine bourgeoise with 'rustic leanings'.

Basic price	£25
Phone	020 7584 4477

The River Café, Thames Wharf, Rainville Rd, Hammersmith, W6 9HA.

One of the trendiest spots in London for the past decade. Jamie Oliver started here and Ruth Rogers and Rose Gray still run the kitchens. Seasonal fare, with strong Italian influence. Much use of wood ovens and chargrill. One of London's great restaurants. Try wood roasted Dover sole with marjoram and capers with fresh baked borlotti beans. Any dessert is enough to give the whole ensemble that wow factor.

Basic price	£50
Phone	020 7386 4200
Internet	www.rivercafe.co.uk

Smollenskys, Bradmore House, Queen Caroline St, W6 9BW.

This may sound contradictory, but it's true: Smollensky's is family-friendly yet trendy. An American diner, it is one of the rare places that has something for everyone. As popular with drinkers as with eaters there is informal seating on several levels and there are some fine Art Deco murals and chandeliers in this fine Georgian house.

Phone	020 8741 8124

La Trompette, 5-7 Devonshire Rd, Chiswick, W4 2EU.

Down river, near Turnham Green tube, stands a sophisticated and accomplished corner of France. Owned by the same people who run the Michelin-starred Chez Bruce on Wandsworth Common, you would expect no less. Popular with locals, just about everything is recommended. Fine wine list

Basic price	£32.50
Phone	020 8747 1836

Mr Wing, 244 Old Brompton Rd, SW5 0DE.

Family-run neighbourhood Chinese, combining elements of Thai and Mongolian cooking. There's a waterfall and a ten-metre reef aquarium. Smart but inexpensive, with live jazz at weekends. Try the crispy duck and the Szechwan beef with chilli.

Phone	020 7370 4450

Utsav, 17 Kensington High St, W8 5NP.

Food from all across India in this three storey, stylish restaurant. Good choice for vegetarians and plenty to keep the carnivore happy. Everything from light pani poori, cabbage vada, fish curry to Hyderabadi lamb biriani with rose scented rice.

Basic price	£20
Phone	020 7368 0022
Internet	www.utsav-restaurant.co.u

Wodka, 12 St Albans Grove, Kensington, W8 5PN.

Sister restaurant to the Baltic, and Chez Kristof in Hammersmith, Wodka attracts a lively young crowd and has the same menu of good food plus excellent cocktails. Does the East European stuff with panache – herrings, Moldavian aubergine with peppers and minted yoghurt, pork belly with horseradish.

Basic price	£24
Phone	020 7937 6513
Internet	www.wodka.co.uk

HOTELS

Knightsbridge, South Kensington, Chelsea, Fulham, Chiswick & Hammersmith

LUXURY

Ascott Mayfair, 49 Hill St, W1J 5NB.

Luxury apartments: £265 (studio – sleeps 2); £610 (2-bed sleeps up to 6); £825 (3-bed, sleeps 8). Green Park.

The complex has a gym, sauna and steam room plus a Club lounge in which complimentary breakfast is served. Well positioned for shopping.

Phone	020 7313 6188
Email	enquiry.london@the-ascott.com
Inernet	www.the-ascott.com

Baglioni Hotel London, 60 Hyde Park Gate, Kensington, SW7 5BB.

66 rooms. S/d/t/ £350 up to £460. Suites £590 to £2,240. Hyde Park Corner. Overlooks Kensington Gardens and Palace.

A personal butler service is available on all floors. There's also an IT butler for those mixing work with pleasure. Last letter in pampering.

Phone	020 7368 5700
Email	info@baglionihotellondon.com
Internet	www.baglionihotellondon.com

Peace of the country: Amid all London hustle and bustle, Kensington Gardens are a haven of tranquility

Capital, 22-24 Basil St, Knightsbridge, SW3 1AT.

48 rooms. From £200. Knightsbridge. Charming and comfortable town house (boutique hotel).

Rooms are furnished with antiques, a private art collection and the finest linen. The restaurant has two Michelin stars.

Phone	020 7589 5171
Email	reservations@capitalhotel.co.uk
Internet	www.capitalhotel.co.uk

Chelsea Village Hotel, Stamford Bridge, Fulham Rd, SW6 1HS.

291 rooms. From £160 s/d/t. Fulham Broadway.

Spread over 12 acres, Chelsea Village is a business, leisure and entertainments complex built around the Chelsea Football Club. Five restaurants and bars. A wide range of food and wines. Parking is available for up to 180 cars (charges apply).

Phone	020 7565 1400
Email	reservations@chelseavillage.com
Internet	www.chelseavillage.com

Hotels: West London (cont)

Colonnade, 2 Warrington Crescent, W9 1ER.
43 rooms. Single: £153. D/t from £185. Family rooms from £250. Breakfast £15. Paddington.
A fine Victorian setting in the quiet backwater of Little Venice. Two houses are linked to make a decent sized hotel.

Phone	020 7286 1052
Email	rescolonnade@theetoncollection.com
Internet	www.theetoncollection.com

Cranley, 10 Bina Gardens, South Kensington, SW5 0LA.
From £125. Gloucester Rd. In the leafy heart of the Royal Borough of Kensington and Chelsea, the Cranley is one of London's most charming town house hotels. Brings together tradition and service with 21st century expectations.

	020 7373 0123
	info@thecranley.com
	www.thecranley.com

Hilton London Kensington, 179-199 Holland Park Avenue, Holland Park, W11 4UL.
602 rooms. From £118 s/d/t. Holland Park. Fashionable spot in a leafy part of west London. Comfortable four star stuff.

Phone	020 7603 3355
Email	sales.kensington@hilton.com
Internet	www.hilton.co.uk/kensington

Hilton London Metropole, Edgware Rd, Maida Vale, W2 1JU.
1033 rooms. From £110. Edgware Rd. Big, busy and popular convention centre. Has the usual refinements plus lively bar and bustling restaurant. Living Well Health Club free to residents and includes a 12.5m swimming pool, sauna and fully equipped gym. Just what you don't need after a day on the tiles.

Phone	020 7402 4141
Email	cbs_londonmet@hilton.com
Internet	www.hiltonlondonmet.com

Lanesborough, Lanesborough Place, SW1X 7TA.
95 rooms. From £300 a night s/d/t.
Palm trees, fountains and lavishly furnished rooms. Glass roofed dining room. Whole place restored to its Regency grandeur. Butler service. This is one of London's luxiest hotels.

Phone	020 7259 5606
Email	info@lanesborough.com
Internet	www.lanesborough.com

Mandarin Oriental Hyde Park, 66 Knightsbridge, SW1X 7LA.
177 rooms from £345 s/d/t.
Rooms look over Hyde Park. Former Gentleman's Club, it is one of London's very grandest hotels. Immaculate service. Recent £50 million restoration. World famous.

Phone	020 7235 2000
Email	molon-reservations@mohg.com
Internet	www.mandarinoriental.com

Marriott Hotel Maida Vale, Plaza Parade, NW6 5RP.
238 rooms. From £130 s/d/t. Maida Vale. Guests can use the indoor heated swimming pool, two state of the art gymnasiums, aerobics studio, sauna and steam room. Bring your own trouser press.

Phone	020 7543 6000
Email	reservations.maidavale@marriotthotels.co.uk
Internet	www.marriott.com/marriott/lownh

Novotel London West, 1 Hammersmith International Centre, Hammersmith, W6 8DR.
629 rooms from £70 s/d/t to £170 s/d/t. Your rate will depend, as with all London hotels, upon demand. There are two bars, two restaurants, fitness centre, beauty salon, business centre and on-site parking.

Phone	020 8741 1555
Email	H0737@accor.com
Internet	www.novotel.com

Park Inn Hyde Park, 66 Lancaster Gate, W2 3NZ.
180 rooms, from £120 s/d/t. Set in a Georgian terrace and close to Kensington Gardens, the Park Inn Hyde Park is convenient for theatres and museums.

Phone	020 7262 5090
Email	info.hydepark@rezidorparkinn.com
Internet	www.parkinn.co.uk

Royal Garden Hotel, 2 Kensington High St, W8 4PT.
S/d/t from £150. Rack rate is much higher.
After its £30 million refurbishment the hotel now has 396 rooms, most offering spectacular views over Kensington Palace, its gardens or Hyde Park.

Phone	020 7937 8000
Email	sales@royalgardenhotel.co.uk
Internet	www.royalgardenhotel.co.uk

Royal Lancaster Hotel, Lancaster Terrace, W2 2TY.
From £290 a room. Standing opposite the 600 acres of Kensington Gardens and Hyde Park, yet only minutes away are the bustling shopping areas of Knightsbridge, Oxford Street and Bond Street.

Phone	020 7262 6737
Email	book@royallancaster.com
Internet	www.concorde-hotels.com

Sheraton Park Tower, 101 Knightsbridge, SW1X 7RN.
From £248. Directly across from Harvey Nichols with Sloane Street shopping and the world famous Harrods just a stroll away. Butlers on call.

Phone	020 7235 8050
Email	central.london.reservations@sheraton.com
Internet	www.sheraton.com/parktower

Thistle Kensington Park, 16-32 De Vere Gardens, W8 5AF.
353 rooms. From £80 single and £94 d/t. Peaceful spot in De Vere Gardens, just off Kensington High Street.

Phone	0870 333 9112
Email	kensingtonpark@thistle.co.uk
Internet	www.thistlehotels.com

MODERATELY PRICED

Ambassadors Hotel, 16 Collingham Rd, SW5 0LX.
140 rooms. From £60 s/d/t. Gloucester Rd, Earl's Court
Quiet location just off the Cromwell Rd. Reasonable price and comfortable.

Phone	020 7373 1075
Email	ambassadorshotel@crystalhotels.co.uk
Internet	www.crystalhotels.co.uk

Hotels: West London (cont)

Basil Street, 8 Basil St, Knightsbridge, SW3 1AH.
80 rooms. From £170 s/d/t. Knightsbridge.
The Basil was built in 1910 and has now been privately owned by the same family for three generations. Sandwiched between Harrods and Harvey Nichols, it is handy for the shops. It offers all the ambience and comfortable style of a country house, but also all the amenities of a modern international hotel. Has an exclusive ladies only lounge.

Phone	020 7581 3311
Email	info@thebasil.com
Internet	www.thebasil.com

Berjaya Eden Park Hotel, 35-39 Inverness Terrace, W2 3JS.
135 rooms. From £100.
Victorian town-house hotel dating from 1860, in a quiet tree-lined terrace, a few minutes from Oxford Street.

Phone	020 7221 2220
Email	reservations@berjayaeden.co.uk
Internet	www.berjayaresorts.com

Burns Hotel (Best Western), 18-26 Barkston Gardens, Kensington, SW5 0EN.
From £120 s/d/t. Earl's Court, Gloucester Rd.
Grade II listed building in a tree-lined garden square in Kensington and also close to Knightsbridge.

Phone	020 7373 3151
Email	burnshotel@vienna-group.co.uk
Internet	www.bw-burnshotel.co.uk

Corus Hotel Hyde Park, 1-7 Lancaster Gate, W2 3LG.
From £125 s/d/t. Hyde Park Corner.
'All room types come with powerful hairdryer, trouser press and coffee and tea facilities,' says the blurb. What more could you want? Also looks over Hyde Park

Phone	020 7262 5022
Email	londonhydepark@corushotels.com
Internet	www.corushotels.com/londonhydepark

Five Sumner Place Hotel, 5 Sumner Place, South Kensington, SW7 3EE.
13 rooms. Single £100. £155 d/t. South Kensington.
Awarded the accolade of the best small hotel in London. Privately owned, it is part of an impressive, white Victorian terrace built around 1848 on the borders of South Kensington and Knightsbridge. Broadband access etc.

Phone	020 7584 7586
Email	reservations@sumnerplace.com
Internet	www.sumnerplace.com

Hilton London Olympia, 380 Kensington High St, W14 8NL.
602 rooms. From £100 s/d/t to £160. Kensington Olympia, Kensington High Street.
Big and busy and popular with business people. Very handy for everything and also offers good weekend rates.

Phone	020 7603 3333
Email	rm_olympia@hilton.com
Internet	www.hilton.co.uk/olympia

Hilton London Paddington, 146 Praed St, Paddington, W2 1EE.
335 rooms. From £100 s/d/t. Suites from £170.
Railway hotel built in Victorian times but sympathetically upgraded over the years. Just 15 minutes by rail from Heathrow, the hotel has recently been refurbished to its former art deco glory. Fully equipped Business Centre, Brasserie Restaurant, and Steam Bar.

Phone	020 7723 8064
Email	paddington@hilton.com
Internet	www.hilton.com

Hotel Ibis London Earl's Court, 47 Lillie Rd, Earl's Court, SW6 1UD.
502 rooms. From £70 s/d/t. Suites from £150.
Opposite Earls Court Exhibition Centre and two minutes walk from West Brompton station, the hotel offers a restaurant, a cafe bar and an undercover paying car park.

Phone	020 7610 0880
Email	h5623-re@accor-hotels.com
Internet	www.ibishotels.com

Kensington Premier Travel Inn, 11 Knaresborough Place, Earl's Court, SW5 0TJ.
From £75 s/d/t.
Two minutes from Earl's Court Underground station and also close to Knightsbridge and the big museums. Free breakfast for children and all the extras you would expect in a business hotel.

Phone	0870 238 3304
Internet	www.premiertravelinn.com

My Place Hotel, 1-3 Trebovir Rd, Earl's Court, SW5 9LS.
50 rooms, £65 s, £85 d/t, £110 3 bed family.
Handsome Victorian town house in the quiet side street. Air conditioning, en-suite, complete with trouser press and cable TV. Sound-proofed nightclub.

Phone	020 7373 0833
Email	info@myplacehotel.co.uk
Internet	www.myplacehotel.co.uk

BUDGET ACCOMMODATION

Delmere Hotel (Best Western), 130 Sussex Gardens, Paddington, W2 1UB.
From £95 s/d/t. Lancaster Gate, Paddington Victorian town house hotel close to Hyde Park, Oxford Street and the West End. Offering reasonable standards of comfort and friendliness. Also featuring a lounge, Jazz Bar and a French/Italian styled restaurant.

	020 7706 3344
	delmerehotel@compuserve.com
	www.delmerehotels.com

Hotel Earl's Court, 28 Warwick Rd, SW5 9UD.
17 rooms, from £30 s to £50 d/t to £60 family. Earl's Court.
Opposite Earl's Court exhibition centre and conveniently close to the Underground. Handy and comfortable as well as cheap.

Phone	020 7373 7079
Email	info@hotelearlscourt.com
Internet	www.hotelearlscourt.com

Lord Jim Hotel, 25 Penywern Rd, Earl's Court, SW5 9TT.
46 rooms, from £40 s, £55 d/t, £72 tpl, £120 5-bed room. Earl's Court. Newly refurbished en-suite shower rooms make this basic hotel a perfectly reasonable base in central London.

Phone	020 7370 6071
Email	ljh@lgh-hotels.com
Internet	www.lgh-hotels.com

Hotels: West London (cont)

Merlyn Court Hotel, 2 Barkston Gardens, Earl's Court, SW5 0EN.
17 rooms from £40 s to £75 d/t. £85 for family rooms (4 beds). A good-value, well-established, family-run hotel in a quiet garden square in Kensington. Close to Earls Court and Olympia exhibition centres, with direct underground link to Heathrow and the West End.

Phone	020 7370 1640
Email	london@merlyncourthotel.com
Internet	www.merlyncourthotel.com

CITY

City, Blackfriars, Farringdon, Holborn, Clerkenwell & Shoreditch

BARS

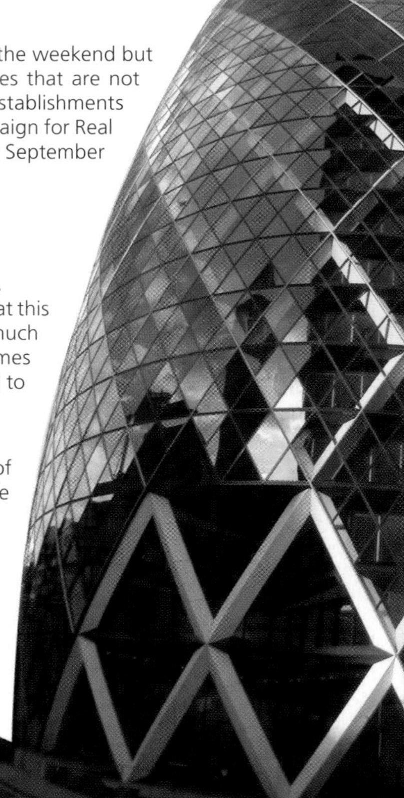

In the City many establishments close at the weekend but you don't have to travel far to find places that are not only open, but heaving. Most of these establishments are recommended by CAMRA, the Campaign for Real Ale group whose 2006 guide came out in September £13.99 – www.camra.org.uk.

TRADITIONAL PUBS

City

Dirty Dicks, 202 Bishopsgate, EC2 4NR.
This place is named after a man who lived at this address for many years without paying much attention to personal hygiene. My, how times have changed. Those in Armani suits tend to be well scrubbed. Good Young's pub.

Counting House, 50 Cornhill, EC3 3PD.
Yet another converted bank with lots of interesting prints and paintings of olde London towne. Fuller's beers.

Crosse Keys, 7 Gracechurch St, EC3Y 0DR.
Wetherspoon's pub in a converted bank. Good space, ideal for a party. Very ornate with a marble oval shaped bar.

Finsbury

White Lion, Central St, EC1V 8AB.
Adnams beer and a large screen for sports. What more could you want?

Old Mitre, 1 Ely Court, Ely Place, EC1N 6SJ.
Historic pub first mentioned in Shakespeare's Richard III. Queen Elizabeth danced around a maypole here. Closed weekends so make it for a pint on Friday or Monday.

Blackfriars, Clerkenwell, Holborn & Farringdon

Calthorpe Arms, 252 Gray's Inn Rd, WC1X 8JR.
Straightforward locals' pub serving Youngs.

Cittie of York, 22 High Holborn, WC1V 3ES.
Famous landmark next to Gray's Inn. Splendid rear bar.

Coach & Horses, 26-28 Ray St, EC1R 3DJ.
Right behind the Guardian building, this pub retains its old charm whilst also becoming one of London's top gastropubs. See restaurant entry.

Cockpit, St Andrews Hill, EC4V 5BY.
Tucked away around the corner from St Paul's, it is popular with bell ringers and city workers, staying open until later than most city establishments. Cosy little bolt hole.

Eagle, 159 Farringdon Rd, EC1R 3AL.
Another pub whose main fame lies in its food (also close to the Guardian). It is one of the very first gastropubs and has been blazing a trail now for 14 years.

Phone	020 7837 1353

Harrow, 22 Whitefriars St, EC4Y 8JJ.
Atmospheric old journalists' haunt round the corner from the old Daily Mail offices. On three levels with a restaurant at the top.

Phone	020 7427 0911

Jerusalem Tavern, 55 Britton St, EC1M 5UQ.
St Peter's Suffolk Ales served in an 18th century setting on the site of a much older pub in a delightful, historic part of town.

Lamb, Lamb's Conduit St, WC1N 3LZ.
Stunning old pub with a wide variety of beers. Great piece of Victoriana with an island bar and 'snob' screens to protect tap room privacy.

Old China Hand, 8 Tysoe St, EC1 4RQ.
Grand old pub recently made over by the new rugby fan owners (see p391). The theme is East meets West, so you can enjoy a variety of real ales, dim sum and other eastern specialities. Right by Exmouth Market near Roesebury Avenue and Sadler's Wells, there are TVs and a big screen for match day.

Phone	020 7278 7630

Old Bank of England, 104 Fleet St, EC4A 2LT.
Slap on the boundary between the City and the beginnings of the West End, the Old Bank is a grand piece of banking pomp now serving a wide variety of well kept ales next to the Royal Courts of Justice. Fullers.

Pakenham Arms, 1 Pakenham St, WC1X 0LA.
A Fuller's pub serving five different real ales. A proper locals' pub not far from Gray's Inn Rd.

Peasant, 240 St John St, EC1V 4PH.
Very busy pub/restaurant near the Angel. Excellent gastronomic pub fare, ideal if you want to combine the pleasures of the hop with the benefits of lumpy stuff.

Phone	020 7336 7726

Princess Louise, 208-209 High Holborn, WC1V 7EP.
Good Beer Guide rightly has this one as a 'must see' – Grade II listed with all the Victorian fixtures and fittings. Gilt mirrors, stained glass etc.

: Built on the site
ld Baltic Exchange
omb attack;
ingly a London
rk

Rugby Tavern, 19 Great James St, WC1N 3ES.
On the ancient site of Rugby school, home of the Game. Great little bar serving good food plus televisation of matches.

Phone	020 7405 1384

Sekforde Arms, 34 Sekforde St, EC1 R0HA.
Young's beers, including Special and Bitter. This is a traditional old boozer in a trendy part of town. It has remained unchanged by change and remains a pub to which the locals are faithful.

Sutton Arms, 6 Carthusian St, EC1M 6EB.
Between Smithfield and Charterhouse Square this pub serves some great beers whilst running a very good little restaurant upstairs. Closed on Sunday.

Phone	020 7253 0723

Smithfield

Butcher's Hook & Cleaver, 61 West Smithfield, EC1A 9DY.
This Fuller's Ale & Pie house could scarcely be any closer to London's ancient meat market. Also close to the Old Bailey law courts – fascinating part of town.

BARS

All Bar One, 91-93 Charterhouse Street, EC1M 6HR.
There are few surprises with this All Bar One; it's where the less style conscious go to drink in this area and it gets crowded when the offices wrap up business. As with the other All Bar Ones in the area, it's open at the weekend, which is uncommon in the city.

Phone	020 7553 9391

The Banker, Cousin Lane, EC4R 3TE.
A spacious bar, well lit and with a great conservatory area overlooking the river, also reasonable outside seating area with river views. Fills up quickly should the sun shine, so it is advisable to arrive early to secure a decent seat.

Phone	020 7283 5206

Barley Mow Freehouse, 50-52 Long Lane, EC1A 9EJ.
A very welcoming pub with attentive and friendly staff, well-kept beer and genial clientele make this an excellent pub. It has a range of guest ales on tap also and they keep the beer fastidiously.

Phone	020 7606 6591

The Barley Mow, 127 Curtain Rd London, EC2A 3BX.
A small pub normally populated by the designer types from the surrounding executive dwellings. Not for everyone.

Phone	020 7729 3910

Berries Wine Bar, 167 Queen Victoria St London, EC4V 4DF.
Berries displays a glow of competence and fine detailing, far from your ordinary City lunchroom. In the back of the wine bar, you can choose a bottle from the small but excellent selection of wines (Louis Latour Corton Grand Cru and Chateau Chasse-Spleen, for example). A fee of just £2.50 corkage over the shelf-price is payable for the wine, at which point you'll be salivating at the prospect of an all-you-can-eat buffet of quiches, salads, pates and cheeses.

Phone	020 7329 4759

The Blackfriar, 174 Queen Victoria St, EC4V 4EG.
A visually interesting pub with good selections of both lagers and real ales, during the week it gets very busy when the surrounding offices empty. Situated on the site of an old monastery and hence the name. Worth bearing in mind this is a smoke free pub so be prepared to stand on the pavement should you be a smoker.

Phone	020 7236 5474

The Cheshire Cheese, 48 Crutched Friars, EC3N 2AP.
This is a large two-storey pub located underneath Fenchurch Street station and very close to the Tower Of London. Similar to a lot of City pubs, it can be quite empty outside of lunch and immediate post-work hours. An older pub for the area, it has an upstairs game room; friendly staff and satellite sports TV, music. It's a bit average, but that's not to say you can't find a decent pint of Bass there.

Phone	020 7265 5141

The Devereux, 20 Devereux Ct, WC2R 3JJ.
Well off the beaten track in one of the tranquil, picturesque alleyways which are feature of the Inns of Court, Devereux is a pretty average sort of pub which is only made by its location.

Phone	020 7583 4562

Nylon, 1 Addle St, EC2 V7EU.
Run-of-the-mill city bar populated by city boys and secretaries alike, large cocktail and shooter list and the usual premium lager brands. Food is served at lunch times and bar snacks are available in the evenings. Prices are inflated due to its location.

Phone	020 7600 7771

CLUBS

City, Blackfriars, Farringdon, Holborn, Clerkenwell & Shoreditch

Fabric, 77a Charterhouse Street, EC1 M6HJ.

One of the largest clubs in the centre of London with an eclectic mix of both music and people. It has been the benchmark against which other London clubs have been judged for the past few years so be sure to arrive before the pubs close otherwise you'll be in for a long wait to get in.

Phone	020 7336 8898

RESTAURANTS

City, Blackfriars, Farringdon, Holborn, Clerkenwell & Shoreditch

Abacus, 24 Cornhill, EC3 3ND.

The most versatile and flexible choice for any celebration. Divided into eight distinct areas, each with its own design, style and personality; Onanon (great name) offers a choice of bars and music until 3am. The lounge, loft, lodge, cocktail, booth, studio, glam, and club offer cool contemporary and sophisticated surroundings for your party, not forgetting the stunning views of Piccadilly Circus.

Basic price	£22
Phone	020 7337 6767
Internet	www.latenightlondon.co.uk

Bleeding Heart, The Cellars, 3 Bleeding Heart Yard, Holborn, EC1N 8SJ.

A great place to while away an afternoon (in the days of nearby Fleet St, when expense accounts existed, it was a favoured haunt of journalists). Now it is the haunt of the suits – lawyers, accountants and merchant bankers. You might try Cornish crab and fresh seaweed sushi with sweet mustard dressing, followed by tournedos of Orkney salmon with creamed parmesan potato and wasabi-washed flying fish roe, or maybe roasted broadside farm suckling pig 'four ways,' with thyme jus. Also a courtyard with pub and wine bar in this 'olde worlde' setting.

Basic price	£36
Phone	020 7242 8238
Internet	www.bleedingheart.co.uk

Café Naz, 46-48 Brick Lane, Spitalfields, E1 6RF.

Café Naz is a well presented contemporary restaurant providing good Indian cuisine in an imaginative setting. Specialities: chingri jhol (small prawns cooked in a light spicy sauce), garlic chilli king prawn with green chillies and fresh garlic, blended with onion and capsicum or rupchanda masala - a whole fish grilled and cooked in a medium hot sauce.

Basic price	£16
Phone	020 7247 0234
Internet	www.cafenaz.co.uk

Caravaggio, 107-112 Leadenhall Street, EC3A 4AA.

Caravaggio is set in a converted banking hall, retaining its original character with added deco glamour. This Italian restaurant, opened by Pavarotti in 1996, offers Modern Italian cuisine. Mixed reports about main courses and service but a great setting. Starters and puddings come highly praised. Aldgate & Bank tubes.

Basic price	£30
Phone	020 7626 6206
Internet	www.etruscagroup.co.uk

Restaurants: City (cont)

Cicada, 132-136 St John St, EC1V 4JT.

A Thai-based restaurant with a fantastic bar. Beyond is the attractive eating area, with a pan-Asian menu: Thai salads and Japanese sushi and tempura. Chilli salt squid, beef san chau bau (roll your own starter). It can be hectic in this restaurant, sister to Notting Hill's E&O and Hoxton's Great Eastern Dining Room (see entry), so book early to grab one of the brown leather eating booths.

Phone	020 7608 1550
Internet	www.cicada.nu

Coach & Horses, 26 Ray St, EC1R 3DJ.

Winner of Time Out's Gastropub of the year, this traditional boozer has been converted without ruining any of its London pubby feel. Just up the side street by the offices of the Guardian newspaper, the food is very good. Mains range from roast haddock, smashed peas and tartare sauce – 'good fish, great chips' says Charles Campion, a noted London critic - plus leafy broccoli-and-lemon risotto or miso braised pork belly with vegetables and English mustard with highly flavoured broth. Highly commended puddings.

Phone	020 7278 8990
Internet	www.thecoachand-horses.com

Club Gascon, 57 West Smithfield, EC1A 9DS.

Temple to South West France, and with a Michelin-star. Does its foie gras in more ways than you could shake a stick at. It is bold and experimental, offering a French take on (albeit very upmarket) tapas. Dishes like duck with creamed caviar and sardine sorbet make one think of Heston Blumenthal. Others include chips cooked in goose fat as at that wonderful Bordelais institution, La Tupina. Portions are small so you get to do some tasting, opt for a tasting menu. Wine list good, service patchy.

Basic price	£38
Phone	020 7796 0600

Clerkenwell Dining Room, 69-73 Street John St, EC1M 4AN.

Clerkenwell has been one of London's most exciting gastronomic areas since Fergus Henderson opened St John (see entry) ten years ago. The chefs are not afraid of challenging the taste buds: citrus and honey marinated salmon, sprouts, shaved vegetables and summer fruits (one dish) to start, followed by fillet of belly pork, apple and shallot tatin, crisp sage or perhaps grilled monkfish with razor clams, saffron potato puree and crispy chorizo. Iced raspberry soufflé with passion fruit is a popular dessert. Cool modern décor grey and blue. Good cocktails.

Basic price	£35
Phone	020 7253 9000
Internet	www.theclerkenwell.com

Coq d'Argent, No 1 Poultry, EC2.

Another of Sir Terence Conran's restaurants. The menu is based on regional French cooking with a wine list to complement. The bar serves salads, grills and crustacea. The restaurant and bar have private terraces and a garden. Bank tube.

Basic price	£35
Phone	020 7395 5000
Internet	www.conran.com

CRU Restaurant, Bar & Deli, 2-4 Rufus Street, N1 6PE.

In a warehouse off Hoxton Square. The wine list is fundamental (as the restaurant's name hints) and has been selected by consultant, Vincent Gasnier. Wine and food are also available from the onsite deli. Smoked chicken salad with pink grapefruit and balsamic vinegar suggests a boldness of flavour, or chicken breast stuffed with taleggio, chorizo and tarragon bean stew. Eclectic fare in a typical Hoxton set-up.

Basic price	£25
Phone	020 7719 5252

East Bar, 54-58 Kingsland Rd, E2 8DP.

Shoreditch, on the edge of the City. Chairman Mao peers benignly on. Suddenly the dictator has become fashionable. One feels he would have approved of the City. He rubs shoulders with that more classical of Chinese takeaway icons, the omnipresent dragon. Menu has Vietnamese influences. Try paper-wrapped prawn with sweet and sour chilli sauce, chicken feet in blackbean sauce, and fresh asparagus in garlic with scallops.

Basic price	£15
Phone	020 7729 6655

Eyre Bros, 68-70 Leonard St, EC2A 4QX.

Forget chic, there's a new phenomenon: Shoreditch rich. Now that most of the artists have gone, the monied classes have arrived. This is a good example of what has sprung up to cater for these tastes. Mediterranean cooking with strong flavours, many informed by Spain and Portugal. Worth trying are the Mozambique prawns with piri-piri, lamb marinated in anchovy, or fillet of Iberico pork marinated with thyme and garlic. Or Bacalhau à Gomes de Sá – salt cod baked with potatoes, onions, garlic and bay, olives, soft-boiled egg, and parsley. Cuttlefish with aioli and escabeche of quail also feature. Everything here has attitude, right down to the chocolate and prune terrine.

Basic price	£30
Phone	020 7613 5346

Fifteen Restaurant Ltd, 13 Westland Place, N1 7LP.

Thumpingly expensive food factory where the sainted chef Jamie Oliver set up an experiment training underprivileged kids to become masterchefs. Ground-floor trattoria and basement restaurant where your evening meal will cost £50 to £60, depending upon whether you opt for meat. Seasonal produce with Mediterranean themes. Dishes such as 'kinda sashimi' and other Jamie epiphanies. Profits go to JO's charity. Nearest tube is Old Street.

Basic price	£28-£60
Phone	0871 330 1515
Internet	www.fifteenrestaurant.com

Fish Shop, 360-362 Street John St, EC1V 4NR.

Excellent fish and chips as well as more sophisticated fish and shellfish from the people who used to be the Upper Street Fish Shop. Whatever you choose will be straight from Billingsgate Market. Pan fried red snapper, pak-choy, sweet soya sauce, wild mushroom and egg noodles. Or maybe roast native lobster, brandy butter and hand cut chips or salad, half or whole. This is a minimalist take on the chippy with floor to ceiling windows flood the two floored listed building with light.

Basic price	£30
Phone	020 7837 1199.
Internet	www.thefishshop.net

Great Eastern Dining Room, 54 Great Eastern St, EC2A 3QR.

The Great Eastern Dining Room is the lively brainchild of Will Ricker, the Antipodean who created Cicada in Clerkenwell (see above) and E & O in Notting Hill. A favourite with the design set, the GEDR is noisy and the crowd is young, fashionable and well-washed bohemian. The new Pan-Asian menu is packing the restaurant out every night and proving popular with the Shoreditch clientele. Waiting staff are friendly and the appealing reasonably priced menu delivers everything it should, while the two bars add to the substantial appeal as a party venue. Dinner for two with a bottle of wine costs around £60.

Basic price	£30
Phone	020 7613 4545
Internet	www.greateasterndining.co.uk

Restaurants: City (cont)

Hanoi Cafe Ltd, 98 Kingsland Road, E2 8DP.
Family run restaurant with over a hundred fresh homemade authentic Vietnamese dishes to chose from, Hanoi's fresh ingredients, relaxed atmosphere and happy atmosphere create an authentic Vietnamese experience. Attracts artists, musicians and business people.

Basic price	£10
Phone	020 7729 5610

Lahore One Restaurant, 218 Commercial Rd, E1 2JT.
Charcoal-fired ovens produce a pungent and accurate taste for many Indian dishes such as spicy lamb kebabs. Very good meat and vegetable biryanis or karahi wok dishes are popular main course dishes. Just off the famous Brick Lane.

Basic price	£10
Phone	020 7791 0112

Mafizs, 28 Osborn St, E1 6TD.
Bangla Town in the East End of London is reckoned to be the epicentre of Indian and Bangladeshi cuisine and Ajwan is one of the best examples. Modern, creative Indian and Bangladeshi food seven days a week. Try the kakra aloo kebab (fresh minced crab meat starter mixed with mashed potatoes, finely chopped onions and ginger rolled on cashew nuts and fried until golden) or golda chingri morrisha (tender pieces of grilled king size prawns in a hot sauce cooked with capsicum, onions and fresh green chillies).

Basic price	£10
Phone	020 7247 1100

The Light, 233 Shoreditch High Street, E1.
The Light is a stunning new venue in the city offering global cuisine. This restored power station houses the restaurant as well as a bar, cocktail lounge, landscaped courtyard and roof terrace. Shoreditch newcomer attracting lots of attention. The funky decor and French/Mediterranean menu, attract a young, vivacious crowd. London Eating awards top marks for food.

Basic price	£30
Phone	020 7247 8989

Mehek, 45 London Wall, EC2 M5TE.
Upmarket contemporary Indian cuisine to pull in the City high-rollers. Small menu based on authentic Indian dishes - plenty of delicate spices without lashings of artificial colouring. Recommended is the boro chingri pardanashi (medium, hot & spicy king prawns cooked Goan style and served in a baby coconut shell) and the Raan-e-Mehek (sliced roast leg of lamb marinated in Indian spices and cooked over a gentle flame in a rich onion and tomato gravy, flavoured with nutmeg).

Phone	020 7588 5044
Internet	www.mehek.co.uk

Moro, 34-36 Exmouth Market, EC1R 4QE.
Spanish/Moorish: plain walls and zinc topped bar, on which they serve excellent tapas (the bar, that is). Kitchen does much of its cooking in wood burning ovens. Popular with creative media types (the Guardian and Observer newspapers are just round the corner). Try: calves kidneys with farika and cinnamon yoghurt, home made labneh (cream cheese) with crudites, pickles and then charcoal grilled mackerel with patatas pobres or Moroccan mezze with flat bread. Near Farringdon tube.

Basic price	£30
Phone	020 7833 8336
Internet	www.moro.co.uk

The way of all flesh: With Smithfield market so close, City restaurants are often great places for those who like their food meaty.

Miyabi, Great Eastern Hotel, Liverpool Street, EC2M 7QN.
Situated in Sir Terence Conran's Great Eastern Hotel on Liverpool Street, Miyabi offers some good Japanese food. A wide selection of sushi, sashimi and tempura are served in tranquil, 'zen-like' surroundings. Chic set up, dark woods and smart furniture, very nice suits. This is no less than you would expect; this is the epicentre of the City.

Basic price	£35
Phone	020 7618 7100
Internet	www.great-eastern-hotel.co.uk

Potemkin, 144 Clerkenwell Rd, EC1R 5DP.
Russian cuisine: great spot for serious eating AND drinking. What's more, it's cheap. But this depends largely upon whether you dip into the caviar or how much you spend at the bar. Voted by an Evening Standard critic as one of the five best places in London for dumplings and number one for Bloody Marys. Food-wise, try Cossack lamb casserole, a spiced tender lamb dish from southern Russia with potatoes, garlic, fresh coriander, and black pepper. Then the pancakes. 80 different vodkas, one for every hour of the day in the gulag.

Basic price	£25
Phone	020 7278 6661

The Real Greek, 14-15 Hoxton Market, N1 6HG.
Theodore Kyriakou has opened The Real Greek to showcase Greek regional cuisine to great critical acclaim. Many of the home-style dishes haven't been seen on restaurant menus in the UK before. A real delight is the smaller mixed mezedes offering dishes such as octopus casserole and rocket, leek, caper and filo pie. There is also tapas-style food at the more casual Mezedopolio café attached.

Basic price	£30
Phone	020 7739 8212

Royal Exchange Grand Cafe & Bar, The Courtyard, Royal Exchange Bank, EC3V 3LR.
The Grand Café & Bar occupies three areas of this Grade I listed building which dates back to 1565. In 2001 when LIFFE vacated the building it was sympathetically remodelled to become the home of the worlds' finest fashion retailers. The Courtyard offers an all-day dining area serving a selection of crustacea, salads, sandwiches, charcuterie, rillettes and terrines, home-made tarts and patisserie. The two mezzanine bars specialise in cocktails and offer a full range of wines, beers and champagnes.

Phone	020 7618 2480
Email	info@conran-restaurants.co.uk
Internet	www.conran.com

Restaurants: City (cont)

St John, 26 St John St, EC1M 4AY.

This is a temple for alll carnivores. Original, simple and well executed dishes using much offal and other under-exploited resources, chef Fergus Henderson did much to enliven this part of town, not to mention the modern British scene. St John is a former smokery close to Smithfield Market. Soothing minimalist interior (with lively downstairs bar) suits the menu. Let us list a few treats and unusual juxtapositions. For starters – pressed pork gizzard or roast bone marrow and parsley salad. For mains, there's calf's liver and chicory; chitterlings (intestines) and radishes; pigeon and pea puree. Or perhaps pig's nose and tail and deep fried calf's brain? Farringdon tube (for transport).

Basic price	£30
Phone	020 7251 0848/4998
Internet	www.stjohnrestaurant.com

Searcy's, Level 2, Barbican Centre, EC2Y 8DS.

Searcy's overlooks the 'lake' and fountains of the Barbican Centre, an arts centre with a diverse programme of events, exhibitions and performances. Offers Modern British cooking in a contemporary setting. Wide range of choice from the exotic and expensive to the more robust and down to earth lamb shank (albeit perched atop a pile of parsnip mash served with root vegetable cappuccino). Desserts come in for praise.

Basic price	£25
Phone	020 7588 3008
Internet	www.barbican.org.uk

Song Que, 134 Kingsland Rd, E2 8DY.

It is a truth universally acknowledged that a good ethnic restaurant will be full of people of the same ethnicity eating in it. So it is at the Song Que. This particular part of Hoxton - Kingsland Road - is sometimes referred to as "Little Vietnam" and there are similar restaurants all around, but Song Que seems to be the locals' favourite. Time Out goes overboard in praise, but counsels eaters to avoid Chinese dishes. Old Street tube then a quick taxi drive.

Basic price	£15
Phone	020 7613 3222

South, 128-130 Curtain Rd, EC2 A3AQ.

Hoxton meets the South of France. This former artists' quarter is now the flavour amongst the nouveau riche and restaurants have followed in their wake. This is good quality French cooking without airs and graces: things like crab and avocado salad adorn the starters list, while duck with red chicory and fig sauce prove popular among the mains. Puddings traditional, all ingredients organic.

Basic price	£22
Phone	020 7729 4452
Email	southrestaurant@aol.com

Les Trois Garcons, 1 Club Row, E1 6JX.

So fabulously opulent it could have been the setting for The Cook, The Thief, His Wife and Her Lover. Full frontal Chandaliers and glass beading drip down gilded walls. Stuffed beasts adorn the place, and to set the scene, a giraffe wearing a tiara and a crocodile greet you at the door. Hard to believe this was once a London boozer. Very French in style, it's the kind of place that attracts celebrities who really want to be noticed. Great French wine list and imaginative menus at top prices. Check out the website.

Basic price	£40 upwards
Phone	020 7613 1924
Internet	www.lestroisgarcons.com

HOTELS

City, Blackfriars, Farringdon, Holborn, Clerkenwell & Shoreditch

LUXURY HOTELS

Chamberlain, 130-135 Minories, City, EC3 1NU.
64 rooms, from £80 to £190 s/d/t. Monument, Cannon Street.
Air-conditioning, plasma screen in the bathroom and the full range of facilities. Near London's West End and the South Bank. Pub style bar.

Phone	020 7680 1500
Email	thechamberlain@fullers.co.uk
Internet	www.thechamberlainhotel.com

Grange City, 8-10 Coopers Row, City, EC3N 2BD.
234 rooms, from £80 s/d/t. Rack rate £280. Bank.
Exceptional deals possible for weekend via internet at this 5-star. Good view of the Tower of London, great sport and leisure centre, plus pool. Restaurants offer Japanese and Italian food. Smart choice.

Phone	020 7863 3700
Email	city@grangehotel.com
Internet	www.grangehotels.com

Great Eastern Hotel, 40 Liverpool St, EC2M 7QN.
264 rooms. From £225 s/d/t. Liverpool Street.
Only large hotel within the City's Square Mile. Interior design by Conran & Partners, the Grade II Listed Hotel four restaurants, three bars and a gym. Victorian exterior, bright and spacious and extremely convenient for trendy Hoxton and Shoreditch.

Phone	08700 600 100
Email	sales@great-eastern-hotel.co.uk
Internet	www.great-eastern-hotel.co.uk

Novotel London Tower Bridge, 10 Pepys St, City, EC3 2NR.
199 rooms, from £100 to £190. Tower Hill.
Purpose built and comfortable with good transport links.

Phone	020 7265 6060
Email	h3107@accor-hotels.com
Internet	www.accorhotels.com

Threadneedles, 5 Street, City, EC2 R8AY.
63 rooms, from £165 s/d/t to £245. Liverpool Street .
Threadneedles (pictured right) is located in the financial district of London. A beautifully converted Banking Hall built in 1856, it creates a feeling of luxury and tranquillity whilst echoing its colourful past. Overlooking the Bank of England and The Stock Exchange, Threadneedles is within minutes of The Strand, Tate Modern, St Paul's Cathedral and the Tower of London. Bonds, the bar, is a popular local hang out. The restaurant offers 'Modern French' cuisine.

Phone	020 7657 8080
Email	resthreadneedles@theetoncollection.com
Internet	www.theetoncollection.com/hotels/threadneedles

Hotels: City (cont)

MODERATELY PRICED

Express by Holiday Inn, 275 Old St, Hoxton, EC1V 9LN.
224 rooms. From £60. Old Street Good value on the doorstep of the city and trendy Hoxton.

Phone	020 7300 4400
Email	reservationsfc@holidayinnlondon.com
Internet	www.holidayinnlondon.com

Thistle City Barbican, 120 Central St, EC1V 8DS.
463 rooms, from £80 s/d/t to £200. Old Street A modern hotel within easy walking distance of the Barbican Centre and the historic City of London. The hotel has conference rooms, restaurant, bar, coffee shop and full leisure centre.

Phone	0870 333 9101
Email	barbican@thistle.co.uk
Internet	www.thistlehotels.co.uk

Travelodge, 1 Harrow Place, City, E1 7DB.
142 rooms, from £89. Liverpool Street Opposite Liverpool St Station, the rooms are spacious and bright – family friendly with all the facilities at a reasonable price.

Phone	08700 850950
Email	duty.manager@travelodge.co.uk
Internet	www.travelodge.co.uk

NORTH LONDON

Islington, Camden, Highgate & Hampstead

BARS

The Alma, 59 Newington Green Rd, Islington, N1 4QU.
Modern foodie pub: no more dartboard, just a blackboard with voguish dishes on the daily menu.

Barnsbury, 209-211 Liverpool Rd, Islington, N1 1LX.
Ropey old boozer that has undergone a metamorphosis following its scrub down. Good food. Fuller's and Taylors.

Compton Arms, 4 Compton Avenue, Islington, N1 4DX.
Warm and intimate hidey hole tucked away between Highbury Corner and Canonbury. Very much a locals pub. Big with Arsenal fans. Greene King.

Duke Of Cambridge, 30 St Peters St, Islington, N1 8JT.
This was the first organic gastropub in London. Everything here (even the lager) is organic.

Phone	020 7359 3066

Duke of Hamilton, 23 New End, Hampstead, NW3 1JD.
Great sporting pub – has its own cricket and rugby teams. A real haven. Voted local CAMRA Pub of the Year 2002 and 2003. Named after the Civil War royalist, the Duke is 200 years old, has a cellar bar, terrace, cobbled yard and larger main bar. Hampstead Heath tube, Fuller's beer.

Phone	020 7794 0258

Flask, 14 Flask Walk, Hampstead, NW3 1HE.
Beautiful, old fashioned pub easily accessible by tube. A real north London institution.

Head of Steam, 1 Eversholt St, Euston, NW1 1DN.
For those stepping off the train at Euston, a good welcome to town. Traditional pub with no pretensions and a wide variety of beers.

Holly Bush, 22 Holly Mount, Hampstead, NW3 6SG.
A lot bigger than it looks at first sight, there are several rooms in these converted Grade II listed stables near the Heath. A cracking pub. Adnams, Fullers and Harveys.

Island Queen, 87 Noel Rd, Islington, N1 8HD.
Great pub tucked away near the canals of Islington near the Angel. This one is on the up: London Pride, Taylor's Landlord and Deuchars, plus Kolsch, Fruli, Leffe, Hoegaarden, Staropramen and de Konninck.

King's Head, 115 Upper St, Islington N1 8JT.
Bustling theatre pub (there is a theatre at the back) with a pre-decimal till. Great Islington landmark, there has been a pub here since the turn of the 17th century. Weekend late license. Adnam, Tetley and Youngs.

Red Lion & Sun, 25 North Rd, Highgate, N6 4BE.
The Red Lion is reckoned to be the best pub in Highgate. It is a 'secret treasure,' according to the Good Beer Guide. Greene King.

Spread Eagle, 141 Albert St, Camden Town, NW1 7NB.
Unchanged by interior designers who over the generations have wrecked a huge number of pubs. Young's. Camden Rd tube.

Wenlock Arms. 26 Wenlock Rd, Islington, N1 7TA.
This is a great pub with lots of character and lots of different and very fine beers. It has barely changed for generations, though came near to a makeover in 1940, thanks to the Luftwaffe. No matter how much money breweries throw at pubs, they can't make them like the Wenlock. Jazz and quizzes. Locals and beer nuts. Not far from Old Street tube/rail, go up the City Road and turn into Windsor Terrace.

Phone	020 7608 3406
Internet	www.wenlock-arms.co.uk

Wrestlers, 98 North Rd, Highgate, N6 4AA.
There has been a pub here since 1547. Dark and cosy and does generous portions of simple food.

TRENDY BARS

Islington, Camden, Highgate & Hampstead

THESE ARE ALL SERIOUSLY LATE NIGHT VENUES

Belushis Bar, 48-50 Camden High Road Camden, NW1 0LT.
Belushi's sits well in the vibrant heart of Camden. Only minutes away from Camden Market and Regents Park, it is part of Camden's groovy night scene. Like all the Belushi's venues, it has a late license, cocktails, food and great music.

Phone	020 7388 1012
Internet	www.belushis.com

Elbow Room, 88-91 Chapel Market, Islington, N1 9EX.
Still remains a top choice for late-night action. Relaxed, good food and action.

Mac Bar, 105-107 Camden Road, Camden, NW1 9EA.
Cocktail bar – comes with top marks. The staff really know their stuff.

Medicine Bar, 181 Upper St, Islington, N1 1RQ.
The only medicine you will see in here is unlikely to have been prescribed by a GP. This is a great DJ venue and has a reputation in North London as being the place to be. Their cocktails are terrific

Salmon and Compass, 58 Penton Street, N1 9PY.
No-one has yet fathomed – or indeed tried to fathom – why maps and fishes enter into the late night equation. This is a hard drinking wild spot for untamed action-seekers bored with the meandering throng on Upper Street. The music is good and the crowd is hip. If you like this kind of thing, you'll like the Salmon.

Social, 33 Linton St, Islington, N1 7DU.
Owned by the trendy record label, Heavenly, Social is tucked away in a distant corner of the borough so consult your A-Z or take a taxi. This is a hip joint for early 20-somethings with a yen for Japanese lagers. There's a wide selection of food and some great tunes. Take note of the phone number in case you get lost:

Phone	020 7354 5809

RESTAURANTS

Islington, Camden, Highgate & Hampstead

Islington is well blessed with restaurants. Decent chains in the area, which we have not listed below, include Carluccio's Caffe, Gallipoli (Turkish), Nando's, Pizza Express, Masala Zone, Strada, Wagamama, Yo! Sushi!

Almeida Restaurant, 30 Almeida Street, Islington, N1 1AD.

Good, robust French regional cooking – classic, simple dishes – in trendy Islington. This is a Conran restaurant, one of Sir Terence's reliable stable, overseen in this instance by the Michelin-rated Orrery. Good but expensive wine list, excellent dessert trolley (there's even a terrine trolley). Fixed price menus good value, a la carte starts to rocket. Tapas menu in the bar available for 1200-2300.

Phone	020 7354 4777
Email	diviere@conran-restaurants.co.uk
Internet	www.almeida-restaurants.co.uk

Angel Mangal, 139 Upper St, Islington, N1 1PQ.

Turkish food has overtaken Greek as the Aegean food for the masses. The Islington area is where much of the Turkish community has settled so you have plenty of choice. The Angel Mangal is probably the best of these on Upper Street. Patlican soslu – aubergine salad with onions and tomatoes cooked on a charcoal oven – is very worthwhile, as are the kebabs and mixed grills, all served with masses of salad. You can eat well at any of these Turkish outlets (we have yet to have a dud).

Basic price	£22
Phone	020 7359 7777

Asakusa, 265 Eversholt St, Camden NW1 1BA. £25.

Japanese – good on fried and grilled, fine list of sashimi and sushi. Reports suggest it is especially good on raw produce such as yellowtail tuna. Other dishes of the day pinned up – usually in Japanese. Good range of sakes. Not the smartest but the food more than compensates. Camden Town or Mornington Crescent tubes.

Basic price	£22
Phone	020 7388 8533/8399

Bierodrome, 173-174 Upper Street, Islington, N1 1XS

Bierodrome has over 200 Belgian beers and numerous Belgian schnapps. Lunch and dinner is available from the restaurant, with traditional Belgian regional cuisine. Simple but effective formula for killing two birds with one stone: drinking beer and taking aboard some lumpy stuff.

Basic price	£20
Phone	020 7226 5835
Internet	www.belgo-restaurants.com

The House, 63-69 Canonbury Rd, Islington, N1 2DG.

Busy bar but you can head straight for the restaurant and dive into risotto of calamari with mascarpone and salt cod mariniere, as well as a good range of starter salads, such as peppered beef fillet, stilton and red onion. Created by Michelin-starred chef Jeremy Hollingsworth and front man Barnaby Meredith, who have both worked for the Marco Pierre White group. Trundling trolley of fine liqueurs. Near Highbury and Islington tube.

Basic price	£33
Phone	020 7704 7410
Internet	www.inthehouse.biz

Gaucho Grill, 64 Heath Street, Hampstead, NW3 1DN.

The Gaucho Grill's Argentinean concept specialises in high quality, free-range Argentinian meat. The restaurant also offers London's largest selection of Argentine wines, not your Mendozan plonk and 30oz T-boners. Sophisticated chain specialising in cocktails to prepare the palate. There's also one in Chancery Lane, Holborn and another in Gracechurch Street in the City.

Phone	020 7376 3222
Internet	www.thegauchogrill.co.uk

Huong Viet, 12-14 Englefield Rd, Islington, N1 4LS.

Very busy 'canteen', as the sign above the door of this Vietnamese community centre states. Cheap and exceedingly cheerful, tables are cheek by jowl and the noise can get a bit oppressive. The busier the place, the slower the service, but worth the wait – and you can take your own booze. BBQ operating in the evening. Cooking is light and subtle, the flavours authentic. Try: cat fish fillet in a hot clay pot, lamb gallangal (chargrilled and tender), the prawn and chicken satay (giant prawns chargrilled on wooden skewers) or chicken and cashew nuts.

Basic price	£16
Phone	020 7249 0877

Jin Kichi, 73 Heath St, Hampstead, NW3 6UG.

It is small, a little scruffy and cramped, the Jin serves genuine Japanese food from sushi to sashimi and tempura, to the humble grilled mackerel. The staff are friendly, courteous and genuine and some have been there a long time. According to some locals, it is 'without doubt' the best restaurant in Hampstead, a wealthy suburb largely bereft of good eateries.

Basic price	£25
Phone	020 7794 6158

Le Mercury, 140A Upper St, Islington, N1 1QY.

This place has been around for donkey's years, always busy and bustling, Bohemian, romantic and cheap. You get, as one guide put it, champagne style on a beer budget. However the cuisine can be hit and miss, serving French/Modern British with good fish and meat options, and desserts. 'Fellow diners will range from young professionals on first dates to new money locals with a taste for value,' according to one guide. Just by the Almeida Theatre, it looks great, with its bright shining windows and crisp white napery.

Basic price	£11
Phone	020 7354 4088

Le Mignon, 98 Arlington Rd, Camden, NW1 7HD.

Lebanese: try the warak inab bizeit, a Lebanese version of stuffed vine leaves. Or the foul moukala, green broad beans cooked in olive oil, fresh coriander and garlic. Moujadara is a house speciality and consists of lentils and rice topped with fried onions. Main courses include a lot of lamb and chicken on skewers, all around the £10, plus charcoal grilled quail. Great little restaurant in a downbeat neighbourhood.

Basic price	£30
Phone	020 7387 0600

Lola's, The Mall/359 Upper St, Islington, N1 0PD.

It wasn't like this in the old days. This converted tram shed provides very chi-chi attic space for Islington's smart set. During daytime the light is wonderful: pink walls under a glass roof, complete with North African mosaic. The food is striking and eclectic – duck cooked three ways to start, slow cooked shoulder of lamb, Challans chicken with harissa-spiced couscous. That sort of thing. Gets its name from the author of a bundle of letters the owners found when they took over the lease seven years ago: in them, Lola, the author, boasts of a successful career as a fraudulent wine critic and thief.

Phone	020 7359 1932

Restaurants: North London (cont)

Metrogusto Islington, 13 Theberton St, Islington, N1 0QY.
Progressive Italian cooking with great attention to detail, this is the younger sibling of the original Metrogusto in Battersea, South London. There's a strong local following because of quality and reasonable prices. Very popular with the locals. Veal escalope with fennel sauce, ravioli of fresh ginger and tuna, stuffed baby squid etc. Fine spot. Mid-way between Angel and Highbury and Islington tubes.

Basic price	£20
Phone	020 7226 9400
Internet	www.metrogusto.co.uk

Morgan M, 489 Liverpool Rd, Islington, N7 8NS.
Superb French cuisine from Morgan Meunier, who used to be head chef at the Admiralty, Somerset House and the Michelin-Starred Monsieur Max in Twickenham. Starters include light cream of pumpkin infused with rosemary, wild mushroom beignet, or foie gras poêlé from 'Les Landes', with an apricot coulis and toasted brioche. Main: fillet of Iken Valley venison, pot roasted, with hare ravioli, glazed apple and chestnut purée, sauce Grand Veneur. Tasting menu £39 (£34 for vegetarians). Totally French wine list Top notch. A five minute walk from Highbury & Islington tube.

Basic price	£35 plus
Phone	020 7609 3560
Internet	www.morganm.com

Le Monmartre Bistro, 196 Essex Rd, Islington, N1 8LZ.
Pub conversion with solid bare-top tables, Le Montmartre is a no-nonsense local bistro that every neighbourhood ought to have. Regional French food at decent prices. Frogs legs and snails in garlic butter, Toulouse sausages in red wine, entrecote steak in a wild mushroom sauce with chips. You get the picture.

Basic price	£17
Phone	020 7688 1497

Odettes, 130 Regent's Park Rd, Primrose Hill, NW1 8XL.
Charming little place with gilded mirrors and very good bistro cooking. Recommended are tronchon of turbot with tartare sauce and deep fried parsley, casserole of sea bass, red mullet and mussels or spit-roast milk-reared lamb cooked with vine tomatoes, courgettes and feta. All good fare. Great setting and not cheap. Chalk Farm tube.

Basic price	£35
Phone	020 7586 5486

Pescador, 23 Pratt St, Camden Town, NW1 0BG.
First class Portuguese fish restaurant. Recommended dishes include Cataplana, a stew of monkfish, clams and prawns cooked in a chilli sauce with rice. Also the pasteis de bacalhau (deep fried potato and cod balls), and the arroz de marisco (clams, squid, prawns, mussels and fish in a soupy rice) are thoroughly recommended by the redoubtable inspectors at Time Out. At around £80 for two (including two bottles of the basic vinho verde) Pescador is a slightly more expensive cousin to Lemonia and Marine Ices - good quantities of simple food done well, with genuine service.

Basic price	£25
Phone	020 7482 7008

Seraphin, 341 Upper Street Islington, N1 0PB. Around £25.
Relaxed but decadent setting. Exotic and eclectic menu (fish and chips, confit of pork belly with crocodile tail etc). Upstairs is the vibey Jade Bar, with its array of cocktails. Ultra-trendy.

Phone	020 7359 7374
Email	michael@seraphin-n1.com
Internet	www.seraphin-n1.com

Viet Garden, 207 Liverpool Rd, Islington, N1 1LX.
Great soft shell crab, barbequed pork, seabass in fish sauce and red chilli and mango are all very good. The seafood is all fresh each day and the recipes often home-grown. Traditional Vietnamese hot soups such as Bun come served with chilli and lemon on the side. Crispy fried noodles with green vegetables were excellent side orders, and for dessert there are delicate yoghurts, flavoured with lavender.

Basic price	£15
Phone	020 7700 6040

Zamoyski Restaurant & Vodka Bar, 85 Fleet Rd, Hampstead, NW3 2QY.
Polish cooking. Three course lunch of soup, main and pudding for under a tenner. That's cheaper than Warsaw. Tortes of beetroot, smoked salmon, smoked trout and dill, veal cutlets and lots of red cabbage are staples. Desserts are good and filling. Lots of tempting vodkas and interesting beers and Russian music.

Basic price	£22
Phone	020 7794 4792

HOTELS

Islington, Camden, Highgate & Hampstead

LUXURY HOTELS

Euston Plaza, 17-18 Upper Woburn Place, WC1 H0HT.
150 rooms. From £120 s/d/t. Euston Light interiors reflects Scandinavian ownership. Well connected for everywhere in town.

Phone	0207943 4500
Internet	www.euston-plaza.com

Hilton London Islington, 53 Upper St, N1 0UY.
178 rooms. From £120 s/d/t. Angel. Next to the Business Design Centre at the bottom end of Upper St, this is a fine and functional hotel in a swinging part of town.

Phone	020 7354 7700
Email	res_islington@hilton.com

Marriott Regents Park, 128 King Henry's Rd, Regents Park, NW3.
298 rooms. From £120 s/d/t. Regents Park. Great location with an impressive leisure centre for working off the weekend's excesses. The Park itself offers a less traumatic alternative.

Phone	020 7722 7711

Novotel London Euston, 100-110 Euston Rd, NW1 2AJ.
311 rooms. From £120 s/d/t. Euston. Large modern hotel not far from the West End and Islington, with Bloomsbury on the doorstep. Some good eating and drinking in Clerkenwell.

Phone	020 7666 9000
Email	h5309@accor-hotels.com
Internet	www.accor-hotels.com

MODERATELY PRICED

Holiday Inn, 215 Haverstock Hill, Hampstead, NW3 4RB.
140 rooms. From £109 s/d/t. Hampstead. Near the centre of Hampstead with its pubs, cafes and smart shops. Business style but none the worse for that.

Phone	0870 4009037
Email	reservations-hampstead@6c.com

Hotels: North London (cont)

Holiday Inn London - Regent's Park, Carburton St, W1 W5EE.
333 rooms. From £100 s/d/t. Great Portland Street Modern accommodation including 35 'Executive' rooms, with a range of amenities. The Junction restaurant serves modern British cuisine from an a la carte menu.

Phone	0870 400 9111
Email	londonregentspark@ichotelsgroup.com
Internet	www.london-regentspark.holiday-inn.com

The House, 2 Rosslyn Hill, Hampstead, NW3 1PH.
23 rooms. From £90 s/d/t. Belsize Park, Hampstead. Boutique hotel in a large Victorian town house, there is a strong period flavour. Each bedroom is differently styled. Much effort has gone into this.

Phone	020 7433 1755
Internet	www.thehousehotel.co.uk
Email	reception@thehousehotel.co.uk

Jury's Inn London, 60 Pentonville Rd, N1 9LA.
229 rooms. Standard rate £104. From £70 s/d/t. King's Cross, Angel.
One of a large chain but nothing wrong with that. Rooms well equipped and there's a good bar. Also the fleshpots of Islington are just round the corner.

Phone	020 7282 5500
Email	jurysinnlondon@jurysdoyle.com
Internet	www.jurysdoyle.com

Langorf Hotel, 20 Frognal, Hampstead, NW3 6AG.
31 rooms. From £80 s/d/t. Apartments sleeping up to 5: £150. Up to 4: £130. Up to 3: £100. Finchley Rd.
Charming Edwardian house in the leafy suburbs with a big, walled garden. Very good value for money. 15 minute walk to the Heath.

Phone	020 7794 4483
Internet	www.langorfhotel.com
Email	info@langorfhotel.com

Premier Travel Inn London Euston, 1 Dukes Rd, WC1 H9PJ.
220 rooms from £75 s/d/t. Euston.
Functional and more than adequate accommodation aimed at the businessman on a low budget account. Plenty of good things in the area.

Phone	0870 2383301
Email	London.euson.mti@travelinn.co.uk
Internet	www.premiertravelinn.com

Premier Travel Inn London King's Cross, Yorkway, King's Cross, N1 9DZ.
276 rooms from £70 s/d/t. King's Cross. Premier tries to offer the kind of comforts you get at more expensive hotels and to a large extent succeeds.

Phone	0870 990 6414
Email	info@premierlodge.co.uk
Internet	www.premierlodge.com

BUDGET ACCOMMODATION

Europa Hotel, 60-62 Anson Rd, Tufnell Park, N7 0AA.
30 rooms, from £35 s to £49 d/t. Tuffnell Park.
Georgian house in a quiet road 15 minutes from the centre of town. Full English breakfast included.

Phone	020 7607 5935
Email	info@europahotellondon.co.uk
Internet	www.europahotellondon.co.uk

Queen's Hotel, 33 Anson Rd, Tufnell Park, N7 0RB.
48 rooms from £25 s to £50 d/t. Tufnell Park.
Large detached Georgian house accessible for buses and tubes.

Phone	020 7607 4725
Email	queens@stavrouhotels.co.uk
Internet	www.stavrouhotels.co.uk

White Lodge Hotel, 1 Church Lane, Hornsey, N8 7BU.
16 rooms, from £32 s, £42 d/t, family 3 £58, family 4 £68, family 5 £78. Turnpike Lane.
Small, friendly family hotel offering personal service and easy access to the rest of the capital.

Phone	020 8348 9765
Email	info@whitelodgehornsey.co.uk
Internet	www.whitelodgehornsey.co.uk

SOUTH LONDON

London Bridge, Southwark, South Bank, Waterloo

This whole area has sprung up as a centre of gastronomic excellence, stretching from the area around Borough Market, down past the Young Vic theatre as far as Waterloo. There are some great pubs and what was once a desolate backwater is now worth a serious detour. Indeed, it is an exciting and highly accessible part of town to base yourselves.

BARS

Belushis Bar, 161 Borough High Street, SE1 1HR.
Always something happening at this place. Party hard into the early hours and then if you like you can book a bed and crash. Three rooms on two floors all open late, three big screens and 12 small screens for sporting events, outside terrace are and BBQs.

Phone	020 7939 9700
Internet	www.belushis.com

All Bar One, 34 Shad Thames Butlers Wharf, Spice Quays, SE1 2YG.
Scenic location situated under Butler's Wharf, right on the Thames and overlooking Tower Bridge. This bar is popular with the surrounding office workers and tourists alike. Its location means that it can become very busy at times and the patrons often spill out onto the promenade.

Phone	0871 223 4003

All Bar One, 1 Chichley St, Waterloo, SE1 7PY.
Much the same as above although without the scenic location.

Phone	0871 223 4010

Auberge, 1 Sandell Street, Waterloo, SE1 8UH.
Busy throughout the week with extensive drinks list, plain interior but with lots of seating so unless the place is really busy you'll find a seat. Diverse range of spirits and reasonable prices for the area.

Phone	0871 223 2588

The Banana Store, 1 Cathedral Street, Southwark, SE1 9DE.
Serves a choice of mixed bar snacks as well as beers, wines and spirits. They show all major international sporting events on a big screen and private functions can be catered for during the weekends.

Phone	0871 223 5209

Clubs: South London (cont)

The Arches, 53 Southwark Street, London Bridge, Southwark, SE1 1TE.
A nightclub as well as a bar so can be a single destination for a night out. All the usual trappings of bars in this part of town - deep leather sofas, high quality sound and lighting system. Well known for having a good atmosphere and friendly crowd.

Phone	0871 223 6043

The Fire Station, 149 Waterloo Road, Waterloo, SE1 8SB.
Good atmosphere for international rugby games. You can sit on long old wooden tables in separate area with big screen. Frequented by a rugby loving crowd with plenty of noise and singing, although beer is slightly more expensive than surrounding venues.

Phone	0871 223 6024

The Bridge Bar, Unit 13, London Bridge Station Railway Approach, London Bridge, SE1 9SP.
A convenient meeting place for friends who might coming to town, fairly standard drinks list and not much to make it stand out.

Phone	0871 223 6241

CLUBS

London Bridge, Southwark, South Bank, Waterloo

The Ministry of Sound, 103 Gaunt Street, SE1 6DP.
Its name precedes it: this is one the most famous clubs anywhere in the world and the queues are there to prove it. If you have the patience to get in, then you can expect a great experience but be warned, a dress code applies with no jeans or trainers allowed. There is also a 21+ age rule. Unlikely to affect most of you.

Phone	020 7378 6528

The Drome, 11 Stainer Lane, London Bridge.
This is one of the more 'out there' clubs on the London scene. It attracts a varied crowd and some events run for a straight 24 hours non-stop. It has none of the pretension that you find at a lot of the other London clubs so the people you find here tend to be more friendly and laid back than at some rival establishments.

Phone	0871 223 2841

Club Wicked, 4 Tooley Street, London Bridge, SE1 2SY.
Without any shadow of a doubt, Cynthia's is one of the more bizarre and outlandish bars in the whole of London. It occupies the middle ground between the seriously kitsch and terribly tacky, with mirrored passages creating disorientation for the already confused clientele.

Phone	0871 223 0940

RESTAURANTS

London Bridge, Southwark, South Bank, Waterloo

Anchor & Hope, 36 The Cut, SE1 8LP.

One of the best pub restaurants in London. Boasts the traditional gastropub uniform of bare floorboards, ochre walls and wood furniture, but retains a strong pub feel. The Good Food Guide awards it 5 out of 10 (only Gordon Ramsay scores 10, and only 42 establishments in the UK score 7 or more). Slow cooking a speciality as is fish and pudding. Good wine list and excellent service. Tube: Waterloo or Southwark.

Basic price	£25
Phone	020 7928 9898

Baltic, 74 Blackfriars Rd, SE1 8HA.

Across the road from Southwark tube. Baltic is a successful and stylish bar, all brushed steel, amber, art works and fibre-optic lighting. Great list of vodka from this Polish establishment, the menu is rugged Polish and Russian. If you have a hankering for Latvian, Lithianian, Georgian or Ukrainian specialities, these are also available. Beetroot, sour cream, blinis, caviar, smoked salmon etc. play their part. According to Time Out, this is London's 'best and most innovative' East European restaurant.

Basic price	£25
Phone	020 7928 1111
Internet	www.balticrestaurant.co.uk

Bermondsey Kitchen, 194 Bermondsey St, SE1 3TQ.

Modern European cooking right in your face: the kitchen stands centre stage, providing a lively floor show for those whose conversation is flagging. The starters are sensational – subtle barigoule of baby artichokes lightly dressed with an exotic olive oil, white anchovy salad with a dollop of aioli and quails eggs. Mains of crab Parmentier and roast suckling pig lived up to expectations.

Basic price	£23
Phone	020 7407 5719
Internet	www.bermondseykitchen.co.uk

Blueprint Café, Design Museum, 28 Shad Thames, SE1 2YD.

Another excellent spot near London Bridge. And another Sir Terence Conran success story. Great views up the Thames to Tower Bridge and Canary Wharf beyond, with its weird winking light. The plain interior accentuates the view, which is actually more memorable than the food – delicious though are the jellied pork with pickles, the parsley crusted razor clams, the salt-cured tuna, the roast loin of rabbit and other house specialties.

Phone	020 7378 7031
Internet	www.conran-restaurants.co.uk/ restaurants/blueprint

Cantina Vinopolis, 1 Bank End, SE1 9BU.

Part of the Vinopolis wine museum, shop and wine bar, this multi-functioning enterprise, which lies at the heart of Borough Market, is a focal point for the local corporate card-carrying suits. It serves some good food to go along with its immense and far from cheap wine list Good steaks and tunas, robust starters.

Basic price	£30
Phone	020 7940 8333
Internet	www.curestaurant .co.uk

Restaurants: South London (cont)

Champor-Champor, 62-64 Weston St, SE1 3QJ.

This Malaysian restaurant has taken off with a bang. So much so they've knocked the wall through to next door to make room for the throngs who now flock here. Exotic and funky. Even has the oriental equivalent of amuse bouche, such as beetroot with Indian salsa. Centre stage, for some reason, is a large scarlet cow and a Buddha. The bar is gold-lacquered and the duck longan and fried soft-shell crab are great, as is the Laotian warm beef salad and lamb fillet with aubergine mousse. Great spot. Near London Bridge (PS: the name means 'mix and match')

Basic price	£25
Phone	020 7403 4600
Internet	www.champor-champor.com

Fina Estampa, 150 Tooley St, SE1 2TU.

Within a few hundred yards of each other, and near to London Bridge station, there are two Peruvian restaurants. This is the place to come if you want a taste of the Andes. Try some Peruvian cocktails then lomo saltado – strips of glazed beef stir fried with chips, red onions and tomatoes. Or perhaps the ceviche – raw marinated fish.

Basic price	£20
Phone	020 7403 1342

Fish!, Cathedral St, Borough Market, SE1 9AL.

Voted runner up in the Time Out Best Family Restaurant award, kids portions are a merciful £6.95 (2 courses). Not quite so cheap for the adults, though. Try grilled or steamed fish of the day, served with salsa, herb and garlic butter or hollandaise. Very fresh and simple, nicely executed. Big and busy, good puddings.

Basic price	£25
Phone	020 7407 3803
Internet	www.fishdiner.co.uk

Georgetown, 10 London Bridge St, SE1 9SG.

Housed in what used to be one of the Simply Nico chain hard by London Bridge, Georgetown is an upmarket recreation of colonial days: chandeliers, gilt, starchy linen, high prices. Marinated rack of pork ribs with lemon grass and mild chilli, served with 'roti chanl' - Malay layered bread, and ladies fingers went down very well, as did a delicious 16th century Portuguese-influenced dish of spicy tiger prawns with Coconut milk and aubergines.

Phone	020 7357 7359
Internet	www.georgetownrestaurants.co.uk

Konditor & Cook, 10 Stoney St, SE1 9AD.

Upmarket café, stylish and top quality sandwiches and soups, tagines, pizzas and kedgeree. Good place to eat if you are visiting Borough Market. If the match is on a Sunday, a visit to the market on the Saturday is a must for foodies.

Basic price	£5
Phone	020 7407 5100

Lightship X, 5a St Katherine's Way, St Katherine's Dock, E1 W1LP.

This seagoing lighthouse served in the North Sea off the coast of Denmark and was captured by the Germans during World War II, who covered its decks with cobblestones to protect the crew from machine gun fire in British air raids. A magnificent place in a great setting, you can eat Scandinavian – all the usual suspects: fish, meat and poultry cooked any number of ways. Good fare at a reasonable price.

Basic price	£25
Phone	020 7481 3123
Internet	www.lightshipx.com

Livebait, 41-45 The Cut, Waterloo, SE1 8LF.

Handy for the theatres – the New and Old Vics are nearby, not to mention the South Bank arts centre. Livebait arrived trailing glory a decade ago when folk were wowed by the idea of a specialist piscatorial emporium. It even looks like a fishmongers, with its tiling and scrubbed interior. Simple and unaffected.

Basic price	£20
Phone	020 7928 7211
Internet	www.santeonline.co.uk/livebait

Lobster Pot, 3 Kennington Lane, Kennington, SE11 4RG.

There's no mistaking this place for a steak house. The Breton chef wears a signature stripy Breton T-shirt, there's a ship-to-shore phone, shells and portholes behind which fish watch as you tuck into their relatives. Good place to dive into lobster, perfectly cooked scallops or langoustines. Straightforward French cooking.

Basic price	£25
Phone	020 7582 5556
Internet	www.lobsterpotrestaurant.co.uk

Meson Don Felipe, 53 The Cut, Waterloo, SE1 8LF.

Tapas joint very popular with locals and those who work nearby. Victim of its own success – often too busy for the in-house guitarist to sit and play. Good range of reasonably priced wines. Popular with MI6, the locally-based spy outfit.

Phone	020 7928 3237

Oxo Tower, Oxo Tower Wharf, South Bank, SE1 9PH.

You would have to try hard to ruin this spot. It's on the 8th floor and once you are up there, it is breathtaking. Since it opened in 1996 the food has been pretty good, if expensive. Both the formal restaurant and more relaxed Brasserie and Bar command views across the Thames to Charing Cross and the City. The menu features a series of 'classics with a twist', as well as a sprinkling of dishes combining Mediterranean/Pacific Rim and French/Asian ingredients. There are 350 wines on the list. A unique louvred ceiling with blue neon lights creates a beautiful moonlit effect in the evenings.

Basic price	£45
Phone	020 7803 3888
Internet	www.oxotower.co.uk

Le Pont de la Tour Bar and Grill, Butlers Wharf Building 36d Shad Thames, SE1 2YE.

Great location, in the shadow of Tower Bridge. Grills, salads and wonderful crustacea: the plateau de fruits de mer is a speciality and a great treat. It also has outdoor seating and a pianist every evening and Sunday lunchtime. Try the tuna carpaccio with baby beetroot and sevruga caviar, or poached turbot, cucumber and sevruga beurre blanc (they do not stint on their caviar), or a meat dish like roast loin of rabbit, haricot blanc and truffle cappuccino.

Basic price	£50
Phone	020 7403 8403
Email	info@conran-restaurants.co.uk
Internet	www.conran.com

Restaurants: South London (cont)

RSJ, 33 Coin St London, SE1 9NR.
Just round the corner from the Oxo Tower, this solid French institution (with a British twist) offered the first decent dining in what was once a benighted culinary area. But that was a quarter of a century ago. RSJ has not changed but the area has. Gressingham duck with a confit of leg, creamed cabbage cooked with smoked bacon is a typically assured staple. Superb wine list. Handy for the South Bank arts centre and the New and Old Vic theatres. Near Waterloo.

Basic price	£30
Phone	020 7928 4554

Tas, 72 Borough High St, SE1 1XF.
Efficient and friendly, Tas offers a wide range of Turkish specialities. Has a big local following. Last time we checked it, the main course was crap but this was the first mishap in 8 years of occasional use. Great salads and grilled meats, plus a decent and reasonably priced wine list

Basic price	£20
Phone	020 7403 7200
Internet	www.tasrestaurant.com

Tito's, 4-6 London Bridge St, SE1 9SG.
Right next to London Bridge station above a sandwich bar, Tito's offers Peruvian cuisine (see also Fina Estampa just round the corner) in fairly unpromising surroundings. You will find it passes the ethnicity test – it's usually full of Latin Americans eating marinated heart or corn flour patties wrapped in banana leaf. Pork and beef dishes well executed and refried beans a speciality.

Basic price	£20
Phone	020 7407 7787

La Spezia, 35 Railway Approach, London Bridge, SE1.
Italian. Occupying an old railway arch, La Spezia is a charming Italian trattoria offering old favourites and an excellent variety of fresh fish and meat dishes. Cheap.

Phone	020 7407 0277

Riviera, Gabriel's Wharf, 56 Upper Ground, SE1.
Mediterranean Riviera, at Gabriel's Wharf, offers the varied cuisine of the Mediterranean region and a wine list to match. It has a great location right by the River Thames.

Phone	020 7401 7314

HOTELS

London Bridge, Southwark, South Bank, Waterloo

LUXURY HOTELS

London Bridge, 8-18 London Bridge St, SE1 9SG.
138 rooms, from £100 s/d/t. London Bridge. Privately owned in the old Edwardian era Post Office building, recently refurbished to a high standard. Restaurant serves Malay cooking in a 'colonial' setting.

Phone	020 7855 2200
Email	sales@london-bridge-hotel.co.uk
Internet	www.london-bridge-hotel.co.uk

London Marriott Hotel, County Hall, SE1 7PB.
200 rooms, from £200 s/d/t. Waterloo, Westminster.
One of the best locations in London with great views of Parliament and the river, particularly from the dining room. Big and comfortable rooms.

Phone	020 7928 5200
Email	Salesadmin.countyhall@marriotthotels.co.uk
Internet	www.marriott.com/lonch

Plaza on the River, 18 Albert Embankment, SE1 7TJ.
66 apartments from £180. 3-bed apartment £480. Vauxhall, Waterloo.
'Plaza on the River Club and Residence' offers a river location with views of Parliament, London Eye, Millbank etc, and a great sunset. A 24-hour concierge service, a river taxi to key locations, extensive on-site facilities because it adjoins the four star Riverbank Park Plaza Hotel. Eat in the oriental restaurant (very good indeed).

Phone	020 7769 2525
Email	info@plazaontheriver.co.uk
Internet	www.plazaontheriver.co.uk

Riverbank Park Plaza, 18 Albert Embankment, SE1 7TJ.
394 rooms, Vauxhall, Waterloo. Opposite Tate Britain art gallery.
Views of the Houses of Parliament, Big Ben and the London Eye, it shares the same building as Plaza on the River. Boasts the Chino Latino Brasserie, Bar and Lounge. River taxi takes you to key locations around the capital.

Phone	020 7958 8000
Email	rpp@parkplazahotels.co.uk
Internet	www.parkplaza.com

MODERATELY PRICED

Days, 54 Kennington Rd, SE1 7BJ.
162 rooms, from £89 s/d/t. Lambeth North. Three star without frills but with a restaurant and bar. Good base opposite the Imperial War Museum.

Phone	020 7922 1331
Email	waterloores@khl.uk.com
Internet	www.dayshotellondonwaterloo.co.uk

Express by Holiday Inn, 103-109 Southwark St, Southwark, SE1 0JQ.
88 rooms, from £90 to £120 s/d/t. Functional with good facilities and location.

Phone	020 7401 2525
Email	stay@expresssouthwark.co.uk
Internet	www.highexpress.com/lon/southwark

London County Hall Travel Inn Capital, Belvedere Rd, SE1 7PB.
313 rooms, £86.95 fixed rate s/d/t. Waterloo, Westminster
Budget part of the famous old County Hall building. Next to the London Eye, represents very good value.

Phone	0870 2383300
Internet	www.premiertravelinn.com
Email	countyhall@travelinn.co.uk

Mercure, 71-79 Southwark St, Southwark, SE1 0JA.
144 rooms, from £80 s/d/t to £165. London Bridge, Southwark. Contemporary look to this converted office block with bright rooms and all the usual business facilities.

Phone	020 7902 0800
Email	h2814@accor-hotels.com
Internet	www.mercure.com

Hotels: South London (cont)

Novotel London City South, 53-61 Southwark Bridge Rd,
Southwark, SE1 9HH. 182 rooms, from £90 to £160 s/d/t. London Bridge. AA 4 star 'New Generation Novotel' near Tate Modern, Millennium Bridge, Shakespeare's Globe Theatre, Vinopolis and St Paul's and Southwark Cathedrals. Garden Brasserie restaurant, Clinks Bar and a rooftop Leisure and Fitness Suite.

Phone	020 7089 0400
Email	h3269@accor-hotels.com
Internet	www.novotel.com

Premier Travel Inn, Anchor, Bankside, 34 Park St, SE1 9EF.
56 rooms, from £85 s/d/t. London Bridge. Good value for money in a happening part of town. Well equipped.

Phone	0870 990 6402
Email	info@premierlodge.co.uk
Internet	www.premierlodge.com

Premier Travel Inn London Tower Bridge, 159 Tower Bridge Rd.
SE1 3LP. 196 rooms £74.95 s/d/t. Well maintained, comfortable and good value.

Phone	0870 2383303
Email	London.tower.bridge.mti@whitbread.com
Internet	www.premiertravelinn.com

Southwark Rose, 43-47 Southwark Bridge Rd, SE1 9HH.
84 rooms, from £80 to £140 s/d/t. Near Shakespeare's Globe Theatre, this modern and quiet establishment combines modest style with good value.

Phone	020 7015 1480
Email	info@southwarkrosehotel.co.uk
Internet	www.southwarkrosehotel.co.uk

S-WEST LONDON

Battersea, Clapham, Putney, Barnes, Richmond and Twickenham

BARS

Brixton

Beehive, 405-407 Brixton Rd, SW9 7DG.
Wide range of quality beers at this Wetherspoon outlet. Equally ranging variety of drinker in this characterful hostelry.

Trinity Arms, 45 Trinity Gardens, SW9 8DR.
Right in the centre of Brixton, handy for the Trinity Asylum. Great beer. Young's.

Clapham & Balham

Bread & Roses, 68 Clapham Manor St, SW4 6DZ.
Owned by the trade union-backed Workers Beer Company. Right-on kind of place to read The Guardian. Adnams & Budvar on tap.

Manor Arms, 128 Clapham Manor St, SW4 6ED.
Several televisions in this sports obsessed, old fashioned pub. Good spot to hunker down for the match. Close to the El Rincon tapas place and Clapham Manor Baths. Adnams, Fullers, Taylors.

ENGLAND

Rose & Crown, 2 The Polygon, SW4 0JG.
Great little local pub to which people are happy to travel, so well kept is the Greene King ale. Adjacent to the Polygon restaurant. Good place to watch the game.

Nightingale, 97 Nightingale La, Balham, SW12 8NX.
A fine award winning pub serving excellent Youngs beer. It has signally failed to follow pub trends, catering simply for people who like to pour beer down their gullets. Great spot to watch the game.

Phone	020 8673 1637

Windmill on the Common, Windmill Drive, SW4 9DE.
Midway between Clapham Common and Clapham South tubes this London landmark has been around for nearly 300 years (founded 1726). Another place to watch the match. Also a hotel (see hotels).

Phone	020 8673 4578

Battersea

Beehive, 197 St John's Hill, SW11 1TH.
Good, honest locals' pub close to Clapham Junction. Fuller's.

Castle, 115 Battersea High St, SW11 3HS.
From the outside this place is very unpromising. But it combines good drinking with excellent eating so it is well worth strolling over from Clapham Junction station. The reviewer from Fancyapint suggests having a mini-crawl, taking in the Woodman and Le Quecumbar across the road.

Wandsworth

Alma Tavern, 499 Old York Rd, SW18 1NN.
Handily opposite Wandsworth Town rail station, this is a rugby pub which makes the most of the big day. Big screens and big lunch to go with it. Very busy and very successful open-plan set up. Great spot and the food is good.

Phone	020 8870 2537

The Brewers Inn, 147 East Hill, SW18 2QB.
Close to Wandsworth Town station, this pub doubles as a hotel (see mention) serving food in the brasserie.

Phone	020 8874 4128

Crane Inn, 14 Armoury Way, SW18 1EZ.
On Armoury Way in Wandsworth, a short distance from the Thames Path. A great little pub well worth a visit.

Grapes, 39 Fairfield St, SW18 1DX.
According to the Good Beer Guide, this is a hidden gem. We must concur. Naturally, being next to the Young's Brewery, it serves their beer. A piano in the corner gets the occasional impromptu outing.

Queen Adelaide, 35 Putney Bridge Rd, SW18 1NP.
Real period piece from the early 19th century. Big garden and keen on sports, so another place to watch if you are ticketless. East Putney tube.

Spread Eagle, 71 Wandsworth High St, SW18 2PT.
Antique mirrors and furnishings lend the Spread a charming old-fashioned atmosphere. Also has a pool table and dart board. Stunning to look at. Young's.

Ship, 41 Jew's Row, SW18 1TB.
Great pub right next to the Thames. Well run, excellent beer (Young's) and good food. It is the sister pub of the Alma, and though not quite as rugby loving, you can still watch the game here.

Phone	020 8870 9667

Tir Na Nog, 107 Garratt La, SW18 4DW.
No plastic Paddy place, this: it's the real thing – full of genuine Irishmen, doing what Irishmen do best. It's a good place for a drink, too, if you can get a glass in edgeways. The live music on Saturday is famed.

Bars: South London (cont)

Putney

Hare & Hounds, 216 Upper Richmond Road West, SW14 8AH
A fine all-round pub. Keen on sports and has large screen TVs.

Dukes Head, 8 Lower Richmond Rd, SW15 1JN.
A great riverside pub offering sport on TV. The boat race starts from outside. Young's property and real locals' pub.

Phone	020 8788 2552

Green Man, Putney Heath, SW15 3NG.
Sponsors of London Cornish RFC, so this is a definite if you are looking to watch the game on TV or do some drinking in rugby company. It's just up the hill from the High St and has been beautifully refurbished.

Phone	020 8788 8096

Ye Olde Spotted Horse, 122 Putney High St, SW15 1RG.
Tardis effect, the pub is actually much larger than it looks from the front. Sports on TV and good beer (yet again, Young's – this is their area). Popular with tourists because it lives up to its name (or at least the 'Ye Olde' bit).

Wimbledon

Fox & Grapes, Camp Rd, SW19 4UN.
Big screen TV next to Wimbledon Common, this pub covers all bases pretty well. Several real ales.

Phone	020 8946 5599

Crooked Billet, 14-15 Crooked Billet, SW19 4RQ.
Cosy in the winter and fine in the summer, this is a smart and stylish pub.

Brewery Tap, 68-69 High St, SW19 5EE.
One of the last genuine pubs left untouched. Shows all major sporting events on TV. Home-cooked food and several real ales.

Barnes

Coach & Horses, 27 Barnes High St, SW13 9LW.
Great pub, impressive beer garden. Barnes's best pub, which is saying something because the others are lovely, too. No concession to passing trends. Young's.

Sun Inn, 7 Church Rd, SW13 9HE.
A superb 'village' pub opposite a duck pond. Spoiled by the interior stylists who have given it an unsympathetic makeover. But they have not ruined the setting.

Kew

Coach & Horses Hotel, 8 Kew Green, TW9 3BH.
17th century coaching inn on Kew Green, opposite the Royal Botanical Gardens. Home-cooked breakfast, lunch, dinner and Young's real ales. Also a hotel and somewhere to watch the game. A great part of London (see hotels).

Richmond

Britannia, 5 Brewers Lane, TW9 1HH.
Good food, fair drink and tellies to watch the game if you are travelling without a ticket.

Dysart, 135 Petersham Rd, TW10 7AA.
Just down the road from the polo club, this is a family pub with beer garden. Large and well run.

Red Cow, 59 Sheen Rd, TW9 1YJ.
Close to the station, there are 4 bedrooms for overnighting. Good, stylish local pub. Young's.

Phone	020 8940 2511.
Internet	www.redcowpub.activehotels.com

Triple Crown, 15 Kew Foot Rd, TW9 2SS.
Near Kew Gardens and Old Deer Park this is a splendid rugby pub with four excellent and changing real ales. Jazz on Sundays, a lively spot.

White Cross, Riverside, Water Lane, TW9 1TJ.
Perched above the river on Richmond's elegant waterfront. Young's.Pictured right.

Isleworth

Coach & Horse.
Proper old coaching inn. Great beers including Smiles and Young's.

Red Lion.
Busy and good local pub. Loads of different beers.

Royal Oak.
Great little pub with a riverside patio and TV area at the back for sports.

Twickenham, Middlesex

Cabbage Patch, 67 London Rd, TW1 3SZ.
Twickenham was built on allotments and the pub commemorates this. Traditional watering hole on match day. You might have to do a bit of queuing. Brakspear, Fuller, Greene King, Speckled Hen.

Eel Pie, 11 Church St, TW1 3NJ.
Good home-made food in this former wine bar. Wide range of beers.

Prince Albert, 30 Hampton Rd, TW2 5QB.
Well rounded local pub serving great beer and good Thai food.

St Margaret's Tavern, 107 St Margaret's Rd, TW1 2LJ.
Former Temperance hotel the Tavern is now a thriving concern having been through the doldrums for many years. Adnams, Deuchars IPA, Fullers, Marstons.

White Swan, Riverside, Twickenham, TW1 3DN.
Good English riverside pub.

Teddington

Lion, 27 Wick Rd, TW11 9DN.
Excellent beer and food that matches. Fullers, Greene King.

Queen Dowager, 49 North Lane, TW11 0HU.
Solid food and drink in a fine century old tavern which commemorates the widow of William IV. Young's.

Hampton Hill

Roebuck, 72 Hampton Rd, TW12 1JN.
Five handpumps. Traffic lights indicate last orders. Good food and excellent beers.

Hampton

Jolly Coopers, 16 High St, TW12 2SJ.
Has been a pub for 300 years. Bigger inside than you would think, serving lots of different beers and good food.

Kingston Upon Thames

Albert Arms, 57 Kingtson Hill, KT2 7PX.
Good big pub doing fine ales and good food. Young's.

Park Tavern, 19 New Rd, KT2 6AP.
Close to Kingston Gate in Richmond Park, this pub is a discreet little gem. Great place for a reviver after the Sunday stroll in the Park. Fuller's.

Wych Elm, 93 Elm Rd, KT2 6HT.
Traditional and welcoming pub. Recently won CAMRA Local Pub of the Year. Good food and excellent beer. Fuller's.

TRENDY BARS & CLUBS

Much of this sort of activity seems to be around Clapham and Brixton.

Clapham

Sand, 156 Clapham Park Rd, SW4 7DE.
Highly rated trendoid bar with suede cube seating. Also serves ambitious food which, we gather, was working well at time of going to press. Lots of different beers and cocktails, loads of good looking girls and boys.

Phone	020 7622 3022

The White House, 65 Clapham Park Rd, SW4 7EH.
Great combination of bar, restaurant and night club in the heart of Clapham. The music is a mix of both current and classic house favourites. First hit the headlines five years ago for being a cool combination of bar, restaurant and night club. Modern British cooking. Big-time DJs (Wednesday to Sunday) and cocktails are mentioned in dispatch.

Phone	020 7498 3388

Brixton

Bug Bar, St Matthew's Church, SW2 1JF.
Bar, lounge and restaurant in the crypts of St Matthew's Church. Bug restaurant is a collection of candlelit coves and arches – romantic and snug. Bug Bar next door has a garden terrace, where you can eat a la carte or from the bar menu. Or just drink if you don't fancy wading through one of those Modern British menus.

Phone	020 7738 3366

Dogstar, 389 Coldharbour Lane, SW9 8LQ.
Not for the faint-hearted. This is where you go to feel the vibe. You'll have to push your way through the huge downstairs bar of this converted pub to get to the house-music club upstairs, but anyone used to a rugby club bar will have no problem. It's spread over three floors, and you can play pool, grab a bite, relax in the 'chillout room' or break onto the dancefloor and compete with the local talent to the sound of house, breaks, retro party and hip hop.

Phone	020 7733 7515

Fridge Bar, Town Hall Parade, SW2 1RJ.
From African Gospel and Cuban salsa to reggae and punk, the fridge has survived for many years on a culturally eclectic diet. It may be small and cramped but it does the business. Probably best for those under 30.

Phone	020 7326 5100

The Telegraph, 228 Brixton Hill, SW2 1HE.
Good spot to mix the three most unmixable pastimes: eating, dancing and drinking, in an old fashion Victorian pub.

Phone	020 8678 0777

Putney

Fez Club, 200b Upper Richmond Road, SW15 2SH.
Part of the Po Na Na chain (there is also one in Hammersmith) of bars with live music, cocktails, and a young, buzzing atmosphere. The Fez Club hosts a variety of themed nights throughout the week. This venue can be hired out for private parties of up to 350 guests on Mondays and Tuesdays.

Phone	020 8780 0123

RESTAURANTS

Clapham & Brixton

Bamboula Jerk Kitchen, 12 Acre Lane, Brixton, SW2 5SG.

Afro-Caribbean: Hardough bread patties, plantain, oxtail with butterbean, ackee, saltfish, goat curry and vegetables with lashings of coconut informed sauces. Bamboo everywhere and sunshine leaps out of the décor. You could be in a Caribbean beach hut, except that the food is too good for that. Authentic and flavoursome, for those who might wish to recreate a summer holiday during a London winter. Brilliant atmosphere.

Basic price	£17
Phone	020 7737 6633

Le Bouchon Bordelais, 5-9 Battersea Rise, SW11 1HG.

French bistro style successful enough for there to be another in the same coin, Le Bouchon Lyonnais. Mousse of avocado and shellfish with a tomato sauce, steak frites and salad, escargots with garlic and parsley butter are amongst the long list of classics available.

Gastro, 67 Venn St, Clapham, SW4 0BD.

Opposite the picture house in Clapham, this brasserie is fine for anything from coffee and croissants in the morning, to a proper sit-down meal in the evening. Utterly Gallic in flavour, right down to the arty and intellectual conversations, among the clientelle Gastro cuts the mustard across a wide variety of dishes from well selected charcuterie to precisely executed fish stew, or gigot d'agneau, or even the French take on the Sunday fry-up. This is among the coolest places to hang out if you are a beret owner.

Basic price	£28
Phone	020 7627 0222

Lavender Restaurant, 171 Lavender Hill, SW11 5TE.

Large and comfortable family brasserie. Relaxed and informal, mix-'n-match furniture and lavender growing up the front. Part of a small local chain covering The Oval, Putney, Embankment and Battersea. Good value. The blackboard menu changes twice daily and includes a range of modern European cooking, with occasional Asian dishes thrown in. Braised shoulder of lamb with borlotti bean cassoulet, buttered spinach and red wine jus. White chocolate and pistachio mousse with bitter chocolate shavings.

Basic price	£20
Phone	020 7978 5242

Numero Uno, 139 Northcote Rd, Clapham. SW11 6PX.

Robust and unpretentious Italian cooking. White truffles enliven home-made pasta and risotto. Ricotta and spinach fillings given life by walnut sauce, or perhaps you'll go for lobster with spaghetti (but save the wild boar sauce for something else). A local family favourite. Locals in 'Nappy Valley' are quite discerning.)

Basic price	£30
Phone	020 7978 5837

Polygon Bar & Grill, 4 The Polygon, Clapham, SW4 0JG.

One of the best positions in Clapham – glass fronted and cool, with leatherette banquettes and clean design. Outside eating is possible, looking towards the Common. Food has always been up and down since this place opened a decade ago. When it's good, it's excellent; but it has never been cheap. Good atmosphere and great pubs either side. International cuisine. Moroccan dishes generally work well.

Basic price	£30
Phone	020 7622 1199
Internet	www.polygon.co.uk

El Rincon, 148 Clapham Manor St, SW4 6BX.

Great spot for a party, very good Spanish cooking in a jolly atmosphere near the traditional real ale pub, the Manor Arms.

Basic price	£20
Phone	020 7622 0599

Restaurants: South West London (cont)

Scoffers, 6 Battersea Rise, Battersea, SW11 1ED.
They don't mind if you are wearing a suit, so long as you don't behave as if you are wearing a suit. Battersea end of South London's green lung, the frequently-changing menu is largely British, but expect international influences such as Thai spring rolls, mezze, bouillabaisse, or fajitas.

Basic price	£20
Phone	020 7978 5542

Tiger Lils Flaming Woks, 16A Clapham Common South Side, SW4 7AB.
We include this because it's a fun place to take the family: select your own ingredients, build your own meal and a tame Mongolian will slap it over the gas and create a one man stage show as your brilliant selection gets cooked to perfection. Asian beers to go with your Asian-style creation. Cocktails available.

Basic price	£15
Phone	020 7720 5433

Tsunami, 4-7 Voltaire Rd, SW4 6DQ.
Never mind the name. Hidden gem that won the Time Out Best Japanese Restaurant Award (2002) and is still on cracking form. Fashionable interior (ie not much) and melt-in-the-mouth sushi and sashimi. Exhibits the style and taste you'd expect from an ex-Nobu chef. Unusual dishes like ebi prawns wrapped in Greek pastry and butternut squash, tuna tataki in miso sauce and especially the mint-tea duck with pear and sweet honey miso, that will really bowl you over.

Basic price	£23
Phone	020 7978 1610

Putney

Enoteca Turi, 28 Putney High St, SW15 1SQ.
A recommended wine for every dish, available by the glass. Owner Giuseppe Turi has 300 to pick from and pays equal attention to his food. Try the warm salad of girolle mushrooms with focaccia di Recco, black and white tagliolini with seafood, and mains such as breast of duck with braised radicchio, roasted pumpkin and balsamic reduction, and puds of Tuscan chocolate cake with pine nuts served with plums. The decor is modern and airy with Tuscan-toned walls and a relaxed feel.

Phone	020 8785 4449

Ma Goa, 242-244 Upper Richmond Rd, SW15 6TG.
Their speciality is the Portuguese-influenced cuisine of Goa, served up in terracotta bowls by cheery staff. Sausages may not be what springs to mind when you think of Goa but the cinnamon-infused pork snags are worth the booking alone. You'll soon understand why this restaurant is repeatedly voted Putney's favourite Indian.

Phone	020 8780 1767

Phoenix Bar & Grill, 162-164 Lower Richmond Rd, SW15 1LY.
Great family-friendly place, ideal for a Sunday lunch (£17.50). Typical dishes: home cured bresaola with rocket and parmesan, scallops with endive salad and beetroot dressing – for the main courses, monkfish rolled in prosciutto and pappardelle with venison and wild mushroom ragu were mentioned in dispatches.

Basic price	£25
Phone	020 8780 3131

Redmonds, 170 Upper Richmond Road West, SW14 8AW.
Excellent neighbourhood restaurant run by a husband and wife team. Redmond Hayward is owner/chef, while Pippa runs front of house. Signature dishes include seasonal game, roast cod with mussel, spinach and saffron risotto, chicken and foie gras terrine, red onion marmalade, roast seabass, crushed new potatoes with smoked salmon and creme fraiche, sauce vierge, seared scallops, Granny Smith and rosemary fritters, cider soup and maple syrup ice cream. Highly rated.

Basic price	£31
Phone	020 8878 1922

Wimbledon

Dalchini Hakka, 147 Arthur Rd, Wimbledon, SW19 8AB.

Indo-Chinese fusion in deepest suburbia. Deep fried fish in a salt-pepper batter, spring chicken lollipops, green plantain fritters or red pumpkin fritters flavoured with ginger served with several dipping sauces. The clear soups can be had before or after the main course to settle the meal. There are no beef or pork dishes which means there's a fair variety of fish and seafood, such as prawn Manchurian or Bengali pomfret served in Kolkata Chong Yee. A bit different.

Basic price	£20
Phone	020 8947 5966

Sarkhels Indian Cuisine, 199 Replingham Rd, SW18 5LY.

Southfields: former head chef of the Bombay Brasserie Udit Sarkhel trips the light fantastic across the whole subcontinent, with assured cooking of everything from Kashmiri specialities to dishes from Karnataka. Always busy and possibly the highest rated Indian in London, worth a diversion.

Basic price	£25
Phone	020 8870 1483

Barnes

The Depot, Tideway Yard, 125 Mortlake High St, SW14 8SN.

Great location, on the Barnes bend of the Thames, the Depot is a long-established brasserie tucked away in Tideway Yard, a renovated Victorian cobbled courtyard with fabulous views. Brick arches link three dining areas and a conservatory runs the length, looking over the river. Sweet figs stuffed with Gorgonzola, wrapped with smoked pancetta to start, and bacon-wrapped monkfish, cannelini bean stew with sun-dried tomato ravioli as a main course is one recommendation.

Basic price	£25
Phone	020 8878 9462

Jim Thompsons, 408 Upper Richmond Rd, SW15 6JP.

Indonesian potato cakes, green chicken curry and all manner of noodles. This Oriental palace, housed in a large former pub, is family friendly, with a menu for the kids. The place is packed with eastern 'treasures', most of which are for sale so it's like being in a Bangkok bazaar.

Phone	020 8788 3737

MVH, 5 White Hart Lane, Barnes, SW13 0PX.

The owner, the eponymous Michael Von Hruscka, sets his standards high: ground floor is called 'Heaven' – all white and ethereal, while upstairs, decked out in gash red, is 'Hell.' You can be the judge of quite how heavenly his boudin blanc with truffle brioche and garlic leaves, or his lemon sole with beetroot mash and munster asparagus actually is. Truly eclectic menu, very high standards and excellent if expensive wine list.

Basic price	£35
Phone	020 8392 1111

Pizza Express, 14 Barnes High St, SW13 9LW.

Great setting opposite the Thames. If you don't want to spend a fortune and merely wish to soak up the excesses of a long day this place, sandwiched between some of London's finest hostelries, is ideal.

Basic price	£17
Phone	020 8878 1184

Riva, 169 Church Rd, SW13 9HR.

This small and elegant family restaurant is rated by many as the best Italian in London. It is something of a Barnes institution and you are unlikely to go wrong. First class salads and starters and well executed fish dishes and a full and generous array of desserts.

Basic price	£35
Phone	020 8748 0434

Restaurants: South West London (cont)

Sonnys, 94 Church Rd, SW13 0DQ.

Airy and elegant with a constantly changing collection of modern art, the chef is a Finnish woman who trained with Pierre Gagnaire in Paris before working for Pierre Koffman in Chelsea. As you would expect, the food at this other Barnes culinary temple is very, very good. Foie gras fricasseed with cinnamon glazed turnips, tender Midde White pork loin with camargue red rice and marinated cranberries, pan-fried sea bass in lobster minestrone. Rhubarb and almond tart. Gagnaire's inventiveness has rubbed off on Helena Puolaaka.

Basic price	£30
Phone	020 8748 0393

Richmond, Surrey

Burnt Chair, 5 Duke St, TW9 1HP.

Modern international cooking with an acclaimed California and Burgundy-biased wine list. Proximity to Richmond Theatre means there are good cheaper menu options. The fusion of global tastes and ingredients makes for great variety of flavour. Alongside spiced rice and pork sausages, ginger and soy vinaigrette expect to see foie gras bon-bon, red onion marmalade and hazelnut brioche. Or try the tarte tatin of lamb, apples, parsnips and tabbouleh.

Basic price	£26
Phone	020 8940 9488

Canyon, The Tow path, Richmond Riverside, TW10 6UJ.

Arizona on the banks of the Thames, Canyon has a terrific location. This is a small patch of America and the theme is Arizona, with the garden done over to look like the Wild West. The words America and 'cuisine' may seem contradictory, but there is enough modern European in the kitchen to overcome Stateside excess.

Basic price	£23
Phone	020 8948 2944

Chez Lindsay, 11 Hill Rise, TW10 6UQ.

A taste of Brittany: crepes and gallettes, fish and seafood, lots of cider informs the cooking. Oysters cooked in cider with cream, spinach and chopped shallots was singled at by Time Out. Our man enjoyed his andouillette (tripe sausage) but he is a Frenchman so can be excused. Generous and genuine.

Basic price	£25
Phone	020 8948 7473

Don Fernando, 27F The Quadrant, Richmond, TW9 1DN.

The genuine Spanish article, set up 15 years ago by the Izquierdo family from Andalusia. All sorts of paellas, excellent tapas and a wide choice of seafood – this is a tiny patch of Spain on the fringes of Surrey. The wine and sherry list are very good.

Basic price	£20
Phone	020 8948 6447
Internet	www.donfernando.co.uk

Origin Asia, 100 Kew Road, SW9 2PQ.

Good neighbourhood restaurant attractively done out on four levels. Good nans and excellent tandooris. Try the lamb chops marinated in yoghurt and garlic and impregnated with chillies and rum, then grilled on charcoal. Lots of flavours.

Basic price	£20
Phone	020 8948 0509

Twickenham, Middlesex

A Cena, 418 Richmond Rd, TW1 2EB.

The focus is purely on food in this simply laid-out Italian, hard by Richmond Bridge. Recommended: grilled sardines with salsa verde, crab salad with fennel, while such staples as pasta and risotto are excellent. Other classics such as osso bucco on the menu. Good value lunch venue: £10 for two courses or £12 for three.

Basic price	£15
Phone	020 8288 0108

The A Bar & Restaurant, 93 Colne Rd, TW12 6QL.

Many will remember this place as the Duke's Head. Some will lament the change. Those with good sense will avail themselves of its excellent menu. The cooking is Mediterranean, lots of pesto and tangy flavours which are precisely put together. Scallops with mango, lime, chilli and mint salsa was highly commended, plus a good lunch time selection of tapas. And you can still get a first class pint of British beer.

Basic price	£23
Phone	020 8898 8000

Brula, 43 Crown Rd, TW1 3EJ.

Fantastic cooking and great value for money, Brula was runner-up in the Time Out Best Local Restaurant awards, and has won several other prizes. Main courses could include chargrilled chicken with pea and mint risotto, tortilla with guacamole, bean salad and tomato salsa, cod roasted with a herb crust and served on a bed of spinach with a red pepper sauce. Or roast pork and Szechwan aubergine. Three course lunch for £10. Amazing place. Book now.

Basic price	£21
Phone	020 8892 0602

McClements, 2 Whitton Rd, TW1 1BJ.

Since winning a Michelin star in 2004 McClements has been much in demand. Its prices reflect that. Between the station and the rugby ground, it would be as well to book now for the year after next. Langoustines with pork belly, light lobster ravioli with black pudding and apple in a foam sauce are singled out for praise. As is John Dory with fennel puree, roast loin of veal and braised pig's head with pickled vegetables, as were the panoply of desserts and puddings.

Basic price	£48 to £60
Phone	020 8744 9610

Ma Cuisine, 6 Whitton Rd, TW1 1BJ.

Basic looking bistro whose food is as highly acclaimed as it is inexpensive: for a fiver or less you can get starters which include fresh tuna and foie gras (separately). Main courses are Modern European in style. 'If the dishes are of bourgeois origins, they have nonetheless been to finishing school,' says the Good Food Guide. 'As witness the discreet bed of choucroute underlying sticky-sweet, slow-cooked belly pork.' High praise indeed. Main courses come with truly garlicky dauphinois potato and the puddings are excellent.

Basic price	£22
Phone	020 8607 9849

Pallavi, Unit 3, Cross Deep Court, Heath Rd, TW1 4QJ.

Never judge a book by its cover. The same often applies to restaurants. The Pallavi is set in a concrete bunker of a shopping precinct but its food is both authentic and highly praised. It specialises in delicate but spicy dishes from Kerala – delicious dosa – rice pancakes, accompanied by coconut and chilli chutney. Then try a cochin prawn curry or any of the other seafood dishes. Book early as there could be competition.

Phone	020 8892 2345
Internet	www.mcdosa.com

ENGLAND

HOTELS

Battersea, Clapham, Putney, Barnes, Richmond and Twickenham

LUXURY

Cannizaro House, West Side, Wimbledon Common, SW19 4UE.
43 rooms. £190 s/d/t. Wimbledon then taxi, or 93 bus.
Formal gardens next to magnificent Georgian mansion on Wimbledon Common.

Phone	0870 333 9124
Email	cannizarohouse@thistle.co.uk

Carlton Mitre, Hampton Court Rd, Hampton Court, KT8 9BN.
34 rooms. From £115 s and £165 d/t.
Built for guests of nearby Hampton Court in 1665, it was designed for those with Royal connections. Many rooms have views of either the palace or the river.

Phone	020 8979 9988
Email	salesmitre@carltonhotels.co.uk
Internet	www.carltonhotels.co.uk

Kingston Lodge, Kingston Hill, KT2 7NP.
63 rooms. From £116 s/t/d. Waterloo to Norbiton.
Close to the Royal Parks and university. Quiet, cosy and relaxed.

Phone	0870 400 8115
Internet	www.swallowhotels.com
Email	swallow.kingston@swallowhotels.com

Petersham, Nightingale Lane, Richmond, TW10 6UZ.
61 rooms. From £110 s to £235 d/t.
Big, elegant Gothic pile, the England team used to stay here before switching to Pennyhill Park in Bagshot, Surrey. Spectacular views of the Thames.

Phone	020 8940 7471
Email	enq@petershamhotel.co.uk
Internet	www.petershamhotel.co.uk

Richmond Gate Hotel, 152-158 Richmond Hill, Richmond, TW10 6RP.
68 rooms. From £120 s to £150 d/t. Richmond station or tube, 1 mile.
Left from station, through town centre. Left again to reach top of Richmond Hill. Four elegant 18th Century Georgian town houses. To the right is Richmond Terrace its views over Thames Valley and to the left 2,500 acres of Royal Richmond Park.

Phone	020 8940 0061
Email	res.richmondgatehotel@foliohotels.com
Internet	www.foliohotels.com

MODERATELY PRICED

136 London Road, Twickenham, TW11.
4 rooms from £35 s, £55 d/t. Large Edwardian house with spacious rooms. Close to all amenities and the station. Twenty minutes to Waterloo by train. 40 minutes to Heathrow by train and bus. Rugby stadium 10 minutes walk. Local attractions include Kew Gardens, Hampton Court and Richmond Park.

Phone	020 8892 3158
Internet	www.accommodation-in-twickenham. co.uk

Chase Lodge, 10 Park Rd, Hampton Wick, KT1 4AS.
13 rooms. From £55 s to £80 d/t. 20 minutes from Waterloo by train.
Individual feel to this family run Victorian house. Well run and easily accessible.

Phone	020 8943 1862
Email	info@chaselodgehotel.com
Internet	www.chaselodgehotel.com

Comfort Inn London Vauxhall, 87 South Lambeth Rd, Vauxhall, SW8 1RN.
94 rooms, from £64 s/d/t (internet only). Otherwise from £80 s/d/t. Vauxhall. Spacious rooms with sofas, coffee table, electronic laptop-sized safe, air conditioning, work desk, fridge and microwave. Free use of mini-gym. Satellite TV, PC points for fax/modem. Good value for money.

Phone	020 7735 9494
Email	stay@comfortinnvx.co.uk
Internet	www.comfortinnvx.co.uk

Doughty Cottage, 142A Richmond Hill, Richmond, TW10 6RN.
3 rooms. £75s - £103 double/twin. Richmond. Elegant Georgian house set above the river behind a walled garden. Lovely spot. Will need early booking.

Phone	020 8332 9434
Email	deniseoneill425@aol.co.uk

Georgian splenour: Richmond and architectucal elegance seem to go hand in hand

Lavender Guest House, 18 Lavender Sweep, Clapham Junction, SW11 1HA.
8 rooms, from £60 d/t. Clapham Junction.
Greek hospitality from the owner, John, who is proud of his garden. His Bed & Breakfast has featured on the BBC.

Phone	020 7585 2767 or 020 7223 1973

Liongate Hotel, 1 Lion Gate, Hampton Court Rd, East Molesey, KT8 9DD.
32 rooms. From £90 s, £100 d/t.
Handsome 18th century house near the Liongate entrance to Hampton Court Palace overlooking Bushy Park. Two buildings and 16 of the bedrooms are in the historic mews. The ground floor restaurant serves good 'modern British' cuisine.

Phone	020 8977 8121
Internet	www.dhillonhotel.co.uk
Email	lionres@dhihotels.co.uk

Park Lodge Hotel, Park Road, Teddington, TW110AB.
43 rooms, from £80 s/d/t.
18th century Grade II listed with contemporary restaurant. Also has a large contemporary bar and restaurant and ample free parking. Near the main line station with frequent connections to central London and is an ideal base for visiting not just Twickers but Hampton Court, Bushy Park, Kingston and Richmond-upon-Thames.

Phone	020 8614 9700
Internet	www.galleongroup.co.uk
Email	Parkadmin@theparklodge.co.uk

Hotels: South-West London (cont)

Premier Travel Inn London Putney Bridge, 3 Putney Bridge **Approach, Putney, SW6 3JD.** 154 rooms, from £70 s/d/t.
Putney Bridge. Budget accommodation with refinements. Just across the River on the north bank. Great spot with plenty of good pubs and excellent restaurants nearby.

Phone	0870 238 3302
Internet	www.premiertravelinn.co.uk

Premier Travel Inn London Kew, 52 High St, Kew, TW8 0BB.
141 rooms, from £60 s/d/t. Kew Bridge rail station. Close to Kew Gardens, comfortable king sized beds plus all the other facilities you would expect (though the blurb makes no mention of a trouser press – you might have to take your own).

Phone	0870 990 6304
Email	info@premierlodge.co.uk
Internet	www.premierlodge.com

Quinns Hotel, 48 Sheen Rd, Richmond, TW9 1AW.
38 rooms from £40 s, £60 d/t to £90 (4-bed family).
Ideally located, simple accommodation only five minutes walk from Richmond station.

Phone	020 8940 5444
Email	quinnshotel@hotmail.com
Internet	www.quinnshotel.com

Riverside Hotel, 23 Petersham Rd, Richmond, TW10 6UH.
20 rooms, from £50 s, £85 d/t. Richmond. Take a taxi from the station.
A rural setting in the town centre, the Riverside Hotel is two linked Victorian townhouses. At the rear, it looks directly onto the River Thames. Wireless and internet services available in all rooms. Convenient for central London, Kew Gardens, Hampton Court, Windsor and numerous local historic houses. Not to mention Twickers.

Phone	020 8940 1339
Internet	www.riversiderichmond.co.uk

Travelodge London Battersea, 200 York Rd, Battersea, SW11 3SA.
86 rooms from £60 s/d/t. Clapham Junction.
Low-cost, comfortable en-suite rooms. Clean and simple – best prices to be found online.

Phone	0870 191 1688
Internet	www.travelodge.co.uk

Victoria, 10 West Temple Sheen, Sheen, SW14 7RT.
7 rooms, £100 s/d/t. Simply but stylishy furnished rooms with a good restaurant. Quiet location, car park, garden, conservatory.

Phone	020 8876 4238
Email	bookings@thevictoria.net
Internet	www.thevictoria.net

Windmill on the Common, Clapham Common South Side, SW4 9DE.
29 rooms. From £80 s/d/t. Clapham South or Clapham Common.
A splendid and busy Victorian pub right on the Common. Well run and comfortable establishment with good transport links.

Phone	020 8673 4578
Internet	www.windmillclapham.co.uk

Irish rugby

Green is for go

By Brendan Fanning
Rugby Correspondent,
Sunday Independent

SHORTLY before the Wales–Ireland game in Cardiff's National Stadium, a colleague and I got down to the serious business of the day: predicting the margin of Ireland's defeat. It was March 1993, and while Cardiff had become a happy hunting ground for us since 1985, Ireland was on the cusp of a uniquely awful statistic in its history. For weeks, we had been looking under rocks and shaking trees searching for old soldiers with a different take on the plight of Irish rugby – veterans who had once known success and could suggest a way of recapturing it. It was hard going. So there we were, as the teams concluded their warm-up, trying to put a figure on what would be Ireland's 12th defeat in a row.

And then they won.

Did it herald the dawn of a new and wondrously successful era of Irish rugby? Er … no. But it looked overwhelmingly positive at the time, and it seemed to be confirmed when, a fortnight later, they beat England at home. And that was the way things were – up for a bit; down for a lot more; then back up again. The only certainty was that you could never be sure when and where Ireland would pull off a headline win.

Those random victories – some moral, some actual – would be presented by the IRFU as evidence that our place in the game was valued by all others, but it just didn't wash. And if the game hadn't staggered into the blinding light of professionalism in the summer of 1995, then we'd still be listening to the same mantra about swings and roundabouts. The advent of above-the-table cash allowed us to get off the merry go round, and figure out how to get back on again as paying customers.

Nowadays, Ireland are no longer considered to be passionate, hopeful and headless. There is a structure to the way the team plays – mainly because there is a structure to the way it prepares. In the dark days of the 1990s, we went from hit or miss amateurs to reluctant professionals. By the end of the decade, the IRFU had copped on that they had to spend if they were to survive in the new order. Thankfully, there is no going back.

The darkest hour actually came in Lens on October 20th, 1999. It was the World Cup quarter-final play off, and the winner got to play France in Lansdowne Road in the quarter-final. Ireland had lost to France by a solitary point eight months earlier in the Six Nations Championship so they felt good about their chances if

Irish Rugby (cont)

they got to that semi. It was the perfect script. Then Argentina shredded it and Ireland went into freefall. In the aftermath, the IRFU resolved to get serious about professionalism. Enough was enough.

The country were blessed to have a ready-made structure on hand. The four provinces have always been part of the Irish game and were the perfect vehicle to take us into the European Cup. If Lens had been the catalyst for the IRFU joining the real world, then the club tournament was what drove Ireland back to international respectability. That's what allowed Munster to conquer their fears away from home: winning away when previously they could only thrive at home. In 1999/2000 they were on another roll, and after getting hammered by England in the opening round of the Six Nations in 2000, Ireland coach Warren Gatland sent for the cavalry from down south.

Ball's away: Peter Stringer has been part of the success, story, but can Ireland keep it going?

Perhaps the biggest lesson Munster had learned from their travels in Europe was not to panic when things went against them. They backboned the team for the next championship game – against Scotland in Lansdowne Road – and got a chance to put their new found patience to the test. Scotland raced into a 10-0 lead, yet Ireland ended up winning the game, 44-22.

Before that, we couldn't buy a win against the Scots, but since then the roles have reversed emphatically. Going into this season's Championship, the only changes have seen Scotland getting worse and Ireland levelling off after back-to-back seasons where they won four out of five matches, picking up a Triple Crown in 2004.

But the way the balloon burst in 2005 will have sobered up a few of the fans. That was billed as the Grand Slam season. On the face of it, things looked good, with opening wins away against Italy and France, and then the mood rocketed when they beat England for the second season running. But the grand design was always predicated on keeping key players fit, and two of them – Brian O'Driscoll and Gordon D'Arcy – missed far too much.

It wasn't, in the end, much of a struggle to understand how an ageing pack, and a backline short of its two best attackers, were leaving the Grand Slam behind them. The same pair will be the focus of much attention again this time round. For O'Driscoll the Lions tour ended in a nightmare, when he was upended by New Zealand, and the worst part of it is that he won't know for sure when it's over. For rugby players – especially those as physical as O'Driscoll – a shoulder dislocation is very bad for business. These things can come back to haunt you, and while the surgery seemed to have gone according to plan, he won't be certain where he stands until he goes back to work.

The issue with D'Arcy may be more mental than physical. Evidently there was no effort by Lions coach Clive Woodward to disguise his annoyance that D'Arcy wasn't available for the third test in New Zealand. To be classed as suffering from "chronic fatigue" in a season where he had played 30 minutes of Six Nations rugby was bizarre. D'Arcy's form on tour had lurched from uninvolved to uncontrolled to outstanding. And then he missed the chance of a test cap. His ability hasn't been diminished by the experience but we'll have to wait and see about his attitude.

The reliance on this pair tells you a great deal about Ireland's resources. In some positions it's as deep as a puddle. Aside from the midfield, the greatest area of concern is in the front row where tight head John Hayes is the only realistic option. While Hayes was away with the Lions, Ulster's Simon Best wore the jersey in the two test series against Japan. Coach Eddie O'Sullivan will be hoping he can get Hayes through to the World Cup by which stage he will be closing in on 34. It looks a long way away.

Elsewhere, O'Sullivan has a greater cushion. He has a raft of good young back rowers who will have gained a lot of useful experience when France '07 comes along. Munster's Denis Leamy, Ulster's Roger Wilson, and Johnny O'Connor of Wasps are leading the charge in this area, and the second row too is not short of options. The Lions pair of Paul O'Connell and Donncha O'Callaghan should be world class by then.

Because of rugby's place in the pecking order in Ireland, where it comes behind Gaelic games and football, it's imperative to keep it in the shop window. So if the national side isn't challenging for honours in the Six Nations, then at least one of the provinces needs to be flying the flag in Europe.

Since they first qualified for the knock out stages in 1998/99 Munster have never been stuck in their pool. Still, despite two appearances in the final, they haven't lived the dream. Last season they played above themselves in losing away to Biarritz in the quarter-final, but what happened the previous day in Dublin was at the other end of the scale. Leinster didn't just lose to Leicester, at the same stage of the competition, they bombed. Not for the first time in their history, they have some amends to make to their fans who also had to endure seeing their team lose dismally in a home semi-final to Perpignan back in 2003 when everything was set up for them to go for the crown at Lansdowne Road. It seems that no sooner have the knock out stages been set up for Leinster, with money-spinning home draws, than they unravel it all on the pitch.

Ulster, whose ground at Ravenhill is scheduled for major recontruction, face a more challenging season. The days when David Humphreys and Kevin Maggs won games for them are over. One of the northern side's most exciting prospects is centre Andrew Trimble, still just 20, but 2005-6 may also finally see Paddy Wallace emerge as a mainstay fly half. Ulster can certainly look forward to vigorous support; for their first friendly, in August, nearly 6,500 fans turned out at Ravenhill.

Poor Connacht, though improving rapidly from its Galway base, it can only go green with envy.

In Dublin, the sight of Leinster – and Irish – leisure wear on the streets of Dublin is common, unthinkable when the national team lurched from defeat to defeat in the miserable 1990s. The price the game has paid for this success is that club matches, as distinct from provincial, have slipped into the small print. Below national level, the provinces soak up the interest, and will continue to do so until the IRFU gets another rush for radical change. Come to think of it, we're due one of those.

FIND YOUR WAY AROUND

DUBLIN'S FAIR CITY

Anyone who has read James Joyce, or even J.P.Donleavy, will know what to expect when they arrive in Dublin. Except that they'd be wrong. The Irish capital has changed so much in the last 20 years that even it's own mother, Anna Livia, wouldn't recognise it.

The city always had charm and swagger – and something of an aggressive edge to it. The bone structure was good and the people living in the slums and tenements, surrounded by the vestiges of empire, took pride in their heritage, their achievement, even their poverty. But modern Dublin is somewhere else entirely.

Since the release of the Celtic Tiger, some two decades back, Ireland has risen from being the poorest member of the old EEC to being the second richest state in the new European Union, beaten only by Luxembourg.

Dublin, as you might expect, has always been at the centre of the revolution. Today, it is an important financial centre, a hub for the telecommunications and computer industry and a retail and leisure capital to rival any large city in the world.

It has also grown. More than 1.1 million people can now call themselves "Dubs," and with their new-found wealth and international outlook, they expect only the best for themsleves and their guests. The city's many historic buildings have nearly all been restored; the finest architects in Europe compete to win contracts for museums, company headquarters, banks, hotels and restaurants. An expanding rapid transit system whisks commuters and visitors in and out of the suburbs, while the new ring road struggles to contain the weight of BMWs, Mercedes, Jaguars and Alfa Romeos.

Dubliners are proud and brash and self-confident. They don't have the time they once enjoyed to sit down and have a quiet pint or three and put the world to rights. But when the work is done and they're finally off the leash, watch out – they'll drink you under the table, then skin you alive.

Lansdowne Road may, as it stands, be a tumbledown shack, but even before its scheduled redevelopment, its location is the envy of the other five nations. The city centre is three stops away on the train, and there are scores of pubs and restaurants within handy walking distance. If your day starts in the city centre, then walking to the game down Baggot Street is the best way to get some atmosphere on the way there, and back. The choice of places to stop off is endless. If you manage no more than three, you'll be doing well.

TRAVEL

Although close to the edge of Europe, Dublin is now a hugely important European business centre and is thus very easily accessible by air or by ferry. The city centre is small and traffic is very congested, but there is a comprehensive public transport system with buses, trams and a light railway. The taxis, which can take the bus lanes, are cheap, friendly and efficient.

AIR

Dublin Airport is an ever growing international airport serving all of Ireland, Europe and beyond, particularly North America. Ryanair, the "no frills" airline was born here and has had an incredible effect on Irish life, opening Europe to Irish people of all ages. The airport's growth has not kept pace with the growth of the country's economy but a second terminal is soon to be built.

The present, one-stop terminal building is on two levels, departures above, arrivals below. The facilities include a bar, food outlets, enormous and comprehensive shopping facilities in the departure area, bureaux de change, ATMs and as many car rental companies as you could wish. Security checks are very strict and it is sensible to arrive in good time prior to departure. There are facilities for disabled passengers.

Movement to and from the airport is, for the moment, by road only. The route to and from the city is well signposted, but the seemingly eternal roadworks are a pain and are such from early morning till late evening. One tip (and keep it quiet) is to take a short detour to the Malahide Road. Just follow signs for the city centre when leaving the airport, then take the second motorway exit, following the signs for COOLOCK. Go past the North Side Shopping Centre and turn right at the next major traffic lights, following the signs for the city centre.

Airport Transfers

Regular Airlink bus services – 746, 747, 748 to the city centre just outside Arrivals. €5 each way. Journey time is given optimistically as 35 minutes to the city centre. Massive taxi presence outside arrivals – journey time to the city centre varies hugely, especially if you're heading to the south side of the Liffey, but a good run would see you in the city centre in half an hour. Cost to the city centre between €20 and €30. The top hotels provide a shuttle service by limousine or minibus.

RAIL

Dublin is the hub of the Irish rail. It is served by two main stations; Connolly in the city centre, behind O'Connell Street, and Heuston, a couple of miles to the west, just south of the Liffey. These two stations are linked by the Luas tramway Red Line. Ferries arriving at Dublin Port from Holyhead have no rail link to the city centre, and passengers must use shuttle buses to the main bus station (Busaras) close to Connolly Station. Passengers arriving at Dun Laoghaire can, however, take a DART train (see below) to the city centre. Those arriving in Belfast off the catamaran from Stanraer can take a train direct to Connolly, a can those arriving at Rosslare from Pembroke, Fishguard, Cherbourg, Le Havre and Roscoff.

The DART (Dublin Area Regional Transport) is a line which runs along Dublin Bay from Howth in the north to Bray in the south, serving Pearse Street, Tara Street and Connolly stations in the city centre. Supporters arriving in Dublin on match day can take a DART from Connolly direct to Lansdowne Road. The DART station is situated next to the old East Stand.

RAIL INFORMATION

Phone:	1850 366 222
Internet:	www.irishrail.ie

Light Rail

The recently open Dublin light railway – the Luas (pronounced "Lewis," so was quickly dubbed the "Jerry Lee") - runs on two tramlines: The Green Line, connecting St Stephen's Green to Sandyford in the south of Dublin, has a total journey time of about 22 minutes. The Red Line, linking Connolly Station in the city centre to Tallaght (via Heuston Station) to the west, takes approximately 48 minutes from end to end.

CAR

Dublin can be a bore by car. Renting a vehicle from the airport is probably value for money if several of you are sharing the costs. The roads are extremely congested and although distances are small, a lot of time is lost. The Irish motorway system is still only half-finished, but the major rugby cities of Ireland, (Cork 250km, Limerick 180km, Belfast 160km, and Galway 150 kms) can all be reached within 3 hours from Dublin. The capital is now almost entirely circled by the M5O, an outer (toll) ringroad with links to all of Ireland's major trunkways.
The bus system covers the whole of the city and there are a number of late night bus routes. Once relaxed, the Gardai (Police) are ferociously strict on drink driving.

BUS INFORMATION

Phone:	873 4222
Internet:	www.dublinbus.ie

Local Taxis

Taxis generally abound, but it is a good idea to book a cab before a late finish. Fares are cheap compared with London and cabs are generally available at all times. If you don't know where you're going, this is the best way to move around the city. Your hotel or B&B will have lists of taxi companies they use regularly, but here are some recommended city centre firms:

Taxi 7	460 0000
Pony Cabs	661 2233
Cab 2000	890 0900
City Cabs	872 7272
Metro Cabs	668 3333
Taxi 24	456 0000
Express Taxis	855 3333
Trinity Taxis	708 2222
Euro Cabs	872 7272

Chauffeur Driven

Liberty Limousines	457 8466 www.libertylimousines.ie
Carey Car	614 2880
Massey Limousines	490 9586
New Ireland Limousines	816 6666
PR Limousines	086 336 1276
Silver Limousines	086 881 9010

TRAVEL IN THE CITY

In the city centre – walk. Lansdowne Road is just 25 minutes on foot from Trinity College. If you wish to move further afield, use taxi, DART, Luas (tramway) or the excellent bus system.

REACHING THE GROUND

Lansdowne Road is about 2km from the city centre. On a nice day (ie if it isn't raining), it is a pleasant walk. There is a DART station under the East Stand with frequent trains on match day. Several bus routes – 5 and 7 from O'Connell Street, 18 from Appian Way-Leeson Street, and 45 from Clare Street – take you from the city centre to Ballsbridge and its pubs before a 10-minute final stroll to the ground. It is now possible to enter the stadium at either the North or South Terraces and make your way to any other part of the ground. This recent change avoids the tiresome walk from the pubs and bars of Ballsbridge along the canal to the North Terrace.

Taxis are a good bet from all parts of town but as kick off approaches you will be dropped further and further from the ground leaving at least a ten minute walk to your seat or terrace.

VITAL STATISTICS

Population: 1,100,000+

Phone Code: 00 353 1 (followed by a 7 figure number); 01 outside Dublin

Time Zone: GMT (one hour behind Central European)

Language: English, Irish.

Average temperature: (winter) 4-7°C

Electrical current: 230 volt, 50 cycles (3 pin square plug as in UK)

Tipping: Not obligatory in taxis or bars, but be wary in restaurants. Most include 12.5% service charge for groups of 6 or more.

Shopping: Dublin is a shopper's paradise. All the top international and Irish designers have outlets. And it doesn't have to be blisteringly expensive. Most of the action is centred around the block of Grafton Street, Kildare Street and Dawson Street. Out of town is the Dundrum Shopping Centre, the largest shopping mall in Europe, served by the Luas light rail from St Stephens Green. Most shops in Dublin are open from 09.00 till 18.00 Monday to Saturday with late opening on Thursday. City centre shops open from 12.00 till 18.00 on Sunday. Shopping centres outside town have different late-opening days.

HOSPITALS

St James Hospital, St James Street, Dublin 8	410 3000
Rotunda Hospital, Parnell Street, Dublin 1	873 0300
Mater Misericordiae Hospital, Eccles Street, Dublin 7	803 2000
St Vincent's University Hospital, Elm Park, Dublin 4	269 4533
Dublin Dental School and Hospital, Lincoln Place, Dublin 2	612 7200

USEFUL CONTACTS

Fire or Coastal Guard	999 or 112
Tourist Information Centre	(Main centre) **Suffolk Street, Dublin 2**
Tourist Information Centre	**Failte Ireland, Baggot Street Bridge, Baggot Street, Dublin 2**
Tourist Information Centre	**14 Upper O'Connell St, Dublin 1**
Tourist Information Centre	**Arrivals Hall, Dublin Airport**
Tourist Information Centre	**Ferry Terminal, Dun Laoghaire Harbour**
British Embassy	**29 Merrion Road, Ballsbridge, Dublin 4** Open: Monday-Thursday: 09.00-12.45 - 14.00-17.15 Friday: 09.00-12.45 - 14.00-17.00 205 3700
Ambassade de France en Irlande	**36 Ailesbury Road, Dublin 4** Heures d'ouverture du Service Consulaire :Lundi-Vendredi : 09h30-12h30 Service téléphonique : 14h00-15h30 277 5000
Ambasciate d'Italia in Irlanda	63/65 Northumberland Road, Dublin 4
Apertura al publico della sezione consulare	L/M/M/V 10.00-12.00 G14.30-16.00 660 1744

IRELAND

PLACES OF INTEREST

Dublin Bus City Tour

A great way to get to know the city quickly. The tour lasts about 75 minutes and visits all the main tourist attractions, including the many literary statues such as James Joyce,right. You can hop off and visit any of the sites you wish before rejoining the bus tour. An adult ticket costs €12.50 and is valid for 24 hours.

Dublin Bus, 59 Upper O'Connell Street, Dublin 1.

Phone:	873 4222
Internet:	www.dublinbus.ie

Historical Walking Tours of Dublin

Starting at the front gate of Trinity College, you receive a 'seminar on the street' from graduates of the university. This award winning and entertaining tour explores the main topics of Irish history; Dublin's development, the influence of the American and French revolutions, the Potato Famine 1845-49, the 1916 Rising, the Wars of Independence, partition and concludes with the ongoing Northern Ireland Peace Process.
November-March: Friday, Saturday, Sunday at 11am. April and October: Daily at 11am. May-September: Daily at 11am and 3pm. Tickets: Adults €10. Students and Seniors €8. Pay on the day.

Historical Walking Tours of Dublin, 64 Mary Street, Dublin 1

Phone:	878 0227
Internet:	www.historicalinsights.ie

Places to visit: (cont)

Dublin Literary Pub Crawl

A tour lasting over two hours of four great Dublin pubs, guided by Irish actors who perform extracts from the works of Dublin's best known writers, and some of the unjustly lesser-known Irish figures such as Patrick Kavanagh, whose statue by the Grand Canal is pictured right. A literary quiz is held with prizes for the winner. "An excellent and organised pub crawl. The actors reminding you that the literature of Dublin has always been constructed out of great jokes," observed the Observer. The pub crawl starts from The Duke on Duke Street, tickets available 30 minutes before the start. Times: 1st December – 24th March: Thurs, Fri, Sat at 7.30, Sunday at 12.00. 26th March – 27th November: Nightly at 7.30, Sunday at 12.00 and 7.30pm. No 12.00 pub crawl on Sunday 1st January 2006.

Phone:	670 5602
Internet:	www.dublinpubcrawl.com

Trinity College and Library

Founded in 1592 by Elizabeth I of England, Trinity College is Ireland's oldest and probably its most prestigious university. It is perfectly acceptable to stroll around the grounds and savour the atmosphere of the gardens, cobbled walks and the ancient and modern architecture. A visit to the Old Library is a very enriching experience. The Long Room houses more than 200,000 of Trinity's oldest books as well as the Book Of Kells, a spectacular ninth century manuscript of the Gospels. In a more modern mode, The Dublin Experience is a multi media audio-visual presentation of the history of Dublin.

Adult entry for Book of Kells and Old Library €7.50. The Dublin Experience €4.20
Trinity College and Library, College Street, Dublin 2.

Phone:	608 2320
Internet:	www.tcd.ie/Library

The Guinness Storehouse

This is Dublin's top visitor attraction. Discover the history of the most famous stout in the known universe. You will also learn how it's made and, finally, in the Gravity Bar which offers a staggering panorama of the Fair City, enjoy the complimentary pint of the local brew. Adult entry €14.
The Guinness Storehouse, St James's Gate, Dublin 8.

Phone:	408 4800
Internet:	www.guinness-storehouse.com

The GAA Museum

In April 2005 the Gaelic Athletic Association voted, in principle, to allow Croke Park to be used to host soccer and rugby matches during the demolition and redevelopment of Lansdowne Road. Go and have a look at the treat in store for rugby fans. This is a magnificent stadium, the fourth largest in Europe. You can visit dressing-rooms, corporate suites, VIP section and media centre. You can stand pitch-side but will not be allowed onto the sacred turf. In the museum you can gain an insight into the importance of the GAA in Irish culture and heritage. The specially designed interactive screens allow you to try out your hurling and gaelic football skills. Adult entry to museum €5.50. Museum + Stadium tour €9.50 The GAA Museum and Croke Park Stadium Tour, St Joseph's Avenue (off Clonliffe Road), Dublin 3.

Phone:	819 2323
Internet:	www.gaa.ie

Dublin Castle

A fortification has stood on this site since the very origins of the city as a Gaelic settlement. The Vikings built a fortress here, a portion of this, the Undercroft, is on view to visitors, as are the State Apartments, once the residential quarters of the viceregal court when Dublin was the second city of the British Empire. Dublin Castle is the venue for the inauguration of Ireland's presidents. State Functions and summits of the European Union also take place here. The Chapel Royal is also open to visitors. Adult entry €4.50

Dublin Castle, Dame Street, Dublin 2.

Phone:	677 7129
Internet	www.dublincastle.ie

Kilmainham Jail

Visited on a bleak February day, this remnant of British occupation gave a tiny insight into what it was like to be incarcerated in a purpose-built Irish prison from the 18th century. The door of every cell is visible from the ground floor. Leaders of Irish rebellion since the Rising of 1798 to the Easter Rising of 1916 were held and some executed here. The guided visit is chillingly fascinating. Adult entry €5.

Kilmainham Jail, Inchicore Road, Kilmainham, Dublin 8.

Phone:	453 5984
Internet:	www.heritageireland.ie

ATTRACTIONS OUTSIDE TOWN

Wild Wicklow Tour

A daylong (09.00 – 17.30) tour of Dublin and the beautiful countryside of neighbouring Wicklow, including the Dublin Mountains, in small Mercedes coaches. Hug the coastline past Dun Laoghaire and the exclusive villages of Killiney and Dalkey (the Beverly Hills of Dublin), then inland to the 6th century monastic settlement at Glendalough. After visiting the Sally Gap – mountain lakes, wild heather and barren boglands (the location for the film Braveheart, you will be offered coffee and craft shopping at Avoca Handweavers - also see the Shopping section for details of Avoca's store in the city) and home-cooked lunch in a traditional Irish pub.

Adult price €28, including all admission charges but not morning coffee or lunch.

Phone:	280 1899
Internet:	www.discoverdublin.ie

Places to visit: (cont)

The Irish National Stud

In charge of promoting the interests of the bloodstock industry in Ireland (and not a reference to hearthrob actor Colin Farrell). So successfully has this been done that the breeding of thoroughbreds is one of the most lucrative industries in Ireland today. The stud covers 958 acres and there are 288 boxes on the farm for mares, foals and stallions. Guided tours of the National Stud take place most days day between February 12th and November 12th from 09.30 till 18.00, with last visitors admitted at 17.00. These last about 35 minutes and you are advised to allow about 45 minutes to see the museum and to take a stroll along Tully Walk to see any mares or foals. In the main yard there is a ten-minute video, "The Birth of a Foal." You can also visit two wonderful gardens in contrasting styles: the Japanese Gardens and St Fiachra's Garden – the latter dedicated to the patron saint of gardeners. Bus from Busaras 9.30 Monday to Saturday. 10am and 12noon Sunday. Train to Kildare from Heuston Station every 35 minutes

Take the N7 following signs for Cork/Limerick, 40-60 minutes drive to Kildare.

Phone:	045 522396 or 045 521617
Internet:	www.irish-national-stud.ie

RACING

You may wish to see the thoroughbreds in action and savour the conviviality and craic of an Irish race meeting, as well as experiencing the renowned generosity of Irish bookmakers. There are several courses around Dublin. Here are three.

Leopardstown

Beautiful course 6 miles south of Dublin city centre in the foothills of the Dublin mountains. Top class flat and National Hunt racing.

Taxi from city centre approximately €20. Luas light rail from St Stephens Green in the city to Sandyford / Brewery Road, then a short walk to the course. Entry to the course: Grandstand Ticket: €12 to €16 depending on meeting. Reserved Enclosure Ticket: €25 to €30 Top Level Seat: €30 to €55.

Phone:	289 0500
Internet:	www.leopardstown.com

The Curragh

Out in horse-obsessed Kildare, the Curragh is the headquarters of flat racing in Ireland and the setting for the Irish Derby.

Car: M50 and take Exit 9, heading on the N7 to Cork/Limerick. Take exit 10 and follow signs to the course. Bus: There is a race-day service from Busaras. The last return bus 30 minutes after the last race. Call Bus Eireann 836 6111. Train: Mainline trains from Heuston Station stop at the Curragh on Classic race days. On other days, take a train to Kildare Town and a complimentary shuttle bus to the course.

ENTRY TO THE COURSE

Regular meetings: €15
Group One days: €18 Classic meetings: €20
Reserved enclosure (Derby day): €50
West End enclosure: €25
Premier Level access: €15 (regular) €25 (Classic/Group One) €75 (Derby)
With seating: €25 (regular) €45 (Classic/Group One) €150 (Derby)

Punchestown

Another great racecourse in County Kildare. Access from central Dublin:

Car: Exit 9 of the M50 and N7 following for Cork/Limerick. Branch left onto R445 (signpost for Naas), continue on R441. Turn left at first lights following sign for Blessington and Punchestown. After 2 miles turn right at the crossroads. The racecourse is one mile from here. Entry From €15. Bus: Race-day service from Busaras. Call Bus Eireann 836 6111

GOLF

Golf is a huge sport and tourist attraction in Ireland. Many retired rugby stars play, and golf matches between former 6 Nations rivals are held regularly on the eve of internationals (keep an eye on the local press for details). There are many wonderful links and parkland courses close to Dublin and here is a small selection.

Parkland Courses

The K Club, Straffan, County Kildare.
(Venue for the 2006 Ryder Cup) 17 miles due west of Dublin. Two 18 hole championship courses designed by Arnold Palmer.

Phone:	601 7200
Internet:	www.kclub.ie

Green Fees per person

1st Jan – 31st March	€115 (non-residents)	€ 75 (residents).
1st April – 30th April	€165	€ 95
1st May – 30th Sept	€250	€115
1st Oct – 31st Oct	€165	€ 95

Druids Glen and Druids Heath, Newtownmountkennedy, County Wicklow.
Two eighteen hole courses. 25 miles south west of Dublin.

Phone:	287 3600
Internet:	www.druidsglen.ie

Green Fees per person

Druids Glen	€ 85
Druids Heath	€ 70

Links courses

County Louth Golf Club, Baltray, County Louth.
Championship links course. 35 miles north of Dublin Airport.

Phone:	41 988 1530
Internet:	www.countylouthgolfclub.com

Green Fees per person

Weekdays	€110	Weekends	€130

The Island Golf Club, Corballis, Donabate, County Dublin.
Course that is used for The Open qualifying competition from 2005-2010. 20 miles north of Dublin.

Phone:	843 6205
Internet:	www.theislandgolfclub.com

Green Fees per person

All week	€110
Early bird (before 7.30)	€ 80
Twilight (after 17.30)	€ 75

Pormarnock Golf Club, Portmarnock, County Dublin.
Championship links (has staged the Irish Open). 8 miles north east of Dublin.

Phone:	846 2968
Internet:	www.portmarnockgolfclub.ie

Green fees per person

Weekdays	€165
Weekends	€190

Golf (cont)

Portmarnock Golf Links, Strand Road, Portmarnock, County Dublin.
Hotel and Links complex. The course was designed by Bernhard Langer, the former Masters champion and 2004 winning Ryder Cup captain. 8.5 miles from Dublin Airport, north east of Dublin city. **Green Fees per person:** €60

Phone:	846 0611
Internet:	www.portmarnock.com

The Royal Dublin Golf Club, Dollymount, County Dublin.
Championship links. 3 miles north east of Dublin city centre.
Green fees per person: €120

Phone:	833 6346
Internet:	www.theroyaldublingolfclub.com

OTHER PLACES OF INTEREST

James Joyce Martello Tower, Sandycove

The Martello towers, along the coast from Dublin, were built as a protection against invasion by Napoleonic forces. This tower, the fictional home of "stately plump Buck Mulligan,", was the setting for the first chapter of James Joyce's "Ulysses," and has been converted to a museum devoted to the writer and his works. Though Joyce sought exile from Ireland for almost all of his adult life, he is still the writer most identified with Dublin. Non-Joyceans may enjoy a trip down here to savour the panoramic view of Dublin Bay and Mountains and breathe some fresh sea air.

Phone:	280 9265
Internet:	www.visitdublin.com

Powerscourt Springs Health Farm and Spa

Only a 30-minute drive from Dublin, this is the place for pure relaxation. The majestic surroundings of the Wicklow Mountains let you escape the hustle and bustle of the city. Even the journey itself is breathtaking as you pass the famous waterfall and go through the scenic Wicklow Way. Powerscourt Springs offers a range of programmes, including the Pampering Day and the De-Stress Weekend. The Health farm was the inspiration of two ladies, Fiona Hanby and Patricia Kinsella.

Phone:	276 1000

THEATRE & THE ARTS

The Abbey Theatre, Lower Abbey Street

Founded by Nobel Laureate WB Yeats and Lady Augusta Gregory, Ireland's National Theatre celebrated its centenary in 2004. It has been the creative cradle for some of Ireland's finest playwrights and actors. It has two stages, the Abbey and the Peacock and backstage tours are available on Thursdays if schedules allow. Tickets at €15 to €30 represent good value for money. Matinees and previews €12.50.

Hours:	Monday – Saturday 10.30am-7.30pm.
Prices:	Matinee €12.50, €15 to €30 all else
Phone:	878 7222
Internet:	www.abbeytheatre.ie

National Concert Hall, Earlsfort Terrace

Home to the RTE Smphony Orchestra. Reckoned by those who play here to be one of the finest halls in Europe. Regular concerts as well as jazz events and traditional and Irish music. Facilities include a Terrace Café, music store, internet kiosk and interactive ticket collection booth, are open from 10am till 7pm Monday to Saturday and for two hours before concerts on Sundays. Box office: 10.00am-7.00pm.

Phone:	417 0000
Internet:	www.nch.ie

The National Gallery, Merrion Square West

Free admission to the extensive permanent exhibition, which includes important works from all of the major European schools as well as those of Irish artists. Also visit the Yeats Museum, devoted to the work of this famously creative family, especially the painter Jack B. Next to the National History Museum and Leinster House, the Irish parliament. Open Monday to Saturday 9.30am-5.30pm (Thursday till 8.30pm) Open Sunday 12noon to 5.30pm.

Phone:	661 5133
Internet:	www.nationalgallery.ie

Royal Hibernian Academy, Ely Place

The Royal Hibernian Academy is an artist-based and artist-orientated institution that has promoted the fine arts in Ireland since 1823. It is dedicated to developing, affirming and challenging the public's appreciation and understanding of traditional and innovative approaches to the visual arts. This is a beautiful, modern gallery situated close to St Stephens Green. It houses regular temporary exhibitions alongside the excellent permanent collection and organises talks, tours, evening lectures, and children's workshops which reflect the Academy's dynamism and dedication to its mission. Open Tuesday – Saturday 11am – 5pm (Thursday open to 8pm) Sunday – 2pm – 5pm. Closed Monday.

Phone:	661 2558
Internet:	www.royalhibernianacademy.com

Dublin Writers Museum

It could be said that the whole of Dublin is a memorial to its great writers with the literary tours, literary pubs, wonderful bookshops and theatres. Four Irishmen have been awarded the Nobel Prize for Literature. Three of them were born in Dublin; G.B. Shaw, W.B. Yeats and Samuel Beckett (the fourth, Seamus Heaney, now lives in Sandymount). The museum has letters, portraits and artefacts of these and other mighty Dublin pens, including Sheridan and Swift, Wilde and Joyce. The museum also organises other temporary exhibitions, lunchtime theatre and readings. There is a permanent exhibition devoted to children's literature. (The museum's café is considered by many to be the best in Ireland). Open Monday – Saturday 10.00am-5.00pm (June, July and August to 6.00pm).

Phone:	872 2077
Internet:	www.writersmuseum.com

SHOPPING

The Blarney Woollen Mill, Nassau Street

Match weekend this shop close to Trinity College selling Irish clothing and artefacts (brooches, pendants, necklaces, crystal glasswear), is packed with foreign fans calls irresistibly to mind Max Boyce's words: "And we all bring our wives back a present, So we can go next time again." The goods on sale are of high good quality and the prices are reasonable.

IRELAND

The Kilkenny Design Centre & Shop, Nassau St

This is Ireland's most exclusive craft and design store. The Kilkenny Shop's focus on design is obvious when you browse through the collections on display by the leading Irish designers. The Art of Dressing range is based on beautiful textures in soft fabrics made into relaxed tailored clothes. The shop also has the largest range of designer knitwear in Dublin. Other products include blown glass, hand turned wood, beautiful lights and Celtic jewellery.

Phone:	677 7066
Internet:	www.kilkennygroup.com

Louise Kennedy, Merrion Square

Louise Kennedy is one of Ireland's best-known and most successful fashion designers. Her career took off with her tailored clothes but she is now also a leading crystal designer whose versatility and flair is best illustrated in her home in Merrion Square – Dublin's most splendid example of 18th century Georgian architecture. The house acts as her headquarters and as a boutique for her fashion and crystal creations.

Phone:	662 0056

Avoca, Grafton Street/St Stephen's Green

Avoca is a seven-level mini-department store and has been described as ' the most exciting retail development in Dublin in years'. Avoca is a family run business originating 280 years ago in a small village in County Wicklow (see attractions outside the city) of the same name. Avoca's café, food-hall and cookbooks have all won prestigious awards. Its designer clothes range is eclectic and colourful. This flagship store is in the heart of the city centre at the bottom of Grafton Street.

Phone:	677 4215
Internet:	www.avoca.com

Powerscourt Centre, South William Street

Inside this splendidly restored 1774 town house you will find the Design Centre. Clothes by Ireland's top designers such as John Rocha, Lyn Mar, Lainey Keogh, and Patrick Sweeney are all stocked here. It is a four storey complex made up of a central courtyard and over 60 boutiques, craft shops, art galleries, wine bars and restaurants. Paintings, jewellery, farmhouse cheeses, clothes and crafts are some of the treasures you will find here.

Dundrum Town Centre, Dundrum, Co Dublin

An enormous shopping centre, one of the largest in Europe, has been built and recently opened in Dundrum, south Dublin, transforming, in a gestation period of eight years, a village into a town. The centre, constructed on four levels, houses restaurants and places of entertainment, large stores; Marks and Spencer, House of Fraser, Harvey Nichols, Tesco, Virgin Megastore, Penney's as well as almost innumerable outlets of Irish and international renown selling almost every type of product or service from hairgrips to holidays. If you fall ill there is a medical centre, if you have a baby there's a crèche. Not quite shop until you drop, however. There's no undertaker.

Directions:	From Dublin city centre: Luas Light Rail Green Line from St Stephen's Green.
Hours:	Monday – Friday: 9am – 9pm. Saturday: 8.30am – 7.00pm. Sunday 10.00am – 7.00pm Tesco is open 24hours.
Phone:	299 1700
Internet:	www.dundrum.ie

EAT, DRINK & SLEEP

BARS

The designation "beer garden" is very important in Dublin. There is a strictly enforced smoking ban in pubs and restaurants, but the beer garden indicates that there is an outdoor area where smoking is allowed.

TRADITIONAL PUBS

O'Connell Street Area and North Quays

O'Neill's Pub and Guesthouse, 37 Pearse Street, Dublin 1. Dark, cosy Victorian pub with many nooks and crannies. Excellent food, reasonably priced.

The Boar's Head, Capel Street, Dublin 1. Tiny pub close to O'Connell Street. Take time for gentle conversation over a few well pulled pints.

South Quays and Temple Bar

The Palace Bar, 21 Fleet Street, Dublin 2.
Journalistic / literary pub. Close to the offices of the Irish Times, a great favourite with Dubliners of a conversational bent. It is therefore always full, particularly early to mid-evening. Frosted glass and mahogany fittings make it a cosy place to sit quietly (mid-afternoon) and read or just listen to the craic.

The Porterhouse, 16-18 Parliament Street, Temple Bar, Dublin 2.
Micro-brewery pub. Ten different beers, each unique, are produced here and these can be sampled from a specially created tasting tray. Savour this place, this is one of the best pubs in Ireland. Take your time over the beer and enjoy a meal - pub food at its best - in carefully and tastefully created decor.

John Mulligan, 8 Poolbeg Street, Dublin 2.
A great pub – allegedly the best pint of Guinness in Dublin (therefore the world). Victim of its own success, it gets jammed in the evening but at lunchtime and mid-afternoon the craic, which the customers generate as there is no music, food or decor to talk about, is brilliant. It was a Mulligan's barman who, when asked by a student for six pints of Guinness and a seventh with a drop of blackcurrant, replied: "What do you think this is? A fuckin' cocktail bar?"

The Long Hall Bar, 51 South Great Georges Street, Dublin 2.
There is a long, narrow bar before the room widens at the back. This pub is always packed quite simply because it is a wonderfully attractive old boozer with a great atmosphere.

St Stephen's Green and Grafton Street area

The International Bar, 23 Wicklow Street, Dublin 2.
Going up Grafton Street with Trinity College behind you, turn right into Wicklow Street, at Brown Thomas. No food but a great spot for a quiet lunchtime or mid-afternoon pint while reading the newspaper. Much livelier in the early evening before giving over to music.

MacDaid's, Harry Street, Dublin 2.
Great literary pub just off Grafton Street at the Stephen's Green end. Usually quiet during the day and at lunchtime as they don't serve food, so a good place to have a quiet pint watched by Joyce, Behan, Beckett, Flan O'Brien and the rest. Gets packed early evening and stays that way. Upstairs room with music takes the overspill from the groundfloor bar.

Bruxelles, Harry Street, Dublin 2.

Used to offer a trendy alternative to MacDaid's opposite. No longer as groovy as it was, but still caters for a younger crowd. Food OK and fairly good value. Happy hour.

Davy Byrne's, Duke Street, Dublin 2.

Go up Grafton Street towards Stephen's Green and turn left into Duke Street. Quality, good value pub grub. A Dublin institution. Great stop-off during a shopping expedition to Grafton Street. Decorated with scenes from Ulysses (the pub and its original owner figure in the book – Bloom has his lunch here). Early evening the pub fills with prosperous Dubliners, young and old. Relatively quiet on match day, but the game is shown on TV. Smokers' terrace summer and winter.

The Duke, Duke Street, Dublin 2.

Dark, wood panelled, traditional Dublin pub. Serves OK pub grub. No tourist trap this, good atmosphere with an older clientele. TV on match day.

The Bailey, Duke Street, Dublin 2.

Justifiably famous Victorian pub. Great place to restore the tissues during an exhausting wrestle with the shops of Grafton Street. Daytime, early doors and late evening drinking before setting off clubward.

Foley's Bar and Restaurant, Merrion Row, Dublin 2.

Wonderfully lively pub, music, conversation. The pub grub is of good quality and reasonable price. With all matches shown on TV this is a very good spot on match day for the ticketless. The restaurant upstairs means that once settled in for the game, there is no need to risk the wilds of Dublin for the rest of the day.

Kehoe's, 9 South Anne Street, Dublin 2. Great, unspoilt, traditional Dublin pub. Quieter drinking during the day, very lively in the evening.

O'Rourke's Bar, Corner of Merrion Row and Merrion Street, Dublin 2. Good, atmospheric, traditional Dublin bar. Rugby fans very welcome.

Merrion Square to Ballsbridge

The Bar At the Mont Clare Hotel, Merrion Square, Dublin 2.

Very pleasant "Gallery" bar. Convenient starting point from city centre on the trek to Lansdowne Road (exit the side door of the hotel, turn left and go straight on). Alternatively don't move, and enjoy the game on the big screen.

Larry Murphy's, 43 Lower Baggot Street, Dublin 2.

Traditional woodpanelled Dublin pub. Thirty minutes walk from Lansdowne Road but too many obstacles on the way to make this timescale remotely feasible.

Toner's or James Toner, 139 Lower Baggot Street, Dublin 2.

Wonderfully atmospheric, traditional and unspoilt Dublin pub. They serve soup and sandwiches at lunchtime. Said to be the only pub ever visited by the poet and yetanotherdublinnobellaureate, W.B.Yeats.

Maguire's Pub, Lower Baggot Street, Dublin 2.

Sound, solid Dublin pub serving hearty pub grub. Good place for pre, during (all big rugby games are shown on TV here), or post-match drinking. Within comfortable walking distance (about 25 minutes) to Lansdowne Road if (and this is a big if) you resist all the temptations on the way.

TRADITIONAL MUSIC PUBS

O'Connell Street Area and North Quays

O'Shea's Hotel and Bar, 19 Talbot Street, Dublin 1.

This is a warm, welcoming pub, popular with construction workers for the quality and, more importantly, quantity of the food. Very good place to feed a hungry bunch. Close to O'Connell Street and on the northside of the Liffey, we predict this pub will become very popular if the rugby moves to Croke Park, just 20 minutes walk away. Free traditional Irish music and ballads nightly.

South Quays and Temple Bar

The Ha'penny Bridge Inn, Dublin 2.

Great, scruffy little pub offering tremendous fun. Regular entertainment with an open comedy night every Tuesday.

The Temple Bar, 47-48 Temple Bar, Dublin 2.

Rather a Temple Bar tourist trap. Live traditional Irish music twice daily. Claims to have Ireland's largest collection of whiskey. Beer garden. Sound pub grub.

The Oliver St-John Gogarty, Fleet Street, Temple Bar, Dublin 2.
Traditional Irish music and dance – sessions daily 2.30pm to 2.30am. Beer garden and good pub food. Restaurant on 2nd floor.

The Vat House at Blooms Hotel, Anglesea Street, Temple Bar, Dublin 2.
So called because the timber for the floor was salvaged from the vat house at Guinness brewery. Good selection of wines alongside a large collection of Irish whiskies. Spontaneous music sessions. Food available.

St Stephen's Green and Grafton Street

M.J. O'Neill's, 2 Suffolk Street, Dublin 2.
Just opposite the main Tourist Office. Large pub with lots of little nooks and corners. Offers very good value pub grub, carvery, sandwich and salad bar every lunchtime. Music Sunday and Monday nights. Wireless internet connection. Sky sports TV. Good place to watch a game if you don't have a ticket.

Whelan's, Wexford Street, Dublin 2.
Arguably Dublin's most popular live music pub while not particularly touristy. Some great bands and brilliant fun.

The Dame Tavern, Dame Lane, Dublin 2.
Tucked away in a little side street parallel with Dame Street, this pub has a happy, lively atmosphere. Regular live music has generated a large, faithful following.

O'Donohue's,15, Merrion Row, Dublin 2.
For fans of Irish music but perhaps more particularly of Dublin ballads (the Dubliners started here) this scruffy, easy pub is a must as there is live music every night. The pub is very attractive in the daytime; quiet and dark. Good pint, good conversation.

SUPERPUBS AND CLUBS

O'Connell Street Area and North Quays

Zanzibar, Lower Ormond Quay, Dublin 1.
Situated next to the Liffey on the O'Connell Street side between the Ha'penny and the Millennium Bridges. Decorated in a Turkish style, this was one of Dublin's first so-called Superpubs, which developed with new licensing laws which have, to some extent, brought about the demise of night clubs. Zanzibar usually attracts a good crowd.

The Bar at the Arlington Hotel, Bachelor's Walk, Dublin 1.
Immense bars with organised mayhem on match day (and most weekends, too). Music, song, Irish dancing before the match. Giant screen and TVs for the game. As good a place as any to watch the rugby.

Fireworks, Pearse Street, Dublin 1.
Quite possibly the biggest bar in a city of big bars. Fireworks covers three large floors and is always impressively packed.

St Stephen's Green and Grafton Street Areas

Samsara, Dawson Street, Dublin 2.
The upmarket "Superpub" in posh Dawson Street. A place to see and be seen but because of this the atmosphere can perhaps be a little restrained.

COCKTAIL BARS

The Morrison Bar at the Morrison Hotel, Ormond Quay, Dublin 1.
The "dramatic, even flamboyant" public areas of this hotel were created by renowned Irish designer, John Rocha. Excellent, beautifully prepared and presented cocktails before continuing the evening in...

Lobo at the Morrison Hotel , Ormond Quay, Dublin 1
A setting as stylish and as beautiful as the clientele. Or...
The Octogan Bar at the Clarence Hotel , 6-8 Wellington Quay, Dublin 2.
Very trendy. Sometimes the owners, after checking the tills, tarry awhile for afters.

The Odeon, Harcour Street, Dublin 2. Formerly a railway station, the conversion into a modern, smartly decorated and stylish bar has been particularly successful. The same adjectives could be used to describe the crowd.

Cocoon, Duke Lane, Dublin 2.
Situated in a side street between Grafton Street and Dawson Street, this is one of Dublin's classiest modern bars, a hang-out for the beautiful people, lots of understated style.

Bars (cont)

TRENDY BARS

Q Bar, O'Connell Bridge, Dublin 2.
Dublin veterans may remember the notorious Harp bar whose sign could be seen for miles and would attract punters like flies to an old pork pie. Well, it has been gutted and replaced by the extremely stylish Q Bar, which attracts a similarly fashionable crowd. Usually pretty busy.

Boomerangs, Temple Bar, Dublin 2.
This basement club is one of the most popular night spots in town. It is very busy every night of the week (there is a strict dress code at weekends) and offers commercial dance music.

Dublin's Left Bank Bar, 18-21 Anglesea Street, Temple Bar, Dublin 2.
It's on the right bank but so what, you get the idea? Late night. DJ music from the 70s, 80s, and 90s. Food available too.

Club M at Blooms Hotel , Anglesea Street, Temple Bar, Dublin 2.
Commercial dance music on several floors in this very popular Temple Bar club. It is busy every night, don't go badly dressed as there is a strict dress code. Don't go drunk either.

Bob's, Temple Bar, Dublin 2.
This enormous, recently restored Temple Bar institution (formerly known as Bad Bob's) takes up four floors. It is always very lively and always very full.

The Temple Theatre, Temple Street, Dublin 2.
This large (room for 75 rugby teams and a girlfriend each), popular club close to Temple Bar on two floors, puts out music according to the night and the floor. No particular dress code, the usual no runners (trainers) is all.

Lillie's Bordello, Grafton Street, Dublin 2.
Favourite hang-out of the celebs. Expensive if you manage to get in. It was here that some rough boys from Bath, in the company of the monarch's grand-daughter, dealt out some rough justice to soccer player Stan Collymore. Security can be pretty hostile. But if it's celebs you want...

The Clarendon, Chatham Row, Dublin 2 Trendy cocktail bar.
DJ's live, with late closing Friday, Saturday and Sunday. Then go back for brunch.

The Pod, Harcourt Street, Dublin 2.
The premises also holds the Red Box and Chocolate Bar. The music changes according to the evening and the venue. One of Dublin's most popular and well-known clubs.

Café en Seine, 40 Dawson Street, Dublin 2.
Very fashionable French-style brasserie. Fine art-deco interior. Terrace seating 30. Open 10.30am till late (NB tills programmed to increase prices by 50c per drink every hour on the hour from midnight). Coffees and pastries. Self-service lunch. All day café food. Sunday brunch. Live swing and jazz bands. (Recommended by Parisians).

WINE BARS

Ely Wine Bar, Ely Place, Dublin 2.
Sophisticated wine bar selling an excellent and continually varying range of wines by the bottle or glass. The food here is exceptional so try it. (See restaurant entry).

PRE AND POST MATCH BARS

The Inkwell (at the Schoolhouse Hotel), 2-8 Northumberland Road, Ballsbridge, Dublin 4. Attractive meeting place for pre and post-match drinks. Easy strolling distance to Lansdowne Road and on the route back to the fleshpots of the city centre after the game. Younger clientele. The Canteen bistro and Satchel's restaurant are in the same building if you feel the need to eat.

The Dubliner Pub at Jurys Ballsbridge Hotel, Pembroke Road, Ballsbridge, Dublin 4. The Dubliner Pub, part of the huge Jurys Hotel in Ballsbridge, is a famous meeting place. However, on match day virtually the whole of the ground floor of the hotel is devoted to entertaining fans, with or without tickets, for the big game just down the road. Improvised bars, filling, easy-to-eat food (the hot roast-beef sandwiches are sensational), ballrooms given over to music and dancing and open to all.

Madigan's, Morehampton Road, Donnybrook, Dublin 4.
Relatively quiet Dublin pub just outside the rugby village of Donnybrook. Good place to drink away from the hurly-burly of Donnybrook or Ballsbridge.
Kiely's of Donnybrook, Donnybrook Road, Donnybrook, Dublin 4.
Large pub geared for match day catering. Serving sound pub food this is good spot to meet, eat and drink before moving towards Ballsbridge and Lansdowne Road. Quite a good place to watch if you don't have a ticket.
Longs, Donnybrook Road, Donnybrook, Dublin 4. Meeting place for the older set before moving on to the match. Pleasantly atmospheric bar.
Bellamy's, Ballsbridge Terrace, Dublin 4.
In amongst restaurants at the Ballsbridge terrace. Minutes walk from Lansdowne Road. Last watering-hole before the game. TV screen for the match and all the pre and post match blarney.

Paddy Cullen's	Ballsbridge	Dublin 4
Mary Mac's	Ballsbridge	Dublin 4
Crowe's	Ballsbridge	Dublin 4

The three pubs are interconnected. All three are jammered on match days. Great atmosphere but get there early if you want a real glass. Great sports pubs – not just rugby but soccer, GAA, racing etc. Sound pub food during the week but not on match day. There is a SPAR next door for cheap snacks, sandwiches etc. There are TV screens everywhere, including a giant screen in the upstairs bar. Minutes' walk to Lansdowne Road, so a renowned meeting place before and after the game.
The Bar At The Berkeley Court Hotel, Lansdowne Road, Dublin 4.
One of Dublin's choicest hotels opens up on match day. Great pre and post match meeting place and just an O'Gara punt to the stadium. If he could swing a leg.
The Bar at the Mount Herbert Hotel, Herbert Road, Dublin 4.
This excellent bar in the Mount Herbert Hotel, just 100m from the South Terrace turnstile at Lansdowne Road, is the place to be if you don't have a ticket but want the match atmosphere. The bar is jammered but there is a giant screen, lots of noise direct from the stadium; in short, everything without actually being there. You also get clean and accessible toilets and, of course, all the pre and post match craic. A Guinness tent in the car park for late-comers or claustrophobics.

Old Wesley, Donnybrook Stadium, Donnybrook, Dublin 4.
The Donnybrook Stadium is the home of Leinster Rugby but is also the home ground of two great Dublin clubs, Bective Rangers and Old Wesley. The stadium often hosts an 'A' international on the eve of the main game. On big match day Bective and Old Wesley open to visitors for a pint and rugby chat. You would be about a mile and a half from Lansdowne Road. There is TV coverage for the ticketless. Check with the club for any other types of entertainment during the weekend.

Bective Rangers, Donnybrook Stadium, Donnybrook, Dublin 4.

Phone:	283 8254

Old Belvedere RFC, Anglesea Road, Ballsbridge, Dublin 4.
Another great Dublin rugby club, cradle of some great Irish stars, opens it doors to visitors during big match weekend. Ten minutes walk to Lansdowne Road. Coverage of the big games on giant screen, friendly atmosphere and maybe an evening match. Contact the club for details of events.

COFFEE SHOPS

Insomnia (Coffee House chain), Unit 2 Lower Mayor Street, Custom House Quay, IFSC, Dublin 1. Top quality coffee in all its forms, from electric shock espresso to iced coffee via American coffee. Take them with a pastry, croissant, muffin or biscotti or a Bendini and Shaw sandwich. Special teas, hot chocolate and cool drinks are available. Other outlets can be found in **Charlotte Way, Dublin 1, Dawson Street, Dublin 2.**

Panem, Ha'penny Bridge Hotel, 21 Lower Ormond Quay, Dublin 1.
Everything presented here is done so with style. From the traditional and fruit breads, sweet and savoury croissants , brioches, soups. All are prepared on the premises with the best possible ingredients, down to the specially imported Sicilian coffee and the hot dark chocolate from Belgium.

Coffee shops (cont)

Butlers Chocolate Café Bar, 24 Wicklow Street, Dublin 2.
Here you can enjoy two special pleasures, your favourite coffee and a delicious handmade Butlers chocolate. The hot chocolate drink Decadence by Decadence is a must. The interior is bright and welcoming. Other Butlers Chocolate Cafés at:

31 Henry Street Dublin 1	18 Nassau Street, Dublin 2
51a Grafton Street, Dublin 2	9 Chatham Street, Dublin 2

IRELAND

The Queen of Tarts, 4 Cork Hill, Dame Street, Dublin 2.
Not just tarts, but cooked breakfasts (from 7.30), sandwiches and desserts, scones and chocolate fudge cake, cookies and breads, from the kitchen of this charming café near Dublin Castle. All at a reasonable price and beautifully presented.

Bewleys Coffee, Waterstone's Bookshop, Dawson Street, Dublin 2.
Unfortunately the great Bewleys coffee shops of Dublin have all closed due to high ground costs and low turnover. The exception is this coffee bar in Waterstone's bookshop which bears the old name but doesn't quite have the old atmosphere. However, one can browse through the shop, find a book and retire to the coffee shop. A calm spot to while away an hour or so.

Café@cocoon, Royal Hibernian Way (shopping mall linking Dawson Street and Grafton Street), Dublin 2. Cocoon is famous more for the cool, stylish ambience of its bar created by the young and beautiful people who frequent it. However, the café is open in the morning and is a pleasant spot to spend an hour or so in some comfort and style.

RESTAURANTS

Chapter One, 18-19 Parnell Square, Dublin 1.
Located in the basement of the Dublin Writers' Museum, the creative inspiration of the great men honoured there has seeped downstairs. Restaurant manager Martin Corbett and chefs Ross Lewis and Garrett Byrne created one of Dublin's finest restaurants. No detail is overlooked. Ingredients have been carefully sourced (Lewis is influential in a pan-European commission for the promotion of quality produce) and are presented – a wonderful charcuterie trolley – or prepared with a strong French influence. There are eight or nine choices for every course. The wine list has been expertly concocted. The best plan is to sit back and let the experts choose, the tasting menu (for whole parties, at €48.50 incredible value) will prepare you for your inevitable second visit.

Phone:	873 2330
Internet:	www.chapteronerestaurant.com

101 Talbot Restaurant, 100-102, Talbot Street, Dublin 1. €30.
Just off O'Connell Street and close to the trendy eateries of the 21st century IFSC (Dublin's new financial area), the 101 has been a deservedly popular restaurant for over ten years. There is a strong Mediterranean and Middle-Eastern influence on the cooking with superb vegetarian options, courteous and efficient service (all dietary requirements are unfussily met) while a lively, bohemian atmosphere is created by the constantly renewed art exhibitions and the crowds from the nearby Abbey and Gate theatres. Not expensive.

Phone:	874 5011

Condotti, 38 Lower Ormond Quay, Dublin 1. The interior belies the exterior. From generally dreary Ormond Quay into light, bright stylish and modern Condotti for a good old fashioned Italian nosh-up. Pastas and gourmet pizzas, simply prepared meats, massive portions. Early dinner menu is particularly good value. Service could be better but the atmosphere is youthful and friendly. There is outside dining for smokers and jazz on Friday. Simple, cheap, good fun.

Phone:	872 0004

D'One, North Wall Quay, IFSC, Dublin 1. €30. A modernist glass cube right on the wall of the river Liffey, furnished in simple style. Efficient service (very necessary as lunch time is hectic, particularly in the week) and value for money, are the house trademarks. The cooking is contemporary and if you keep to the basics all goes well. Short but well constructed wine list with house wines reasonably priced, at least for Dublin, from €15.

Phone:	856 1622

The Vaults, Harbourmaster Place, IFSC Dublin 1. €35.
10 vaulted chambers, built under Connolly station in the mid 19th century to support a railway track, were converted in 2002 to form a multi-purpose events venue. With each vault a separate entity, decorated and furnished in its own style, different events can take place simultaneously. Some of the vaults have plasma screens which are ideal for ticketless fans looking for a lively place to watch a game. Unsurprisingly, seats have to be reserved. The food, supervised by Michael Martin, formerly of the Clarence Hotel's Tea Room (see entry), is simple; pizzas, pastas, grilled meats, ice-cream. Everything is prepared on the premises, is well executed and stylishly presented.

Phone:	605 4700
Internet:	www.thevaults.ie

Monty's of Kathmandu, 28 Eustace Street, Temple Bar, Dublin 2. €25.
High quality, fairly priced, Indian sub-continent cooking with a strong leaning towards Nepal, which is where the chefs are from. Vegetable curry is prepared to taste (mild, medium or hot), cochlea (a sort of lamb tartare served with a shot of whiskey), and Moo (dumplings). The tandoori food is very good and there is an extensive wine and drinks list, including a beer, 'Shiva', which is brewed specially for Monty's.

Phone:	670 4911
Internet:	www.montys.ie

The Tea Room, The Clarence Hotel, 6-8 Wellington Quay, Dublin 2. €55.
One of the most impressive, and sexiest dining rooms in Dublin (this has been described as the city's great date restaurant). The linen, cutlery, glasswear, service of drinks and menus establish a professional tone. The menu, constructed around fine Irish produce, is strong yet not overpowering. The European style of the cooking develops the seasonal ingredients most inventively: caramelised halibut, monkfish with Savoy cabbage, partridge with green beans and lentil vinaigrette, and a slow-cooked neck of lamb with potato, carrot and onions - unrecognisable from the version Scousers eat across the water. The tasting menu at €65 gives full rein to chef Anthony Ely's rare talents.

Phone:	407 0813
Internet:	www.theclarence.ie

Les Frères Jacques, 74 Dame Street, Dublin 2. €45.
Les Frères Jacques has been a bastion of high quality cooking in Dublin since 1986. A feast of French food with strong seafood and fish offerings (all from Irish waters), with game in season. The set lunch is incredible value at €22 with three choices on each course enhanced with options from the à la carte menu. Dinner takes things into another dimension with cuisine bourgeoise classics, an excellent cheese board (featuring some Irish poduce), and fine desserts. Choose from an extensive, well conceived and mainly French wine list.

Phone:	679 4555

Tulsi Indian Restaurant, 17a Lower Baggot Street, Dublin 2. €25.
Advisable to reserve because it is popular and not just for its prices. You are quickly into the thick of things, service is slick and the menu offers the full range of Indian cuisine including some good vegetarian options. The decor is refined, the food carefully prepared so not really a place best appreciated after too many pints.

Phone:	676 4578

Jacob's Ladder, 4 Nassau Street, Dublin 2. €55.
A smart, modern restaurant on Nassau Street (which runs along the wall of Trinity College), from the dining-room you can look over the playing fields. The seasonally adapted menu leans towards fish, but rabbit and other game can feature and the vegetarian options are thoughtful and of high quality. Service is good, polite and helpful, but can appear slow because mains are cooked to order. The cheese selection comes from Sheridans cheesemongers.

Phone:	670 3865

Salamanca, 1 St Andrews Street, Dublin 2. €25.
A lovely, warm, friendly tapas restaurant in the heart of Dublin. The style of Salamanca is simplicity and conviviality, service is quick, without being impersonal. The decor is redolent of Spain, warm yellows, reds and oranges.

Phone:	670 8628
Internet:	

One Pico Restaurant, 5/6 Molesworth Place, Dublin 2. €55.
Discreetly located in a quiet lane close to Dail Eireann (Parliament) and Grafton Street. This defies categorisation as chef Eamon O'Reilly's influences range far and wide, though he's strong on Irish ingredients. A tendency to over-virtuosity but certain dishes, ballotine of foie gras de canard with pomme maxime and sauternes dressing for example, deserve classic status. You may think such well sourced cooking would cost the earth, but not here. Lunch and dinner set menus are excellent value and the wine list is long on choice and reasonably priced.

Phone:	676 0300
Internet:	www.onepico.com

Trumans Restaurant, Kildare Street, Dublin 2. €45.
Can be entered from the adjoining Buswells Hotel on Molesworth Street. There is a pleasant, elegant yet unassuming atmosphere and the menu reflects this. Sophisticated starters of baked crab with sweet chili sauce or prawn and saffron rissotto can be followed by such basic staples as fish and chips, steaks or rack of lamb. An excellent selection of Irish cheese and some very moreish desserts.

Phone:	614 6558

Ely Wine Bar and Café, Ely Place, Dublin 2. €45.
This rarity, a wine bar which is genuinely concerned with wine and which also offers high quality food, occupies a ground floor and basement in the heart of Georgian Dublin. Many of the exceptional selection of wines are sold by the glass to accompany foods among which organic meats, sausages and savoury puddings from the family farm in County Clare are a strong feature. You are not required to eat a full meal. A glass of red to accompany a selection of mature cheeses, or a coffee and hand-made chocolate. Understandably, this is one of the most popular quality eateries in Dublin and has recently been extended. Reservation recommended.

Phone:	676 8986

The Cellar Restaurant, Merrion Hotel , Upper Merrion Street, Dublin 2. €35.
Everything is spot on. The location, in the basement of the Merrion Hotel, is one of Dublin's best. The service is friendly and truly professional. The food is unpretentious and beautifully presented. Highlights include ham hock terrine and calf's liver in onion gravy. Locals know. It offers tremendous value for money and if you want a great end to a short weekend in Dublin, reserve now for Sunday brunch.

Phone:	603 0600

Restaurant Patrick Guilbaud, 21 Upper Merrion Street, Dublin 2. €105.
Imagine a centre made from the combined talents of Brian O'Driscoll and Didier Cordoniou. He doesn't exist, but imagine. Now imagine a restaurant combining perfect Irish ingredients, French imagination and technique and hey presto! It does exist, and naturally enough, it has two Michelin stars (why not three?) At €130 the nine course Land and Sea tasting menu is inspired and fun: Molly Malone Cockles and Mussels (marinière of shellfish), Bacon and Egg (braised crubeen, hock and bacon, the egg is a poached quail's egg), Irish Whiskey (cold coffee and whiskey jelly with warm white chocolate mousse). Cheeses come from Sheridan's cheesemongers, to the work of which family John McKenna dedicated his Irish Food Guide. If this is too daunting, try the set lunch, astonishing value at €30 (the vegetarian menu is €24). The restaurant opens onto a delightful terrace and landscaped garden and is decorated with works by Irish artists.

Phone:	676 4192
Internet:	www.restaurantpatrickguilbaud.ie

IRELAND

Roly's Bistro, 7 Ballsbridge Terrace, Dublin 4. €55.
A bustling and boisterous bistro-brasserie which has been serving the burghers of Ballsbridge for many a year. The cooking is an imaginative blend of mainly European influences. The house classics - and there are many - include Kerry lamb pie, Dublin Bay Prawns, fillet of beef with black pepper potato cake, summer pudding. The cheese-board is excellent, the desserts highly commended and the wine list is reasonably priced. Lunch and dinner set menus are good value, à la carte can be steep.

Phone:	668 2611
Internet:	www.rolysbistro.ie

The French Paradox, 53 Shelbourne Road, Ballsbridge, Dublin 4. €40.
Many will walk past this tiny wine bar-restaurant close to Lansdowne Road. Although The French Paradox was originally principally concerned with wine, the food is simple but effective. Perfectly combined salads, cured hams from the Basque country, terrines and pâtés, farm produced cheeses and house baked bread. And it's all good for you. There's the paradox. The winelist is extensive, with nearly seventy labels available by the glass.

Phone:	660 4068

Furama, Eirpage House, Donnybrook Road, Donnybrook, Dublin 4. €45.
Just opposite the rugby ground in Donnybrook, this sleek stylish restaurant offers some authentic Chinese cooking as well as such westernised dishes are prawns with black bean sauce. Furama, although quite large (100 covers), is said to be a popular dating venue so reservation is advised at weekends.

Phone:	283 0522
Internet:	www.furama.ie

O'Connell's in Ballsbridge, at the Bewleys Hotel, Merrion Road, Ballsbridge, Dublin 4. €30. The O'Connell in question has nothing to do with the famous street or even Munster's second-row, but Tom O'Connell, a brother of Darina Allen who from her base in Ballymaloe, County Cork, has devoted her life to the simple cooking of excellent local ingredients. The same philosophy is continued here. The menu states that produce in a dish is sourced from suppliers using Bord Bia (the Irish Food Board) Quality Assurance schemes (thus the beef comes the Irish Hereford Prime Beef Society) or names the artisan producer of an ingredient in a dish (Bill Casey of Shanagarry Co. Cork supplies smoked salmon). The wine list too reads like an oenology lesson. The propoganda can be a little wearing but what is undeniable is that O'Connell's provides excellent food, in a most pleasant setting, at very reasonable prices.

Phone:	647 3304
Internet:	www.bewleyshotels.com

QUICK BITE

IRELAND

Café Bar Deli, 12-13 South Great George's Street, Dublin 2.
Formerly a Bewley's Café, once the by-word in Dublin for stylish self-indulgence, the ambience continues here today albeit with basic continental style lunch dishes, friendly service and very reasonable prices.

Phone:	677 1646

Café en Seine, Dawson Street, Dublin 2.
Dead trendy art deco Parisian style bar-cum-brasserie. The self-service-pay at the till restaurant seems out of place but once installed enjoy the good value offerings and the astonishing decor and setting.

Phone:	677 4369

Sheridan's Cheesemonger, 11 South Anne Street, Dublin 2.
Cheese suppliers to Ireland's top restaurants. But this is Ireland's finest cheesemonger, so no surprise there. St Stephen's Green and Merrion Square are invitingly close so all you need is some crusty bread for the perfect picnic.

Phone:	679 3143

Nude, 21 Suffolk Street, Dublin 2.
Self-service, pay at the cash-desk. Wide choice of fresh food, much of it organic. Excellent fresh fruit and vegetable, soups, salads, freshly baked breads, juices, coffees and teas.

Phone:	672 5577

RESTAURANT ROUND-UP

Italian

Romano's,	12 Capel Street, Dublin 1	872 6868
Balducci's,	27 Westmoreland Street, Dublin 2	679 8849
Bellissimo,	34 Wicklow Street, Dublin 2	672 5480
Le Caprice,	12 St Andrew's Street, Dublin 2	679 4050
Da Pino,	38 Parliament Street, Dublin 2	671 9308
Dunne and Creszenzi,	14 South Frederick Street, Dublin 2	677 3815
Boccaccio,	18 Dame Street, Dublin 2	679 7049
Bianconi's,	232 Merrion Road, Dublin 4	219 6033

Good Pub Grub

O'Shea's Hotel	19 Talbot Street, Dublin 1	836 5670
O'Neill's Guesthouse and Pub	36-37 Pearse Street, Dublin 2	677 5213
The Oliver St-John Gogarty	57-58 Fleet Street, Temple Bar, Dublin 2	671 1822
The Vat House at Blooms Hotel	Anglesea Street, Temple Bar, Dublin 2	671 5622
The Porterhouse	16-18 Parliament Street, Dublin 2	679 8847
Davy Byrne's	Duke Street, Dublin 2	677 5217
Kiely's of Donnybrook	Donnybrook, Dublin 4	

Thai/Oriental

Lobo at The Morrison Hotel	Ormond Quay, Dublin 1 www.morrisonhotel.ie	887 2400
Papaya Thai Restaurant	Ely Place, Dublin 2	676 0044
Tiger Becs	35 Dawson Street, Dublin 2	677 4444
Siam Thai	St Andrew's Street, Dublin 2	677 3363
Siam Thai	Ballsbridge (opposite RDS), Dublin 4	660 1722
Kites	15-17 Ballsbridge Terrace, Ballsbridge, Dublin 4	660 7415
Baan Thai	16, Merrion Road, Ballsbridge, Dublin 4	660 8833

French

L'Ecrivain	109a, Lower Baggot Street, Dublin 2 www.lecrivain.com	661 1919
La Mère Zou	22 St Stephen's Green, Dublin 2	661 6669
Brownes Brasserie	22 St Stephen's Green, Dublin 2 www.brownesdublin.com	638 3939
Thornton's Restaurant	28, St Stephens Green, Dublin 2 www.fitzwilliamhotel.com	478 7008
The Old Mill	14 Temple Bar Merchants Arch, Dublin 2	671 9672
Peploe's Wine Bistro	16 St Stephen's Green, Dublin 2	676 3144
Pearl Brasserie	20 Merrion Street Upper, Dublin 2	679 2402

Other recommended bistros

Contemporary International

Synergie at The Clarion Hotel	IFSC, Excise Walk, Dublin 1 www.clarionhotelifsc.com	443 8800
"Halo" at The Morrison Hotel	Ormond Quay Lower, Dublin 1 www.morrisonhotel.ie	877 2400
The Harbourmaster Bar and Restaurant	IFSC, Dublin 1 www.harbourmaster.ie	670 1688
The Paramount Bistro at the Paramount House	Parliament Street and Essex Gate, Temple Bar, Dublin 2 www.paramounthotel.ie	417 9900
Chatham Brasserie	Chatham Street, Dublin 2	679 0055
The Riverside Restaurant at The Fitzsimons House	21-22 Wellington Quay, Temple Bar, Dublin 2 www.fitzsimonshotel.com	677 9315
Bleu Bistro Moderne	Joshua House, Dawson Street, Dublin 2 www.onepico.com	676 7015
La Stampa	35 Dawson Street, Dublin 2 www.lastampa.ie	677 8611
The Canteen at the Schoolhouse	2-8 Northumberland Road, Ballsbridge, Dublin 4 www.schoolhousehotel.com	667 5014
Ernie's Restaurant	Mulberry Gardens, Donnybrook, Dublin 4	269 3300

Restaurant round up (cont)

Irish

The Aberdeen at the Gresham	O'Connell Street Upper, Dublin 1 www.gresham-hotels.com	874 6881
Avoca Café,	11-13, Suffolk Street, Dublin 2 www.avoca.ie	672 6021
Fitzers	40 Temple Bar Square, Dublin 2 www.fitzers.ie	679 7000
Fitzers	51 Dawson Street, Dublin 2 www.fitzers.ie	677 0440
The Grill Restaurant at Buswells Hotel	25 Molesworth Street, Dublin 2 www.quinnhotels.com	614 6500
Foley's Restaurant	Merrion Row, Dublin 2	
The Pie Dish	at the St Stephen's Green Hotel, Dublin 2 www.ocallaghanhotels.com	607 3600

The Lobster Pot	9 Ballsbridge Terrace, Dublin 4 www.thelobsterpot.ie	668 0025

Indian

Shalimar	Great George's Street South, Dublin 2	671 0738
Khan's Balti House	51 Donnybrook Road, Dublin 4	269 7664

Chinese

Fans	60 Dame Street, Dublin 2	679 4263
Good World	18 South Great George's Street, Dublin 2	677 5373

Cuban

Bella Cuba	11 Ballsbridge Terrace, Dublin 4 www.bella-cuba.com	660 5539

Quick Bite

Beshoffs (Fish and Chips)	6 O'Connell Street Upper, Dublin 1	872 4400
Beshoffs (Fish and Chips)	14 Westmoreland Street, Dublin 2	677 8026

Dublin would not be Dublin without a one and one (cod and chips). These are as good as any, and you can eat in or take away.

Kylemore Café	O'Connell Street, Dublin 1	872 2138
Kylemore Café	St Stephen's Green, Dublin 2	478 1665

Self-service, pay at the till restaurants, offering Full Irish Breakfast all day, pastries, tea, (good) coffee, meat and veg lunches, sandwiches and snacks.

HOTELS

LUXURY

O'Connell Street Area and North Quays

Gresham Hotel, Upper O'Connell Street, Dublin 1.
282 rooms, from €100-€310 s/t/d. Rack €360 t/d.
One of Dublin's great hotels. It offers considerable comfort and excellent service. The Aberdeen Restaurant, or the slick, modern '23' offer quality Irish/ international cooking. Unfortunately O'Connell Street, pictured left, is not one of Dublin's prettiest, but that hardly matters in a city this compact since you can quickly reach the trendier IFSC, South Quays or Grafton Street areas.

Phone:	874 6881
Internet:	www.gresham-hotels.com

Morrison Hotel, Ormond Quay, Dublin 1. 84 rooms, from €285-€450 rack s/d/t.
Trendy with range of bars and restaurants. Café Bar for light meals, the Morrison Bar for cocktails, Lobo for sushi and cocktails and open till 3.00am Friday and Saturday. Halo restaurant offers French fusion cooking.

Phone:	887 2400
Email:	info@morrisonhotel.ie
Internet:	www.morrisonhotel.ie

Clarion Hotel, International Financial Services Centre (IFSC), Custom House Quay, Dublin 1. 145 rooms, from €190-€245 s/d/t. Rack: €265. Stylish, high class international hotel in Dublin's new IFSC development on the Custom House (North Wall Quays). This place exudes rude health. Synergie restaurant with its light oak, glass, and white linen offers simple, light fusion cooking. The Kudos bar, with a strong Oriental ambience, offers three wok stations.

Phone:	433 8800
Email:	info@clarionhotelifsc.com
Internet:	www.clarionhotelifsc.com

South Quays and Temple Bar

The Clarence Hotel, 6-8 Wellington Quay, Dublin 2. 43 rooms. Rack €330 s/d/t. Owned by Bono, lots of money has been lavished on the conversion of this building and although this is no guarantee of success, everything oozes High Chic. The hotel's Tea Room restaurant is one of the best tables in Dublin (see entry). Drink in the "Octagon Bar" or "The Study", a 24 hour residents' lounge.

Phone:	407 0800
Email:	reservations@theclarence.ie
Internet:	www.theclarence.ie

Hotels: (cont)

St Stephen's Green and Grafton Street area

The Westbury, Harry Street (off Grafton Street), Dublin.
205 rooms. Rack from €357 to €442 s/d/t.
These rates do not include 15% service charge. Breakfast extra. Luxurious place just off Grafton Street, Dublin's shopping and theatreland. There is a Westbury Mall – fashion, food, gifts, Irish craft shops, hair and beauty salons plus a swanky cocktail bar and lounge lizards' terrace.

Phone:	679 1122
Email:	westbury@jurysdoyle.com
Internet:	www.jurysdoyle.com

Buswells Hotel, 25 Molesworth Street, Dublin 2.
67 rooms, from €175 s. Rack €225 d/t. €245 tpl.
Very comfortable hotel close to the Irish Parliament and good drinking in Buswells Bar, plus reasonably priced food in the Grill Restaurant offering breakfast and lunch carvery. Around the corner, in Kildare Street, the excellent Truman Restaurant offers an interesting variety of modern and traditional Irish cooking.

Phone:	614 6500
Email:	buswells@quinn-hotels.com
Internet:	www.quinnhotels.com

La Stampa Hotel, 35 Dawson Street, Dublin 2. 49 rooms.
€200 d/t room only.
Chic hotel bang in the centre of town. Celebrity guest book includes Gareth Edwards, Jonah Lomu and the New Zealand Rugby Team, the Welsh Rugby Team, Bill Beaumont. Samsara café-bar, La Stampa Brasserie, Tiger Becs Thai restaurant, offer good eating and drinking.

Phone:	677 4444
Email:	dine@lastampa.ie
Internet:	www.lastampa.ie

Merrion Square to Ballsbridge

Merrion, Upper Merrion Street, Dublin 2.
125 rooms, from €370 to €470 s/d/t.
One of the very best hotels in Dublin, attentive service of the highest quality. The leisure complex comprises the Tethra Spa, swimming-pool, steam room, gym, treatment rooms and gym plus beautifully designed gardens. Former guests include the French rugby team. Try the restaurants – Morningtons, for contemporary Irish, Restaurant Patrick Guilbaud (Michelin 2 Stars) or the Cellar Restaurant, and you'll see why the FFR committee men chose this place.

Phone:	603 0600
Email:	reservations@merrionhotel.com
Internet:	www.merrionhotel.com

The Burlington Hotel, Upper Leeson Street, Dublin 4.
504 rooms, from €256 s to €288 d/t.
Dublin's biggest hotel, and a self-contained micro-economy - gift shop, newsagent, etc. Restaurants: the Sussex Room for fine dining in an 'old world' ambience; then there's the Diplomat for more modern and informal cuisine; the Lobby Lounge for coffee and light snacks. Bars: Buck Mulligan's, in traditional Irish pub, and the Mespil Lounge for residents. The Ana night club and the Burlington Cabaret are open from May to October, Sunday – Thursday. On match day a focal point for pre and post-match meetings. Easy stroll to your seat or terrace at Lansdowne Road.

Phone:	660 5222
Email:	burlington@jurysdoyle.com
Internet:	www.jurysdoyle.com

Mont Clare Hotel, Clare Street / Merrion Square, Dublin 2.
80 rooms, from €185 s to €240 d/t (12.5% service charge may apply).
Gallery Bar. Sister hotel to the Davenport (you can use the gym at the Davenport across the street) and the St Stephen's Green Hotel (see entries). Comfortable hotel offering good service. Excellent location at Merrion Square and close to Trinity College area. Easy access to Lansdowne Road.

Phone:	607 3800
Email:	montclareres@ocallaghanhotels.ie
Internet:	www.ocallaghanhotels.ie

The Davenport Hotel, Clare Street / Merrion Square, Dublin 2. 115 rooms, from €185 s to €240 d/t (12.5% service charge may apply).
Facilities include a gym and Lanyon's Restaurant. Quality hotel in a superb location, ideal for exploring of the south side of central Dublin. Culture, shopping, top eateries on the doorstep.

Phone:	607 3500
Email:	davenportres@ocallaghanhotels.ie
Internet:	www.ocallaghanhotels.ie

IRELAND

The Schoolhouse Hotel, 2-8 Northumberland Road, Ballsbridge, Dublin 4.
31 rooms, from €165 to €250 s/d/t.
Converted schoolhouse offers quietly efficient service. Its Canteen restaurant does reasonably priced bistro food. The Inkwell Bar is popular with Dublin's younger, rugby crowd. Recommended spot to meet for a drink before strolling to a game.

Phone:	667 5014
Email:	reservations@schoolhousehotel.com
Internet:	www.schoolhousehotel.com

Ballsbridge and Lansdowne Road Area

The Berkeley Court Hotel, Lansdowne Road, Dublin 4.
186 rooms, from €383 s/d/t. Rack €450 s/d/t.
A favourite luxury hotel. It has a boutique and gift shop and the Berkeley Room restaurant serves highly rated lunches and dinners. The Palm Court Café, a more informal eatery, is open all day. The bar and lounge get jammed on match day as Lansdowne Road is just a punt away. Good fun if you like crowds.

Phone:	665 3200
Email:	berkeley_court@jurysdoyle.com
Internet:	www.jurysdoyle.com

Four Seasons Hotel, Simmonscourt Road, Ballsbridge, Dublin 4.
259 rooms, from €295 to €520 s/d/t.
Arguably Dublin's greatest hotel. Set in the Royal Dublin Society show grounds (international trade fairs, world class show-jumping) it is very sylish and luxurious. Guests have included Bill Clinton, Nelson Mandela, and the England rugby team.

Phone:	665 4000
Internet:	www.fourseasons.com

Herbert Park Hotel, Ballsbridge, Dublin 4.
154 rooms from €135 s/d/t. Rack €275 s/d/t.
Pavillion Restaurant. Close to Lansdowne Road, 2km south of the city centre. Glass walls and grand vistas plus large exhibition of contemporary Irish art.

Phone:	667 2200
Email:	info@herbertparkhotel.ie
Internet:	www.herbertparkhotel.ie

Hotels: (cont)

Jurys Ballsbridge Hotel, Pembroke Road, Ballsbridge, Dublin 4.
303 rooms, from €159 to €195 s/d/t. Rack €320 s/d/t.
Luxury place opposite the American Embassy. Match day meeting place, given over to live music and entertainment. To be bulldozed, so enjoy while you can.

Phone:	660 5000
Email:	ballsbridge@jurysdoyle.com
Internet:	www.jurysdoyle.com

IRELAND

Jurys Ballsbridge, The Towers, Lansdowne Road, Ballsbridge, Dublin 4.
107 rooms, from €215 s/d/t. Rack €390.
Cannot be accessed by general public, boasts a cinema room and Hospitality Lounge offering complimentary bar Monday-Thursday. All the facilities at the bigger Jury's Ballsbridge Hotel are available to The Towers' guests.

Phone:	667 0033
Email:	towers@jurysdoyle.com
Internet:	www.jurysdoyle.com

MODERATELY PRICED

O'Connell Street Area and North Quays

Jurys Custom House Inn, Custom House Quay, Dublin 1.
239 rooms, from €127 s/d/t. Rack €225.

Bright, clean and comfortable hotel in the chic IFSC area overlooking the Liffey. Innfusion restaurant serving breakfast, lunch and dinner, the Inntro bar also serving food, and "Il Barista" café are lively meeting points.

Phone:	607 5000
Email:	jurysinncustomhouse@jurysdoyle.com
Internet:	www.jurysdoyle.com

Royal Dublin Hotel (Best Western), O'Connell Street, Dublin 1.
117 rooms, from €79 s/d/t. Rack €239 (minimum 2 nights).
Formulaic but reasonably priced. Its brasserie is open all day. Well away from Dublin rugby life, but easy for the airport and walkable to Temple Bar or Grafton Street.

Phone:	873 3666
Email:	enq@royaldublin.com
Internet:	www.royaldublin.com

Academy Hotel, Findlater Place (off O'Connell Street), Dublin 1.
100 rooms, from €189 s, €238 d/t. Rack €255.
A short stroll to the livelier areas of Dublin across O'Connell Bridge. If the rugby moves to Croke Park this will prove a handy address.

Phone:	878 0666
Email:	stay@academy-hotel.ie
Internet:	www.academy-hotel.ie

North Star Hotel, Amiens Street, Dublin 1.
123 rooms, from €89 s/d/t. Rack €170 d/t.
Bianconi Restaurant offers good Irish/international cooking and McCoy's Bar serves food all day. There is a beer garden for smokers. Close to Connolly DART station for easy access to Lansdowne Road.

Phone:	836 3136
Email:	norths@regencyhotels.com
Internet:	www.regencyhotels.com

Arlington Hotel, 23-25 Bachelor's Walk, O'Connell Bridge, Dublin 1.
116 rooms, from €99 s, €150 d/t. Rack €240 d/t.
Free live Irish music and dance every night. Lively hotel with match day and night turned into a major event with music, and comprehensive TV coverage of the game. Probably more suited to the younger crowd travelling without tickets.

Phone:	804 9100
Email:	info@arlington.ie
Internet:	www.arlington.ie

South Quays and Temple Bar

Bloom's Hotel, Anglesea Street, Temple Bar, Dublin 2.
86 rooms, from €79 s to €200+ d/t.
Comfortable hotel, amiable staff right in the middle of the Temple Bar action. The bar has daily live music open to all, but there is an exclusive residents' bar. Attached is a night club – M Club – which one of Dublin's more popular night spots.

Phone:	671 5622
Email:	info@blooms.ie
Internet:	www.blooms.ie

The Parliament Hotel, Lord Edward Street, Temple Bar, Dublin 2.
62 rooms, from €115 s, €190 d/t.
Unpretentious Edwardian building. Two bars: Forum 1 – in a traditional Dublin style; and Forum 2 – in a trendy new conservatory. Historic Dublin (Christ Church, the Castle) and bustling Temple Bar, pictured left, are on the doorstep.

Phone:	670 8777
Email:	parl@regencyhotels.com
Internet:	www.regencyhotels.com

The Paramount Hotel, Parliament Street and Essex Gate, Temple Bar, Dublin 2.
66 rooms, from €120 s, €260 d/t.
Sombre ground floor corridors belie lighter, airier bedrooms. Good stepping stone for night life of Temple Bar, shopping, Dublin Castle, Trinity College. There is a bar and the Paramount Bistro offers solid continental bistro food.

Phone:	417 9900
Email:	paramount@iol.ie
Internet:	www.paramounthotel.ie

The Fitzsimons Hotel, 21-22 Wellington Quay, Temple Bar, Dublin 2.
30 rooms, from €130 to €220 d/t. Triple rack €252.
Lively hotel's Riverside Restaurant (modern Irish and European cooking) transforms into a late night cocktail bar. Live music bars on all three floors Spacious ground floor pub/bar serving pub food. Fitzsimons Ballroom Niteclub – pop, dance and chart music - free entry for hotel guests. Set in the heart of Temple Bar.

Phone:	677 9315
Email:	info@fitzsimonshotel.com
Internet:	www.fitzsimonshotel.com

Hotels: (cont)

Temple Bar Hotel, Fleet Street, Dublin 2.
129 rooms from €120 to €200 d/t.
Comfortable hotel close to Trinity College and Grafton Street. Buskers bar does food and there's a giant screen for match day. DJ music and late closing Friday, Saturday and Sunday. The Rendezvous Bar allows access to residents only.

Phone:	677 3333
Email:	reservations@tbh.ie
Internet:	www.towerhotelgroup.com

IRELAND

St Stephen's Green and Grafton Street area

Stephen's Green Hotel, St Stephen's Green, Dublin 2.
75 rooms from €210 s/d/t. Rack €240 d/t.
Chic and stylish in the business area around St Stephen's Green. Pleasant stroll to central Dublin's shops, culture, bars, restaurants and night life. Magic Glasses bar. Pie Dish bistro does contemporary Irish-bistro cooking.

Phone:	607 3600
Email:	stephensgreenres@ocallaghanhotels.ie
Internet:	www.ocallaghanhotels.ie

Albany House, 84 Harcourt Street, Dublin 2.
43 bedrooms, from €120s to €150 d/t. Rack €130s €200 d/t.
In the heart of Georgian Dublin. Harcourt Street is full of hotels (see below) and they are busy every weekend because of proximity to shopping areas around Grafton Street, nightlife of Great St George's Street, Leeson Street and Temple Bar.

Phone:	475 1092
Email:	albany@indigo.ie
Internet:	www.byrne-hotels-ireland.com

Harrington Hall, 70 Harcourt Street, Dublin 2.
30 rooms, from €133, €173 to €268 d/t.
Highly recommended, good value hotel in a Georgian street near St Stephen's Green, which means a good central location, ideal for shopping, nightlife and rugby. Fan assisted air conditioning in the rooms is unlikely to be tested by a wet February night.

Phone:	475 3497
Email:	harringtonhall@eircom.net
Internet:	www.harringtonhall.com

Trinity Lodge, 12 South Frederick Street, Dublin 2.
16 rooms, from €110 to €115 s, €150 to €200 d/t. Extra bed €50.
Comfortable Georgian townhouse in a quiet street close to Trinity College, Grafton Street. Good restaurants, bars and Dublin's nightlife are very close.

Phone:	617 0900
Email:	trinitylodge@eircom.net
Internet:	www.trinitylodge.com

Jackson Court Hotel, 29/30 Harcourt Street, Dublin 2.
25 rooms, rack €110 s, €155 d/t. Triple €190. Family €210.
Cheap and cheerful accommodation. Close to more raucous temptations of Great George's Street and Leeson Street. Free entry for guests to Copper Face Jacks nightclub in basement.

Phone:	475 8777
Email:	info@jackson-court.ie
Internet:	www.jackson-court.ie

The Harcourt Hotel, 60 Harcourt Street, Dublin 2.
100 rooms, from €105s, €240 d/t.
Comfortable lodgings near St Stephen's Green. Little Caesar's restaurant is part of an Italian pizza and pasta chain. It's location means it is handy for the bright lights of the city whilst also offering easy access to the rugby areas of Ballsbridge and Donnybrook.

Phone:	478 3677
Email:	reservations@harcourthotel.ie
Internet:	www.harcourthotel.ie

Merrion Square to Ballsbridge

Roxford Lodge Hotel, 46 Northumberland Road, Ballsbridge, Dublin 4.
20 rooms, from €80 s, €120 d/t. €135 tpl. €160 fam. Rack €100 pppn.
Large Victorian house proud of its amiable service just a gentle stroll from Lansdowne Road. There is a residents' lounge, some rooms are equipped with a jacuzzi.

Phone:	668 8572 or 01 660 8813
Email:	reservations@roxfordlodge.ie
Internet:	www.roxfordlodge.ie

MODERATELY PRICED

Ballsbridge and Lansdowne Road Area

Mount Herbert Hotel, Herbert Road, Lansdowne Road, Dublin 4.
180 rooms, from €99s, €129 d/t. Rack €220 d/t.
Excellent spot with a large, light and a large, airy bar popular on match day,mainly because it is just 100m from the South Terrace. Large screen and TVs to watch games if you can't get into the ground. About as close as you can get to being there without actually being in the ground.

Phone:	668 4321
Email:	info@mountherberthotel.ie
Internet:	www.mountherberthotel.ie

Ariel House, 50-54 Lansdowne Road, Ballsbridge, Dublin 4.
37 rooms, from €130 s/d/t. Rack €250 d/t.
Convivial guesthouse so close to Lansdowne Road that you could nip to your en-suite bathroom at half-time.

Phone:	668 5512
Email:	reservations@ariel-house.net
Internet:	www.ariel-house.net

Jurys Montrose Hotel, Stillorgan Road, Dublin 4.
180 rooms,from €139 to €164 s/d/t.
Modern spacious hotel on a main road south of Dublin, opposite the campus of University College and close to the HQ of RTE - Ireland's national television and radio broadcaster. From here, there is very easy access to Donnybrook and Ballsbridge for the rugby (ten minutes by taxi to Lansdowne Road), but you are also within range of both the city centre to the north and the bracing fresh air of the Dublin mountains to the south.

Phone:	269 3311
Email:	montrose@jurysdoyle.com
Internet:	www.jurysdoyle.com

BUDGET

O'Connell Street Area and North Quays

Mount Eccles Court (Hostel), 42 North Great Georges Street, Dublin 1.
27 rooms, 130 beds, from €13 - €30 (dorms). €30 to €38pp for private room.
Fine Georgian buildings to the north of Dublin city centre. Facilities, private bedrooms or dormitory, all en-suite, TV and music lounges, a fully fitted kitchen. Short walk to the city centre nightlife, convenient for the airport, public transport etc.

Phone:	873 0826
Email:	info@eccleshostel.com
Internet:	www.eccleshostel.com

Celtic Lodge Guest House, 81-82 Talbot Street, Dublin 1. 29 rooms, from €65 s., €45-€50 per person sharing for d/t/tpl.
Cheap and cheery close to O'Connell Street. Attached to the Celt Pub with music seven nights a week and free admission for guests.

Phone:	878 8810 or 878 8732
Email:	celticguesthouse@eircom.net
Internet:	www.celticlodge.ie

O'Shea's Hotel, 19 Talbot Street, Dublin 1.
35 rooms from €60 pppn.
Unusually for Dublin, the owners do not change prices just because of a rugby match. Attached to a pub which does good grub and folk music. Good address for a family on a budget and one to note if the rugby moves to Croke Park. Easy stroll to all parts of central Dublin with good public transport links to Lansdowne Road.

Phone:	836 5670 or 836 5665
Email:	osheashotel@eircom.net

Jacobs Inn Hostel Accommodation, 21-28 Talbot Place, Dublin 1.
From €26.25 to €41 d, €18 to €39pp in dorms.
Minimum three night stay during "event" weekends. Includes light breakfast. Self-catering facilities, internet and bike storage. Boca J's Restaurant. Friendly cosmopolitan atmosphere. Sister hostel to Isaacs Hostel, below.

Phone:	855 5660
Email:	jacobs@isaacs.ie
Internet:	www.dublinbackpacker.com

Isaacs Hostel, 2-5 Frenchman's Lane, Dublin 1.
From €26.25 d, €14pp in dorms. €1-€2 pp extra on match weekends.
Has single rooms and rooms with 12-16 beds, self-catering facilities, bike storage, restaurant, video shows and live music. Good spot for student teams and large groups and social sides on a budget. Close to O'Connell Street and so just over the bridge to Temple Bar.

Phone:	855 621
Email:	hostel@isaacs.ie
Internet:	www.dublinbackpacker.com

South Quays and Temple Bar

Gogarty's Budget Accommodation, 18-21 Anglesea Street, Dublin 2.
Twin to 10-bed en-suite rooms from €50 to €90 d/t. Dorms from €15 to €40pp.
Hostel style offering self-catering facilities, continental breakfast, laundry facilities, TV room, towel hire and international payphones.

Phone:	671 1822
Email:	info@gogartys.ie
Internet:	www.gogartys.ie

Barnacles Temple Bar House, 19 Temple Lane, Temple Bar, Dublin 2. Twin, double and multi-bedded en-suite rooms. €65-€94.00 d/t. Dorm from €14pp.
Breakfast included. Hostel offers laundry service, left luggage, safe deposit box, 24 hour reception, self-catering, internet, international payphones. Cheap and simple in the heart of Temple Bar.

Phone:	671 6277
Email:	tbh@barnacles.ie
Internet:	www.barnacles.ie

O'Neill's Guesthouse and Pub, 36-37 Pearse Street, Dublin 2.
8 rooms. €35 - €75pp.
Recently restored, tastefully furnished twin, double and four bed rooms, above one of Dublin's oldest and finest family run pubs (the grub is very good) in a superb location close to Trinity College.

Phone:	671 4074
Email:	oneilpub@iol.ie
Internet:	www.oneillsdublin.com

St Stephen's Green and Grafton Street area

The Earl of Kildare Hotel, Kildare Street, Dublin 2.
30 rooms, from €55 s, €75 d/t. Rack €120.
Cheap comfortable accommodation in a great location close to Trinity College. Comfortable wood panelled bar with TV for sport. Snug bar without TV for those seeking a quiet drink. Serves basic carvery lunch and evening menu.

Phone:	679 4388
Email:	eok@iol.ie
Internet:	www.iol.ie/eok

Kilronan House, 70 Adelaide Road, Dublin 2.
15 rooms. Rack €85pp.
In a quiet area of Dublin area but close to the shopping and party areas of St Stephen's Green and Grafton Street, this is a well run and friendly establishment.

Phone:	475 5266 or 475 1562
Email:	info@dublinn.com
Internet:	www.dublinn.com

Inishowen Guesthouse, 199 South Circular Road, Dublin 8.
8 rooms (4 en-suite), from €38 to €60pp.
Very close to the city centre and easy access to Ballsbridge and the rugby. Comfortable and good value for the budget tourist.

Phone:	453 6272
Email:	mcterry1@aol.com
Internet:	www.inishowen-guesthouse.com

Ballsbridge and Lansdowne Road Area

Bewley's Hotel Ballsbridge, Merrion Road, Ballsbridge, Dublin 4.
304 rooms, from €89 d/t.
Highly recommended for several reasons: level of comfort for price is unmatched in Dublin, especially in this area; tariffs stay same even on international weekends; it is very close to Lansdowne Road and is also opposite the Four Seasons, where a room can cost ten times as much.

Phone:	668 1111
Email:	bb@BewleysHotels.com
Internet:	www.BewleysHotels.com

French rugby
Singing les blues

by Ian Borthwick
L'Equipe rugby writer

FRANCE

IT IS perhaps all too easy when talking about le rugby français to trot out the old cliché "unpredictable." But despite significant progress in many sectors of the game, in their own inimitable fashion les Tricolores have done nothing in recent years to remove that particular tag from their CV. At times unstoppable, at others pedestrian, for their home supporters the French still have the infuriating ability of playing sublime rugby one week, and of descending to the depths of mediocrity the next.

French clubs might have dominated the Heineken Cup club competition for the second year running last season, but on the international front the French national side failed to reflect not only this dominance, but also the ambitious, attractive and ultimately successful rugby being played by their top clubs Toulouse, Stade Français and Biarritz. And with the next World Cup being held in France, if the host nation is to have the slightest chance of making the final at the Stade de France on October 20th 2007, and of repeating the exploit of the French soccer team in 1998, the major challenge facing les Bleus is to improve their consistency and their ability to string together a series of hard-edged encounters against their principal Anglo-Saxon opponents.

To be fair, France's current national coach Bernard Laporte has gone a long way towards rectifying this flaw, and if his professorial tone is heeded by France's international players, the 2005-06 season ought to see significant progress on the errors of the preceding year. A balding bespectacled former Bègles scrum-half with a sharp wit and a sharper tongue, the 41 year-old is currently, and by a long stretch, the longest serving national coach in Europe, having taken over the reins of the French XV in November 1999. Laporte has successfully instilled a greater degree of discipline in the French and instead of concentrating, like some of his predecessors, on the grand theories of space and movement, he has taken a far more nuts-and-bolts approach to the game, focussing on the smaller details and, while continuing to cultivate France's

Break from the past: Yann Delaigue, escaping Italian atention, was one of many experiments of last season ulike Fabien Pelous, bottom left, who has become an institution in the side

traditional attacking flair, simultaneously morphing les Tricolores into the best defensive team in Europe.

The 2006 season however sees the team at a critical crossroads, and though the end of year tour to the Southern Hemisphere in June 2005 – a suicidal excursion with two tests against South Africa and one against Australia in the space of three weekends – left a considerable glimmer of hope, the challenge facing Laporte and his men is firstly to show that they have learned from the bitter lessons of 2005, and secondly that they are once again capable of footing it with the best the Southern Hemisphere has to offer.

Though French domestic rugby has never been as vibrant, with their leading clubs, Stade Toulousain, Biarritz, and Stade Français continuing to dominate the European club scene, and although the national side is favourite to win the 2006 Six Nations, France's record against their Southern Hemisphere rivals in the 2004-05 shows one victory, one draw and four defeats. One of these was a resounding 45-6 thumping on their home ground at Stade de France. Indeed, despite starting with a promising 27-14 win over the Wallabies in Paris in November 2004, the international season was far from a success, and from 11 matches, they could only scrape 5 wins, for 5 losses and a draw.

There were nevertheless two turning points in the season. The first was undoubtedly the crushing 45-6 loss to New Zealand in Paris on November 27th giving the All Blacks their biggest ever victory over the French. And the second was the stumbling, stuttering win over Scotland in the opening game of the Six Nations, a win which owed more to refereeing errors than anything constructive from the French, but which was to prove a watershed in the way they approached the game.

Admittedly, against Graham Henry's New Zealanders, the French were on the receiving end of one of the great All Black performances, a game which set the benchmark for the team that seven months later was to humiliate the 2005 British and Irish Lions, before going on to win the Tri-Nations tournament. But, coming as it did two weeks after beating Australia and a week after succumbing 24-14 to Argentina in Marseilles, it came as a timely reminder to Laporte that if France is to have any chance of competing in 2007, he had to enlarge his squad and to increase the ability of his players to compete with the intense physical challenge thrown down by New Zealand, South Africa and Australia, and, to a certain extent, Argentina. "The aim is to have 40 players capable of performing at the international level by the start of

Singing Les Bleus (cont)

the 2007 season," insisted Laporte, who immediately started to delve into the huge untapped resources of the Top-16, developing some of the raw talent on display week after week at club level.

The other turning point was the unflattering 16-9 win against Scotland in the opening round of the Six Nations. The lowly-ranked Scots clearly deserved to win this game, and not for the first time at Stade de France, the home crowd were quick to show their disapproval by loudly booing the hapless French side. In response to this reaction and to the plodding and unimaginative nature of France's performance, Laporte decided to inject some new blood into the squad.

This came notably in the form of the fullback from Brive, Julien Laharrague, who has this season transferred to Perpignan. Having long been considered a dilettante in the game, the 26 year-old Laharrague had finally decided to take it seriously, and with his devil-may-care attitude and daring counter-attacks, carving up the opposition from deep in his own territory, he had been the revelation of the early part of the season in France. Drafted into the French team for the game against England at Twickenham, Laharrague's presence became a sort of catalyst for the French, and although their 18-17 victory against England was largely due to Charlie Hodgson's failure with the boot, it was enough to enable 'les Bleus' to start expressing themselves with some of the flamboyance of old.

Indeed the following game against Wales, was one of the most thrilling and spectacular tests ever at the Stade de France, and although won (24-18) by a splendid Welsh side which went on to claim the Grand Slam, it laid the pattern for what was to follow. And for what, in theory, should be the template for France's game plan. Laharrague was just the tip of the iceberg, however, and by the end of the season, Laporte would introduce a whole new raft of thrilling young players, the 21-year-old flanker Yannick Nyanga and the 22 year-old hooker Dimitri Szarzewski from Béziers, exciting centres Benoît Baby (22) and Florian Fritz (21) from Toulouse, and the hard-nosed 25 year-old flanker from Paris with the intoxicating name, Rémi Martin. Dynamic, inventive and irrepressible, by injecting their youth and vigour into a team which already features such gnarled veterans as Fabien Pelous (101 caps) and Olivier Magne (83 caps), and such potential stars as Frédéric Michalak and Yannick Jauzion, France's latest group of recruits are certain to play a key role in the coming season. At club, European, and international level.

On the club level, French rugby has never been as healthy or as vibrant. Last season saw an unprecedented level of interest for the national club competition, with a total of 1.9 millions spectators, an average of 7,334 paying punters per match. Stade Toulousain continue to blaze a pioneering trail, averaging a total of 13,725 for club games at stadium Ernest-Wallon. Furthermore, the 40,558 who turned up to watch them play Stade Français at the Parc des Princes set a new record for a club game in France (excluding semi-finals and finals), the average number of season tickets per club soared to 8,306 and at the time of writing continues to rise. Having reduced the number of clubs by two, France's gruelling national championship now goes by the name of 'Top-14'. But once again the favourites are the big three, who between them have monopolised the "Bouclier de Brennus" over the past decade: Stade Toulousain (1996, 97, 99, 2001) Stade Français (1998, 2000, 2003, 2004) and Biarritz (2002, 05).

These three super-powers will also lead France's challenge in the European (Heineken) Cup, and with a total of seven teams (Stade Toulousain, Stade Français, Biarritz, Perpignan, Bourgoin, Clermont-Auvergne, Castres) it is difficult to see France relaxing the vice-like grip it has held on this competition in the past few years. Last year's record against English clubs showed 12 French wins for one draw and six defeats, and with the tightening of France's élite to 14 clubs, and the intense recruitment campaigns in the off-season, they will be just as competitive, if not more, in the 2005-06 Heineken Cup.

Champions Toulouse for instance have snapped up Irishman Aidan McCullen as well as rising French star Yannick Nyanga, while last year's unlucky finalists Stade Français have recruited Italian N° 8 Sergio Parisse and two promising young centres Thibault Lacroix from Biarritz and Geoffroy Messina from Clermont. Biarritz, as current champions of France will be keen to cement their place on the European stage, and Perpignan, reinforced by the brilliant Julien Laharrague, and Scotsman Nathan Hines, will always represent a threat to the opposition. Beware also of sleeping giants Castres, now coached by Laurent Seigne, and of Clermont-Auvergne, the perpetual under-achievers of French rugby who have not only changed their coach, but thrown the recruitment net wide, snaring Springbok star Breyton Paulse, the Argentinean hooker and captain Mario Ledesma, Tongan international Sione Kiole, and former Crusaders back-rower Sam Broomhall.

FRANCE

Finally, on the international level, as early as November 2005, les Tricolores will be able to measure themselves against the spectre of Southern Hemisphere superiority when they take on Australia, in Marseilles, and the impressive South Africans in Paris. As for the Six Nations Championship, despite their disappointing performances last year, the French, having won back-to-back Grand Slams in the 2003 and 2004 editions must once again be favourite to finish at the top of the table. The two major hurdles of the 2006 Championship, England and Ireland, will be encountered on their home pitch at Stade de France, and there is little in the recent performances of either of these teams, or of the British Lions, to suggest that they will be in a position to threaten France in the giant cauldron at Saint-Denis.

What is clear, however, is that when France travels to Cardiff to meet the current Grand Slam champions, given the expansive and ambitious style of play favoured by both sides, the game against Wales at the Millennium on March 18th will undoubtedly be the highlight of the season. If not the Grand Slam decider. To get that far, however, and to have a chance of challenging Wales on their hallowed home turf, Bernard Laporte, Fabien Pelous and their men will have to draw on the lessons of the past twelve months. There is no doubt that French rugby has all the ingredients, the talent, the passion and the instinct for the game, to claim a place at the summit of the world rugby hierarchy. The new generation of players is already there, an exciting new brand of expansive play is in place, all that remains is for the French to turn their backs on their old demons. And to surprise everyone...by becoming consistent and predictable.

• *Originally from New Zealand, Ian Borthwick is a rugby writer for French sports daily L'Equipe. Based in Paris, he has been reporting on French and world rugby for more than two decades.*

FIND YOUR WAY AROUND

FRANCE

CITY OF ROMANCE

THIS is the city of romance and the one place your partner would probably most relish (though Rome puts in a serious challenge). Its charms, though plentiful, are most likely to bypass an all male assault party, to whom the expression 'the other half' is another beer.

Divided in two by the mighty river Seine, there is the Right Bank (rive droite) and the Left Bank (rive gauche). For those unfamiliar with these iconic locations, *'la rive gauche est l'endroit ou on pense, la rive droite ou on depense.'* Your other half will understand the distinction immediately.

What can one say about such an *embarras de richesses*? Stay for a month and work your way through all that we recommend, or just dive in. Whiz to the top of the Eiffel Tower, climb to the lofty summit of Notre Dame, visit the Sacre Coeur and see the whole vista spread out before you. Take in the fabulous shops and sweeping boulevards on the right bank, delve in amongst the trinkets, bars, bookshops and galleries of the left bank. You could spend a lifetime exploring Paris. The Louvre alone, with its Napoleonic plunderings, is a lifetime's work. And then there's the Musée d'Orsay.

Or just take it easy and watch life roll by from the terrace of a café. It is a mistake to try and take in too much. After all, you would not go for lunch at the Restaurant Guy Savoy if you only had 15 minutes to spare.

Paris is not just a marvellously preserved medieval theme park. Much has been done in recent years. Under de Gaulle's successors, Georges Pompidou and Valéry Giscard d'Estaing, Paris underwent major redevelopment. The Centre Pompidou was built along with the ultra-modern complex at La Villette (originally an abattoir, now a science museum). Some absolute stinkers were also accreted to the city, such as the hideous skyscraper at Montparnasse and the hellish underground mall at Les Halles, where once an elegant and historic market had been for centuries.

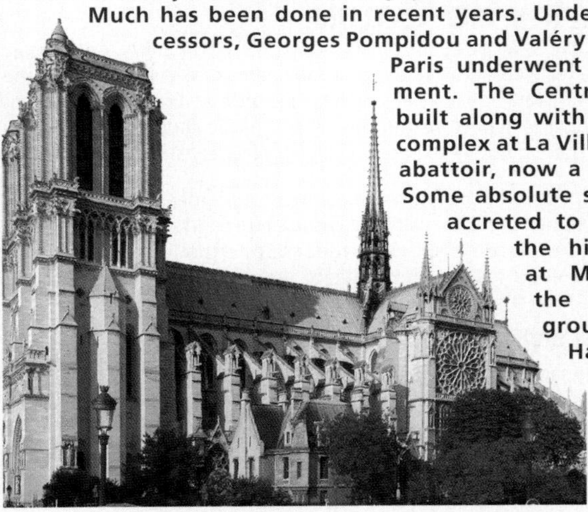

A popular misconception is that Parisians are haughty and cold-hearted, refusing to speak English when confronted by a monoglot Brit. That's wrong. They do communicate. They have to if they want your business. The wallet outweighs prejudice. There is no evidence that the average Parisian lives up to his reputation and they are certainly no ruder than your average New Yorker.

Political scandal has mired France for some years, mainly surrounding Chirac, who allegedly granted favours for relatives and party supporters when he was Mayor of Paris. His election in 1995 protected him from further enquiry, but not for much longer. The city also acquired its first openly homosexual Mayor with the election of Bertrand Delanoë in 2001. His approach to the job has added some genuine gaiety to street life.

TRAVEL

Paris is the most visited city in the world and has a transport system to handle it. It is served by two major international airports; Roissy-Charles-de-Gaulle, to the north, and Orly to the south. Both have excellent links to the centre of Paris by road and rail. Several "no-frills" airlines use Paris-Beauvais airport, about 80km north of the city, connecting by shuttle bus with Porte Maillot near the Champs-Elysées.

Travel inside the city is cheap and quick if you use the underground métro and RER network, which operate from about 5.30am until 1am. Buses are slower but cheap and allow you to see the innumerable sights.

The taxi companies provide a patchy service, excellent during work hours and the early evening, but poor late at night or in the early morning.

AIR

Every major airline in the world, and many smaller ones, fly to Paris.

From the UK:	British Airways and BMI, as well as Air France, fly direct to Paris from the major UK hubs.
From Ireland:	Aer Lingus has direct flights to CDG from Cork and Dublin. Ryanair flies to Paris-Beauvais. Easyjet runs to CDG terminal three from Belfast, Liverpool, Luton and Newcastle.
From Italy:	Alitalia operates to CDG from Roma Fiumicino and Milano.

Of the "no frills" airlines, BMI and Easyjet fly to Charles-de-Gaulle.
Easyjet fly to Orly, with flights from Milano Linate, Napoli, Torino and Pisa.
Ryanair fly into Paris-Beauvais from Prestwick, Dublin and Rome Ciampino.

Roissy-Charles-de-Gaulle

Flights from the UK arrive at all three terminals. Terminals 1 and 2: BA, Aer Lingus, BMI, Air France. These terminals are circular and can seem complex, but follow the signs for taxis, coach transfers, rail links etc. Most signs have an English translation. The shopping facilities in the departure lounges are not particularly good. Alchohol and perfume, for example are more expensive than in ordinary shops.

EasyJet fly to and from Terminal 3, which has a very simple design, with arrivals and departure on the same floor. You will find a bureau de change, ATM, post box, self-service café-bars, a newsagent and car hire facilities – though the latter may be closed, requiring travellers to take the shuttle to terminal 2. There is a taxi rank outside and a short walk to the railway station for trains into the city.

GETTING INTO TOWN

TRAIN

From Airport to central Paris	Rail and Metro via RER Line B: From Terminal 1, take the Aéroport de Paris shuttle bus to the station and then take RER line B to central Paris where you can link up with the Metro.
	From Terminal 2A: Take the Aéroport de Paris shuttle bus from Sortie 8 (departures) to Gare TGV – RER
	From Terminal 2B: Take the shuttle bus from Sortie 6 to the station and again take RER line B and do as above.
	From Terminals 2C, 2D, 2E, 2F: Follow the signs "Paris par train" and again take the RER line B.
	From Terminal 3: Turn right (leaving the terminal on your right) and take the covered walkway following signs to the station. Once you've walked the 500 metres or so, again take the RER line B, as above. A single combined ticket (valid for RER and Metro) to central Paris €7.30. CDG is a maze of a place so take heed of the tables below if you are keen to make a clean exit.

"ROISSYBUS" TO CENTRAL PARIS (OPERA GARNIER)

The coach arrives at the angle of the rue Auber and the rue Scribe close to the Opera Garnier in the 9th arrondissement. Close to Metro Opera (lines 3, 7, 8)

From:	Terminal 1	Sortie 1 (arrivals)
	Terminals 2A and 2C	Sortie 9 Terminal 2A
	Terminals 2B and 2D	Sortie 11 of Terminal 2D
	Terminals 2E and 2F	Sortie 5 from the galerie
	Terminal 3	Arrivals hall exit
Price:	€8.30	

CARS AIR FRANCE – COACH SERVICES TO CENTRAL PARIS

Line 2 goes to Place Charles-de-Gaulle - Arc de Triomphe (Metro lines 1,2, 6 and RER A) and Porte Maillot (Metro line 1 and RER C).

From:	Terminal 1	Sortie 2 (arrivals)
	Terminals 2A , 2B, 2D	Sortie 6 Terminal 2A
	Terminals 2C	Sortie 5 of Terminal 2D
	Terminals 2E and 2F	Sortie 3 from the liaison gallery
	Terminal 3	Take a shuttle bus to one of above

Coach Line 4 goes to Gare de Lyon (Metro lines 1 and 14, RER A and D) and Gare Montparnasse (Metro lines 4, 6, 12, 13).

From:	Terminal 1	Sortie 32 (arrivals)
	Terminals 2A and 2C	Sortie 2 Terminal 2C
	Terminals 2B and 2D	Sortie 1 of Terminal 2B
	Terminals 2E and 2F	Sortie 3 from the liaison gallery
	Terminal 3	Take a shuttle bus to one of above
Price:	€12	

TAXI RANKS

Terminal 1	Sortie 20 (arrivals)
Terminals 2A and 2C	Sortie 6
Terminals 2B and 2D	Sortie 7
Terminals 2E and 2F	Sortie 1
Terminal 3	Arrivals hall exit
Fare to central Paris	€35 - €50

Orly

About 20km south of the city. Two terminals, Orly Ouest and Orly Sud. Mainly for internal flights and no flights from the UK or Ireland arrive here. The Bar de l'Arrivée at Orly Oeust is the meeting point for the French rugby team.

Rail and Metro via RER C: At Orly Sud go to Sortie G quai 1, or at Orly Ouest Sortie G (arrivals level) and take the Aéroports de Paris shuttle bus to the station Pont de Rungis-Aéroport d'Orly. Then take the train to central Paris.

Rail and Metro via RER B: Take the Orlyval train from Orly Sud or Orly Ouest to Anthony. Change to RER B to Paris, then change to appropriate Metro services. Single combined ticket (valid for RER and metro) €5.30.

"Orlybus" shuttle coach service: From Orly Sud Sortie H or Orly Ouest Sortie J, to Denfert-Rochereau (Metro lines 4, 6 and RER B) in central Paris. Single ticket: €5.40.

Cars Air France – coach service to central Paris: From Orly Sud Sortie J and Orly Ouest Sortie D (arrivals level) to Invalides (Metro lines 8, 13 + RER C) and Montparnasse (Metro lines 4, 6, 12, 13) in central Paris. Single ticket €8.

Taxis: Ranks at Orly Sud Sorties M or L. Ranks at Orly Ouest Sorties H ou I. Cost to central Paris approximately €35.

Paris-Beauvais

Ryanair fly here from Rome, Dublin and Prestwick. The airport is pretty basic but growing all the time. There is a self-service restaurant, newsagent and the gift shop. Inside the departure lounge is a combined alchoholic drinks, perfume and chocolate shop. Everything is on one floor, which adds to the convenience of this curiously rustic facility.

GETTING INTO TOWN

COACH

Takes you to the Porte Maillot in north-west Paris, close to the Arc-de-Triomphe. Tickets are on sale from a small office inside the airport building just outside the arrivals door. Buy your ticket before you get on the bus. The price of a single ticket is €13. For your return journey, you can buy your ticket on the coach at the Porte Maillot. The coach park is close to Metro Porte Maillot (Metro line 1 and RER C). If you want to continue your journey by taxi, there is a rank at the Concorde-Lafayette Hotel, an enormous building just across the road from the coach park.

TAXI

There are usually taxis waiting outside the airport, but watch out, they are very expensive for 80km journeys.

CAR HIRE

There are several car hire companies at the airport. The rental car park is within a couple of hundred yards of the terminal. The Stade de France is also on the north of the city, so it is a reasonably easy drive and you don't have to go anywhere near the city centre.

TRAINS

Eurostar from London Waterloo or Ashford International to Gare-du-Nord.

Overnight train from Roma Stazione Termini to Gare de Bercy.

Daytime Trains from Milano and Torino to Gare de Lyon.

Overnight trains from Milano Gare de Bercy.

Eurostar-Gare du Nord:
For Londoners and those living in south-east England, this is probably the quickest and the most convenient way of travelling to Paris. The journey time from Waterloo to the Gare-du-Nord, pictured right, is around 3 hours – and will soon to be down to two and a half.

From Ashford International station in Kent:
The journey currently takes two hours 20 minutes. The Gare-du-Nord is also one of the main métro stations, from which all parts of Paris are quickly reached, as well as being on line B of the RER (suburban rail network) and just one stop from the Stade de France.

Gare de Bercy / Gare de Lyon - Italy:
There is a direct link between the Gare de Bercy in central/east Paris to the main stations in Milan, Turin and Rome. There are further direct services from Milan and Turin to the Gare de Lyon. All main line stations in Paris have excellent links with the city's métro system and/or the RER (suburban rail network).

CAR

From UK:	Ferry from Dover to Calais.
	Ferry from Newhaven to Dieppe.
	Ferry from Portsmouth to Le Havre.
	Ferry from Hull to Zeebrugge (Belgium)
	Eurotunnel from Folkestone to Calais
From Ireland:	Ferry from Rosslare to Cherbourg (not recommended for onward journey to Paris)
	Ferry from Cork to Rosscoff (not recommended for onward journey to Paris)
Landbridge:	Ferry Dublin/Dun Laohaire to Holyhead or Liverpool
	Belfast to Liverpool, Rosslare to Pembroke or Fishguard, Cork to Swansea
From Italy:	Via Switzerland, Basel, and Mulhouse. Via Tunnel de Fréjus Via Menton, Côte d'Azur, Avignon, Lyon.

All roads in France seem to lead to Paris (the distance signs you see are measured from a point just outside the main door of Notre-Dame). The main motorways from all points of the compass (A1 from the north, A15 from Normandy, A10 from the south-west, A6 from the south-east, A4 from the east) join the notorious Boulevard Périphérique, the ring-road which hugs the edge of the city and which seems to be choc-a-bloc most of the time. Once on the périphérique, you find the "porte" (gate, corresponding with the gates in the now lost-city walls) closest to your destination and leave the périphérique to head into the heart of the city .

There is no central bus station. Instead, a number of individual route terminuses, which often extend to the "portes" of the périphérique. Most of the main arteries of Paris now have a bus lane which makes for relatively quick travel around the city, the advantage over the métro being that one is able to see the sights.

Local Taxis

G7 Horizon	01 47 39 00 91 (Specialists for handicapped)
Les Taxis Inter	01 55 07 89 40
Abeille Radio Taxis	01 45 83 59 33
Airport Cab	01 49 00 00 00
SOS Taxis	0800 698 294 (Airports) 0892 698 294 (All destinations)
Alpha Taxis	01 45 85 85 85
Taxis Bleus	08 25 16 10 10
Taxis G7	01 47 39 47 39
Taxis Parisiens	08 73 68 75 92
Airport Connection Services	01 43 65 55 55

Chauffeur Driven

Modern Travellers	01 34 29 00 80
Baron's Limousines	01 45 30 21 21
Golden Air	01 34 10 12 92
Service Prestige	01 74 37 77 77
American Limousine	08 20 09 09 99
LD Mobilité Concept	01 41 10 81 98

TRAVEL

Paris 'intra muros' (within the périphérique) is a relatively small city. It is divided administratively into 20 arrondissements but is thought of more as a series of quartiers (quarters), each with their own unique atmosphere. We have selected six quarters, five of which form a chain running closely along the left and right banks of the Seine from the Bastille in the east, to the Porte Maillot in the West, plus Montmartre, in the north of the city. Each of these areas is easily explored on foot.

Movement to and from the different quarters is easy because of the brilliant Métro and bus services. Buying tickets for the bus (aka the RATP) is simple. You can buy an individual ticket (€1.30) which is valid for the whole of your journey no matter how long (or short). A cheaper option is to buy a "carnet" of ten tickets, for €10.50. You can also buy "Paris Visite" travel cards for 1, 2, 3 or 5 days. The passes are valid on the Metro, buses, RER and trains in the appropriate zones. Individual tickets and carnets can be bought as you get on a bus or from métro stations. The Paris Visite pass is available from metro stations or RATP travel offices. It is useful to know that métro tickets are valid on the suburban train network (RER lines A, B, C, D, and E) inside Paris. For example the closest station to the Eiffel Tower is "Champs de Mars" on RER line C. One can travel there using the métro and the RER on the same ticket.

Getting to the ground

CAR

The stadium is most easily reached from Paris from the Porte de la Chapelle exit of the Boulevard Périphérique. The exit for the Stade de France is about 1.5km from here. There is very limited car parking (spaces for only 4,000 cars for a stadium that holds nearly 80,000 people), but you can reserve a space on the internet and since they are under the stadium itself, they could scarcely be more convenient. Leave plenty of time to get in and out as the entrances are always congested.

Internet:	www.ffr.fr

PUBLIC TRANSPORT

RER

Lines B and D from the city centre (line B leaves you closer to the stadium). Line B takes you from the Latin Quarter (Cluny-Sorbonne and St-Michel, Châtelet-Les Halles, and Gare du Nord). Line D takes you from Gare de Lyon, St-Michel, Châtelet-Les Halles, and Gare du Nord.

Metro

Line 13 – get off at the Porte de Paris. One train in two on this line goes to Porte de Paris, so make sure you are on a train going to St-Denis-Université (if your train is empty you are on the wrong one). The trains are very regular but get packed from 90 minutes before kick-off, so it is advisable to get to the ground early. There is not a lot to do in or around the ground, however: the food on offer is very basic, served from catering marquees, and the beer is usually alchohol lite.

VITAL STATISTICS

Phone Code: Country code 33 (ignore '0' outside France)

Paris Area code: 01 (this is required for local calls)
Beginning with 08 – business numbers
Beginning with 06 – mobile numbers

Population: 2,300,000 City of Paris

Time zone: GMT + 2 from last Sunday in March to Saturday before last Sunday in October. GMT + 1 from Saturday before last Sunday in October to last Sunday in March

Electricity: 220 volts AC, 50Hz; round two-pin plugs are standard.

Average temperatures:

	Max	Min
January	6°C	1°C
February	7°C	1°C
March	11°C	3°C

Tipping: Not expected as restaurants and bars must include a service charge in their bill. Rounding up is common, but amounts are totally at the customer's discretion. Same for taxis.

HOSPITALS

Hertford British Hospital	**3, rue Barbès, 92300 Levallois-Perret.** 01 46 39 22 22
Hôpital Hôtel Dieu	**1, place Parvis Notre Dame, 75004 Paris.** 01 42 34 82 34
Hôpital Pitié Salpétrière	**47 boulevard de l'Hôpital, 75013 Paris.** 01 42 16 00 00
Hôpital Lariboisière	**2, rue Ambroise Paré, 75010 Paris.** 01 49 95 65 65
Dental emergencies	**12, rue St-Antoine, 75004 Paris.** 01 48 04 56 70

FRANCE

POLICE

Address:	Préfecture de Police 7, boulevard du Palais, 75004 Paris.
Phone:	01 53 71 53 71

USEFUL CONTACTS

Ambulance	15
Police	17
Fire	18
European Emergency Call	112

OFFICE DE TOURISME ET DES CONGRÈS

Main Office	25, rue des Pyramides, 75001 Paris	08 92 68 30 00
Opéra – Grands Magasins	11, rue Scribe, 75009, Paris	08 92 68 30 00
Gare de Lyon-Grandes Lignes	20, boulevard Diderot, 75012, Paris	08 92 68 30 00

EMBASSIES

British Embassy	35, rue du Faubourg-St-Honoré 5008 Paris
Hours:	Monday-Friday: **09.30-13.00, 14.30-19.00**
Phone:	01 44 51 31 00
Irish Embassy	4, rue Rude, 75016 Paris
Phone:	01 44 17 67 00
Italian Embassy	51, rue de Varenne, 75007 Paris
Phone:	01 49 54 03 00

PLACES OF INTEREST
CITY SIGHTSEEING

Open top bustour
A simple way of seeing all the major sites in the city. A complete tour lasts 5 hours 15 minutes. Your ticket, however, is valid for 24 or 48 hours and you can hop on and off at the dozen or so stops close to the major attractions. There is commentary in English and Italian and headphones for each passenger. Tickets available from RATP sales offices, Paris Tourist Offices, major hotels or as you get on the bus (vivid yellow and green stop signs).

Price:	€25 (24 hours), €28 (48 hours)

FRANCE

Eiffel Tower
Gustave Eiffel's creation for the World Fair of 1889 which was supposed to be a temporary structure but now seems to be the eternal symbol of Paris. 324 metres high, weighing 10,100 tonnes, the views from all three stages are tremendous. It is no longer possible to walk to the top (the stairs from the second to the third stage were taken out twenty years or so ago) but you can go as far as the second stage under your own steam before taking a lift to the top.
There are two restaurants; Altitude 95 on the first stage for lunch and dinner and whose bar is open all day for snacks, and Le Jules Verne (one Michelin star and 16 / 20 from Gault et Millau), on the second stage.
Every hour on the hour after dark, the tower sparkles and this spectacular show can of course be seen from all over the city.

Eiffel Tower, Champs de Mars, 75007

Lift Price:	€4.10 to first stage, €7.50 to second stage, €10.70 to third stage	
Stairs Price:	€3.80	
Hours:	Open every day: Spring, Autumn, Winter : **09.30-23.45** (Stairs open until **18.30**) Summer : **09.00-00.45** (Stairs open till **00.30**)	
Restaurant:	**Altitude 95**	01 45 55 20 04
	Le Jules Verne	01 45 55 61 44
Directions:	RER Line C – Champs de Mars-Tour Eiffel.	
Phone:	01 44 11 23 23	
Internet:	www.tour-eiffel.fr	

Musée d'Orsay

Once a railway station (the Gare d'Orsay), it was built by the architect Victor Laloux and was opened in its origianl form in 1900 but closed to railway traffic in 1939. A project to redevelop the site as a museum was first mooted in 1973 and brought to fruition in 1986 when the new exhibition space opened to the public.

It owes its undeniable success (around 4 million visitors a year) to its exceptional collections, (Manet, Degas, Monet, Renoir, Van Gogh, Gauguin, as well as Millet, Courbet, Puvis de Chavannes, or Carpeaux, Rodin and Maillol), its interior architecture (designed by Gae Aulenti), with its outstandingly effective lighting, and its location – overlooking the Seine from the Left Bank across to the Tuileries Gardens and the Louvre.

Musée d'Orsay, 1 rue de la Légion d'Honneur, 75007	
Hours:	**Tuesday to Sunday** 09.00-18.00 (summer) **Tuesday to Saturday** 10.00-18.00 **Sunday** 09.00-18.00 (winter) **Late opening Thursday** to 21.15
Price:	€7
Directions:	Ⓜ : **Solférino** or **RER Line C** – Musée d'Orsay
Phone:	01 40 49 48 14
Internet:	www.musee-orsay.fr

FRANCE

Centre Georges Pompidou

The project to construct a museum on the then derelict Beaubourg site near the old Paris markets of Les Halles was launched by President Georges Pompidou in 1972. An international architectural competition was organised to find a design team to work according to criteria established by Pompidou and his adviser Sébastien Loste. The winning team of architects, Renzo Piano, Richard Rogers and Gianfranco Franchini designed the building on the lines of an "evolving spatial diagram". The priority was to optimise functional movement and flow inside the building by placing technical ducting (water conduits, air conditioning, electricity cables) and conveyance systems (stairs, elevators etc.) on the outside of the building.

In 1974, a proposal was launched to transfer the collections of the Musée national d'art moderne in the avenue Président Wilson to the new museum. The Centre Pompidou was inaugurated in 1977 by President Giscard d'Estaing, Pompidou having died in 1975. The museum now houses the largest permanent collection of modern art in Europe. But Beaubourg, as the centre is more usually called, is much more than a museum. It is a living, vibrant space. Cinemas, shows, concerts, temporary exhibitions, conferences and debates animate the museum, while outside, street artists, buskers, escapologists, fire-eaters and caricaturists bring the streets to life.

Georges Pompidou, place Georges Pompidou, 75004	
Hours:	**Open Daily** 11.00-22.00
Adult entry:	€7 to Museum and permanent exhibitions). €10 One day Centre pass – everything. €7-€9 for temporary exhibitions.
Directions:	Ⓜ : **Hôtel de Ville** (lines 1, 3, 11), **RER** lines A, B, D – Châtelet Les Halles.
Phone:	01 44 78 12 33
Internet:	www.centrepompidou.fr

City sightseeing (cont)

Boat trips along the Seine

Several types of trip are available from various departure points along the river. "**Bateaux Mouches**" departs Pont de l'Alma (right bank), Ⓜ : **Pont de l'Alma** (line). Standard cruise – Adults €7 (regular departures between 10.15 and 21.30) Cruise with lunch Saturday, Sunday and public holidays at 1.00pm. €50 Cruise with dinner every evening at 7.45 (departs 8.30) Set €95. A la carte €125

Phone:	01 42 25 96 10

Bateaux Parisiens Tour-Eiffel, Port de la Bourdonnais (left bank), Ⓜ : **Trocadéro** (line). Standard cruise – Adults €9.50 (regular departures between 10am and 10pm) Cruise with lunch – every day at 12.15 from €50 Cruise with dinner – every day at 8.00pm from €92.

Phone:	08 25 01 01 01

Batobus. You can hop on and off the waterbus along the Seine. 8 ports of call; Eiffel Tower, Musée d'Orsay, Saint-Germain-des-Prés, Nôtre-Dame, Jardin des Plantes, Hôtel de Ville, Louvre, Champs-Elysées. Adults : €11
Combined ticket with entry to Musée d'Orsay : €12.50

Phone:	08 25 05 01 01
Internet:	www.batobus.com

FRANCE

Nôtre-Dame de Paris

The construction of the cathedral, one of the great masterpieces of Gothic architecture, began in 1163 with the laying of the first stone by Maurice de Sully, Bishop of Paris. In 1182, the High Altar was consecrated and the demolition of the ancient cathedral completed by the end of the century. During the 13th century the facade was erected and the transept was enlarged with the construction of the north and south arms. The wondrous north and south rose windows were next to be installed. From the middle of the 13th century to the beginning of the 14th, chapels were constructed between the buttresses of the nave. The first half of the 14th century also saw the construction of the gothic choir. This choir was replaced by one in the Baroque style in the early 18th century.

Between 1792 and 1793, during the Revolution, the cathedral was closed due to violent anti-clericalism of the ruling authorities. Paintings and statues were removed or destroyed. However, the Concordat between Napoleon and Rome saw the cathedral rededicated for worship according to Roman Catholic rites.

Between 1845 and 1864, the cathedral was restored by architects Baptiste Lassus and Viollet-le-Duc. The side chapels have been adorned by works by seventeenth century masters such as Le Brun and Jouvenet. These works were commissioned by the guilds of gold and silversmiths and were presented to the church each year on May 1st (this tradition, which lasted between 1630 and 1707 was know as the "Mays") – May being a month dedicated by the church to Our Lady – Notre-Dame. The cathedral is open seven days a week but access is forbidden 15 minutes after the start of mass.

Mass times:	Weekdays: 8.00 9.00 12.00 18.15 Sunday: 8.00 8.45 10.00 (Latin mass): 11.30 12.46 18.30
The Towers of Notre Dame:	Daily: 09.30–19.30
The Crypt	Daily: 10.00-18.00 (closed Monday)
Museum	Wed, Sat, Sun: 14.30-18.00

Nôtre-Dame de Paris, 6 place du Parvis Nôtre-Dame, 75004 Paris.

Directions:	Ⓜ : **Cité** (line 4). **RER C** - St Michel.
Phone:	01 42 34 56 10
Internet:	www.cathedraledeparis.com

Louvre Museum

The largest museum in the world, this awe-inspiring building was once a residence of the Kings of France. There is too much to see and absorb in a single visit, so you need to be selective. Decide on a few things you would like to see and concentrate on them. The choice is admittedly difficult as the Louvre presents comprehensive collections of western art from the Middle Ages to 1850, as well as of the antique civilisations that preceded and influenced this art. They are divided into eight departments: Oriental Antiquities, Islamic Art, Egyptian Antiquities, Greek, Etruscan and Roman Antiquities and, for the modern period, paintings, sculptures, art items, prints and drawings until 1848. In addition to these departments, the museum has a section devoted to the history of the Louvre itself, including the medieval moats erected by Philippe Auguste in 1190. Twenty one new rooms have been dedicated to collections of Italian and Spanish paintings dating back to the XVIIth and XVIIIth centuries.

And, of course, there is the Mona Lisa, its eternal appeal given a renewed popularity after the astonishing success of the Da Vinci Code.

Hours:	**Closed on Tuesday.** Open 09.00-18.00
Late opening:	**Wednesday and Friday**: 09.00 – 21.45
Price:	Adults €8.50 €6.00 (6-9.45pm Wednesday and Friday) €8.50 (exhibitions in Hall Napoléon) €13.00 (Unlimited access)
Directions:	Ⓜ : **Palais Royal Musée du Louvre** (Line 1)
Phone:	01 40 20 53 17
Internet:	www.louvre.fr

Arc de Triomphe

Commissioned in 1806 by Napoleon, shortly after his victory at Austerlitz, it was not finished until 1836. There are four huge relief sculptures at the bases of the four pillars. These commemorate the Triumph of 1810 (Cortot); Resistance and Peace (both by Etex); and the Departure of the Volunteers, more commonly known by the name La Marseillaise. Engraved around the top of the Arch are the names of major victories won during the Revolutionary and Napoleonic periods. The names of less important victories, as well as those of 558 generals, are to be found on the inside walls. Generals whose names are underlined died in action.

Beneath the Arc is the Tomb of the Unknown Soldier and eternal flame commemorating the dead of the two world wars.

On 14 July – the French National Day (referred to as Bastille Day everywhere except in France) – a military parade down the Champs Elysées begins at the Arc. For important occasions of state, and national holidays, a huge French tricolore is unfurled and hung from the vaulted ceiling inside the Arc, which also houses a small museum documenting its history and construction.

From the top there are spectacular views of Paris, along the Champs-Elysées to the Tuileries Gardens and the Pyramid at the Louvre, along the Avenue de la Grand Armée and the Arche de la Défense. Look south-west to the Bois de Boulogne. Enjoy a wonderful panorama of the whole of the ville lumière, particularly exciting at sunset.

Arc de Triomphe, place Charles-de-Gaulle, 75008 Paris.

Price:	€8 for stairs or lift to the top of the Arc and access to the museum.
Directions:	Ⓜ : **Charles-de-Gaulle-Etoile** (lines, 1, 2, 6). **RER A**.

FRANCE

FRANCE

The Basilica of Sacré-Coeur (Sacred Heart) stands at the top of Montmartre. Montmartre means "the mount of martyrs" because tradition has it that this was the site of the martyrdom of Saint Denis, the first bishop of Paris, and his companions. Since then the hill has been considered a holy place and has been visited by St Germain, St Clotilde, St Bernard, St Joan of Arc, St Vincent de Paul and the Society of Jesus was founded here in 1534 by Saint Ignatius of Loyola and St Francis-Xavier. A huge Benedictine Abbey occupied the hill until the revolution when the nuns were guillotined and the abbey destroyed.

In 1870 war broke out between France and Prussia and France faced military defeat and occupation. According to church leaders France's ills of the time stemmed from spiritual weakness and sinfulness. A vow was made to build a church consecrated to the Sacred Heart in reparation. In 1872, Cardinal Guibert, archbishop of Paris, chose Montmartre as the site. The work was financed by gifts, often very modest, from all over France. The names of the donors are carved in the stonework.

The foundation stone was laid in 1875 after Paul Abadie was chosen as the architect. The style was Romano-Byzantine, taking Saint Sophia in Constantinople and St Mark's in Venice as models. Six other architects succeeded Abadie before work was completed for the consecration in 1914. This was postponed until 1919 because of another outbreak of Franco-German hostilities. The edifice is often held to be vulgar, even garish, but its principal architectural features are impressive. The dome is 83 metres high and the Cupola, 55 meters high and 16 metres across. The views over Paris from the steps in front of the building are worth the visit.

Sacré Coeur – Montmartre, parvis du Sacré-Coeur, 75018

Hours:	**Basilica**: 6am – 10.30pm (visits are free)
	Dome and Crypt: 10am – 5.45pm (€5.00)
Mass times:	**Monday–Saturday**: 11.45am, 6.30pm, 10.00pm (no 6.30 pm mass Saturday) **Sunday**: 11.00am, 6.00pm and 10.00pm (11 o'clock mass is sung and it is possible to attend the choir's rehearsal between 9.45 and 10.45)
Directions:	Ⓜ : **Anvers** (line 2) + **Funiculaire**.
Phone:	01 53 41 89 09.
Internet:	www.sacre-coeur-montmartre.com

PARKS AND GARDENS

Paris is both compact and densely populated. Most people live in apartments so the local parks have, de facto, become their garden. You will find many small parks or public gardens as you walk around the city, but three parks in particular are larger spaces in which to stroll, relax or picnic.

Le Parc de Monceau

Situated in the 17th arrondissement, Monceau is a short walk along the avenue Hoche from the Arc de Triomphe. It has a structured design, contrasting pleasantly in style to the formal design of the Luxembourg or the Tuileries. The trees are allowed to grow naturally, and amongst them you will statues, temples and follies, shaded walks, "natural" springs rather than fountains.

Les Jardins du Luxembourg

A large, historic park in which the Senate building is located. The gardens, where the birds are pictured being fed, right, are situated to the south of St-Germain-des-Prés, close to the Latin Quarter, Sorbonne, Panthéon. The place par excellence to promenade on Sundays. Statues, fountains, tennis courts and an excellent children's play area.

Les Tuileries

Bordered on one side by the rue de Rivoli (the main east-to-west thoroughfare from the Bastille to the Concorde), the place de la Concorde, the Seine and the Louvre. Wonderful statues, a triumphant arch built by Napoleon, fountains, the Orangerie and Jeu de Paume museums.

OUTSIDE THE CITY

Monet's Garden

Claude Monet, one of the leaders of the Impressionist school, lived in the tiny village of Giverny, north-west of Paris on the edge of Normandy, for the last 43 years of an eventful life. The garden he created there is famous through his work, particularly his views of the Japanese bridge, and the water lilies in the water garden.
Vernon is the nearest station, on the main Paris-Rouen-Le Havre line. Take the métro to the Gare-St-Lazare (which has not changed much since Monet painted it). Take the "SNCF – Grandes Lignes" exit and get a return to Vernon. The fastest trains complete the journey in less than 45 minutes. At Vernon there is a complimentary shuttle to Monet's house.

Monet's Garden, Fondation Claude Monet, rue Claude Monet 27620, Giverny.

Hours:	Daily except Mondays from 9.30am to 6.00pm from April 1st to November 1st.
Prices:	House and Garden: €5.50.
	Gardens only: €4.00
Phone:	02 32 51 54 18
Internet:	www.giverny.org

FRANCE

Sights outside the centre (cont)

Disneyland Resort Paris

A good forty minutes east of Paris, but the trains are very frequent and regular. Paris's most visited attraction has two principal parks – the Disneyland Park and the Walt Disney Studios. All kinds of offers are available, so it is best to call or consult the website for details.

Disneyland Resort Paris, 77 Marne-la-Vallée.

Prices:	Adults €41 Children €33
Day ticket:	Adults €49 Children €39
Phone:	08 25 30 60 30
Internet:	www.disneylandparis.com

Stade de France

Daily guided visits to the stadium every hour from 10am till 5pm. Visits in English at 10.30 and 2.30. You will see the dressing rooms, warm-up areas, get to run out onto the pitch, visit the museum and the Presidential box, see the incredible technical and logistical work that goes into organising and running a major event (eg the lower tier of the East and West stands can be moved back to provide space for athletics, car racing on ice, ski-ing etc). The stadium has also housed rock concerts and operas. No visits on match days or the eve of matches. But if you are in Paris for a few days before the game, a trip will give a fascinating insight into everything that goes on in the build-up.

Stade de France, ZAC du Cornillon Nord, 93216 Saint-Denis-la-Plaine.

Price:	€10
Directions:	Ⓜ : **St-Denis-Porte-de-Paris**. **RER B** – La-Plaine-St-Denis Stade de France.
Phone:	08 92 70 09 00

Château de Versailles

At one time Versailles was just a tiny hamlet, lost in a wood. Then the Gondi family constructed a small château which Louis XIII liked so much he made it his hunting lodge. In 1661, Louis XIV, who had been immensely impressed by the pomp and splendour of the aforesaid Vaux-le-Vicomte, gave the architect Louis le Vau the task of adapting and enlarging the hunting lodge at Versailles. Louis, the Sun King, who sought to demonstrate his absolute power with this grandiloquent architectural gesture, played a part in its conception and employed the greatest artists of the era to achieve his dream.

Apart from the château itself, there are 2,000 acres of ornate gardens containing 80km of trees. Every year 210,000 flowers are planted. The Trianon area is where Louis had an entire village demolished to make way for a quiet retreat in which he could "partake of light meals".

Château de Versailles, 78000 Versailles.

Directions :	**Métro RER C**: Versailles-Rive Gauche-Château de Versailles. Rail from Gare Montparnasse to Versailles-Chantiers. Rail from Gare Saint-Lazare to Versailles-Rive Droite. **Bus** (RATP) n°171 - Pont de Sèvres to Versailles-Place d'Armes.
Hours:	**Tuesday to Sunday:** 9am-6.30pm (1st April – 31st October). 9am – 5.30pm (Ist November- 31st March)
Prices:	Adult €7.50 (+ €4.50 with audio guide).
Phone:	01 3083 78 00
Internet:	www.chateauversailles.fr

FRANCE

Musée de l'Air et de l'Espace

Located at Le Bourget airport, 8 km north of Paris, the Musée de l'Air et de l'Espace offers an exceptional covered exhibition of over 150 original aircraft along with artefacts from 18th and 19th century ballooning. It covers everything from the early experimental days of aviation to space flight – notably life-size models of the Ariane 1 and Ariane 5 rockets. Also on view are military machines, acrobatic and record-breaking aircraft, prototypes and helicopters. The Paris Air Show in June is a spectacular event, when the movers and shakers of the aeronautic industry meet to exhibit, view, buy and sell state-of-the-art aircraft.

Musée de l'Air et de l'Espace (Aviation and Space museum), Le Bourget Airport, BP 173, 93352 Le Bourget cedex.

Directions :	**RER B** (north) and **Bus 152**
Hours:	**Tuesday to Sunday:** 1st April-30th September: 10am-6pm 1st October-31st March: 10am-5pm
Prices:	Adult 7€, Visit of Boeing 747 €2 Concorde €2
Phone:	01 49 92 70 95
Internet:	www.mae.org

GOLF

(**Centre National de Golf**), **78180 St-Quentin-en-Yvelines.** 30km south-west of Paris. Two 18 hole courses. (Albatros course – venue for French Open). 6 hole compact.

Phone:	01 30 43 36 00
Internet:	www.golf-national.com

Fees

Albatros	€70 - €90.
Aigle	€57-€66.
Compact	€27-€28

St-Nom-la-Bretèche, Hameau de la Tuilerie Bignon, 78860 St-Nom-la-Bretèche. 8km south of St-Nom-la-Bretèche. Formerly venue of the Lancôme Trophy. 2 x 18 hole courses.

Phone:	01 30 80 04 40

Racing Club de France, Golf de la Boulie, 78000 Versailles. 1km east of Versailles. 2 x 18 hole courses. 1 x 9 hole course.

Phone:	01 39 49 04 16
Internet:	www.racingclubdefrance.org

Golf de Bussy-Saint-Georges, promenade des Golfeurs, 77600 Bussy-Saint-Georges. 30km east of Paris. 18 hole course.

Phone:	01 64 66 00 00
Internet:	www.golf-bussy.com

Fees

€28-32 (week)	€44-€57 (weekend)

Golf Stade-Français Courson, Ferme de la Gloriette, 91680 Courson-Monteloup. 18-hole course.

Phone:	01 64 58 80 80

Fees

€47 (week)	€70 (weekend)

Things to do: Golf (cont)

Golf de Saint-Cloud, 60, rue du 19 janvier, 92380 Garches. 6km west of Paris. 2 x 18 hole courses. Green fees: €90. Closed to non-members at weekends. Proof of membership of a club required.

Phone:	01 47 01 01 85

THEATRE & ARTS

Ballet

Opéra National de Paris, Palais Garnier, place de l'Opéra, 75009, Paris.

Phone:	08 92 89 90 90
Internet:	www.opera-de-paris.fr

Ballet and Opéra

Opéra Bastille, place de la Bastille, 75011 Paris.

Phone:	08 92 89 90 90
Internet:	www.opera-de-paris.fr

Museums

Musée Picasso, Hôtel Salé, 5 rue de Thorigny, 75003 Paris.
In order to meet death duties, Picasso's family made this donation of works to the French state. A wonderful collection in this grand Marais palace.

Hours:	**Wednesday to Monday:** 9.30am to 6pm
Phone:	01 42 71 25 21

Dali Espace Montmartre, 11, rue Poulbot (nr place du Tertre), 75018 Paris.
Sculptures, illustrations and etchings. One of the most comprehensive collections.

Hours:	**Open daily:** 10am to 6.30pm.
Phone:	01 42 64 40 10

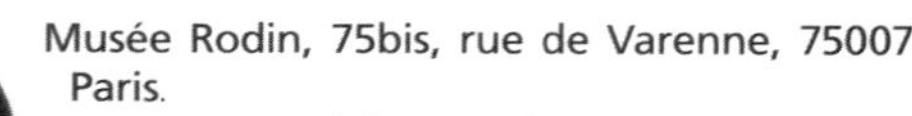

Musée Rodin, 75bis, rue de Varenne, 75007 Paris.
Permanent exhibition of some of the great works of Rodin; the Kiss, the Thinker, Balzac, the Burghers of Calais. There is also a room devoted to the work of his pupil and mistress, Camille Claudel.

Hours:	Tuesday to Sunday: 9.30am to 5.45pm
Phone:	01 44 18 61 10

Musée Carnavalet, 23, rue de Sévigné, 75003 Paris.
Traces the history of Paris from pre-historic time to the present day.

Hours:	Tuesday to Sunday: 10am to 6pm
Phone:	01 44 59 58 58

Musée Cognacq-Jay, 8, rue Elzévir, 75003 Paris.
Collection of Ernest Cognacq's eighteenth century artworks; paintings, marquetry furniture, porcelaine, small utensils and ornaments.

Hours:	Tuesday to Sunday: 10am to 6pm
Phone:	01 40 27 07 21

Musée du Vin, rue des Eaux, square Charles Dickens, 75016 Paris.
The museum covers the history of wine in France. Tools, bottles, corkscrews, objets d'art are exhibited in fifteenth century vaulted cellars. Regular lectures are given and lessons in oenology are available on request. The glass of wine at the end of the visit is included in the entry fee of €8. Lunch in the restaurant.

Hours:	**Tuesday to Sunday**: 10am to 6pm
Phone:	01 45 25 63 26

Latin Quarter Arthouse Cinemas

Note that all the films will be shown in the original language with French sub-titles.

Studio Galande, 42, rue Galande, 75005 Paris.
Latest movies, older classics and every Friday at midnight, *The Rocky Horror Picture Show* with full audience participation.

Phone:	01 43 26 94 08

Le Champo, 51, rue des Ecoles, 75005 Paris.
Two screen cinema first opened in 1938. It is on the same street as the Sorbonne.

Phone:	01 43 54 51 60

Action Christine, 4, rue Christine, 75006 Paris.
Renowned for showing new prints of old films, Hollywood classics and American independents.

Phone:	01 43 29 11 30

Moulin Rouge, 82, boulevard de Clichy, 75018 Paris.
The film has injected a new lease of life into this tired old flapper. Now she's alive and kicking again. Champagne and show – €85-€95. Dinner and show €135 - €165.

Phone:	01 53 09 82 82

Le Club 79, 22, rue Quentin Chaubart / 79 avenue des Champs-Elysées, 75008 Paris. Tea-dance every day from 2.30pm to 7.00pm.

Phone:	01 47 23 68 75

Bouglione Circus, Cirque d'Hiver, 110 rue Amelot, 75011 Paris. The wonderful "cirq d'hiv" built in 1852 is the setting for the great Bouglione family's latest show. Times and dates vary. Please consult the web or box office.

Phone:	01 47 00 12 25
Internet:	www.cirquedhiver.com

Comedy in English

The French love British comedy. When their all-time favourite, The Benny Hill Show (his death made the number one item on French news bulletins), was finally removed from its peak time slot, he was replaced by Mr Bean.

Laughing Matters, Hôtel du Nord, 102, quai de Jemmapes, 75010 Paris.
The promoter Karel Beer manages to attract strong acts from Britain and America.

Phone:	01 53 19 98 88
Internet:	www.anythingmatters.com

The Bowler, 13 rue d'Artois, 75008 Paris.
An English pub, close to the Champs-Elysées hosts comedy evenings. Good home-from-home atmosphere, chips, darts, and rugby on TV.

Phone:	01 45 61 16 60

SHOPPING

The big stores on the Champs-Elysées are allowed to open on the Sabbath, unlike their rivals elsewhere. France is a country which treasures tradition and Sunday is sacred. And in fashionable shopping areas like the Marais, the non-chain boutiques will flout such niceties and take the Sunday trade. See shopping section.

High fashion

Avenue Montaigne, off the Champs-Elysées, 75008, Paris.
Chanel, Gucci, Krizin, Escada, Jil Sander, Gianfranco Ferré, Salvatore Ferragamo, Max Mara, Christian Dior, Nina Ricci, Inès de Fressange.

Gastronomy

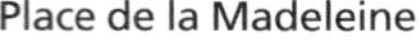

Place de la Madeleine
A veritable paradise for foodies. Around this square you will find La Maison de la Truffe, truffle specialists. They do a truffle tasting menu for €65 and a remarkably good set lunch for €20.

Hédiard and Fauchon
Grocers to the rich, pastries (a particular speciality), fine wines, cutlery, glassware. Hédiard has a top class restaurant as does Fauchon, which also boasts a salon de thé. **Caviar House & Prunier**, and Caviar Kaspia. Pâtisserie Japonaise, delicate Japanese pastries, and at number 9, the 3 Michelin starred Lucas-Carton restaurant.

Boulevard Raspail, St-Germain-des-Pres, 75006 Paris.
Ⓜ **Rennes** on Boulevard Raspail, between rue du Cherche-Midi and rue de Rennes, is the city's major organic market, bursting with offerings, fish, and eco-friendly produce. It's open Tuesday and Friday.

Pierre Hermé, 72 rue Bonaparte, Latin Quarter, 75006, Paris.
Ⓜ **Odéon**. Pierre Hermé is the man known as the 'Picasso of pastry.' Even though the store is only named after him, it is fabled for its creations. All sorts of weird and wonderful creations and, according to Fodor's critic 'the exotic macarons sparked a major buzz, as more familiar flavours like hazelnut and lemon were joined by white truffle and olive oil.' Lesser things have sparked revolutions.

Phone:	01 43 54 47 77

Markets

Marché aux Fleurs de l'Ile de la Cité, place Louis Lépine, 75004 Paris.
Ⓜ **Cité (line 4)**. Beautiful flower market close to Notre Dame. Open every day 8am-7pm.

Rue de Buci, 75006 Paris.
Ⓜ **Odéon (lines 4 and 10)**. Small food market every day on this lively street in the St-Germain-des-Prés quarter.

Marché Couvert St-Germain. Rue Mabillon, 75006 Paris.
Ⓜ **Mabillon (line 10)**. In the same quarter there is the covered Marché St-Germain. Food dominates, but there are other offerings; clothes, household goods. Open Tuesday to Saturday 8.30am-1pm, then 4pm-7.30pm. Sunday **8.30**am to **1**pm.

Setting out their stall: Wherever you go in France fruit and veg markets flourish, and Paris is no exception

FRANCE

Marché de la Création "Bastille", boulevard Richard-Lenoir, 75011 Paris.
Ⓜ Bastille (lines 1, 5, 8). Large and lively food market with some clothes stalls. Butchers, bakers, wine producers, fishmongers, delis. On Sunday morning there is an excellent news stall with same day papers from all over Europe. Open Thursday and Sunday, 8.30am and 1.30pm. Every Saturday from 9am to 7pm.

Marché Couvert Monge, rue Monge, 75005 Paris.
Ⓜ Monge (line 5). Another covered market, mainly food but other shopping. This is a very lively place in a truly Parisian part of the Latin Quarter.
Open Wednesday, Friday and Sunday, 8.30am to 1pm.

Flea Market (Marché des Puces de Saint-Ouen).
Ⓜ Porte de St-Ouen (line 13) and Ⓜ Porte de Clignancourt (line 4). Enormous flea market in northern Paris close to the boulevard Périphérique, between Porte de St-Ouen and Porte de Clignancourt. Antiques, objets d'art, porcelaine etc. Open Saturday, Sunday and Monday 10am-6pm.

Department stores

Bon Marché, 24, rue de Sèvres, 75007 Paris.
Ⓜ Sèvres-Babylone (lines 10 and 12). Bon Marché means cheap in French. This place is anything but. However there is free skin care advice and consultations in the cosmetics department and free alterations on clothes purchased. Open Monday, Tuesday, Wednesday and Friday 9.30 to 7.00. Thursday 10.00am to 9.00pm. Saturday 9.30am to 8.00pm.

Phone:	01 44 39 80 00

Galeries Lafayette, 40 boulevard Haussmann, 75009 Paris.
Ⓜ Chaussée d'Antin-Lafayette (line 9) and Auber - RER A. There are 75,000 brand names stocked in this cornucopia of indulgence, which claims to be the only department store where you will find ALL the most prestigious designers on recently refurbished floors around the store's famous dome. Europe's largest space devoted entirely to men's fashion. Two fine restaurants. The store is spectacularly decorated at Christmas. Fashion shows are held every Tuesday of the year at 11am and Saturday at 2.30 from Easter to October. Open Monday to Saturday 9.30 to 7.30. Late open Thursday (9.00pm).

Phone:	01 42 82 34 56
Internet:	www.galerieslafayette.com

Shopping: Department stores (cont)

Le Printemps, 64 boulevard Haussman, 75009 Paris.
Ⓜ **Havre-Caumartin**. Specialists in fashion and perfume and prides itself on being the trendiest store in town. Apart from being at the cutting edge of fashion for men, women and children it also has a truly and unashamedly expensive section, boasting the biggest perfume department in the world. It commands some stunning views and has an attractive 1920 art nouveau cupola, eight restaurants. From Mondays to Saturdays **9.35**am to **7**pm (10pm on Thursdays).

Phone:	01 42 82 50 00
Internet:	www.printemps.com

Madelios, 23 boulevard de la Madeleine, 75001.
Ⓜ **Madeleine** (lines 8, 12, 14). High class shop of around 50,000 square feet dealing only with men's fashion. All the big labels. Open Monday to Saturday **10**am to **7**pm.

Phone:	01 53 45 00 00
Internet:	www.madelios.com

Décathlon, 17, boulevard de la Madeleine, 75001 Paris.
Ⓜ **Madeleine** (lines 8, 12, 14).

Phone:	01 55 35 97 55

Décathlon, 26, avenue Wagram, 75008 Paris.
Ⓜ **Ternes (line 2)**. Each store has several specialist workshops providing, for example, golf club re-gripping or re-alignment, racket (badminton, tennis, squash) restringing, bike repairs. If one shop can't help you, they will point you in the direction of colleagues in another store who can. Brilliant sports complex.

Phone:	01 45 72 66 88

Antiques

St-Germain-des-Prés. Predominantly up-market selection of dealers and galleries which covers a very large range of art forms and styles and also quite a large territory. From the Musée d'Orsay in the west and close to the river to the institut de France to the east and south to the Luxembourg gardens.

Village St-Paul, 75004 Paris.
Not quite a village but a grouping of antique dealers, restorers and galleries in cobbled backstreets and courtyards in the southern part of the Marais district.

Books

These are expensive commodities in Paris. But this is not often the case if you visit the bouquinistes who run the rows of bookstalls perched against the parapet of the Seine. Here, if you're lucky, you might find a valuable first edition that has escaped the eagle eye of the owner. But you are more likely to witness an Italian Grand Slam. FNAC is the biggest and best known of the chains. There's a big one in the Forum des Halles.

Supermarkets

These are sprouting everywhere in Paris as the pace of Parisian life changes. Ideal spots to pick up foie gras, decent wine and other delicacies for those in a rush. Chains include ED, Franprix, Leader Price, and Monoprix.

Eclectica

Au Vase de Delft, 19 rue Cambon, 75001. 01-42-60-92-49.
Ⓜ **Concorde**. Specialises in fine vintage jewellery, ivory sculptures from China and Japan, gold boxes, watches, and Russian-made silverware (some by Fabergé).

Comptoir de l'Image, 44 rue de Sévigné, 75003, Paris.
Books/Printed Matter, (English-Language), Le Marais. Métro: St-Paul. Designers John Galliano, Marc Jacobs and Emanuel Ungaro stock up on old copies of Vogue, Harper's Bazaar, and The Face. Also on sale are trendy magazines like Dutch, Purple, and Spoon, designer catalogues from the past and rare photo books.

Phone:	01 42 72 03 92

Carré Rive Gauche, between St-Germain-des-Prés and Musée d'Orsay, 75006, Paris. Ⓜ **St-Germain-des-Prés**, Rue du Bac. Antiques, Art Gallery. It is in the streets between rue de Bac, rue de l'Université, rue de Lille, and rue des Saints-Pères. Here more than 100 associated shops, marked with a small blue banner on their storefronts, are linked and provide some museum quality works, as you can see, right. You could find anything from a 12th-century bronze Byzantine treasure to an 18th century doll's house in this veritable Aladdin's Cave.

Jean-Paul Gaultier, 44 av. George V, 8e, Paris.
Ⓜ **Bourse or George V.** Women's fashion. This is the man who moulded Madonna's iconic corset and did for her breasts what Seb Coe has done for London. Sumptuous, over-the-top haute couture. Designer Philippe Starck is responsible for the fantastic look of the place, with its quilted cream walls and Murano mirrors. Also to be found at : 6 Galerie Vivienne, 2, Opéra/Grands Boulevards.

Phone: | 01 44 43 00 44

Mare, 23 rue des Francs-Bourgeois, Le Marais, 75004, Paris.
Ⓜ **St-Paul.** Ⓜ **St-Sulpice.** Shoes. Heels R Us is the watchword: square, round, pencil-thin, transparent, you name it. Also some brilliant bargains with best-selling brands often at half-price and other more esoteric designers getting a foothold by selling for a song. Also **4 rue du Cherche-Midi, 6, St-Germain-des-Prés.**

Phone: | 01 48 04 74 63

Prada, 8-10 av. Montaigne, 75008, Paris.
Ⓜ **Alma-Marceau.** Fashion. Shoes, bags and other accessories which cause trans-continental queuing are the hallmarks of this amazingly successful outfit. Elegant long skirts, cardigans, sweaters, retro prints. Also to be found at:
6 rue du Faubourg St-Honoré, 8, Louvre/Tuileries. Ⓜ **Concorde.**
5 rue de Grenelle, 6, St-Germain-des-Prés, Ⓜ **St-Sulpice.**

Phone: | 01 53 23 99 40

EAT, DRINK & SLEEP

BASTILLE

BARS

BRITISH – IRISH PUBS

Kitty's, place de la Bastille / rue de la roquette, 75011 Paris.
Small pub specialising in pints, cocktails and TV for sports. Can get crowded. Launch pad for other adventures because of the area, it closes at 1am.

Falstaff, 10/12 place de la Bastille, 75011 Paris.
Large brasserie style specialising in beer, cocktails and pizzas baked in a wood fire. Late night opening: 4.30am weekdays and 5am weekends.

COCKTAIL BARS

L'An Vert du Décor, 32, rue de la Roquette, 75011 Paris.
Stylish modern decor in trendy night club bar. Darkness illuminated only by the glow from the screens giving the very latest music videos.

Iguana Café, 15, rue de la Roquette, 75011 Paris
A place to be seen. Round bar gives the boys plenty of room to wield the shaker. Look down on the style setters from the mezzanine floor.

Barrio Latino, 46-48 rue du Faubourg Saint-Antoine, 75012 Paris.
Large place with a variety of bars and a restaurant serving "nuevo latino" cuisine. Opens late and closes late.

SanZ SanS, 49, rue du Faubourg Saint-Antoine, 75012 Paris.
Dark and sultry atmosphere where the trendy drink cocktails and champagne and nibble tasty amuse-bouches.

La Distillerie, 50, rue du Faubourg Saint-Antoine, 75012 Paris.
West Indian bar specialising in rum punches with a restaurant offering good creole cooking at a good price (3 courses €25). Work it all off in the dance hall to hip-hop, rock and R'n'B.

JAZZ

Le Café du Passage, 12, rue de Charonne, 75011 Paris.
Old world jazz feel and specialises in cognacs, eaux de vie, cured and smoked hams and cheeses. Sort of place you might meet Ken Clarke.

WINE BARS

L'Ecluse Bastille, 13, rue de la Roquette, 75011 Paris.
Excellent wines sold by the bottle or glass to accompany (or not) very good French bistro food.

CLUBS: DANCING

La Scène, 2bis, rue des Taillandiers, 75011 Paris.

La Chapelle des Lombards, 19, rue de Lappe, 75011 Paris. (Latin, souk, salsa)

La Fabrique, 53, rue du Faubourg-St-Antoine, 75012 Paris. (DJ)

Le Caveau de la Huchette, 5, rue de la Huchette, 75005 Paris. (Jazz, Rock)

RESTAURANTS

Bastille

La Galoche d'Aurillac, 41 rue de Lappe, 75011 Paris. €40.
La Galoche d'Aurillac is an anachronism among the trendy bars, a slightly old-fashioned, warm and welcoming family-run restaurant offering home cooking in which produce from the Auvergne features strongly. Charcuterie and cheese are staples, the foie gras is very good. Generous portions contradict the Auvergnats' reputation for meanness and this is a place for true trenchermen, unsuited to the weak of heart or liver.

Phone: | 01 47 00 77 15

Le Repaire de Cartouche, 8 boulevard des Filles du Calvaire, 75011 Paris. €23.
Between the Place de la Bastille and the Place de la République and close to the refuge of "Cartouche", a notorious Parisian ne'er-do-well who would hide here and whose adventures are recounted in the many frescoes dotted around the place. Renowned locally for the quality of its wines and its regional produce, the atmosphere is convivial and the food is pan-French. The wine list is extensive, with some real gems from little known production areas. Excellent value for money.

Phone: | 01 47 00 25 86

Le Capricorne, 3 Boulevard Richard Lenoir, 75011 Paris. €35.
Quiet dining across the Bastille from the Opéra. Comfortable French family cooking in a friendly, open environment. Reasonably priced menus du jour with a mainly southern flavour. The menus offer exactly the sort of comfort food, with personal style, that mark out a true bistro. Open late.

Phone:	01 47 00 25 00

Chez Paul, 13, rue de Charonne, 75011 Paris. €30.

Wholesome food: Chez Paul is a traditional Paris bistro.

As the name suggests, a traditional Parisian bistro, located off a splendid city square. Wholesome and unpretentious food, sound wine, and excellent value for money. Outdoor seating also available.

Phone:	01 47 00 34 57

HOTELS

(Bastille)

MODERATE

Hôtel Paris-Bastille, 67, rue de Lyon, 75012 Paris. Ⓜ Bastille.
37 rooms. €149 s. €156 d. €192 tpl. €225 suite. Recently renovated in exotic woods and warm colours the hotel is located opposite the Opera Bastille and just a stone's throw from the increasingly happening Bastille area.

Phone:	01 40 01 07 17
Email:	infosbastille@wanadoo.fr
Internet:	www.hotelparisbastille.com

BUDGET

Hôtel Les Sans Culottes, 27, rue de Lappe, 75011 Paris. Ⓜ Bastille.
9 rooms. €53.50 s. €61 d/t. Cheap but pleasant accommodation in a lively little street. The establishment also has a bar with happy hour and cocktails.

Phone:	01 49 23 85 80
Email:	hotel.lessansculottes@wanadoo.fr
Internet:	www.lessansculottesfr.com

FRANCE

Hôtel Lyon-Mulhouse, 8, boulevard Beaumarchais, 75011 Paris. Ⓜ Bastille. 40 rooms. €60 to €75 s/d/t, €90 tpl. Comfortable, friendly, perfectly adequate hotel offering a great location next to the Bastille and close to the flesh-pots of the Marais.

Phone:	01 47 00 91 50
Email:	hotellyonmulhouse@wanadoo.fr
Internet:	www.1-hotel-paris.com

Le Pavillon Bastille, 65, rue de Lyon, 75012 Paris. Ⓜ Bastille. 25 rooms. €130 d/t. Privately owned boutique accommodation opposite the Opera Bastille. Contemporary decor and furniture within easy reach of the Bastille and the Marais.

Phone:	01 43 43 65 65
Email:	hotel-pavillon@akaMail.com
Internet:	www.paris-hotel-pavillonbastille.com

FRANCE

LE MARAIS & BEAUBOURG BARS

CAFÉ + SIMPLE FOOD

Bistro des Vosges, boulevard Beaumarchais, 75004 Paris.
Bar and restaurant serving good, simple food. They have an underused large screen and are always happy to show sport. Ask and the screen will be made available.

APÉRITIF AND LATER

Café Martini, 11 rue du Pas de la Mule, 75004 Paris.
Atmospheric little bar very close to chic Place des Vosges. They serve potent cocktails and Happy Hour is from 6 till 8. Good apéritif venue.

Phone:	01 42 77 05 04

Le Vieux Comptoir du Cap Horn, 8, rue de Birague, 75004 Paris.
Small bar on a side-street between the rue de Rivoli and the place des Vosges. Louche latin-american atmosphere. Rum cocktails a speciality. Try the Créole food.

Phone:	01 42 72 34 50

L'Etoile Manquante, 34, rue Vieille du Temple, 75004 Paris.
Bar with small terrace. Very good cocktails. This is a relaxed, friendly bar on perhaps the trendy Marais' trendiest street.

Phone:	01 42 72 48 34

BRASSERIE

Le Royal Turenne, rue de Turenne, 75003 Paris.
Friendly place to drink either at the bar, where prices are low and measures large, or on the terrace where prices are slightly higher but the street spectacle good fun. Quality bistro food served all day.

PARISIAN BISTRO

Le Bûcheron, 14, rue de Rivoli, 75004 Paris.
Lumberjacks would feel at home in this rough and ready drinking den. True Parisian bistro tradition. Good cooking too.

Phone:	01 48 87 71 31

Le pick-clops, 16, rue Vieille-du-Temple, 75004 Paris.
Bar – restaurant. Ever lively place to drink and the food is copious and of good quality. Small terrace area to watch the Marais boulevardiers go by.

Phone:	01 40 29 02 18

Au petit fer à cheval, 30, rue Vieille du Temple, 75004 Paris.
Café – restaurant. Famous Marais watering hole, its name coming from its horseshoe shaped bar. Space is limited inside and only a small terrace area. Good food served lunchtime and evenings till late.

Phone:	01 42 72 47 47

Au Rendez-Vous des Amis, 10, rue Ste-Croix de la Bretonnerie, 75004 Paris.
Old gnarled wood, smoky, "bo-bo" (bohemian-bourgeois) atmosphere. Good food at reasonable prices.

Phone:	01 42 72 05 99

TAPAS

La Perla, 26, rue François Miron, 75004 Paris. Principally a tequila cocktail bar (they sell Margaritas by the jug) they also do tasty tapas. Relaxed and convivial atmosphere, a good spot for early doors.

Phone:	01 42 77 59 40

BRITISH / IRISH PUB

The Auld Alliance, 80, rue François Piron, 75004 Paris.
Scottish pub that keeps Edinburgh hours - open till 2am every night. They do brunch Saturday and Sunday. Huge collection of pure malt whisky and some staff are expert enough to guide you through a tasting. Beer served by the pint. Good spot for the ticketless. TV for sports.

Phone:	01 48 04 30 40

The Single Malt, 4, rue Caron, 75004 Paris.
Neat, cosy little Scottish boozer which also sells pints. Good place to see the game and good for post-match philosophising. Closes 2am.

Phone:	01 42 76 03 77

TERRACE CAFÉ

Le Café des Phares, place de la Bastille, 75004 Paris.
Large terrace area. Occasionally they organise Sunday lunch-time philosophical debates chaired by Sorbonne professors on themes such as «Referees, a necessary evil?»

RESTAURANTS

(Marais and Beaubourg)

Bofinger, 5-7, rue de la Bastille, 75004 Paris. €45.
A Parisian institution. Go through the revolving doors into a cosy bar area where you can take an apéritif (try the white wines from Alsace or the house champagne) before being led to your table in this wonderful belle époque brasserie. Oysters, seafood platters, choucroutes are exceptional, especially if accompanied by Alsace whites. Service is quick, quietly humourous and professional. Open all day with excellent value fixed lunch menus for €24 and €35. Popular with Parisians and tourists wanting a treat, so if you want to eat at a relatively conventional time, reserve and don't let them put you in the Petit Bofinger across the street.

Phone:	01 42 72 87 82
Internet:	www.bofinger.com

Ma Bourgogne, 19, place des Vosges, 75004 Paris. €50
All day brasserie. Traditional French food in copious portions in a lively and convivial ambience in a great spot under Place des Vosges. Skate and steak tartare served with great chips. The wine list is perhaps too conventional and expensive. Three courses for about €50. No credit or debit cards. Reservation recommended.

Phone:	01 42 78 44 64

Au Bourguignon du Marais, 52, rue François Miron, 75004 Paris. €35.
Once chief propagandist for Burgundian gastronomy in the Marais, proprietors Jacques and Christine Bavard have recently moved towards a menu embracing a more international range of offerings. It is wisest however to stick to what they are best at, namely traditional Burgundy specialities; oeufs Meurette (eggs poached in red wine with bacon and mushrooms), andouillette (chitterling) in aligoté, jambon persillé, (ham in its jelly with parsley). The very good wine list obviously has a strong Burgundian leaning, (the Bavards are wine retailers and tastings are regularly organised).

Phone:	01 48 87 15 40

Le Pamphlet, 38, rue Debelleyme, 75003 Paris. €40.
Beamed, spacious and well presented dining room. The chef, Alain Carrière, seems to have a low boredom threshold so the menu is ever changing (the standard of cooking is consistently good, however), with subtle takes on traditional cuisine bourgeoise or bistro staples. Rabbit confit with aubergine, parmentier de canard (cottage pie made with duck), a pig's cheek and vegetable tajine. The service is friendly, efficient and helpful. The wine list is cleverly composed of solid favourites and well selected smaller AC or Vin de Pays bottles.

Phone:	01 42 72 39 24

FRANCE

Caves St-Gilles, 4, rue Saint-Gilles, 75003 Paris. €30
Unsophisticated but lively and convivial tapas restaurant. You cannot reserve so you may have to wait for a table, but this is time well spent at the lively bar, tasting the olives, watching Spanish soccer on TV, and enjoying the insults traded between supporters of the opposing teams. Excellent choice once at the table, the planchas of grilled fish or meats are simple, copious and effective, there is a good paella at weekends, while the house wines from Spain are perfectly adequate.

Phone:	01 48 87 22 62

L'Excuse, 14, rue Charles V, 75004 Paris. €50.
Sophisticated, delicious French cooking in a quiet southern Marais street running parallel with the rue de Rivoli. The room is intimate, the decor refined, ideal for tête-à-tête dining. Classic dishes include giant prawn ravioli in a shellfish and whisky jus, noisette of lamb roasted with wild cherries. For starters try oysters in soured apple juice with chives and shallots. The sauces in particular are very well balanced. There is an excellent wine list. The à la carte prices can be a little steep but there are excellent value-set menus €20 - €35.

Phone:	01 42 77 98 97

L'Ambassade d'Auvergne, 22, rue du Grenier-St-Lazare, 75003 Paris. €35.
Authentic, rustic Auvergnat auberge, very popular locally and a haunt of showbiz personalities who are here solely for the simple, filling and genuine food. The house speciality is the "aligot", a creamy mashed potato to which tomme cheese is added, which when served (here with great ceremony and aplomb) creates a web of cheese strands as it delicately lands on the plate. The aligot is served with chunky, meaty saucisse d'Auvergne. Other favourites include boudin noir with apple, a salad of green lentils, lardons and challots, cured hams, ox cheek in a gribiche vinaigrette (chopped eggs, gherkins, capers and herbs). Auvergnat wines, Chanturgue, Boudes and Madargues will best accompany these. Ask the friendly, enthusiastic waiting staff for advice.

Phone:	01 42 72 31 22
Internet:	www.ambassade-auvergne.com

Le Bar à Huitres, 33, Boulevard Beaumarchais, 75003 Paris. €40.
Avoid this establishment if you don't enjoy life, or cuisine, in the raw. But should you savour the sensation of a bivalve going down your throat or regard lunch as an extension of carpentry, this is the place for you. Oysters. Seafood platters. Lightly cooked fish.

Phone:	01 48 87 98 92
Internet:	www.lebarahuitres.com

Auberge Chez Rosito, rue du Pas de la Mule, 75003 Paris. €25.
A traditional Corsican restaurant, where you are welcomed rather than ransomed. Game in season; lots of fish dishes from the Mediterranean, including a "catch of the day". Expect to pay around €25 a head, plus wine, much of it from the etraordinary island from which Napoleon launched his ambition for a French-led European Union. Charcuterie a speciality.

Phone:	01 42 76 04 44

L'Ambroisie, 9, place des Vosges, 75004 Paris. €250.
Three Star Michelin. Extreme luxury, perfect service, romantic setting. You are made to feel very special. The food, it is said, was intended for the Gods - though even they would struggle for a parking space around here. When you enter, you feel rich; two hours later, after presentation of 'l'addition,' less so. An experience to remember – not least when your bank statement arrives. Exceptional wine cellar. Reserve well in advance (two months is recommended).

Phone:	01 42 78 51 45

Chez Janou, 2, rue Roger-Verlomme, 75003 Paris. €30.
Very popular with locals young and old. Good French cooking in jovial atmosphere. Very small terrace at the front, which fills quickly in a competitive environment. Cooking is fast and furious. The kitchen is small and the staff move at an incredible pace. Never have so many been served so much by so few.

Phone:	01 42 72 28 41

La Guirlande de Julie, 25, place des Vosges, 75003 Paris. €45.
Classy restaurant of the Tour d'Argent stable with a suitably classic French menu. The vaulted interior apes the square itself. There is also a small terraced area under the arcades where you might find yourself being serenaded by talented buskers.

Phone:	01 48 87 94 07
Internet:	www.latourdargent.com

La Chaise au Plafond, 10, rue du Trésor, 75004 Paris. €30.
All day café. Traditional French cooking in the tradition begun by the mythical Maman. Small outside terrace. Long wooden benches, purloined from old Metro carriages, create convivial atmosphere inside.

Phone:	01 42 76 03 22

Le Petit Picard, 42, rue Ste-Croix de la Bretonnerie, 75004 Paris. €28. Lively restaurant serving French cooking that features specialities from Picardy. Get ready to scrum down. If you eat early you will not be allowed to linger as the restaurant easily fills for a second sitting, particularly at weekends. Big helpings should satisfy all but the most discerning diners.

Phone:	01 42 78 54 03

Vin des Pyrénées, 25 rue Beautreillis, 75004 Paris. €30. Traditional French bistro just off the Rue de Rivoli. Leans towards the South-West in its cooking style. Bustling and confident, it's important to book. Young, friendly staff and there are some excellent wines from the South. Great fun but can get noisy.

Phone:	01 42 72 64 94

Gaspard de la Nuit, 6 rue des Tournelles, 75004 Paris. €55.
Smart, comfortable restaurant for one to one dining. Lot of men with jumpers over their shoulders. Dégustation menu at €72 per person. Service soigné, which means the waiters know what they're doing and expect the same from their customers. Simpler, reasonably priced bistro food at lunchtime.

Phone:	01 42 77 90 53
Internet:	www.legaspard.com

L'Area, 10, rue des Tournelles, 75004 Paris. €40.
Rather young Bo-Bo (bourgeois-bohème), with cuisine to match. Open for lunch, then in the evenings from five until the early hours – so good for a ruck between the bar and the disco. "DJ – mix – food – friends". Sunday brunch till five.

Phone:	01 42 72 96 50

Caffé Boboli, 13, rue du Roi de Sicile, 75004 Paris. €35.
Small, very fashionable Italian designer atmosphere in the Marais. The cuisine here claims to be transalpine, which refers less to the rarefied atmosphere of the dining room than the blend of Savoy French and nouvelle Italian cooling. Offers a good, reasonably priced brunch.

Phone:	01 42 77 89 27
Internet:	www.caffeboboli.com

Le Jardin du Marais, 35, rue du Roi de Sicile, 75004 Paris. €25. Good place for a family on a budget with hungry kids. Fast food with finesse in an area once known for its aristos, then notorious for its revolutionary fervour. Great pizzas, simple pastas, and try the escalope bolognaise if particularly hungry.

Phone:	01 42 78 80 98

L'Escale du Liban, 1, rue Ferdinand Duval 75004 Paris. €25. Much appreciated by its varied clientele, one of whom recently described it as "the best Lebanese restaurant in Paris". Its specialities include kebbé nayé – delicately perfumed meats served in crushed rice – and flakey sweet pastries.

Phone:	01 42 74 55 70

FRANCE

HOTELS

(Le Marais and Beaubourg)

LUXURY

Le Pavillon de la Reine, 28, place des Vosges, 75003 Paris. Ⓜ Chemin-Vert. 41 rooms, from €345 to €495 d/t. Extremely comfortable, warm, luxury hotel on the beautiful and chic Place des Vosges. The setting is calm, the welcome friendly and intimate.

Phone:	01 40 29 19 19
Email:	contact@pavillon-de-le-reine.com
Internet:	www.pavillon-de-la-reine.com

MODERATE

Libertel Grand Turenne, 6, rue de Turenne, 75004 Paris. Ⓜ Saint-Paul. 41 rooms, from €172 to €220 s/d/t. Promotional offers available. Comfortable hotel of the Libertel chain although the decor is sufficiently unique that this is not obvious. Pleasant atmosphere and a great location.

Phone:	01 42 78 43 25
Internet:	www.libertel-hotels.com

Grand Hôtel Malher, 5, rue Malher, 75004 Paris. Ⓜ Saint-Paul. 31 rooms, from €90 to €132. Family run hotel for three generations, full of character, it offers a warm and friendly welcome. The hotel was completely renovated during 2004 without losing its old, soft comfort.

Phone:	01 42 72 60 92
Email:	ghmalher@yahoo.com

Hôtel Saint-Paul Le Marais, 8, rue de Sévigné, 75004 Paris. Ⓜ Saint-Paul. 28 rooms, from €115 to €210 s/d/t. €170 to €195 tpl.
Very good value hotel, recently and very successfully renovated. The present building is on the site of a 16th century convent. The basic harshness of the nuns' cells has not been retained. This is modern comfort in an authentic style.

Phone:	01 48 04 97 27
Email:	reservation@hotelsaintpaullemarais.com
Internet:	www.hotelsaintpaullemarais.com

Hôtel Saint-Louis Marais, 1, rue Charles V, 75004 Paris. Ⓜ Saint-Paul. 19 rooms, from €91 to €125 s/d/t. €140 tpl. Neat little hotel in a pleasant side street in the southern part of the Marais.

Phone:	01 48 87 87 04
Email:	slmarais@noos.fr
Internet:	www.saintlouismarais.com

Hôtel de la Place des Vosges, 12, rue de Biragues, 75004 Paris. Ⓜ Saint-Paul. 16 rooms, from €107 s/d/t. Small, friendly family run hotel between the Place des Vosges and the rue de Rivoli.

Phone:	01 42 72 60 46
Email:	hotel.place.des.vosges@gofornet.com
Internet:	www.hotelplacedesvosges.com

Castex Hôtel, 5, rue Castex, 75004 Paris. Ⓜ Bastille. 30 rooms. From €85 to €140 s/d/t. Hotel completely renovated in 2003. High level of comfort situated in a calm street in the southern Marais close to the Bastille and close to a safe car park.

Phone:	01 42 72 31 52
Email:	info@castexhotel.com
Internet:	www.castexhotel.com

Hôtel Bastille Speria, 1, rue de la Bastille, 75004 Paris. Ⓜ Bastille. 42 rooms, from €98 to €145 s/d/t. Modern, comfortable hotel in the Marais near the place des Vosges and very close to the Bastille for access to the rest of the city.

Phone:	01 42 72 04 01
Email:	info@hotelsperia.com
Internet:	www.hotel-bastille-speria.com

BUDGET

Hôtel Jeanne d'Arc, 3, rue de Jarente, 75004 Paris. Ⓜ Saint-Paul. 36 rooms. €58-€96 s/t/d, €115 tpl, €145 qd. Reasonably priced, comfortable accommodation in a great location close to the Place du Marché-St-Catherine in the middle of the Marais.

Phone:	01 48 87 62 11
Email:	information@hoteljeannedarc.com
Internet:	www.hoteljeannedarc.com

Hôtel Sévigné, 2, rue Malher, 75004 Paris. Ⓜ Saint-Paul. 30 rooms, from €65 to €85 s/d/t, €100 tpl. Recently renovated hotel offering reasonable comfort at a reasonable price. Excellent location in a busy area just off the rue de Rivoli in the centre of the Marais, within easy striking distance of Notre-Dame and the Bastille. All the rooms are double-glazed and air-conditioned.

Phone:	01 42 72 76 17
Email:	contact@le-sevigne.com
Internet:	www.le-sevigne.com

Le Compostelle, 31, rue du Roi de Sicile, 75004 Paris. Ⓜ Hôtel-de-Ville 25 rooms en-suite. €63 s, from €93 to €100 s/t. Close to the Tour St-Jacques, a starting point for the pilgrimage to Santiago de Compostella in northern Spain. But that's for another day. You'll miss the match if you try that. Cheap yet comfortable accommodation in the heart of the Marais.

Phone:	01 42 78 59 99

Grand Hôtel du Loiret, 8, rue des Mauvais Garçons, 75004 Paris.
Ⓜ Hôtel-de-Ville. 29 rooms (21 en-suite), from €45 to €70 s. €60 to €80 d/t, €90 tpl, €100 qd.
Cheap, basic but comfortable accommodation in a great location.

Phone:	01 48 87 77 00
Email:	hotelduloiret@hotmail.com

MADELEINE, OPÉRA & TUILERIES
BARS

WINE BARS

L'Ecluse Madeleine, 15, place de la Madeleine, 75008 Paris.
High quality wine bar. Vintages by the glass. Great location on the Madeleine - a real foody's paradise.

Phone:	01 42 65 34 69

FRANCE

TERRACE CAFÉS

Café de la Paix, avenue de l'Opéra, 75002 Paris.
One of the most famous bars in Paris just next to the Palais Garnier Opera House. Very smart. They say that if you stay on the terrace here long enough, you will see everyone you know in the world. But that's true of any bar, as George Best once observed.

IRISH PUBS

Kitty O'Shea's, rue des Capucines, 75002 Paris.
Probably the most famous of Paris's Irish pubs, it is well known to the local rugby crowd. (French TV has used the place for late-night post match analysis programmes).
Carr's, rue Mont Thabor, 75002 Paris.
Very pleasant, wood panelled pub with tasteful artefacts on an Irish theme. There's a basic but charming restaurant and an open fire and piano. RTE coverage of rugby, soccer, GAA. Connal Carr, the Irish owner who has been in rue Mont Thabor for years, is a font of wisdom for generations of Daily Telegraph Paris correspondents, whose office on the rue de Rivoli is just around the corner.

RESTAURANTS
(Madeleine, Opéra & Tuileries)

"10 Le J.Go", 4, rue Drouot, 75009 Paris. €40.
A newish restaurant whose roots are firmly set in South-West France (there is a sister restaurant of the same name in Toulouse) with very strong rugby links. The great Fabien Galtié is a shareholder and you might catch sight of him after the game. The restaurant has quickly established itself as a sympathetic lunchtime meeting point for the quarter's auctioneers and antique dealers. The convivial atmosphere is aided by the long bar and narrow tables; the young serving staff are friendly, quick and attentive. The kitchen's offerings are classic south-west: cassoulet, duck confit, ham – cured or grilled with shallots – foie gras, leg of lamb (gigot), best accompanied by light reds of the region. Busy and animated at lunchtime, relaxed and intimate in the evening.

Phone:	01 40 22 09 09
Internet:	www.lejgo.com

Le Céladon, 15 rue Daunou, 75002 Paris. €90.
Attached to the Hôtel Westminster. One Michelin star. Charming restaurant with an elegant atmosphere created by regency style furniture and exquisite Chinese porcelaine. The food is classic (duck terrine with spiced quince, cod with Guijuelo ham, fillet of John Dory in green paprika and oil of grilled peppers, Limousin beef roasted in tarragon with a confit of potatoe and pepper). The desserts are perfect, if not particularly imaginative. The lunchtime "Retour de Marché" set menu is astonishing value for money at €51. The cellar boasts a list of classics from the main French production areas.

Phone:	01 47 03 40 42
Internet:	www.leceladon.com

Le Gavroche, 19, rue Saint-Marc 75002 Paris. €25.
Nothing to do with the famous restaurant in London, this is quite another world. True Parisian bistro food eaten cheek by jowl in a convivial atmosphere. Much appreciated as a late night eatery where a huge rib of beef can be washed down with a Beaujolais or a Côtes-du-Rhône by those who believe it is bad to eat on an empty stomach. Close to the Opera Garnier.

Phone: 01 42 96 89 70

Dell'Orto, 45, rue Saint-Georges, 75009 Paris. €40.
So popular, even locals have trouble finding a table. The food is a heady mixture of Italian flair added to French invention. Choice amongst them: salade of squid with fennel grains, potatoes in paprika with cream of anchovy with balsamic vinegar, lamb with aubergine and pistachio polenta, ravioli of pigeon with morille mushrooms. The wine list does not quite match the quality of the food and the decor is unremarkable. But who cares?

Phone: 01 48 78 40 30

FRANCE

Lescure, rue de Mandovi, 75001 Paris. €35.
Family owned since 1919, you will find yourself elbow to elbow in this tiny but highly hospitable and atmospheric restaurant, close to the Place de la Concorde. The lunchtime menu comes with wine. Game in season. Note that the restaurant is closed Saturdays and Sundays.

Phone: 01 42 60 18 91

Le Soufflé, 36 rue du Mont Thabor, 75001 Paris. €40.
Every course from starter to dessert can be a soufflé (there are a few other options) in a cosy, fun atmosphere. There is room – just – for two soccer teams, but with only 22 covers it is not the ideal location for the annual club dinner.

Phone: 01 42 60 27 19

La Maison de la Truffe, 19, place de la Madeleine, 75008 Paris. Pure luxury. Even the lunchtime €20 menu. A special truffle tasting menu is available at €65. Foie gras and caviar are other specialities. Lots of delicious goodies to take away from the shop. Parking available.

Phone: 01 42 66 10 01

Le Bar Romain, rue de Caumartin, 75009 Paris. €40. Neat little restaurant in the showbiz Olympia area. The food is predominantly French, the Roman bit refers to the paintings on the wood panels – scenes of Imperial excesses...

Phone: 01 42 68 07 89

Les Bacchantes, rue de Caumartin, 75009 Paris. €35.
Pleasantly atmospheric restaurant, simple food, good wine, warm welcome.

Phone: 01 42 65 25 35

Le Clos Bourguignon, rue de Caumartin, 75009 Paris. €25.
A local Parisian bistro – brasserie par excellence. Rapid service, usually packed. the menu du jour is good value.

Phone: 01 47 42 56 60

Les Comédiens, 9 rue Volney, 75002 Paris. €30.
Comédien in French usually means actor and this restaurant is decorated in homage to the 7th Art. Good food, nice atmosphere particularly in the evening.

Phone: | 01 42 61 78 77

Il Lotti, 9 rue de Castiglione, 75001 Paris. €55.
Smart and luxurious Italian. Ideal for tête-à-tête dining or for ladies who lunch – the excellent set menu at €22 allows savings to be made before an attack on the jewellers of the place Vendôme.

Phone: | 01 42 60 40 62

Au Pied de Cochon, 6 Rue de Coquillière, 75001 Paris. €40.

A genuine French chop house, this over-the-top brasserie is one of the most famous in Paris. Just the place to fall into in the middle of the night when you have a craving for pork chops, steaks or oysters, washed down with lashings of beer and wine. Open 365 days a year.

Phone: | 01 40 13 77 00

Le Dauphin, 167 Rue St. Honoré, 75001 Paris. €35. A smart address, fit for a prince. Gourmet menus, supervised by a chef from the Michel Guérard stable, offering delicacies from France's South West, including laperau (young rabbit) de grande mere and magret de canard.

Phone: | 01 42 60 40 11

Dilan, 13 Rue Mandar, 75002 Paris. €10. Superb value Kurdish food. Wonderful starters, offerings include stuffed aubergines, fish wih yoghurt and spiced courgettes, plus the usual barbecued suspects. Closed Saturday and Sunday lunch.

Phone: | 01 40 26 81 04

Kitty O'Shea's, 10 Rue des Capucines, 75002 Paris. €15.
This is a perfect, if idealised, re-creation of a Dublin city pub, where, as an accompaniment to Guinness, Smithwick's and Jameson, you can enjoy seafood flown in from Galway. Traditional Irish music on Sundays (see Irish Pubs).

Phone: | 01 40 15 08 08

HOTELS

(Madeleine, Opéra & Tuileries)

LUXURY

Vendôme, 1, place Vendôme, 75001 Paris. Ⓜ Tuileries.
18 rooms. 11 suites. From €370 to €690 s/d/t room only. Suites from €390 to €1210. Member of the Small Luxury Hotels of the World group. High luxury and good taste in a wonderful 18th century location.

Phone:	01 55 04 55 00
Email:	reservations@hoteldevendome.com
Internet:	www.hoteldevendome.com

Crillon, 10, place de la Concorde, 75008 Paris. Ⓜ Concorde.
103 rooms. 44 suites. From €500 to €880 s/d/t room only. Suites from €985 to €8080. The epitome of French luxury, the Crillon exudes style, taste, impeccable service. Two Michelin starred restaurant, Les Ambassadeurs, and the excellent L'Obélisque.

Phone:	01 44 71 15 00
Email:	crillon@crillon.com
Internet:	www.crillon.com

Hotel Meurice, 228 rue de Rivoli, 75001 Paris. Ⓜ Tuileries. 121 rooms €294 (lowest rate deal) to €6270. Empire and Napoleon scream out from this magnificently gilded peacock of a hotel. Queen Victoria, Tchaikovsky and Ginger Rogers were visitors. For 200 years it has been a corner of Angleterre in a foreign land, attracting the writers Thackeray and Kipling, not least because of its Anglophonic disposition. If you want to do some celebrity spotting, book in or simply take a coffee in the Jardin d'Hiver, or aperitifs in the Fontainebleu Bar.

Phone:	01 44 58 10 10
Internet:	www.lemeurice.com

Hôtel Scribe, 1, rue Scribe, 75009 Paris. Ⓜ Opéra. 206 rooms, from €390 to €500 d/t. Suites from €565 to €1300. A by-word for comfort and discretion, Parisian art-de-vivre and savoir-faire. Rooms decorated and furnished in Louis-Philippe style while being extremely well equipped for the modern international traveller.

Phone:	01 44 71 24 24
Email:	HO663@accor-hotels.com
Internet:	www.sofitel.com

Intercontinental – Le Grand Hôtel, 2, rue Scribe, 75009 Paris. Ⓜ Opéra. 478 bedrooms. 72 suites. From €610 to €680 d/t. Suites from €710 to €3000. This famous hotel's Second Empire luxury and style has recently been fully restored. Enjoys an excellent reputation in an area where luxury accommodation abounds. The world famous Café de la Paix is part of the complex.

Phone:	01 40 07 32 32
Email:	legrand@ichotelsgroup.com
Internet:	www.paris.intercontinental.com

Hôtel Le Péra, 17, rue Caumartin, 75009 Paris. Ⓜ Opéra. 47 rooms, from €225 to €285 s/d/t. Oasis of comfort and calm. Warm, friendly welcome, tastefully decorated rooms. An attractive glass ceilinged bar with a wood fire serves excellent cocktails. Steps away from the Opéra Garnier and the retail therapy of the Grands Boulevards.

Phone:	01 53 43 54 00
Email:	hotellepera@wanadoo.fr
Internet:	www.hotellepera.com

Hôtel Westminster, 13, rue de la Paix, 75002 Paris.
Ⓜ Opéra. 80 rooms, from €420 to €570 d/t.

Named in 1846 after its best client, the Duke of Westminster. Sumptuously decorated. The Duke's Bar is redolent of a London gentleman's club and the Céladon restaurant (one Michelin Star – see entry) has an excellent reputation.

Phone:	01 42 61 57 46
Email:	resa.westminster@warwickhotels.com
Internet:	www.hotelwestminster.com

The Ritz, 15, place Vendôme, 75001 Paris.
Ⓜ Tuileries. 107 rooms. 55 suites. From €610 to €770 s/t room only. Suites from €1180 to €8500. Extra bed €100 per night.

Ernest Hemingway did some unwitting self-PR by writing: "When I dream of the afterlife in heaven, the action always takes place in the Ritz Hotel, Paris." He was rewarded by one of the bars being named after him, which will probably be remembered for longer than the writer himself.

Phone:	01 43 16 30 30
Email:	resa@ritzparis.com
Internet:	www.ritzparis.com

FRANCE

Hôtel Opéra-Richepanse (Best Western Premier), 14, rue du Chevalier de Georges, 75001 Paris.
Ⓜ Concorde. 35 rooms, from €230 to €350 d/t. Extra bed €50.

Recently renovated in art deco style and decorated in warm, relaxing colours. Very comfortable rooms and luxurious bathrooms.

Phone:	01 42 60 36 00
Email:	richepanseotel@wanadoo.fr
Internet:	www.richepanse.com

MODERATE

Hotel Mansard, 5, rue des Capucines, 75001 Paris. Ⓜ Métro Madeleine. 57 rooms, from €120 to €305 s/d/t. Extra bed €17.

Recent renovation includes a pictorial homage to Louis XIV's great architect Jules Hardouin-Mansart, whose works include the Château de Versailles and the Place Vendome, which is just 50m from the hotel. Friendly welcome and atmosphere.

Phone:	01 42 61 50 28
Email:	hotel.mansart@esprit-de-france.com
Internet:	www.esprit-de-france.com

Hôtel Saint-Petersbourg, 33-35 rue de Caumartin, 75009 Paris.
Ⓜ Opéra. 100 rooms, from €145 to €225 s/d/t. Extra bed €43. Buffet breakfast.

Spacious and comfortable bedrooms decorated and furnished a la Louis XVI. Similarly elegant lounge, while Le Relais restaurant serves refined French cooking.

Phone:	01 42 66 60 38
Email:	hotel.st-petersbourg@wanadoo.fr
Internet:	www.hotel-st-petersbourg.com

Hotel Brighton, 218 rue de Rivoli, 75001 Paris.
Ⓜ Tuileries. 60 rooms, from €110 s/d/t to €230 suite.

Opposite the Tuilerie Gardens on the Rue de Rivoli, this is spectacular value. Its junior suites command views of the Louvre, the gardens, the Pantheon and the Eiffel Tower. Ideal base for exploring the Latin Quarter, the Opera area and the great shopping streets.

Phone:	01 42 60 41 78
Internet:	www.esprit-de-france.com

Church square: The spectacular Eglise St Marie Madeleine dominates its quarter of Paris

Libertel-Caumartin, 27, rue de Caumartin, 75009 Paris. Ⓜ Opéra. 40 rooms, from €151 to €190 s/d/t. The decor is light wood panelling, 1930's club armchairs in the foyer set the tone for the rest of the hotel. Paintings, sculptures and lithographs litter this elegant establishment.

Phone:	01 47 42 95 95
Email:	H2811@accor-hotels.com
Internet:	www.libertel-hotels.com

FRANCE

Hotel Madeleine Plaza, 33, place de la Madeleine, 75008 Paris. Ⓜ Madeleine. 52 rooms, from €180 to €275 s/d/t. Stylish and comfortable establishment in a great location behind the church of the Madeleine. Within easy striking distance of the lively Opera area to one side, straight ahead to the Concorde and the Champs-Elysées with the gastronomic delights of the Madeleine outside the door.

Phone:	01 43 12 92 60
Email:	mp@hotels-emeraude.com
Internet:	www.hotels-emeraude.com

Hôtel des Capucines, 6, rue Godot-de-Mauroy, 75009 Paris. Ⓜ Madeleine. 45 rooms, from €119 to €205 s/d/t room only. Rooms for three or four available. All are individually furnished. Art deco fittings decorate the public rooms. Quiet hotel in a side street close to the shopping areas of the Grands-Boulevards, the Opera, and the showbiz streets around the Olympia theatre.

Phone:	01 47 42 25 05
Email:	infos@hotelcapucinesparis.com
Internet:	www.hotelcapucinesparis.com

BUDGET

Hotel Volney Opéra, 11, rue Volney, 75002 Paris. Ⓜ Opéra. 31 rooms. €90 s , €105 d/t. Comfortable, well-decorated rooms in this quiet street in a busy, bustling quarter. Good value accommodation, save your money for the shopping (department stores, jewellers) nearby.

Phone:	01 42 61 85 24

Hôtel de l'Athénée, 19, rue Caumartin, 75009 Paris. Ⓜ Opéra. 20 rooms, from €70 s/d/t, rack €117. Extra bed €17. The only two-star hotel in this area. Offers reasonable comfort in an area renowned for the variety of its attractions.

Phone:	01 47 42 85 26
Email:	contact@hotel-athenee.com
Internet:	www.hotel-athenee.com

ST GERMAIN DES PRÉS, LUXEMBOURG & MONTPARNASSE

BARS

PARISIAN BISTRO-CAFÉ

Le Comptoir des Canettes (aka Chez Georges), rue des Canettes, 75006 Paris.
Louche drinking den. Place to drink, listen to jazz, play chess, drink and talk in May '68 ambience. Wonderfully hospitable, scruffy, eccentric.

Birdland Café, 8, rue Guisarde, 75006 Paris.
Jazz and rugby are the themes here in this convivial drinking den. Good place to watch a big game with the advantage of a place at the bar before the crowds arrive from the Stade-de-France. Happy hour, but not at the weekend.

Phone: | 01 43 26 97 59

FRANCE

BRASSERIE

Les Deux Magots, 6, place St-Germain-des-Prés, 75006 Paris.
Along with its neighbour "Le Café Flore", one of the landmarks of this quarter. Wonderful, if expensive, Parisian brasserie. Sit on the terrace and observe fellow drinkers or the boulevardiers of St-Germain. Unfortunately a hedge blocks the view of the church. The cream of street entertainers can often be enjoyed here.

Phone: | 01 45 48 55 25

TERRACE CAFÉ

Le Café de Flore, 172, boulevard St-Germain, 75006 Paris.

Next door to "Les Deux Magots" this great Parisian café was the haunt of 'l'élite intellectuelle'. Gide, Sartre, de Beauvoir, Camus, all drank here and it still holds an annual Literary award.

Le Bar du Marché, rue de Buci, 75006 Paris.
Lively, convivial bar with large terrace overlooking the daily street market. Excellent launch-pad for an evening in St-Germain-des-Prés or the Latin quarter. Or you could end the evening here, it is always lively.

Phone: | 01 45 48 55 26

COCKTAILS

La Rhumerie, boulevard St-Germain, 75006 Paris.

Smart bar with great terrace area looking out on the fauna of St-Germain-des-Prés. As the name suggests, they specialise in rum based cocktails and serve spiky Créole snacks to accompany if you wish. Try the Hemingway Special – it makes you wonder why he ever needed a shotgun.

BRITISH – IRISH – MICRO

O'Neill's, rue des Canettes, 75006 Paris

Beers brewed on the premises. Pub-style establishment serving robust grub.

The Frog and Princess, 9, rue Princesse, 75006 Paris.

Pub and micro-brewery with a restaurant serving okay pub-grub. Happy hour. Pints. Cocktails. "Jazzy Brunch" on Saturday before settling in to watch the game on the giant screen.

Phone: | 01 40 51 77 38

Coolin, 15, rue Clément, 75006 Paris.

Irish pub selling generous Irish pub-grub. Sports mad bar. Although home to the Paris Celts GAA teams, rugby is not only tolerated but encouraged. Giant screen, good atmosphere on match days. Happy hour and Sunday brunch. Good sized terrace. Regular live music.

Phone: | 01 44 07 00 92

Corcorans, 28, rue St-André-des-Arts, 75006 Paris.

Irish pub. Serving Irish food – fish and chips, beef in Guinness – all day at remarkably low prices. Happy Hour except weekends. Live music and DJs. Screens for sports fans.

Phone: | 01 40 46 97 46

Le Galway, 13, quai des Grands-Augustins, 75006 Paris.

Long established Irish pub, close to Notre-Dame, next to the Seine. They advertise themselves thus "Tunes and Talk – No TV". Pints. Simple lunches. Open until 5am Friday and Saturday.

Phone: | 01 43 29 64 50

BEER BAR

La Pinte, carrefour de l'Odéon, 75006 Paris. Specialist beer bar. Large selection of draught and bottled beers. Rather expensive, so more a place for the langourous connoisseur than the swiller of pints. Cold meats and cheese platters served.

Au Chai de l'Abbaye, Rue de Buci, 75006 Paris. Beer bar also serving sound brasserie food. Pleasant decor - light oak wood panels and mirrors. Ideal watering-hole during a shopping expedition, or good for a beer or two before heading to a restaurant.

LATE BAR – NIGHT SPOT

Eden Park, rue Princesse, 75006 Paris.

Bar-club created by the Eden Park team lead by former French international Frank Mesnel, who created the eponymous clothing line. Good bar, cellar bar, music, and gets pretty packed on match nights. Definitely for the younger crowd.

Le pouce au crime. Rue Guisarde. 75006 Paris.

A late-night haunt of French international rugby stars in the heart of St-Germain-des-Prés', aka "Vallée de la Soif" (valley of thirst).

Le Pub St-Germain, 17, rue de l'Ancienne-Comédie, 75006 Paris.

Trendy 24/24 bar with food served from noon till 5am. Happy hour. Cocktails. Large selection of whiskies.

Phone: | 01 56 81 13 13

The Mazet, 61 rue St-André-des-Arts, 75006, Paris.

Self-styled "Old English Pub." Happy Hour Monday to Friday. Late closing (5am) weekends. Loud and lively spot with live music every night. And TV screens for live sports.

Phone: | 01 43 25 57 50

CLUBS: DANCING

La Mezzanine de l'Alcazar, 62 rue Mazarine, 75006 Paris. (DJ)
(St-Germain-des-Prés) Wagg, 62 rue Mazarine, 75006 Paris. (Very cool)
Bateau Concorde Atlantique, on river opposite 25, quai Anatole-France, 75007 Paris. (Mainstream but not midstream - it's moored)
La Scala, 188bis, rue de Rivoli, 75001 Paris.
Le Cab, 2, place du Palais-Royal, 75002, Paris.
Rex Club, 5 boulevard Bonne Nouvelle, 75002 Paris. (House - Techno)

RESTAURANTS

(St Germain des Prés, Luxembourg & Montparnasse)

"14 L'Atelier de Joël Robuchon", 5, rue Montalambert, 75007 Paris. €85.
This is contemporary chic writ large. On entering, settle at a Japanese style bar, take an apéritif and ponder the menu. Very high quality ingredients sometimes presented rather than cooked, sometimes prepared under Mediterreanean influence with precise technique. Always exciting. There is an exceptionally good wine list, with many good examples available by the glass. The service from a young staff is elegant and precise. The menu "découverte" at €98 is sensational.

Phone:	01 42 22 56 56
Internet:	www.hoel-pont-royal.com

FRANCE

Au Bon Saint-Pourçain, rue Servandoni, 75006 Paris. €42.
A restaurant set in a cobbled side street near the Luxembourg gardens and the Senate. Fittingly, everything is done at senatorial pace. If you want the epitome of the expression "leisurely meal," this is it. This is fine cuisine bourgeoise served with courtesy and charm. Old fashioned values in a superb setting. Excellent value for money. Very good cellar.

Phone: 01 43 54 93 63

André Allard, rue St-André-des-Arts, rue de l' Epéron, 75006 Paris. €50.
Wonderful example of great French bistro cooking. The atmosphere is true Parisian, helped by the zinc bar, the busy white-aproned waiters and the large presence of enthusiastic locals. The walls are decorated with scenes of life in Burgundy, and the food is dominated by specialities of that region: boeuf bourguignon, challans duck with olives, Burgundy snails, roast Bresse chicken with sauteed cepes. Very good value set menus at €24 - €34.

Phone: 01 43 26 48 23

Joséphine – Chez Dumonet, 117 rue du Cherche-Midi, 75006 Paris. €60.
Glorious epitome of rich, bourgeois cooking. A restaurant where the enjoyment of food is not accompanied by any sense of guilt: you are expected to wallow in the experience, not count the calories. The portions are so large that most dishes are offered in a half-size option. The cooking is enhanced with luxury ingredients (in season, truffles are often in evidence), wild duck, top-notch andouillette, tenderest tournedos, with goose fat sauteed potatoes – rarely so good outside the south-west. The very good wine list is unashamedly obvious.

Phone: 01 45 48 52 40

La Muraille de Jade, 5, rue de l'Ancienne-Comédie, 75006 Paris. €30.
A happy mix of Chinese, Vietnamese and Thai cooking in a setting which brings together the ancient features of this listed building with Oriental art. This place is popular with the locals (who can also indulge in a little star-spotting), the food

is unfailingly pleasing; bo bun, saigon prawn pancake, or Thai chicken curry, the options are large and varied. The service is courteous and efficient, the wine list reasonable.

Phone: | 01 46 33 63 18

Le Balzar, 49 Rue des Ecoles, 75005 Paris. €30.
Founded in 1920, this brasserie has been a favourite with generations of teachers and students from the Sorbonne. The intellectual atmosphere is perfect Latin Quarter left-bank chic, though cynics might suggest that Pseud's Corner was born here.

Phone: | 01 43 54 13 67

Les Deux Magots, 6 Place St Germain des Prés, 75006 Paris. €15.
Simple café fare, but famous links to the lives and excesses of the literary gang led in the 1940s and '50s by Jean-Paul Sartre and Simone de Beauvoir. Looked down upon by present-day literary types, who prefer to maintain their slates at the neighbouring Le Flore.

Phone: | 01 45 48 55 25

La Closerie des Lilas, 1571 Boulevard du Montparnasse, 75006 Paris. €35.
This upmarket brasserie has been a legend in other people's lunchtimes for as long as anyone can remember. The generally high prices did not put off Verlaine, Mallarmé, Modigliani, Léger, Strindberg, Hemingway – or even Lenin. Food with a dash of history thrown in for free.

Phone: | 01 40 51 34 50

Lipp, 151 Boulevard St-Germanine, 75006 Paris. €40.
A temple to Paris's literary and political Establishment and a Left Bank must. The food is good, but that's not the point: One goes to Lipp to see and be seen. Once, you couldn't book and it was left to the discretion of the head waiter as to who got a table and who did not. Now, a phone call is de rigueur.

Phone: | 01 45 48 53 91

FRANCE

"Au 35", 35, rue Jacob, 75006 Paris. €30.
Smart, cosy and reasonable restaurant offering classic French dishes.

Phone: | 01 42 60 23 24

Le Mâchon d'Henri, 8 rue Guisarde, 75006 Paris, €40.
Lyonnais/Beaujolais specialities served with Beaujolais wines. The "mâchon" being the traditional silk workers' meal in Lyon. Small, jolly, good food.

Le Bistro d'Henri, 16, rue Princesse, 75006 Paris. €40.
Brother to Henri's « Mâchon » around the corner. Generous bistro food in small, intimate room.

Phone: | 01 46 33 51 12

Le Séraphin, 5, rue Mabillon, 75006 Paris. €25.
Bar–Restaurant. Pleasant student atmosphere. Young, friendly and attentive staff. Simple food at reasonable prices. Pleasant watering hole in the heart of St-Germain-des-Prés.

Phone: | 01 56 24 41 00

La Grille St-Germain, 1 rue Guisarde, 75006 Paris. €35.
Old fashioned bistro food in atmospheric "black and white cinema" decor.

Phone: | 01 43 54 16 87

Institute de France: 17th Century splendour in the St Germain quarter

Chez Maître Paul, 12 rue Monsieur le Prince, 75006 Paris. €45.
Quintessential Paris. Simple, pleasant décor. Accomplished French cooking, courteous if distant service. Cosmopolitan French wine list.

Phone:	01 43 54 74 59

Santa Lucia, 22 rue des Canettes, 75006 Paris. €30.
Lively, convivial Italian restaurant whose pizzas are generous and tasty. A good starting point for a long evening in this happening corner of a vibrant quarter.

Phone:	01 43 26 42 68

La Méditerranée, 2 place de l'Odéon, 75006 Paris. €45.
Specialist, quality fish restaurant which nevertheless serves a few meat dishes. Pleasant, light décor.

Phone:	01 43 26 02 30

L'Arbuci, 25 rue de Buci, 75006 Paris. €40.
Very chic, modern restaurant specialising in oysters, seafood platters and fish. Also a jazz club.

Phone:	01 44 32 16 00
Internet:	www.arbuci.com

FRANCE

HOTELS

(St Germain des Prés, Luxembourg & Montparnasse)

LUXURY

Hôtel Pont Royal, 7, rue de Montalembert, 75007 Paris.
Ⓜ Rue du Bac. 65 rooms, rack rates from €380 to €430 d/t.
Literary hotel - Gide, Degas, Apollinaire, Malraux, Scott and Zelda Fitzgerald stayed here. Comfortable, padded luxury. Signature bar, midday till midnight, library. Gastronomic L'Atelier de Joel Robuchon restaurant is attached.

Phone:	01 42 84 70 02
Email:	hpr@hotel-pont-royal.com
Internet:	www.hotel-pont-royal.com

Lutetia, 45 boulevard Raspail, 75006 Paris.
Ⓜ Sevres Babylone. 206 rooms, from €480 s/d/t.
Old chic. Built during the belle epoque in 1910, the Lutetia is well run, helpful and a magnet for the Rive Gauche's shakers. Painters and writers like Picasso, Matisse and Gide were regulars, and President de Gaulle spent his honeymoon here. Most of the rooms have a commanding view of the Eiffel Tower.

Phone:	01 49 54 46 46
Email:	lutetia-paris@lutetia-paris.com
Internet:	www.lutetia-paris.com

Hôtel Luxembourg Parc, 42, rue de Vaugirard, 75006 Paris.
Ⓜ Saint-Sulpice. 23 rooms,from €200 to €475 s/d/t.
Individually decorated rooms in Louis XV, Louis XVI and Napoleon III styles. Close to the senate and the Luxembourg gardens. A little gem.

Phone:	01 53 10 36 50
Email:	booking@hotelluxparc.com
Internet:	www.hotelluxparc.com

Relais Saint-Germain, 9, carrefour de l'Odéon, 75006 Paris.
Ⓜ Odéon. 22 rooms, from €210 to €360 s/d/t.
Classically decorated and furnished (antiques, classic fabrics, original beams) in the centre of the historic St-Germain-des-Prés and Odéon areas. "Le Comptoir du Relais", attached to the hotel, is an archetypal Parisian intellectuals' bistro.

Phone:	01 43 29 12 05
Email:	hotelrsg@wanadoo.fr
Internet:	www.hotelrsg.com

MODERATE

Libertel Bellechasse, 8, rue Bellechasse, 75007 Paris.
Ⓜ Solférino, RER C Musée d'Orsay. 41 rooms, from €150 to €190 s/d/t.
Contact them directly for promotional offers. Comfortable if formulaic hotel in the Mercure-Accor style. Good location for culture vultures (on the doorstep of the Musée d'Orsay and a pleasant stroll accross the Seine to the Tuileries and the Louvre) but the immediate locality may be a little quiet for the party animal.

Phone:	01 45 50 22 31
Email:	h2762@accor.com
Internet:	www.libertel-hotels.com

Duc de Saint-Simon, 14 rue St-Simon, 75007 Paris.
Ⓜ Rue du Bac. 34 rooms, from €250 s/d/t.
Beautiful and ever so slightly faded elegance. One of the city's most charming spots with impeccable service and crammed full of fine antiques. Despite being in the heart of one of Paris's most lively locations, it is an oasis of calm, tucked into a tiny medieval backstreet. Little wonder that it is Lauren Bacall's favourite Parisian hotel (ask politely and you could have her bed).

Phone:	01 44 39 20 20
Email:	duc.de.saint.simon@wanadoo.fr
Internet:	www.hotelducdesaintsimon.com

Hôtel d'Angleterre, 44, rue Jacob, 75006 Paris.
Ⓜ St-Germain-des-Prés. 24 rooms. 3 suites. From €135 to €260 s/d/t. Suite €290 rack. Extra bed €45. Breakfast included.
So called because this building once housed the British Embassy, it is appropriately furnished. A charming, higgledy-piggledy affair offering huge charm for good value. The rue Jacob, running parallel with the Boulevard St-Germain, offers easy exploration of galleries great and small, antique dealers, fashion creators, restaurants and cafés.

Phone:	01 42 60 34 72
Email:	reservation@hotel-dangleterre.com
Internet:	www.hotel-dangleterre.com

Hôtel du Danube, 58, rue Jacob, 75006 Paris.
Ⓜ St-Germain-des-Prés. 35 rooms. 5 apartments.
From €114 to €164 d/t room only. Apartments €230. Extra bed €50.
Dating from the Napoleon III era, this is a comfortable estalishment. Rooms are individually decorated in Chinese, colonial or Victorian style. Stroll to the centre of St-Germain, across the river to the Louvre, or down the street to the musée d'Orsay.

Phone:	01 42 60 34 70
Email:	info@hoteldanuble.fr
Internet:	www.hoteldanube.fr

Hôtel L'Académie, 32, rue des Saints-Pères, 75006 Paris.
Ⓜ St-Germain-des-Prés. 26 rooms, from €199 to €229 d/t room only. Suites from €299 to €458.
Restored former residence of the Duc de Rohan, beams and stonework are features. The surrounding area is full of small galleries and antique dealers and the Musée d'Orsay is only a short stroll away, while the Louvre is just across the river.

Phone:	01 45 49 80 00
Email:	academiehotel@aol.com
Internet:	www.academiehotel.com

Hôtel St-Germain-des-Prés, 36, rue Bonaparte, 75006 Paris.
Ⓜ St-Germain-des-Prés. 30 rooms, from €180 to €255 d/t. Extra bed €15.
Breakfast included. Luxurious hotel in an 18th century building hard by the Eglise St-Germain, after which the quarter is named, and also close to the renowned Café des Deux Magots and the Café du Flore. Each room is individually decorated. Residents' bar and salon. Wintergarden.

Phone:	01 43 26 00 19
Email:	Hotel-Saint-Germain-des-Pres@wanadoo.fr
Internet:	www.hotel-saint-germain-des-pres.com

Hôtel La Perle, 14, rue des Canettes, 75006 Paris.
Ⓜ Mabillon. 38 rooms, from €160 to €230 s/d/t room only.
Renovated 17th century building in the epicentre of action-packed St-Germain-des-Prés becomes a magnet on a big match day. Great food, bars and clubs within a 100m radius of this hotel.

Phone:	01 43 29 10 10
Email:	booking@hotellaperle.com
Internet:	www.hotellaperle.com

Hôtel Jardin de l'Odéon, 7, rue Casimir-Delavigne, 75006 Paris.
Ⓜ Odéon. 41 rooms. From €80 to €300 s/d/t.
Recently renovated (spring 2005). This is a charming, friendly hotel in a perfect location for the Luxembourg gardens, Latin quarter, St-Germain-des-Prés and the Odéon.

Phone:	01 53 10 28 50
Email:	hotel@jardindelodeon.com
Internet:	www.jardindelodeon.com

Artus Hôtel St-Germain-des-Prés, 34, rue de Buci, 75006 Paris.
Ⓜ Odéon. 27 rooms, from €190 to €235 d/t.
Recently renovated hotel in African art theme. Rue de Buci is a hustle-bustle street – bars, restaurants, food outlets and a daily street market. Cosmopolitan atmosphere where St-Germain meets and greets the world.

Phone:	01 43 29 07 20
Email:	info@artushotel.com
Internet:	www.artushotel.com

BUDGET

Hôtel Michelet Odéon, 6, place de l'Odéon, 75006 Paris.
Ⓜ Odéon. 40 rooms, from €80 s/d/t. Rack €115, €135 tpl, €150 qd. Suites €170.
Reasonably priced, comfortable spot tucked into a corner of the lovely place de l'Odéon. Calm of the Luxembourg gardens behind you, fleshpots of the Odéon and St-Germain-des-Prés to the fore.

Phone:	01 53 10 05 60
Email:	hotel@micheletodeon.com
Internet:	www.hotelmicheletodeon.com

Hôtel Récamier, 3, bis place Saint-Sulpice, 75006 Paris.
Ⓜ Saint-Sulpice. 40 rooms, from €117 to €144 s/d/t.
Small, reasonably priced and comfortable hotel tucked into a corner of the place Saint-Sulpice. Excellent position for the restaurants and bars of St-Germain-des-Prés and the Latin Quarter.

Phone:	01 43 26 04 89

ST MICHEL & PANTHÉON

BARS

BRITISH – IRISH PUBS

L'Irlandais, place de la Contrescarpe, 75005 Paris.
This Irish style pub has been going for years. TV for sports but probably better for post-match drinking, it attracts lots of French rugby people. Late closing (2am).

The Fifth Bar, 62 rue Mouffetard, 75005 Paris
Scruffy Irish bar runs a Happy Hour. All the best sport on TV (including the Irish GAA). This is a good place for the livelier crowd because there is so much going on nearby. Regular live music.

Connolly's Corner, rue de Mirbel / rue des Patriarches, 75005 Paris
Irish pub. Happy Hour and regular live Irish music. A feature is a collection of ties. This is an unofficial clubhouse of the SCUF rugby club – one of Paris' oldest teams whose fame resides in the fact that a former player and president presented the FFR with a shield to be presented to the winner of the French rugby championship. The "Bouclier de Brennus" is still presented today. After a few pints go the whole hog and finish your evening in Paris at the Indian restaurant up the street.

The Long Hop, 25-27 rue Frédéric Sauton, 75005 Paris.
Pub on three floors. DJ weekends. Young clientele. A real "party, party" pub; pints, cocktails, and DJ's at weekends. With Sports on TV screens this is a good spot for the ticketless and later for the post-match party.

Phone:	01 43 29 40 54

The Bombadier, 2, place du Panthéon, 75005 Paris.
English pub, serving, and this must be highlighted, Real Ale. Robust pub grub lunches from 12 till 4. Happy Hour 4-9. Try the cocktails. Live TV sports coverage makes this a home from home, especially for the ticketless on match day.

Phone:	01 43 54 79 22

Pub St Hilaire, rue des Carmes /rue Valette, 75005 Paris
Good spot for the those without tickets with full TV sports coverage. For the competitive there is pool, darts, chess and board games.

LATE BAR – NIGHT SPOT

The Shebeen, rue du Pot de Fer, 75005 Paris
Irish "clandestine" bar. In the heart of the lively, cosmopolitan and bohemian, Mouffetard – Contrescarpe area. Late closing (5am) offering DJ music in variety of styles.

Tantra Lounge, rue Mouffetard, 75005 Paris
Lots of worn wood and leather create a slightly louche ambience. Early doors happy hour is enjoyable for pints and cocktails.

PARISIAN BISTRO

Les Arts, place de la Contrescarpe, 75005 Paris
Very typical, Parisian « bistro de quartier ». Heavy with smoke, pinball, cheap beer and pastis at the bar accompanied by locals' loud opinions on Paris and politics. Great fun if you speak French but still very friendly if you don't.

La Méthode, rue Descartes, 75005 Paris

Restaurant and bar. Cheap, simple food lunch and dinner. They also do cocktails. There is a small terrace looking out onto the rue Descartes and the gates of the Ecole Polytechnique.

TERRACE CAFÉ

Cafe society: St Michel is famous for its street cafes, many with links to famous characters from literature and history.

Café Delmas, place de la Contrescarpe, 75005 Paris.

Dark wood panelling inside and with a glass frontage, this is a smart café. No beer swilling joint this. Relax on the large terrace. Be cool. Be seen.

Le Départ, place St-Michel, 75005 Paris.

On a corner next to the hectic RER / metro station at St-Michel, close to Notre-Dame, large terrace, all the ingredients are here for a comfortable spot of people-watching.

RESTAURANTS

St Michel & Panthéon

La Tour d'Argent, 15 quai de la Tournelle, 75005 Paris. €180.

A Parisian institution since the 16th century, La Tour d'Argent is said to be the most famous restaurant in the world. It is also said to be in decline after the loss of its third Michelin star a few years ago. The slide has been halted and though the great signature dishes (scrambled eggs with truffles and the canard au sang) remain, the menu has been adapted to modern tastes: sea bass with caviar and artichoke, veal sweetbreads with girolle mushroom. If possible, reserve close to the bay windows which allow wonderful views over the Seine and Nôtre-Dame. The building houses a museum to gastronomy and the cellar has no less than 500,000 bottles, many reasonably priced. There is an excellent value lunch menu. Reservation essential.

Phone:	01 43 54 23 31
Internet:	www.latourdargent.com

La Truffière, 4 rue Blainville, 75005 Paris. €90.

As the name suggests, the star of the show is the truffle. You can select foie gras with truffle, a duck parmentier with truffle, veal quasi with truffle, and many more. But don't worry, there are truffleless options (often from south-west France) which receive as much care and attention from chef Jean-Christophe Rizet and his team. The wine list is 60 pages long, with some rare classics (the Cheval Blanc goes back in a direct line to 1947), but many are affordable. There are tasting menus at 55€ and 82€ per person, with a guided selection of wines at €80. This is a restaurant which exudes the qualities of luxurious eating and drinking, so the set lunch menu for 19€ seems ridiculous, as if the figures should be reversed – but they are indeed correct.

Phone:	01 46 33 29 82
Internet:	www.latruffiere.com

Le Pré Verre, 8, rue Thénard, 75005 Paris. € 30.
Now, if you want a really, really good meal at absolute rock bottom prices, try and get into this young restaurant in quiet rue Thénard close to the Sorbonne. The decor is light and modern, the food is prepared with easy skill; spiced suckling pig, praline mousse with grilled sesame seeds. The wine list is a masterpiece of cleverly researched bottles offering high quality for low price. The restaurant has been a thoroughly deserved overnight success.

Phone	01 43 54 59 47

Mavrommatis, 42, rue Daubenton, 75005 Paris. €45.
Bright, airy, restaurant offering high quality Greek cuisine in a quiet corner of the Latin quarter at the bottom of the rue Mouffetard, a million miles from the overgrown kebab houses of the rue de la Huchette and the rue Saint-Sévérin. Simple but perfect moussaka, a wonderful caviar of aubergine, stuffed calamares in a shellfish jus, baked apples in filo pastry. The choices are extensive - pick and mix is a good option, the service is efficient and affable and the wine list interesting. Lovely terrace in the summer. They say Turkish is the new Greek, but Mavrommatis strikes a mighty blow for hellenic cuisine.

Phone:	01 43 31 17 17

Le Cosi, 9, rue Cujas, 75005 Paris. €40.
Tucked away in a small side street between the Panthéon and the Sorbonne, this is a warm and welcoming little Corsican restaurant. The proprietors are from the Ile-de-Beauté and the menu abounds with the products and influences of the island. The charcuterie is excellent and the famous Corsican cheese brocciu features with cannelloni and in an astonishing cheesecake. Other traditional dishes include a fine Corsican soup, a veal and olive casserole (stuffatu), cabri à l'istrettu (kid in a stew of tomato, olive, capers, garlic and white wine). The wine list is again strongly Corsican but none the worse for this.

Phone:	01 43 29 20 20

L'Atelier de Maître Albert, 1, rue Maître Albert, 75005 Paris. €50.
A restaurant strongly influenced by 3 starred Michelin chef Guy Savoy; strong on service, friendly and attentive, and very high quality ingredients, skilfully prepared. The centrepiece is an elaborate roasting spit on which free-range fowl, duck, beef and fish (monkfish) are skewered before your very eyes. There is an excellent choice of desserts and the generally reasonable priced wine list has been intelligently assembled for the food. The set lunch menus at €23 and €25 represent remarkable value for money.

Phone:	01 56 81 30 01
Internet:	www.guysavoy.com

La Table Corse, 8 rue Tournefort, 75005 Paris. €45.
Corsican and Mediterreanean. Local produce. Small, intimate restaurant. Chunky country furniture. Three courses à la carte €40.

Phone:	01 43 31 15 00

Le Volcan, 10 rue Thouin, 75005 Paris. €22.
Opposite the Mayflower pub. Reasonable meals at reasonable prices. Traditional French cooking, with some Greek classics added to the mix.

Phone:	01 46 33 38 33

Bistro des Cygales, 12, rue Thouin, 75005 Paris. €28.
Mediterreanean and Provençal specialities served without fuss in a proper French manner. Small, cosy.

Phone:	01 40 46 03 76

Auberge le Pot de Terre, 22 Rue Pot de Fer, 75005 Paris. €20.
The restaurant, part of an ancient religious foundation, dates back to 1539. Its heart-warming menu features such classics as cassoulet et moules à la crème, souple a l'oignon gratinee and carré d'agneau, with an excellent tarte aux pommes to follow.

Phone:	01 43 31 15 51

La Rôtisserie du Beaujolais, 19, quai Tournelle, 75005 Paris. €40.
Annexe to La Tour d'Argent, home base of the great Claude Terrail. Specialities of Lyons and as the name suggests, fowl and meats roasted on the spit.

Phone:	01 43 54 17 47

Les Bugnes, 11, rue du Pôt de Fer, 75005 Paris. €30.
Small, wood-panelled restaurant, perfect for a winter's evening, offering Basque – Landaise cooking.

Phone:	01 43 31 80 82

Gaudeamus, 47, rue de la Montagne Ste-Geneviève, 75005 Paris. €20.
Cheap but nourishing food for the student budget. The double-fronted premises, with token tables on the slanted pavement, stages exhibitions of art and photography.

Phone:	01 40 46 93 40

Le Berthoud, 1 rue Valette, 75005 Paris. 01 43 54 38 81. €27.
Small, neat bistro, tucked away on a quiet Latin Quarter corner. Pleasant food. Good value.

Le Bar à Huitres, 33, rue St-Jacques, 75005 Paris. €45.
Oysters. Seafood platters. Fish. Pleasant Parisian brasserie designed by the celebrated Jacques Garcia. Open 1am.

Phone:	01 44 07 27 37

HOTELS

St Michel & Panthéon

MODERATE

Hôtel Sully – St Germain, 31 rue des Ecoles, 75005 Paris.
Ⓜ Maubert Mutualité. 61 rooms. from €150 to €220 s/d/t.
One of three of the Sequana group of hotels (Sequana is the Latin root of "Seine") on the rue des Ecoles a street which divides the Latin quarter in two, north from south. Each hotel provides a high level of comfort and a good base from which to explore this historic part of Paris, its intellectual centre. The Hôtel Sully's theme is the middle ages. Suits of armour, coats of arms adorn the lobby.

Phone:	01 43 26 56 02
Email:	sully@sequanahotels.com
Internet:	www.sequanahotels.com

Hôtel Moderne – St Germain, 33 rue des Ecoles, 75005 Paris.
Ⓜ Maubert Mutualité. 45 rooms, from €150 to €220 s/d/t.
The second of the Sequana hotels on the rue des Ecoles. A feature is the trompe l'oeil image of the Luxembourg gardens on the wall of the lounge. The real thing is only a few minutes walk away.

Phone:	01 43 54 37 78
Email:	moderne@sequanahotels.com
Internet:	www.sequanahotels.com

Hôtel California – St Germain, 32, rue des Ecoles, 75005 Paris.
Ⓜ Maubert Mutualité. 44 rooms, from €150 to €220 s/d/t.
The third Sequana hotel features a pleasant collection of antiques and a conservatory giving onto a pleasant courtyard.

Phone:	01 46 34 12 90
Email:	california@sequanahotels.com
Internet:	www.sequanahotels.com

Hôtel du Panthéon, 19, place du Panthéon, 75005 Paris.
Ⓜ Luxembourg. RER B. 36 rooms, from €168 to €243 s/d/t, €198-€264 tpl.
Elegant hotel beautifully situated next to the Panthéon. High level of courteous service in this elegant hotel, close to the Luxembourg gardens and the other delights of the Latin quarter.

Phone:	01 43 54 32 95
Email:	hotel.pantheon@wanadoo.fr
Internet:	www.hoteldupantheon.com

Hôtel des Grands Hommes, 17, place du Panthéon, 75005 Paris.
Ⓜ Luxembourg. 31 rooms. From €168 to €243 s/d/t, €198-€264 tpl.
Sister of the Hôtel du Panthéon next door, offering similar high level of comfort and service. The superior rooms look over the Pantheon where lie the remains of the great men of France (and one great woman – no, not Mme Spanghero - the Polish scientist, Marie Curie). Standard rooms look onto the courtyard.

Phone:	01 46 34 19 60
Email:	reservation@hoteldesgrandshommes.com
Internet:	www.hoteldesgrandshommes.com

Hôtel Mercure Paris La Sorbonne, 14, rue de la Sorbonne, 75005 Paris.
Ⓜ Luxembourg. RER B. 45 rooms, rack €185 s, €200 d/t, €223 tpl, €250 suites.
Modern Accor chain-style comfort. The location is the attraction, next to the Sorbonne, close to the Luxembourg gardens, the Pantheon and the rest of the Latin quarter.

Phone:	01 56 24 34 34
Email:	H2897@accor-hotels.com
Internet:	www.mercure.com

Select Hôtel, 1, place de la Sorbonne, 75005 Paris. Ⓜ Cluny-La Sorbonne. 67 rooms, from €139 to €175 s/d/t, €179-€189 tpl, €212 duplex.
Completely renovated in a modernist style during early 2005. Very comfortable and friendly establishment, featuring an indoor garden. Superb location with easy access to the Latin quarter and across the boulevard St-Michel into St-Germain-des-Prés.

Phone:	01 46 34 14 80
Email:	info@selecthotel.fr
Internet:	www.selecthotel.fr

BUDGET

Hôtel des Grandes Ecoles, 75, rue Cardinal Lemoine, 75005 Paris.
Ⓜ Cardinal Lemoine. 51 rooms, from €105 to €130. Extra bed €20
Brilliant location in the University area of the Latin Quarter. Lovely hotel with friendly staff representing quite incredible value for money. Set in pleasant garden.

Phone:	01 43 26 79 23
Email:	hotel.grandes.ecoles@wanadoo.fr
Internet:	www.hotel-grandes-ecoles.com

Hôtel St-Jacques, 35, rue des Ecoles, 75005 Paris.
Ⓜ Maubert Mutualité. 35 rooms, from €52 to €118 s/d/t, €145 tpl.
Comfortable if slightly faded hotel close to the Sorbonne in the centre of the Latin quarter. 19th century style, murals, original staircase lend a certain charm.

Phone:	01 44 07 45 45
Email:	hotelsaintjacques@wanadoo.fr
Internet:	www.paris-hotel-stjacques.com

Hôtel du Collège de France, 7, rue Thénard, 75005 Paris.
Ⓜ Maubert Mutualité. 29 rooms, from €70 s/d/t. Rack €110.
Lovely little family run hotel in a quiet street close to the boulevards St-Germain and St-Michel. Excellent location and very good value for money.

Phone:	01 43 26 78 36
Email:	hotel.du.college.de.France@wanadoo.fr
Internet:	www.hotel-collegedefrance.com

Hôtel de la Sorbonne, 6, rue Victor Cousin, 75005 Paris.
Ⓜ Cluny-La Sorbonne. 39 rooms, from €110 to €130 d/t.
Wonderfully quirky place close to the Sorbonne. Wooden floors, exposed beams, open fire in the lounge and an equally warm welcome.

Phone:	01 43 54 58 08
Email:	reservation@hotelsorbonne.com
Internet:	www.hotelsorbonne.com

FRANCE

CHAMPS-ELYSÉES & PORTE MAILLOT

BARS

BRITISH – IRISH PUBS

The James Joyce Pub, 71, boulevard Gouvion Saint-Cyr, 75017 Paris
Very popular Irish pub. Giant screen for SkyTV sports coverage with RTE for GAA. Upstairs restaurant for pub grub lunch and dinner but snacks served all day throughout the pub. Sunday brunch. Live music and discos at the weekend. Don't expect Dublin drink prices, however. This is even dearer.

Phone:	01 44 09 70 32

Cottage Elysée (Irish pub), rue Lincoln, 75008 Paris
Just off the Champs-Elysees this bar offers pints alongside good wines and cocktails.

The Freedom, rue de Berri, 75008 Paris
English pub just off the Champs-Elysées. Pints and cocktails and happy hours. Live music every Thursday and a DJ Friday and Saturday. TV screens for sports coverage.

TERRACE CAFÉS

Fouquets, avenue des Champs-Elysées, 75008 Paris
Great people-watching spot at one of Paris's most celebrated addresses. Pricy brasserie food on ground floor. The very smart restaurant upstairs is a regular venue for showbiz parties.

Le Paris, avenue des Champs-Elysées, 75008 Paris
Smart bar with extensive terrace. Snack on simple brasserie food. Take a cocktail or a coffee while watching the world go past.

Le Deauville, avenue des Champs-Elysées, 75008 Paris
Waiters dressed as matelots attempt to recreate a seaside atmosphere. Cocktails and champagne are what these sea dogs mostly serve up.

LATE SPOTS

Budda Bar, 8, rue Boissy-d'Anglas, 75008 Paris.
Fashionable bar-bistro-night-club with hedonism presided over by an enormous statue of the Buddha.

La Cantine du Faubourg, rue du Faubourg-St-Honoré, 75008 Paris.
Chic, stylish and very trendy eatery – night spot. Young, very affluent crowd. You might spot some French soccer stars, off duty from the English Premiership (there aren't any in the French championship).

CLUBS: DANCING

Régine's, 49-51 rue de Ponthieu, 75008 Paris.
Queen, 102, avenue des Champs-Elysées, 75008 Paris.
Le Baron, 6, avenue Marceau, 75008 Paris. (Very retro)
La Suite, 40, avenue Georges V, 75008 Paris. (Fashion setters)

RESTAURANTS

Champs-Elysées & Porte Maillot

The 8th arrondissement is home to what must be the greatest concentration of top class restaurants anywhere in the world. Here is a list of the establishments which have received the highest accolades:

FRANCE

Alain Ducasse au Plaza Athénée	25 avenue Montaigne, 75008 Paris. www.alain-ducasse.com	01 53 67 65 00
Le Cinq, au George-V	31 avenue George-V, 75008 Paris www.fourseasons.com/paris	01 49 52 71 54
Ledoyen	1,avenue Dutuit, carré des Champs-Elysées, 75008 Paris	01 53 05 10 01
Taillevent	15 rue Lamennais, 75008 Paris	01 44 95 15 01
Lucas-Carton	9, place de la Madeleine, 75008 Paris. www.lucascarton.com	01 42 65 22 90
Pierre Gagnaire – Hôtel Balzac	6, rue Balzac, 75008 Paris.	01 58 36 12 50
Les Ambassadeurs au Crillon	place de la Concorde, 75008 Paris. www.crillon.com	01 44 71 16 16
Apicius	20, rue d'Artois, 75008 Paris	01 43 80 19 66
Bristol – Hôtel Bristol	112 rue du Faubourg St-Honoré, 75008 Paris. www.hotel-bristol.com	01 53 43 43 40
Lasserre	17, avenue Franklin - Roosevelt, 75008 Paris.	01 43 59 53 43
Laurent	41, avenue Gabriel, 75008 Paris.	01 42 25 00 39

Restaurant Guy Savoy, 18 rue Troyon, 75017 Paris. €260.
We had to pick one Michelin three star and chose Guy Savoy because he is a rugby fan. He has fed the All Blacks and innumerable French stars (helping some to establish themselves in the restaurant trade). In houses of similar standing one can feel as if one is entering the holy of holies, but here the atmosphere is relaxed and convivial. The service is supremely attentive yet humour abounds (Guibert, the maitre d', is a scream). The wine list contains all the classics but M. Savoy is not afraid to go off piste to unearth some real treasures. The other great restaurants above (we tested five of them) will also give you a lasting memory.

Phone:	01 43 80 40 61

Le Bristol, Hôtel Bristol, 112, rue du Faubourg-St-Honoré, 75008 Paris. €130.
Everything here combines to make a perfect gastronomic experience. The setting is exceptional – one of the most sumptuous in Paris. In winter, you are shown into a stunning oak panelled and chandeliered oval dining room; in summer, the setting is a white and gold dining room or else al fresco in the breathtaking summer garden. It is generally agreed that chef Eric Fréchon is an artist of the highest calibre, and he will not fail you. The great traditions of French cooking are maintained within hyper-modern technique and international inspiration. The many famous dishes on offer include veal sweetbreads or lobster in a bouillon of ginger and lemon grass . A signature dish – poularde cooked in a pigs bladder (for four hours at 60°C - not 59° or 61° but 60°) in a Jura vin doux jus – is served with great ceremony. Desserts too are a homage to the past – Grand-Marnier soufflé – or contemporary: an intricate interweaving of strawberry and candy-floss. A fine cellar of classics with some unexpected curiosities.

Phone:	01 53 43 43 00

Le Cap Vernet, 82 avenue Marceau, 75008 Paris. €55.
Stephane Marcuzzi, who is self-taught and passionate about his trade, used to play for the Stade-Français. His restaurant has recently undergone a complete refurbishment. The house specialises in fish and seafood. Excellent shellfish, especially oysters, are available throughout the year. Chic, impeccable service, a well constructed wine list, conviviality. An excellent place to treat yourself to a fine meal in a very smart setting – in the shadow of the Arc de Triomphe – without breaking the bank.

Phone:	01 47 20 20 40

FRANCE

La Table du Lancaster, 7 rue de Berri, 75008 Paris. €90.
Three starred chef Michel Troisgros has come to Paris from the backwaters of Roanne to inspire and supervise this young restaurant in the luxurious and discrete Hôtel Lancaster, close to the Champs-Elysées. The result was an immediate success. The menu is by theme rather than by course; the 'wit' of the tomato (small snails in a spiky sauce); the burst of lemon and citrus fruit (scallops as an incredible melba); the bite of condiments and spices (sole meuniere with dried ceps and capers); the green of fresh vegetables (voluptuously blended leek and potato with mussels in saffron). The desserts, which you order at the start of the meal, are sensational: apple charlotte with cinnamon ice-cream, cold coconut soufflé with a maple heart. The wine list is irreproachable.

Phone:	01 40 76 40 18
Internet:	www.hotel-lancaster.fr

Findi, 24, avenue George V, 75008 Paris. €30.
Just to prove that even in the 8th arrondissement you don't have to re-mortgage to live "la dolce vita", there is Findi, an elegant Italian restaurant in the heart of Paris's "golden triangle". The atmosphere is 40's decorated baroque palazzo and the food is classic Italian with a three course set menu for €30. Yes, €30. Excellent options of a dozen cold starters; salad of green asparagus with smoked salmon and poached egg, Parma ham with Buffalo Mozzarella in basil sauce. Pastas; tagliatelli with calamar and shellfish, beef ravioli in a truffle gravy. Fish; fillet of red mullet with lemon and potatoes with parsley. Meat; fillet of beef with chicory fondue, gorgonzola and walnuts. There is a selection of Italian cheeses or choose one of around ten fine desserts such as Lasagne de Fruit de Saison Lasagna of summer fruits, sorbetto alla grappa. The house wine is perfectly acceptable and some great bottles are tucked away.

Phone:	01 47 20 14 78
Internet:	www.findi.net

Chez Georges, 273 Boulevard Pereire, 75017 Paris. €40.
Good quality fish and impressive seafood platters are the order of the day here. Smart, efficient restaurant looking out over the Palais des Congrès at the Porte Maillot. A pleasant after dinner stroll on the wide pavements of the avenue de la Grande-Armée towards the Arc-de-Triomphe and the Champs-Elysées.

Phone:	01 45 74 31 00

Grand view: The Grand Palais is one of many architectural masterpieces to be found around the Champs-Elysées

FRANCE

Le Fouquet's Barriere, 99 Ave des Champes-Elysées, 75008 Paris. €65.
In the setting of his large, luxurious dining room, re-designed by Jacques Garcia, chef Jean-Yves Leuranguer offers his well-heeled, high-profile clientele a broad sweep of dishes from every corner of France. Charolais beef bearnaise in a gratin of macaroni vies on the menu with tartare césar, roast chicken, prawns and lobster. The building itself is a National Monument.

Phone:	01 47 23 50 00

Le Congrès, 80, avenue de la Grande-Armée, 75016 Paris. €40
Light, airy restaurant specialising in fish, oysters and seafood platters. Excellent value set menu available. 600m from the Arc de Triomphe.

Phone:	01 45 74 17 24

Le Ballon des Ternes, 103, avenue des Ternes, 75017 Paris. €35.
Traditional Parisian brasserie, lunch, dinner, supper. Oysters and seafood platters a speciality along with reliable French bourgeois cooking.

Phone:	01 45 74 17 98

Dragons Elysée, 11 Rue de Berri, 75008 Paris. €35.
This is the restaurant Dr No would have built for himself. Essentially a dining room inside an aquarium, the talented Asian chefs offer Thai and Chinese specialities, including dim sum and curried seafood. A la carte meals can run expensive, but there is an excellent lunchtime and weekend menu for just €13.

Phone:	01 42 89 85 10

Le Restaurant W, Hôtel Warwick, 5 rue de Berri, 75008 Paris. €80
Warm welcoming atmosphere, contemporary cooking in exquisite decor, the restaurant is tucked away inside the luxurious hotel close to the Champs-Elysées. Excellent set menus €45-70.

Phone:	01 45 61 82 08
Internet	www.warwickparis.com

Chez Catherine, 3 rue Berryer, 75008 Paris. €45.
Elegant, glass ceilinged room which offers high quality contemporary cooking. Calm, unhurried atmosphere.

Phone:	01 40 76 01 40

Restaurants: Champs-Elysées & Porte Maillot (cont)

Al Ajami, 58, rue François 1er, 75008 Paris. €40.
Long established family restaurant which offers a largely local clientele a comfortable menu of well prepared Lebanese specialities.

Phone:	01 42 25 38 44

Shin Jung, 7, rue Clapeyron, 75008 Paris. €32.
Very Zen. Decorated with calligraphic prints, Korean specialities include raw fish and other oriental delicacies.

Phone:	01 45 22 21 06

La Terrace du Jazz, (Hôtel Le Méridien Etoile), 81, boulevard Gouvion Saint-Cyr, 75017 Paris. Sumptuous international buffet. Set in an oasis close to the interior garden of the Méridien hotel. The evening later turns to the music provided by the Jazz Club Lionel Hampton – big band, swing, blues. Sunday brunch.

Phone:	01 40 68 30 85

HOTELS

Champs-Elysées & Porte Maillot

FRANCE

LUXURY

Hôtel Le Méridien L'Etoile, 81, boulevard Gouvion Saint-Cyr, 75017 Paris.
Ⓜ Porte Maillot. 1008 rooms, from €385 to €450 d/t.
Huge hotel opposite the Palais des Congrès, venue for trade fairs, conferences and big time entertainment. Two restaurants: L'Orénoc (trendy, sophisticated) and La Terrace du Jazz, with its famous buffet. The hotel also houses the Jazz Club Lionel Hampton. Close to the Arc de Triomphe and the Champs-Elysées.

Phone	01 40 68 34 34
Email	guest.etoile@lemeridien.com
Internet	www.lemeridien.com

Hotel Plaza Athenee, 25 avenue Montaigne, 75008.
Ⓜ Alma Marceau. 143 rooms, from €555 to €750 s/d/t.
Erstwhile favourite of the Vanderbilts, Rockefellers and Jackie Kennedy Onassis. Its American 30s-style Relais Plaza restaurant has signed photos of guests, including Rudolf Valentino, Fred Astaire and Grace Kelly. Its cavernous cocktail bar featured prominently in the last episodes of Sex and the City and regulars guests include Meg Ryan, Keanu Reaves and Jack Nicholson. Also houses Alain Ducasse's signature restaurant.

Phone	01 53 67 66 65
Email	reservation@plaza-athenee-paris.com
Internet	www.plaza-athenee-paris.com

Hôtel Concorde Lafayette – Paris Champs-Elysées, 3, place Général Koenig, 75017 Paris.
Ⓜ Porte Maillot. 950 rooms, from €119 to €518 s/d/t.
Ultra modern hotel rising into the sky above the Porte Maillot offering wonderful panoramic views of the ville lumière. Great hustle and bustle in the lobby, important meeting place of movers and shakers, being close to La Défense business district, the Paris Palais des Congrès and the Champs-Elysées. Excellent place for celebrity spotting and the post-match banquets are often held here. Check the local press for details.

Phone	01 40 68 50 50
Email	booking@concorde-hotels.com
Internet	www.concorde-lafayette.com

Hôtel Warwick, 5, rue de Berri, 75008 Paris.
Ⓜ Georges V. 122 rooms.
Luxurious hotel just off the Champs-Elysées. Has welcomed the Wales and New Zealand rugby teams. The Warwick boasts a multi-lingual staff, the 'W Lounge' – open 7/7 and the 'W Restaurant' for lunch and dinner Monday to Friday.

Phone	01 45 63 14 11
Email	resa.whparis@warwickhotels.com
Internet	www.warwickhotels.com

Hôtel Lancaster, 7, rue de Berri, 75008 Paris.
Ⓜ Georges V. 49 rooms, from €390 to €590 d/t.
Luxurious and elegant hotel close to the Champs-Elysées. It boasts an impressive art collection, the highly regarded Michel Troisgros restaurant, La Table du Lancaster, and a top floor fitness centre with view towards Montmartre.

Phone	01 40 76 40 76
Email	reservations@hotel-lancaster.fr
Internet	www.hotel-lancaster.fr

Hôtel Bristol, 112, rue du Faubourg-St-Honoré, 75008 Paris.
Ⓜ Miromesnil. 116 rooms. 46 suites. From €550 to €780 d/t. Suites from €800 to €7600.
Immaculate marble lobby illuminated by an enormous crystal chandelier by Baccarat sets the tone. Wonderful piano bar attracts the great and good for coffee or aperitif. Louis XV and Louis XVI bedrooms, two Michelin starred restaurant, beautiful garden, and a rooftop swimming-pool with wonderful views of nearby St-Augustin and beyond to Sacré-Coeur and Montmartre.

Phone	01 53 43 43 00
Email	resa@lebristolparis.com
Internet	www.lebristolparis.com

Four Seasons-George V, 31, avenue George-V, 75008 Paris.
Ⓜ Georges V. 184 rooms. 61 suites. From €650 to €890 d/t. Suites from €1250 to €9000.
Recent, massive investment has brought what is possibly Paris's most famous hotel back to the very top of the tree. Three Star Michelin restaurant Le Cinq, the Pierre-Yves Rochon designed public rooms are elegant and bathed in a gentle light. Highly luxurious rooms, marble bathrooms, every detail has been considered and cared for. Even the gym is beautiful. Amazing flower arrangements.

Phone	01 49 52 70 00
Internet	www.fourseasons.com/paris

MODERATE

Hôtel Villa des Ternes, 97, avenue des Ternes, 75017 Paris. Ⓜ Porte Maillot. 39 rooms, from €140 to €260 s/d/t. Extra bed €30.
Comfortable hotel. Convenient for the Champs-Elysées, but away from its hustle and bustle. Close to good restaurants and bars. Car parking at Le Méridien.

Phone	01 53 81 94 94
Email	hotel@hotelternes.com
Internet	www.villadesternes.com

Hotel du Ministère, 31, rue de Surène, 75008 Paris.
Ⓜ Madeleine.
28 rooms, from €120 to €209 s/d/t. Long established, friendly hotel in a side street near the Elysée Palace and the US and British embassies. High level of comfort, lots of wood panelling and one of those old-fashioned lifts with a folding cage door. Close to the Madeleine and the Champs-Elysées.

Phone	01 42 66 21 43
Email	hministere@aol.com
Internet	www.ministerehotel.com

FRANCE

Hotels: Champs Elysées & Porte Maillot (cont)

Claridge Bellman, 37 rue Francois 1er, 75008.
Ⓜ Alma Marceau. 42 rooms, from €230 to €390 s/d/t.
Just round the corner from the Plaza Athenee and the George V, this smart establishment is tucked away behind the Champs Elysees and the Avenue Montaigne, amongst the couturiers and perfumers of the ultra chic 8th arrondissement.

Phone	0147 23 54 42
Internet	www.hotel-claridge-bellman.com

Hôtel Mayflower, 3, rue Chateaubriand, 75008 Paris.
Ⓜ Georges V. 24 rooms, from €128 to €175 s/d/t.
Neat little hotel in a side street close to the Champs-Elysées. Comfortable rooms decorated in pastel tones, marble en-suite bathrooms. The breakfast room is decorated with frescoes of the voyages of the Pilgrim Fathers.

Phone	01 45 62 57 46
Email	mayflower@escapade-paris.com
Internet	www.escapade-paris.com

FRANCE

BUDGET

Hôtel Saint-Cyr Etoile, 101, avenue des Ternes, 75017 Paris. Ⓜ Porte Maillot. 30 rooms, from €75 to €110 s/d/t. Comfort for a reasonable price and in the Porte Maillot area. Easy access to the Champs-Elysées and close to the métro Porte Maillot for West to East exploration of the rest of the city.

Phone	01 45 74 87 42

Hôtel Alison, 21, rue de Surène, 75008 Paris.
Ⓜ Madeleine. 35 rooms, from €78 to €140 s/d/t, €160 tpl, €215 or €285 fam.
Light, bright, modern decor is a feature of this comfortable family run establishment located in a quiet street near the Madeleine.

Phone	01 42 65 54 00
Email	hotel.alison@wanadoo.fr
Internet	www.hotelalison.com

GARE DU NORD & MONTMARTRE

Picture perfect: Montmartre lies at the heart of the Paris art community

BARS

BRASSERIES

Le Falstaff, 15,rue de Dunkerque, 75010 Paris.
Late closing (4am week, 5am weekend) beer bar which also serves traditional French food in large portions. Just opposite the Gare du Nord. Easy access to the Stade de France, just one stop on RER Line B.

Phone	01 42 85 12 93

Paris Nord Café, 17, rue de Dunkerque, 75010 Paris.
Open 7/7 has good value set menus of traditional French food from €12 - €20. Good steaks, choucroute or big salads will fill you up. Good draught lagers and some Belgian beers.

Phone	01 42 85 23 61

Café du Nord, 19, rue de Dunkerque, 75010 Paris.
Open from 5am till 2am this is a friendly brasserie which like its neighbours serves copious portions of traditional French regional dishes for reasonable money. Brunch also served if you miss breakfast. Rugby fans are particularly welcome.

Phone	01 48 78 93 49

BRITISH-IRISH PUBS

O'Sullivan's Pub, 92, boulevard de Clichy, 75018 Paris.
Large pub of the O'Sullivan's chain, very close to the Moulin Rouge. All day pub grub, cocktails and pints. Modern decor for a younger crowd. TV screens for spots coverage.

Phone	01 42 52 24 94

PARISIAN BISTRO

Au Baroudeur, 30, rue Yvonne Le Tac, 75018 Paris.
Very much the Parisian bistro de quartier. Lively conversation, heavy smoking, robust wines accompanying authentic bistro cooking. Few tourists.

Phone	01 46 06 00 79

BRASSERIES

Le Vrai Paris, rue des Abbesses, 75018 Paris.
Pleasant watering hole which does tearoom, cocktail bar, aperitifs and draught beers.

Le Sancerre, rue des Abbesses, 75018 Paris.
Another jack-of-all trades brasserie, tearoom and cocktail bar, which also provides OK traditional bistro food and a brunch. Good selection of draught and bottled beers.

La Divette de Montmartre, 136 rue Marcardet, 75018 Paris.
Eclectically decorated bar in the backstreets of Montmartre. There is a red telephone box, table football, posters, album covers.

Phone	

Autour de Midi, 11 rue Lepic, 75018 Paris.
Full programme of jazz nightly except Monday. There is also a café-restaurant. Atmospheric, for the serious jazz fan.

Phone	01 55 79 16 48

La Nouvelle Eve, 25, rue Fontaine, 75009 Paris.
Revue bar with dinner or champagne.

Phone	01 48 75 69 25

CLUBS: DANCING

Folies Pigalle, 11, place Pigalle, 75009 Paris.

Le Hammam, 94, rue Amsterdam, 75009 Paris.

La Loco, 90, boulevard de Clichy, 75018 Paris (House, dance, charts)

COFFEE SHOPS

Queen Ann, 5 rue Simon-le-Franc, 75004 Paris.
Neat little coffee shop in a side street in the Marais. Hot and cold savoury tarts a speciality.

FRANCE

Bars: Gare du Nord & Montmartre (cont)

Le Loir dans la Théière, 3, rue des Rosiers, 75004 Paris.
Ever so laid-back tea-shop (the name means the "dormouse in the teapot") on perhaps the most famous street in the Marais. Leather armchairs, bookshelves, lazy comfort.

La Madeleine de Proust, 4 rue Descartes, 75005 Paris.
Not dedicated to a lover of the great Marcel but to the moist, orange flavoured sponge cake so closely associated with him. Savour the romantic Latin quarter atmosphere...

Jean-Paul Hévin, 3 rue Vavin, 75006 Paris.
Quite wonderful chocolates, ice-creams and pastries from Monsieur Hévin, a true artist.

DESSERT AND PASTRY RESTAURANTS

Ladurée, 75, avenue des Champs-Elysées, 75008 Paris

**Ladurée, 64 boulevard Haussmann, 75009 Paris.
(in the Primtemps department store)**

Ladurée, 16, rue Royale, 75008 Paris.

Ladurée, 21 rue Bonaparte, 75006 Paris.

Belle époque setting for exquisite croissants, breads and jams for breakfast, desserts and pastries later. The house products can be bought to take away as presents...

Fauchon, 26 place de la Madeleine, 75008 Paris.
Treat yourself to a break from the shopping and a coffee or tea and pastry in this Parisian bastion of gastronomic style and luxury.

Mariage Frères, 260 rue du Faubourg-St-Honoré, 75008 Paris.
High quality tea merchant who also sells by the cup in an elegant room close to the Champs-Elysées.

Bagel Co, 31, rue Ponthieu, 75008 Paris.
Bagels, coffee, tea, sandwiches, ice-cream and pastries in a side street close to the Champs-Elysées.

RESTAURANTS

Gare du Nord & Montmartre

30 Le Relais Gascon, 6, rue des Abbesses, 75018 Paris. €20.
Great value for money. The €18.50 set menu gives an extremely difficult choice of eight or nine traditional south-west France specialities, starters and mains. Foie-gras, terrines, saucisses, cured hams, enormous salads to start. Mains include leg of lamb, magret of duck, cassoulet. Then cheese or home-made desserts (tartes, flans, crème bruléé) and coffee. Robust Cahors, Bordeaux or Buzets to accompany. Wonderful relaxed atmosphere induces easy conversation with one's neighbours. Non-stop service 10am till 2am.

Phone	01 42 58 58 22

A la Pomponette, rue Lepic, 75018 Paris. €35.
Face the Moulin Rouge, pictured right, and look up the street to the right – the Rue Lepic. The street turns to the left and on the right is "À la Pomponette." Here there is a nostalgia inducing atmosphere of the old Montmartre "bistro de quartier" as locals come to chew the fat over a prolonged apéritif. The faded but comfortable restaurant area offers sturdy traditional French dishes: pig's trotters, rib of beef, at very fair prices, washed down with unpretentious wines direct from selected vineyards. Good cheeses; the desserts are all alchohol based. Weight watchers, wowsers and vegans desist.

Terminus Nord, 23, rue de Dunkerque, 75010 Paris. €35.
Large, Belle Époque brasserie, specialising in seafood. The oysters are particularly good. Situated directly opposite the Gare-du-Nord, this glass-fronted brasserie has been the first port of call of British visitors for generations. The menu consists of classic bistro cooking from the foie gras to the crème brulée. Seafood platters and fish are specialities. The oysters (eaten in or outside on the pavement) are in a class of their own.

Phone	01 42 85 05 15

La Table d'Anvers, 2 Place d'Anvers, 75009 Paris. €40.
At the foot of Montmartre, surrounded by theatres and other places of entertainment, the Table d'Anvers, under the direction of masterchef Christian Conticini, is now recognised as one of France's culinary glories. The desserts, in particular, are unforgettable. These include chocolate soufflé with a coffee sorbet; baked apple stuffed with quince; and crepes with almonds and caramel.

Phone	01 48 78 35 21

Chartier, 7 Rue du Faubourg, 75009 Paris. €15.
Famous for its huge cooking pot that has bubbled continuously for more than a century, chartier is a jewel of the Grands Boulevards. The fin de siecle décor makes a fitting setting for the solid, traditional cooking.

Phone	01 47 70 86 29

Chez Grisette, 14, rue Houdon, 75018 Paris. €30
Wonderful Montmartre bistro. Close seating encourages easy conviviality, and fuelled by the robust food (good raviolis, sautéed veal, and superb farm produced boudin) and the excellent, predominantly Loire Valley wines, the atmosphere warms as the evening proceeds.

Phone	01 42 62 04 80

Le Bouquet du Nord, 85, rue de Maubeuge, 75010 Paris.
North central Paris is a hidden jewel. It may lack high culture and, outside of the railway stations and Montmartre, obvious tourist locations, but it is full of unexpected charms and is a place much valued by discerning Parisians. The Bouquet du Nord is pleasant and unpretentious, with an attractively decorated bar offering good beers and live jazz on Friday evenings. Oysters are a speciality.

Phone	01 48 78 29 97

La Maison Blanche, 21, rue de Dunkerque, 75010 Paris.
This modest, but accomplished establishment, known far outside its immediate area, offers choucroute, grills, moules marinières and a reliable steak-frites. What is particularly good to know (especially if you are a reveller) is that, like London's Windmill, it never closes.

Phone	01 48 78 15 92

Restaurants: Gare du Nord & Montmartre (cont)

Au Quai de L'Espérance, 25, rue de Dunkerque, 75010 Paris.
Specialities of the Aveyron; great cheeses and cured hams, copious quantities, good house wines.

Phone	01 48 78 09 90

La Divette du Moulin, 98, rue Lepic, 75018 Paris. €25
One of the great Montmartre addresses, once a drinking den, now a wine bar and restaurant offering food straight from the market, a warm bohemian atmosphere.

Phone	01 46 06 34 84

La Maison Rose, 2, rue de l'Abreuvoir, 75018 Paris. €30.
Close to the Place du Tertre, a famous Montmartre landmark, the walls decorated with photos of film stars and music hall artists who once frequented the place.

Phone	01 42 57 66 75

Le Relais Savoyard, 13 Rue Rodier, 75009 Paris. €15.
You reach the dining room through a busy bar to discover a range of fare that runs from fondues and tarts to serious gastronomic offerings. Sound as a bell.

Phone	01 45 26 17 48

Al Caratello, 5, rue Audran, 75018 Paris. €25.
A neat little trattoria, offering good food in a cosy, family atmosphere. A cool, switched-on chef and friendly service.

Phone	01 42 62 24 23

FRANCE

HOTELS

Gare du Nord & Montmartre

LUXURY

Terminus Nord - Hôtel Mercure, 12, boulevard de Denain, 75010 Paris.
Ⓜ Gare-du-Nord. 236 rooms, from €227-€298 d/t. (Check for offers).
Favourite with generations of journalists and rugby fans. After major renovation work the dear old Terminus Nord retains its allure. Opposite the Gare-du-Nord for boat train, Eurostar, Charles-de-Gaulle airport and one stop to the Stade de France. Attached is the Terminus Nord, a belle époque Parisian brasserie known for its oysters, seafood platters and no-nonsense traditional cooking.

Phone	01 42 80 20 00
Email	h2761@accor.com
Internet	www.mercure.com

MODERATE

Comfort Hotel Place du Tertre, 16, rue Tholozé, 75018 Paris.
Ⓜ Abbesses. 46 rooms. Rack €95 s, €100 d/t.
Don't be fooled by the name, there's still a good a climb to the top of the hill. Formula hotel, but the basics are well provided in this perennially lively spot.

Phone	01 42 55 05 06
Email	comfort.placedutertre@wanadoo.fr
Internet	www.comfort-placedutertre.com

Hôtel Prima-Lepic, 29, rue Lepic, 75018 Paris.
Ⓜ Blanche. 38 rooms, from €98 to €164 s/d/t, €186 tpl, qd.
Recently converted, close to the Moulin Rouge, at the bottom of the hill at Montmartre. Rue Lepic retains an authentic Montmartre atmosphere with plenty of local colour and a strong cosmopolitan presence.

Phone	01 46 06 44 64
Email	reservation@hotel-prima-lepic.com
Internet	www.hotel-prima-lepic.com

BUDGET

Hôtel Montana Lafayette, 164, rue Lafayette, 75010 Paris.
Ⓜ Gare-du-Nord. 23 rooms, from €48 to €75 s/d/t, €75-€90 tpl.
Cheap but adequate. Lots of hearty eating and drinking around the area. Easy for the Stade de France and Eurostar.

Phone	01 40 35 80 80
Email	hotelmontana@wanadoo.fr
Internet	www.hotelmontanalafayette.com

Hôtel Plaza-Lafayette, 175, rue Lafayette, 75010 Paris.
Ⓜ Gare-du-Nord. 48 rooms, from €113 to €140 d/t.
Luxurious yet moderately priced three star hotel. Features include an English style pub, Parisian brasserie, and terrace with balcony.

Phone	01 44 89 89 10
Email	reservation@hotelplazalafayette.com
Internet	www.hotelplazalafayette.com

FRANCE

Albert 1er – Best Western, 162, rue Lafayette,75010 Paris.
Ⓜ Gare-du-Nord. 55 rooms, from €95 to €116 s/d/t, €140 tpl.
Recently renovated, the rooms are clean and bright and comfortably furnished. Close to the Gare du Nord for easy access to the Eurostar and Stade de France. Uninspiring area but good value for money.

Phone	01 40 36 82 40
Email	paris@albert1erhotel.com
Internet	www.albert1erhotel.com

Hôtel Regyn's Montmartre, 18, place des Abbesses, 75018 Paris.
Ⓜ Abbesses. 22 rooms, from €42 to €92 s/d/t. Extra bed €20.
Very friendly and comfortable home-from-home in a superb location. Outstanding value for money with all the attractions of Montmartre on the doorstep.

Phone	01 42 54 45 21
Email	hrm18@club-internet.fr

Comfort Hotel Sacré Coeur, 57, rue des Abbesses, 75018 Paris.
Ⓜ Abbesses. 41 rooms. €75 s, €80 d/t.
Cheap yet comfortable hotel on a great Montmartre street full of bars, restaurants, cafés, and local trades people. A bit rich to call it Sacré-Coeur though.

Phone	01 42 51 50 00
Email	comfort.sacrecoeur@wanadoo.fr
Internet	www.choicehotels.com

Hôtel Utrillo, 7, rue Aristide Bruant, 75018 Paris. Ⓜ Blanche.
30 rooms, from €64 to €82 s/d/t. Extra bed €14.
Cheap and cheery accommodation in a quiet backstreet in Montmartre, close to all the action, however.

Phone	01 42 58 13 44
Email	adelutrillo@wanadoo.fr
Internet	www.francehotelreservation.com/utrillo

Scottish rugby

Slide of the saltire

By Alasdair Reid
Chief rugby writer, The Sunday Herald

The doctrine of permanent revolution was Leon Trotsky's most significant contribution to socialist theory, so you would hardly expect the famously conservative rulers of Scottish rugby to adopt its principles with much enthusiasm. Yet turmoil has been the almost ever-present backdrop for the sport north of the border in the 10 years since rugby abandoned amateurism in 1995, and there are few indications of a more settled future ahead as professional rugby enters its second decade of existence.

A quick survey of the landscape of the sport in Scotland in recent times would highlight an underachieving international team, professional sides that consistently fail to meet their targets in European and Celtic competitions, and declining standards and crowds at the amateur club level. If there is any hope at all for the sport in the years ahead, it rests all-too-precariously on the fact that season 2004-05 was such an unequivocally dismal experience that things can surely only get better.

Before reviewing that season of travails, it is worth casting the mind back to where Scotland stood 10 years ago in the months immediately prior to the momentous decision of the game's governors to usher in the era of pay-for-play. For it is all too easily forgotten that the Scottish team of the time was comfortably the best of the Celtic nations – Scotland were just pipped at the post by England for the 1995 Five Nations title in a Grand Slam showdown at Twickenham – and the sport's wider popularity could be measured by the huge success of the debenture issue that had funded the redevelopment of Murrayfield Stadium into the glistening new arena it had just become.

Jim Telfer, the Border shepherd's son whose language never lost its robustly agricultural edge on his rise to become one of the most respected coaches in the world game, once said that Scotland would be disadvantaged by the arrival of professionalism in comparison with other nations, and even his detractors would acknowledge the astuteness of that observation. Of all the game's traditional powers, Scotland has struggled hardest, and with least success, to unshackle itself from the old way of doing things and boldly embrace the new.

Although the channelling of resources into quasi-provincial professional sides in Edinburgh, Glasgow and the Borders (and, in the early years, the North as well) was attractive on paper, those sides have rarely looked too impressive on grass. Edinburgh are still the only Scottish side to have reached the last-eight stage of the Heineken Cup (in the 2003-04 tournament, when they were crushed by a merciless Toulouse team in a brutally one-sided quarter-final), while Celtic League progress has been painfully slow at times. In comparison with the amalgamated sides of Wales and Ireland, Scotland's representatives have been trailing far behind.

It is easy to argue – and many have – that the men who ran Scottish rugby throughout the 1990s were guilty of a series of catastrophic misjudgements that laid the road to ruin for the sport they were meant to be tending. Yet even if senior SRU figures of the time displayed a collective arrogance and an appetite for the perks of office that would make their counterparts on the International Olympic Commission seem almost monastic, it was also true that they required the support of their traditional constituencies, the clubs, to push through their policies. A handful of top clubs argued that they, not the Scottish districts, should be the engine rooms of professional rugby's future, but their ambitions were crushed in a series of resounding defeats when they sought approval to represent Scotland in Europe.

The clubs-versus-district debates that raged then are mere history now, for even their former champions would concede that sides like Melrose, Watsonians and Stirling County, the powerful Scottish clubs of a decade ago, have lost too much ground to be able to offer a realistic challenge to their professional counterparts from England and France. Yet nobody who had witnessed the rise of Scottish club sides over the previous 20 years – in 1973, Scotland became the first of the home nations to implement a truly national league championship – could be immune to poignancy as some of the great club institutions go into sharp and seemingly irreversible decline. Scottish rugby may never have produced a more depressing document than the press release that was issued by Hawick at the start of the 2005-06 season, in which the club that was, historically, Scotland's most successful, appealed for supporters to get behind their side and rescue it from a dangerous slump.

How the powers behind Scotland's national team must have been tempted to come up with similar sort of statement for their side. At the dawn of the 2005-06 season, Scotland's international stock is as low as it has been since that dreadful sequence of results between 1951 and 1955 when they managed to lose 17 international matches on the trot. Indeed, while the percentage success rate has been better over the past two years than it was during that catastrophic streak half-a-century ago, it ought to be remembered that Scotland's only recent international victories have been against Samoa, Japan, Italy and Romania, countries that would not have merited Test status in that earlier era.

The decline has been sudden as well as depressing. In 1999, Scotland won the last Five Nations title – Italy brought the numbers up to six when they joined the tournament the following year – with a bold attacking style that had its most flamboyant reward on a remarkable afternoon in the Stade de France when they put five tries past France in the space of only 17 minutes. A year later, they claimed

Side of the Saltire (cont)

a rapturously received 19-13 victory over England, albeit in a season when another whitewash loomed, taking advantage of some memorably vicious Edinburgh weather to snatch the dream of Grand Slam glory away from opponents who were left ashen by the whole experience. Since then, though, international successes have been rare.

It was only by the skin of their teeth, and a last-minute try by Tom Smith, that Scotland squeezed past Fiji to reach the quarter-finals of the 2003 World Cup in Australia. Their next match brought defeat by the host nation, and marked the departure from the job of the then national coach Ian McGeechan at the end of a four-year reign in which he had rarely seemed to be the inspirational figure he had been during his first stint in charge, a period that had been highlighted by the Grand Slam Scotland achieved in 1990.

Enter Matt Williams: he of the nice hair, the nice teeth, the friendly manner and the inconveniently catastrophic record as an international coach. The Australian boasted a winning smile, but winning anything else went out of the window as he led Scotland to a Six Nations whitewash in his first season in charge, a campaign that was improved upon only slightly the following year when he somehow coaxed them past an underpowered Italian side at Murrayfield. By then, though, the patience of Williams's SRU paymasters was already exhausted; at the end of the season, and after a mercifully brief review of his self-evidently hopeless performance, Williams was sacked from the job.

Which brings us to where we are now, for at the dawn of the new season Scotland have just annointed a successor to Williams. Frank Hadden, the long-serving Edinburgh coach, has taken the mantle after successfully caretaking the team to friendly wins against the Barbarians and Romania. Despite Williams's best efforts, it seems that others in the field of elite coaching (Hadden's opposition was strong) still considered the Scotland job to be something other than a poisoned chalice.

Perhaps that owes something to the belief that it would be hard to disappoint a Scottish audience whose expectations are close to rock bottom after two thoroughly depressing seasons. Yet it may also rest on the suspicion that there is far more individual talent in the Scotland squad at the moment than Williams was ever able to reveal. Some of the most vivid performances of the 2005 RBS Six Nations Championship were provided by Scotland players who had decided to unshackle themselves from the tight tactical strictures imposed by Williams and allow their true abilities to shine through.

In that regard, Scottish supporters are entitled to feel excited about the potential their side could yet fulfil. When Sir Clive Woodward selected all his old England mates – and you can stress the 'old' there – for the 2005 Lions tour to New Zealand, he overlooked a host of rising Scottish stars who could yet light up the firmament of European rugby. Some commentators have suggested that the only advantage that Wales have over Scotland at the moment is the collective confidence of their players: that may be overstating things, but not by a huge margin.

Certainly, the spine of a very useful side could be found if form and fitness are maintained by number 8 Simon Taylor, scrum-half Chris Cusiter, and Chris Paterson, the accomplished and versatile footballer who seems to have settled at full-back. The lack of a truly outstanding fly-half remains a concern, but if Scotland can somehow plug that gap then they will not be short of talent in the wider positions. The Lamont brothers, Rory and Sean, can both bring power and physical presence to the backline, while Scottish supporters will be praying that Tom Philip, the young centre who was a revelation in his first senior season, can soon recover from the injury problems that have kept him out of the game for more than a year. Donnie Macfadyen, the compact but wonderfully effective Glasgow flanker, is another who should return to top-flight action after missing the entire 2005 Six Nations with a knee problem.

Where Scotland might struggle is in the area of tight forward play. Tom Smith and Gordon Bulloch, both Lions, announced their retirements from the international arena at the end of the 2004-05 season, and Scotland's stock of hard-nosed experience has also been diminished by the decision of Stuart Grimes, the amiable Newcastle lock, to take a one-year sabbatical from Test rugby. Those three players could boast almost 200 caps between them, and their departures will surely be felt. There is promise aplenty in such figures as Euan Murray, Scott Lawson and Craig Hamilton, but they will be on steep learning curves if they are to fill the vacated front-five roles.

It is probably true to say that Scotland's status as a top-class Test nation has looked decidedly rickety of late. Throughout rugby history, however, the Scots have demonstrated remarkable powers of regeneration, with some of their greatest successes coming hard on the heels of sequences of depressing defeats. Scotland supporters will be praying for another revolution.

FIND YOUR WAY AROUND

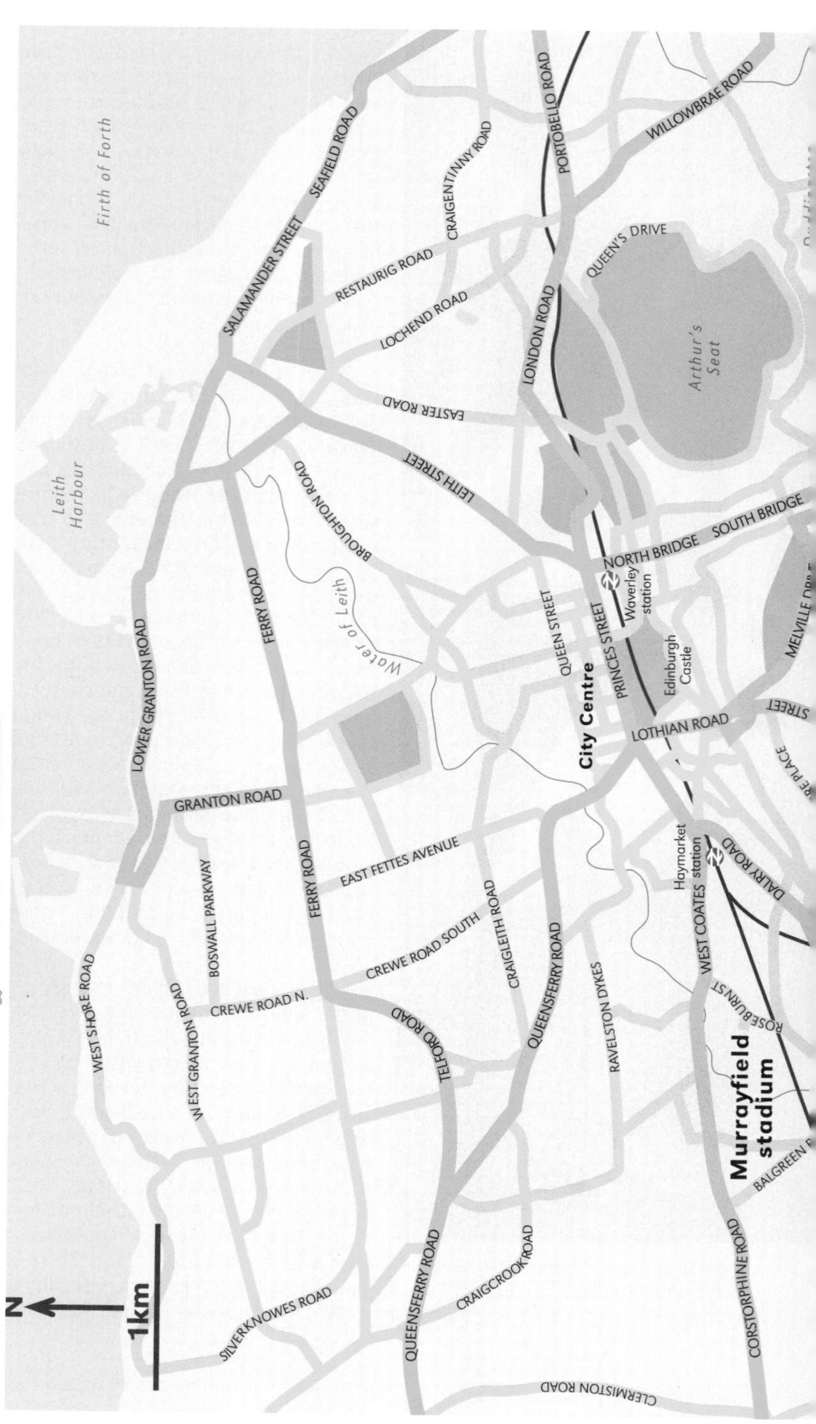

SCOTLAND

NORTHERN STAR

Like Rome, Edinburgh is built on seven hills. Unlike Rome, however, the weather fronts often blow in from Siberia, so wrap up warm. Known as the Athens of the North, this is a reference to the great thinkers of the 18th century Enlightenment and thus has more to do with David Hume and Adam Smith than the weather.

Edinburgh has, in recent years, made huge leaps as a destination. It is now brimming with seriously good restaurants and vibey bars, good hotels. Long gone is its dour image (well deserved though it was) of the past. It was here, beneath the Doric temples of Calton Hill – Edinburgh's very own Acropolis – that the controversial parliament opened its portals to debate in 2000 for the first time since the 1707 Acts of Union.

As most of you will already know, it is one of the most stunning cities in the world and every summer it hosts the world's finest arts festival, when the city's population swells like a well fed python to double its normal size. But this elegant and ancient metropolis, with its beautifully crafted Georgian New Town and its gnarled yet grandiose Old Town, accommodates them effortlessly as stunning new productions exceed the superlatives of the previous year's affair.

Two features dominate the city: the Crags, of which Arthur's Seat is the crowning geological glory, and the Castle. The latter sits atop the Royal Mile on a dead (we hope) volcano, a louring tribute to the city's past when a few hundred ragged Highlanders led by Bonny Prince Charlie strolled into town and shunted the feeble money men and lily livers aside as the first step of the 1745 Catholic uprising.

The New Town is full of shops and bars, hotels and restaurants as is the Old Town just across the way. You can walk everywhere in Edinburgh – yes, even down to Leith, taking in the slightly shabby depths of Leith Walk. Leith is the city's latest triumph – it has risen from the ashes of a grubby port into being one of the city's hottest nightspots. There's a riot of entertaining bars and some really good little restaurants. Indeed, the city's first Michelin-starred restaurant, Martin Wishart, is on The Shore amongst the crow-stepped establishments that give the water's edge a truly continental feel.

Just south of the centre is the Meadows, a great green lung amongst the elegant Victorian tenements. Taking the air there you suddenly happen upon a wonderful view of Arthur's Seat rising like Table Mountain above Cape Town. Cosmopolitan Edinburgh has come a long way from the days of Auld Reekie, when it was probably the most revolting city on the European landscape.

TRAVEL

AIR

Edinburgh International Airport is 12km (8 miles) west of the city centre and is easy to reach thanks to an excellent – and regular – Airlink Coach and good taxi services. It takes about 20 minutes to get from the airport to the city centre.

There are more than 40 flights from London to Edinburgh every day and the average flight time, capital to capital, is about an hour. There are also regular services to Edinburgh from other major UK airports and frequent scheduled flights from 40 European airports - from Amsterdam to Zurich.

To and from Dublin:	Ryanair and Aer Lingus
To and from Cardiff:	bmibaby
To and from Rome:	Eurofly, FlyGlobespan and British Airways
To and from Paris:	Air, France and British Airways do the business, while easyjet flies to Charles de Gaulle from Newcastle.
To and from London City:	ScotAirways, British Airways
To and from London Stansted:	easyjet, FlyGlobespan.
To and from London Gatwick:	easyjet, British Airways
To and from London Heathrow:	bmi British Midland, British Airways
To and from London Luton:	easyjet

For further details try www.edinburghairport.com

RAIL

Edinburgh is easy to reach by train. The Great North Eastern Railway (GNER) line is the fastest intercity railway in the UK, with a journey time of just 4 hours between Edinburgh (Waverley) and London (King's Cross).

ScotRail operate an overnight service, the Caledonian Sleeper, between London (Euston) and Edinburgh 6 nights a week.

Edinburgh has great rail links to other major cities too: York, Newcastle, Inverness and Aberdeen are all about 2 hours away by train, and Glasgow is just 50 minutes away on the First ScotRail shuttle service which leaves Waverley every 15 minutes.

The following companies can provide more information.

Linking Edinburgh and London via the east coast main line:

GNER:	08457 48 49 50

Linking Edinburgh to towns and cities in England:

Virgin:	08457 222 333

Travelling to and from Edinburgh around Scotland:

First Scotrail:	08457 48 49 50

For all your timetables and fares UK wide:

National Rail Enquiries:	08457 48 49 50

For all your rail travel requirements:

Traveline:	0870 608 2 608

CAR

Because Edinburgh is at the heart of the Scottish motorway network, it can be quick and easy to get here by car. If you're travelling from the north of Scotland, for example, Edinburgh is only 3 hours from Inverness and just over 2 hours from Aberdeen and less than an hour from Glasgow. Journey times from England are just as good; you can get here from Birmingham in about 5 hours, from Manchester and York in about 4 hours, and the city is just 2 hours from Newcastle. However once in the city, it can get congested at peak times and parking is policed with zealous enthusiasm by the so-called Blue Meanies, the dreaded Edinburgh traffic wardens.

To help plan your journey you might find the following route planners useful:

RAC	www.rac.co.uk/routeplanner
AA	www.theaa.com/travelwatch/planner_main.jsp

BUS

If you're on a budget then buses are a great travel option. And because Edinburgh is well placed on the Scottish motorway network, getting here by bus or coach could be quicker than you might think. There are regular coach services to Edinburgh from all major UK cities.

The following companies can provide more information:

Linking Edinburgh to England:

National Express	08705 80 80 80

Linking Edinburgh to England and to cities across Scotland:

Mega Bus	01738 639 095

Linking Edinburgh to towns and cities across Scotland:

Scottish Citylink	08705 50 50 50
Stagecoach	0870 608 2 608

FERRY

It's easy to get to Edinburgh by sea. An overnight Superfast ferry service operates between Zeebrugge and Rosyth every day, with a crossing time of 17.5 hours.

Rosyth is about half an hour's drive from Edinburgh, so getting to the city is plain sailing. You can also reach Edinburgh easily by road from the continental ferry ports of Newcastle and Hull and the Irish ferry ports of Stranraer and Cairnryan.

The following companies can provide more information.

FROM ZEEBRUGGE

Superfast	www.superfast.com

FROM IRELAND

P&O Ferries	www.poferries.com
Stenaline	www.stenaline.co.uk

VITAL STATISTICS

Population: 443,600

Phone Code: country code 44, area code 0131

Time zone: GMT (GMT + 1 from last Sunday in March to Saturday before last Sunday in October).

Electricity: 220 volts AC, 50Hz; square three-pin plugs are standard.

Average January temp: 3°C (40°F).

Language: English and Gaelic

Tipping: A tip of around 10% is customary in restaurants. Round up for taxis. Tipping in bars is rare.

Airport Transfers: Airlink Coach service and taxi. About 20 minutes.

Getting around the city: Edinburgh has an amazingly comprehensive bus service. The city is often clogged with buses – indeed there are so many that we refer you to the website of the main server - Lothian Buses.

Phone:	0131 555 6363
Internet:	www.lothianbuses.co.uk

There are also plenty of very reasonably priced taxis prowling the streets.

Shopping: 7 days a week, normal hours. See shopping section.

Getting to the ground: it's just over 20 minutes from the centre of town – most people tend to walk. If you don't fancy that, check with Lothian Buses (above).

HOSPITALS

Eastern General Hospital	Seafield St, EH6 7LN **0131 536 7000**
Western General Hospital	Crewe Rd South, EH4 2XU **0131 537 1000**
Royal Infirmary of Edinburgh	51 Little France Crescent, EH16 4SA **0131 536 1000**
BUPA Murrayfield Hospital	122 Corstorphine Rd, EH12 6UD **0131 334 0363**

SCOTLAND

USEFUL CONTACTS

Police	Headquarters, Lothian and Borders Police Force Headquarters, Fettes Avenue, EH4 1RB
Telephone:	0131 311 3131
E-Mail:	enquiries @ lbp.pnn.police.uk
CrimeStoppers	0800 555 111
Information Centre:	188 High Street, Edinburgh EH1 1QS
Telephone:	0131 226 6966

VISITOR INFORMATION

Main Information Centre	3 Princes St, EH2 2QP www.edinburgh.org
Tourist & Airport Information Desk	International Airport, EH12 9DN.
National Booking	0845 2255121 info@visitscotland.com
Weather information	www.edinburgh.org/practical/weather

FACTS 'N STATS

(courtesy of Edinburgh & Lothians Tourist Board)

1. Edinburgh's population is over 460, 000. But that figure swells to well over 1 million during its August festivals.

2. Edinburgh hosts the biggest New Year street party in the world. (Edinburgh's Hogmanay).

3. JK Rowling, author of the famous Harry Potter books, wrote her first novel 'Harry Potter and the Philosopher's Stone' at the Elephant House Café, 21 George IV Bridge, Old Town (see entry).

4. Sean Connery grew up in Edinburgh and as a boy, delivered milk to Fettes School, where the fictitious character of James Bond was educated. (UK Prime Minister, Tony Blair, was also educated at Fettes.)

5. The city's Scotch Whisky Heritage Centre, dedicated to Scotch whisky, features both sound effects and aromas! For the real thing visit Scotland's Southern most whisky distillery, Glenkinchie, thirty minutes drive from Edinburgh

6. Edinburgh University was established in 1583.

7. Edinburgh Castle, which dominates the city skyline, is the most popular visitor attraction in Scotland with over 1 million visitors each year.

8. The word 'caddie' originated from the men who were hired to carry pails of water up the tenement flats in the Old Town of Edinburgh. Golf caddies are thought to stem from Mary Queen of Scots who was a keen golfer. Apparently, she christened the students who carried her clubs 'cadets' and, given the French pronunciation of the word, some people believe that this is how the modern meaning of the term developed.

9. Sir Arthur Conan Doyle, the creator of Sherlock Holmes, was born in Edinburgh. A statue of Sherlock Holmes is in Picardy Place celebrates the birthplace of Arthur Conan Doyle, and is the only statue of its kind in the UK.

10. In the Old Calton Burial Ground, in the centre of Edinburgh, there is a memorial to the Scottish soldiers who died in the American Civil War and a statue of Abraham Lincoln – the first erected outside the USA.

11. The Royal Yacht Britannia served the Royal Family for forty four years and is the last in a long line of Royal Yachts. Its permanent home is at Ocean Terminal in the historic port of Leith

12. Alexander Graham Bell, the inventor of the telephone, was born in Edinburgh. Bell, like his father, was an educator of the deaf. He went first to Canada and then to the United States, where in 1873 he was appointed a professor in the School of Oratory, Boston University.

13. Robert Louis Stevenson lived at 17 Heriot Row in the New Town. His poem '*Leary the Lamplighter*' was written about the local lamplighter, who Stevenson could see from his window. Famous landmarks with RLS connections include the Jeckyll & Hyde pub, Deacon Brodie's Tavern and The Hawes Inn in South Queensferry which features in 'Kidnapped'.

14. While Princes Street Gardens, situated in the city centre, boasts the world's oldest floral clock, the Royal Botanic Garden contains Britain's tallest Palm House in The Glasshouse Experience.

15. The founder of America's National Parks, is commemorated at the John Muir House & Country Park, just outside Edinburgh

16. Some of the movies to have been filmed in Edinburgh and the surrounding district include 'The 39 Steps', 'The Prime of Miss Jean Brodie', 'Jude', and 'Mary Reilly'.

17. The story of 'Greyfriar's Bobby', the faithful Skye terrier, hails from Edinburgh, and the statue to the little dog is located on George IV Bridge, opposite Greyfriar's Bobby pub.

18. Edinburgh, along with Bath, Rome and Venice, has been designated a World Heritage Site.

PLACES OF INTEREST

(This is just a brief summary – the point about Edinburgh is that just about everything is of interest.)

Museum of Scotland, Chambers St

This striking new building holds more than 10,000 of Scotland's most precious artefacts dating from before the country's first primordial grunts to the present day. See how much has changed. Free.

Phone:	0131 247 4422

Royal Museum, Chambers St,

Outstanding collections and varied visiting exhibitions, covering Decorative Arts, Science and Industry, Archaeology and the Natural World, such as the insect show that has so captivated this young visitor.
Free.

Phone:	0131 247 4422

Edinburgh Castle, Castlehill, Royal Mile

History has given the Castle a rough ride - sacked and burned by invaders, the current louring edifice represents several architectural rethinks over the years. It makes its first historical appearance after the death of Queen, later Saint, Margaret, the wife of Malcolm Canmore, in 1093. The oldest remaining part - St Margaret's Chapel – dates from the 12th century. The Great Hall was built under James IV around 1510. The Scottish National War Museum was added after World War I. Scotland's crown jewels (Honours of Scotland) are kept here, as is the Stone of Destiny, upon which kings of Scotland were traditionally crowned. The One O'clock Gun fires from the ramparts every day. Multi-lingual guided tours available.

Hours:	Apr - Oct: 9.30 - 18:00 (last entry 17:15). Nov - Mar: 9.30 - 17:00 (last entry 16:15).
Prices:	Adult: £9.50 Concession: £7.00 Child: £2.00
Contact:	0131 225 9846

Palace of Holyroodhouse, Canongate, Royal Mile

Founded as a monastery in 1128, the Palace of Holyroodhouse is the Queen's official residence in Scotland. Situated at the east end of the Royal Mile, the palace is closely associated with Scotland's turbulent past, especially the time of Mary, Queen of Scots, who lived there between 1561 and 1567 and whose secretary David Rizzio was murdered there.

Later, it survived being taken over by Oliver Cromwell's troops during the Civil War and was the base for Bonnie Prince Charlie during the Jacobite Uprising a century later in 1745.

Successive kings and queens have made the Palace of Holyroodhouse their main royal residence in Scotland. Today, the Palace is the setting for State ceremonies and official entertaining. Its modern-day comfort owes much to Charles II, who built the spacious upper floor where the Royal Family's private apartments are still located. This magnificent baroque Palace stands opposite a rather newer and highly controversial monument – the Scottish Parliament. The two are, architecturally, unusual bedfellows.

Hours:	Apr - Oct: 9:30 - 18:00 (last entry 17:15) Nov - Mar: 9:30 - 16:30 (last entry 15:45)
Prices:	Adult: Queen's Gallery £5.00, Palace £8.00, Both £11.00. Over 60 / Student (With ID): QG £4.00, P £6.50, Both £9.00 Under 17: QG £3.00, P £4.00, Both £5.50 Under 5: Free Family Ticket (2+3): QG: £13.00, P £20.00, Both £27.50
Facilities:	Shop, Disabled Access, Café
Contact:	0131 556 5100

Scotch Whisky Heritage Centre

Tucked in beside Edinburgh Castle, the whisky centre reveals the history, mystery and romance of Scotch whisky making. Tour guides take guests through the amazing difference between whiskies from the Highlands, Lowlands, Speyside and Islands. Watch a short film on the making of whisky, visit the distillery and learn the subtleties of the process, meet the ghost of a master blender who passes on some trade secrets and go on a barrel ride through the 300-year history of the "water of life". Whisky Barrel Restaurant offers food and drink.

Scotch Whisky Heritage Centre, 354 Castlehill, Royal Mile, EH1 2NE.

Hours:	10:00 - 18:00. Last tour 17:00.
Prices:	Adult: £7.95, Concession: £5.95, Child: £4.25 Family Ticket (up to 4 children): £18.00.
Contact:	0131 220 0441

The Royal Yacht Britannia

Yet another attraction down in the Port of Leith. You commence this worthwhile tour in the Visitor Centre where you can discover Britannia's fascinating history. The audio tour is self-led (available in 13 languages with a special handset for children in English) which takes you around five decks, giving a unique insight into what life was like for the Royal Family, Officers and Yachtsmen. You can see the Royal Marine Barracks, the Laundry and the Sick Bay. What is most amazing is how utterly ordinary the Royal quarters are – it's like a smart 1950s house.
The Royal Yacht Britannia, Ocean Terminal, Leith, EH6 6JJ

Hours:	January - February: Daily: 1000 - 1530; March - October: 0930 - 1630; November - December: 1000 - 1530. Closes 1.5 hours after last admission.
Disabled Facilities:	Full Wheelchair Access, Audio Handset, Written Script.
Prices:	Adult: £9.00 Senior (60+): £7.00 Child (5-17): £5.00 (under 4's go free) Student (in full-time education, with ID): £5.00 Family (2 adults and up to 3 children): £25.00.
Phone:	0131 555 5566
Internet:	www.royalyachtbritannia.co.uk

SCOTLAND

Museum of Flight

Take the A1 and come off at Haddington, 17 miles from the city centre. It's just off the A199. Two massive hangars, part of a World War II airfield, are packed with aeroplanes, rockets, models and memorabilia. Hangar 4 is the home of Concorde G-BOAA following her epic final voyage by land and sea from Heathrow. G-BOAA became the first of the British Airways fleet to operate commercially when she flew from London to Bahrain in January 1976. **Museum of Flight Museum, East Fortune Airfield, East Fortune, East Lothian, EH39 5LF.**

Hours:	16 March to 30 October: daily 10am to 5pm. 31 October to 31 March: weekends only or by prior arrangement 10am to 4pm.
Prices:	Adult: £5.00; Concession: £4.00 ; Child under 12: free.
Contact:	01620 880 308
Internet:	www.nms.ac.uk/flight

National Gallery of Scotland

The National Gallery of Scotland, oldest of the five Galleries, is in the heart of Edinburgh on The Mound, between the Old and New Towns. It is home to Scotland's greatest collection of European paintings and sculpture ranging from the Renaissance to Post-Impressionism, and is one of the finest galleries of its size in the world. At the heart of its collection are works by Jacopo Bassano, Van Dyck and Tiepolo plus Gauguin's *Vision after the Sermon*, Velázquez's *Old Woman Cooking Eggs*, El Greco's *Fábula*, Bernini's sculpture of *Carlo Antonio dal Pozzo*, Botticelli's *Virgin Adoring the Sleeping Christ Child* and Antonio Canova's *Three Graces*, shared with the Victoria & Albert Museum in London. It has the largest and most comprehensive collection of Scottish paintings in the world, including Ramsay, Raeburn, Wilkie and McTaggart. Among the best-loved works are Raeburn's *Reverend Robert Walker Skating on Duddingston Loch* and Ramsay's portrait of his second wife, Margaret Lindsay.

National Gallery of Scotland, The Mound, Edinburgh, EH2 2EL.

Phone:	0131 624 6200
Internet:	www.nationalgalleries.org

Edinburgh Zoo

Home to over 1,000 rare and beautiful animals and the daily penguin march, pictured, is always a hit with the children. Gift shop, cafeterias and hilltop safari ride. **Edinburgh Zoo, Murrayfield, EH12 6TS.**

Hours:	April -September: Daily: 0900-18:00; October & March: Daily: 0900-17:00; Nov-Feb: Daily: 0900-16:30.
Price:	Adults: £9.00 Children: (3-14) £6.00 Family Ticket (2 adults + 2 children): £28.00 Family Ticket (2 adults + 3 children): £31.50 Family Ticket (3 adults + 4 children): £35.00 Family Ticket (2 adults + 4 children): £33.00 Extra children (Family Ticket): £2.50 Disabled people (helper free, if required): £5.50 UB40 card holders: £6.00 Senior Citizens: £6.00 Students / Young people: £6.50.
Contact:	0131 334 9171
Internet:	www.edinburghzoo.org.uk

Hotels: (cont)

Dynamic Earth Science Centre

Dynamic Earth is the most exciting attraction to have opened in Edinburgh in recent times. Housed in a striking, tented structure (like a smaller version of a certain dome in London), there is plenty of interactive entertainment for both children and adults, such as its pre-historic, volcanic, tropic, Antarctic and dynamic galleries. It explores the extremes of planet Earth, travelling back in time to the Big Bang. You can feel the earth moved by an erupting volcano, and you can fly over glaciers, feel the chill of polar ice, and get caught in a tropical rainstorm, all of which might prove a light diversion after Murrayfield.

Our Dynamic Earth Science Centre, Holyrood Road, EH8 8AS.

Hours:	November - March: 1000 - 1700 Wed to Sun (closed Mon & Tue) - last entry at 1550. April - October: 1000 - 1700 daily (open seven days) - last entry at 1550 July and August: 1000 - 1800 daily (open seven days) - last entry at 1650
Disabled:	The attraction is fully accessible - Assisted Wheelchair Access
Prices:	Adult: £8.95; Children (5 - 15)/Senior: £5.45; Student/UB40/Disabled: £6.50; Family tickets from: £16.50.
Contact:	0131 550 7800
Internet:	www.dynamicearth.co.uk

SHOPPING

ANTIQUES

Causewayside Antiques

Exciting cluster of shops selling curios, furniture, theatre props and military bits and bobs. It's like a small market place and is somewhere to pick up something unusual. Well worth a mooch around.

Causewayside Antiques, 67-189 Causwayside, Southside.

Phone:	0131 662 0557

Edinburgh Architectural Salvage Yard (EASY)

Creaking old warehouse jam packed with wonderful and interesting reclamation, you can get anything from a stuffed elephant to a cast iron drain cover. Again, a fascinating place for a mooch. It is not cheap, however. Edinburghers are into this kind of thing, so demand has driven the prices up.

Edinburgh Architectural Salvage Yard (EASY), 31 West Bowling Green St, Leith.

Phone:	0131 554 7077
Internet:	www.easy-arch-salv.co.uk

Princes Mall

Over 60 shops offering a selection of quality designer fashion, food and gifts - including Scottish arts and crafts. A newly improved Food Court, coffee shop and outdoor kiosk offer a wide range of food and refreshments throughout three levels of the Mall.
Princes Mall, Princes Street, City Centre.

Phone:	0131 557 3759
Internet:	www.princesmall-edinburgh.co.uk

CRAFT AND KNITWEAR

Anta Scotland Ltd

Handpainted stoneware and 100% woollen textiles, all designed and made in the Highlands. Ceramics include four tartan designs, a thistle, bluebell and a children's range. Throws, cushions, cloth and carpet, produced in tartan.
Anta Scotland Ltd, Crockets Land, 91-93 West Bow, Victoria Street, Old Town.

Phone:	0131 225 4616
Internet:	www.anta.co.uk

Ragamuffin

The very best of designer knitwear and original clothes, inspired in-house design. Also heaps of hats, funky scarves, sparkly jewellery.
Ragamuffin, 278 The Canongate, Royal Mile.

Phone:	0131 557 6007
Internet:	www.ragamuffinonline.co.uk

GLASSWARE

The Glasshouse at Edinburgh Crystal Shop

Guided factory tours, exhibition room, video presentation, factory shop, crystal showroom, Scottish craft gift shop. Free coach and car parking, picnic tables, play area.
The Glasshouse at Edinburgh Crystal Shop (factory shop), Visitor Centre Eastfield, Penicuik, Midlothian, EH26 8HB. Ask for directions.

Phone:	01968 675128

COFFEE SHOPS

Elephant House Café, 21 George IV Bridge, Old Town, EH1 1EN
One of the most extensive ranges of fine quality teas and coffee in Edinburgh. Large selection of cakes and hot food. Great views of the castle. JK Rowling wrote much of the first Harry Potter book here.

Phone:	0131 220 5355
Internet:	www.elephant-house.co.uk

Black Medicine Coffee Company Coffee Shop, 2 Nicolson Street, EH8 9DH.
A distinctive, individual coffee shop a short distance from the Royal Mile serving the best Italian coffee and a range of quality bagles, paninis, pastries and cakes.

Phone:	0131 622 7003

Coffee shops: (cont)

Café Hub, Castlehill, Royal Mile, EH1 2NE.
Large yellow building more famous for being the HQ of the Edinburgh International Festival. Gaining a reputation for its food.

Phone:	0131 473 2067
Email:	cafehub@eif.co.uk
Internet:	www.thehub-edinburgh.com

Café Newton, Dean Gallery, 72 Belford Rd, West End.

Tucked away in the grounds of the gallery pictured above this is a good and cheap joint for simple food and excellent coffee.

Phone:	0131 624 6273

Filmhouse Café Bar, 88 Lothian Rd, Tollcross. Busy and bustling gathering point, and not just for filmgoers. Just as popular with drinkers as with café society.

Phone:	0131 229 5932

Gallery Café, Scottish National Gallery, 74 Belford Rd, West End. Good and cheap food, renowned for its healthy salads and imaginative dishes.

Phone:	01 31 332 8600

Spoon, 15 Blackfriars St, Old Town.
One of Edinburgh's best. Everything is done well here from the fresh and tasty soups to the giant sandwiches and frothing cappuccinos.

Phone:	0131 556 6922

Terrace Café, Royal Botanic Garden, Inverleith Row, New Town.
Great setting in the gardens commanding some tremendous views of the city. The menu is as attractive as the setting.

Phone:	0131 552 0616

Valvona & Crolla, 19 Elm Row, City Centre.
A veritable institution. Brilliant deli, accomplished restaurant and wine merchant, they still find time to accommodate the humble caffeine addict (see restaurants).

Phone:	0131 556 6066

TEA ROOMS

The café in Edinburgh has all but replaced the city's fabled tearooms, where once the fur coated denizens of Morningside cocked their genteel fingers over a cuppa. They have done for the tea swilling sorority what the grey squirrel did to the red. So at the bottom of our café list are a couple of remaining tearooms.

Forsyth's Tea Room, 81 High St, Old Town. The sort of place you might expect to encounter Miss Jean Brodie, or her creator, Dame Muriel Spark.

Phone:	0131 557 5150

Clarinda's Tea Room, 69 Canongate, Old Town. This is a wonderfully traditional tea room with all the charm and high level of service you would expect.

Phone:	0131 557 1888

EAT, DRINK & SLEEP

OLD TOWN BARS

TRADITIONAL PUBS

Blue Blazer, 2 Spittal St.
Close to the Castle in a former brew house, this is a well run and friendly pub that attracts trippers and locals alike. Good range of Scottish beers.

Phone:	0131 229 5030

Bow Bar, 80 West Bow, Grassmarket.
On one of Edinburgh's prettier streets linking the Grassmarket with George IV bridge, the Bow Bar is a great little pub. One-roomed bar with lots of ales. Deuchars, the 2002 Champion Beer of Britain, was brewed specifically for this pub. Lots of interesting features and a lively, friendly atmosphere.

Phone:	0131 226 7667

Doctor's, 32 Forrest Rd.
Big screen. Traditional and friendly pub, good range of beers, food and a very decent wine list, it is amongst the top places to go on big match day – assuming, of course, you don't fancy joining the massive scrummage or don't have a ticket.

Phone:	0131 225 1819

Ensign Ewart, 521 Lawnmarket.
Hilariously unwelcoming – you need a PIN code to visit the toilet – the Ensign, named after the Waterloo hero, might have a reputation as curmudgeon central but its regulars love the place. Great beer, great atmosphere and, if you're lucky, great entertainment as it's a regular haunt of some of Scotland's finest folk musicians.

Phone:	0131 2257440

Milne's Bar, 35 Hanover St.
Situated on the corner of Rose St, Edinburgh's most famous drinking alley, Milne's is another classic with literary connections. Hugh McDairmid and Norman McCaig, Scotland's leading poets in their time, regularly took the waters here while discussing revolution. The old rhymers might birl in their graves to see the business-suit crowd it now attracts, but still a fine boozer for all that.

Phone:	0131 225 6738

Three Sisters, 139 Cowgate.
A theme pub, apparently, although you might struggle to identify the theme from its mix of Western, Irish and Gothic influences. Still, becoming well established as a rugby pub, albeit one for the students and the kilts-and-Caterpillar-boots brigade. Good service, decent beer and strong hormones on offer.

Phone:	0131 622 6801

TRENDY BARS

Bar Union, 253 Cowgate.
Late and cheap drinking in roughish and ready surroundings. Good pitstop for anyone wishing to add icing (or carrots) to the cake after a day on the tiles.

Phone:	0131 557 2780

Ego, 14 Picardy Place.
The Mirrorball Preservation Society would love the place. But so would anyone after a few jars elsewhere, as Ego has a friendly atmosphere and a generally happy crowd. Not one for the style fascists (thankfully) but choose your evening carefully as theme nights might not be to everyone's tastes.

Phone:	0131 478 7434

Opium, 71 Cowgate.
In the heart of Edinburgh's stag night zone (the Cowgate), Opium offers an upmarket take on the traditional rock pub. Open until 3am most nights, it stages regular clubs and entry is free, with the occasional drink offers thrown in. Offers a more metal alternative to the traditional student haunts in the area.

Phone:	0131 225 8382

El Barrio Latin Bar, 104 West Port.
If you fancy immersing yourself in 'The Rum-Soaked Nightspot of Latin Rhythm!' this is the (self-styled) place. El Barrio is the only purpose built Latin/Hispanic bar in the whole of Scotland. Open until indecent hours, there's a fair chance of uninhibited fun to be had here.

Phone:	0131 229 8805
Internet:	www.elbarrio.co.uk

Espionage, 4 India Buildings, Victoria St.
A labyrinthine hotbed of covert liaisons. The Lizard Lounge is the main infiltration point to Espionage's lowest levels. In the late 1950s, the doorman was none other than Sean 'Big Tam' Connery. Big, wild last-port-of-call kind of place.

Phone:	0131 477 7007
Internet:	www.espionage007.co.uk

It's a Scream, The Tron, 9 Hunter Sq.
11 Big screens. Bright yellow three level den offering a variety of fun themes, from the quieter toned down ground level bar to the noisier student magnet in the basement.

Phone:	0131 226 0931
Internet:	www.screampubs.co.uk

Medina, 45-47 Lothian St.
Located underneath Negociants restaurant this is a Moroccan themed nightclub offering live acoustic performances, DJs playing Hip Hop, R&B, Funk, Soul and House music plus 'interactive' salsa classes.

Phone:	0131 225 6313
Internet:	www.medinaedinburgh.co.uk

The Scotsman Lounge.
Open at 6am every morning except Sunday, this pub is ideal for hard core evening drinkers still on the batter, or those coming off a night shift. Occupies the rather grand former residence of The Scotsman newspaper, there is more going on there now than during the era of hot metal.

Phone:	0131 225 7726

Bar Oz, 14 Forrest Rd.
Big screen. Geared up for watching all things sporty, this pulls in phalanxes of Aussie ex-pats. Set in a massive Masonic hall, Bar Oz has a large central bar and a balcony with lots of seating. The beer is all keg and there are lots of types of bottled beers. Food is surprisingly cooked in-house and perfectly acceptable at reasonable prices.

Phone:	0131 220 1816

Biddy Mulligans, 94-96 Grassmarket.
Big screen. A popular Grassmarket pub with a mixed crowd and decked out in a gothic style with occasional live acts. Does an excellent breakfast and Sunday roasts.

Phone:	0131 220 1246

Black Bull, 12 Grassmarket.
Big screen. An enormous black bull's head with flashing red eyes announces that you have got to the right place. Thanks to its close proximity to the Venue and Studio 24, it's definitely the place to head if you like to wash your beer down with a healthy dose of Guns 'N Roses and Aerosmith.

Phone:	0131 225 6636
Internet:	www.myedinburgh.net

Finnegan's Wake, 9b Victoria St.
Big screen. Irish theme pub that does live bands and great Irish music. Inside there is a large circular bar and small booths around the perimeter. The floors and walls are all wood with a small raised area to one corner where the bands play. Bar food is served during the day and, of course, Guinness is on tap.

Phone:	0131 226 3816

Liquid Room, 9C Victoria Street.
Liquid Room is one of Reekie's most talked about venues where groovy new bands such as Dawn of the Replicants play. One of Joe Strummer's last gigs, this is where middle class kids like to hang out. They also have regular drinks promotions and a late license, which might, of course, explain its popularity with the younger shakers.

Phone:	0131 225 2564

RESTAURANTS
(Old Town)

David Bann, 56-58 St Mary St, EH1 1SX. £20.
Very reasonable wine list at this new and exciting vegetarian addition to the scene. Walnut and hazelnut haggis or fennel risotto come in for praise. For those who like their puddings, the assiette for two sounds fun: hot chocolate pudding with white chocolate sauce, cognac chocolate truffle, tartlet of date and kiwi topped with homemade vanilla ice cream and homemade raspberry ice cream with raspberry coulis. Go easy on the starters and mains if you are going to take this option.

Phone:	0131 556 5888
Internet:	www.davidbann.com

The Doric Tavern, 15/16 Market Street, EH1 1DE
Unpretentious and jolly wine bar/pub opposite the side entrance of Waverley station offering good, honest Scottish and European food. The menus can change twice daily depending on the popularity of the meals, so you can guarantee that everything is totally fresh. An excellent selection of wines from the Old and New World.

Phone:	0131 225 1084
Internet:	www.thedoric.co.uk

La Garrigue, 31 Jeffrey St, EH1 1DH. £23.
A small parcel of Edinburgh's Old Town which shall, for the foreseeable future, be a corner of Languedoc. A cross between an up-market restaurant and a French bistro, the ambience is friendly and relaxed. The cool hyacinth walls and original Tim Stead tables and chairs create a light and airy space in which to sample Jean Michel Gauffre's south western cooking. Straight from Castelnaudary comes le cassoulet aux trois viandes, the famous baked bean casserole with pork, lamb, duck and Toulouse sausage, served with a walnut salad, or the tender breast of French duck with mango and peaches, raspberry vinegar jus. Vaux le detour, as they say in some quarters.

Phone:	0131 557 3032
Email:	jeanmichel@lagarrigue.co.uk
Internet:	www.lagarrigue.co.uk

Restaurants: Old Town (cont)

Off the Wall, 105 High St, Old Town, EH1 1SG. £35.
Hidden from view on the first floor above the Royal Mile the chef/owner David Anderson keeps things simple but well executed and has built up a deserved reputation. First class seafood and good game.

Phone:	0131 558 1497
Internet:	www.off-the-wall.co.uk

Petit Paris, 38-40 Grassmarket, EH1 2JU. £21.
The Auld Alliance is alive and well. It's also cheap, cheerful and tasty in this authentic restaurant. Great value food, served with friendliness and charm. Chequer table cloths and bare whitewashed walls are a soothing counterbalance to the frantic bustle of the Grassmarket. Genuinely Gallic, down to the carefully choreographed chaos.

Phone:	0131 226 2442
Internet:	www.petitparis-restaurant.co.uk

Le Sept Restaurant, 5 Hunter Square, EH1 1QW. £20.
In the heart of Edinburgh's Old Town, this friendly and informal restaurant is still run by the man who set it up nearly a quarter of a century ago. Le Sept offers a varied, French-based menu, and crepes are a particular speciality.

Phone:	0131 225 5428
Internet:	www.lesept.co.uk

Viva Mexico, 41 Cockburn St, EH1 1BS. £18.
Classic Mexican diner run by the Gonzalez family since 1984. It's on two levels: upstairs is quiet and intimate; downstairs the décor and ambience are more boisterous. Billy Connolly once said Mexicans only make one dish, they just fold it different ways. True or not, they do it well at Viva Mexico, as well as serving the best margaritas in town.

Phone:	0131 226 5145
Internet:	www.viva-mexico.co.uk

SCOTLAND

Witchery, Castlehill, Royal Mile, EH1 2NF (see also hotel listing opposite)

Located in a spectacular sixteenth century merchant's house only a few doors down from the gates of Edinburgh Castle. It is only a few yards from the Whisky Heritage Centre and opposite the Camera Obscura. The Witchery is one of the city's most atmospheric dining spots. Inside enjoy the stunning décor from the same team that did Prestonfield (see entry), the wine list is spectacular and there's some very fine Scottish produce. Its ideal location means it is often a good spot for celebrity spotting.

Phone:	0131 225 5613
Internet:	www.thewitchery.com

Tower Restaurant, Museum of Scotland, Chambers St, EH1 1JF. £30.
Upmarket rooftop brasserie with a commanding view across the city. The food tries hard and often succeeds - rolled suckling pig, warm bean salad, Dijon mustard dressing, or organically reared Shetland salmon, cardamom rice, onion fritters. Highly praised starters include warm pear and Dunsyre blue cheese gallette with rocket salad or pressed fish terrine with home made piccalilli.

Phone:	0131 225 3003
Internet:	www.tower-restaurant.com

HOTELS
(Old Town)

LUXURY HOTELS

Carlton, 19 North Bridge, EH1 1SD.
184 rooms, rack £195 s/d/t. From £135.
Big rooms in a bustling part of town between the Royal Mile and Princes St. Good, comfortable base camp.

Phone:	0131 472 3000
Email:	carlton@paramount-hotels.co.uk
Internet:	www.paramount-hotels.co.uk/carlton

Radisson SAS, 80 High St, EH1 1TH.
238 rooms, from £110 s/d/t. Rack £225.
Modern yet in keeping with the vernacular baronial style of the Royal Mile. Pubs, restaurants, the Castle and just about everything at your door.

Phone:	0131 557 9797
Email:	reservations.edinburgh@radissonsas.com
Internet:	www.radissonsas.com

Scotsman, 20 North Bridge, EH1 1YT.
58 rooms, from £250 s/d/t. Rack £295.
Former home of the eponymous newspaper, the Scotsman Hotel opened in 2001 and quickly became known for its relaxed comfort and style. Boasts the usual fitness facilities, with an unusual stainless steel pool. Central location and spectacular views from some rooms.

Phone:	0131 556 5565
Email:	reservations@thescotsmanhotel.co.uk
Internet:	www.thescotsmanhotel.co.uk

Witchery by the Castle, 352 Castlehill, The Royal Mile, Edinburgh, EH1 2NF.
7 suites, from £295.
16th century merchant's house in the heart of the Old Town near the top of the Royal Mile. Sumptuous and extravagant luxury. Some rooms have galley kitchens while downstairs is one of Edinburgh's best restaurants (see restaurants).

Phone:	0131 225 5613
Email:	mail@thewitchery.com
Internet:	www.thewitchery.com

MODERATELY PRICED HOTELS

Apex International City Hotel, 31-35 Grassmarket, EH1 2HS.
175 rooms, from £130 s/d/t. Rack £240.
Big glass front and open-plan design, beautifully situated at the foot of Edinburgh's castle rock. Nicely positioned, too, for the bustling nightlife of the Grassmarket area, where good pubs and restaurant abound. No great character to the place, but you won't be staying in for the evening anyway. Rooms with castle views slightly pricier.

Phone:	0131 243 3456
Email:	reservations@apexhotels.co.uk
Internet:	www.apexhotels.co.uk/edinburgh

Hotels: Old Town (cont)

Apex City Hotel, 61 Grassmarket, EH1 2JF.
119 rooms, from £130. Rack £240.
Bland businessman's bunkhouse at the foot of Edinburgh's castle rock. No great character to the place, but that's not the point. Location is all.

Phone:	0131 243 3456
Email:	reservations@apexhotels.co.uk
Internet:	www.apexhotels.co.uk/edinburgh

Point Hotel, 34 Bread St, EH3 9AF.
138 rooms, from £55. Rack rate £145.
Once a Co-op store the Point is now one of the city's grooviest joints, designed by architect-owner, Andrew Doolan, who died unexpectedly in 2004. There is a cocktail bar and good but inexpensive restaurant. Magnet for arty folk.

Phone:	0131 221 5555
Email:	reservations@point-hotel.co.uk
Internet:	www.point-hotel.co.uk

BUDGET

Ibis, 6 Hunter Square, Old Town, EH1 1QW.
99 rooms from £52.95 s/d/t to £95 s/d/t.
Tucked away in the heart of the Old Town just off the Royal Mile. Cheap and cheerful, provides a solid and functional base for any visit to the city.

Phone:	0131 240 7000
Email:	H2039@accor-hotels.com
Internet:	www.accor-hotels.com

Travelodge Edinburgh Central Hotel, 33 St. Mary's Street, EH1 1TA. 193 rooms, from £70 to £90 s/d/t. Modern hotel just off the Royal Mile. Does all you need and is right in the thick of things. Good value for money.

Phone:	0870 191 1637
Internet:	www.travelodge.co.uk

SCOTLAND

NEW TOWN

BARS

TRADITIONAL PUBS

Barony Bar, 81-3 Broughton St
Despite being in the most bohemian and trendy street in Scotland, the Barony somehow contrives to be an unpretentious straight-up drinking haunt where folk gather for a grown up pint and a chat. Cosy fireplace but beware: can get packed at night.

Phone:	0131 557 0546

Café Royal, 19 West Register St.
An Edinburgh classic and probably the most famous bar in the city. The Café Royal is architecture-in-aspic, a perfect example of an upmarket Victorian watering hole. Generally classy ambience is suspended for the Six Nations – the only time the TV is switched on – when things can become a little more boisterous.

Phone:	0131 557 4792

Cask & Barrel, 115 Broughton St.
Mostly locals drink here. Always busy, especially so on 'match day.' It is a very popular stop off pub en route to either of Edinburgh's football grounds, not to mention Murrayfield. An old traditional style circular bar is the central attraction and a large selection of guest ales can be changed on a daily basis.

Phone:	0131 556 3132

Cumberland Bar, 1-3 Cumberland St.
Serves excellent Taylor's Landlord and Caledonian Deuchars in a smart wood-panelled bar with green leather seating to the edges. This is a stylish drink station dispensing the amber from traditional Scottish beer founts.

Phone:	0131 558 3134

Guildford Arms, 1 West Register St.
Spectacular internal features – plasterwork, cornices and friezes offset by a garish carpet that belongs on a skip. There's a gallery room and a good number of ales. Usually very busy and has big screens. Next door to the rather classier Café Royal.

Phone:	0131 556 4312

Oxford Bar, 8 Young St.
Tucked away in a New Town side street, the Oxford has gained worldwide fame as the boozer of choice of Ian Rankin's fictitious Inspector Rebus. Once enjoyed a reputation for eccentricity; now just a solid and respectable Edinburgh bar. Good beer, but watch out for the literary tourists. And Ian Rankin.

Phone:	0131 539 7119

Kays Bar, 39 Jamaica Street West.
Rugby fans' heaven. This is a delightful little pub in a converted wine importer's office just off India St, a very smart part of town. Almost everyone who drinks in Kays is a rugby nut and the games will be shown on TV. Get there early, for a camel stands more chance of passing through the nozzle of a beer engine than you will of squeezing in. Great list of impeccably presented ales. Edinburgh's finest.

Phone:	0131 225 1858

SCOTLAND

TRENDY BARS

Bar 38, 126-8 George St.
Forget about the blond wood fittings, the cloth sculptures and the pricey drinks (not to mention the good food and lively atmosphere): this place made a splash by introducing unisex toilets, so plumbing is a major topic of conversation in some quarters.

Phone:	0131 220 6180

Browns, 131-3 George St.
Bustling, relaxed and friendly atmosphere which makes this unpretentious brasserie an ideal place to sit, chat, eat and drink. Good cocktails and safe from Goths and other strange types who flit around the darker recesses of Auld Reekie.

Phone:	0131 225 4442
Internet:	www.browns-restaurants.com

Living Room, 113-5 George St. (see restaurant entry)
This place seems to appeal to a wide cross-section of the city and seems to have got the balance between food and flashy drinks just about right. Colonial style setting.

Madogs, 38a George St.
Live entertainment every day of the week until 3am. Featuring live groups and entertainers established on the European Piano Bar circuit, An intimate venue best known as the launch pad of former Genesis front man, Ray Wilson. Cheap drink and friendly service.

Phone:	0131 225 3408

Bars: New Town (cont)

Opal Lounge, 51a George St

If the neuron-scrambling cocktails don't floor you then their price-tags certainly will in this glitzy monument to conspicuous consumption. Still, not a bad place to perfect your lounge-lizard look, if that's what you want to do. But remember – glamour doesn't come cheap.

Phone:	0131 226 2275
Internet:	www.opallounge.co.uk

Penny Black, 15 West Register St.

Good place to end the night or start the morning if you're feeling especially energetic. Whilst it's not the smartest of chic venues it does open at 5am and caters for those who like to party while the rest of the city sleeps.

Phone:	0131 556 1106

Fingers Piano Bar, 61a Frederick St.

See out the night or see in the dawn with some laid-back ivory tinkling at this popular piano bar. Fingers is famed as the place to wind down after the serious activity elsewhere, and regular queues outside bear witness to its popularity.

Phone:	0131 225 3026

Yo! Below, 66 Rose St.

Itchy Edinburgh describes YB being 'done out like a dojo with cushions,' like a Jackie Chan movie set full of Pokemon fanatics. There's a DJ, and a beer tap on each table that counts how many pints you're overdrawn at the bar. Worth a trip for the curious.

Phone:	0131 220 6040
Internet:	www.yobelow.com

RESTAURANTS
(New Town)

SCOTLAND

Bar Roma, 39a Queensferry St, EH2 4RA. £27.

Long-established ristorante, with a lively atmosphere and even livelier waiters. Bar Roma can occasionally irritate by camping up the pastiche Italian theme, but it can also serve stonkingly good and authentic fare. Generous pasta portions.

Phone:	0131 226 2977
Internet:	www.bar-roma.co.uk

Café St Honore, 34 NW Thistle Street Lane, EH2 1EA. £30.

More French than most of Paris, this corner of foreign Edinburgh, just off Frederick St, will forever be fin de siecle France. Another example of the auld alliance still at work. Bustling and personally run bistro. You can hardly go wrong with such favourites as boeuf bourgignon, navarin of lamb or duck leg confit.

Phone:	0131 226 2211
Internet:	www.cafesthonore.com

Ducks at Le Marche Noir, 2-4 Eyre Place, EH3 5EP. £30.

Good and willing service and some imaginative cooking in this comfortable Franco-Scottish establishment where the owner's name (Duck) has given rise to a riot of avian themes. Sir Sean Connery, not given to gushing praise, has marked the visitors' book with the less than immortal words: 'Good – very good, very very good.'

Our critic enjoyed pan fried salmon with spicy lentils, coriander creme fraiche and deep fried wonton, followed by a robust fillet of Aberdeen Angus beef on sweet onion compote with crispy parsnip curls and wild mushroom sauce.

Phone:	0131 558 1608
Email:	booking@ducks.co.uk
Internet:	www.ducks-le-marche-noir.co.uk

Fishers in the City Restaurant, 8 Thistle Street, New Town, EH2 1EN.
Slick seafood city centre restaurant. Off-shoot of the original Fishers in Leith (see p 246). Everything from Arbroath smokies to monkfish pakora, Edinburgh-style bouillabaisse to fillet steak cooked with a brandy sauce. Range of vegetarian options.

Phone:	0131 225 5109
Internet:	www.fishersbistro.co.uk

Howies Waterloo Place, 29 Waterloo Place, EH1 3BQ. £20.
One of a chain of four serving fresh Scottish produce in a modern and innovative style. Relaxed service and atmosphere with a very reasonable wine list.

Phone:	0131 556 5766
Internet:	www.howies.uk.com

Hadrian's, Balmoral Hotel, 2 North Bridge, EH1 1TR. £25.
British New Wave in an art deco setting, Hadrian's was recently refurbished with 'a palette of lime and walnut and a splash of African violet'. The combination of colours was inspired by the natural landscapes of Edinburgh, taking the Salisbury Crags, sea and sky as influences. Uncomplicated menu cleanly executed: pan seared salmon, rib eye with Roquefort butter, pan seared tune Nicoise sort of thing.

Phone:	0131 557 5000
Internet:	www.thebalmoralhotel.com

Henderson's Salad Table, 94 Hanover Street, EH2 1DR.
Henderson's is now in its 40th year of providing good, innovative vegetarian food. Freshly prepared salads, quiches and savouries are available all day along with Henderson's breads. All ingredients are organically grown and local. Interesting vegetarian cuisine.

Phone:	0131 225 2131
Internet:	www.hendersonsofedinburgh.co.uk

Living Room Restaurant, 113 - 115 George Street (see trendy bar entry).
One of a groovy chain of places that has had the bright idea of making eating and drinking a subsidiary of being seen. It's a human zoo without bars. Sit there and you cannot avoid looking at others, who themselves are cricking their necks. Decent food and cocktails. Ingenious concept. The place has a cool, colonial feel, and the service is pretty good. 0870 4422718 www.thelivingroom.co.uk

Phone:	0870 44 22 718
Internet:	www.thelivingroom.co.uk

Number One, Balmoral, 1 Princes St, EH2 2EQ. £50.
Edinburgh's chintziest fine dining is the city's second place to get a Michelin star. Chef Jeff Bland has an original approach and showcases Scottish ingredients with dishes such as white crab meat layered with pasta, avocado and vine tomato and mango jelly, or truffle poached duck egg, with sautéed (Scottish) frog's legs, petit pois veloute and garlic oil. These are signature starters, while poached Scottish lobster with scallops, mussels and shellfish nage or Gressingham duck breast with cumin spiced butternut squash and pak choi are typical mains, all showing a precise focus and high level of technical expertise.

Phone:	0131 557 6727
Internet:	www.roccofortehotels.com

Roti, 70 Rose St North Lane, EH2 3DX. £25.
This is a restaurant that serves Indian cuisine, not a curry house. In the building that once housed Martin's, once of Edinburgh's best little restaurants. Tucked away to the side of Princes St, it is owned by Tony Singh, who runs Oloroso (see entry) and former head chef on the Royal Yacht Britannia.

Phone:	0131 225 1233
Internet:	www.roti.uk.com

Valvona & Crolla Caffe Bar, 19 Elm Row, EH7 4AA. £25.
V&C could have been transported wholesale from Milan: you walk into an Aladdin's Cave of cheeses and hams to a waft of fresh baked bread and myriad other Italian delicacies. Great list of wines. Beyond the long food counter is the restaurant where the Contini family continue to serve up oak-smoked salmon, pork, beef and pine-nut meatballs in a tomato Vitale tomato sauce and sundry other dishes. Cheerful and busy. Closes at 6pm weekdays and Saturdays and at 4.30pm Sundays (lunch: 12-3).

Phone:	0131 556 6066
Internet:	www.valvonacrolla.com

HOTELS
(New Town)

LUXURY HOTELS

Balmoral, 1 Princes Street, EH2 2EQ.
167 rooms, from £145 s/d/t. Rack rate from £330 d/t.
From £280 s. An Edinburgh institution and landmark, and one of the world's great rugby hotels. Pricey, but suitably swish. The Balmoral is that great granite pile at the east end of Princes Street, but it comes alive on international match days, when some of rugby's most famous faces can usually be spotted in the foyer.

Phone:	0131 556 2414
Email:	thebalmoralhotel@rfhotels.com
Internet:	www.thebalmoralhotel.com

Glasshouse, 2 Greenside Place, EH1 3AA.
65 rooms from £215 to £395. Internet deals possible.
Roof garden at the foot of Calton Hill with some great city views. The rooms are thoughtfully designed in a U shape around the garden above a modern shopping mall and you enter this ultra-modern space through the portals of an erstwhile church.

Phone:	0131 525 8200
Email:	resglasshouse@theetongroup.com
Internet:	www.theetoncollection.com

Howard, 34 Great King St, EH3 6QH.
13 rooms (5 suites) from £190. Rack rate from £240 for rugby weekends.
Discreet and luxy 5-star Georgian townhouse. Crystal chandeliers and opulent furnishings plus a 'team' of butlers (is there a collective noun?) Hotel also boasts 'lifestyle managers'.

Phone:	0131 557 3500
Email:	reserve@thehoward.com
Internet:	www.thehoward.com

Parliament House Hotel, 15 Calton Hill, EH1 3BJ.
53 rooms, from £80. Rack £180 t/d. £120 s.
Comfortable and quiet retreat just round the corner from the madding crowds. Got its name when the fledgling parliament was poised to move into the Royal High School next door. Then plans changed...

Phone:	0131 478 4000
Email:	info@parliamenthouse-hotel.co.uk
Internet:	www.parliamenthouse-hotel.co.uk

Roxburghe, 38 Charlotte Sq, EH2 4HG.
197 rooms, from £160. Rack £250 s/d/t. £210 s.
Fine Georgian building in one of the classic New Town squares in the city centre. Exterior is Adam. Smart and very period without being showy.

Phone:	0131 240 5500
Email:	roxburghe@esmm.co.uk
Internet:	www.theroxburghe.com

Royal Terrace Hotel Edinburgh, 18 Royal Terrace, EH7 5AQ.
108 rooms, from £85 s/d/t. Rack £175 to £240.
Quintessential Edinburgh, set in a tranquil row of Georgian houses with a charming garden, conservatory restaurant and lively cocktail bar.

Phone:	0131 557 3222
Email:	reservations@royalterracehotel.co.uk
Internet:	www.roaylterracehotel.co.uk

MODERATELY PRICED

10 Glenfinlas St, Charlotte Sq, EH3 6AQ.

2 rooms, from £85 to £90. Also 3 apartments, minimum 3 nights.
Immaculate Georgian house. B&B plus ground floor 5 star apartment in just off the square, pictured. Family run with 2 further apartments on the Lothian Rd.

Phone:	0131 225 8695
Email:	rugby@edinburghholidays.com
Internet:	www.edinburgh-holidays.com

Brunswick Hotel, 7 Brunswick St, Edinburgh, EH7 5JB.
10 rooms, from £35 s, £60 d/t.
Georgian townhouse designed by William Playfair, architect of the National Gallery of Scotland. Traditional decor but comfortable and unfussy. Good base for a remarkably reasonable price.

Phone:	0131 556 1238
Email:	info@edinburghbrunswickhotel.co.uk
Internet:	www.edinburghbrunswickhotel.co.uk

Hotels: New Town (cont)

Christopher North House Hotel, 6 Gloucester Place, New Town EH3 6EF.
15 rooms, from £98 - £140 s/d/t.
Down in Stockbridge, a village on the edge of New Town. Great spot and a charming little hotel. Area abounds with good shops, pubs and restaurants.

Phone:	www.christophernorth.co.uk
Internet:	reservations@christophernorth.co.uk

George Hotel, 19-21 George St, EH2 2PB.
195 rooms from £120 – £150 s/d/t.
One of the New Town's grandest buildings built by Robert Adam in the late 18th century. Splendid and unspoilt Georgian period piece – quintessential Edinburgh.

Phone:	0131 225 1251
Email:	Edinburgh@interconti.com
Internet:	www.principal-hotels.com

Rick's Restaurant with Rooms, 55a Frederick St, EH2 1LH.
10 rooms, fixed £130 s/d/t.
Comfortable and sophisticated rooms above a successful restaurant. Popular with celebrities.

Phone:	0131 622 7800
Email:	info@ricksedinburgh.co.uk
Internet:	www.ricksedinburgh.co.uk

BUDGET

SCOTLAND

Ailsa Craig Hotel, 42 Royal Terrace.
14 rooms, from £35pp. £70-£100 d/t. Dorm for 7 or 8: £30 a head.
Georgian family townhouse near the Playhouse Theatre, at the foot of Calton Hill.

Phone:	0131 556 1022
Email:	ailsacraighotel@ednet.co.uk
Internet:	www.townhousehotels.co.uk

Elm Row, 42 Elm Row, EH7 4AH. 2 rooms, £35 s, £60 d.
Luxury B&B only a few minutes' walk from most of the city's attractions. Good attention to detail. Continental and Scottish meat-free breakfasts.

Phone:	reservations@elmview.net
Internet:	www.elmview.net

Six Mary's Place, Raeburn Place, Stockbridge, EH4 1JH.
8 rooms, from £70 to £90 s/d/t. Fam £125 to £150 (2d & 1s).
Sympathetically modernised Georgian townhouse with free internet access for guests. Great part of town and close to that tiny rugby Mecca, Kay's Bar in Jamaica St. For rugby historians it is only a few steps from the site of the first rugby international, when Scotland defeated Engalnd by a goal and a try to a single try on 27 March 1871. Mind you, it was 20-a-side and hacking (kicking the shins to persuade your opponent to release the ball) was allowed, so it is not just the scoreline that has changd over the centuries.

Phone:	0131 332 8965
Email:	info@sixmarysplace.co.uk
Internet:	www.sixmarysplace.co.uk

WEST END
(Southside, Tollcross, Marchmont & Fountainbridge)
BARS

TRADITIONAL PUBS

Athletic Arms, 1-3 Angle Park Terrace, West End.
AKA the Diggers (it is opposite a cemetery) this is a first class pub just a few minutes' walk from Murrayfield. It's also very close to the Caledonian Deuchars brewery and many fans find it following the full-time Diaspora from the ground.

Phone:	0131 337 3822

Bennet's Bar, 1 Maxwell St, Morningside.
Belhaven beers plus four guest ales this is a real gem of an old-fashioned Edinburgh pub that has been run by the eponymous family for several generations. Lots of Edwardiana.

Phone:	0131 447 1903

Bennets Bar, 8 Leven St, Marchmont. Truly wonderful piece of Victorian pub architecture – lots of tiling and leaded windows and a great range of real ales, malts and a good wine list. Big screen available. Busy and friendly.

Phone:	0131 229 5143

Bert's Bar, 29-31 William St, West End. Old-fashioned, traditional bar designed for standing rather than sitting. This is a no frills ale house designed with drinking in mind. And it is none the worse for that.

Phone:	0131 225 5748

The Canny Man's, 239 Morningside Rd, Morningside.
Great food and tremendous beer in a very special pub. The Canny Man's is a warren of fascinating rooms and a treasure trove of antiquities. It is expensive but money around here does not seem to be a problem.

Phone:	0131 447 1484

Cloisters, 26 Brougham St, Tollcross.
Good range of real ales in this converted monastery. Popular with beer connoisseurs, mature students, lecturers and other bearded types for whom the number of beers on offers is usually more than ten. They also do a 'malt of the month' for hardy souls who indulge in 'chasers.'

Phone:	0131 221 9997

Drouthy Neebors, 1-3 West Preston St, Southside.
As you might guess from the name, this is a Scottish theme pub. Either that or a Peter Sellers invention. Appeals to the older generation of beer swiller. Shouldn't be too crowded.

Phone:	0131 662 9617

Film House, 88 Lothian Rd, Tollcross.
One of Edinburgh's best cinemas, almost as many people come here to eat and drink. The bar fulfils both of these functions with aplomb. Not far from Shakespeare's, as well as two theatres and the Usher Hall.

Phone:	0131 228 2688

Golden Rule, 30 Yeoman Place, Fountainbridge.
This pub has been in the Good Beer Guide for the last 10 years. But then it is only a hop and a skip from the brewery, so it should be. Split level bar serving a wide range of guest beers as well as the staple Deuchars and Harviestoun.

Phone:	0131 229 3413

Bars: West End (cont)

Junction, 24-6 West Preston St, Southside.
Great counter-balance to the expensive style bars, the Junction is popular with penny counting students and others who don't like paying a tenner for a glass of sugar. Beer is usually well under £2. Big screen and American style food.

Phone:	0131 667 3010

Maltings, 81-85 St Leonard St, Southside.
Cosy retreat for winter evenings and popular with students (Southside is where they usually live) Maltings offers good and cheap beer in an unfussy setting.

Phone:	0131 667 5946

Pear Tree House, 38 West Nicolson St, Southside.
Not the smartest bar in the world but it does have a pleasant garden which proves a magnet to the city's drinkers on the odd occasion when the sun peeps out. Popular with students and those seeking a cheap bowl of soup.

Phone:	0131 667 7533

Roseburn Bar, 1-5 Roseburn Terrace, West End.
Heading out from the city centre, the Roseburn is the last bar on the way to Murrayfield, so gets a tad busy on match day. Still, its three bars and slick staff can handle the ruck and keep the beer flowing. Not in the Café Royal league, but nicely appointed with good architectural features. Big screen.

Phone:	0131 337 1067

Shakespeare's, 65 Lothian Rd, Tollcross.
Defies the cultural tone of the area (Shakespeare's is bang next door to the Traverse and Lyceum theatres and Usher Hall) you can watch sport on the telly or just wolf down pints of well kept ale. Great position.

Phone:	0131 228 8400

The Sheep Heid Inn, 43-45 The Causeway, Duddingston.
The village of Duddingston has been swallowed by Edinburgh's expansion, but it retains a distinct and pleasant character, best enjoyed in the warmth of the Sheep Heid, which is said to date from 1360. Past customers have allegedly included Mary Queen of Scots and Bonnie Prince Charlie (the only revolutionary to be named after three separate sheepdogs). Lovely atmosphere.

Phone:	0131 656 6951

TRENDY BARS

Berlin, 3 Queensferry St Lane.
Hidden away in a West End alley this comfy basement has a list of more than 50 different beers and 30 cocktails. Despite being a night dive, Berlin is a place to go for drinking and talking – it is not dominated by the dance floor or oppressively loud music.

Phone:	0131 467 7215

Favorit, 30-2 Leven St, Tollcross.
Ideal post pub pitstop, good food, agreeable atmosphere – ideal if you're not the night-clubbing type but fancy a late drink. Can get packed at weekends, however. There is a second Favorit in Bristo Square but this is the one that stays open latest.

Phone:	0131 221 1800

Caley Sample Room, 58 Angle Park Terrace, Gorgie. Has a bierkeller atmosphere and is owned by the Caledonian brewery just along the street. Probably serves the best 80/- in town, there are 26 beer taps, wooden floors and an agreeably functional feel to the place.

Phone:	0131 337 7204

The Fountain, 131 Dundee St, Fountainbridge. Big screen. Ideal place to watch the game if you are lacking a ticket, it's not far from the ground. The Fountain has a massive screen along with an exhaustive drinks list and good beer. There is also robust pub grub.

Phone:	0131 229 8338

All Bar One, Exchange Plaza, Lothian Rd.
There are two branches of this reliable chain in Edinburgh (the other one being in George St New Town). This cavernous edifice is next to the smart new Sheraton hotel and has the advantage of not being as crowded as its younger sister.

Phone:	0131 221 7951

RESTAURANTS

(West End, Southside, Tollcross, Marchmont & Fountainbridge)

Atrium, 10 Cambridge St, EH1 2ED. £35.
Could be forgiven for allowing complacency to creep in, but the Atrium maintains its status as one of Edinburgh's finest eateries. The menu is eclectic, modern and imaginative, the service smooth and the presentation impeccable. Good value, too (it has been awarded the coveted Michelin 'Bib Gourmand' for quality at reasonable price) but watch out for the price tickets on the wine list. It is just as calm and easy going as its sister, Blue (upstairs) is hectic and noisy.

Phone:	0131 228 8882

Bonham, 35 Drumsheugh Gardens, EH3 7RN. £30.
Classically trained chef Michel Bouyer cut his teeth in his native Brittany before going to the Jules Verne restaurant in the Eiffel Tower. Try the seared hand dived scallops with crab cannelloni, pear and caper dressing or the pan fried fillet of halibut with saffron risotto, mango salsa and vanilla sauce. Adventurous diversions from the classical canon, not for the pre-pubcrawl carbo-loaders.

Phone:	0131 623 9319
Internet:	www.thebonham.com

La Bruschetta, 13 Clifton Terrace, Haymarket, EH12 5DR. £28.
Great saucier at work, achieving an intensity of flavour to accompany the freshly prepared pasta. Seafood is highly recommended as is the veal (cotoletta alla Milanese, for example). The proprietor Giovanni Cariello does the cooking and service is exemplary. Opposite Haymarket station, you will pass it if walking to the ground from the town centre.

Phone:	0131 467 7464
Internet:	www.labruschetta.co.uk

Channings, Channing Hotel, 12-16 Learmonth Gardens, EH4 1EZ. £24.
Modern cooking in stylish, minimal surroundings. Mackerel escabeche, roast chicken leg stuffed with tarragon mousse and creamy polenta, followed by a peach puree vanilla fromage frais and biscotto would be a typical three courser at this simple and unpretentious restaurant. Good value and decent wine list.

Phone:	0131 315 2225
Internet:	www.channings.co.uk

Grill Room, Sheraton Grand Hotel, 1 Festival Sq, EH3 9SR. £42. The Grill Room is an Edinburgh landmark, an award winning fine dining restaurant. Starched white tablecloths, silver, crystal, and fine china create the atmosphere, while the cuisine, using the finest Scottish ingredients, has a following of locals and visitors. Ornate ceilings and dark woods and modern glass set the stage for some good European cooking.

Phone:	0131 221 6422

Kalpna, 2/3 St Patrick's Square, EH8 9EZ. £15. Potentially life-changing for hardcore carnivores, Kalpna offers the best of Indian vegetarian cooking in comfortably understated surroundings. Opened more than 20 years ago, but still going strong as one of the city's most celebrated dining establishments. Gujarat cuisine is the predominant influence on this eclectic kitchen.

Phone:	0131 667 9890

Marque Central, 30b Grindlay St, EH3 9AX. £27.
We have tried this place several times over the years and have yet to find it wanting. Chef John Rutter is still at the helm. Reasonable prices and exciting dishes in a splendidly central location – ideal for concerts, theatre and the Old Town. Typical starters: cod wrapped in pancetta, piperade, roquette, shaved parmesan; duck rillet, wild mushroom and roast onion crostini. For mains, try the chargrilled lamb loin with basil crust, merguez, pea & chanterelle fettucine, or perhaps the seabass baked with gremolata, roast king prawn and plum tomatoes, crushed new potato. It's all very yummy.

Phone:	0131 229 9859
Internet:	www.marquecentral.co.uk

Pompadour Restaurant, Caledonian Hotel, Princes Street, EH1 2AB.
Inspired by the court of Louis XV and named after his mistress, this is a rich and pampering experience, with teams of penguins theatrically lifting Prussian helmets from steaming platters of classic French cuisine. Such dishes as sea bass with crispy leeks and caviar-butter sauce, whole lobster with mustard and cheese, and loin of venison with potato pancakes are the living evidence of a continuing alliance between Scottish ingredients and French know-how.

Phone:	0131 222 8888

Oloroso, 33 Castle St, EH2 3DN. £32.
Strong Asian influence to this 3rd floor international restaurant. Good wine and cocktail selection and the a la carte menu changes twice daily. Terrace snack menu also available (the terrace is stunning).

Phone:	0131 226 7614
Internet:	www.oloroso.co.uk

Orchid Chinese Restaurant, 33-35 Castle Terrace, EH1 2EL.
Fine and unpretentious home to Canton, Peking and Szechuen cuisine. Vegetarian and seafood dishes a speciality. Reasonably priced and right in the heart of theatre and concert land, below the castle crags.

Phone:	0131 229 1181
Internet:	www.orchidedinburgh.co.uk

Rhubarb, Prestonfield, Priestfield Road, EH16 5UT.
Its interior is extravagant and could easily have done for the filming of such sumptuous costume dramas as Tony Richardson's Tom Jones, or perhaps even Marco Ferreri's La Grande Bouffe. Stuffed with ancestral portraits, silk wall covering and theatrical regency grandeur. Isle of Skye scallops, Lindisfarne oysters, Black Gold beef from Angus and the finest artisan produce ensure exceptional food to match the splendour of the surroundings, whilst a list of over 500 wines offers great wines by the glass to the most famous names (also see hotels).

Phone:	0131 225 1333
Internet:	www.rhubarb-restaurant.com

Santini, 8 Conference Sq, EH3 8AN. £35.
Tucked away behind the Sheraton, of which it is a part, the menu offers Italian classics put together with flair and served charmingly by a thoroughly professional team. This is Pavarotti territory, a trencherman's paradise. Typical dinner might include chargrilled baby cuttlefish with peppers and rucola, taglioni with fresh crab, followed by roast duck and cured bacon, chestnuts and honey. The desserts are highly rated if you can manage a third course.

Phone:	0131 221 7788

HOTELS
(West End, Southside, Tollcross, Marchmont & Fountainbridge)

LUXURY HOTELS

Bonham, 33 Drumsheugh Gardens, EH3 7RN.
46 rooms, from £110 d/t and 80 s. Rack: £205 d/t, £150 s.
Highly original styling – contemporary interior in a 19th century building. Very good food in a tremendous setting.

Phone:	0131 226 6050
Email:	reserve@thebonham.com
Internet:	www.thebonham.com

Caledonian Hilton, Princes St, EH2 2EQ.
251 rooms, from £190 s/d/t. Rack £250 - £275
The grand old lady of grand old Edinburgh hotels. Safe and steady, efficient and comfortable, the Caley sits in the shadow of the castle and is warmly panelled in dark wood behind a sandstone Victorian exterior.

Phone:	0131 222 8888
Email:	ednchhirm@hilton.com
Internet:	www.hilton.co.uk/caledonian

Prestonfield, Priestfield Rd, EH16 5UT.
29 rooms from £195 per night for a luxury room, £225 for a large luxury room and £275 for a suite. Rates do not vary.
Prestonfield is the ultimate retort to minimalism: it is maximalism. Writ large. Which probably explains why Lord Watson, former Labour member of the Scottish Parliament and driving force in the anti-foxhunt bill, tried to burn it down by setting fire to the curtains and got 16 months inside for his pains. Filled with exquisite chinoiserie, leather wallpaper, objets d'arts, cherubs bearing fruit and sundry celebrations of bacchanalia. Sitting at the foot of Arthur's Seat, the extinct volcano near the centre of Edinburgh, it is an imposing 17th century house built for the Lord Provost by the same chap who created Holyroodhouse a mile or so down the road.

Phone:	0131 668 3346
Email:	info@prestonfield.com
Internet:	www.prestonfield.com

Sheraton Grand, 1 Festival Sq, EH3 9SR.
243 rooms, from £140 - £170 s/d/t. Rack £270.
Very central and ultra modern with a sophisticated spa. Luxurious with a panoramic view across Festival Square. Its spa is the city's centre for pampering – open rooftop hot pool.

Phone:	0131 229 9131
Email:	grandedinburgh.sheraton@sheraton.com
Internet:	www.sheraton.com/grandedinburgh

MODERATELY PRICED

Apex European Hotel, 90 Haymarket Terrace, EH12 5LQ.
66 rooms from £100. Rack rate £220.
Handy for the ground. The rack rate is expensive for what you get. But this is what you have to pay when demand is high.

Phone:	0131 474 3456
Email:	reservations@apexhotels.co.uk
Internet:	www.apexhotels.co.uk/edinburgh

Hotels: (cont)

Borough, 72-80 Causewayside, EH9 1PY. 12 rooms, from £70 d/s/t. A former snooker hall, the rooms are framed by enormous warehouse windows and high ceilings. Two double twin rooms ideal for a small group or family. The stylish king-sized beds have the highest quality duck-down duvets and pillows for you to sink into. You'll find modern art on the walls and a TV and DVD. There's even a daily cocktail happy hour.

Phone:	0131 668 2255
Email:	bookings@boroughhotel.com
Internet:	www.boroughhotel.com

Links Bar, 4 Alvanley Terrace, Marchmont, EH9 1DU. 19 rooms, from £80 d/t. Small intimate hotel adjacent to Brunswick links. Bright and modern in décor, complimentary tea and coffee, satellite television, trouser press, hair dryer and telephone. The Links Bar, with its sporting theme, is popular with locals and visitors alike. Licensed from 9am until 1am daily, you are guaranteed a view of all major sporting events shown on a big screen. Bar meals are served daily.

Phone:	0131 229 3834

BUDGET

Green House, 14 Hartington Gardens, Bruntsfield, EH10 4LD. 6 rooms, from £35pp. Vegetarian/vegan family home offering serious breakfast and comfort. Award winning and friendly but discourages groups. Close links to local yoga centres.

Phone:	0131 622 7634
Email:	greenhouse_edin@hotmail.com
Internet:	www.greenhouse-edinburgh.com

Grosvenor Gardens Hotel, 1 Grosvenor Gardens, EH12 5JU. 9 rooms, £65 s. From £66 d/t to £110 d/t. Just across the road from Haymarket station and close to the ground. Good amenities surround this traditional and comfortable establishment.

Phone:	0131 313 3415
Email:	info@stayinedinburgh.com
Internet:	www.stayinedinburgh.com

Heatherlea Guest House, 13 Mayfield Gardens, EH9 2AX. 10 rooms, from £27 s, £57 d/t. Family rooms available. Near the foot of Arthur's Seat, this is a well run and friendly B&B popular with the cycling fraternity who come up from Newcastle doing the Coast & Castles route. Bring your bike.

Phone:	0131 667 3958
Email:	al@heatherlea-guesthouse.co.uk
Internet:	www.heatherlea-guesthouse.co.uk

Murrayfield Hotel, 18 Corstorphine Road, EH12 6HN. 32 rooms, from £40 s/d/t. The hotel itself is a comfortably nondescript Victorian affair, but its proximity to the stadium across the road lends a certain convenience on Six Nations weekends (when Scotland are at home, though some might think this debatable). Nice bar, nice staff, nice short walk to the game.

Phone:	0131 337 1844

Original Raj, 6 West Coates, EH12 5JG. 17 rooms, from £60 d/t to £80 d/t. Strategically positioned between Murrayfield and Haymarket station, this place is stylish and cheap. It belongs to Tommy Miah, who owns the Raj restaurant in Leith. Takeaways by arrangement. Take a look at the rooms using the weblink below. They are swish for the price.

Phone:	0131 346 1333
Email:	rajhotel@btconnect.com
Internet:	www.rajempire.com

Premier Lodge Hotel, 82 Lauriston Place, EH3 9HZ. 112 rooms £74.95 s/d/t.
Next door to the Edinburgh College of Art and close to the Meadows this place is good value for your money and even has the trendy Bar Est attached.

Phone:	0870 990 6610
Internet:	www.premiertravelinn.co.uk

WATERFRONT
(Leith)

BARS

TRADITIONAL PUBS

Cameo Bar, 23 Commercial St.
Since its refurbishment, the Cameo now sports scarlet walls and a giant angel sculpture, with funky artwork on the walls. *'Happily it's none of it skank chic and is still littered with boys who've fallen out of bed and girls doing peroxide-with-roots: this is the spiritual home of still-skint artists and Leith's younger meeja crowd,'* says a review in the Guardian. By day, there's a putting green out the back - competitions are held every Sunday afternoon - while excellent bistro food is available (game pie for a fiver). Cheap drinks (£3.60 for a pint plus a JD and Coke) keep everyone happy at night.

Phone:	0131 554 9999

Carriers Quarters, 42 Bernard St.
Small frontage belies an extensive rear room. Building pub dates from 1785. To one side of the bar is a tiny nook where 'ladies of the night' would sit and await customers. The bar itself is well stocked with a good choice of ales, whiskies and wines. Homemade food is cooked in a tiny kitchen at lunchtimes. There is a lovely stone walled back room with booths and tables. Live music is held in this back room once a week. The pub has a very friendly atmosphere and attracts all types of clientele.

Phone:	0131 554 4122

Kings Wark, The Shore.
A fine bar on the corner of Commercial St, it serves good food and is a very popular eating place, especially on Sunday afternoons. The bar has a warm and cosy ambience with a rustic feel with old wooden floors. A good selection of cask ales and malt whiskies are available. Historic setting.

Phone:	0131 554 9260

Malt & Hops, 45 The Shore.
An old pub overlooking the water with good service and a friendly landlord. There are around eight cask ales, dozens of malt whiskies and cask conditioned cider. The pub is decorated with many beer mats and old mirrors. The roaring fire and low beamed ceiling make this a very cosy pub on a cold winter night.

Phone:	0131 555 0083

Ship on the Shore, 24-6 The Shore.
Bright purple pub overlooking the Water of Leith which has become a popular eating place. Offers 'haute cuisine' and the usual pub food. The interior walls are painted in crimson with lots of boat related pictures. In fine weather tables are outside the pub on the pavement.

Phone:	0131 555 0409

Shore, The Shore.
Good locals' pub with an excellent restaurant attached (see restaurant entry), a popular venue for live folk music. Small, dark wood bar and well kept Caledonian and Deuchars ales. On a sunny day people throng onto the quayside.

Phone:	0131 553 5080

TRENDY BARS

Club Java, Commercial St.

Cool address, cool place. Cool everything, in fact, at a venue that is handily placed for some post-prandial pop (er, sorry, sophisticated grooves) after a visit to one of Leith's many fine restaurants. A recent venture, one of a growing number of churches converted by the entertainment industry. Opportunity John Knox, as they say in Presbyterian circles.

Phone:	0131 467 3810

Port o' Leith, 58 Constitution St.

This not a theme pub based on nautical artefacts. The adornments in this bar have been brought from far and wide by the many irregular visitors when in the Port. Open from early morning for shift workers and sailors from the docks, this is a wee pub with a big reputation. Sailors like this place and there is a steady regular local crowd who, along with the bar staff, are famous for making everyone welcome. They have one cask ale, half a dozen malts and a standard range of bottled beers.

Phone:	0131 554 3568

Lighthouse, 32-4 The Shore.

Great addition to the vibey shoreline, Lighthouse gets very busy and does a brisk trade in exotic lagers, cocktails and glamour. If it gets too packed try any of the marvellous pubs in the vicinity.

Phone:	0131 554 9465
Internet:	www.lthse.com

Ocean Bar, Ocean Terminal, Ocean Drive.

Great setting in front of the panorama windows above the Royal Yacht Britannia. This place could be really cool if more people ventured down to Ocean Terminal. So it's a quiet place of repose if you fancy watching the sun setting over the Firth of Forth with a glass of champagne. Ideal Sunday lunch spot to chill out.

Phone:	0131 553 8073
Internet:	www.ocean-bar.co.uk

RESTAURANTS

(Leith)

Fishers, 1 The Shore, Leith,

Laid-back bistro down on the waterfront. Daily specials chalked up in this charming and bustling street corner eaterie: seafood soup, gamba prawns the size of a sea-dog's crusty hand or perhaps soft shell crab in a tempura batter. Simple and safe, lively and reasonable. Same menu as its sister restaurant (see New Town).

Phone:	0131 554 5666
Internet:	www.fishersbistro.co.uk

Restaurant Martin Wishart, 54 The Shore, Leith EH6 6RA. £50.
It came as some surprise that Martin Wishart, a consummate proponent of haute cuisine a la Francaise, didn't get his second Michelin star in 2005. This is a formal French restaurant run by a Scot who has worked for both Roux brothers and Marco-Pierre White. You will not go wrong, whether you go for the squab pigeon with oysters or the roast loin and braised cheek of Ibericho pork coucroute, saucisse Morteau in a champagne and mustard sauce. Groaning cheese board et al, and a wine list to rob for.

Phone:	0131 553 3557
Internet:	www.martin-wishart.co.uk

Shore Bar and Restaurant, 3 Shore , Leith, EH6 6QW. £28.
A charming pub bar to be found on the Leith waterfront, full of lively locals, plays joint first fiddle with a discreet and solid restaurant in an adjoining room. This is a competitive eating zone and the Shore has a daily changing menu offering some good seafood and game options.

Phone:	0131 553 5080
Internet:	www.theshore.biz

Skippers Bistro, 1a Dock Place, Leith, EH6 6LU. £25.
Edinburgh's oldest seafood restaurant is tucked away in a quiet corner of Leith, between the Water and the Scottish Executive. It is also one of the capital's finest and has a loyal following, so try and book early. Homely nautical theme and fine ingredients simply presented.

Phone:	0131 554 1018
Email:	info@skippers.co.uk
Internet:	www.skippers.co.uk

Ristorante Tinelli, 139 Easter Road, EH7 5QA. £22.
Genuine old fashioned Italian neighbourhood restaurant in a far-from-fashionable part of town, just a quick taxi ride from the centre. This place has been preserved in a time capsule and Giancarlo Tinelli has been cooking up the dishes of his native Lombardy for more than 20 years opposite the Hibs ground. Family run and as far from the trendsetting town centre places as it is possible to get. Solid and inexpensive wine list.

Phone:	0131 652 1932

Vintners Rooms, The Vaults, 87 Giles St, Leith, EH6 6BZ. £30.
The cooking of Patrice Ginestiere has only improved since taking joint ownership in 2004. This is one of Edinburgh's great restaurant settings in 18th century vaults below the Scottish Malt Whisky Society (see entry). This is the old wine merchants' auction room with the striking vaults warehouse. Try scallops with pancetta, rocket and parmesan, marinated tuna with artichokes barigoule and basil. Among the mains, turbot and caviar croustillant with sauce antiboise and pavé of venison with blackberry sauce are excellent, as are the desserts and cheese board. Excellent wine list.

Phone:	0131 554 6767
Internet:	www.thevintnersrooms.com

Waterfront Wine Bar & Bistro, 1c Dock Place, Leith, EH6 6LU.
Quayside conservatory situated in the heart of Leith's historic dockland. Serving a wide selection of fresh seafood, shellfish, game, steaks, chicken and vegetarian, with an extensive wine list and real ales. Booking advised.

Phone:	0131 554 7427
Internet:	www.waterfrontwinebar.co.uk

HOTELS

(Leith)

MODERATELY PRICED HOTELS

Malmaison Edinburgh, 1 Tower Place, Leith, EH6 7DB.
100 rooms, from £135 - £165 s/d/t.

Boutique hotel in Leith's increasingly trendy harbour area. The hotel is housed in an old port building right on the waterfront and although imitators have made its style looks less individual, it still has real class. Good deals possible via their website.

Phone:	0131 468 5001
Email:	Edinburgh@malmaison.com
Internet:	www.malmaison-edinburgh.com

BUDGET

Bar Java, 48/52 Constitution St, EH6 6RS.
9 rooms 5 of which are ensuite, from £25 s, £50 d/t. £70 d/t en-suite.

Busy bar down in Leith with a small but cosy hotel upstairs. Fairly basic but cheerful and friendly in one of Edinburgh's liveliest areas.

Phone:	0131 553 2020

OUTSIDE EDINBURGH

Many fans visiting Murrayfield have rugby links outside the metropolis and opt to stay, for instance, in the Borders or on the outskirts of town. Melrose, in the heart of the rugby playing Borders, is a popular destination. Peebles, with its fine hotels, is only 22 miles from Edinburgh and is fast becoming the most favoured alternative.

Peebles and Surrounding Area

Peebles has an 18 hole golf course, swimming pool, fishing, mountain biking and walking in the forests of Tweeddale or on the challenging Southern Upland Way, which is easily accessible.

South west is Tweedsmuir, 500 metres above sea level on an old coaching route. The church spire is an unmistakable landmark in the remote and peaceful upland area, once the haunt of Covenanters. The River Tweed rises in these hills and a lay-by and sculpture on the A701 mark the site. Broughton village is noted for its gallery and the John Buchan Centre, which recreates the life of the famous writer, soldier and politician.

Innerleithen is home to Traquair, Scotland's oldest continually inhabited house, pictured at the top of the next page, and is surrounded by the scenic hills and forest of the Tweed Valley. St. Ronan's Well Interpretative Centre depicts the era of the 19th century when the town was famed as a spa. Robert Smail's Printing Works give a fascinating insight into the printing processes of the past.

Gardening fans are well placed to enjoy a visit to Dawyck, one of the National Botanic Gardens of Scotland, at Stobo, or Kailzie Gardens with its formal walled garden, stocked trout pond and 18-hole putting green. Peebles' spacious High Street offers interesting boutiques and welcoming tearooms for a spot of shopping, then round off the day with a visit to Peebles Eastgate Theatre; opened in 2004 with a varied year-round selection of theatre, music and art exhibitions.

Call in at the Visitor Information Centre for a free copy of a historic town trail, and view Peebles by foot.

Phone:	0870 6080404
Email:	bordersinfo@visitscotland.com
Internet:	www.scot-borders.co.uk

BARS

Bridge Inn, Port Brae, Peebles, EH45 8AW.
Known locally as the 'Trust', this popular one room local serves either Deuchars IPA or Caledonian 80/- on tap. Good prices. Ideal for a 4-pub crawl of Peebles real ale outlets. Check out the porcelain in the gents.

County Inn, 35 High St, Peebles EH45 8AN.
Restored coach house serving fresh produce in a lively atmosphere. Good selection of real ales and whiskies.

Cross Keys Hotel, 24, Northgate, Peebles, EH45 8RS.
One of the oldest establishments in Peebles and reputedly haunted. Used to be a dog hole but has improved dramatically since a refurb. Occasional ale on tap.

Crown Hotel, 54, High St, Peebles EH45 8SW.
Recently refurbished, this small friendly spot used to be the bar of choice of the late actor and truly heroic tippler, Oliver Reed. His chair is still to be found in the bar.

Neidpath Inn, 25 Old Town, Peebles EH45 8JF.
Great food and a welcoming atmosphere. Impromptu folk nights, all the sporting events and great beer. Usually one or two ales on tap, including Caledonian 80/-.

Traquair Arms Hotel, Traquair Rd, Innerleithen EH44 6PD.
Just down the road in the former spa town of Innerleithen, this charming bar with bustling restaurant serves up, inter alia, Traquair Ales, brewed across the way at Scotland's oldest inhabited house. Traquair (itself a real must for a visit). Log fires, beer garden and comfortable rooms.

Phone:	01896 830229

RESTAURANTS
(Peebles and Surrounding Area)

Cringletie House Hotel, Edinburgh Rd, Peebles EH45 8PL.
For a long time Cringletie has been renowned for its cooking (see hotel entry). It has two AA rosettes and specialises in local produce and has won many awards. A class act in an area not blessed with the finest cooking in the world.

Restaurants: Peebles & srrounding area (cont)

Glentress Hotel, Innerleithen Rd, Peebles EH45 8NB.
Privately run hotel next to the Glentress forest's wonderful walks and cycle routes. Reliable cooking in a great spot.

Phone:	01721 720100
Internet:	www.glentresshotel.co.uk

HOTELS

(Peebles and Surrounding Area)

Cardrona Hotel Golf & Country Club Hotel, Cardrona, Peebles, EH45 6LZ.
99 rooms, from £70 s/d/t.
Set in the Tweed Valley, there is a good balance between modern extras and traditional hospitality. Good leisure facilities and comfortable rooms, plus grand mountain and River Tweed views. Renwicks restaurant specialises in local produce and is acquiring a good reputation. Golfers must pre-book on 01896 833701 if they want a crack at the fairway.

Phone:	01896 833600
Internet:	www.cardrona-hotel.co.uk

Castle Venlaw Hotel, Edinburgh Road, Peebles, Peebleshire, EH45 8QG.
12 rooms, from £125 s/d/t.
A magnificent castle built in 1782 standing on Venlaw Hill with panoramic views over Peebles, River Tweed and countryside. The castle development has retained its old character whilst sensitively adding modern touches. All rooms have private facilities.

Phone:	01721 720384
Internet:	www.venlaw.co.uk

Cringletie House Hotel, by Peebles, Peebleshire, EH45 8PL.
12 rooms, from £100 s/d/t.
Cringletie House is a stunning baronial mansion, situated in the rolling hills of the Scottish Borders. The House is grade B listed and sits in 28 acres of gardens and woodlands. There are large rooms, smaller rooms and romantic turret rooms. Has a deserved reputation for its food (see entry).

Phone:	01721 725750
Internet:	www.cringletie.com

Peebles Hotel Hydro Hotel, Innerleithen Road, Peebles, EH45 8LX.
128 rooms, from £100 s/d/t.
Peebles Hotel Hydro is set within 30 acres in the stunning Scottish Borders and commands a magnificent view over the Cademuir Valley from its hilltop position. Peebles Hydro has been awarded Four Stars with the AA and is now in the top 40 AA hotels in Scotland. Indoor pool and leisure complex.

Phone:	01721 720602
Internet:	www.peebleshotelhydro.com

Tontine Hotel, High Street, Peebles, Tweeddale, EH45 8AJ. 36 rooms, from £60 s/d/t. Built in 1808, this elegant family run hotel overlooks the River Tweed. Friendly, personal service, 36 tastefully furnished en-suite bedrooms and good cooking in the Adam Room Restaurant. Great for golf with the championship Roxburgh and new Cardrona courses.

Phone:	01721 720892
Internet:	www.tontinehotel.com

MELROSE

One hardly needs to introduce Melrose in a rugby guide, the ancient home and birthplace of the 7-a-side form of the game. It's the most picturesque of the pretty Borders towns. Robert the Bruce's heart is buried in a lead casket at the spectacular abbey, pictured above. Abbotsford, Sir Walter Scott's home is just a couple of miles away. Melrose is just off the A68, 38 miles from Edinburgh. You can also get there driving down the A7 through Galashiels. There are bus links and plans to reopen the old Waverley line – which got its name from Scott's series of novels and in turn gave its name to the main Edinburgh station – thus re-establishing a rail link with this picturesque part of the world.

BARS

Burts Hotel, Market Square, Melrose, Roxburghshire, TD6 9PL.
Although more geared to eating, the bar also serves some cracking real ale and if you don't mind munchers it is a thoroughly civilised spot to take a jar or a dram.

Kings Arms Hotel, High Street, Melrose, TD6 9PB.
Melrose's best pub – a real, bustling locals' local with a wide range of well kept beers. The landlord is a lively chap and hell will freeze over before you get a pint at the King's that has been lying around in the tap.

RESTAURANTS

Burts Hotel, Market Square, Melrose, Roxburghshire, TD6 9PL.
For a long time the restaurant here has been one of the better spots to dine in the Borders. Locals say the food has improved since the new chef took over.

Phone:	01896 822285
Internet:	www.burtshotel.co.uk

Dryburgh Abbey Hotel, Dryburgh Village, St Boswells, Melrose, TD6 0RQ.
See hotel entry. Imported a top French chef who spent three years on the banks of the Tweed training up a local team who have now taken over. Great local produce and some excellent game.

Phone:	01835 822261
Internet:	www.dryburgh.co.uk

Hoebridge Inn, Gattonside, Melrose TD6 9LZ.
Modern British and Mediterranean cuisine in a popular setting, the Hoebridge has pulled locals in for years during its various incarnations. The new owners are doing a fine job.

Phone:	01896 823082

Restaurants: Melrose (cont)

Marmions Brasserie, Buccleuch St, Melrose TD6 9LB.
Oak panelled interior with large mirrors and stylish décor, Marmions has been around for aeons. Imaginative, inexpensive and unpretentious cooking. Generous portions. This place really takes off at weekends and is great fun. It's also a fine coffee house, serving home made cakes and scones.

Phone:	01896 822245

HOTELS

(Melrose)

Buccleuch Arms Hotel, St Boswells, Melrose, Roxburghshire, TD6 0EW.
20 rooms, from £75 s/d/t.
Family run establishment with ace golfer Billy Hamilton leading the team. Comfortable rooms, much improved cooking and now some real ale in the bar, this is a good and inexpensive spot to retreat to after the hurly burly of Edinburgh.

Phone:	01835 822243
Internet:	www.buccleucharmshotel.co.uk

Burts Hotel, Market Square, Melrose, Roxburghshire, TD6 9PL.
20 rooms, from £90 d/t.
For more than 30 years Burts has been owned by Graham and Anne Henderson, whose friendly personal attention has built the hotel's excellent reputation. Now joined by their son Nicholas and his wife Trish, they provide each guest with every comfort and the ultimate in service. Set in Melrose's picturesque 18th century Market Square, it was built in 1722 for a local dignitary and still reflects much of the period charm of that time. Ninety single malt whiskies on offer.

Phone:	01896 822285
Internet:	www.burtshotel.co.uk

Dryburgh Abbey Hotel, Dryburgh Village, St Boswells, Melrose, TD6 0RQ.
38 rooms, from £60 s/d/t.
Fantastic setting on the banks of the Tweed, bang opposite the famous Abbey where Sir Walter Scott is interred. Ten acres of ground and family run.

Phone:	01835 822261
Internet:	www.dryburgh.co.uk

Kings Arms Hotel, High Street, Melrose, TD6 9PB.
7 rooms, from £65 d/t. £44s.
One of Melrose's finest attractions, the Kings Arms is a pub with rooms and serves solid fare. The former coaching inn dates back more than 300 years and has been lovingly restored, losing none of the original character and charm.

Phone:	01896 822143

Townhouse Hotel, Market Place, Melrose, TD6 9PQ.
11 rooms, from £88 s/d/t.
Owned by the same family who run Burts just across the square, the Townhouse provides relaxing and comfortable surroundings, good food and a hearty traditional Scottish breakfast.

Phone:	01896 822245
Internet:	www.thetownhousemelrose.co.uk

Station Hotel, Market Sq, Melrose, TD6 9PG.
The emphasis lies very much upon serving innovative food in a 'relaxed and friendly' atmosphere. The hotel forms part of chef Gary Moore's small restaurant chain.

Phone:	0870 242 4453
Internet:	www.garymoorerestaurants.com

Welsh rugby

Dragon's great test

By Graham Clutton

THERE are those in Wales who are still pinching themselves. After all, in the wake of so many international calamities in recent seasons, a Triple Crown, Grand Slam and Six Nations Championship in one season, came, quite literally, out of the blue. Years of watching and waiting, months of hoping rather than expecting and campaigns which ended in disbelief rather than delight, had left the national game on its knees. Admittedly, the investment in Graham Henry, the New Zealander, and his sidekick Steve Hansen, had provided some hope for a nation which had, until this year, been forced to live off its success during the Halcyon Days of the 1970s.

But even their significant contribution had failed to convince the desperate supporters that a new dawn was awaiting around the corner. Still, with the arrival of Mike Ruddock, the Gwent-born Welshman with a desire as deep as anyone's, and with Hansen having invested so heavily in youth during his two-year reign in charge of the national team, the faint hopes of a nation gave way to a realistic ambition.

Last season's autumn series of games saw Wales lose out by a score to New Zealand and South Africa, whilst the arrival on the scene of new faces such as Ryan Jones and Gavin Henson underpinned that belief. When England came and perished in Cardiff on the opening day of last season's Championship – thanks, of course, to Henson's last gasp long range penalty – a sporting nation was reborn. Six weeks later, captains Gareth Thomas and Michael Owen were parading the Championship trophy after Wales, in decisive fashion, had ditched Ireland at their £125 million citadel on the banks of the River Taff.

Reborn? Yes. After 27 years of frustration and failure, four relatively modest World Cup campaigns (1987 they finished third) and numerous humiliating defeats at the hands of the big five - France, England, South Africa, Australia and New Zealand, Welsh rugby had etched its name, indelibly, on the rugby map.

Now comes the difficult part. Maintaining that push towards the top and proving that 2005 was not simply a flash in the pan, will be significantly tougher for the

Dragon's greatest test (cont)

aforementioned Ruddock and his players. The regional structure that underpins that national drive, is still flawed in terms of limited finance, whilst the loss of the Celtic Warriors at the start of last season, has done little other than drive a wedge between a considerable number of Welsh rugby enthusiasts and the governing body that is the Welsh Rugby Union.

Thankfully in David Moffett (chief executive) and Steve Lewis (WRU manager), the Union has two belligerent characters with an eye for success. Of course there are knives in their backs, but the very fact that the WRU has wiped out a £10million overdraft in the space of 12 months and successfully restructured its £60millon debt in order to assume a modicum of financial stability, should not be forgotten.

It's up to the four regions now (Scarlets, Blues, Dragons, Ospreys) to show the same level of foresight and dedication. If they do, well, Welsh rugby can take the next significant step on the long road to consistency at the highest level. The first step for that quartet will be to arrest a collective decline in Europe. After all, despite an appearance from Cardiff in the inaugural Heineken Cup final, the contribution of the Principality's clubs, and more recently the regions, has been modest to say the least. Yes, the Scarlets left their mark with successive appearances in the semi-finals, but last season, all four failed to escape the pool stages. This season should be different, although the grouping for the Ospreys, arguably Welsh rugby's best hope, has hardly been kind. Still, with Henson, Jones and Brent Cockbain set to make their return to regional duty after playing for the British and Irish Lions in New Zealand, there is a genuine air of expectancy around the region's new £30 million stadium in Swansea.

Adam and Duncan Jones, as well as captain Barry Williams, provide the front row brawn, whilst the brain behind the scrum will come from New Zealander Jason Spice, the gutsy, outstanding scrum half who was arguably the region's most influential player last season. Amongst the young players to watch out for, are centres Andrew and David Bishop and outside half Matthew Jones, who made his senior Wales debut in the summer tour to North America.

Matthew Rees, the Scarlets hooker, also took his international bow on that tour, but at Stradey Park this season, all eyes will be on the arrival of overseas stars Hottie Luow and Regan King - amongst others. The southern hemisphere influence will be significant for the Scarlets who have lacked a cutting edge over the past 18 months. Former Scarlets scrum half Michael Phillips has left for the Blues where Wales legend Rob Howley has taken over as backs coach. Xavier Rush arrives from New Zealand to bolster the back row, whilst Andrew Powell moves in at no.8 and Mark Stcherbina at centre. Watch out for the returning youngster Nicky Robinson who missed eight months of last season with glandular fever.

His presence at outside half will give the Blues more balance, whilst Tom Shanklin's return from knee surgery will give a considerable boost to the midfield. Rhys Williams and Craig Morgan are two of the outside backs with something to prove, whilst loose head prop Gethin Jenkins and last season's captain and flanker Martyn Williams start the campaign with a Lions tour under their belts.

The toughest task this season falls on the Dragons where Paul Turner comes in as head coach to replace Aussie Chris Anderson who had his contract cut short after last season's disappointing campaign. With money tight as Rodney Parade, there have been no major signings although former Pontyrpidd wing Richard Fussell is amongst a group of youngsters hoping to make an impression. Scrum half James Ireland is another whilst Andrew Hall, who arrives from Glasgow, is arguably the leading new name to touch down in Gwent.

The emphasis on that top tier has dominated Welsh rugby since Moffett's arrival although the implementation of regional rugby has meant the virtual death of club rugby as we knew it. The days of 45,000 watching Cardiff and Newport and the Boxing Day bashes between the capital club and Pontypridd have long gone. These days, the two self-styled "greatest clubs in the world", attract just a few hundred as the second tier struggles to compete in the brave new world.

Thankfully, with those clubs being forced to cut their cloth accordingly, and with young players being given a chance to display their talents at a new level, the Union is confident that in time, the paying public will understand that the tough measures taken two years ago were necessary.

Lewis said: "We have moved onto a different stratosphere in the space of two years and although there are many people who are not impressed and certainly not supportive, I am sure that in another couple of years, we will have seen even greater development in this great game of ours."

That, of course, will be measured by the success of a national team whose fixtures this season began with New Zealand, South Africa and Australia. The three southern hemisphere Super Powers arrived in Cardiff with understandable concern. After all, in recent seasons (last year apart) a trip to the Welsh capital was pretty straightforward. Welsh rugby has rediscovered its passion and power and as England struggles to rebuild after the 2003 World Cup, Ireland face the inevitable job of rebuilding too and Scotland and Italy continue to decline at an alarming rate, this season's Championship could come down to a straight scrap between the current Champs and last season's Jeckyll and Hyde outfit from across the Channel.

Graham Clutton writes for the Daily Telegraph.

Break time: Shane Williams shows his paces against Scotland. Above: Gavin Henson leads the title celebration.

FIND YOUR WAY AROUND

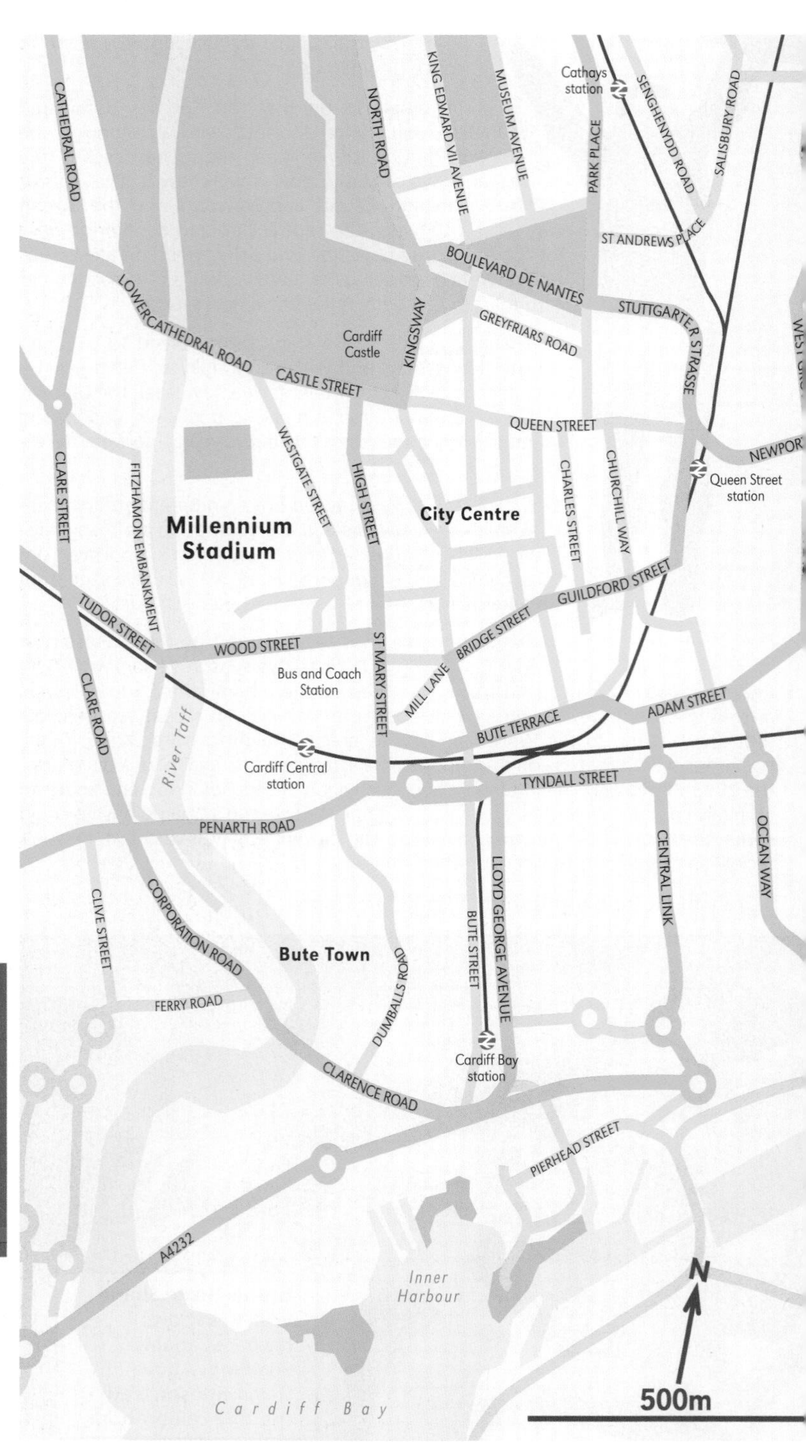

WALES

CITY BY THE BAY

CARDIFF is Europe's youngest capital. It was only in 2005 that it celebrated its centenary as a city, and its 50th year as Wales' capital. Before 1955, the Principality's governing city was London. Little wonder the Welsh still summon up so much sound and fury when playing their neighbours from the other side of Offa's Dyke. Visiting Cardiff now, this seems hard to swallow, so self-assured has it become, with its parliament and its fine Millennium Stadium.

Cardiff is the geographical opposite of London. It is so centrally defined as to be almost a village, and this makes for a unique atmosphere during big match weekend. You will not get lost in the madding crowd; you are that crowd.

Nowhere else in Britain has made so much municipal progress during the last few years. As the European leaders congregated in the Welsh capital for the G7 summit in 1998, the cranes, bulldozers and men in hard hats were busily turning Tiger Bay from slum dwellings into one of the world's leading waterside developments. That project is now virtually finished and as we go to press, the final touches are being applied to the National Assembly for Wales building down in Cardiff Bay. Shops, clubs, bars and numerous up and coming businesses are now located down there, including the Wales Millennium Centre and the International Sports Village.

Hotels have sprouted, as have swish new restaurants. The pubs have been cleaned up and the high streets are full of smart shops and arcades. Not since the days of King Coal has the city burgeoned with such pride and pomp. Llandaff Cathedral is one of the oldest sites in Britain, dating from the 6th century. The Bay is one of the newest. Cardiff Castle, meanwhile, straddles history: its ancient roots were thoroughly made over by the Bute family in Victorian times, when veins of coal poured unimaginable riches into the pockets of the captains of industry and landowners. The Castle, in 146 acres of Bute Park, was one of the most sumptuous abodes in Europe, as the picture of the great hall shows.

Another great reflection of coal and steel wealth is Cathays Park and the Civic Centre, built in dazzling white Portland stone. Just take a stroll around the university, Law Courts, City Hall, Alexandra Hall and the National Museum and Gallery. They match any of the architectural grandiloquence of Paris.

You could do worse than spend half a day at the National Museum, which houses one of the largest collections of impressionist paintings in Europe, as well as a whole gallimaufry of Welsh art and heritage.

TRAVEL

This is an easy city to get to with more and more flights coming through Cardiff International Airport, which has direct links to Europe, Ireland and Canada, as well as many other major British cities. The city is also well wired for rail and road links and once you are here, transport is mercifully easy. Compared to London and Paris, Cardiff is little more than a village (we are only talking size here). However, with the rugby ground being sited right in the middle of town, only a few yards from the busiest shopping streets, the place can get very busy on match days. It is usually a good idea to arrive early (before the crowd) and leave late (after the inevitable congestion has died down).

AIR

CIA (Cardiff International Airport)

Twelve miles south west of the city and ten miles from J33 of the M4. Fast growing and now user-friendly, with comfortable new facilities. CIA offers 13 direct flights to major cities across the UK and Europe, while it is the only airport in southwest UK to offer trans-Atlantic services.

The single terminal building houses check-in desks on the first floor and arrivals on the ground floor. Airport facilities include three Travelex bureaux de change, an ATM, baby change rooms, two games zones, and a children's play area.

A food court overlooks the runway (open **05:00 - 22:00**). There are also two pubs offering food and beer and open for all departing flights. Facilities for disabled passengers include a minicom system at the information desk, dedicated parking, specially designed toilets, lifts, and use of airport wheelchairs. There are bus and taxi connections to Cardiff Central Station, from where there are rail links to everywhere in the UK. Eventually, there will be a rail link to town and life will become a lot simpler for air travellers.

When it comes to driving there, the airport is well signposted from the A4232, which connects with the M4 at Junction 33. The car park has 24-hour CCTV surveillance

CONTACTS

Information	01446 711111
Car park	0800 128 128 (to pre-book)
Taxis	01447 710693
Internet	www.cardiffairportonline.com

GETTING INTO TOWN

BUS

The Airbus Xpress (X91) to Cardiff Central Station runs every half hour Monday to Friday from 05.20 – 23.35 and hourly on Saturdays (two hourly Sundays). A rail link is expected to be completed in spring 2005.

Cost	£3 single, £5 return

TAXI

There is a taxi stand near the arrivals hall, and usually plenty of drivers hanging around waiting for a fare. However, there are a limited number of them and the round trip to the centre of the city can easily take more than an hour, so at busy times queues build up.

Cost	£15-£20

RAIL

Central Station is the bigger and busier of the two stations servicing the capital. There are frequent InterCity links to London Paddington, West Wales and the north. The station has been restored to its former glory. The other station, Queen Street, provides local and Valleys services.

On match days, Cardiff Central station obviously gets extremely busy, and crowd control measures are in place, both before and after the game. Customers are specifically advised to take note of the following points: after the match admittance to Cardiff Central will be limited for safety reasons and a queuing system will be in place. Left Luggage facilities are not available at Cardiff Central Station for security reasons.

Customers who need special assistance should speak to the stewards dealing with queues in order to gain assistance in accessing the platforms, which are up a flight of steps. In addition, seat reservations for all trains leaving Cardiff Central station are suspended after a major event, and spaces on trains for return journeys are on a first come first served basis.

Rail Enquiries	08457 48 49 50

ROAD

The **M4** is the main artery into South Wales and it skirts the northern fringes of the capital, sweeping on to west Wales via Swansea. London and the South East are only a couple of hours away and the M4 links with the M32, M5, M48, M49 and M50. These roads link Cardiff with all four points of the compass. Cardiff's bus station is just in front of Central Station.

Cardiff bus	www.cardiffbus.com
Traveline	08706 082608 **7am-9pm** (7 days a week)

TAXIS

STANDARD TAXIS

Cab Auto Centre	029 2033 3666
Capitol Black Cabs	029 2077 7777
Castle Private Hire	029 2034 4344
Celtic Cars	029 2045 2045
Delta Cars	029 2020 1010
Dragon Taxi	029 2046 4646 029 3033 3333
Premier Cars	029 2055 5555 029 2056 5656
St David's Cars	029 2054 9999

LIMO

Executive Car Hire	029 2052 9907
TMC Chauffeur Services Ltd	029 2074 7868
Wilson & Wilson Executive Cars	029 2056 1531
Mints Limousines	0800 0717718
My Limos	029 2040 3936
Just4You.co.uk	0781 712 6832
LimoScene	01443 436118

VITAL STATISTICS

Population: 315,000, 10% of which are students

Phone Code: **country code 44, area code:** 029

Time zone: GMT (GMT + 1 from last Sunday in March to Saturday before last Sunday in October).

Electricity: 220 volts AC, 50Hz; square three-pin plugs are standard.

Average January temp: 4.5°C (40°F).

Language: English and Welsh

Twinned with: Nantes – France, Stuttgart – Germany, Xiamen – China, Hordaland – Sweden, Lugansk - Ukraine

Tipping: A tip of around 10% is customary in restaurants. Round up for taxis. Tipping in bars is rare.

Getting around: Cardiff is a very compact city and can easily be explored on foot. Regular shuttle buses run between the city and Cardiff Bay and a waterbus runs from the Millennium Stadium to Cardiff Bay. Pedal powered taxis can be found at pick up points around the city and can take 2 passengers free of charge around the city centre.

Shopping: Most shops are open from 9am – 5pm with late night shopping on Thursdays. Sunday opening from 10am– 4pm

Getting there: BMI Baby flies to Cardiff from numerous European destinations. Zoom airlines operate a Toronto – Cardiff flight. Cardiff is linked to London and the rest of the UK via the M4. Trains from London Paddington to Cardiff run every half hour and take around two hours.

Getting to the ground: It's smack in the middle of town. You can't miss it. Unless you are staying outside town, in which case follow the signs...

HOSPITALS

St David's Community Hospital	**0.5 miles W - Cowbridge Rd East, Cardiff, CF11 9XB** 029 2053 6666
Cardiff Royal Infirmary	**0.8 miles NE - Newport Rd, Cardiff, CF24 0SZ** 029 2049 2233
Lansdowne Hospital	**1.5 miles W - Sanitorium Rd, Canton, Cardiff, CF11 8PL** 029 2023 3651

Other useful contacts

Cardiff Visitor Centre	The Old Library, The Hayes, Cardiff, CF10 1WE, 0870 909 2005.
Cardiff Visitor Centre	The Tube, Harbour Drive, Cardiff Bay, Phone 02920 463833
Police headquarters	61 Norbury Road, Cardiff, CF5 3AT, 029 2022 2111

WALES

PLACES OF INTEREST

Wales Millennium Centre

Visitors are escorted around the centre by 'Arts Sherpas', who guide visitors through front and backstage areas, drop in on the dressing rooms and even catch a glimpse of a rehearsal. Visitors are also free to roam the ArtsExplorer area, with its interactive games, or peruse the art galleries. (Tours take about one hour and run daily at 11am and 2pm. Book in advance, £4 adults, £3 concessions)

Phone	08700 40 2000
Internet	www.wmc.org.uk

Millennium Stadium

Home of Welsh rugby and football, the stadium has hosted FA Cup Finals, the Rugby World Cup, supercross and numerous supergroups, including Robbie Williams and the Manic Street Preachers. Visitors can take a tour and walk through the player's tunnel, visit the dressing rooms, the pitch, and even try out the Queen's seat in the Royal Box. (tours throughout the day, some tours available on match days: adult £5)

Phone	029 2082 2228
Internet	www.millenniumstadium.com

Cardiff Castle

Cardiff Castle contains over 2,000 years of history, with Roman walls and a Norman keep, pictured, next to the refurbished Victorian elegance of the Bute home. The 3rd Marquis of Bute, possibly the richest man in the world at the time, transformed the castle into an extravagant palace. Visitors can tour the interior, discovering the multi-cultural influences of the décor, and also explore the castle grounds. (Open every day, except Christmas and New Year's Day, tours run throughout the day, adult £6, grounds only £3)

Phone	029 2087 8100
Internet	www.cardiffcastle.com

National Museum and Gallery of Wales

Thanks to the two Davies sisters, who collected art in the early 20th century, the National Gallery has one of the finest collections of Impressionist paintings outside Paris – and here at least you won't have to queue to see them. The audio guide will take you around the archaeological and art exhibitions, and prepare to be impressed with what you will find. Free entry, closed Mondays, deposit required for audio-guide.

Phone	029 2039 7951
Internet	www.nmgw.ac.uk

City Sightseeing Bus

Tour the City Centre and the Bay. Live commentary will guide you around 11 stops including; Cardiff Castle, The Civic Centre, Cardiff Bay & The Millennium Stadium, and you can 'hop on and hop off' at will. (Adults £7, concessions £5)

Phone	029 2038 4291
Internet	www.city-sightseeing.com

ACCESSIBLE FROM THE CITY

Middle ground: Cardiff's ornate centre is the starting point for adventure

Llanerch Vineyard

Vale of Glamorgan

The 3rd Marques of Bute was the first to create a vineyard in the Vale of Glamorgan, but now Llanerch Vineyard produces award winning Welsh wines. The 20 acre estate of vineyard, gardens and woodland can be explored for a small admission charge, which includes wine tasting. Coffee shop for light refreshments. Open 10am to 5pm.

Phone	01443 225877
Internet	www.llanerch-vineyard.co.uk

Cosmeston Medieval Village

An authentic medieval village in 110 hectares of Welsh countryside. Explore meadows, lakes, woodland and wetland and visit the 14th century, or simply enjoy the lakeside restaurant.

Phone	029 2070 1678

Rhondda Heritage Park

Lewis Merthyr Colliery, Cardiff owes much of its heritage to the coal industry in Wales, and the Rhondda Heritage Park gives an insight into the culture and character of the Rhondda Valleys, which were at the heart of the industry. Experience life as a 1950's coal miner with underground tours, a reconstructed 1950's village street and interactive exhibitions.

Phone	01443 682036
Internet	www.rhonddaheritagepark.com

Museum of Welsh Life

At St Fagan's. They took down historic buildings from all round Wales, mainly the industrial valleys, including a mansion house, a quarryman's cottage, farmhouses, a six-cottage terrace and a Victorian shop complex and rebuilt them stone by stone in this attractive park on the western edge of the city. All this can be explored in this 100 acre open air museum. Open every day with regular seasonal events. Free entry.

Phone	029 2057 3500
Internet	www.nmgw.ac.uk

Dyffryn Gardens, St Nicholas, Vale of Glamorgan

10mins from the centre of Cardiff, in the heart of the Vale of Glamorgan countryside, this Edwardian garden is being restored with Heritage Lottery support. Great lawns, herbaceous borders, intimate garden rooms and an arboretum of rare and unusual trees can be explored.

Phone	029 2059 3328
Internet	www.dyffryngardens.org.uk

ART & CULTURE

St David's Hall, The Hayes

St David's National Concert Hall is the most broadcast concert venue in Britain, probably due to its wide range of productions. Best known for classical concerts, including The Welsh Proms, and attracts major international orchestras and soloists. Schedule ranges from the BBC Cardiff Singer of the Year competition to samba drumming and stage fighting . (Tickets range from free to around £30).

Phone	029 2087 8444
Internet	www.stdavidshallcardiff.co.uk

New Theatre, Greyfriars Road

Since opening in 1906, this recently restored Edwardian Playhouse, has played host to stage legends. The stars of today are in good company, with Laurel and Hardy, Sarah Bernhardt and Anna Pavlova all having taken to the boards here. Specialises in musicals. (Tickets range from £6 - £30).

Phone	029 2087 8889
Internet	www.newtheatrecardiff.co.uk

Wales Millennium Centre, Cardiff Bay

Dominating the Cardiff Bay skyline, above, the centre is just as impressive close up with its huge inscription, pictured left, in both Welsh and English (*Creu Gwir/ Fel Gwydr/ O Ffwrnais Awen* or *In These Stones/ Horizons/ Sing*). It is home to seven major arts organizations, including the Welsh National Opera, and aims to present international opera, ballet, dance and musicals, mostly at affordable ticket prices. (Tickets £10-£35).

Phone	08700 40 2000

SHOPPING

St David's Centre

Right in the heart of Cardiff, St David's Centre has over 40 stores offering fashion, shoes, toys, jewellery, furniture books, computers and lots of exciting places to eat or enjoy a coffee.

Mermaid Quay

A selection of shops, restaurants and services right on the waterfront at Mermaid Quay.

Cardiff Bay Retail Park

A collection of large department stores, including Ikea, can be found in the new bay development.

Cardiff Arcades

Chic, elegant, now, sexy, hip, happening – all the words that sound kind of trendy, but quite simply, that's the way it is. The arcades on Cardiff's High Street and St Mary's Street offer all this amongst a multitude of quirky and fashionable outlets, not forgetting the more traditional shopping experiences. These include Castle Arcade; High Street Arcade; Morgan Arcade; Royal Arcade; Wyndham Arcade; Duke Street Arcade; Dominions Arcade; Andrews Arcade.

Shopping: Cardiff (cont)

Queens Arcade and Capitol Shopping Centre. A juxtaposition of glossy new shopping centres against the authentic Edwardian and Victorian arcades harbour some of Cardiff's specialist stores, where you can find special gifts, designer clothes, sample a smoothie and find a bargain in a second hand store. Queen's Arcade has more than 40 stores offering fashion, shoes, toys, jewellery, furniture, books and computers while Capitol is a modern and well designed centre with a younger and more bustling atmosphere.

ANTIQUES

Cardiff Antiques Market	Royal Arcade	(029) 2039 8891
Jacobs Antique Centre	West Canal Wharf	(029) 20390939
The Pumping Station	Penarth Road	(029) 2022 1085

BOOKSELLERS

Booksale	Church Street	(029) 2022 8422
Capitol Bookshop	Morgan Arcade.	(029) 2038 8423.
Fopp Bookshop	Queen Street.	(029) 2037 4090
The Sports Bookshop	Royal Arcade.	(029) 2066 7756
The Works	St David's Centre.	(029) 2022 4669
Troutmark	Castle Arcade.	(029) 2038 2814
TSO Bookshop	High Street.	(029) 2039 5548
Waterstones	The Hayes.	(029) 2066 5606

CARDIFF MARKETS

Bessemer Road Market	Bessemer Road.	(029) 2037 3653
Cardiff Indoor Market	St Mary Street.	
Riverside Market	Fitzhamon Embankment.	(029) 2022 7982
Splott Market	Ocean Park.	(029) 2077 7123

CRAFT AND HOBBY SHOPS

Antics	High Street.	(029) 2022 9065
Cardiff Comic Guru	Wyndham Arcade.	(029) 2022 9119
Games Workshop	High Street.	(029) 2064 4917
Forbidden Planet	Duke Street.	(029) 2022 8885

DEPARTMENT AND VARIETY STORES

BHS	41/47 St Davids Way.	(029) 2039 0167
Debenhams	46/50 St Davids Way.	(029) 2039 9789
Ikea	Cardiff Bay Retail Park. 0845 3552267	

GALLERIES

Capsule Gallery	Charles Street.	(029) 2038 2882
Castle Galleries	Capitol Shopping.	(029) 2022 2020
Gallery 66	Royal Arcade.	(029) 2022 7822
Honzou Corporation	Castle Arcade.	(029) 2034 4111

FASHION

@ Fab	Castle Arcade.	(029) 2064 1727
A G Meek Ltd	16 St Davids Way.	(029) 2039 5101
Accessorize	41/47 St Davids Way.	(029) 2022 0782
Adams	29/31 Town Wall.	(029) 2022 6682
Ann Harvey	21 Cathedral Walk.	(029) 2039 9442
Austin Reed	Capitol Shopping.	(029) 2022 8357
Bay Trading	31 St Davids Way.	(029) 2022 1805
Benetton	Capitol Centre.	(029) 2037 3250
Calders	Duke Street.	(029) 2022 0616
Cardiff Jeans Co	St Mary Street.	(029) 2022 4130
Chessman	Castle Arcade.	(029) 2025 6140
The Designer Room	Mermaid Quay.	(029) 2048 5626
Gap	Queen Street.	(029) 2034 0464
High & Mighty	High Street.	(029) 2022 7925
Jaeger	Capitol Shopping.	(029) 2022 6898
Karen Miller	Capitol Shopping.	(029) 2066 6515

GIFTS AND SOUVEINEERS

Cardiff Visitor Centre	The Hayes.	(029) 2022 7281
Castle Welsh Crafts	Castle Street.	(029) 2034 3038
Discovery	13 St Davids Way.	(029) 2038 8925
Gadget Shop	Capitol Centre.	(029) 2039 4355
Kaleidoscope	Wyndham Arcade.	(029) 20255542
The Entertainer	Queens Arcade.	(029) 2066 6513

HEALTH AND BEAUTY

Bauhaus	St Mary Street.	(029) 2022 8749
Classic Eyes Optician	Mermaid Quay.	(029) 2049 2121
Constantinou Brothers	Bridge Street.	(029) 2022 8222
Frayne and Jones	Royal Arcade.	(029) 2066 7733

Internet	www.wmc.org.uk

EAT, DRINK & SLEEP

BARS

Big-screen bars

The Eli Jenkins, 7 Bute Terrace, Cardiff Bay.
Big ale house overlooking the bay. Surrounded by attraction, good place to hunker down for the match and then go exploring the Bay.

Dewi's, Unit 1, UCG Building, Mary Anne St.
Three big screens and one plasma, this tavern – previously known as the Springbok Bar – sprawls over two floors and is still a popular spot with stray South Africans.

Sports Café, Graving Docks, Cardiff Bay.
As its name implies, this bar is keen on sport and you'll be unlikely to get ice hockey on match day. Doubles as a restaurant, dance floor and general hang-out centre.

Toucan Club, 95 St Mary's St.
Good food and atmosphere on match day.

Kiwis, 21-27 Wyndham Arcade.
Popular rugby meeting place.

Real ale

Butcher's Arms, High St, Llandaff, at top of Cathedral Road.

About half an hour's walk, or a short taxi ride, from the city centre this gem of a pub, pictured left, is just round the corner from Llandaff Cathedral. Regulars include Barry John, Jonathan Davies, Gareth Davies and John Dawes. It's a bar for the giants of recent rugby history and serves a cracking pint of draught bitter.

Cayo Arms, 36 Cathedral Rd. Canton area near city centre.

This pub only opened in 2000 and but has already won the CAMRA Pub of the Year award twice. Homely atmosphere (it once was a home), it keeps its beers very well and is popular amongst locals, professionals and guzzlers alike. Lots of choice of ales.

Chapter Arts Centre, Market Rd, Canton.

Former school now a thriving arts centre also has some value added: a contemporary and characterful bar which also doubles as an art gallery. There are four pumps dispensing a variety of local brews, including some fine German wheat beers. Twenty minutes walk from the city centre, there are German beerfests here in May and October. Worth a visit if you don't fancy the belch and heave of Munich.

The City Arms, 10 Quay St, City Centre.

Great little pub but you'll have a tough time of it rucking your way to the bar on match day as it's right next to the ground. And it's not going to get any quieter as the night progresses – it's a favourite night-spot, staying open until 2am on Thurs, Fri and Sat.

Cottage, St Mary's St, City Centre.

Non-smoking. Good cheap food in a quiet, relaxed, light and stylish old pub. However it will not be so quiet on international day as it is close to the Millennium Stadium and the railway station. So get in early. Specialises in the local Brains Dark Bitter. The local guide book 'Itchy Cardiff' says 'Best avoided if you are under 50'.

Gatekeeper, 9-10 Westgate, City Centre.

This is a Wetherspoon pub in an old auction house. It is a haven from noise (Wetherspoon's do not play 'music'), a tranquil retreat from the ear-shattering racket you will get in most pubs (though it will hardly be quiet on match day). There are two bars on an upper and lower level and there are eight guest beers. Also handy for the Stadium, so get in early. Cheap and cheerful with bargain price food.

Glamorgan Council & Staff Club, 17 Westgate, City Centre.

Not the most glamorous sounding establishment, this is a great stop for a cheap pint of good beer. It's also close to the Stadium. This place survives the demise of Glamorgan County Council and has been turned into a private club which allows (almost) anyone access.

Goat Major, 33 High St, City Centre.

Lovely, unspoilt, Victorian town centre haven for folk seeking award-winning ale away from the blare of the disco beat. Its name reflects connections with the Prince of Wales regiment. Indeed, the regimental goat is an occasional visitor and enjoys a tipple of Brains Dark.

New Dock Tavern, 188 Broadway, Roath (1 mile NE of the City Centre)

This could be a good bolt hole if you wish to flee the throng. About 15 minutes brisk walk up the Newport Road and you are into an unspoilt, proper old-fashioned boozer. As the Good Beer Guide says: 'Excellent example of a traditional street corner local in Cardiff.'

Old Arcade, Church St, City Centre

Handy for the shops and very rugby friendly (as you'd expect in Cardiff). Lots of rugby memorabilia.

Owain Glyndwr, 10 St. John's St

Named after famous Welsh prince from the middle-ages, the Owain Glyndwr (pronounced Owen Glen-Dower) in St John's St is in the centre of Cardiff's shopping district and celebrates everything Welsh. While still open and welcoming to English visitors, expect a cheeky pun or two about the rugby. Looks a bit ropey from the outside, but a recent refit means that it is comfortable and contemporary.

The Robin Hood, 16 Severn Grove, Pontcanna.

About 15 minutes walk from the centre this is a fine real ale haunt and welcomes fans with open arms.

Westgate, 49 Cowbridge Rd East.

Just outside the city centre and owned by Brains, the big local brewery and sponsor of the Welsh team. Popular and big. There is even a map inside showing where all the other pubs are. Entry is likely to be restricted on match day.

The Yard, Brewery 1/4.

If its Brains you want, then the Yard is the place to go. As the brewer's flagship pub it offers the whole range of Brains beers as well as fine food and a good atmosphere.

Phone	029 2022 7577

White Hart, 66 James Street, Cardiff Bay.

A traditional pub on James Street down in what used to be called Tiger Bay, now an increasingly upmarket purlieu of swinging Cardiff. Only a short journey from the town centre, the pub serves a wide selection of Brains beers, as well as other lagers, ciders and bottled drinks and also hot snacks. There is a pool table and a big screen TV.

Packet, 96 Bute Street, Cardiff Bay.

Popular little community pub situated on Bute Street in the heart of the vibrant Cardiff Bay area. Recently renovated, the Packet is now attracting a wider range of clientele – no longer the scrapings of downtown. Live entertainment at the weekend and pub grub available.

The Wharf, Schooner Way, Atlantic Wharf, Cardiff Bay.

A Waterside venue with regular live music and comedy. The 60-seat restaurant on the first floor serves an interesting variety of dishes with many fish specials and can also be hired for private functions and business conferences. The ground floor bar is relaxed and friendly and the bar menu is served throughout the day. There is disabled access and facilities. Good range of fluids.

Non-smoking bars

Bar En Route, Cathays Terrace.

Cardiff's first non-smoking bar is a small and cosy affair, tucked neatly into the outer edge of Cathays, the main student area. It offers continental lagers and wines all personally recommended by the chatty owner; an ideal location for a quiet and relaxed night away from the crowds, as long as you go early. Later on it tends to fill up (open 11am-11pm).

Phone	02920 404444

Dewi's, Mary Ann Street.

Occupying what was once Springboks sports bar next to the UGC cinema, Dewi's has kept the sporting theme, as it is part owned by ex-English test cricketer, Andy Caddick. Non-smoking throughout, Dewi's serves exotic Thai food throughout the day and cocktails at night. DJ's liven up the evenings and the big screen shows the all the big rugby and football games.

Phone	02920 395899

Non-smoking bars (cont)

Cwtch Bar, 5 Bute Crescent, Cardiff Bay.
Cwtch is Welsh for cuddle and, curiously enough, cupboard under the stairs. Hidden beneath Jolyons Hotel, this Cwtch comes complete with fireplace, deep sofas and huge pieces of local art. Offering an extensive wine list and friendly service, the owner also makes an effort to source his ingredients locally.

Phone	02920 488775

33 Windsor Place, Windsor Place.
Formally known as Bar Essential, this is yet another bar that has been given a complete refit and reborn as a clean air bar. Its stylish design provides a contemporary feel and is located away from the main drinking area of St Mary street.

Phone	02920 383762

Trendy bars

CITY CENTRE

Floyds Bar, St. Mary St.
A small, privately run bar, found nestled above the clothes shop of the same name and one of Cardiff's best-kept secrets. Live jazz on Thursdays. Reckoned to be Cardiff's coolest hangout – media types and hip 20 somethings come here to be seen. Sangria and cocktails, an ideal pre-club venue. Open 7.30pm – 2am.

Phone	029 2022 2181

Café Jazz, 21 St. Mary St.
Cardiff's only fully-fledged jazz spot. Predictably, it looks like a dive from the outside but inside, is tickety-boo. Sunday lunch revival session, piano to go with the remedy of your choice. Welcomes talented jammers, so bring your sax and swing!

Phone	029 2038 7026

City Arms, 10 Quay St, City Centre (see also under Pubs).
Great little pub but you'll have a tough time of it rucking your way to the bar on match day as it's opposite the ground. It is not going to get any quieter as the night progresses – a favourite night-spot, staying open until 2am on Thurs, Fri and Sat.

Phone	029 2022 5258

Copa, 4 Wharton Street.
Formerly the Glassworks, this place was popular with rugby fans: worry not. There is a large overhead projector screen plus many smaller TVs. Real ale has been replaced by 'Euro beers'. Italy's Nastro Azzuro, Germany's Erdinger and Belgium's Leffe, all on tap. The most interesting offering of all is Belgium's Kriekbier which is best described as alcoholic cherryade, but tastes surprisingly good. 1am Fri & Sat.

Phone	029 2022 2114

WALES

Detox, Harlech Court, Bute Terrace.
Gay club and coffee bar open 7 days a week. 2am on Thurs.

Phone	029 2034 2429
Internet	www.dnacardiff.com

Oz Bar, 12 St. Mary St.
Most bars these days seem to be run by Australians so it makes sense for them to open one of their own. Good place to crack a tube or two and strut your Barry Humphries impressions. Open until 1am at weekends. Entry charge: £1 - £3.

Phone	029 2066 8008

Model Inn, Quay St.
Top pre-club spot next door to the City Arms. Traditional Welsh boozer which has remodelled itself and now doubles up as a groovy spot for later in the day, closing at 2am on Fri & Sat depending on events.

Phone	029 2023 3128

Moloko, 7 Mill Lane.

Cool hangout for vibey types. Combination of bar and club. Small dance floor full of hip-hop 'classy types – no skanky stag nighters or dodgy hen partyers here,' according to Itchy guide (for about a fiver, Itchy is pretty good). Vast range of flavoured vodkas and some interesting booths upstairs, ideal for making new friends (assuming that the booty shaking dance routine succeeds).
Open until **2**am.

Phone	029 2022 5592

BSB, Windsor Place.

Patio provides open space for balmy Cardiff nights. If one of these coincides with a match we'd be surprised. This is Cardiff's glamour centre – this is where the capital's beau monde congregate for speed dating, DJs, open mic and vast quantities of modestly priced fuel.
Open until **2am** weekends.

Phone	029 2023 8228

Clwb Ifor Bach, Womanby St.

Goldie Lookin' Chain were regulars here until they took off big-time. Good mixture of live music performed here. Old favourite.
Open late every night.

Phone	029 2023 2199
Internet	www.clwb.net

La Tantra, Westgate Street.

Located directly opposite the Millennium Stadium, this Turkish themed bar and club serves a wide range of drinks and cocktails and is quickly becoming popular with the local 20-somethings who want something different. DJ's in the club downstairs play funky jazz and chilled beats (open **11**am – **12**pm **2**am downstairs).

Phone	029 2039 9400

Fontanan Wine Bar, 12 Church St.

Pricy but stylish downstairs bar, below Topo Gigo restaurant. Cosmopolitan feel, swanky décor. Prices should keep most of the hoi polloi elsewhere. **2am**.

Phone	029 2034 5903

Bar Cuba, Unit 9, The Friary.

Cheap cocktails – absurdly good value at happy hour. This is the place to 'dance and pull' according to the city's Itchy Guide. 'Music is a mixture of cheese, RnB and old classics.' Open until **2**am. Closed Sundays.

Phone	029 2039 7967

Barfly, Kingsway.

Barfly works on the ethos of supporting the best new music by filling its 5 Britain-wide venues with the stars of tomorrow seven days a week. Check the website to find out what's on in the venues which helped launch the careers of Coldplay, The Darkness, Franz Ferdinand and many more. Doubles as a club.

Phone	029 2039 6589
Internet	www.barflyclub.com

BSB The Place, 11 Windsor Place.

A 'relaxed-atmosphere-bar' serving cocktails and world beers, daily changing menu. Live music. Hip-hop, drum and bass and break beat. Closed Sun & Mon. Open to **2am** Thur-Sat.

Phone	029 2023 8228

Hard Rock Cafe, Brewery Quarter, St. Mary St.

Cardiff's own Hard Rock Café is part of the brewery quarter – the redeveloped site of the old Brains Brewery. The outdoor area is ideal for summer drinks. Happy hour between **5**-**7**pm Mon-Thur. Open until **1**am.

Phone	029 2037 3403
Internet	www.hardrock.com

The Funky Buddha Lounge, 34 Woodville Road.
On the edge of Cardiff's main student strip, the Buddha lounge continues the trend for independent venues with a quirky feel. Serving cocktails and good food, it fills up quickly in the evenings. A cosy place to hang out with friends, and great for a Sunday roast.

Phone	02920 665353

La Tantra, Westgate Street.
Directly opposite the Millennium Stadium, this Turkish themed bar and club serves a range of drinks and cocktails and is quickly becoming popular with the local 20-somethings who want something different. DJ's downstairs play funky jazz and chilled beats (open 11am – 12pm 2am downstairs).

Phone	02920 399400

Toucan Club, 95 St. Mary's St.
Funk, world and Latin music served up alongside wholesome food. Has restorative powers for those making a post-match day visit. Voted best place for live music. Also offers open-mic nights.

Phone	029 2037 2212

Kiwis, 21-27 Wyndham Arcade, City Centre.
Popular spot for post-match meetings, could provide both the starting and finishing point for a wild night out. (See also under clubs).

Bar M, 31 Westgate St.
Next to the Millennium Stadium. A civilised spot for late-night boogying, though the music is mainstream. Low-level sofas and chromium bars on both floors.

Phone	029 2034 3330

The Philharmonic, 76 St. Mary St.
Thursday night is medic's night so don't get injured on a Friday. St Mary St, for strangers to Cardiff, is the main drag – both sides of the street are lined with pubs and restaurants. Be warned.

Phone	029 2023 0678

Soda Bar, 41 St. Mary St.
The place to go into the wee small hours. 4am on Saturday (Sunday) and 3am Friday (Saturday). If you want the whole weekend to appear on the memory board as a blur, this is the place. Not cheap, which discourages the rabble.

Phone	029 2023 8181
Internet	www.thesodabar.com

CARDIFF BAY

Ba Orient, Unit 27, Mermaid Quay, Cardiff Bay.
One of the most stylish options in Cardiff Bay, Ba Orient serves wide range of cocktails and good dim sum in smart and sophisticated surroundings. Minimalist décor and swanky VIP areas. (open 12pm-12am weekdays, 12pm – 1am weekends).

Phone	02920 463939
Internet	www.baorient.com

Bar 38, Stuart St, Mermaid Quay.
Much like the above, but without quite the style or the dim sum. A good enough spot for a cocktail and late session. Closes 1am.

Phone	02920 494375

City Canteen, 1-2 Mount Stuart Square.
Smart and sophisticated. Another choice of media types, CC is right on the quay and is about as different as it's possible to get from the old Tiger Bay.

Terra Nova, Stuart St, Mermaid Quay.
Smart spot near the even smarter St David's Hotel. Not particularly late-night venue, but the food is good and it's a place to people-watch. Closes 1am at weekend.

Phone	02920 450947

ROATH & CATHAYS

Bar Billabong, Wellfield Rd.

Good mixture of students and locals at this big, inexpensive and cosmopolitan venue. Great for big screen sport (there are lots of screens so you won't miss anything, even in a crush). No late opening.

Phone	02920 252042

Journeys, 1-2 Upper Clifton St.

One of the more interesting night-spots. Poetry, reggae, story telling, world music and cheap wine and food. Popular with old hippies, students and lots of others. Raffles offering sea sponge prizes kind of place. Open until 2am weekends.

Phone	029 2049 1061
Internet	www.journeysbar.co.uk

The Social, 7-9 Miskin St.

In the heart of student land – Cathays – a great and cheap place to drink everything from real ale to exotic cocktails. No late opening.

Phone	02920 25200

Callaghans, Castle Street.

A popular Irish pub within a stones throw of the Millennium Stadium and plenty of Guinness on tap Bar food is served throughout the day including the 'All Day Irish Breakfast'.

Phone	02920 347247

CLUBS

These are all open until dangerously late.

Addiction	Harlech Court, Bute Terrace Internet www.dnacardiff.com	029 2034 2429
Bar Ice	4 Churchill Way	029 2023 7177
Bar Risa	Millennium Plaza	029 2023 8228
Club Latinos	11 Mill Lane, Café Quarter	029 2064 5000
Club X	35-39 Charles St	029 2040 0876
Creation	Park Place	029 2037 7014
Cuba Bar & Grill	Unit 9 The Friary	029 2039 7967
Evolution, Atlantic Wharf	Hemingway Rd, Cardiff Bay	029 2046 4444
Exit Club	48 Charles St	029 2064 0102
Fantasy Lounge	93 St Mary St www.thefantasylounge.co.uk	029 2038 2201
Flares Nightclub	96-97 St Mary St	029 2023 5825
Fontana Wine Bar	12 Church St	029 2034 4794
Inncognito	29 Park Place	029 2041 2190
Jumpin's Jak's	Millennium Plaza www.jumpinjaks.com	07000 352352
Kiwis	21-29 Wyndham Arcade	029 2022 9876
La Tantra	Westgate St	029 2039 9400
Liquid	Imperial Gate, St Mary St	029 2064 5646
Lush	Caroline St	029 2035 9123

Clubs: (cont)

Minsky's	Cathedral Walk	029 2023 3128
The Philharmonic	76 St Mary St	029 2023 0678
Rioja Bar	La Brasserie, Mill Lane	029 2023 4134
Sam's Bar	63 St Mary St	029 2034 5189
Toucan Club	95-97 St Mary St www.toucanclub.co.uk	029 2037 2212
The Union	3 Churchill Way www.unioncardiff.com	029 2064 1010
University Union	Park Place	029 2078 1400

COFFEE SHOPS

A Shot in the Dark, 12 City Road.
Serving soup bowl size fair-trade cappuccinos and mochas, and tempting you with huge, squashy sofas, Shot in the Dark is an ideal venue for a chilled out coffee break. Apart from eco-friendly coffee, fresh food and friendly staff, the café also has its own writers' group and opens until late.

Capsule, 48 Charles St.
Part café, part gallery, relax on the comfy chairs while contemplating contemporary art. Capsule also serves Italian food and offers free Wi-Fi connection. Run by Acid Casuals, who include members of Super Furry Animals, it is a given that there will be something good on the stereo.

Europa, 25 Castle St.
Licensed and open until late, this small but perfectly formed city centre coffee house offers a great alternative to the drunken revelry of St.Mary St. Live DJ's and poetry nights liven up the evenings, and local artists often decorate the walls (with the owner's consent).

Café Brava, 71 Pontcanna St.
Neatly tucked in Cardiff's media land is this lively café. Contemporary art lines the walls and its smart interior is often full of smart suited clientele. Also serves breakfast lunch and three course evening meals.

Coffee 1, 9 Wood St.
Big leather sofas downstairs and a balcony terrace, complete with heaters and umbrellas. Ideal for people watching as the throngs file down Wood Street. A good selection of cakes and pastries are available along, with caramel mochas and all the other incomprehensibles that foam society throws up.

RESTAURANTS

Armless Dragon, 97 Wyeverne Street.
This restaurant claims to offer the true taste of contemporary Wales, and with a menu including Brecon lamb, Welsh black beef, skate wing in cockle and leek sauce and of course, bara brith bread and butter pudding, you're unlikely to fault with the claim. Using locally sourced and organic ingredients where possible, they have featured in the Good Food Guide since 1985. (open Tues-Fri and Sat evenings, three courses less than £25 per head).

Phone	029 2038 2357
Internet	www.armlessdragon.co.uk

Da Castaldo, 5 Romilly Crescent, Canton.

The eponymous chef Antonio Castaldo sets out to 'uphold authentic Italian traditions within a modern style' in this bright restaurant set amidst a jungle of Edwardian streets off Cathedral Road. One of its specialities is pasta al fagioli, a robust bean and pasta dish from the southern Med. Another is spaghetti al cartoccio (shellfish, cherry tomatoes and white wine) and pork fillet in a chestnut and honey sauce with roast vegetables. Desserts include perfect pannacotta, precise tiramisu, torta di mela and then there are the cheeses: some two dozen fine varieties.

Basic Price	£25 plus
Phone	029 2022 1905
Internet	www.dacastaldo.com

Le Gallois, 6-10 Romilly Crescent, Canton.

This is a smart Gallo-French fusion of talent and ingredients – fine fare cooked with French panache in Cardiff's highest ranking restaurant. Bizarrely, many of the ingredients come from the markets of Paris, while the chef is Welsh. You would not necessarily expect this combination to work, but it does. Set up in 1998 by the Dupuy and Jones families, the restaurant floor is run by the French but you are likely to hear French, English and Welsh spoken. According to the Good Food Guide, which scores it above the six other establishments it lists, *"The smart dining room …is a worthy setting for a starter such as sautéed scallops with belly pork, boudin noir, quail's egg, confit tomato and honey jam: each element perfectly cooked and a perfect foil to the others"*. Other imaginative combinations include oxtail bourguignon with monkfish, and a mascarpone sorbet and rhubarb, orange and champagne sorbet with a hot Szechuan pepper informed tuile. Fine service.

Basic Price	£35 plus
Phone	029 2034 1264
Internet	www.legallois-ycymro.com

Bosphorus, 31 Mermaid Quay, Cardiff Bay.

This glass-fronted Turkish restaurant has one of the best positions in Cardiff, sitting, as it does on its own peer, in the middle of Cardiff Bay. There is some pretty sharp and authentic cooking – triangular borek pastries and paplican-biber kizartma (fried aubergines with peppers and garlic) plus colourful salads and protein packed grills and fish specials. Owned and run by three Turkish brothers, they also serve such staples as moussaka, seafood and lamb casserole. Wine list is good and for the hungry, there is the Sultan's feast for £19.50. Lunch and dinner served daily.

Basic Price	£25, approx
Phone	029 2048 7477
Internet	www.bosphorus.co.uk

Brazz Wales, Millennium Centre.

If you want to eat in the marvellous new Wales Millennium Centre, Brazz is the place. The Triangle bar offers a large range of wines and cocktails, while the restaurant tempts with roasted skate wing or braised shoulder of lamb. Three course dinner for two will cost around £40-60. Open for lunch and dinner 7 days a week.

Basic Price	£20
Phone	029 2045 9000
Internet	www.brazz.co.uk

Celtic Suite Restaurant, UWIC Campus, Colchester Ave.

Amazing value for those happy to be guinea pigs for local catering students. The Times reviewed it very favourably ('Cardiff's best-kept secret…using top ingredients' etc.) Said students are supervised by teachers, some of whom have cooked their way through the kitchens of the Savoy and the Connaught. Lunch £8 for three courses. Dinner is four courses for £15 while house wine is £7.95. Book now!

Basic Price	£15
Phone	0845 201 3358

Restaurants (cont)

The Inn at the Elm Tree, St Brides, Nr Newport.

This is a restaurant with rooms and sets out to be a *"21st century inn with traditional values,"* according to owner Shaun Ellis. British cooking with a European take – renowned for its seafood. Game is also a feature, from local estates. Sourcing is organic and Welsh.

Basic Price	£30
Phone	0845 201 3390
Internet	www.the-elm-tree.co.uk

La Tasca The Brewery Quarter.

Part of the Old Brewery Quarter development in Cardiff city centre, La Tasca offers a range of tapas, paellas, and Spanish wines and beers, which can all be enjoyed to the strains of Latin music, Mediterranean décor and the occasional Spanish speaking waiter. Fun place and for those staying on (or arriving early), there are also salsa lessons on Wednesdays (8-10pm).

Tapas £2-£4 per dish, paella, £8.95 per person.

Basic Price	£20
Phone	029 2023 0087
Internet	www.latasca.co.uk

The Old Post Office, Greenwood Land, St Fagans, Cardiff.

Conservatory dining in pleasingly minimalist surroundings – crisp white, oak floorboards, brown leather seats and terracotta give warmth. Part of Choice Products (along with Woods and Cutting Edge). Good enough to feature in the Good Food Guide. A terrine of rabbit and foie gras with grape chutney and toasted brioche won praise, "while main courses of pan-fried turbot are accompanied by a saffron and mussel broth, and fillet of Welsh Black beef comes with fondant potato, spinach, asparagus and a rich red wine jus."

Phone	029 2056 5400
Internet	www.old-post-office.com

Pearl of the Orient First Floor, Mermaid Quay, Cardiff Bay.

With Cantonese, Peking, Szechuan and Malaysian dishes, and the opportunity to eat lunch, high tea, set meals and a la carte, there's certainly no shortage of choice. Apart from its acclaimed cooking, it's worth going just to see the tropical fish tank built into the entire length of the bar. The set menus range from £14-£28 per person, high tea £4.50 per person.

Basic price	£14-£28.
Phone	029 2049 8080
Internet	www.thepearloftheorient.com

Izakaya Japanese Restaurant, Mermaid Quay, Cardiff Bay.

Cross between a restaurant and a canteen, the Izakaya is a welcoming spot. The menu is helpful – the exotica on offer are helpfully illustrated with photographs so even a Martian could make an informed choice from the many exotic dishes on offer. Try the yakitori (on skewers), sushi and sashimi in individual portions or as part of packaged platters, not to mention the tempura and noodle dishes. One of the advantages to this kind of eating is that you don't have to order everything at once: just amble through the menu, stopping off where your palate takes you, washing down the various tastes with different Japanese beer and sake (there's quite a choice). The GFG recommends that those who know anything about Japanese food are probably better going off-piste, and ordering dishes separately.

Basic Price	£14-£50.
Phone	029 2049 2939
Internet	www.izakaya-japanese-tavern.com

Woods Brasserie, The Pilotage Building, Stuart St, Cardiff Bay.

Some of the best cooking to be had in Cardiff is served in this stylish and informal setting on the edge of the Bay area. The building is light and airy, with a distinctly contemporary feel. The cooking is European: crab and basil linguini with roasted scallops, Asian crispy duck leg with beansprout and chilli salad should whet the appetite before baked canon of lamb on a bed of rosti potato, with a cherry and garlic dressing. Desserts are a speciality and the wine list is solid and medium priced. Woods is part of Choice Produce, which also owns the Old Post Office in nearby St Fagans (see entry) as well as the Cutting Edge bistro in Discovery House, just round the corner. Head chef Sean Murphy joined Woods and has previously worked at 2 and 3 star Michelin restaurants, including Chez Nico and Gordon Ramsay.

Basic price	£35-£55
Phone	029 2029 2400
Internet	www.old-post-office.com/woods

Da Venditto, 7-8 Park Place, City Centre.
Swish establishment housed in the centre of Cardiff, stainless steel and mahogany compete to give this grand old Victorian building a modern feel. Recently awarded AA Restaurant of the year for Wales, it is also in the Good Food Guide and has been voted one of the top five Italian Restaurants in the UK by Martini magazine. Terrine comprises confit of duck, foie gras, lentils, balsamic vinegar and is served up with roasted red onion confit. Roast rump of salt marsh lamb served up with buttered spinach, another speciality. Desserts are also highly prized. Strong wine list.

Basic Price	£30-£60
Phone	029 2023 0781
Internet	www.vendittogroup.co.uk

Café Naz, Mermaid Quay, Cardiff Bay.
Upmarket and contemporary Indian restaurant on the upper level of Mermaid Quay with obliging and courteous service. An offspring of the Café Naz in London's Brick Lane. There's another in Cambridge; another in Horsham. They're springing up all over – because this formula of Bangladeshi cooking is a couple of levels up from your average high street curry shop. The wine list is very reasonable.

Basic Price	£15-£20
Phone	029 2049-6555
Interrnet	www.cafenaz.co.uk

Restaurants (cont)

QUICK BITE

Crockerton's Deli, Caroline Street.

Taking full advantage of Cardiff status as the world's first FairTrade capital, this funky deli is successfully introducing ethically traded and locally sourced products to the mainstream. Blending a sustainable approach with a contemporary design, they offer fine foods that are good for karma as well as your health. Sandwiches from £3, anti-pasta from £4.50.

Phone	02920 220 088
Internet	www.crockertons.co.uk (FairTrade)

Celtic Cauldron, Castle Arcade, Castle Street.

A small but busy café, this friendly restaurant is open throughout the day to provide a true taste of Wales. Mainly vegetarian, you can try traditional Welsh favourites such as rarebit, faggots, or a bowl of cawl – a Welsh soup with lamb and vegetables. Takeouts available. £5 for lunch.

Phone	02920 387 185

The New York Deli, High Street Arcade.

For those with a monstrous appetite, head over to the New York Deli, where you can find vast hoagies, hot-dogs, filled bagels and grinders (meatballs in a long roll). Try the Sinatra Special or the Alamo Hoagie for a treat, soups and salads also available. (hoagies £4, bagels £2.60, bagel burger £2.75).

Phone	02920 388388

Zushi, The Aspect, Queen Street.

Wales' first conveyor belt style sushi restaurant has recruited chefs directly from Japan to create a modern Japanese experience in the heart of the Welsh capital. Select dishes from the e-menu at the computer terminals or surf the net while your sashimi snakes its way round on the 'kaiten'. Breakfasts, sample menus and vegetarian options all available, and takeaway bento boxes start from £3.50.

Phone	02920 669 911
Internet	www.zushi-uk.com

The Plan, Morgan Arcade.

Nearly everything here is organic from egg and cress sandwiches, continental breakfasts and scrummy cakes to organic milkshakes, hot chocolates and herbal teas. There is also a large selection of coffees from around the world, so you can choose an Ethiopian Mocha or a Kenyan Peaberry to satisfy your caffeine needs. (sandwiches £4.50, coffee £2.10 pot for one, herbal teas, £1, pot for one).

Phone	02920 398 764

OTHERS TO TRY

INDIAN

Balti Cuisine	103 Woodville Rd, Cathays 029 2022 8863
Balti Empire	157-159 Albany Rd, Roath 029 2048 5757
Balti-Wallah	72 Cowbridge Rd East, Canton 029 2039 5959
The Cinnamon Tree	Kings Rd, Pontcanna 029 2037 4433
Juboraj	Lakeside, Lake Rd West 029 2045 5123
Juboraj II	10 Mill Lane 029 2037 7668

CHINESE

Crispy Duck Café	The Millennium Plaza, Wood St 029 2039 4543
Fortune House Cantonese	43-45 Salisbury Rd 029 2064 1311
Happy Gathering	233 Cowbridge Rd 029 2039 7531
Noble House	St David's House, 9 Wood St 029 2038 8430
Phib's	98 Crwys Rd, Cathays 029 2039 8352

ITALIAN

Ana Bela	5 Pontcanna St 029 2023 9393
Cibo's	83 Pontcanna St, 029 2023 2226
Da Enrico	53 Crwys Rd 029 2037 4757
Gio's Giovannis	38 The Hayes 029 2022 0077
Lorenza's Ristorante Italiano	153-155 Crwys Rd 029 2023 2261
Positano	9-10 Church St 029 2023 5810

FRENCH

La Brasserie	60 St Mary St 029 2037 2164
Le Monde	62 St Mary St 029 2038 7376

MEXICAN

El Paso	120 City Rd 029 2046 2054
Las Iguanas	8 Mill Lane 029 2022 6373
Chiquito	The Brewery Quarter, Caroline St 029 2038 7465

PORTUGUESE

Portos	40 Mary St 029 2022 0060

THAI

Thai House	3 Guildford Crescent 029 2038 7404
Thai Thai	2-4 Elms Rd 029 2049 4007
Tiger Bay Restaurant	Mermaid Quay, Cardiff Bay 029 2048 3388

WELSH

Buffs	8 Mount Stuart Square, Cardiff Bay 029 2046 4628
Salt	Mount Stuart Square 029 2049 4375

HOTELS

In and around Cardiff

Angel Hotel, Castle Street, Cardiff, CF10 1SZ
102 rooms. £220 s, £240 d/t. From £46 at other times.
Traditional rugby haunt opposite the castle and immediately across the road from the stadium. Well used on match days, both by ordinary punters and corporate hospitality guests. The Angel has been expensively refurbished and the prices reflect this. Air conditioned rooms and free parking.

Phone	029 2064 9200
Email	angelreservations@paramount-hotels.co.uk
Internet	www.paramount-hotels.co.uk

Arnedd Lon Guest House, 157-159 Cathedral Road, Pontcanna, Cardiff, CF11 9PL.
6 rooms. £60 d/t. £30 s. Double room £30 at other times.
Cosy guest house close to city centre, there are six bedrooms. Mike and Maria Tucker, both of them Welsh speakers (don't worry: they speak English, too) have been running the place for more than a decade. They are – it almost goes without saying in this city – keen rugby fans. Free car park.

Phone	029 2022 3349

Austins Guest House, 11 Coldstream Terrace, City Centre, Cardiff, CF11 6LJ.
11 rooms. From £75 d/t. £40 s. Normal: £45 d/t, £35 s.
Just 300 metres from the Castle, this small, friendly hotel/B&B overlooks the River Taff. Everything is on hand and the bus and train stations are just minutes' walk away.

Phone	029 2037 7148
Email	austins@hotelcardiff.com
Internet	www.cardiffhotel.com

The Big Sleep, Bute Terrace, Cardiff, CF10 2FE.
81 rooms. From £99 d/t to £110.
Very good value indeed. Hardly any mark-up for the big occasions. ***'Super cheap but sexy-chic'*** according to one style magazine. ***'1 of the 25 coolest hotels in the world'*** – according to Conde Nast Traveller. Housed in a 60s block on the Cardiff Bay edge of the city with spectacular views towards the sea, John Malkovich, the actor, is a shareholder. Cosmo Fry, the chocolate magnate, owns it. The Big Sleep means death in Raymond Chandler parlance. You should sleep well.

Phone	029 2063 6363
Email	bookings@thebigsleephotel.com
Internet	www.thebigsleephotel.com

Brecon Lodge, 6 Kymin Terrace, Penarth, Cardiff, CF64 1WW.
From £27.50. 15 minutes drive from Cardiff City Centre but only minutes' walk to the sea.
Brecon Lodge offers a warm welcome. You can look across to the Somerset coastline, just 13 miles away. Buses into the centre of Cardiff itself run every 8 minutes throughout the day, dropping off outside the Millenium Stadium or the St. David's Shopping Mall. There is also a good train service.

Phone	029 2070 2111
Email	info@breconlodge.co.uk
Internet	www.breconlodge.co.uk

Cardiff Backpacker, 96-98 Neville Street, Riverside, Cardiff, CF11 6LS.
Dorm: Backpackers hostel offering 80 beds in a variety of room configurations.

Phone	029 2034 5577
Email	info@cardiffbackpacker.com
Internet	www.hostelswales.com

Cardiff Marriott, Mill Lane, Cardiff, CF10 1EZ.
184 rooms. From £295 d/t. £245 s. Normal price: from £72.50 to £135.
In the city centre opposite the colourful Cafe Quarter within walking distance of the city's central attractions. Full leisure facilities.

Phone	029 2039 9944
Internet	www.marriotthotels.com/cwldt

Cardiff University, Southgate House, Bevan Place, Cardiff, CF14 3XZ.
From: £22.50 to £27 NB: Useless for the rugby because it's closed during term time, but handy between June and September if you are here for any other reason. Since this is also a general travel guide, we have chosen to include it. Standard and en-suite rooms in the centre with catering, parking, sporting and social facilities. 908 rooms.

Phone	029 2087 4702
Email	conference@cardiff.ac.uk
Internet	www.cardiff.ac.uk/res

Churchills Hotel, Cardiff Rd, Llandaff, Cardiff, CF5 2AD.
From: £100 d/t to £80 s. Normal: from £75 d/t. Big, handsome townhouse near the perfect village of Llandaff, with its stunning cathedral, pubs and postcard pretty houses. Busy bar and friendly service just five minutes by taxi from town. Popular, no-frills venue. 35 rooms of which 13 are suites housed in mews cottages

Phone	029 2040 1300

Church Hotel, 126 Cathedral Road, Cardiff, CF11 9LQ.
£50. Possible concessions for groups. Normal cost: £25
Set amidst the Victorian charms of Pontcanna, within just a few minutes of the city centre, the Church – which is owned by the parents of Charlotte Church, the singing star and, at the time of going to press, girlfriend of Gavin Henson – offers a relaxing atmosphere. And a very fair rate.

Phone	029 2034 0881
Email	enquires@churchhotelcardiff.com
Interrnet	www.churchhotelcardiff.com

Copthorne Hotel, Copthorne Way, Culverhouse Cross, Cardiff, CF5 6DH.
From £195 s/d/t. Normal tariff: from £100 s/d/t.
Culverhouse Cross is about eight miles (roughly 15 minutes) from the city centre with quick and easy access to the M4 and all of South Wales. Excellent leisure facilities. Another advantage: price.

Phone	029 2059 9100
Email	sales.cardiff@mill-cop.com
Interrnet	www.millenniumhotels.com

Court Colman Manor, Pen-y-Fai, Bridgend, CF31 4NG.
From £85 d/t to £50 s. Normal price: £70 d/t.
Twenty miles and about £30 by taxi (but there is a rail link from the centre of Bridgend) from the action. But a neat escape from the throng at an elegant Grade II listed Georgian country house. Panelled halls, fine Italian Renaissance fireplaces and sweeping staircases set in six acres of gardens. Built on the site of an ancient abbey, the owner Vijay Bhagotra also provides classy Indian cooking. 10 rooms.

Phone	01656 720212
Email	experience@court-colman-manor.com
Internet	www.court-colman-manor.com

Hotels (cont)

Egerton Grey Hotel, Porthkerry, Rhoose, CF62 3BZ.
9 rooms. From: £95 s/d/t. Normal price – same.
Gem of a 17th century country house and former rectory full of antiques and paintings set in seven acres. Restored Edwardian bathrooms, open fireplaces, ornate mouldings and oak panelling. Secluded valley with views and walks down to the sea. Near Cardiff Airport.

Phone	01446 711666
Email	info@egertongrey.co.uk
Internet	www.egertongrey.co.uk

Express by Holiday Inn, Longueil Close, Off Schooner Way, Atlantic Wharf, Cardiff Bay, Cardiff, CF10 4EE.
87 rooms. From: £120 s/d/t. £145 (fam room sleeping 4). 50% non-refundable deposit payable up front. Normal: from £69 d/t.
Between the city and the Bay, it's about 10 minutes walk to either and easy to get to from the M4. Clean and businesslike, its character owes much to the proximity of the waterfront. Clearly designed with the business traveller in mind, it has everything you need – ie bed, bar, hose down room and Wireless LAN for those in need.

Phone	029 2044 9000
Email	info@exhicardiff.co.uk
Internet	www.hiexpress.com/cardiffbay

Future Inn, Cardiff Bay, Hemingway Road, Cardiff Bay, Cardiff, CF10 4JY.
198 rooms. From: £100 d/t to £59.50 (sharing a suite). Otherwise, rooms £99 - £119. (Hotel does say, at time of going to press, it is prepared to allow 4 to a room for same price.) Normal price: rooms from £69.
Looks like a leisure centre but it is hard to miss, with its garish Future sign. Good value rooms and spacious suites. In the heart of the vibrant dining and entertainment Mecca of Cardiff Bay. Handy for the Wales Millennium Centre, the Welsh National Assembly, County Hall and the business community. Not to mention the Millennium Stadium. 198 rooms.

Phone	029 2048 7111
Email	reservations@furtureinns.co.uk
Internet	www.futureinns.co.uk

The Glendale, 10 Plymouth Rd, Penarth, Vale of Glamorgan.

20 rooms. From: £75 d/t to £48 s. Family room for 4: £105. Normal: from £30 to £36.50. Down in delightful Penarth, a seaside town looking across Cardiff Bay to the city, as shown above. Right opposite the hotel is the bus and railway station and nearby, a water taxi takes you across the water to Cardiff Bay. Run by Tony Apollonio and his family, the Glendale's big bar is geared up on match day with big screen. Italian restaurant. Great atmosphere.

Phone	029 2070 6701

Hilton Cardiff, Kingsway, Cardiff.

From: £280 d/t. £270 s. 50% non-refundable deposit payable up front. Normal: from £55 (sharing).

Luxury hotel in the heart of the city with spectacular views over Cardiff Castle. Five minutes from the Millennium Stadium. Five star treatment at stellar prices. This same hotel offers dinner, bed and breakfast for TWO for £149 – that's £121 less than a single room during the internationals. But that's market forces for you. 197 rooms.

Phone	029 2064 6300
Internet	www.hilton.co.uk/cardiff

Holiday Inn, Castle Street, Cardiff, CF10 1QZ.

From: £280 d/t to £270 s. Full payment up front. Non-refundable. Normal: from £40 sharing.

The hotel overlooks Cardiff Castle, Bute Park and the Millennium Stadium. Callaghan's Irish Bar with live music seven nights a week is part of the hotel. Popular fan destination, despite prices. 155 rooms.

Phone	0870 400 8140
Internet	www.holiday-inn.co.uk

Holiday Inn Cardiff North, Pentwyn Road, Pentwyn.

From: £175 s/d/t. Normal: from £80 s/d/t.

Easy to get to both the city centre to the southwest and the Valleys to the north. Health and fitness club plus indoor play area for children at weekends. Useful for those combining sport with exercise or a trip to the Brecon Beacons. 142 rooms.

Phone	0870 400 8141
Internet	www.holiday-inn.co.uk

Holland House Hotel, 24-26 Newport Road, Cardiff, CF24 0DD.

From: £200 s/d/t. Normal: from £100 s/d/t.

Leisure club and spa provide a tonic to over-indulgence. One of Cardiff's new luxury hotels within staggering distance of the Millennium stadium and the shops. Yet another establishment which sees fit to double its prices for match day, it does at least have a pool, sauna, steam room and 'techno' gym.

Phone	0870 122 0020
Email	sales.holland@macdonald-hotels.co.uk
Internet	www.macdonaldhollandhouse.co.uk

Jolyon's Hotel, 5 Bute Crescent, Cardiff, CF10 5AN.

From: £85 to £155 s/d/t.

Elegantly restored Georgian town house in the oldest terrace in Cardiff Bay, Jolyon's has been converted to a (non-smoking) and very comfortable boutique hotel. Bedrooms lavishly furnished, king-sized beds, broadband facilities, free-to-view TV, some with views of Cardiff Bay. The owner does not believe in charging you more for your room just because some guys are kicking a bladder of wind around a nearby park. Downstairs bar has log fire. Jolyon also runs a dating agency for Gallophones.

Phone	02920 488775
Email	info@jolyons.co.uk
Internet	www.jolyons.co.uk

Hotels (cont)

Jurys Cardiff Hotel, Mary Ann Street, Cardiff, CF10 2JH.
From: £122.50 to £230. Normal: from £40.
Beside the Cardiff International Arena and the city's prime shopping districts, Jury's is one of a big chain providing reasonable value for money.

Phone	029 2034 1441
Email	info@jurysdoyle.com
Internet	www.jurys-cardiff-hotels.com

Lincoln House Hotel, 118/120 Cathedral Road, Cardiff, CF11 9LQ.
From £85 s/d/t.
On Cathedral Rd, dotted with reasonable family run hotels, the odd pub and charming Victorian architecture, Lincoln House was recently refurbished. This is a family run and friendly place with four-posters for those who like to swank.

Phone	029 2039 5558
Email	reservations@lincolnhotel.co.uk
Internet	www.lincolnhotel.co.uk

Llanerch Vineyard B&B, Hensol, Pendoylan, Vale of Glamorgan, CF72 8GG.
From: £34.50 to £55 pp. Price does not vary.
Farmhouse B&B on a commercial vineyard near Cardiff. Easy access from M4. Has 5-star self-catering and 4-star B&B accommodation. The 21 acre estate is set in the Vale of Glamorgan, one of the most beautiful parts of the UK, with lovely villages and bustling market towns, only a short drive from the city centre. Has featured on TV as is one of the country's 'Great Little Places.'

Phone	01443 225877
Email	enquiries@llanerch-vineyard.co.uk
Internet	www.llanerch-vineyard.co.uk

Miskin Manor Country Hotel, Pendoylan Road, Pontyclun, CF72 8ND.
From: £126 d/t to £99 s. Normal: £110 d/t to £94 s.
Grade II listed building in 22 acres of undisturbed and sculpted parkland, a peaceful and exclusive setting only 8 miles from city centre. Grand enough to have hosted Edward VIII before he and Mrs Simpson went Stateside. Hall big enough to seat a rugby club. Conference rooms and three helipads, should you require.

Phone	01443 224204
Email	info@miskin-manor.co.uk
Internet	www.miskin-manor.co.uk

Novotel, Schooner Way, Atlantic Wharf, Cardiff Bay, CF10 4RT.
156 rooms. From: £150 Normal: £89. Half-way between the Bay and the City Centre, this is a 4-star businessman's hotel with all the usual refinements – parking, ironing board, modem, multi-channel telly for those not needing the modem, and bar for those not needing either. Swimming pool and hairdryers. Ideal for families.

Phone	029 2047 5000
Email	H55982@accor.com
Internet	www.novotel.com

Plaza Park Hotel, Greyfriars Road, Cardiff, CF10 3AL.
From: £220 d/t. to £120 s. Normal: from £99 d/t to £79 s.
Slap in the centre of Cardiff, this oddly shaped building has been imaginatively done – light and airy, warm and yet cool, a series of log fires flicker in the lobby (they can't crackle because they are gas). Rooms well appointed, bar very well run and restaurant switched on. Service a plus. Health club and pool, massage and beauty treatment. Internet access in all 129 rooms.

Phone	029 2011 1111
Email	ppcinfo@parkplazahotels.co.uk
Internet	www.parkplaza.com

Premier Travel Inn, Cardiff Ocean Park, Keen Rd, CF24 5JT.
77 rooms. Fixed price: £51.95 s/d/t.
No tricks, price hikes or hidden extras on this industrial estate, with its taxi rank, buses and train. service What you see is what you get – which is internet access, remote telly, king size bed, parking and efficient service. Be warned, though. It seems to be company policy. Exit M4 at J29 and follow A48M.

Phone	08701 977 050
Internet	www.premiertravelinn.com

Premier Travel Inn, Cardiff Roath, David Lloyd Leisure Club, Ipswich Rd, Roath, Cardiff, CF23 9AQ. 75 rooms. Fixed price: £51.95 s/d/t. No tricks, price hikes or hidden extras on this industrial estate (see above), just a mile from the centre. What you see is what you get – which is internet access, remote telly, king size bed, parking and efficient service. Leave M4 at J30 and take A4232 to A48 and follow signs to docks.

Phone	08701 977 049
Internet	www.premiertravelinn.com

Quality Hotel, Merthyr Road, Tongwynlais, Cardiff, CF15 7LD.
95 rooms. From £160 d/t to £115 s. Normal: from £70 d/t to £60 s.
Near the fairytale scene of Castell Coch, yet another of the Bute family's Victorian follies, with easy access to city centre (and South Wales), the hotel is situated just off Junction 32 on the M4 so it could not be more convenient by car. Designed, like so many of these Legoland hotels, with a view to mixing business with leisure. Trouser presses and hairdriers in every room.

Phone	029 2052 9988
Email	admin@gb629.u-net.com
Internet	www.qualityinn.com/hotel/gb629

Saco Apartments, Cathedral Rd, Cardiff.
One bedroom apartment: £85 per night, Two bedroom apartment: £125 per night. Comfortable serviced apartments in city centre. Living/dining area (some with sofa beds), fully equipped kitchen, master bedroom with king size beds and separate bathroom. Two bedroom apartments also have additional en-suite shower rooms.

Phone	0845 122 0405
Email	info@sacoapartments.co.uk
Internet	www.sacoapartments.co.uk

St Mellons Hotel, Castleton, Cardiff, CF3 2XR.
41 rooms. From £115 s, £130 d, £150 t.
Converted manor house with squash courts, pool, gym and leisure club. Seven miles from town on the Newport road, the hotel is on the outskirts of St. Mellons.

Phone	01633 680355
Email	reception@stmellonshotel.co.uk
Internet	www.stmellonshotel.co.uk

The St David's Hotel & Spa, Havannah Street, Cardiff Bay, Cardiff, CF10 5SD.
132 rooms. From: £175 to £275 s/d/t. Normal: £100 to £275.
Cardiff's swishest hotel with stunning views. A striking five star landmark on the waterfront of Cardiff Bay with all bedrooms commanding views over Cardiff Bay. Excellent health spa and first class restaurant.

Phone	029 2045 4045
Email	reservations@thestdavidshotel.com
Internet	www.roccofortehotels.com

Hotels (cont)

B&B: The Town House, 70 Cathedral Rd, Pontcanna, Cardiff, CF11 9LL.
8 rooms. From: £80 d/t. £55 s. Normal £60 d/t and £45 s.
Elegant Victorian house in a handsome suburban setting 10 minutes walk from the centre. Rooms are en-suite. Strictly no smoking. The owner, Charles Mullins, is a keen rugby fan and ex-smoker.

Phone	029 2023 9399
Email	thetownhouse@msn.com
Internet	www.thetownhousecardiff.co.uk

Thistle Cardiff, Park Place, Cardiff, CF10 3UD.
120 rooms. From: £167 d/t, £147 s. Normal £100 d/t.
Modern 4-star in a Victorian building. Geared up for rugby, with big screen in the bars and function room. The Park Vaults pub is part of the hotel, as well as a Sports Bar, Harlech Bar and Oval Brasserie. Caters well for the ticketless.

Phone	029 2038 3471
Internet	www.thistlehotels.com

Vale Hotel Golf & Spa Resort, Hensol Park, Hensol, CF72 8JY.
143 rooms. From: £195 d/t and £175 s. Packages from £400.
Luxury Hotel, Golf and Health Resort set in 450 acres of beautiful countryside with two championship golf courses. Wales's largest health spa and leisure facilities. A short drive to Cardiff city centre.

Phone	01443 667800
Internet	www.vale-hotel.com

Victoria Hall, Blackweir Terrace, Cardiff, CF10 3EY.
Quality en-suite self-catering flats located within a 5 minute walk of the city centre. Typical 5-bed flat has one double and four single rooms, all with self-catering essentials provided and 24-hour manned security. Check web for 2006 prices.

Phone	029 2035 9500
Email	cardiff@victoriahall.com
Internet	www.victoriahall.com

25 Great Ormes House, Cardiff Bay, CF11 0JD.
Newly completed waterfront property. Peacefully located for travel either to Cardiff Bay or the City Centre. The self catering studio flat accommodation is 4 star Welsh Tourist Board approved.

Phone	07880 795639
Internet	www.cardiffstay.co.uk

The Old Post Office, Greenwood Lane, St Fagans, Cardiff, CF5 6EL.
6 rooms. From: £40 to £70 s/d/t. Normal: Same. £135 for two nights.
Stylish conversion of a grand old post office. St Fagans is where the Museum of Welsh Life is – a short taxi ride to and from town, but set in the countryside. French and Spanish spoken and the food is good enough to feature in the Good Food Guide (see restaurants). One of the city's best all-round hotels. Gold Award in True Taste of Wales. Dinner B&B packages.

Phone	029 2056 5400
Internet	www.old-post-office.com

Greendown Hotel, Drope Rd, St George's, Nr Cardiff, CF5 6EP.
15 rooms. From: £50 to £75 (sharing – no singles).
15th century inn in a quaint village. Near St Fagans, Culverhouse Cross and junction 33 of the M4). Lots of car park space.

Phone	01446 760310
Email	enquiries@greendownhotel.co.uk
Internet	www.greendownhotel.co.uk

Best Western Mount Sorrel Hotel, Porthkerry Road, Barry, South Glamorgan, CF62 7XY.42 rooms. From: £130 d/t and £70 s. Normal: £90 d/t and £60 s.
Seven miles from Barry (not to be confused with Barry Island), this is a traditional hotel. Ideal for the airport and an easy run into town. The nearby seaside, pictured, is great for fossil hunting. Free entry to leisure club, swimming pool and sauna. Trouser-press to room ratio is not yet 100% but they are working on it.

Phone	01446 740069
Internet	www.mountsorrel.co.uk

The Celtic Manor Resort, Coldra Woods, Newport, NP18 1HQ.
400 rooms. From: £240 d/t. Normal: from £144. Buses laid on to go to and from the games (£13 return).
Only 90 minutes from London and just inside Wales, the 5-star hotel lies in 1400 acres of the Usk Valley, with convention centre, spa, golf and leisure facilities including four restaurants, two health clubs and three championship gold courses (one of which will stage the Ryder Cup in 2010). Owned by Terry Matthews, a billionaire electronics magnate who was born in a nursing home on the site.

Phone	01633 413000
Email	postbox@celtic-manor.com
Internet	www.celtic-manor.com

The Inn at the Elm Tree, St Bride's Wentloog, Nr Newport, NP10 8SQ.
10 rooms. From: £90 d/t and £80 s. Price does not vary.
Charming spot known as Little Holland because of the flat river meadows of the Severn estuary. Contemporary style mixed with tradition. Great reports about the seafood (see restaurants), comfortable rooms and generally very well run. An easy commute to the matches. Likely to be fully booked well in advance.

Phone	0871 995 8230
Email	inn@the-elm-tree.co.uk
Internet	www.the-elm-tree.co.uk

The Great House, Laleston, Bridgend, CF32 0HP.
16 rooms. From: £130 d/t and £100 s. Normal: from £100 d/t and £80 s.
16th century Grade II listed midway between Cardiff and Swansea. Flagstone floors and oak beams, inglenook fireplaces. Stephen and Norma Bond have lovingly restored the Great House. There is also a bungalow which sleeps six. Ideal for golf at Royal Porthcawl and Southerndown. Great food and serious wine list.

Phone	0871 995 8224
Email	enquiries@great-house-laleston.co.uk
Internet	www.great-house-laleston.co.uk

Premier Travel Inn, Cardiff West, Port Road, Nantisaf, Cardiff, CF5 6DD.
76 rooms. Fixed price: £51.95 weekend rate s/d/t. £54.95 mid-week.
See descriptions for other Premier Travel Inns. No price hikes or hidden extras at this pleasant establishment near Culverhouse Cross. Internet access, remote telly, king size bed, parking and efficient service. Exit M4 at J33 and head south of A4232, following signs for airport. On the Barry Road (A4050).

Phone	08701 977 052
Internet	www.premiertravelinn.com

Italian rugby
Against all odds

by Emanuele Palladino
Freelance writer and player

IN A country where football is revered, and the infamous red scuderia of Ferrari is granted mythical status in the hearts of the Italian people, rugby - 'the game with the funny shaped ball' as it is affectionately known - remains almost anonymous.

Since Italy was granted entry into the 6 Nations in 2000, rugby's popularity has grown significantly, with attendance figures at club and international games rising annually. However when compared to other sports, rugby's impact registers as a ripple rather than a shockwave on the media radar. Italy's premier sports newspaper, the Gazzetta dello Sport, dedicates up to fifteen pages to football, and several pages to other popular sports such as Formula One racing, cycling and even volleyball on a daily basis. Rugby can expect a mere paragraph or perhaps a full page on Six Nations match day; club rugby passes by almost unnoticed. How can rugby compete in such a climate of ignorance?

Where England claim 'Fortress Twickenham' as their spiritual rugby home, Rome's Stadio Flaminio is the Italian rugby team's equivalent, a poor relation in comparison. Despite near sell-out crowds in Italy's home 6 Nations games, rugby passes almost unnoticed in a city where 'calcio' monopolises the fans' attention. Indeed, with many of Italy's leading clubs such as Treviso and Padova nestled in the north-east of Italy, many see this as the true heartland of Italian rugby and an ideal venue for the national team to play. Although many in the rugby fraternity support this view, it will require a prodigious feat to wrestle the home matches away from Rome where the FIR (Italian Rugby Federation) is based. As debate continues to rage, it is critical that the FIR find a permanent home and power base for Italian rugby to lay its foundations and flourish as soon as possible.

The Italian public has an insatiable appetite for success whatever the sport or event, and only winning will rouse media interest in rugby and attract new sponsors and players to the game. England's World Cup victory generated a wave of interest in the sport in England and a few wins for Italy in the Six Nations would undoubtedly have a similar effect there. The success of any national team is inextricably linked to its club system. Unfortunately in the Italian premiership, the 'Super 10', a two-tier league has developed, driven by financial status. Treviso, champions four times in the past six seasons, Viadana and Calvisano have monopolised the last decade of the Italian championship, boasting far superior budgets and playing squads to other teams. Below them there is a sharp decline in ability, and the chasm is widening every year. Such disparity has compelled the FIR to seek ways of improving things. The Italian Championship was shorn from twelve to ten teams four seasons ago to create the 'Super 10.' Unfortunately the longed-for competitive championship has not materialised. Competition is critical to create a breeding ground for success. A sense of fear and vulnerability is necessary for a team to develop, equipping them with the mental dexterity to pull through tight games. In Italy such an environment does not exist. 'We are not used to being put under that sort of pressure' were the cries emanating from the Treviso camp after their European games. Unlike in the Guinness Premiership, where every game is competitive, in Italy Treviso has not learnt how to fight and play at such a high tempo on a weekly basis, because they have never needed to.

Last season Treviso admirably carried the baton for Italian rugby in the European Cup, with impressive victories over Bath and Bourgoin. Their performances have deservedly earned them many plaudits, and have helped raise not only their own profile but that of Italian rugby. The concern however is that below Treviso there is a staggering dearth of competition. In all other European competitions Italian teams have barely registered a win. Calvisano, Italy's second-placed team in recent seasons, have been the perennial whipping boys of the European Cup and even the emergence of Viadana in recent seasons, has done little to ruffle the feathers of Italy's champions, Treviso.

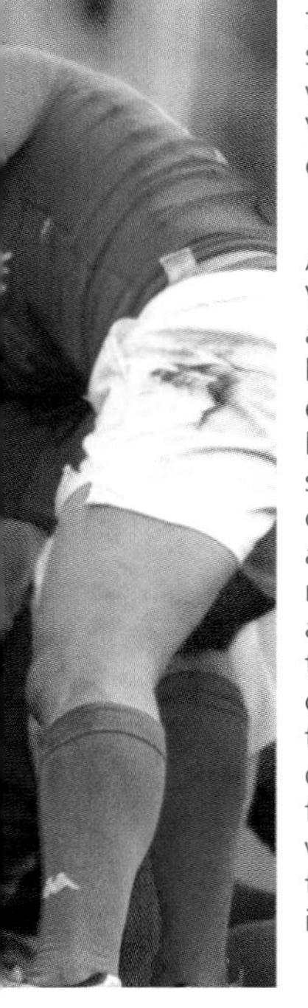

The idea of a 'Rainbow League', including teams from South Africa and the Celtic League, together with Treviso, Calvisano and Viadana is one which has gathered momentum in recent months, and the Celtic connection, at least, has genuine potenital. The benefits for these three Italian sides are clear to see. They would enjoy a more competitive platform on which to test their skills, help attract new sponsors and larger crowds. For the remaining seven teams however, the economic consequences could be catastrophic, undoubtedly increasing the chasm between them and the rest, leaving the poor to get poorer and the rich to get richer. The teams left behind would struggle to find sponsorship and risk falling away altogether, with their only alternative being to seek local sponsorship. Another more likely proposal is the creation of three or four Italian regional super powers to join the Celtic League. Such an alternative may however signal the death knell for club rugby, which is already struggling to survive financially. Ultimately for any such moves to be implemented, it would require the co-operation and agreement of the FIR and all the clubs in the Super 10, and in the present climate in Italy, that is unlikely to happen.

Italy: Against all odds (cont)

With the results of the national team so crucial to the popularity of the sport in Italy, the indiscriminate hiring and firing of the Italian national team coaches is doing little to calm the choppy waters of Italian rugby. In a desperate attempt to find a winning formula, the FIR has dispensed with four coaches since Italy joined the 6 Nations. If the national team is to find consistency, ambition must be tempered by caution and patience.

The long-term solution lies in focusing on coaching, and investing in grass roots rugby now. A glance at the national teams at U21 and U19 levels in particular, suggests that there is cause for optimism, though still much work remains to be done. The current crop of national team players is promising and with a national team with an average age of twenty four and a half, there is time yet. They have developed in maturity and discipline in recent season as they have adjusted to the rigours of playing in the 6 Nations. They boast a formidable forward pack, capable of competing with the best in world rugby. Their natural instinctive aggression and ferocity suggests that they are equipped with a temperament well suited to the demands of rugby. However this must be complemented by equal measures of skill and tactical acumen, which they are lacking at present. Other problems to be addressed include the standard of the refereeing. Many games in Italy have been turned unfairly on a poor refereeing decision, with referees often influenced by the crowd. Consequently in European competitions Italian teams find themselves at a disadvantage as they struggle to adapt to different refereeing styles. Such manageable problems must be swiftly dealt with, even if this means sending referees abroad to train, or importing referees in the short-term.

With the 'Super 10' lacking the intensity and environment to challenge many of Italy's brightest stars, players such as the Bergamasco brothers, their captain Marco Bortolami and Aaron Perscio, have moved abroad to be exposed to a higher level of rugby, and there will be many more to follow in the next season. This is the only way forward if they are to develop as players and ultimately if the national team is to improve.

So what does this mean for Italian rugby? For a start it means that the Italian championship is denied the presence of its most known and marketable players, lost to foreign leagues forever. In their places, many clubs have resorted to importing foreign players in a desperate attempt to improve results in the short term - understandably unavoidable in a climate where relegation carries serious financial implications. This however is harmful to the development of young players, and does little to fill seats or please crowds who would much prefer to pay to watch home grown talent rather than an unknown player fresh off the plane from New Zealand or Australia. As a direct consequence, this season the FIR have implemented a new rule stating that each team must have at least twelve 'Italians' in their match day squad of twenty two. 'Italians' are defined now not as Italian passport holders, as in previous years, but as players who have played in Italy at junior level. Such a move has left teams in disarray as they scramble to find high quality Italian players. However in the long-run it may underline the need to develop Italian players.

The way forward and the future of rugby in Italy depends on their successful integration into Europe at club level. Heineken Cup games never fail to arouse interest from the public and propel players to reach new levels. The question remains however as to the best way to implement this so as to help all, and not just the privileged few.

• *Emanuele Palladino, a freelance journalist, was a wing for Italy in the Six Nations Under-21 and for Roma in the Italian 'Super 10'. He now plays for London Irish.*

HOME FROM ROME

THE Eternal City would be recognisable today to Caligula or Hadrian. Few other cities could boast that level of preservation. Almost everywhere you go you are likely to stumble over some antiquity of monumental importance. Rome is, in fact, rightly considered a living encyclopaedia of the last 3,000 years of western art.

The historical centre is within the limits of the ancient imperial walls and while some central areas were reorganised after the reunification, and some important additions and adaptations made during the Fascist period (the Via dei Fori Imperiali in front of the Vatican, for example) much of its miraculous early Renaissance and Classical architecture has remained untrammelled by planners.

The Tiber weaves its way through the western quarter of the city, dividing the secular from the spiritual. As you stroll northwards along its peaceful banks, under the Palatino, Fabricio, Garibaldi, Sisto, Mazzini and Vittorio Emmanuele II bridges, you will see the Vatican off to the left, protected by the muscular presence of the Castel Sant'Angelo.

The Tiber is a remarkably underexploited asset to the city, a peaceful retreat from the bustling streets and noisy byways. Its wide walkways, shaded by plane trees, are often deserted and you can't help making comparisons with the regenerated Thames and the hugely popular banks of the Seine. Where are the trippers, the pleasure craft, the booksellers and artists? An especially attractive section is the stretch from the Ara Paci Augustae to Piazza Bocca della Verita, near the trading and military ports.

Restful is not how you would describe the honeycomb of streets, squares, churches, temples and wonderful boulevards to the right of the Tiber. The main arteries are clogged with noisy folk and thunderous traffic, though you can find quiet side alleys and places of repose to sit back and take in the spectacular grandeur of the setting.

Rome is compact and you can tackle it on foot. You could spend an entire weekend just looking at the baroque fountains, the most famous of which (partly due to Fellini's La Dolce Vita) is the Trevi Fountain, which dominates the eponymous piazza. Legend has it that if you throw a coin in you are destined to return. Stroll on, via the Pantheon, to the fountains in the Piazza Navona, where the Fountain of the Four Rivers by Bernini, takes the breath away. From here, wander up to the Spanish Steps and look at Bernini's father's Fontana della Barcaccia. There are hundreds more.

And of course, there's the Colosseum, St Peter's Basilica, the Foro Romano excavation sites, Capitol Hill, priceless galleries and the 1400 rooms of the world's largest museum at the Vatican. If you get time, the bars and restaurants are pretty good, too. Check out our list and book your return ticket

FIND YOUR WAY AROUND

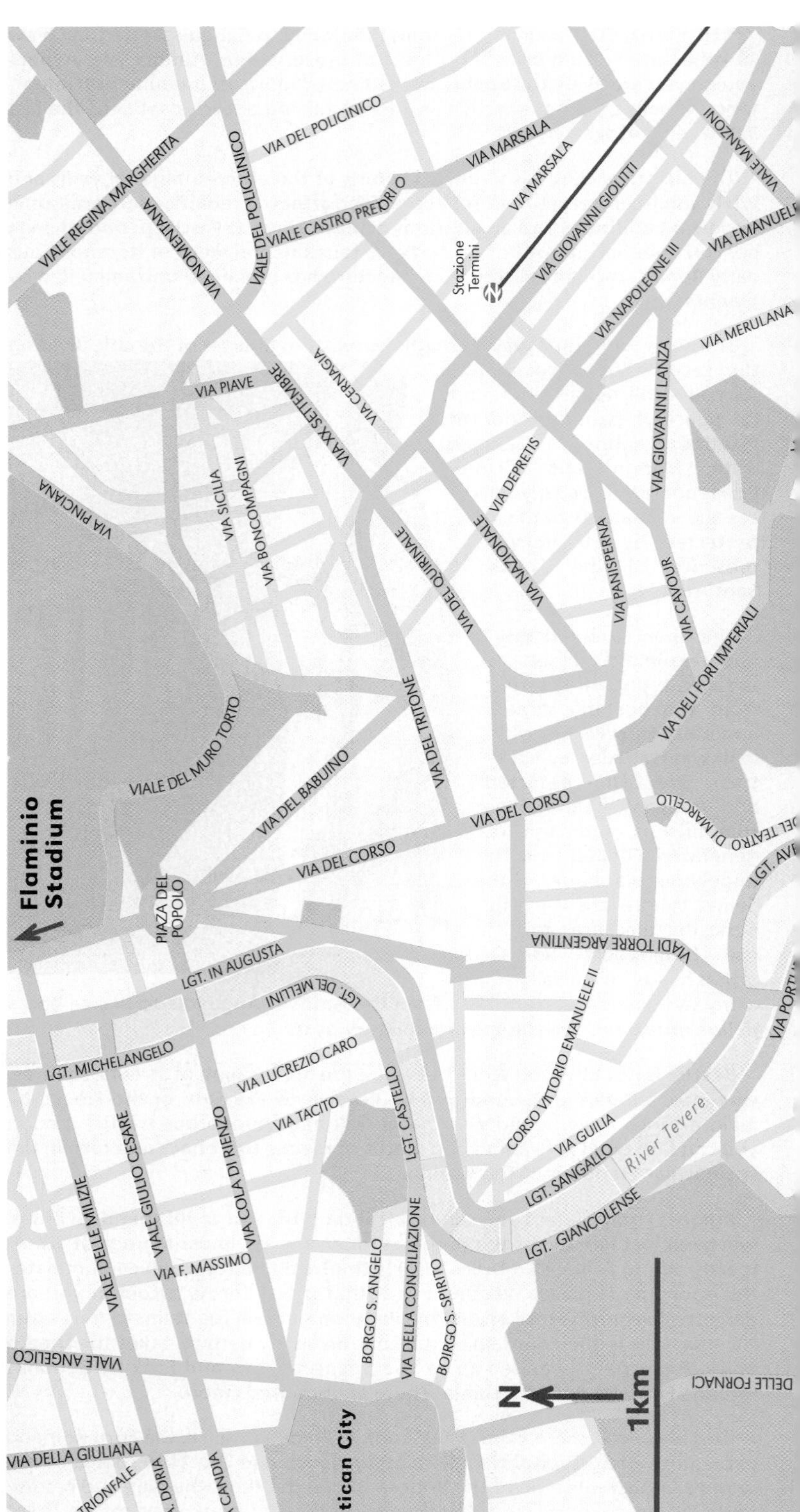

ITALY

TRAVEL

AIR

Leonardo Da Vinci – Fuimicino Airport

There are three terminals. A – domestic flights. B – domestic and international flights (member countries of the Schengen Agreement) and Terminal C – International flights (countries outside the Schengen Agreement). The airport offers all the standard facilities.

Phone:	06 65951

Ciampino

The smaller of Rome's two airports is used principally by the no-frills airlines, Ryanair and bmibaby from the UK and Ireland. Arrivals and departures are on the same level and facilities include an information desk, post office, bank, bureau de change, ATM, chemist, medical care and services for disabled passengers.

Travel to Italy

From Ireland:	
Aer Lingus	Dublin to Roma-Fiumicino (Leonardo da Vinci)
	Cork to Roma-Fiumicino (Leonardo da Vinci)
Easyjet	Belfast to Roma Ciampino
Ryanair	Dublin to Roma Ciampino

From UK:	
BA	London Heathrow to Roma Fiumicino (Leonardo da Vinci)
	London Gatwick to Roma Fiumicino (Leonardo da Vinci)
	Birmingham to Roma Fiumicino (Leonardo da Vinci)
	Manchester to Roma Fiumicino (Leonardo da Vinci)
Alitalia	London Heathrow to Roma Fiumicino (Leonardo da Vinci)
Easyjet	Bristol to Roma Ciampino
	London Gatwick to Roma Ciampino
	Newcastle to Roma Ciampino
	Nottingham East Midlands to Roma Ciampino
Ryanair	Durham Teeside to Roma Ciampino
	Nottingham East Midlands to Roma Ciampino
	Glasgow – Prestwick to Roma Ciampino
	Liverpool to Roma Ciampino
	London Luton to Roma Ciampino
	London Stansted to Roma Ciampino

FRANCE	
Air France	Paris Charles-de-Gaulle to Roma Fiumicino (Leonardo da Vinci)
	Marseille to Roma Fiumicino (Leonardo da Vinci)
	Lyon to Roma Fiumicino (Leonardo da Vinci)
Ryanair	Paris Beauvais to Roma Ciampino

RAIL

Most French, British and Irish visitors will arrive by plane and there are excellent links by rail and coach between the two airports and Stazione Termini, Rome's main railway station.

Termini is the hub of Rome's public transport system. It is the main inter-city rail station at which the city's two metro lines (A and B) meet. In front of the station is a busy taxi rank and the Piazza dei Cinquecento, the city's main bus terminal. There you will find a tourist office, banks and ATM's, newsagents selling international press, bars, restaurants and shops, and points at which you can buy travel tickets.

Tiburtina is Rome's second railway station, reached by Metro (line B) and bus. The slower, cheaper night buses to Fiumicino airport leave from here. There is a 24/7 supermarket and a bureau de change. Also on the 492 bus route.

THE LEONARDO EXPRESS

Fiumicino to Roma-Stazione Termini Every 30 minutes daily from 6.37 to 23.37
Roma-Stazione Termini to Fiumicino Every 30 minutes daily from 5.52 to 22.52
Journey time 35 minutes. Adult single €9.50

Travel to Italy

RAIL	
From Paris-Bercy:	There is an overnight train to Roma Termini. The journey time is approximately 15 hours.
From Lyon-Part Dieu:	There is a train link with Roma Termini which requires a change at Chambéry and either Torino or Milano. The journey via Milano is quicker by about two hours, taking approximately 11¼ hours.
From Marseille-St Charles:	There is a train link with Roma Termini and Roma Ostiense. Both require a change at Nice. The journey time to Roma Ostiense is shorter by about 45 minutes (approximately 12 ½ hours) but arrival at Roma Termini leaves you in the very centre of the city.
From Toulouse Matabiau:	There is a train link with Roma Termini and Roma Ostiense. Both require a change at Nice.

COACH

Terravision Shuttle

Fiumicino to Roma-Stazione Termini. Departs national and international arrivals. Arrives 22, via Marsala (next to Stazione Termini).

Hours:	08.30, 10.50, 12.30, 14.30, 16.30, 18.30, 20.30
Prices:	Adult single €9 Adult return €15

Roma-Stazione Termini to Fiumicino. Departs 22, via Marsala (next to Stazione Termini). Tickets available from 3 Terravision ticket booths in the domestic and international arrivals halls and, in Rome, at the Hotel Royal Santina on the via Marsala, opposite the departure point of the coach, or on the web.

Hours:	06.30, 09.20, 10.30, 12.30, 14.30, 16.30, 18.30
Prices:	Adult single €9 Adult return €15
Internet:	www.terravision.it

COTRAL Night Service

Fiumicino to Roma-Tiburtina (via Stazione Termini). Tickets are on sale at arrivals at Ciampino airport, and from the Terravision booth at Stansted Airport. They may be on sale during an Easyjet or Ryanair flight. You can also purchase tickets on the web.

Hours:	Fiumicino: 01.15, 02.15, 03.30, 05.00 Tiburtina: 00.30, 01.15, 02.30, 03.45
Prices:	Adult single €5
Internet:	www.terravision.it

CAR

Rome is well served by taxis and buses. The reputation of Roman drivers as fast and impatient is probably only half correct. The city, particularly in the centro storico, at the main tourist sites, and along the banks of the Tiber in the city centre, is pretty congested so it is difficult to drive quickly. Buses are crowded and generally do not move quickly for the same reason. Use the official white taxis with a meter. Taxi fares are heavily regulated and a copy of the regulations is in every cab with an English translation.

Travel to Italy

ROAD	
From Paris:	Autoroute A6 to Mâcon Nord then A40 to the Tunnel du Mont-Blanc. Once in Italy follow signs for Genova. At Genova, follow signs for Firenze, at Firenze follow signs for Rome. Travelling time is about 13 hours, the distance 1415km.
From Lyon:	Take the Autoroute A42 in the direction of Genève and Milano then join the A40 to the Tunnel du Mont-Blanc. Once in Italy follow signs for Genova. At Genova, follow signs for Firenze, at Firenze follow signs for Rome. Travelling time is approximately 10 hours, the distance 1023km.
From Marseille:	Take the A50 to Aubagne then the A520 to the A8. The A8 takes you to the Italian border. Once in Italy take the A10 for 160km then the A7 to Genova. At Genova, follow signs for Firenze, at Firenze follow signs for Rome. Travelling time is about 9 hours and the distance 886km.

Local Taxis

There are busy taxi ranks at both Fiumicino and Ciampino airports. Use only the official white taxis with a meter. The fare to the centre of Rome should be between €35 and €45. Within Rome the official taxi companies, recommended by the Roman tourist office, can be reached at the following numbers:

06 3570	06 6645	06 8822	06 4157	06 4994	06 5551

There are taxi ranks at strategic points around the city; at St Peter's Square, the Colosseum, the Piazza Venezia, the Piazza del Popolo, the Spanish Steps, Stazione Termini etc. Officially you should not hail taxis but queue at taxi rank, but a lot of drivers will stop for a fare.

Chauffeur Driven

Cooperativa Termini: **Stazione Termini, 1, via Marsala.** 06 481 7979

Cooperativa Airport: **Domestic Arrivals, Fiumicino Airport.** 06 65 953 788

Cooperativa S.A.R.: **Domestic Arrivals, Fiumicino Airport.** 06 659 547 46

Concora – **International Arrivals, Fiumicino Airport.** 06 659 539 34

REACHING THE GROUND

By foot

It is a pleasant walk from the Piazza del Popolo. Leave the piazza under the arch on the northern side. Directly opposite you is the via Flaminia. The Stadio Flaminio is an easy twenty minutes walk away

By tram

The Number 2 tram runs straight to the stadium from the end of the via Flaminia in the city centre.

VITAL STATISTICS

Phone Code: country code 39, area code: 06 (you dial the zero).

Population: 2,665,000

Time zone: GMT +1 (GMT + 2 from last Sunday in March to Saturday before last Sunday in October).

Electricity: 220 volts AC, 50Hz. Round twin plugs, triangular form three pin plugs.

Average temps:

	Average max	Average min
January	13°C	3°C
February	13°C	4°C
March	15°C	6°C

Tipping: A tip of around 10% is customary in restaurants and taxis. Tipping in bars is rare.

Getting around: Rome is a very compact city and can easily be explored on foot. There is something breathtaking around every corner. Mild spring temperatures also help to make walking a pleasure.

There is a two line metro system which does not cover the city well and is probably only useful in the unlikely event of your destination and departure point coinciding with stations. The metro is open from 5.30am till 11.30pm.

The bus system is comprehensive. Even in tiny backstreets you will see small buses. The buses run between 5.30am and midnight.

The Rome public transport system is called Metrebus. If you purchase a Metrebus ticket you can travel on the four means of transport covered by Metrebus – underground (Metro), urban train, tramway and bus. You must validate your ticket whenever you enter the underground, use a bus, tram or an urban train. These tickets are on sale at tobacconists, news stands, travel agencies, hotels, vending machines at bus terminals and Metro stations and with approved dealers at railway stations in Rome and Lazio.

Shopping: Rome is not a city of large department stores; smaller boutique type stores are much more the norm. As a consequence, opening times and rest days vary enormously. In the centro storico shops will open at around 9.30 and stay open until 7 or 8pm. In other areas the times would be 10am to 1pm and 4pm to 7.30pm in winter, 5pm to 8pm in summer. As a general rule, clothes shops are closed on Monday mornings and food stores close on Thursday afternoon.
Credit cards are almost universally accepted, small food shops being the most notable exception.

METREBUS TICKET TYPES

BIT	Valid for 75 minutes	For one journey on the Metro or urban trains. Price €1
BIG	Valid till midnight	Unlimited travel on buses, Metro and urban trains. Price €4
CIS	Valid for seven days	Unlimited travel on buses, metro and urban trains. Price €16.
BTR	Valid for three days	Unlimited travel on buses and Metro in Rome, but also on urban and regional trains. The price varies from €6.50 to €28.50 depending on the number of areas you wish to travel in.

HOSPITALS

Universita Cattolica **del Sacro Cuore 8, largo Gemelli 00168 Roma**	06 30151
Azienda Complesso Ospedaliero **San Filippo Neri 5, piazza Santa Maria Pieta 00135 Roma**	06 33061
Ospedale San Pietro **Fatabenefratelli 600, via Cassia 00189**	06 33581 / 06 33582 644
Aurelia Hospital **860, via Aurelia 00165 Roma**	06 66411 425 / 06 66416 665
Azienda Ospedaliera **Policlinico Umberto I6, via Benevento 00161 Roma**	06 44240 764 / 06 44241 037

POLICE

Municipal police	06 67691
Central Police station	06 4686

USEFUL CONTACTS

Emergencies	118
Carabinieri	112
Police	113
Fire	115
Red Cross Ambulance	06 5510

TOURIST OFFICES

Azienda di Promozione Turistica di Roma Visitor Centre 5	via Parigi (nr piazza della Repubblica) 00185 Roma. Open Monday to Saturday 9am to 7pm (Closed on Sunday)
Information Office Leonardo da Vinci	(Fiumicino) Airport International Arrivals (Terminal B) Open every day 8am to 7pm

Useful Contacts: (cont)

TOURIST INFORMATION CALL CENTRE

Phone:	06 820 59 127

There are tourist information offices strategically placed around the city. These are open daily from 9am till 6pm

CasSan Angelo, Piazza Pia	06 68 80 97 07
Fori Imperiali, Piazza Tempio della Pace	06 69 92 43 07
Stazione Termini, Piazza dei Cinquecento	06 47 82 51 94
Via dei Condotti, Largo Goldini	06 68 13 60 61
Trastavere, Piazza Sonnino	06 58 33 34 57
Fontana di Trevi, Via Minghetti	06 67 82 988
Santa Maria Maggiore, Via dell'Olmata	06 47 40 955

EMBASSIES

British Embassy, Via XX Settembre 80a, I-00187 Roma RM	06 4220 0001 / 06 4220 2603
Irish Embassy Piazza Campitelli 3, 00186 Roma	06 697 9121
Ambassade de France Piazza Farnese 67, 00186 Roma	06 68 60 11
Section Consulaire Via Giulia, 251, 00186 Roma	06 6860 11

PLACES OF INTEREST

St Peter's Square and the Basilica (cont)

The most spectacular approach to St Peter's Square and the Basilica is along the via della Conciliazione, constructed in 1929 to mark the signing of the Lateran Treaty, an agreement between the church and Mussolini which recognised the Pope as sovereign within Vatican City.

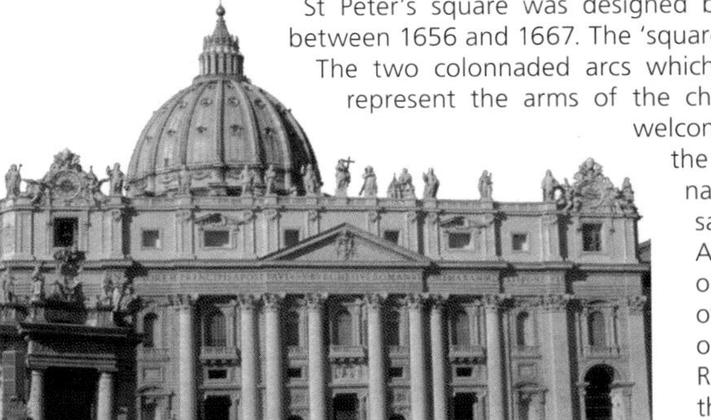

St Peter's square was designed by Bernini and built between 1656 and 1667. The 'square' is actually circular. The two colonnaded arcs which compose its sides represent the arms of the church gathering and welcoming the faithful. At the top of the colonnades are statues of saints and of Pope Alexander VII. The obelisk at the centre of the square was originally brought to Rome from Egypt by the emperor Caligula who had it erected in his circus. Its later encapsulation by the all-embracing arms of the church was meant to symbolise Christian victory over the Islamic Ottoman Empire.

A majestic stairway, flanked by statues of Saint Peter and Saint Paul, rises from the square towards the Basilica. The facade of the Basilica is crowned by a pediment with statues of 11 apostles, (St Peter is not there), St John the Baptist and Christ. It is from the lodge below the pediment that the Pope gives his blessing 'urbi et orbi' (to the city and the world).

To the right of the porch is the Porta Santa, or Holy Door, which can only be opened and closed by the Pope at the beginning and end of a Holy Year. The nave is 211m long and there are 50 altars and 500 statues (perhaps the most famous, La Pieta, the Virgin Mary holding the body of her crucified son, by Michelango) which, along with the paintings, tell the story of the origins and development of Christianity. The dome, a spectacular 132.5m high cupola designed by Michelangelo, draws the eye. Around the dome are Jesus' words (in Latin) from the Gospel of St Matthew which gave St Peter his special place in the history of the Church. Underneath the dome, the Baldacchino – a magnificent canopy of gilded bronze designed by Bernini – under which only the Pope can say mass.

Entry to St Peter's Basilica is free. Queue at the colonnades to the right of St Peter's Square as you look at the front of the Basilica. There is a strict security and dress code before entering the Basilica.

Hours:	Open 7am to 7pm (April to September). 7am to 6pm (October to March).
Entry to the dome:	8am to 5.45pm (April to September) 8am to 4.45pm (October to March).
Prices:	Ticket €4 (stairs) €5 (lift).
To see the Pope:	The Pope holds a weekly audience at 10am (in summer) or 10.30am (in winter) usually on St Peter's Square.

Tickets for an audience are free and can be obtained by sending a written request one or two weeks in advance to **Prefettura della Casa Pontificia, Città del Vaticano, 00120 Roma**.

Phone:	06 6988 3273

Groups must specify numbers requiring tickets (and their place of origin). Tickets can be collected the day before the audience between 3pm and 8pm or from 8am on the day of the audience from the bronze door of the Prefettura at St Peter's Square. Sometimes tickets are available on the day of the audience. The Pope gives a blessing from the library window at the noon Angelus on Sundays and Holy Days.

Places to visit (cont)

Castel San Angelo

Originally constructed by the Emperor Hadrian as a mausoleum for himself and his family. It later became a fortress when it was incorporated into the city walls by Aurelius in 270AD. A chapel was added by Pope Gregory the Great who, during a procession to ask for the cessation of a plague which was decimating the population of Rome, had a vision of an angel who replaced his sword in its sheath. Gregory saw this as a sign of the end of the plague and had the chapel built in gratitude. The great bronze statue of the angel above the castle recalls the vision. During the middle ages, and the seemingly unending strife between the great Roman families and the Popes, the edifice became a true fortified castle. A wall, originally built as a pathway from the papal palaces in the Vatican to San Angelo, was covered for use as a protected passage during a siege. After the Reunification of Italy the building was used as a military prison and barracks. A highlight of a visit to the castle is the views from the terrace across Rome and towards St Peter's.

Hours:	Tuesday to Sunday 9am to 8pm.
Prices:	Adult entry €5

The Vatican Museums – The Sistine Chapel

The Vatican museums contain one of the world's most impressive collections of artworks, dating from ancient Egypt to modern works of religious art. To take everything in during a single visit is out of the question.

The highlights would be the Raphael Rooms, and, of course, the Sistine Chapel. The Raphael Rooms - Le Stanze di Raffaello - were started in 1508, when Pope Julius II decided to hire a young painter by the name of Raphael. He was so taken by the artist's work that the original team were sacked. Their work was erased and replaced completely by that of Raphael, and are considered to be among the greatest masterpieces of Renaissance art.

Cappella Sistina – The Sistine Chapel: The principal chapel of the Vatican Palace was named after Pope Sixtus IV, its founder. The walls were frescoed by some of the greatest artists of the Renaissance period: Perugino, Botticelli, Rosselli, Michelangelo. The twelve paintings on the side walls illustrate episodes from the lives of Christ and of Moses. Michelangelo created "The Last Judgement" on the wall behind the great altar. The ceiling of the Sistine Chapel, along with the Last Judgement, were completely restored over fourteen years between 1980 and 1994. The frescoes can now be seen in all their original glory, having been blackened by centuries of candle smoke.

Michelangelo painted the ceiling of the Sistine Chapel between 1508 and 1512. He was therefore working at the same time as Raphael. His inspiration was the Old Testament; Genesis - The Creation to Noah and the Flood, the Ancestors of Christ, the Prophets, Scenes of Salvation. The exceptions to Old Testament images are those of the Classical Sybils who are included because they are said to have prophesied the birth of Christ, and on these he worked without assistance.

Address:	Viale Vaticano, 00120 Città del Vaticano
Hours:	Monday to Friday: 08.45 – 15.20 Saturday: 08.45 – 12.20 (exit at 13.45) Last Sunday of month: 08.45 – 12.20
Prices:	Adults €12 (Free on Sunday)
Phone:	06 698 838 60

The Colosseum

Building of the Colosseum was begun under the Emperor Vespasian in 72AD on part of the land given over to Nero's "Golden Palace". It was the largest amphitheatre constructed in the Roman world, whose purpose was to provide a fittingly sumptuous setting for the Games – religious festivities designed to maintain good relations between the City and its deities.

In 80AD the Colosseum, although unfinished, was inaugurated by Titus, Vespasian's son. These first games, involving combat between men and wild animals, gladiator fights and races, lasted 100 days. Later the Colosseum was flooded and used to stage mock naval battles. In 249AD, to celebrate the millennium of the founding of Rome, games on a hitherto unheard of scale were held. A thousand pairs of gladiators fought, 32 elephants, tigers and more than 50 lions from different corners of the Empire, were slaughtered. Contrary to popular belief, no Christians were ever martyred in the Colosseum.

Close by is the Arch of Constantine, erected in honour of the great Emperor. Probably the best restored and most magnificent of the great Roman arches.

Open every day from 9am till sunset. Entry €8. This ticket also allows entry to the Palatine hill (Imperial palaces) and the Palatine museum.

Closest Metro: | Colosseo

The Imperial Forums

The sites of the Imperial forums are divided in two by the 30m wide via dei Fori Imperiali, which links the piazza di Venezia and the Colosseum. Originally Rome had a single forum but as the city grew, the forum was no longer big enough to allow proper meetings of the people, the dispensing of justice, the treatment of public affairs or commerce. Julius Caesar began work on a second forum and other forums were added by Augustus, Vespasian, Nerva, and Trajan. They were ostentatious demonstrations of the Emperor's power and prestige and were designed to curry favour with the populace. Today it requires some work of the imagination to picture their full grandeur.

The archaeological digging went on during the 19th century but it was not until the 1920s and 1930s that the medieval buildings, which had been constructed over the site, were removed. One of the best restored forums is dominated by the Column of Trajan, an incredibly complex work of spiralling bas-relief which recounts the military campaigns of great Emperor. The statue at the top of the column is of St Peter, Trajan having been removed and replaced in 1597. Entry to the Markets of Trajan from the via di 4 Novembre.
Entry to the other forums close to the Arch of Constantine opposite the Colosseum. Open from 9am to sunset.

Closest Metro: | Colosseo, line B

Places to visit: (cont)

The Trevi Fountain

At the piazza di Trevi at the foot of the Quirinal hill, the Trevi fountain, a spectacular example of late baroque artistry, is one of Rome's most visited sites. The fountain, already famous, was made even more so by Anita Ekberg's fully clad bathing scene in Fellini's La Dolce Vita (a film also famous for introducing the word paparazzi to common usage). The fountain was constructed at the end of a 20km canal – Aqua Virgo - first built in 19BC by Agrippa to bring fresh water to Rome. The fountain was designed and constructed by Niccolo Salvi in the 1730's. The high relief sculptures show, to the left, Agrippa and, to the right, the Virgin, who originally indicated the source of the canal to Roman soldiers. The central figure is Neptune, God of the Seas, flanked by two Tritons, each riding a marine horse. One horse is placid, the other out of control, symbolising the violently changing moods of the sea.

The tradition here is to turn your back to the fountain and throw two coins into it. One of the coins will ensure you return to Rome, the second you accompany with a wish.

The Spanish Steps and Piazza di Spagna

The area took its name in the 17th century, when the Spanish ambassador to the Holy See took the Palazzo di Spagna as his residence, and the quarter formed by the via del Corso, via dei Condotti and via della Mercede became Spanish territory. Often innocent visitors crossing the area at night would find themselves "enrolled" in the Spanish army.

The quarter became a meeting point for artists and intellectuals: Goethe, Stendhal, de Chirico, Keats and Shelley (there is a museum dedicated to the two English poets at the foot of the Spanish Steps), and later dissolute Englishmen frequented the local drinking dens during the Roman stage of their Grand Tour. Today the quarter is a real meeting point for young Romans and tourists from all over the world. The square, the steps up to the church, Chiesa della Trinita dei Monti, are packed day and night.

The fountain on the piazza di Spagna was created by Bernini's father, Pietro, and represents a barge which the flooded Tiber is said to have carried to the piazza. The steps themselves were constructed between 1723 and 1726.

Chiesa della Trinita dei Monti, the church at the top, was founded in 1495 for the novices of the neighbouring convent. It was badly damaged by the French revolutionary army but was entirely restored in 1816. The property is now French owned and the convent houses the Sisters of the Sacred Heart.

Down below the via dei Condotti and the via Frattini, which descend directly from the Steps, and the piazza di Spagna, are possibly the most famous streets in Rome for high fashion shopping.

The Pantheon

The piazza della Rotonda is dominated by the Pantheon, an astonishing example of Roman architecture and engineering. It is on the site of a temple originally built by Augustus' son-in-law, Marcus Agrippa, as a "temple to all the gods." That was replaced by one designed by the Emperor Hadrian. The real glory of the Pantheon, its huge hemispherical dome, is largely hidden from the outside by the rectangular, colonaded portico, so to appreciate fully the dome, you have to enter the Pantheon. The rotunda's diameter is the same as its height (43m or 140 feet) while the building's only source of light is the oculus, the hole at the summit of the dome.

Hours:	Monday to Saturday: 09.00 – 16.30 (18.00 July and August). Sunday and public holidays: 09.00 – 13.00

Piazza Navona

One of Rome's liveliest squares, its bars and restaurants are bustling day and night. It is on the site of a stadium constructed by the Emperor Domitian in 86AD and is dominated by the works of the great Renaissance and Baroque artists. The great and the good of this period took up residence around the square and inevitably attracted artisans and tradesmen.

The main artistic features of the piazza are the fountains. The largest, the Fontana dei Fiumi (fountain of the rivers) was conceived by Bernini, having been commissioned by Pope Innocent X. Four rivers represent for the four known continents; the Nile for Africa, the Ganges for Asia, the River Plate for the Americas and the Danube for Europe. The obelisk, created during Domitian's reign, was brought from the via Appia and incorporated into the design of the fountain by Bernini.

The fontana del Moro was renovated by Bernini though completed by a pupil. The Fontana del Nettuno was added to at the end of the 16th century. It fell into disrepair and the sculptures were replaced by the present ones in the 19th century.

Trastavere

Trastavere (literally 'across the Tiber') was traditionally a working-class district peopled by those willing to lend their hearts and fists to the latest revolutionary cause. It is becoming a more prosperous area, inhabited by well-off Italians and foreigners. It remains a genuinely Roman quarter, packed with restaurants, bars, trattorias and pizzerias, where one can enjoy simple food in a convivial atmosphere.

The streets are narrow and cobbled, well shaded in the summer when the area is perhaps best appreciated. Every Sunday the Porta Portese neighbourhood becomes an immense market, some of which is given over to a flea market. A short walk (or rapid tram ride) from the largo Argentina, Trastavere can be reached from the Teatro Marcello by crossing the river at the picturesque Isla Tiburina, a small island in the centre of the Tiber.

Circus Maximus

The great circus was constructed at the foot of the Palatine hill and is overlooked by the Imperial palaces. It was the largest circus in Rome, could hold 300,000 people and was reserved for chariot races (as in Ben Hur). Augustus and his successors greatly embellished this circus. In 10BC, at the centre of the arena, a 23m high obelisk was erected (it now stands in the piazza del Popolo) below the Flavian palace, and a magnificent tribune was constructed for the comfort of the Imperial family.

Teatro Marcellus

Julius Caesar began it but Augustus finished the work between 13 and 11BC, and dedicated it to his nephew, Marcellus, son of Octavia. Two levels of arches remain (and this style was adapted for the construction of the Colosseum) but there was almost certainly a third level. The theatre was abandoned and left to rack and ruin at the end of the fourth century AD, and much of the stone was pillaged for other buildings. In the sixteenth century it was reclaimed by the Savelli family who made it their palace, with the architect Baldassare Peruzzi building the quarters we see today above the ancient arches. The palace later became the property of the Orsini family. The ancient theatre was restored to its present condition in the late 1920's when the buildings which then surrounded it were demolished.

Places to visit (cont)

Piazza della Bocca della Verita

A square bordered by the Palatine and Capitol hills and the Tiber. We find here two temples; Tempio di Vesta, an elegant, circular edifice built at the time of Augustus and incorrectly attributed to Vesta (the real temple to Vesta is in the Imperial Forums) and Tempio della Fortuna, possibly erected in honour of Portumnus, the God of Rivers and Ports, in the second century BC.

Santa Maria

The principal landmark opposite these temples is the 12th century church Santa Maria in Cosmedin, whose bell tower is one of the most beautiful in Italy. Restauration work in the 19th century brought it back to its medieval glory. In the porch is the Bocca della Verita – the Mouth of Truth. The plaque is said to represent a water god and legend has it that whoever puts his hand in the mouth while harbouring a lie on their conscience will lose their hand. The crypt of Santa Maria in Cosmedin is open to the public between 9am and 6pm.

Hours:	9am and 6pm
Prices:	Entry €2

Attractions just outside

Ostia Antica

Ostia is situated at the mouth of the River Tiber, 25km south west of Rome. During the Republican era it was Rome's principal commercial port and a military base. The city continued to flourish under the Emperors and at its peak its population would have been in excess of 100,000. The port's main business was the corn trade. Political stability depended on rulers' ability to feed the population, but Italy alone could not meet demand so corn had to be imported from all over the Roman world. Thus for many centuries Ostia played an essential role in the economic and political life of Rome.

It was also the gateway to the Empire so the atmosphere and culture was strongly cosmopolitan, with offices of traders and shipbuilders from Egypt, Tunisia, Sardinia, Greece, southern France. There were also temples to Persian gods, a synagogue and an early Christian basilica.

During the 4th century AD, Ostia's influence began to wane as its harbour silted up and Portus, further up the coast, took over after a devastating malaria epidemic sounded the city's death knell. For centuries Ostia lay preserved, if not in aspic, under a thick layer of sand. Consequently it is immaculately preserved.

A visit to the excavations, where the mask, above, was uncovered, affords a vivid insight into Roman life and, more particularly, into the immense logistical and commercial activity in feeding the world's dominant economic and political power.

A highlight of the tour of the site is the theatre which has been completely restored and which in summer is the venue for productions of classical plays.

Directions:	Take the metro line B in the direction of Laurentina. Get off at Piramide and take a train to Ostia Antica.
Journey time:	40 minutes approx.
Hours:	Tuesday to Sunday: 8.30am - 7.30pm – April-October. 8.30am-5.30pm – November-March

Frascati

A small town 20 kilometres from Rome, Frascati is most famous for its crisp white wine. It is also a highly picturesque town, surrounded by 16th and 17th villas constructed by wealthy Roman families seeking a restful space away from the bustle of the city. Many are now hotels or the headquarters of cultural institutes.

The central piazza affords a wonderful view as far as Rome and an excellent perspective of the town's most famous landmark, the Villa Albobrandini. Constructed towards the end of the 16th century, the villa possesses an ornate garden of great beauty, with alleys, terraces and fountains. The garden is open to the public on weekdays from 9am till 1pm and 3pm till 6pm (5pm in winter). A free pass must be collected from the tourist office at 1 piazza Marconi.

At 6 piazza Marconi, the former stables of the villa Albobrandini have been converted to house the Museo Tuscolano (open Tuesday to Saturday 10am-6pm), in which archaeological remains and maquettes of the Tuscolano villas are exhibited. Close to the town, on the road to Monte Porzio Catone you will find the Museo del Vino, dedicated to the art of the production of the local wines. You could also try local produce during lunch on the terrace of one of Frascati's fine but unpretentious restaurants.

Getting there:	Regular trains from Stazione Termini to Frascati. Last train back to Rome around 8.30pm
Journey time:	30 minutes
Price:	Return fare €3.40

Lake Bracciano

A haven of tranquillity 40km north-west of Rome. The Emperor Trajan constructed an aqueduct to supply the Trastavere quarter of Rome with drinking water from the lake. The aqueduct was destroyed several times before being rebuilt by Pope Paul V in 1609, who gave the aqueduct his name. There are some wonderful walks through the forests and villages which surround the lake.

Anguillara-Sabazia is a small medieval town perched on a rocky promontory overlooking the lake. There is an imposing gate to the town. crowned by a 16th century clock. From the square there are wonderful views across the water and a charming walk down to the lake's edge through the exquisite medieval streets.

Trevignano Romano is another medieval town, lined with fishermen's cottages, clinging to a rock dominated by the ruins of the Orsini family's fortress (the family was a pre-eminent dynasty throughout the Middle Ages). The Church of the Assumption is decorated with frescoes by the school of Raphael and beyond the clock tower is the piazza Vittorio Emanuele III.

Bracciano itself is joined to Rome by the via Claudia, just as it was two millennia ago. All roads in Bracciano lead to the piazza 1° Maggio but the town is dominated by its castle, the Castello Orsini-Odescalchi, with its mighty cylindrical towers. Originally a medieval fortress of the Prefetti di Vico, its control was wrested by the Orsini family, who maintained their dominance for several centuries before selling the castle to the Odescalchi family. It moved on to the Torlonia family at the beginning of the 19th century before returning to the Odescalchis, who own it today.

Hours:	Tuesday to Sunday
Prices:	Guided visit €5
Phone:	06 998 04348

There are regular trains from Rome, Stazione Termini and Stazione Tiburtina, to Bracciano. Journey time is 60 minutes. Return ticket €5. During the summer period the "Sabazia II" motorboat makes scheduled excursions of about one and a half hours on the lake, stopping at Bracciano, Anguillara, and Trevignano.

Information:	**Consorzio Lago di Bracciano, Via IV Novembre 119/a - Rome 06 67661**
	Ex Idroscalo degli Inglesi, Bracciano 06 998 05462

THEATRE & ARTS

The Gallery of the Villa Borghese

An astonishing collection of masterpieces, particularly the from the Renaissance and Baroque periods, with works by Raphael, Titian, Caravaggio, Bernini and Canova, with the gallery's most famous piece being the latter's sculpture of Paolina Borghese.

The collection was the work of Cardinal Scipione, a member of the immensely powerful Borghese family who commissioned the great artists of his era to produce original works or wonderful restorations. This is not the complete original collection because part of it was sold to Napoleon and is exhibited in the Louvre in Paris, where much of the Emperor's booty has resided for the last two centuries.

It is compulsory to book at least two days in advance.

Address:	Piazza Scipione Borghese
Hours:	09.00 – 19.00 (Visits at 09.00, 11.00, 13.00, 15.00, 17.00) 09.00 – 23.00 (Saturday)
Prices:	€8.50
Phone:	06 32810

The National Roman Museum

Construction of the palazzo Altemps began towards the end of the 15th century for Giolamo Riario, a nephew of Pope Sixtus IV (founder of the Sistine Chapel). It was acquired in 1568 by Cardinal Marcus Sitticus Altemps who had the palace rebuilt by Martino Longhi the Elder. Today the palace is the property of the Holy See and one of its principal attractions is the Ludovisi-Boncompagni collection of ancient statues. Some of the statues were renovated in the 17th century by that era's greatest sculptors (Algard, Bernini etc). This collection, apart the palace, is worth a visit on its own merits; the frescoes which adorn the walls of the chambers, its magnificent ceilings and the 15th and 16th century remains of the original palace.

Hours:	Tuesday to Sunday 9am – 7.45pm
Prices:	€5
Phone:	06 399 677 00
Internet:	www.archeorm.arti.beniculturali.it

The Roman Civilisation Museum

Unfortunately situated off the beaten track, this museum is well worth a detour. The main feature of the museum is a large and incredible reproduction of Imperial Rome which shows exactly what the city looked like at the height of the Empire. There is also a complete set of moulds of the Trajan Column, which tell the story of the emperor's military exploits. The museum also houses reproductions of works from classical antiquity which have been lost or destroyed.

Hours:	Tuesday – Saturday: 9am – 7pm Sunday: 9am – 1pm
Prices:	€6.20

Palazzo Doria Pamphilj

A palace as famous for its architecture as for its art gallery which houses the collection of the Pamphilj family, over 400 paintings dating from the 15th to 18th century. The most famous work is probably Velasquez's portrait of pope Innocent X (a member of the Pamphilj family and great sponsor of the arts – the Fontana dei Fiumi on the piazza Navona). Works by Titian and Caravaggio also feature.

The entrance on the via del Corso allows a view of the 16th century porticoed courtyard constructed by the della Rovere family. The facade of the piazza del Collegio Romano was built by the Pamphilj family while the wonderful chapel and theatre were inaugurated in 1684 by Queen Christina of Sweden.

Open:	Monday – Wednesday & Friday – Sunday 10am – 5pm
Tickets:	€8
Phone:	06 679 7323
Internet:	www.doriapamphilj.it

Ta Matete Living Museum

Situated close to the piazza Venezia this is a museum which doesn't quite follow the usual museum pattern. Here you are encouraged to participate in the art, to explore your response to the art and the artists (there are regular workshops with visiting artists). Experience multi-sensory stimuli and interactive choreography. Even the opening hours are artistic (late start, late finish).

Hours:	Tuesday – Sunday 11am – 9pm
Phone:	06 679 1107
Internet:	www.tamatete.it

OPERA AND BALLET

There is a programme of opera, classical music and ballet all year by the Teatro dell'Opera di Roma. The summer opera season has been presented since 1937 at the Caracalla Baths, Imperial Rome's (inaugurated in 216AD) most important thermal buildings. An astonishing setting. **1, piazza Beniarnino Gigli, 00184 Roma**

Hours:	Tuesday to Saturday: 9am – 5pm (Summer 10am – 4pm). Sunday: 9am – 1.30pm. Day of performance: 9am – 5pm (and 1 hour berfore performance).	
Prices:	Concerts	€11 - €28
	Ballet	€17 - €65
	Opera	€17 - €130
	Caracalla	€25 - €100
Phone:	06 481 60255 or 06 481 7003	
Email:	ufficio.biglietteria@operaroma.it	
Internet:	www.operaroma.it	

SHOPPING

MARKETS

Campo de' Fiori, Centro Storico

Here, on one of Rome's oldest and most popular piazzas, you will find a wonderful array of stalls selling vegetables and fruit (lots of produce from market gardens), fish, poultry, meat, cheeses, cured or baked hams, salamis, sausages, herbs and spices (sometimes premixed to accompany specific types of food), eggs, beans, nuts, breads. The stall holders are very happy for you to try their produce and enjoy trying to sell in English or in French. The atmosphere is relaxed and a tremendous hubbub is created as the bargaining at the stalls joins the noise of conversations from the café terraces which surround the pîazza.

Hours:	Monday – Saturday 8am-2pm

Mercato de Stampe

A market which resembles a conclave of all the bouquinistes of Paris gathered in one place. On sale are prints, antique and secondhand books. For non-Italian speakers there is a superb selection of artbooks, prints of Rome which can make wonderful gifts or souvenirs. You must not be afraid to bargain. You may not speak Italian but you probably do have hands.

Hours:	Saturday 7am-1pm

Porta Portese

An enormous Sunday morning flea market in the Trastavere quarter. It all starts at 6.30am as the local bars open or close. However, even if you don't find a bargain, you will have great fun looking. And haggling. A rough rule of thumb is to divide the asking price by FIVE.

DEPARTMENT STORES

There are no real equivalents in Rome of Harrods, Galeries Lafayette or Arnotts. The closest would be **La Rinascente (189 via del Corso)** in which you find a large and attractive assembly of boutiques selling branded clothing, perfumes and leather goods. **M.A.S., 11 via dello Statuto**, (close to Santa Maria Maggiore) is closer to the Tati stores in Paris in which you can rifle through the racks and shelves in search of THE bargain from a pair of flip-flops to a leather jacket.

Ricordi Mediastore

A chain of 5 stores in Rome selling music, books, DVD, IT and digital equipment. The main store, at 506 via del Corso, (close to the Piazza del Popolo) is vast and has a box office selling tickets for concerts, shows and sports events. The other Ricordi Mediastores are located at:

73 via Orlando (close to piazza della Republica)
120/c via C. Battisti (close to piazza Venezia)
88 via Giulio Cesare (close to the Vatican)
Gallery of the Stazione Termini

ANTIQUES

Rome, with its rich history of artistic endeavour and achievement is a veritable treasure trove of antiques. Close to the Campo de'Fiori are the via Giulia, via del Pellegrino, via dei Cappellari, in which you will find a whole host of small shops selling books, prints, paintings, statues, or the workshops of artisans working (often in the open air) on restoration of furniture, art works or musical instuments.

Close to the piazza Navona is the via dei Coronari, browse through boutiques offering art nouveau and antiques. Be careful, a lot of what is on offer has been imported. And be doubly careful if you decide to ask for a price. You may discover how the street earned its name...

HIGH FASHION

All the great Italian designers and many of the top international names in high fashion clothing, accessories, perfumes, jewellery, have their outlets in a small but perfectly formed area close to the Spanish Steps.

In via dei Condotti, via Frattini, via Borgognona, via Bocca di Leone you will find Max and Co, Max Mara, Dolce & Gabbana, Furla, Burberry, Dior, Eddy Monetti, Celine, Salvatore Ferragamo, Hermès, Max Mara, Gucci, Mont Blanc, Giorgio Armani, Cartier, Bulgari, Prada, Yves-Saint-Laurent, Versace et al. These streets become packed with shoppers, window shoppers, tourists and young Romans heading for the Spanish Steps, and, in the evening, promenaders of an older generation. The conversational racket is phenomenal.

A more tranquil setting for some top-of-the-range retail therapy is the sophisticated Prati area close to Vatican City. Some top designers (especially jewellers) are to be found tucked away in the distinguished streets between piazza Risorgimento and piazza Cavour. The via Cola di Renzo off the piazza Risorgimento is home to high quality food shops and also mid-range brand stores for clothes, books and gifts.

OTHER PLACES OF INTEREST

Il Giardino del Tango

Situated in the 1960 Olympic Village, Il Giardino del Tango is the place for dance afficionados to find the perfect setting and atmosphere in which to dance. 9pm-3am. The last Saturday of each month dancing continues till 5am.

Cine Pub

The place is given over to the owners' love of the cinema with a huge collection of photos of movie greats a major feature. There is balcony bar, separate from the Cine Pub which is the venue for many types of live entertainment; cabaret, rock, jazz, not to mention the drag act. Free pasta dishes for all comers during happy hour. 6pm-3am.

Phone:	06 489 07230

Other places of interest (cont)

New Orleans Café

This café opens in the morning as an excellent breakfast bar. They serve a good lunch and by the evening it has transformed into a fine cocktail bar. Proper draught beers are also a selling point and also good food. All this is followed by a jam session or concert by some of Rome's finest jazz musicians. If only you could sleep there. (Note It moves to Fregene on the coast for the summer).

Hours:	9am–1pm
Phone:	335 842 1367

L'Impiccione Viaggiatore

It is difficult to classify this modern contemporarily furnished café situated in a cobbled street close to Trajan's Markets. It is a unique place in Rome, l'Impiccione Viaggiatore (the travelling busybody) is at once a wine bar (excellent food, wine and coffee are offered in a warm and welcoming atmosphere), and travel agent with bookshelves lined with travel literature for purchase or perusal. The large plasma screen shows images of holiday destinations. Theme weeks are organised during which the owners will hawk the merits of a particular city or region (not necessarily in Italy; Ireland was the theme during St Patrick's week this year) with lectures and videos on its culture with promotion of its gastronomic specialities in the café's menu. In short, a wonderful place to enjoy Rome's food and wine.

Phone:	06 678 6188

EAT, DRINK & SLEEP

CENTRO STORICO

(Piazza Navona, Spanish Steps, Campo de'Fiori, Santa Maria Maggiore, Via Vittorio Veneto, Forums, Trevi Fountain, Pantheon)

BARS

WINE

Il Bicchiere di Mastai, 52 via dei Banci Nuovi.

Elegant wine bar in which to linger over a bottle selected from the 800 labels on offer. Food is available all day. Marinated meats and fish, smoked meats and salamis, cheeses and desserts. There is a businessman's lunch for €12 (including a glass of wine). In the afternoon the place becomes a coffee house before bringing out the cocktail mixers from 7pm.

Phone:	06 681 9228

Antica Enoteca, 76b via della Croce.

A wine outlet since 1720, this perennially busy enoteca maintains an old world charm. The house has more than a thousand wine labels and food which ranges from homemade tarts and local cheeses, light lunches to full blown fine dining.

Il Brillo Parlante, 12 via della Fontanella. Small, welcoming bar between the piazza del Popolo and the Spanish Steps. Four hundred mainly Italian and French wines and, unusually for Rome, the list also includes South American, Australian and New Zealand produce. There is a very good range of whiskies and grappas. Classic Italian dishes, a selection of smoked meats and Italian and French cheeses.

Phone:	06 323 5017

La Petite Chambre, 7 vicolo Cancelleria. Friday and Saturday till 2am. Small tearoom-winebar-bistro in an intimate and romantic French style. There is a choice of more than 50 teas or infusions. Salads and hot and cold savoury dishes are available all day along with an extensive list of exclusively Italian wines. Happy hour from 4 till 6pm.

Phone:	06 681 36267

Al Vino Al Vino, 19 via dei Serpenti.
Three small, artistically decorated rooms. Lots of cold dishes are on offer: Sicilian specialities, cured meats, a selection of cheeses and handmade desserts. There is a difficult choice to be made from a list of 500 wines and the house also sells some fine liqueurs and grappas.

Phone:	06 485 803

Libreria Caffè Bohemienne, 36 via degli Zingari.
Neo-baroque setting which seeks to recreate the atmosphere of bohemian Montmartre. One can leaf through art books, perhaps buy one, or just enjoy one of the (mainly imported) wines while savouring the selection of Italian and French cheeses.

Phone:	328 173 0158

BRITISH / IRISH PUBS

Abbey Theatre, via del Governo Vecchio.
Named after the celebrated theatre in Dublin, this pub offers a warm welcome and a good atmosphere. Some simple food available, (crostini, Roman specialities and Irish pub grub). A lively happy hour till 9pm and Sky TV for sports fans and the ticketless. There is also access to the internet.

Phone:	06 686 1341

Old Bear, 2 via dei Gigli d'Oro.
Atmospheric 17th century convent illuminated by candles and lanterns, a blend of Roman tavern and beer cellar. The food is good, and there's a good selection of wines. Draught beers also feature.

Phone:	06 682 10009

The Bulldog Inn, 107a Corso Vittorio Emanueli II.
Large pub on this main artery and close to the piazza Navona. Lots of draught beers and simple, filling food; hamburgers, hot dogs, bruschettoni etc. All major sport on TV, so a good place for non-ticketholders.

Phone:	06 687 1357

Mad Jacks', 20 via Arenula.
The apostrophe's position in the name might suggests that more than one madman called Jack got together to open an Irish pub in Rome. In fact the pub's business is more steady than mad, based on good food (mainly Italian) draught beers and cocktails. There are TV screens for music channels and sport. Good location close to the lively Campo de'Fiori area and a brief walk across the Tiber into the Trastavere quarter.

Phone:	06 688 08223

The Old Marconi, 9c via Santa Prasseda. Subdued lighting for an intimate atmosphere, draught beers and a long list of cocktails are the main attractions of this English style pub next to Santa Maria Maggiore. Robust Italian and International food is available all day and there is happy hour from noon till 6.30pm.

Phone:	06 474 5186

The Flan O'Brian, 17 via Nazionale.
Large pub of over 4000 square feet which is dominated by three plasma screens showing the latest pop and rock videos. Young, cool clientele. The food is good (Argentinian Angus beef, chicken in Kilkenny Ale), some good cocktails, draught beer and a fine Sunday brunch.

Phone:	06 488 0418

The Nag's Head, 138b via Quattro Novembre.
Named after a famous scene in The Godfather and located close to the piazza Venezia this is a very popular meeting place for young foreigners in Rome. Lively happy hour from 7 till 10pm and sport on TV.

Phone:	06 679 4620

Bars: Centro Storico (cont)

The Shamrock, 1c via del Colosseo.
Close to the Colosseum, this Irish theme bar is one of the best in Rome and is managed by a keen rugby fan. The Shamrock becomes very lively, especially in the evening, with a young international crowd attracted by the good selection of bottled beers, draught Irish stout and lagers and the occasional live rock concert. The food is robust pub grub and all major sport is shown on TV screens.

Phone:	06 679 1729

The Surge, 110 via della Madonna dei Monti.
Owned by the same people as the Shamrock, this one is just across the via Cavour. A quieter place to watch of the match. Pleasant staff who enjoy the rugby craic.

Phone:	06 679 5133

Finnegan's, 66-67 via Leonina.
Irish-owned pub close the the via Cavour and the Imperial Forums. Quite a large place – a good spot for the ticketless, as all top sport is shown on the TV screens. Basic pub grub is available along with draught beer and stout, pool and darts for les sportifs.

Phone:	06 474 7026

The Albert, 132 via del Traforo.
Some draught beers; Guinness, Tennents, Red Stripe and some simple but hearty food such as couscous, jacket potatoes and salads.

Phone:	06 481 8795

Trinity College, 6 via del Collegio Romano.
One of Rome's better Irish pubs just off the via del Corso towards the piazza Venezia end. There is a pleasant, cosmopolitan atmosphere, a small TV for sport and OK draught beers and stout. The restaurant on the first floor offers an extensive international menu.

Phone:	06 678 6472

COCKTAIL BARS

Lot 87, 87 via del Pellegrino.
Designer establishment in a famous medieval Roman street which runs north from the Campo de' Fiori and is full of interesting boutiques, furniture restorers, antique dealers or jewellers. Lot 87 evolves from coffee house to aperitif/cocktail bar as its long day progresses. A large plasma screen flickers all day with Fashion TV, international news or Sky TV.

Phone:	06 976 18344

La Curia di Bacco, 79 via del Biscione. In a small street close to the Campo de'Fiori, you go through a small passage which opens into a cellar (dated 70BC) and you are in the Curia di Bacco. There is a most welcoming candle-lit atmosphere, with a good list of wines, beers and cocktails. Tasty cheeses and cold meats. Happy hour everyday from 4 till 8pm.

Phone:	06 689 3893

Le Grand Bar, at the St Regis Grand Hotel, 3 via V E Orlando.
Elegant 19th century bar in this luxury hotel. Excellent cocktails accompanied by fine piano playing. Jazz concerts are held here every Wednesday from 10pm.

Phone:	06 470 92741

LIVE MUSIC

Rockodile, 8 via delle Tre Cannelle.
Three large rooms provide the venues for live rock, blues and jazz. Hot and cold food is available with Italian wines or draught beers. Lively happy hour from 6 till 9pm.

Gregory's, 54d via Gregoriana.
Live concerts and jam sessions throughout the week in this atmospheric jazz club in a small street just off the Spanish Steps. Beers include John Bull, Guinness, Mc Ewens and 70 plus different whiskies. International food with slight Irish tones is available. There is a happy hour every day from opening time till 9.30pm.

Phone:	06 679 6386

Habana Café, 120 via dei Pastini.
The via dei Pastini, is a lively little street just off the piazza della Rotonda (Pantheon). The Habana Café offers a happy hour and pub grub till about 11pm when the place become the scene for live music; rock, lounge and mainstream pop.

Phone:	06 678 1983

NIGHTCLUBS

Anima, 57 via di Santa Maria dell'Anima.
10pm-3am. A popular cocktail bar which transforms into a night club as the evening takes its course, with dancing to black, hip-hop and R'n'B.

Phone:	347 850 9256

Le Coppelle, 52 piazza delle Coppelle.
6pm-2am. Located on a small square close to the Pantheon and the Piazza Navona, this is a cutting edge space where vibey jet-setters congregate to admire each other. It transforms from cocktail bar (the cocktails are good) to night club with in-house DJ.

Phone:	06 683 2410

RESTAURANTS

(Piazza Navona, Spanish Steps, Campo de'Fiori, Santa Maria Maggiore, Via Vittorio Veneto, Forums, Trevi Fountain, Pantheon)

Piazza Navona

Le Streghe, 13 vicolo del Curato. €45
In a quiet street close to the Tiber, just across from the Castel San Angelo. A pleasant, romantic restaurant offering a well balanced, traditional Tuscan "land and sea" menu which varies according to the season, with some exotic touches such as curried gambas.

Phone:	06 687 8182

Giulio Passami l'Olio, 28 via di Monte Giordano. €25. Traditional.
Some surprisingly good wines at this simple and unpretentious restaurant offering some excellent traditional dishes (the lasagna is very good) and a selection of cured hams, salamis and cheeses. A good little spot.

Phone:	06 688 03288

Before, 18 piazza Nicosia. €35. Traditional.
The decor has been inspired by the proprietor's love of cinema. Classic Italian cooking with some more exotic offerings (an excellent concoction of spaghetti with Indonesian spices, prawns, chicken, pork and vegetables). There is a quite an extensive wine list and possibilities for all budgets with good pizzas from €6.

Phone:	06 688 91458

Spanish Steps

Da Giggi, 94a via Belsiana. €20
A little rough and ready this place, but great fun in a quiet street between the piazza del Popolo and the Spanish Steps. There is an extensive menu of country and Roman specialities (bucatini all'amatriciana, pasta with beans, clams with rustic bread soaked in a white wine and garlic sauce, trippa alla Romana). If in a group, try a large and varied selection of starters, mains and side dishes and pick and mix as if you were in the local Chinese. The prices and generous portions encourage this. Go for the house wines. The service seems off-hand but quickly changes to dead-pan humorous when appreciation of the food and wine begins to flow. It's a good idea to phone or pass by to reserve.

Phone:	06 679 1130

Hostaria dell'Orso, 25c via dei Soldati. €85.
The oldest hostelry in Romè. In the 16th century it became a hotel and guests included Rabelais, Goethe and Montaigne. When it became a restaurant in the mid 20th century, guests included the entire cast of La Dolce Vita, Onassis and Maria Callas, Clark Gable and a host of others. It was recently taken over by Gultiero Marchesi, Italy's first ever Michelin 3-star chef. Classic cooking - ravioli of ewe cheese in a lamb ragout, chicken alla Romana, and a huge international wine list. Music is a strong theme, there is a piano bar and the evening continues after dinner in the chic La night club. Stellar prices for a star establishment.

Phone:	06 683 01192
Internet:	www.hdo.it

Il Convivio-Troiani, 31 vicolo del Soldati. €75.
Located in a little street between Piazza Navona and the Tiber, Il Convivio-Troiani is another Michelin-starred gastronomic address. Duck foie gras 'au torchon' in pastry with figs, pistachios, Marsala and black truffles, reminds us that in ancient Roman days, geese and ducks were fed with figs to give an incomparable sweetness to the liver. Equally tasty is roast pigeon with orange. Sabayon parfait with balsamic vinegar from Modena gives us an ancient take on sweet and sour.

OP LA, 10 via Angelo Brunetti. €40.
Located just a few steps away from the piazza del Popolo and just off the via del Corso, this intimate restaurant offers traditional setting. A well structured menu with high quality ingredients (cured ham with mozzarella, fried sage leaves, spaghetti in Cognac, Sicilian tuna, swordfish with cherry tomatoes) served by enthusiastic staff. An up-and-coming establishment which is developing a following.

Phone:	06 321 9302

Nino, 11 via Borgognona. €30.
Warm and welcoming wood panelled restaurant in the designer shopping area close to the Spanish Steps. The food is high quality, good value, genuine Tuscan: spinach and tomato soufflé, bean soup, smoked meats and very good fish dishes. The service is friendly and attentive and the clientele is a cheerful, crowded mix of well-to-do Romans families and tourists. The wine list is exclusively Italian with several half-bottles available. A real "can't-go-wrong" restaurant in a great location.

Phone:	06 679 5676

Reef, 47 piazza Augusto Imperatore. €60.
Sleek maniera Italiana design, Reef is at the cutting edge of culinary and architectural chic. Quality Italian cooking with a Japanese touch. The signature dish is seared tuna in a sesame seed crust with couscous and spinach. The homemade desserts, and in particular the variations on a chocolate theme, are truly inventive. Décor and quality are reflected in the prices but there is a tasting menu at €45. From Tuesday to Saturday there is a light lunch menu at €12. The wine is extensive, over 300 labels, with some wines available by the glass.

Phone:	06 683 01430

Sant'Andrea, 9-10 via Sant'Andrea delle Fratte. €30.
Small and smart establishment close to the Spanish Steps. Classic Roman cooking backed up with an good list of Italian wines. Closed on Saturday.

Phone:	06 679 3167

Al Vantaggio, 35 via del Vantaggio. €20. Roman
Family restaurant close to the Piazza del Popolo. Good setting for a cheap and cheery carbonara, oxtail stew or roast lamb. Small wine list with fairly priced and reliable house wines.

Phone:	06 323 6848
Internet:	www.alvantaggio.it

Scene from the top: Rome in all its splendour pictured from Gianicolo Hill

Campo de'Fiori

Al Bric, 51 via del Pellegrino. €50.

Warm and welcoming restaurant in the fascinating via del Pellegrino off the Campo de'Fiori. It is worth coming here for the cheese alone (displayed in the window) and/or the wines (more than 1,000 labels on offer, including many half-bottles). The cooking is refined, the homemade gnocchi are sensational as is the beef strogonoff in barolo with slithers of parmesan and velouté of yellow peppers. The service throughout is spot on while the desserts are perfectly adequate, without being exceptional.

Phone:	06 687 9533

TRADITIONAL

Giggetto al Portico d'Ottavia, 21a via del Portico d'Ottavia. €35.

Although the restaurant can take up to 280 covers (200 inside and 80 outside) it is advisable to reserve because this places gets packed and noisy, especially at weekends. Popular with locals and tourists. Expect singers and musicians. Roman specialities are the staples – roast lamb, oxtail, fettucine with artichoke, rigatoni alla carbonara. The wine list is extensive. Despite size, the service is efficient.

Phone:	06 686 1105

ITALIAN

Grappolo d'Oro Zampano, 80 piazza della Cancelleria. €30.

Close to the Campo de'Fiori, this is a traditional Roman trattoria which has been transformed into a contemporary restaurant whose influences go well beyond Rome's boundaries. The decor is bright with lots of light wood and chrome and the service is friendly and well-paced. Try the savoury millefeuille with aubergine flowers, gnocchi in an Alpine cream cheese; or the eggplant flan with gorgonzola. Its adjoining pizzeria is also singled out for praise. The semifreddo (a sort of half-chilled ice-cream) in different flavours and other homemade desserts are recommended. Balanced wine list which matches perfectly the menu.

Phone:	06 689 7080

Ditirambo, 74 piazza della Cancelleria. €35.

Also close to lively Campo de'Fiori, this Ditirambo offers some imaginative twists on traditional Roman dishes. There is a wide choice of meat and fish and the wine list is comprehensive. This is a popular and successful restaurant so it is advisable to book, if possible, for the first dinner sitting because service and cooking can become tired as the evening progresses.

Phone:	06 687 1626
Internet:	www.ristoranteditirambo.com

Grotte del Teatro di Pompeo, 73 via del Biscione. €30.

Family style restaurant in the vaults of the Theatre of Pompey (55BC) close to Campo de'Fiori. Robust Roman cooking, good wine list, a charming place for a good, inexpensive meal.

Phone:	06 688 03686

Restaurants: Centro Storico (cont)

Il Duca, 52-56 vicolo del Cinque. €20.
Informal trattoria offering traditional Roman dishes (oxtail, spaghetti alla carbonara, saltimbocca) and house wines. Close to the Ponte Sisto which crosses the Tiber close to the Campo de'Fiori.

Phone:	06 581 7706

Santa Maria Maggiore

Agata e Romeo, 45 via Carlo Alberto. €75.
Small and refined restaurant boasting one Michelin star. Recent reports, however, suggest that it has become a bit hit and miss, with service lacking and attention to detail occasionally absent from the cooking. The menu, is Agata's domain, and offers both traditional and modern cooking supported by an excellent wine list, handled by her sommelier and maître d' husband, Romeo. When on form, Agata puts an inspired twist on dishes such as crepes with chestnut flour and ewe's-milk ricotta, and breaded lamb chops. A tasting menu, complete with wine, changes monthly to reflect seasonal dishes and allows you to try a range of specialties. Desserts are scrumptious and the wine list is excellent. Please feel free to feed back information on this culinary bastion. Closed on Saturday and Sunday.

Phone:	06 446 6115

Mater Mutata, 47 via Milano. €55.
Light, bright contemporary decor and atmosphere. Two possibilities: fine dining with creatively prepared fusion cooking (the wine list is impossibly long, however) or the winebar menu of cold meats, cheeses and desserts with a cocktail or long drink. The second option is available till 3.30am.

Phone:	06 478 25746

Via Veneto

Harry's Bar, 150 via Vittorio Veneto. €65. One of the temples of the Dolce Vita, Harry's specialises in refined Mediterranean cooking in a suitably elegant and sophisticated atmosphere. The bar is wonderful for aperitifs and cocktails (try to go mid-afternoon when things are quiet - you get the barman's full attention) with sixties music or, later in the day, live piano.

Phone:	06 484 643
Internet:	www.harrysbar.it

Papà Baccus, 32/36 via Toscana. €45. Close to the via Veneto, this charming restaurant has for many years been a bastion of Tuscan cooking, with regional specialities alongside some imaginative piscatorial creations from the Med. The wine list is well researched, with a majority of bottles from small producers.

Phone:	06 427 42808

Al Grappolo d'Oro, 4/10 via Palestro. €35.
Next to the Diocletian Baths, recently refurbished in an elegant classic style, the Grappolo does traditional Italian dishes accompanied by good wines.

Phone:	06 494 1441

T-Bone Station, 29 via Francesco Crispi. €30. Off the via Tritone and the via Sistina, this is a good steak house offering burgers and spare-ribs in a trendy, upbeat atmosphere. Satellite TV, music, hyper-cheerful service. Good idea to reserve.

Phone:	06 678 7650

Trevi Fountain

Piccolo Arancio, 112 vicolo Scanderbeg. €30.
Charming bijou establishment close to the Trevi Fountain but seemingly immune to the hustle and bustle. Attentive service for such a tripper's area. Simple but well executed traditional Italian fish and meat dishes. Splendid desserts.

Phone:	06 678 6139

Water on the rocks: The claim is that throw a coin in the Trevi Fountain and you will be certain to come back to Rome ... seems more than a decent bargain.

Al Moro, 13 vicolo delle Bollette. €40.
Small and genuine Roman restaurant superbly located in a tiny street close to the Trevi Fountain. One of our critics, who eats only spaghetti carbonara (useful for setting a spagehtti gold standard), reckons this is in Rome's top dozen. Excellent fresh fish every day, and all the desserts are homemade.

Phone:	06 678 3495

Pantheon

La Rosetta, 9 viale della Rosetta. €75.
Just off the Piazzo Novona, this Michelin starred restaurant is regarded as THE place to go for fish. Simple but very well executed. The menu varies each day according to the market and the produce is on display at the entrance to the restaurant, in this instance an indication of freshness rather than naffness. The cellar is phenomenally large with a selection of over 700 Italian and French wines. Reservations essential.

Phone:	06 686 1002

Supperclub, 14 via de' Nari. €55.
Very young restaurant which quickly became part of the Roman scene. There's always an exhibition of current artists. A colourful spot with live music and some cutting edge cooking. International chain which grew out of New York.

Phone:	06 688 07207

Da Gino, 4 vicolo Rosini. €35.
In a small backstreet behind the Palazzo di Montecitoria, the Italian parliament building, this is a lively restaurant frequented by journalists and politicians. The menu offers classic Roman dishes and high quality fresh fish and homemade desserts are justly renowned. Advisable to reserve.

Phone:	06 687 3434

Enoteca Corsi, 87/88 via del Gesu. €20.
This is a true Roman trattoria, one for the locals and usually full. Although the sign says "enoteca" the wine list is a little thin, but the food is the real star of the show. Open only for lunch.

Phone:	06 679 0821

Il Bacaro, 27 via degli Spagnoli. €40.
Candlelit and tiny, intimate restaurant close to the Pantheon. The menu of refined Italian cooking is well balanced between surf and turf. Try tender veal rolled around scallions and pine nuts in a green olive sauce. The wine list is good and includes several varieties of after-dinner drinks, a rarity in Rome. Reservations essential.

Phone:	06 686 4110

Il Barroccio, 13 via dei Pastini. €25.
Pleasant restaurant in a lively medieval street close to the Pantheon. Avoid the tourist menus and instead delve deep into the menu with the help of the attentive, friendly waiters. Robust fish and meat dishes and the pizzas are worth it if you just fancy a snack.

Phone:	06 679 3797

Armando al Pantheon, 31 via Salita dei Crescenzi. €30.
Small family restaurant in a tiny street close to the Pantheon. Traditional Roman fare in a jumping atmosphere. Good, mainly Italian, wine list. Best to reserve.

Phone:	06 688 03034

HOTELS

(Piazza Navona, Spanish Steps, Campo de'Fiori, Santa Maria Maggiore, Via Vittorio Veneto, Forums, Trevi Fountain, Pantheon)

LUXURY

Spanish Steps

Hotel d'Inghilterra, 14, via Bocca di Leone.
98 rooms, from €240 to €570 s/d/t. Extra bed €80.
Luxurious service situated between the via del Corso and the Spanish Steps. The rooms are tastefully furnished, antiques and artwork abound. The bar is described as a corner of England in Rome.

Phone:	06 699 81204
Email:	reservation.hir@royaldemeure.com
Internet:	www.hir.royaldemeure.com

Hassler Villa Medici, 6 piazza Trinità dei Monti.
112 rooms from €460 to €880 s/d/t. 31 suites from €1800 to €3550.
Rome's most luxurious and prestigious hotel, according to Michelin (they give it the highest possible grading, and who are we to quibble?) Overlooking the Spanish Steps, the panoramic views of the Eternal City from the roof restaurant at lunch, dinner or Sunday brunch are breathtaking.

Phone:	06 699 340
Email:	booking@hotelhassler.it
Internet:	www.hotelhasslerroma.com

Hotel dei Borgognoni, 126 via del Bufalo.
54 rooms, from €190 to €320 s/d/t.
A beautifully modernised 19th century palazzo located close to the Spanish Steps. Comfortably furnished and finely decorated bedrooms. Service discreet and courteous. Very pretty courtyard and garden and an excellent base for Roman culture and shopping.

Phone:	06 699 41505
Email:	info@hotelborgognoni.it
Internet:	www.hotelborgognoni.it

Grand Hotel Plaza, 126 via del Corso.
215 rooms from, €330 to €540 s/d/t. €620 fam. Extra bed €70.
One of the oldest and most prestigious hotels only a few steps away from Trinità dei Monti (the Spanish Steps) next to Via dei Condotti and the best shopping in Rome. Established at the time of Italy's Unification in 1860, it has been a theatre of important cultural and social events ever since. Guests have included Pope Leone X and Robbie Williams.

Phone:	06 699 21111
Email:	plaza@grandhotelplaza.com
Internet:	www.grandhotelplaza.com

Via Vittorio Veneto

Sofitel, 47 via Lombardia. 111 rooms from, €335 to €500 d/t.
Good view of the Villa Borghese gardens, a mere step away from the Via Veneto and the Vatican Museum. The Sofitel is a 19th century palazzo tucked into a corner just off the via Veneto, refurbished in neo-classical Roman style with sculptures and casts everywhere you would expect a five star hotel to have them. Great terrace with views over the rooftops. The restaurant is in the converted stables.

Phone:	06 478 021
Email:	prenotazioni.sofitelroma@accor-hotels.it
Internet:	www.accor-hotels.it

Marriott Grand Hotel Flora, 191 via Vittorio Veneto. 163 rooms. Rack €380 d/t.
Located at the end of the via Veneto. A recent refurbishment has given the hotel a subtle blend of classic elegance and modern refinement. There is an attractive restaurant for buffet lunch and à la carte dining.

Phone:	06 489 929
Internet:	www.marriott.com

Forums

Forum, 25-30 via Tor de' Conti. 78 rooms, from €145 to €340 s/d/t. €290 to €380 tpl. Splendid old place in a cobbled side street next to the Markets of Trajan. It boasts a rooftop restaurant with views over the Imperial Forums and the Colosseum. The food is slightly overpriced but what a view!

Phone:	06 679 2446
Email:	info@hotelforum.com
Internet:	www.hotelforumrome.com

Hotel Traiano, 154, via IV Novembre. 41 rooms, from €165 to €310 s/d/t. €295-€340 tpl. Family room €390 fam. Smart establishment close to the piazza Venezia, the Markets of Trajan, and the rest of the Imperial Forums. The bedrooms are opulently furnished and decorated. A feature is the nineteenth century dining-room. Courteous and efficient service.

Phone:	06 678 3862 / 06 679 2358
Email:	htraiano@tin.it
Internet:	www.hoteltraiano.it

Hotel Cosmopolita, 5 via di Sant'Eufemia. 47 rooms, from, €250 to €300 s/d/t. Family room – on request. Located in the heart of Rome, close to the piazza Venezia, the Markets of Trajan and the Imperial Forums, the hotel is a calm and comfortable refuge from the hustle and bustle. The bedrooms are pleasantly decorated and offer good modern amenities. Pleasant, welcoming staff.

Phone:	06 699 41349
Email:	info@hotelcosmopolita.com
Internet:	www.hotelcosmopolita.com

Hotels: Centro Storico (cont)

Pantheon

Pantheon, 131 via dei Pastini. 14 rooms from, €200 to €350 s/d/t. €270 to €450 tpl. Small, luxury hotel on the narrow and lively via dei Pastini which joins the piazza della Rotunda (the Pantheon) and the piazza di Pietra. Very high level of comfort, excellent, personal service in an outstanding location.

Phone:	06 678 7746
Email:	info@hotelpantheon.it
Internet:	www.hotelpantheon.it

Grand Hotel de la Minerve, 69 piazza della Minerva. 116 rooms, from €370 to €600 s/d/t. 17th century palazzo which hosted literati – Stendhal, Sartre (and, naturally, Simone de Beauvoir) this is top luxury within reaching distance of Hadrian's Pantheon. The rooms are individually decorated and furnished. The lobby is adorned by a Liberty stained glass windows. La Censa, the hotel's restaurant, cleverly manages to bring some imagination to traditional dishes.

Phone:	06 695 201
Email:	minerva@hotel-invest.com
Internet:	www.hotel-invest.com

MODERATELY PRICED

Piazza Navona

Hotel Portoghesi, 1 via dei Portoghesi. 27 rooms from, €120 to €185 s/d/t. Extra bed €10 or €25. Located next to the church of San Antonio dei Portoghesi in a quiet street in the heart of Rome's centro strorico. A small, family run establishment which was recently renovated to offer a high level of modern comfort.

Phone:	06 686 4231
Email:	info@hotelportoghesiroma.com
Internet:	www.hotelportoghesiroma.com

Hotel Rinascimonto, 122 via del Pellegrino. 19 rooms from, €120 to €200 s/d/t. €220 tpl. €250 quad. Good value, comfortable establishment in a lively quarter of medieval Rome. Easy walking distance to St Peter's and the Vatican and a stone's throw from the bustle of Campo de'Fiori, Piazza Navona and the Pantheon.

Phone:	06 687 4813
Email:	info@hotelrinascimento.com
Internet:	www.hotelrinascimento.com

Genio, 28 via Giuseppe Zanardelli. 60 rooms, from €160 to €230 s/d/t. A comfortable elegantly furnished and decorated establishment in a quiet street close to the Piazza Navona, the Tiber and St Peter's, the dome of which you can see from the relaxing terrace, along with much of the rest of Rome.

Phone:	06 683 2191 / 06 683 3781
Internet:	www.leonardihotels.com

Spanish Steps

Hotel Homs, 71-72 via Della Vite. 48 rooms, €140 s, from €190 d/t. Pleasant rooms decorated in a contemporary style. The hotel is 100m from the Spanish Steps which allows easy exploration of Rome's centro storico. Excellent shopping, eating and drinking nearby.

Phone:	06 679 2976
Email:	info@hotelhoms.it
Internet:	www.hotelhoms.it

Peace of the night: The Barcaccia in the Piazza di Spagna at the foot of the Spanish Steps has its moments of calm, but some of the world's most famous shops lurk nearby

Campo de'Fiori

Hotel Teatro di Pompeo, 8 largo del Pallaro. 12 rooms from, €130 to €190 s/d/t. Wonderfully atmospheric place, built on the site of Pompey's Theatre (built in 55BC). You take breakfast in the vaulted cellar of the original building close to such lively hubs as the Campo de' Fiori and the Piazza Navona. Lots of good bars, restaurants and cafés close by, exuding a very Roman ambience. All rooms are double or twin, with private bathroom and air conditioning. Guests may enjoy breakfasts and drinks in presence of ancient Roman remains.

Phone:	06 687 2812
Email:	hotel.teatrodipompeo@tiscali.it
Internet:	www.hotelteatrodipompeo.it

Santa Maria Maggiore

Raffaello, 3-5 via Urbana. 37 rooms, from €150 to €200 d/t.
Named after the great artist, the reception is decorated with copies of frescoes by the master. A reasonably priced, comfortable hotel in a quiet backstreet but allowing easy exploration of the local attractions - Santa Maria Maggiore, shopping on the via Nazionale and the parco di Traiano.

Phone:	06 488 43 42
Email:	info@hotelraffaello.it
Internet:	www.hotelraffaello.it

Ariston, 16 via Turati. 97 rooms. Rack rates: €170 s, €235 d/t, €270 tpl.
Comfortable, newly refurbished 4 star hotel near Santa Maria Maggiore's Basilica and Termini railway station, the Ariston is a traditional family-run establishment offering a good level of comfort and modern amenities.

Phone:	06 446 5399
Email:	hotelariston@hotelariston.it
Internet:	www.hotelariston.it

Via Vittorio Veneto

Albani, 45 via Adda. 157 rooms from, €150 to €250 s/d/t. Extra bed €52.
Modern hotel in a wonderful location overlooking the park of the Villa Albani and close to the via Veneto. Modern amenities, spacious comfort, courteous and efficient service. Full air conditioning, internet links and fitness centre.

Phone:	06 849 91
Email:	hotelalbani@flashnet.it
Internet:	www.hotelalbani.it

Hotels: Centro Storico (cont)

Fenix, 5 viale Gorizia.
73 rooms from, €95 to €190 s/d/t. €170 to €210 tpl.
Situated a little way from the hustle and bustle of the main tourist sights but an easy stroll to via Veneto and the gardens of the Villa Torlonia. The hotel is tastefully furnished and there is an internal courtyard garden.

Phone:	06 854 0741
Email:	info@fenixhotel.it
Internet:	www.fenixhotel.it

Forums

Hotel Duca d'Alba, 14, via Leonina.
30 rooms from, €100 to €190 d/t.
Family-run business which has recently been renovated to offer comfortable, classically furnished bedrooms. The quarter is well served for historical interest (the Forums and the Colosseum are nearby) and for pleasant bars and restaurants.

Phone:	06 484 471
Email:	info@hotelducadalba.com
Internet:	www.hotelducadalba.com

Hotel Antica Locanda, 84, via del Boschetto.
33 rooms, from €105 to €210 s/d/t. Extra bed €30.
A pleasant and comfortable hotel close to Santa Maria Maggiore. The rooms are tastefully decorated, service is warm and courteous. There is a terrace for a breath of Roman air and a cosy breakfast room / bar.

Phone:	06 484894
Email:	info@antica-locanda.com
Internet:	www.antica-locanda.com

Hotel Madrid, 93-95 via Mario de'Fiori.
26 rooms from, €160 to €220 s/d/t. €235 to €275 tpl.
A comfortable spot ideally located for culture (as the name suggests, it is close to the Spanish Steps), shopping - the via dei Condotti and the via Frattina – are very near. Hotel is surrounded by good bars and restaurants.

Phone:	06 699 1510
Email:	info@hotelmadridroma.com
Internet:	www.hotelmadridroma.com

Forum society: Trajan's column dominates the ancient Roman Forum

Nerva, 3-4 via Tor de' Conti.
19 rooms, from €110 to €220 s/d/t. Extra bed €35 or €45.
Some of the Nerva's walls and foundations date from the 1500s, just a few steps steps from the Roman Forum, this is a family-run hotel in a quiet cobbled side street close to the piazza Venezia. Wood and terracotta tiles and some guest rooms retain the original ceiling beams. You might be reassured to learn that the rooms are soundproofed.

Phone:	06 678 1835
Email:	info@hotelnerva.com
Internet:	www.hotelnerva.com

Pace Elvezia, 104, via IV novembre.
77 rooms from, €150 to €220 s/d/t. €105- €130 s.
Overlooking Piazza Venezia and just a few minutes walk to the historic sites and the shops on the via del Corso. Comfort combined with courteous and efficient service at reasonable prices. Rooms tastefully decorated and furnished. Small terrace with view of the monument to Vittorio Emmanuelli and the Forums.

Phone:	06 868 00116
Email:	info@leonardihotels.com
Internet:	www.leonardihotels.com

BUDGET

Campo de'Fiori

Pomezia, 12-13 via dei Chiavari.
24 rooms from, €90 to €125 s/d/t.
Pleasant, family-run establishment in a lively, very Roman street (lots of small shops, bakeries, cafés) between the Campo de'Fiori and the Largo Torre Argentina. Clean, comfortable rooms and a friendly, hospitable atmosphere.

Phone:	06 686 1371
Email:	h.pomezia@libero.it

Hotel Arenula, 47 via Santa Maria de Calderari.
50 rooms from, €70 to €125 s/d/t. Extra bed €21.
Recently renovated family-run hotel near the via Arenula, linking the historic and lively largo Torre Argentina with ponte Garibaldi across the Tiber to the happening Trastavere quarter. Good location, good value for money. Friendly, helpful service.

Phone:	06 687 9454
Email:	hotel.arenula@flashnet.it
Internet:	www.hotelarenula.com

Santa Maria Maggiore

Saturnia, 4-6, via Ruinaglia.
16 rooms from, €65 to €128 s/d/t.
Good value, basic, family-run accommodation. The hotel's attraction is its location in the lively via Cavour area and its closeness to the Stazione Termini – the hub of the city's transport system. Easy walk to the Imperial Forums.

Phone:	06 482 8499 / 06 484 609
Email:	info@hotelsaturnia.net
Internet:	www.hotelsaturnia.net

Verona, 154, via Santa Maria Maggiore.
34 rooms from, €110 to €130 d/t.
Reasonable comfort close to the sites of Imperial Rome in a recently renovated family run hotel. Pleasant courtyard-garden with palm trees.

Phone:	06 487 1244
Email:	veronaht@tin.it
Internet:	www.hotelverona-roma.com

Hotels (cont)

Hotel Igea, 97 via Principe Amedeo.
42 rooms from, €50 to €150 s/d/t. €90 to €165 tpl.
Clean, comfortable family-run establishment. Basic but the welcome is warm and there is easy access to the rest of the city via the nearby Stazione Termini.

Phone:	06 446 6913
Email:	info@igearoma.com
Internet:	www.igearoma.com

Hotel Canova, 10 via Urbana. 1
5 rooms from, €90 to €120 d/t.
Cheap and cheery hotel close to the lively via Cavour. Lots of bars, restaurants and cafés close by with easy access to the rest of the city's attractions.

Phone:	06 487 3314
Email:	h.canova@tiscalinet.it
Internet:	www.canovahotelroma.it

VATICAN & PRATI

BARS

COCKTAIL BARS

Hemingway, 16 via Tunisi.
On two floors. Dark wood and leather armchairs abound. Drink, eat, smoke (there is a splendid cigar club on the ground floor), listen to music or do them all at once. Live music on Tuesday and Friday, background or DJ on other days.

Phone:	06 390 31046

Morrison's, 88 via E Q Visconti.
All things to all men (and women). First a coffee shop and tearoom, later, as the day progresses, a diner and restaurant which proposes simple pub grub or pasta dishes. For drinkers, draught beers, Italian wines and a good selection of whiskies. The happy hour goes on every day till 10pm which ensures a convivial atmosphere.

Phone:	06 322 2265

LIVE MUSIC

The Place, 27 via Alberico.
American style bar, an elegant and welcoming corner of New York in Rome. There is live music six nights a week and The Place has become renowned for offering some of the best jazz, funk, latin and R'n'B in the city.

Phone:	06 682 15214

RESTAURANTS

MEDITERRANEAN

L'Arcangelo, 59-61 via Giuseppe Giocchino Belli. €45.
Classy establishment in the style of a 1950's trattoria offering classic Mediterranean dishes cooked with care and some original touches. Try the seafood, marinated pumpkin and capers, lamb with a potato and chilli sauce. Excellent cheeseboard, some fine desserts (the caramelised pears are worth a stab) and a large (over 300 labels) wine list. Smoking allowed after 2.30pm and 10.30pm.

Phone:	06 321 0992

TRADITIONAL

La Veranda dell'Hotel Columbus, 73 borgo Santo Spirito. €60.
Refined, elegant establishment near St Peter's. Discreet, professional service with a well-balanced menu. Interesting internal garden which is lit at night. The dining room is a spectacular frescoed affair, so the dilemma is whether to sit inside or outside. The chef offers modern classics and historical dishes, such as a 17th-century recipe for sea bream, baked in an almond crust. Reservations essential.

Phone:	06 687 2973

INTERNATIONAL

La Pergola at the Hotel Cavalieri Hilton, 101 via Cadlolo. €80.

Mediterranean alta cucina (haute cuicsine). High above the city just north-west of the Vatican with spectacular views, this is Rome's most renowned restaurant – the only one to have been awarded 2 Michelin Stars (there are no 3 Stars in the city). As you would expect for such a rating, there is a sophisticated, refined atmosphere, and excellent service. The signature dishes include a carpaccio of sea-bass with Mediterranean vegetables, veal fillet in a vanilla sauce with a purée of squash. The desserts, particularly the chocolate variations, are pure, wicked delight. Two tasting menus are suggested; five courses for €130 or the seven courses for €145. Ther is an excellent and comprehensive list of wines. All this is enhanced by stunning panoramic views over the Eternal City.

Phone:	06 350 9221
Internet:	www.rome.hilton.com

Taverna Angelica, 6 piazza Amerigo Capponi. €35. Creative.

About the only class act in the area surrounding St. Peter's Basilica. Candle lit in the evening, the service is punctilious but discreet. There are only 20 seats available, which allows the chef to give full attention to each dish, and it shows. Recommended dishes include the lentil soup with pigeon breast, chickpeas with a pecorino fondue, and breast of duck in balsamic vinegar. Being so good but so small, reservations essential.

Phone:	06 687 4514

HOTELS

LUXURY

Dei Consoli, 2D via Varrone. 28 rooms from, €200 to €290 s/d/t.

A blend of Empire style decor with 21st century comforts makes this a pleasant base to explore the smart Prati quarter (excellent shopping) and the neighbouring Vatican City.

Phone:	06 688 92972
Email:	info@hoteldeiconsoli.com
Internet:	www.hoteldeiconsoli.com

Cicerone Hotel, 55c via Cicerone.
302 rooms. Rack rates €253 s, €310 d/t.

All is done with a certain style and taste. Located in a quiet area which boasts several stylish restaurants, close to the Vatican, high quality shops and just a short trip to the centro storico of Rome.

Phone:	06 3576
Email:	info@ciceronehotel.com
Internet:	www.ciceronehotel.com

Cavalieri Hilton, 101 via Cadlolo.
371 rooms from, €865 to €920 d/t.

High luxury, excellent service and calm – the Cavalieri is on the hill above the Vatican. You can even browse through their private art collection, for that touch of exra class and culture. Il Giardino dell'Uliveto restaurant in the hotel's park offers dining, with piano, next to the pool. Also attached is the La Pergola restaurant, (see above). There is a fabulous view over the Eternal City from the sun terrace, a great place for a sundowner.

Phone:	06 35091
Email:	concierge.rome@hilton.com
Internet:	www.cavalieri-hilton.it

MODERATELY PRICED

Hotel Arcangelo, 15 via Boezia.
33 rooms from, €110 to €215 s/d/t. €200 to €235 tpl. Extra bed €24.
Charming hotel housed in a converted early 20th century building. Features include a roof garden with a wonderful view of the dome of St Peter's Basilica and a charming wood panelled bar. Close to the Vatican, the shopping of the Prati district and easy access to the sights of the centro storico. Ten minutes walk from the Piazza Novona and the Spanish Steps.

Phone:	06 687 4143
Email:	hotel.arcangelo@travel.it
Internet:	www.travel.it/roma/arcangelo

ISA Hotel, 39 via Cicerone.
42 rooms from, €170 to €200 d/t.
A blend of ancient and modern. Antique furniture and frescoes depicting Ancient Rome adorn the public parts of the hotel and contrast with the contemporary decor and comfort in the bedrooms. Friendly hotel with a terrace offering a great view of the dome of nearby St Peter's.

Phone:	06 321 2610
Email:	info@hotelisa@travel.it
Internet:	www.hotelisa.com

Grand Hotel Olimpic, 2a via Properzio.
51 rooms, from €120 d/t. (Prices depend on dates and availability).
This is an elegant and luxurious hotel, offering a refined atmosphere and high quality service. The location between the piazza del Risorgimento (close to the Vatican Museum) and the piazza del Popolo is excellent. The surrounding streets are generally quiet and offer some pleasant restaurants and bars. The local shopping possibilities are good with some high-class designers of both clothing and jewellery to be found in many of the by-ways near the hotel. Very good value for money.

Phone:	06 689 6650 / 06 689 6652
Email:	info@aurumhotels.it
Internet:	www.aurumhotels.it

Star Hotel Michelangelo, 14 via della Stazione di San Pietro.
171 rooms from, €90 to €330 s/d/t.
Close to St Peter's offering a good level of comfort and modern amenities. The bedrooms, public areas and restaurant are decorated in a sober, classical style which is reflected in the efficient and courteous service.

Phone:	06 398 739
Email:	michelangelo.rm@starhotels.it
Internet:	www.starhotels.com

FLAMINIO

BARS

WINE BARS

La Glissade, 3a via Cinabue.
Bistro in the style of old Montmartre created by three friends whose passion for dance is reflected in the name of the café, the piano and images of ballet stars. There is a small selection of wines to accompany savoury country tarts, cured meats and other cold dishes. The desserts are very good.

Phone:	06 360 03594

BRITISH/IRISH PUBS

Kilmoon Pub, 2 via G.B. Tiepolo.

The ground floor is more in a wine-bar style while above it is an Irish theme pub with a screen for music, videos and sport. Simple food is available; panini, salads, crepes, and unlimited crisps. Quite close to the Stadio Flaminio, so a place to watch the game if you don't fancy a loose maul at the ground.

Phone:	06 321 5457

RESTAURANTS

REGIONAL ITALIAN

L'Ortica, 573 via Flaminia Vecchia. €45.

Fine, atmospheric restaurant which specialises in slightly revamped Neapolitan country recipes. Friendly service and a very good wine list with a decent selection of wines by the glass. Rustic and convivial.

Phone:	06 333 8709

TRADITIONAL

Un Cochon dans Mon Jardin, 30 via Giovanni Antonelli. €35.

The name might suggest that this is a French establishment but the cooking is firmly Italian, (the meat dishes are a strong point), in a friendly, informal atmosphere. Slightly away from the city centre, the Cochon is quite close to the stadium and so convenient for either pre- or post-match solids.

Phone:	06 807 3968

Hostaria Natalino e Maurizio, 115 Corso di Francia. €40.

Located outside the city, not far from the rugby ground and convenient as a meeting point before or after the match. This is a real locals' restaurant. High quality meat and fish cooked with care and one of the best places for such basic staples as spaghetti carbonara in Rome. Good wine list.

Phone:	06 333 2730

Duke's, 200 viale Parioli. €45.

A trendy, Californian-style restaurant a little out of town. There is an excellent cocktail bar in which to acclimatise before settling down to a sturdy supper (the fish dishes are very good and specialities include delicate palate ticklers such as rib-eye steak and beef rib marinated in five herbs).

Phone:	06 806 62455

T-Bone Station, 525-7 via Flaminia Vecchia. €30.

Not the place for our carbonara expert, this is old-fashioned steakhouse fare: burgers, steaks, spare-ribs in a trendy, upbeat atmosphere. You could almost be in the USA the way it feels here, so perhaps it is best avoided. Satellite TV, music, cheerful service. Good idea to reserve.

Phone:	06 333 3297

HOTELS

LUXURY

Duke Hotel, 69 via Archimede. 85 rooms from, €220 to €430 s/d/t.

Luxurious hotel just outside the city centre close to the Galleria Borghese, in the embassy area. The hotel lives up to its name, recreating with enthusiasm the comfort and refinement of an English gentleman's club. Afternoon tea is served in front of an open fire. All mod cons, however.

Phone:	06 367 221
Email:	theduke@thedukehotel.com
Internet:	www.thedukehotel.com

MODERATELY PRICED

Hotel Astrid, 4 Largo Antonio Sarti. 48 rooms from, €120 to €160 s/d/t.
Great spot, just 300m from the Stadio Flaminio. The Astrid, which overlooks the Tiber, offers a good degree of comfort at reasonable prices – like the rest of the city these remain unchanged for rugby international weekends but given the location this fairmindedness is admirable and could be copied elsewhere. There are some interesting restaurants nearby or you could take a tram to the piazza del Popolo, about a mile along the via Flaminia.

Phone:	06 323 6371
Email:	info@hotelastrid.com
Internet:	www.astridhotelrome.it

TRASTEVERE

BARS

WINE BARS

In Vino Veritas Art Bar, 2a via Garibaldi. Pleasant address in the increasingly fashionable Trastavere quarter. Decorated in a minimalist style with low tables and leather covered benches. There is an excellent list of Italian wines to accompany a fine selection of cheeses. Regular live music or DJ.

Phone:	339 446 3371

Il Cantiniere di Santa Dorotea, 9 via Santa Dorotea. A well established wine bar with over 800 labels. The proprietor is happy to guide you through the range. Top wines plus great value produce from less known but talented growers, many of which are available by the glass.

Phone:	06 581 9025

BRITISH / IRISH PUBS

The Dog and the Duck, 70 via della Luce.
A good address in the happening Trastavere quarter offering pub grub, fine single malt whiskies and draught Guinness, Oyster Stout, Young's Double Chocolate and Belgian Tripel Carmeliet. The Dog and Duck is also a bookshop, a sports centre (darts and backgammon) and a meeting place for bikers.

Phone:	339 158 3525

COCKTAIL BARS

Oxygen, 63 vicolo del Bologna.
Two small rooms in contemporary, high-tech style with background chill-out music. Over 70 cocktails as well as the cult beer "Menabrea".

Phone:	328 237 4105

Roma Caput Mundi, 64 via Lucio Manara.
Young clientele. Beer is on offer but the house speciality is the large selection of classic cocktails as well as the ones invented on the spot by the bar staff. TV for national and international sport.

Phone:	06 581 3680

Antilia, 1 via della Scala.
On two floors, one of which is entirely devoted to live music. The decor may be sober but there is no obligation for you to be. Good selection of Italian wines and draught lagers. Happy hour every day till 9pm.

Phone:	06 583 35788

COFFEE SHOPS

Caffè Giolitti, 40 via degli Uffici del Vaticano.
Large salon in the belle epoque style welcomes a lively mix of tourists, office workers and political animals from the Italian parliament just a few steps away in the palazzo di Montecitorio. Elegant service, excellent coffee and pastries.
La Casa del Caffè Tazza d'Oro, 84, via degli Orfani.
Open since 1946, specialises in high quality coffees, roasted on the premises. A wonderfully lively place. This is the place for the serious coffee drinker. Always busy, it is a great place to observe Roman life. You can recreate this at home by internet bean ordering.

Internet:	www.tazzadorocoffeeshop.com

Il Gelato di San Crispino, 42 via della Panetteria.
Close to the Trevi Fountain, this is one of the world's most celebrated ice-cream houses.
Babington's, 23 piazza di Spagna.
One of the more elegant tearooms in Rome, its exclusiveness is reflected in the prices. A haven from the crowds around the Spanish Steps and the exhaustion of decision making in the designer shops of the via dei Condotti. All day brunch.
La Bouvette, 47 via Vittoria.
Elegant coffee shop and tearoom. Excellent buffet breakfast and good lunch.
Cioccolati, 36 via Marianna Dionigi, Prati.
Close to the piazza Cavour in the Prati quarter, this is the place for the true lover of chocolate. The very highest quality is available.
Pellacchia, 103-107 via Cola di Renzo, Prati.
Historic Roman ice-cream parlour to which people have flocked since its opening in 1900. Select from over 25 different flavours and linger at one of the attractive terrace tables.

RESTAURANTS

MODERN ROMAN

Spirito di Vino, 31 via dei Genovesi/13 vicolo dell'Atleta. €45.
Peaceful atmosphere, the service is efficient, courteous and extremely helpful. The cooking takes traditional Roman dishes onto a much higher plain than can be found in most local trattoria though the bill does not reflect this. For each course there is a selection of seven or eight dishes and making a choice is the difficult part. Outstanding, however, is the tuna with spaghetti delicately perfumed with lemon and the pork fillet "alla Mazio", a recipe apparently created by one of Julius Caesar's cooks. The desserts are excellent, as is the 800-strong wine list, through which you are expertly and patiently led by Francesco, the son of the proprietors.

Phone:	06 58 9 6689

ROMAN

Da Enzo, 29 via dei Vascellari. €20
Popular with politicians and journalists, it is therefore surprising to discover that the prices are within everyone's reach. Here you will find top class cooking of traditional local dishes; carbonara, oxtail, saltimbocca, alongside a good selection of non-Roman dishes, all produced and served in a convivial, elbow-to-elbow atmosphere with copious portions and robust local house wines. The dessert menu is studded with classics. The wine choice is pretty much restricted to the house wines.

Phone:	06 581 8355

Fidelio, 5-7 via de' Stefaneschi. €20.
Wonderfully atmospheric wine bar and restaurant in a backstreet of the Trastavere. The regular choice of traditional Roman dishes is augmented each week by a menu which presents specialities of a different Italian region accompanied by wines of the same area. Very warm welcome to everyone.
L'Assinocotto, 48 via dei Vascellari. €45.
Warm and welcoming restaurant in the heart of Trastavere. There are some interesting takes on traditional Roman dishes. The wine list is good without being overly long, with some available by the glass.

Phone:	06 589 8985

HOTELS

MODERATELY PRICED

Santa Maria, 2 vicolo del Piede.
20 rooms from, €135 to €210 s/d/t. €200 to €250 tpl. €220 to €280 quad.
A tranquil haven close to the beautiful church of Santa Maria di Trastavere. Cosy bedrooms and a warm welcome from courteous and efficient staff. Wonderful location in the very Roman Trastavere quarter.

Phone:	06 589 4626
Email:	info@hotelsantamaria.info
Internet:	www.hotelsantamaria.info

River fun: You sleep by day, party by night on the banks of the Tiber.

San Francesco, 7 via Jacopa de'Settesoli. 24 rooms from, €110 to €205 s/d/t. €180 to €230 tpl.
Once a hostel for the adjoining church, now a completely renovated hotel. The bedrooms are comfortable and well equipped.

Phone:	06 583 00051
Email:	hotelsanfrancesco@tin.it
Internet:	www.hotelsanfrancesco.net

BUDGET

Hotel Cisterna, 7-9 via della Cisterna.
19 rooms from, €90 to €130 s/d/t.
Reasonable level of comfort at a reasonable price. The attraction is the location in the Trastavere quarter, which, while retaining its popular, working-class atmosphere, is now becoming one of the trendiest areas of Rome.

Phone:	06 581 7212 / 06 588 1852
Email:	prenotazioni@cisternahotel.it
Internet:	www.cisternahotel.it

Domus Tiberina, 37 via in Piscinula.
10 rooms from, €95 to €140 s/d/t. €130 to €180 tpl. €170 to €250 quad. Extra bed €30.
The Trastavere quarter is not well endowed with hotels. The Domus Tiberina, close to the Tiber, is more than serviceable but its main attraction, it has to be said, is its location. There is a huge choice of bars, cafés and restaurants on the door step. In summer especially, Trastavere sleeps by day and parties by night.

Phone:	06 580 3033
Email:	info@domustiberina.com
Internet:	www.domustiberina.com

Trastavere House, 7 vicolo del Buco.
9 rooms from, €90 s, €105 d/t.
Very quaint setting in a converted 18th century palazzo in a tiny cobbled backstreet in the heart of Trastavere. Reasonable comfort, the breakfast is extra and best avoided, but there are plenty of fine cafés close by. Friendly service.

Phone:	06 588 3774
Email:	trastaverehouse@hotmail.com

EDGE OF THE CITY
RESTAURANTS
ROMAN
Da Ettore, 127 Corso Trieste. €30.
North of the city centre. Close to the Villa Borghese, this is a great place for a good old-fashioned lingering Roman feast cooked with impeccable care. Good antipasti with combinations of cheese, cured hams and artichokes "alla Romana" to the fore. Rigatoni alla carbonara, veal in a tuna fish sauce, meat balls and roulades are delicious (and copious) mains. If particularly hungry, fit in the house's delicious mashed or roast potatoes and finish with a great homemade dessert, panna cotta with chocolate slithers, or the honey pie. Small, but adequate, wine list.

Phone:	06 855 4323

CLASSIC ITALIAN
Giuda Ballerino, 135 via Marco Valerio Corvo. €60 South-west of the city centre. This restaurant has the reputation of being one of Rome's finest. Situated a little away from the city centre in the Tuscolano quarter close to the Lucio Sestio metro station. Service and comfort are excellent, and the wine is expertly matched to the food. Outstanding dishes include a soup, Nonna Papera, based on black chick peas from Alta Tuscia; medallions of sausage and venison with turnip tops; suckling pig stuffed with plums. Wide ranging list of beers, liqueurs, coffees and cigars. Smoking is allowed after 10.30 provided everyone in the room has finished eating. Prices are reasonable given the quality of the food. There are two tasting menus at €46, one offering fish, the other meat dishes.

Phone:	06 715 84807

MEDITERRANEAN
Capo Boi, 80 via Arno. €45. North of city centre.
Mainly fish and seafood dishes cooked confidently. The desserts are good but the wine list is slightly disappointing. Reservation advisable.

Phone:	06 841 5535

Il Leonardo, 29 via Catania. €55.
High class, elegant establishment, most suitable for intimate tête-à-tête dining. Top quality ingredients prepared with assured technique and presented imaginatively. The desserts are superb and the wine list high quality. Located close to the Piazzale delle Provincie, north-west of the city centre.

Phone:	06 442 33705

CREATIVE
Kitchen, 3 via dei Conciatori. €40. Ostiense quarter. South of city centre.
Chic, minimalist, "New York" setting. Very high quality ingredients prepared with a strong Mediterranean leaning. More traditionally, the artisanal salamis and cheeses are excellent and the wine list is good.

STEAK HOUSE
I Butteri, 28/29 piazza Regina Margherita. €30. North of the city centre. Bright, sunny restaurant dominating one corner of the piazza Margherita. Good quality wood grilled meats and pizzas alongside some sound Tuscan antipasti and mains well accompanied by a fine light house red or a good Chianti.

Phone:	06 854 8130

Beef, 54-56 via Basento. €35. Steak house. The carnivore's delight. High quality grilled meats, some slow cooked, good anti-pasti and salads, excellent desserts. The wine list is rather limited but the decor is very pleasant. Close to the Galleria Borghese, to the north of the city centre.

Phone:	06 853 05130

BATH

Founded	1865
Stadium	The Recreation Ground Spring Gardens, Bath, BA2 6PW, 01225 469230
Admin	11 Argyle Street, Bath, BA2 4BQ
Capacity	9,980
Tel	01225 32 52 00
Fax	01225 32 52 01
Website	www.bathrugby.com
Telephone for tickets	0871 721 1865
Club shop	1 Argyle Street, Bath, BA2 4AB
Tel	01225 311 950
Web	www.bathrugby.com
Email	shop@bathrugby.com
Colours	Black, sky blue and white hoops.
Coaches	John Connolly, Mike Foley
Club captain	Steve Borthwick

EUROPEAN RUGBY CUP

ERC 2004/5 Eliminated at pool stage. In Pool 2 with Bourgoin, Leinster and Treviso. Leinster qualified.

How qualified for 2005/6: 6th in English Premiership.

ERC 2005/6: Pool 5: with Bourgoin, Leinster, Glasgow.

FIXTURES

(Consult press for changes and for kick-off times).

Saturday 22nd October 2005 v Leinster	AWAY	17.15
Saturday 29th October 2005 v Bourgoin	HOME	14.15
Saturday 10th December 2005 v Glasgow	HOME	14.15
16/17/18 December 2005 v Glasgow	AWAY	
13/14/15 January 2006 v Bourgoin	AWAY	
20/21/22 January 2006 v Leinster	HOME	

ERC RECORD

Participations 6	Matches 39	Won 28	Lost 11	Drawn 0

REACHING THE CITY

AIR

To Bristol:

British Airways from Edinburgh and Glasgow.

Easyjet from Edinburgh, Glasgow, Belfast, Newcastle, Geneva and Rome Ciampino. Ryanair from Dublin and Shannon.

Aer Lingus from Dublin.

RAIL

Bath Spa station is just a 5 minute walk from the Recreation Ground. It is connected to London and the South West by Intercity services. Bath also has direct rail links to Cardiff, Salisbury and Southampton. Regular services to Bristol Temple Meads connect with services to Birmingham and the Midlands. National Rail enquiries: 08457 48 49 50. (www.nationalrail.co.uk)

REACHING THE GROUND

RAIL

Straight out of the station and cross the road into Manvers Street. Go past the police station on your right then turn right at the traffic lights. Walk over the bridge (you will see the stadium to your left). On the far side of the bridge, go down a covered spiral staircase to the river bank. Walk along the river to the Recreation Ground.

ROAD

The M4 motorway joins Bath to London in the east and Wales in the west. The M5 links the city with the Midlands to the north, with Somerset, Devon and Cornwall to the south. Bath is best accessed from J18 of the M4.

You are asked to use Bath's Park & Ride facilities wherever possible. In addition to Lambridge Park & Ride (see below) there are several Council run Park & Ride sites serving Bath City Centre which is just a few minutes walk from The Recreation Ground. Please note that, as these facilities are not run by Bath Rugby, they can accept no responsibility for them or information relating to them.

To Lambridge Park & Ride: From J18 of the M4 follow the A46 to Bath, then follow the signs for the town centre on the A4. After the first set of traffic lights the Lambridge Park & Ride (Bath Rugby's training ground) is immediately on your left. The Park & Ride is open for all 1st XV weekend fixtures.

To Bath city centre: Follow directions to Lambridge Park & Ride but then continue on the A4. Now follow the map provided and use the parking located around the city centre. Please note that an experimental access system has been implemented recently which restricts access through the centre itself. Parking is at a premium and is not readily available at busy periods.

TOURIST OFFICE

(Consult for rugby weekend breaks)

Bath Tourist Information Centre, Abbey Chambers, Abbey Churchyard, Bath, BA1 1LY. Information Line: 0906 711 2000 (calls cost 50p/min). Overseas Callers Line: + 44 870 444 6442 tourism@bathtourism.co.uk www.visitbath.co.uk

HOTELS

Royal Crescent, 16 Royal Crescent, Bath, BA1 2LS. 34 rooms, from £199 s/d/t. 01225 823333 reservations@royalcrescent.co.uk www.royalcrescent.co.uk

Bath Priory, Weston Rd, Bath, BA1 2XT. 28 rooms, from £245 s/d/t.

01225 331 922 mail@thebathpriory.co.uk www.thebathpriory.co.uk

The Francis on the Square, Queen Sq, Bath BA1 2HH. 95 rooms, from £120 s/d/t.

0870 400 8223 francis@macdonald-hotels.co.uk www.thefrancishotel.co.uk

County, 18-19 Pulteney Rd, Bath, BA2 4EZ. 22 rooms, from £75 s, £110 d/t.

01225 425003 reservations@county-hotel.co.uk www.county-hotel.co.uk

Express by Holiday Inn, Lower Bristol Rd, Brougham Hayes, Bath BA2 2BV.

126 rooms, from £89 s/d/t. 0870 444 2792 bath@ebhi-fsnet.co.uk

BIARRITZ

Founded	1902
Stadium	Aquiléra
Address	Parc des Sports Aguiléra, Rue Cino Del Duca, 64200, Biarritz
Capacity	12,667
Website	www.bo-pb.com
Switchboard	05 59 01 64 60
Fax	05 59 01 64 63

Biarritz (cont)

Telephone for tickets	05 59 01 61 46
Internet tickets	www.billeterie.bo-pb.com
Club shop	Club House Aguiléra, Parc des Sports d'Aguiléra, 64200, Biarritz
Tel	05 59 01 64 71
Fax	05 59 01 64 63
Web	www.bo-pb.com
Colours	Red and white
Coaches	Patrice Lagisquet and Jacques Delmas
Club captain	Thomas Lièvremont

FIXTURES

Ticket office is open from Monday to Friday from **11.00** to **13.00** and from **15.30** till **18.30** and on match days from two hours before kick-off.

Tickets generally go on sale the Monday before the match.

Sunday 23rd October 2005 v Saracens	AWAY	15.00
Saturday 29th October 2005 v Ulster	HOME	16.00
Sunday 11th December 2005 v Trevise	HOME	16.00
16/17/18 December 2005 v Trevise	AWAY	
13/14/15 January 2006 v Ulster	AWAY	
20/21/22 January 2006 v Saracens	HOME	

ERC RECORD

Participations 5	Matches 36	Won 21	Lost 14	Drawn 1

REACHING THE CITY

AIR

Biarritz International Airport, is a short distance from the city centre.

05 59 43 83 83 www.biarritz.aeroport.fr

Direct flights from GB and Ireland with **Ryanair** from Dublin and London Stansted. Ryanair also fly to Pau (about 120km from Biarritz) from London Stansted. Within France there are flights to Biarritz with **Air France** from Paris Charles-de-Gaulle, Paris Orly, Clermont-Ferrand, Lyon and Nice.

RAIL

Biarritz SNCF Station	05 59 50 83 07
SNCF telephone reservation service	08 92 35 35 35
SNCF website address	www.sncf.fr

ROAD

From Dax	N124 to the A63 then take Sortie 6 for Biarritz Centre
From Bordeaux	N10 then the A63 then take Sortie 6 for Biarritz Centre
From Spain	A63 to Sortie 4 for Biarritz Centre

BY SEA

If you don't fancy the drive or flying you can always take your chances on the Bay of Biscay. The closest port to Biarritz is Bilbao in northern Spain. There is a car ferry service to Bilbao with P&O. www.poferries.com

REACHING THE GROUND

From the city centre follow signs for Aguiléra. There is limited parking at the ground. In addition, there is some on-street parking.

TOURIST OFFICE

Office du Tourisme, Biarritz-Tourisme, Square d'Ixelles, 64200, Biarritz.
05 59 22 37 10

HOTELS

Du Palais, 1 avenue Imperatrice, 64, Biarritz.
132 rooms, from €360 s/d/t to €520.
05 59 41 64 00 reception@hotel-du-palais.com www.hotel-du-palais.com
Crowne Plaza, 1 carrefour Helianthe, 64, Biarritz.
150 rooms, from €290 s/d/t to €325.
05 59 01 13 13 reservations@cpbiarritz.fr www.crowneplaza.co.uk
Grand Hotel Mercure Regina, 52 avenue Imperatrice, 64, Biarritz.
58 rooms, from €110 to €362. H2050@accor-hotels.com www.accor-hotels.com
Windsor, Grande Plage, 64, Biarritz.
48 rooms, from €75 s/d/t to €150 s/d/t.
Hotelwindsor-biarritz@wanadoo.fr
Maitagaria, 34 avenue Carnot, 64 Biarritz.
17 rooms, from €55 s/d/t to €75.
www.hotel-maitagaria.com

BOURGOIN

Founded	1898
Stadium	Pierre-Rajon
Address	Avenue du Professeur Tixier, 38300 Bourgoin-Jallieu
Capacity	10,022
Admin	CS Bourgoin-Jallieu, 28, rue de la Liberté, BP 141 Bourgoin-Jallieu
Web	www.csbj-rugby.fr
Telephone for tickets	04 74 19 08 10
Internet tickets	www.francebillet.fr or www.ticketnet.fr
Club shop	Chalet du Stade, 28 rue de la Liberté, 38300, Bourgoin-Jallieu
Tel	04 74 19 08 13
Fax	04 74 19 03 01
Web	www.csbj-rugby.fr
Colours	Claret and Sky Blue
Coaches	Christophe Urios, Guy Tourlonnias
Club captain	Julien Frier

FIXTURES

Consult press for changes and for kick-off times.

Friday 21st October 2005 v Glasgow	HOME	20.30
Saturday 29th October 2005 v Bath	AWAY	14.15
Saturday 10th December 2005 v Leinster	AWAY	17.15
16/17/18 December 2005 v Leinster	HOME	
13/14/15 January 2006 v Bath	HOME	
20/21/22 January 2006 v Glasgow	AWAY	

The winner of each group qualifies for the quarter finals along with the two best second placed teams. Each qualifying club will be seeded according to results of its pool matches. The four top seeds will play their quarter final match at home.

Bourgoin (cont)

Quarter Finals	Saturday 1st April and Sunday 2nd April, 2006
Semi Finals	Saturday 22nd April and Sunday 23rd April, 2006.
Final	Saturday 20th May 2006 at the Millennium Stadium, Cardiff

Tickets are now on sale from www.ticketmaster.co.uk at £15, £25, £35 and £45

ERC RECORD

Participations 5	Matches 30	Won 9	Lost 21	Drawn 0

REACHING THE CITY

BY AIR

Fly to Lyon Saint-Exupéry from GB and Ireland.

British Airways	London Heathrow, Manchester, Birmingham
Air France	London Heathrow
Easyjet	London Stansted
Aer Lingus	Dublin

There are many flights from all over the UK and Ireland to Paris. There are direct flights to Lyon within France with Air France from Toulouse, Bordeaux, Nantes, Strasbourg. Lyon is 2 hours from central Paris (Gare de Lyon) by TGV.

There is a very infrequent bus service – 1460 - from Lyon Airport to Bourgoin-Jallieu. Otherwise, a taxi journey of about 20 minutes.

RAIL

Lyon is a hub of the French railway system – there are frequent TGV's from Marseille, Montpellier, Grenoble and Paris. There are regular services to Bourgoin-Jallieu from Grenoble and Lyon.

SNCF reservation service: 08 92 35 35 35 www.sncf.fr

ROAD

Bourgoin-Jallieu is situated 43km east of Lyon and 66km west of Grenoble. It is linked to these two cities by the A43 motorway. Take the exit signed "Bourgoin centre - Ruy-le Rivet" then follow the signs first for "Centre-Ville" then "Stade Pierre Rajon"

REACHING THE GROUND

15 minutes walk from the railway station. There is a bus service or local taxis. See above for driving directions.

TOURIST OFFICE

Office de Tourisme 1, place Carnot, 38300, Bourgoin-Jallieu.

04 74 93 47 50 ot@bourgoinjallieu.fr www.bourgoinjallieu.fr

HOTELS

Bourgouin-Jallieu is small, with little accommodation, so we have listed four large hotels in Lyon, 47km away, as well as some charming, but small, local inns.

L'Auberge, La Combe Les Eparres, (7km up the N85).
8 rooms, from €25 to €35 s/d/t
04 74 92 01 17

Hotel des Dauphins, 8 rue François Berrier, 38300, Domarin Bourgoin-Jallieu.
19 rooms, from €37 to €47
04 74 93 00 58 www.hoteldesdauphins.com

LYON

Villa Florentine, 25 Montee St-Barthelemy, 69005, Lyon.

20 rooms from €190 s/d/t.
Florentine@relaischateaux.com www.villaflorentine.com

Carlton, 4 Rue Jussieu, 69002 Lyon.
84 rooms, from €80 s/d/t (online deals cheapest).
H2950@accor.com www.mercure.com

La Residence, 18 Rue Victor Hugo, 69002 Lyon.
67 rooms, from €70
Hotel-la-residence@wanadoo.fr www.hotel-la-residence.com

CALVISANO

Founded	1927
Stadium	Centro Sportivo San Michele
Address	102, via San Michele, 25012 Calvisano (Breschia)
Capacity	3000
Website	www.calvisanorugby.it
Tel	030 968 012
Fax	030 968 519
Tickets	030 968 012
Colours	Black and yellow
Coaches	Andrea Cavinato, Deane McKinnel
Club captain	Maurizio Zaffiri

FIXTURES

Consult press for any changes and for kick-off times.

Saturday 22nd October 2005 v Perpignan	HOME	14.00
Saturday 29th October 2005 v Leeds	AWAY	20.00
Friday 09th December 2005 v Cardiff	HOME	14.00
16/17/18 December 2005 v Cardiff	AWAY	
13/14/15 January 2006 v Leeds	HOME	
20/21/22 January 2006 v Perpignan	AWAY	

ERC RECORD

Participations 4	Matches 24	Won 2	Lost 22	Drawn 0

REACHING THE CITY

AIR

Calvisano is a 45 minute drive from Bergamo Airport. This small hub is also known as Milan – Orio al Serio. The next nearest airport is Milan-Linate (1.5 hours away). Milan-Malpensa is two and a quarter hours. You can also fly direct to Brescia from Stansted. Brescia is a charming small town near the ground, with lots to offer.

To	Milan Linate
From	**GB & Ireland** with bmibaby from London Heathrow. With Easyjet from London Gatwick. With Alitalia from London Heathrow. Aer Lingus from Dublin
From	**France** with Air France from Paris CDG. With Alitalia from Paris CDG.

To	Milan Malpensa
From	**GB & Ireland** with BA from London Heathrow, Birmingham and Manchester. With Alitalia from London heathrow, Birmingham, Manchester and Dublin.

Calvisano (cont)

From	France with Air France from Toulouse, Clermont, Lyon, Marseille, Paris CDG and Paris Orly. With Alitalia from Toulouse, Lyon, Marseille, Paris CDG.

ROAD

Calvisano is in the south-eastern corner of the province of Brescia. Coming from the A4 Milan-Venice motorway, take the Brescia Est exit and follow the indications for Montichiari Airport. After the airport, take the turning for Mantua and this will bring you to Calvisano. If you are travelling on the A21 Piacenza-Brescia, it is best to take the Manerbio exit, and follow the State road 668 in the direction of Montichiari and you will find the turning for Calvisano.

RAIL

Change at Brescia on the Milan-Venice line. There are frequent local connections with Calvisano and the Centro Sportivo San Michele is only a few minutes' walk from the station.

TOURIST OFFICE

(Brescia), Corso Zanardelli 38, Brescia 25121
030 280 061 iat.brescia@tiscali.it www.quibrescia.it/entituristici

HOTELS

Calvisano is a small place with little in the way of accommodation so we have chosen five places in Brescia, the nearest sizable place 27km from the ground. There are lots of very fine restaurants. Check your Michelin guide.

Novotel Brescia 2, Via Pietro Nenni 22, 25124 Brescia.
120 rooms, from €130 s/d/t
030 242 5858 Novotel.brescia@accor-hotels.it www.accor-hotels.it

Park Hotel Ca' Noa, Via Triumplina 66, 25123 Brescia.
80 rooms, from €110 s/d/t
030 398 762 info@hotelcanoa.it www.hotelcanoa.it

Vittoria, Via Delle 10 Giornate 20, 25121 Brescia.
64 rooms, from €166 s. €214 d/t.
030 280 061 info@hotelvittoria.com www.hotelvittoria.com

Jolly Hotel Igea, Viale Stazione 15, 25122 Brescia.
87 rooms, from €150 s/d/t
030 44221 brescia@jollyhotels.it www.jollyhotels.it

Impero, Via Triumplina 6, 25123 Brescia.
22 rooms, from €62 s/d/t
030 381 483 algrillosnc@libero.it

CARDIFF BLUES

Founded	1876
Stadium	Cardiff Arms Park
Address	Westgate Street, Cardiff, CF10 1JA
Capacity	13,000
Switchboard	029 20 30 20 00
Fax	029 20 30 20 08
Web	www.cardiffblues.com
Tickets	029 2030 2030
Email for tickets	ticket.office@cardiffblues.com
Club shop	Cardiff Rugby Football Club Shop At Stadium
Tel	029 2030 2018
Web	www.cardiffblues.com

Colours	Navy blue and sky blue
Coaches	David Young, Geraint John, Chris Tombs
Club captain	Rhys Williams

FIXTURES
Consult press for changes and for kick-off times.

Saturday 22nd October 2005 v Leeds Tykes	HOME	13.00
Friday 28th October 2005 v Perpignan	AWAY	20.30
Friday 09th December 2005 v Calvisano	AWAY	14.00
16/17/18 December 2005 v Calvisano	HOME	
13/14/15 January 2006 v Perpignan	HOME	
20/21/22 January 2006 v Leeds Tykes	AWAY	

ERC RECORD

Participations 9	Matches 56	Won 25	Lost 29	Drawn 2

TRAVEL/HOTELS

Please refer to the chapter on Cardiff. Cardiff Arms Park is next to the Millennium Stadium on Westgate Street.

CASTRES

Founded	1906
Stadium	Stade Pierre Antoine
Address	Rue de Bisséous, 81100 CASTRES, France
Capacity	9,423
Website	www.castres-olympique.fr
Telephone for tickets	05 63 35 32 96
Fax	05 63 51 06 81
Club shop	205, avenue Général de Gaulle, 81100 Castres
Tel	05 63 35 32 96
Fax	05 63 35 49 37
Web	www.castres-olympique.fr
Colours	Royal Blue and White
Coaches	Laurent Seigne, Philippe Berot

FIXTURES
Consult press for changes and for kick-off times.

Saturday 22nd October 2005 v Newport-Gwent Dragons	HOME	18.15
Saturday 29th October 2005 v Munster	AWAY	17.15
Friday 09th December 2005 v Sale Sharks	HOME	20.30
16/17/18 December 2005 v Sale	AWAY	
13/14/15 January 2006 v Munster	HOME	
20/21/22 January 2006 v Newport	AWAY	

ERC RECORD

Matches 22	Won 11	Lost 10	Drawn 1

Castres (cont)

REACHING THE TOWN

AIR

From Britain and Ireland: Castres' closest international airport is Aéroport Toulouse-Blagnac, approximately 80km (50 miles) west of Castres.
05 61 71 11 1 www.toulouse.aeroport.fr

You can fly direct to Toulouse from London Gatwick with BA, and Easyjet, and from Bristol and Birmingham with British European.

Carcassonne is 70km south of Castres. Ryanair fly into Carcassonne airport from Dublin, Liverpool and Stansted. Ryanair also fly to Montpellier (180km from Castres) and Perpignan (170km to Castres) from London Stansted. www.ryanair.com

Internal – France: There are direct flights to Castres from Paris and Lyon.

RAIL

Castres has a railway station but is not particularly accessible from mainline stations. The trip from Toulouse takes about 1¼ hours, from Carcassonne or Montpellier you have to travel via Toulouse, and from Paris around 7 hours. For rail information, call 0892 35 35 35 from inside France, the SNCF website www.sncf.fr

All Castres trains arrive and depart from Castres SNCF 05 63 71 37 00

ROAD

For a route planner try www.viamichelin.com. It is 50 miles due west of Toulouse along the N126.

For Motorway conditions (from inside France) call 0892 681 077

TOURIST OFFICE

3 rue Milhau Ducommun, 81100 Castres, France. 05 63 62 63 62
otcastres@wanadoo.fr

HOTELS

Inter-Hotel Imotel, 11 rue Le Chatelier, 81100 Castres.
Double room from €49.
05 63 59 82 99 hi8102@inter-hotel.com

Le Miredames, 1-3 rue Roger Salengro, 81100 Castres.
Double room €64 maximum.
05 63 71 38 18

L'Occitan, 201 avenue Général de Gaulle, 81100 Castres.
Double room €89 maximum.
05 63 35 34 20

Best Western Montagne-Noire, 29 avenue de Castres, 81090 Laguarrigue.
05 63 35 52 00 contact@lamontagnenoire.com

Renaissance, 17 rue Victor Hugo, 81100 Castres.
Double room €95 maximum.
05 63 59 30 42 hotel-renaissance.europe@wanadoo.fr

CLERMONT-AUVERGNE

Founded	1911
Stadium	Stade Marcel Michelin
Address	Parc des Sports Marcel-Michelin, 35 Rue du Clos Four, 63100 Clermont-Ferrand, France
Capacity	13,000
Website	www.asm-rugby.com
Tel	04 73 30 48 66

Fax	04 73 30 20 41
Tickets	0810 55 30 74
Internet tickets	www.francebillet.com www.ticketnet.fr
Club shop	Espace Jaune et Bleu, Parc des Sports Marcel-Michelin, Avenue de la République, 63100 Clermont-Ferrand
Tel	04 73 14 60 26
Web	www.asm-rugby.com
Colours	Yellow and Blue
Coach	Jean Pierre Laparra
Club captain	Pierre Mignoni

FIXTURES

Consult press for changes and for kick-off times.

Saturday 22nd October 2005 v Leicester Tigers	AWAY	15.00
Sunday 30th October 2005 v Neath-Swansea Ospreys	HOME	16.00
Saturday 10th December 2005 v Stade Français	HOME	16.00
16/17/18 December 2005 v Stade Français	AWAY	
13/14/15 January 2006 v Neat-Swansea Ospreys	AWAY	
20/21/22 January 2006 v Leicester Tigers	HOME	

ERC RECORD

Participations 3	Matches 20	Won 10	Lost 9	Drawn 1

REACHING THE CITY

AIR

Clermont-Ferrand-Auvergne. 04 73 62 71 00

There are no direct regular flights from GB and Ireland. You would have to transfer at Paris Charles-de-Gaulle or Paris Orly. Internal flights with Air France from Lyon, Marseille, Nice, Montpellier, Toulouse, Biarritz, Paris CDG and Paris Orly. From Italy with Air France from Milan Malpensa.

RAIL

It is not recommended to travel to Clermont-Ferrand by train. Most services are irregular and slow, there being no TGV line to Clermont-Ferrand. However, if you must make the attempt ...

From Paris	Direct service from the Gare de Lyon or via Moulins.
From Montpellier	via Béziers or Lyon Part-Dieu.
From Lyon	Direct service
From Bordeaux	Direct service or via St-Germain-des-Fosses
From Toulouse	Direct service or via Arvant or Brive.

ROAD

From Paris: A10 then A71 to Clermont-Ferrand. Leave the motorway at Clermond-Ferrand-Nord, then 150 m after the "motorway ends" sign you enter Clermont-Ferrand.

From Montpellier: A75 to Clermont-Ferrand then continue on A710/E70 for 6 km then follow Clermont-Ferrand, Limoges on the A710W for 2.5 km then 150 m after the "motorway ends" sign you enter Clermont-Ferrand.

REACHING THE GROUND

From the Boulevard Edgar Quinet as you leave the autoroute. Continue for 1.5 km. Turn left into Boulevard Léon Jouhaux/N9 for 350 m then right onto the N9 for 0.7

Clermont-Auvergne (cont)

km. Turn right onto the Boulevard Léon Jouhaux/N9 for 250 m, right onto the N9 for 0.8 km. Turn right onto the Rue De Catarou for 250 m then right onto the Rue Du Clos Four sur 90 m and the Parc des Sports Marcel Michelin.

TOURIST OFFICE

Maison du Tourisme, Place de la Victoire, 63000 Clermont-Ferrand.
04 73 98 65 00 www.clermont-fd.com

HOTELS

Mercure Centre,82 boulevard Francois Mitterrand, 63000 Clermont-Ferrand.
123 rooms, from €100 s/d/t.
04 73 34 46 46 H1224@accor-hotels.com www.accor-hotels.com

Novotel, 32-34 rue Georges Besse, Le Brezet, 63100 Clermont-Ferrand.
131 rooms, from €100 s/d/t.
04 34 14 14 H1175@accor.com www.accor-hotels.com

Coubertin, 25 avenue Liberation, 63000 Clermont-Ferrand.
81 rooms, from €80 s/d/t.
04 73 93 22 22 accueil@hotel-coubertin.com www.hotel-coubertin.com

Dav'Hotel Jaude, 10 rue Minimes, 63000 Clermont-Ferrand.
28 rooms, from €45
04 73 93 31 49 contact@davhotel.fr www.davhotel.fr

Albert-Elisabeth, 37 avenue Albert-Elisabeth, 63000 Clermont-Ferrand.
38 rooms, from €46.
04 73 92 47 41 Hotel-albertelisabeth@massifcentral.net

EDINBURGH GUNNERS

	2000
Stadium	Murrayfield
Capacity	67,500
Address	Murrayfield, Edinburgh, EH12 5PJ
Switchboard	0131 346 5000
Fax	0131 346 5269
Web	www.edinburghrugby.com
Telephone for tickets	0131 346 5100
Internet tickets	www.scottishrugby.org/tickets.cfm
Club shop	Scottish Rugby Store, Murrayfield Stadium, Edinburgh,EH12 5PJ.
Tel	0131 346 5044
Web	www.scottishrugbydirect.com
Colours	Black shirts with white and red trim
Coaches	At the time of going topress, the successor to Frank Hadden, who had been promoted to Scotland coach, was still to be named
Club captain	Chris Paterson

FIXTURES

Consult press for changes and for kick-off times.

Sunday 23rd October 2005 v London Wasps	HOME	13.00
Saturday 29th October 2005 v Llanelli Scarlets	AWAY	15.00
Saturday 10th December 2005 v Toulouse	HOME	16.00
16/17/18 December 2005 v Toulouse	AWAY	
13/14/15 January 2006 v Llanelli Scarlets	HOME	
20/21/22 January 2006 v London Wasps	AWAY	

TRAVEL/HOTELS

For all travel and tourist information and directions to Murrayfield, please see the chapter on Edinburgh, who play at the national stadium.

GLASGOW WARRIORS

Founded	2000
Stadium	Hughenden
Address	Hughenden Stadium, 32 Hughenden Road, Glasgow, G12 9XP
Capacity	6,000
Admin	First Floor, 5 Somerset Place, Glasgow, G3 7JT
Switchboard	0141 353 3468
Fax	0141 332 5875
Web	www.glasgowrugby.com
Ticket office	239, Argyle St, Glasgow, G2 8DL. All Virgin Megastores
Telephone for tickets	0131 346 5100
Internet Tickets	www.scottishrugby.eticketing.co.uk
Club shop	On match days at Hughenden
Web	www.scottishrugby.org/onlineshop
Mechandise Hotline	0870 240 1183
Colours	Navy Blue shirts with light blue sleeves.
Coaches	Hugh Campbell
Club captain	Jon Petrie

FIXTURES

Consult press for changes and for kick-off times.

Friday 21st October 2005 v Bourgoin	AWAY	20.30
Sunday 30th October 2005 v Leinster	HOME	13.00
Saturday 10th December 2005 v Bath	AWAY	14.15
16/17/18 December 2005 v Bath	HOME	
13/14/15 January 2006 v Leinster	AWAY	
20/21/22 January 2006 v Bourgoin	HOME	

ERC RECORD

Participations 7	Matches 43	Won 12	Lost 30	Drawn 1

Glasgow Warriors (cont)

REACHING THE CITY

AIR

Glasgow International 0141 887 1111 www.baa.co.uk/main/airports/glasgow

Prestwick 0871 223 0700 www.gpia.co.uk

Directions from the airport to the city centre: Glasgow International – M8 motorway from airport to city centre. Prestwick (Glasgow) – Turn right out of airport on to A79, and then on to A77/M77 to M8 and on to city centre

BY SEA

Local Port: Troon (Seacat from Belfast) 08705 523 523 (ROI) 1800 80 50 55

Stena Line operate crossings from Belfast Port to Stranraer, while P&O offer services to Cairnryan and Troon from Larne.

REACHING THE GROUND

RAIL

Local Railway station: Hyndland Station. Low level services from Glasgow's two major stations - Queen Street and Central. 0845 74 84 950 www.scotrail.co.uk

Directions from the station: Turn left out of Hyndland station up to the top of Novar Drive. Turn left along Hyndland Road, and Hughenden is the left turn directly before the tennis club.

Local taxi telephone numbers	0141 429 7070
	0141 954 2000
	0141 950 1234

ROAD

From the city centre: Head west on Great Western Road (A82 – signed to Dumbarton). After Hilton Grosvenor Hotel (on left) and Botanic Garden (on right), at second set of traffic lights, turn left into Hyndland Road. Turn right down Hughenden Road (beside Western Tennis Club).

TOURIST OFFICE

Glasgow Tourist Information Centre, 11 George Square, Glasgow, G2 1DY
0141 204 4400 enquiries@seeglasgow.com www.seeglasgow.com

HOTELS

Radisson SAS, 301 Argyle St, Glasgow G2 8DL.
246 rooms, from £100 s/d/t. Rack £190.
0141 204 3333 reservations.glasgow@radissonsas.com www.radissonsas.com

Hilton Glasgow, 1 William St, Glasgow G3 8HT.
315 rooms, from £130 s/d/t. Rack £200.
0141 204 5555 glahiltwgm@hilton.com www.hilton.co.uk/glasgow

Glasgow Moat House, Congress Rd, Glasgow G3 8QT.
267 rooms, from £130 s/d/t.
0141 306 9988 cbgla@queensmoat.co.uk www.moathousehotels.com

One Devonshire Gardens, 1 Devonshire Gardens, Glasgow G12 0UX.
35 rooms, from £150 s/t to £495 (luxury suite).
0141 339 2001 reservations@onedevonshiregardens.com www.onedevonshire-gardens.com

ArtHouse, 129 Bath St, Glasgow G2 2SJ.
63 rooms, from £115 s/d/t
0141 221 6789 info@arthousehotel.com www.arthousehotel.com

LEEDS TYKES

Founded	1991
Stadium	Headingley Stadium
Address	St Michael's Lane, Leeds LS6 3BR
Capacity	18,000
Website	www.leedsrugby.com
Tel	0845 0700 881
Fax	0845 0700 882
Telephone for tickets	08700 60 60 50
Email for tickets	tickets@leedsrugby.com
Web	www.seatbooker.net/leedstykes
Club shop	Headingley Retail, St Michael's Lane, Headingley, Leeds, LS6 3BR
Tel	0113 203 3228
Web	www.leedsrugby.com and click on Headingley Retail
Colours	Dark blue with white trim
Coaches	Jon Callard
Club captain	Tom Palmer

FIXTURES

(We have tried to make the information concerning dates, times and venues for the matches listed below as accurate as possible. Dates and times are liable to change for purposes, for example, of television scheduling or postponements due to bad weather. Consult press for changes and for kick-off times).

Saturday 22nd October 2005 v Cardiff Blues	AWAY	13.00
Friday 28th October 2005 v Calvisano	HOME	20.00
Sunday 11th December 2005 v Perpignan	HOME	14.30
16/17/18 December 2005 v Perpignan	AWAY	
13/14/15 January 2006 v Calvisano	HOME	
20/21/22 January 2006 v Cardiff Blues	HOME	

ERC RECORD

Participations 1	Matches 6	Won 1	Lost 5	Drawn 0

REACHING THE CITY

AIR

Leeds-Bradford International Airportis 11 miles from Leeds city centre. Metered taxi service outside the airport. There is a direct train service to Leeds City Rail Station and a flight bus service number 757 to Leeds City Bus Station and Rail Station.

RAIL

Direct services to Leeds City Rail Station from London Kings Cross, Birmingham, Bristol , Edinburgh, Newcastle, Leicester and Manchester. From Cardiff change at Birmingham or Bristol. From Glasgow change at Carlisle or Newcastle.

Headingley is just over two miles from Leeds City Rail Station.

National Rail enquiry service – 08457 48 49 50

ROAD

To get to Headingley Stadium, take the M62, followed by the M621, exiting at junction 2, which is signposted Headingley Stadium. Follow the A643 (A58) Wetherby Road and, at the next roundabout, take the City Centre/Wetherby A58 exit.

Leeds Tykes (cont)

Almost immediately, bear left to Ilkley (A65) and the airport. At the lights, with TGI Friday on your left, turn left onto Kirkstall Road (A65).Proceed ahead for 0.75 miles (Yorkshire Television is on the right). There is a sign at the traffic lights saying "Headingley, 1.5 miles." Stay in the right hand lane.

Turn right and go up the hill to another set of traffic lights at the crossroads. Carry straight on up Cardigan Road (The Co-op is on the left). After the pedestrian lights and bus stop, turn left into St Michaels Lane, signposted Headingley Stadium. The Stadium is on the right.

TOURIST OFFICE

Gateway to Yorkshire Tourist Information Centre, The Arcade, Leeds City Station, Leeds, LS1 1PL.
0113 242 5242 infotour@leeds.gov.uk www.leeds-uk.com

HOTELS

Marriott Hotel Leeds, 4 Trevelyan Square, Boar Lane, LS1 6ET.
243 rooms, from £80 s, £100 d/t. Rack £111 s, £122 d/t.
0870 400 7260 reservations.leeds@marriotthotels.co.uk www.marriott.com/lbadt

Malmaison, Sovereign Quay, LS1 1DQ.
100 rooms, from £79 s/d/t. Rack £135
0113 398 1000 / Central reservation service 0845 3654 247 leeds@malmaison.com www.malmaison.com

Quebecs, 9 Quebec St, LS1 2HA.
54 rooms, from £120 s/d/t - £300 s/d/t.
0113 244 8989 res-quebecs@etontownhouse.com www.theetoncollection.com

42 The Calls, 42 The Calls, LS2 7EW.
38 rooms, from £90 s/d £100 t. Rack 150 d to 180d/t. £395 suite.
0113 244 0099 hotel@42thecalls.co.uk www.42thecalls.co.uk

Novotel, 4 Whitehall, Whitehall Quay, LS1 4HR.
194 rooms, from £50s/d/t. Rack £119. 0113 242 6446
H3270@accor-hotels.com www.novotel.com

LEICESTER TIGERS

Founded	1880
Stadium	Welford Rd
Address	Aylestone Road, Leicester, LE2 7TR
Capacity	16,815
Website	www.leicestertigers.com
Switchboard	0116 254 1607
Telephone for tickets	08701 28 34 30
Fax	0116 2171 263
Email for tickets	tickets@tigers.co.uk
Club shop	Leicester Tigers, Aylestone Road, Leicester, Leicestershire, LE2 7TR
Tel	08701 28 34 30
Web	www.leicestertigers.com
Colours	Green, white & red hoops
Coaches	Richard Cockerill (forwards); Pat Howard (head coach)
Club captain	Martin Corry

FIXTURES

Consult press for changes and for kick-off times.

Saturday 22nd October 2005 v Clermont	HOME	1500
Saturday 29th October 2005 v Stade Francais	AWAY	1400
Sunday 11th December 2005 v Ospreys	HOME	1500
16/17/18 December 2005 v Ospreys	AWAY	
13/14/15 January 2006 v Stade Francais	HOME	
20/21/22 January 2006 v Clermont	AWAY	

ERC RECORD

Participations 8	Matches 60	Won 42	Lost 17	Drawn 1

REACHING THE CITY

AIR

East Midlands Airport runs many international flights throughout Europe. For more information about the airport and timetables see the Leicester tourist office web site. To get to the airport from Leicester take the A6 northbound and join the M1 northbound. Come off at J23A and follow signs to the Airport.

Direct flights are run by:
Bmibaby from Belfast, Cork, Edinburgh, Glasgow and Paris CDG.
Ryanair from Dublin, Shannon and Rome-Ciampino.
Easyjet from Edinburgh and Rome-Ciampino.

The next airport is Birmingham International.

RAIL

Leicester Station is a ten minute walk away, along Waterloo Way.

For more information on the station and train timetables and prices have a look at the links below.

Midland Mainline	www.midlandmainline.com
National Rail Information	www.nationalrail.co.uk

ROAD

From M1 (North and South) and M69 (East): Exit the motorway at Junction 21 (M1). Follow the signs for the city centre via Narborough Road (A5460). After 3 miles, at the cross-road junction with Upperton Road, turn right. Continue over the River Soar, onto Walnut Street, and follow the signs to the city centre. The stadium is approximately ½ mile ahead.

From A6 (South): Follow the signs for the city centre, coming in via London Road. At the main set of lights opposite the entrance to the railway station (on the right), turn left onto Waterloo Way. Continue over the next set of traffic lights onto Tigers Way. The stadium is immediately in front of you.

From A47 (East): Follow the signs for the city centre, coming in via Uppingham Road. At the St George's Retail Park roundabout, take the second exit into St George's Way (A594). Carry on past the Leicester Mercury offices on the right, and then filter off right onto Waterloo Way just before the Railway Station and then onto Tigers Way. The stadium is ¼ mile further on.

TOURIST OFFICE

Tourist Information Centre, 7-9 Every St, Leicester, LE1 6AG.
0116 294 1113 info@discoverleicester.com www.discoverleicester.com

HOTELS

Holiday Inn Leicester, 129 St Nicholas Circle, LE1 5LX.
187 rooms, from £70 s/d/t. Rack £135 s/d/t.

Leicester Tigers (cont)

08704 009048 Reservations-leicestercity@ichotelsgroup.com
www.ichotelsgroup.com
Holiday Inn Leicester West, Braunstone Lane East, LE3 2FW.
172 rooms, from £65 s/d/t. Rack £120 s/d/t.
08704 009051 Reservations-leicestercity@ichotelsgroup.com
www.ichotelsgroup.com
Express Leicester Walkers Stadium, Filbert Way, Raw Dykes Rd, LE2 7FQ.
110 rooms, from £60 s/d/t. £89 Rack.
0116 249 4590 info@exhileicester.co.uk www.ichotelsgroup.com
Belmont House, De Montfort St, LE1 7GR.
77 rooms, £60 s/d/t. rack £70 s £90 d/t.
0116 254 4773 info@belmonthotel.co.uk www.belmonthotel.co.uk

LEINSTER

Founded	1879
Stadium	Donnybrook Stadium, Donnybrook Rd, Dublin 4
Capacity	7,500
For higher profile matches	Royal Dublin Showground, Anglesea Rd, Dublin 4
Capacity	14,000
Admin	Leinster Rugby, 55 Main Street, Donnybrook, Dublin 4
Switchboard	01 269 3224
Fax	01 269 3142
Web	www.leinsterrugby.ie
Telephone for tickets	01 223 5103
Internet tickets	www.leinsterrugby.ie
Club shop	Donnybrook Stadium, Donnybrook, Dublin 4
Tel	01 269 1855
Colours	Royal Blue and Gold
Coaches	Micael Cheika, David Knox, Gerry Murphy, Roly Meates
Club captain	

FIXTURES

Consult press for changes and for kick-off times.

Saturday 22nd October 2005 v Bath	HOME	17.15
Sunday 30th October 2005 v Glasgow	AWAY	13.00
Saturday 10th December 2005 v Bourgoin	HOME	17.15
16/17/18 December 2005 v Bourgoin	AWAY	
13/14/15 January 2006 v Glasgow	HOME	
20/21/22 January 2006 v Bath	AWAY	

ERC RECORD

Participations 10	Matches 59	Won 37	Lost 21	Drawn 1

REACHING THE GOUND

Donnybrook Ground is approximately 2 miles from centre of Dublin City (O'Connell Street) traveling south past St. Stephen's Green and is walking distance from Lansdowne Road.

BUS

The number 10 and 46A bus services O'Connell Street and Trinity College (beside Grafton Street) and both go straight past the ground. (Cost would be in the region of €1.50). From town, the journey is around 15 minutes on a bus.

DART

The DART station at Lansdowne Road is approximately a 15 minute walk from the Grounds. At traffic lights on Lansdowne Road walk up Shelbourne Road to Ballsbridge, bear right over the Bridge over the River Dodder, and cross the road past Old Belvedere RFC on Anglesea Road. At the top of Anglesea Road at the Church turn right, back over the river and you are at the Ground.

Alternatively From Sydney Parade, turn right and walk straight up past the Four Seasons Hotel. Merrion Cricket Club is facing you. Turn left, past Old Belvedere RFC on Anglesea Road. At the top of Anglesea Road at the Church turn right, back over the river and you are at the Ground.

FROM DUN LAOGHAIRE

Number 46A bus or the DART to Lansdowne Road.

FROM DUBLIN AIRPORT

There is an Aircoach service from Dublin Airport which also leaves you at the ground (€7 single/€12 return approx.). You'd be better giving yourself an hour because of road works on the dual carriageway on the Dublin Airport – City Centre road. For further information and for a route map visit www.aircoach.ie

The 746 bus service also departs from Dublin Airport and serves Donnybrook.

WALKING

If you're feeling energetic, Donnybrook is around a half hour southward walk from St. Stephen's Green. Donnybrook is a 10 minute walk from the Burlington Hotel. The ground is also a 10 minute walk from Ballsbridge, past Old Belvedere RFC and covers the R.D.S. & Four Seasons Hotel.

It is also a 15 minute walk to Lansdowne Road (Jury's Doyle Hotel, Tower Hotel and Berkeley Court Hotel).

BOAT

From Dublin Port (North Wall), go into the city centre and follow instructions above. From Dun Laoghaire harbour, the any of the 46 bus routes will leave you at the ground and will take in the region of a half hour.

TOURIST INFORMTION/HOTELS

Please refer to section on Dublin

LLANELLI SCARLETS

Founded	2003
Stadium	Stradey Park
Address	Llanelli, Carmarthenshire, SA15 5BT
Capacity	10,800
Tel	01554 783 900
Fax	01554 783 901
Web	www.scarlets.co.uk
Telephone for tickets	0871 871 8088
Internet tickets	www.scarlets.co.uk
Email Ticket Office	ann@scarlets.co.uk
Club shop	Llanelli Scarlets Shop, Stradey Park, Llanelli, SA15 4BT.
Tel	01554 783 900
Fax	01554 783901

Llanelli Scarlets (cont)

Email	scarletsshop@scarlets.co.uk
Web	www.scarlets.co.uk
Colours	Scarlet shirts, white shorts
Coaches	Gareth Jenkins, Nigel Davies, Paul Moriarty.
Club captain	Simon Easterby

FIXTURES

Consult press for changes and for kick-off times).

Saturday 22nd October 2005 v Toulouse	AWAY	16.00
Saturday 29th October 2005 v Edinburgh	HOME	15.00
Sunday 11th December 2005 v London Wasps	HOME	13.00
16/17/18 December 2005 v London Wasps	AWAY	
13/14/15 January 2006 v Edinburgh	AWAY	
20/21/22 January 2006 v Toulouse	HOME	

ERC RECORD

Participations 9	Matches 61	Won 36	Lost 25	Drawn 0

REACHING THE TOWN

AIR

The nearest International airport is Cardiff International Airport, approximately one hour's drive along the M4 from Llanelli (follow the signs for Port Talbot, Swansea nad Carmarthen). For airport information please refer to the section on Cardiff or call 01446 711111.

The city centre is well signposted from the airport

There is a bus link with the city centre and from there an excllent rail link with Llanelli from Cardiff Central Station, sited next to the bus terminus.

Travellers may choose to fly into Bristol airport, which is 40m miles east of Cardiff. There are direct flights to Bristol from GB and Ireland.

British Airways	Edinburgh and Glasgow
Easyjet	Edinburgh, Glasgow, Belfast, Newcastle, Geneva and Rome Ciampino
Ryanair	Dublin and Shannon
Aer Lingus	from Dublin

RAIL

Llanelli Train Station approximately 20 minutes walk from the stadium. Local Taxis are availible from outside the station gates.

For further information regarding train times contact the National Rail Enquires on 0845 748 4950 or alternatively go to the National Rail Enquiries website. www.nationalrail.co.uk

BY ROAD

Leave the M4 at Junction 48. Turn left on to the A4138, which heads past the village of Llangennech. Follow this road for approximately 3 miles, looking out for signs for Tros-tre Retail Park. You will arrive at a set of traffic lights. You will see a McDonalds situated on a roundabout in the distance. When at the roundabout, stay in the right hand lane and take the fourth exit (signposted Stradey Park). Follow this road for approximately three to four miles passing through the back of the retail park and heading towards the coastal road. This road will take you past the recently developed golf course and beautiful scenic views of the Gower. At the end of this road you will appoach a small roundabout, take the first turning left signposted Stradey Park. Continue over a small bridge, you should now start to see the Stradey Park Floodlights in the distance. Follow this road until you approach a roundabout. Take the second turning on to Sandy Road. There is a turning, signposted 'Stradey Park' approximately 200 metres on your right.

TOURIST OFFICE

Carmarthen Tourist Information Centre, 113 Lammas Street, Carmarthen, SA31 3AQ.
01267 231557 CarmarthenTIC@carmarthenshire.gov.uk
www.camarthenshire.gov.uk

HOTELS

The Diplomat, Felinfoel Rd, Llanelli, Carmarthenshire SA15 3PJ.
51 rooms, from £65. 01554 756 156 reservations@diplomat-hotel-wales.com
www.bw-diplomathotel.co.uk

Stradey Park Hotel, Furnace, Llanelli, Carmarthenshire SA15 4HA.
83 rooms, from £85 s, £110 d/t. 01554 758171 reservations@stradeyparkhotel.com
www.stradeyparkhotel.com

Travelodge Llanelli Cross Hands Hotel, A48, Cross Hands, Llanelli, Camarthenshire, SA14 6NW.
32 rooms, from £53 s/d/t.
0870 191 1729 www.travelodge.co.uk

Ashburnham Hotel, Ashburnham Road, Pembrey, Llanelli, Carmarthenshire SA16 0TH. (4 miles outside town along the A484)
13 rooms, from £60 s, £80 d/t, £95 family.
01554 834 343 / 834455 info@ashburnham-hotel.co.uk
www.ashburnham-hotel.co.uk

MUNSTER

Founded	1879
Stadium	Thomond Park
Address	Thomond Park, Limerick
Capacity	13,200
Stadium for Celtic League matches	Musgrave Park, Ballyphehane, Cork
Tel	021 432 3563
Fax	021 432 3956
Web	www.munsterrugby.ie
Email	info@munsterrugby.ie
Tickets via internet:	www.shop.irishrugby.ie/shop www.munsterrugby.ie
Club shop	Munster Rugby Store, 4 Rutland Street, Limerick
Tel	0613 18080
Fax	061 318081
Email	store@munsterrugby.ie
Web	www.munsterrugbystore.com
Colours	Red shirts, white shorts
Coach	Alan Gaffney
Club captain	Anthony Foley

Munster (cont)

FIXTURES

Consult press for changes and for kick-off times.

Friday 21st October 2005 v Sale Sharks	AWAY	19.30
Saturday 29th October 2005 v Castres Olympique	HOME	17.15
Saturday 10th December 2005 v Newport-Gwent Dragons	AWAY	13.00
16/17/18 December 2005 v Newport-Gwent Dragons	HOME	
13/14/15 January 2006 v Castres Olympique	AWAY	
20/21/22 January 2006 v Sale Sharks	HOME	

ERC RECORD

Participations 10	Matches 68	Won 45	Lost 22	Drawn 1

REACHING THE TOWN

AIR

Direct flights from UK to Shannon International Airport.

Aer Lingus	London Heathrow.
British Airways	Manchester
Ryanair	Bristol, Nottingham-East Mids, Glasgow-Prestwick, Liverpool, London Gatwick, London Luton, London Stansted.
Easyjet	London Gatwick

Direct flights from France with Ryanair from Nantes, Paris Beauvais

SEA AND ROAD

Ferry from Swansea to Cork (crossing takes 10 hours). Limerick is about 2 hours drive from Cork.
Ferry from Pembroke to Rosslare (crossing 3hours 30mins). 4 hour drive from Rosslare.
Ferry from Holyhead to Dublin (crossing 1¾ hours – 3½ hours). 3 hour drive to Limerick.

From Limerick city centre: Turn left at the junction between O'Connell and William Street and go on to Sarsfields Bridge. Continue for about 400m to the Ennis-Shelbourne Road junction. Turn right at the traffic lights and go straight on to the next set of lights, turn left and Thomond Park is opposite.

RAIL

The closest station to Thomond Park is Colbert Station, Parnell Street, Limerick. Direct Intercity service from Dublin and Cork. It's a long hike to Thomond Park from Colbert Station. It's advisable to get a taxi, the cost would be between €5 and €10.

Treaty Cabs	061 415544 or 415566
Economy Cabs	061 411422
Top Cabs	061 417417
Speedi Taxi	061 318844
Set Price Taxi	061 414141

TOURIST OFFICE

Arthur's Quay, Limerick. 061 317522 www.ireland.ie

HOTELS

Jurys Inn Limerick, Lower Mallow Street, Limerick.

151 rooms, from €80 s/d/t.
061 207000 jurysinnlimerick@jurysdoyle.com www.jurysdoyle.com

The Clarion Hotel, Steamboat Quay, Limerick.
93 rooms, from €120 s/d/t.
061 444100 info@clarionhotellimerick.com www.clarionhotellimerick.com

South Court Hotel, Raheen Roundabout, Adare Road, Limerick.
124 rooms, €130s, €160 d/t.
061 487487 www.lynchotels.com

Woodfield House Hotel, Ennis Road Limerick.
27 rooms, rack rates €70 s, €130 d/t.
061 453022 woodfieldhousehotel@eircom.ie

THE DRAGONS

Founded	2003
Stadium	Rodney Parade
Address	Newport NP19, Gwent, Wales
Capacity	11,676
Website	www.newportgwentdragons.com
Tel	01633 670 690
General Enquiries	jon.hall@rodneyparadeltd.com
Ticket Office	01633 674 990
Tickets via internet	www.newportgwentdragons.
Club shop	Pure Rugby Limited, Rodney Parade.
Tel	01633 674 959
Web	www.pure-rugby.com
Colours	Red, black and gold jerseys
Coaches	Paul Turner
Club captain	Jason Forster

FIXTURES

Consult press for changes and for kick-off times.

Saturday 22nd October 2005 v Castres Olympique	AWAY	18.15
Saturday 29th October 2005 v Sale Sharks	HOME	19.30
Friday 09th December 2005 v Munster Rugby	HOME	13.00
16/17/18 December 2005 v Munster Rugby	AWAY	
13/14/15 January 2006 v Sale Sharks	AWAY	
20/21/22 January 2006 v Castres Olympique	HOME	

ERC RECORD

Participations 2	Matches 12	Won 5	Lost 7	Drawn 0

REACHING THE CITY

AIR

Direct Flights To Cardiff

British Airways	Edinburgh
Air Wales	Liverpool and Plymouth
Bmi From	Edinburgh, Prestwick, Belfast, Cork, Paris and Geneva
Ryanair	Dublin

The Dragons (cont)

Direct Flights To Bristol

British Airways	Edinburgh and Glasgow
Easyjet	Edinburgh, Glasgow, Belfast, Newcastle, Geneva and Rome Ciampino
Ryanair	Dublin and Shannon
Aer Lingus	Dublin

RAIL

Rodney Parade is only about five minutes from the railway station. As you leave the station go over the river bridge, turn right by the furniture shop into Rodney Road and the ground is straight ahead of you.

For travel details call National Rail Enquiries. 0845 748 4950.

ROAD

From the North-West and Midlands: M6 to M5 then the M50. At the end of the M50 join the A40 then the A449 to Newport.

From the North-East and Midlands: M1 to the M42. M42 to the M5. M5 to the M50. At the end of the M50 join the A40 then the A449 to Newport.

From London: M4 to Newport.

FERRY

Ferry from Cork to Swansea (10 hour crossing) then M4 to Newport.

Ferry from Rosslare to Pembroke (3¾ hour crossing). A477 to St Clears then the A40 to the A48 at Carmarthen then on to the M4 to Newport.

Ferry from Rosslare to Fishguard (3½ hour or 1¾ hour crossing) then A40 to Carmarthen. At Carmarthen take the A48 to the M4 and on to Newport.

TOURIST OFFICE

Newport Tourist Information Centre, Newport Museum and Art Gallery, John Frost Square, Newport NP20 1PA.
01633 842 962 newport.tic@newport.gov.uk www.newport.gov.uk/tourism

HOTELS

Newport Lodge Hotel, Brynglas Road, Newport NP20 5QN.
Double room £125 maximum.
01633 821 818 info@newportlodgehotel.co.uk www.newportlodgehotel.co.uk

Celtic Manor Hotel, The Coldra, Newport NP6 2YA.
Double room £255 maximum. The adjoining championship golf course is venue for the 2010 Ryder Cup.
01633 413 000 bookings@celtic-manor.com www.celtic-manor.com

Roman Lodge Hotel, Ponthir Road, Newport NP18 3NY.
Double room £80.
0845 658 5900 brian@romanlodgehotel.com www.romanlodgehotel.com

Express by Holiday Inn, Lakeside Drive, Coedkernew, Newport, NP10 8BB. Double room from approx £85.
01633 819 850/0870 990 4083 pippa.walker@ukonline.com
www.ichotelsgroup.com

NB. Please see the Cardiff chapter for other hotels close to Newport.

OSPREYS

Founded	2003
Home Stadiums	Regional Rugby Stadium, Swansea
Addresses	Regional Rugby Stadium, Swansea
Capacity	20,280

Website	www.ospreysrugby.co.uk
Switchboard	0870 9909175
Ticketline	0870 9909175
Email for tickets	info@ospreysrugby.com
Club shop	The Stadium, Landore, Swansea, SA1 2FA
Shop Telephone	01792 616 616
Colours	Black & white
Coaches	Lyn Jones
Club captain	Barry Williams

FIXTURES

Consult press for changes and for kick-off times.

Sunday 23rd October 2005 v Stade Francais	HOME	1500
Saturday 29th October 2005 v Clermont Auvergne	AWAY	1600
Friday 09th December 2005 v Leicester Tigers	AWAY	1500
16/17/18 December 2005 v Leicester Tigers	HOME	1500
13/14/15 January 2006 v Clermont Auvergne	HOME	1500
20/21/22 January 2006 v Stade Francais	AWAY	1600

ERC RECORD

Participations 2	Matches 12	Won 4	Lost 8	Drawn 0

REACHING THE GROUND

BY CAR

Park and Rides: From M4 - Swansea Vale Park and Ride. Come off at Junction 45, take the A4067 and follow signs to 'Stadium Park and Ride'.

Other Park and Ride sites are situated at County Hall and the Recreation Ground. For these take the A4067 and follow the signs.

Disabled Supporters: A drop off/pick up only point is located at the front of the Stadium for disabled supporters.

Information on car-sharing is available at www.swwitch2share.com

BY TRAIN

First Great Western and Arriva Trains operate regular services into Swansea's High Street Station, with frequent bus services to the Stadium.

For train times call National Rail Enquiries on 08457 484950
or visit: www.nationalrail.co.uk

PLUS BUS

When travelling by rail to destinations in Swansea, tickets can be purchased from many train stations covering the combined rail and bus journey. An add-on fare of £3 will give unlimited travel on all participating local bus services in the Swansea Bay area. Ask at your train station for details.

BY BUS

For more details call Traveline Cymru: 0870 6082608. Lines are open from 0700 to 2200, seven days a week or visit: www.firstgroup.com

For First Customer Services, call 01792 572255. Lines are open from 0900 to 1700, Monday to Friday. To find out your bus stop code visit: www.traveline-cymru.org.uk

TOURIST OFFICE

Plymouth Street, Opposite Quadrant Bus Station, Swansea, SA1 3QG.

01792 468321 tourism@swansea.gov.uk www.swansea.gov.uk/tourism

Ospreys (cont)

HOTELS

SWANSEA

Morgans, Somerset Place, Swansea, SA1 1RR.
20 rooms, from £100s/d/t to £250.
01792 484848 fdesk@morganshotel.co.uk www.morganshotel.co.uk

Swansea Marriott, Maritime Quarter, Swansea, SA1 3SS.
122 rooms from £75 s/d/t to £200.
0870 400 7282 www.marriott.com

Beaumont, 72-73 Walter Rd, Swansea, SA1 4QA.
16 rooms, from £60-£90.
01792 643956 info@beaumonthotel.co.uk www.beaumonthotel.co.uk

NEATH

Castle Hotel, The Parade, Neath, SA11 1RB.
29 rooms, from £45 s and £60 d/t.
01639 641119 info@castlehotelneath.co.uk www.castlehotelneath.co.uk

Express by Holiday Inn, Neath Road, Llandarcy, Neath, SA10 6JQ.
91 rooms, from £65 s/d/t.
01792 818700 swansea@expressbyholidayinn.net www.hiexpressswansea.co.uk

Ambassador, 24-42 The Parade, Neath, SA11 1RA.
24 rooms from £30s, £50d/t.
01639 638091 info@ambassador-hotel-neath.co.uk
www.ambassador-hotel-neath.co.uk

PERPIGNAN

Founded	1902
Stadium	Aimé Giral
Address	Stade Aimé Giral, Avenue Aimé Giral, 66000 Perpignan, France
Capacity	13,500
Website	www.usap.fr
Email	infos@usap.fr
Telephone for tickets	04 68 59 60 37
Internet tickets	www.francebillet.fr www.ticketnet.fr
Club shop	Boutique de l'U.S.A.P. 38, rue Mally, 66000 Perpignan.
Tel	08 92 68 66 15
Web	www.usap.fr
Colours	Blood and Gold
Coaches	Philippe Boher, Philippe Ducousso
Club captain	Bernard Goutta

FIXTURES

Consult press for changes and for kick-off times.

Saturday 22nd October 2005 v Calvisano	AWAY	14.00
Friday 28th October 2005 v Cardiff Blues	HOME	20.30
Sunday 11th December 2005 v Leeds Tykes	AWAY	14.30
16/17/18 December 2005 v Leeds Tykes	HOME	
13/14/15 January 2006 v Cardiff Blues	AWAY	
20/21/22 January 2006 v Calvisano	HOME	

ERC RECORD

Participations 5	Matches 35	Won 21	Lost 14	Drawn 0

REACHING THE CITY

AIR

To Perpign an-Rivesaltes

Air France	Paris-Orly. Taxi 6km journey to the centre of Perpignan.
FlyBe	Edinburgh, Birmingham and Southampton
Ryanair	London Stansted

To Carcassonne

Direct flights with Ryanair from Dublin, Liverpool and London Stansted. It is then approximately 120km to Perpigan. By car take the A61 motorway to Narbonne then the A9 to Perpignan. Exit motorway A9 at "Perpignan Nord", follow the signs for Perpignan Centre then leave the dual carriageway at the sign for Aimé Giral. Taxi to the SNCF railway station and direct train to Perpignan or to Narbonne and change there for Perpignan.

RAIL

Direct service from Montpellier, Narbonne, Toulouse, Lyon.

From Paris to Narbonne or Montpellier by TGV then change for Perpignan.

Paris, by TGV direct to Paris Gare de Lyon or Paris Austerlitz (standard train).

ROAD

Exit motorway A9 at "Perpignan Nord", follow the signs for Perpignan Centre then leave the dual carriageway at the sign for Aimé Giral.

TOURIST OFFICE

Office Municipal de Tourisme, Place Armand Lanoux, 66000 Perpignan.
04 68 66 30 30 contact-office@perpignan.fr www.perpignantourisme.com

HOTELS

Villa Duflot, Rond-point Albert Donnezan (Serrat d'en Vaquer), 66000 Perpignan.
24 rooms, from €110-€140.
04 68 56 67 67 contact@villa-duflot.com www.villa-duflot.com

Best Western Park Hotel, 18 Boulevard Jean Bourrat, 66000 Perpignan.
68 rooms from €86-€100.
04 68 35 14 14 contact@parkhotel-fr.com www.parkhotel-fr.com

New Christina, 51, cours Lassus, 66000 Perpignan.
25 rooms, from €70-€85
04 68 35 12 21 www.hotel-newchristina.com cdt66@wanadoo.fr

Mercure Perpignan Centre, 5-5 bis Cours Palmarole, 66000 Perpignan.
55 rooms, €88.
04 68 35 67 66 H1160@accor.com www.accorhotels.com

Hotel L'Eolienne Perpignan, 170, avenue Guynemer, 66100 Perpignan.
04 68 66 00 00 leolienne66@aol.com www.hotel-leolienne.fr

SALE SHARKS

Founded	1861
Stadium	Edgeley Park
Address	Hardcastle Road, Stockport SK3 9DD
Capacity	10,541
Website	www.salesharks.com

Sale Sharks (cont)

Telephone for tickets	08712 220 120
ContactJohn	0161 286 8915
Club shop	Edgeley Park Sports Store (at the stadium)
Tel	0161 286 8899
Web	www.salesharks.com/shop.php
Colours	Shades of blue
Coaches	Philippe Saint-Andre
Club captain	Jason Robinson

FIXTURES

Consult press for changes and for kick-off times.

Friday 21st October 2005 v Munster	HOME	19.30
Friday 28th October 2005 v Newport-Gwent Dragons	AWAY	19.30
Friday 09th December 2005 v Castres Olympique	AWAY	20.30
Friday 16th December 2005 v Castres Olympique	HOME	20.00
Saturday 14th January 2006 v Newport Gwent Dragons	HOME	20.00
Saturday 21st January 2006 v Munster	AWAY	15.00

ERC RECORD

Participations 2	Matches 12	Won 3	Lost 9	Drawn 0

REACHING THE CITY

AIR

To Manchester International Airport. Approximately 20 minutes to Edgeley Park by taxi. There is a rail connection from the airport to Manchester Piccadilly where there are frequent links to Stockport.

Direct Internal Flights To Manchester	
British Airways	London Heathrow, London Gatwick, Edinburgh, Glasgow
BMI baby	Edinburgh, Glasgow, London Heathrow
Direct Flights To Manchester From Ireland	
Aer Lingus	Dublin
British Airways	Cork, Shannon, Belfast
Ryanair	Dublin
BMI baby	Cork, Belfast
Direct Flights To Manchester From France	
British Airways	Paris, Lyon
Air France	Paris
Direct Flights To Manchester From Italy	
British Airways	Rome Fiumicino, Milan, Alitalia, Milan

RAIL

Stockport station is ten minutes walk from Edgeley Park. Leave the station by the rear exit, turn left up Station Road and continue up the hill towards a roundabout. Go straight over the roundabout and turn left into Caroline Street and the stadium is in front of you.

From the South: Stockport is on the main North/South line to Manchester. Most trains from the Midlands, the South and West, and London call at Stockport.

From the East: There is an hourly service from Sheffield, which can originate at Derby, Nottingham, Lincolnshire, Peterborough and East Anglia. There is a Midland Mainline service from London St Pancras which calls at Luton, Wellingborough, Kettering, Market Harborough, Leicester and Stockport.

From the North-East and Yorkshire: There is a very good service from Leeds to Stockport with three or four trains per hour which can originate at Newcastle, Scarborough, York or Hull. All these trains are bound for Manchester Airport so it is necessary to change at Manchester Piccadilly whence there is an excellent service to Stockport. If you are travelling via Bradford, there is a service to Manchester Victoria and you can use your rail ticket on the Metro to transfer between Manchester Piccadilly and Stockport.

From the West: There are frequent services to Stockport from Liverpool, Southport and Blackpool.

From the North: There are services to Manchester Airport from Scotland, the North and the Lake District which entail a change at Manchester Piccadilly. There is a direct, but infrequent, Virgin train from Scotland to Manchester Piccadilly and Stockport.

ROAD

Stockport is easily accessible from the M60 motorway which passes through the town. The M60 can be reached via M62 from Liverpool and Yorkshire.

M6 / M61 from the North, M6 / M56 from the South. A6 from the Peak District, Derby, Nottingham, and East Anglia. From Ireland, take a ferry from Dublin Port or Dun Laoghaire to Holyhead. Then take the A55 to Chester, then M53-M56 to the M60 and Stockport.

TOURIST OFFICE

Stockport Tourist Information Centre, Staircase House, Stockport SK1 1ES.
0161 474 4444 tourist.information@stockport.gov.uk www.visitmanchester.com

HOTELS

Acton Court Hotel, 187 Buxton Road, Stockport SK2 7AB.
Double or Twin room £55
0161 483 6172 www.actoncourthotel.co.uk

County Hotel, Bramhall Lane South, Bramhall, Stockport, SK7 2EB.
Double room £59
0161 455 9988 www.regalhotels.co.uk/countymanchester

Bredbury Hall Hotel and Country Club, Dark Lane, Goyt Valley, Bredbury, Stockport, SK6 2DH.
Double room £79.50.
0161 430 7421 reservations@bredburyhallhotel.co.uk
www.bredburyhallhotel.co.uk

Britannia Hotel Stockport, 67 Dialstone Lane, Offerton, Stockport, SK2 6AG. Double room £60.
0161 930 1000 reservations@britanniahotels.com www.britanniahotels.com

Hilton Moorside Hotel, Mudhurst Lane, Higher Disley, Stockport, SK12 2AP.
Double room £145.
01663 764 151 matthew.plunkett@hilton.com www.hilton.co.uk/moorside

SARACENS

Founded	1876
Stadium	Vicarage Road, Watford, WD18 0ET
Capacity	20,000
Website	www.saracens.com
Ticket Office	4th floor Rigby House, Watford High Street

Saracens (cont)

Tel	01923 475222
Internet tickets	www.saracens.talentarena.co.uk
Club Shop	At Vicarage Road Stadium. Open on match days from 11am.
Tel:	0870 241 6820
Web	www.saracens.com/shop
Colours	Black and white
Coaches	Steve Diamond
Club captain	Hugh Vyvyan

FIXTURES

Consult press for changes and for kick-off times.

Sunday 23rd October 2005 v Biarritz	HOME	15.00
Saturday 29th October 2005 v Treviso	AWAY	14.00
Friday 09th December 2005 v Ulster	AWAY	19.30
16/17/18 December 2005 v Ulster	HOME	
13/14/15 January 2006 v Treviso	HOME	
20/21/22 January 2006 v Biarritz	AWAY	

ERC RECORD

Participations 2	Matches 12	Won 7	Lost 5	Drawn 0

REACHING THE CITY

AIR

The closest airports are London Luton and London Heathrow. Please see the chapter on London for further details.

RAIL

North London Railways: Watford Junction is 20 minutes on a fast train from Euston (and 15 mins walk to ground). Or Watford High Street Station if you take a slow train from Euston (5 mins from ground).

London Underground: Metropolitan Line to Watford Met. Station (10 mins walk) or Croxley.

From the station to the ground: From Watford Junction Station go left down Clarendon Rd. and follow the crowds to Vicarage Rd.

From Watford Junction Station by Bus: Bus Route 321 - to Vicarage Road.

Directions from Watford Metropolitan Line (10-15 minute walk): Turn right out of the station and follow the crowds. If there is no-one else coming to the game, ask for directions.

From Watford Metropolitan Line by Bus: Bus route W4- to Vicarage Road (Sunday service: hourly at 23 minutes past the hour; 26 minutes past the hour from Vicarage Road (General Hospital) back to station.

ROAD

From the North: Exit M1 at Junction 5 and take third exit off roundabout, A4008 (Stephenson Way), signposted Watford Town Centre. Bear left on dual carriageway towards Town Centre. At next roundabout follow signs to Town Centre. Immediately ahead is the Harlequin Centre. Stay in the middle lane of the three-lane carriageway.

After the second set of traffic lights (Watford High Street Station is on your left), move into the left-had lane and bear left at traffic lights to Stadium. Look for parking at Watford General Hospital, where limited spaces are available to non-season ticket holders or stay on the ring round and follow signs for the car park. The Stadium is a ten minute walk.

From the West: Exit M25 at Junction 19 and take third exit off roundabout, A411 (Hempstead Road), signposted Watford. Continue for approximately 2 miles and at roundabout go straight across, then follow signs to Rickmansworth (A412). We strongly recommend parking in the Gade car park, accessed via the first turning on your left, Rosslyn Road.

From the South: Exit M1 at Junction 5 and take first exit off roundabout, then as north. From the East Exit M25 at Junction 21A and then join the M1 Southbound (J6). Exit at Junction 5, then as from North.

COACH TRAVEL

No provision for coach parking at Vicarage Road Stadium, but passengers can be dropped off and collected post-match. For further details phone Saracens clubhouse on: 01923 475222 .

TOURIST OFFICE

Watford Borough Information Service.
01923 226 400 www.watford.gov.uk

HOTELS

The Grove, Chandler's Cross, Watford, WD3 4TG.
211 rooms, from £250 s/d/t.
01923 807807 info@thegrove.co.uk www.thegrove.co.uk

Hilton Watford, Elton Way, Watford, WD25 8HA.
199 rooms, from £130 s/d/t.
01923 235881 Rm_watford@hilton.com www.hilton.co.uk

Watford Moat House, 30-40 St Albans Rd, Watford, WD17 1RN.
90 rooms, from £55.00 s/d/t to £65 d/t.
01923 429988 watford@moathousehotels.com www.moathousehotels.com

White House Hotel, 27 - 31 Upton Rd, Watford, WD18 0JF.
55 rooms, £60 s or £80 d/t.
01923 237316 info@whitehousehotel.co.uk www.whitehousehotel.co.uk

Premier Travel Inn, Water Lane, Watford, WD17 2NJ.
105 rooms, from £56 s/d/t.
01923 205530 www.premiertravelinn.com

STADE FRANCAIS

Founded	1893
Stadium	Jean-Bouin
Address	Stade Jean-Bouin, 26 Avenue du General Sarrail, 75016 Paris
Capacity	12,000
Website	www.stade.fr
Telephone for tickets	01 46 51 00 75
For tickets	www.francebillets.com, any FNAC or Carrefour
Fax	01 46 51 24 24
Club shop	2, rue du Commandant Guilbaud, 75016 Paris or Stade Jean-Bouin on match days.
Tel	01 46 51 00 75
Fax	01 46 51 24 24
Web	www.stade.fr
Colours	Royal blue with red flashes

Stade Francais (cont)

Coaches	Fabien Galtier & Fabrice Landreau
Club captain	David Auradou

FIXTURES

Consult press for changes and for kick-off times.

Sunday 23rd October 2005 v Ospreys	AWAY	1500
Saturday 29th October 2005 v Leicester Tigers	HOME	1400
Saturday 10th December 2005 v Clermont Auvergne	AWAY	1600
16/17/18 December 2005 v Clermont Auvergne	HOME	
13/14/15 January 2006 v Leicester Tigers	HOME	
20/21/22 January 2006 v Ospreys	HOME	

ERC RECORD

Participations 6	Matches 47	Won 33	Lost 14	Drawn 0

TRAVEL/HOTELS

For travel details please see France chapter. The Stade Jean-Bouin is situated in the west of Paris, a little away from the centre. It is most easily reached on the Métro line 9. Get off the train at Porte de Saint-Cloud. Some games will be played at the Parc des Princes stadium just across the road.

STADE TOULOUSAIN

Founded	1907
Stadium	Ernest Wallon
Address	114 rue des Troènes, 31200 Toulouse
Capacity	19,600
Or for higher profile matches	
Stadium	Le Stadium
Address	Allées Gabriel Biènes, 31200 Toulouse
Capacity	38,650
Website	www.stadetoulousain.fr
Telephone for tickets	08 92 69 21 92
Internet tickets	www.stadetoulousain.francebillet.com
Club shop	Espace Stade Toulousain, 75, rue Alsace Lorraine, 31200 Toulouse
Tel	08 92 69 31 15
Web	www.boutique.stadetoulousain.fr
Colours	Black and Red
Coach	Guy Novès, Serge Lairle, Philippe Rougé-Thomas
Club captain	Fabien Pelous

FIXTURES

Consult press for changes and for kick-off times.

Saturday 22nd October 2005 v Llanelli Scarlets	HOME	16.00
Sunday 30th October 2005 v London Wasps	AWAY	15.00
Saturday 10th December 2005 v Edinburgh Rugby	AWAY	15.00

16/17/18 December 2005 v Edinburgh Rugby	HOME	
13/14/15 January 2006 v London Wasps	HOME	
20/21/22 January 2006 v Llanelli Scarlets	AWAY	

ERC record

Participations 10	Matches 72	Won 52	Lost 19	Drawn 1

REACHING THE CITY

AIR

Toulouse is served by an international airport Aéroport Toulouse-Blagnac. For further details 05 61 71 11 1 or visit www.toulouse.aeroport.fr.

You can fly direct to Toulouse from London Gatwick with BA, and Easyjet, and from Bristol and Birmingham with British European. Ryanair fly into Carcassonne airport which is about 80 km east of Toulouse from Dublin, Liverpool and Stansted. Ryanair also fly to Pau, Perpignan and Montpellier from London Stansted. Check their website www.ryanair.com for further information.

RAIL

Toulouse has a mainline station, Gare Matabiau, and is easily accessible from across Europe. The trip from Paris takes around 5 1/2 hours. For rail information, call 0892 35 35 35 from inside France, the SNCF website www.sncf.fr.

All Toulouse trains arrive and depart from Gare Matabiau 05 61 10 10 00

ROAD

For a route planner try www.viamichelin.com. For Motorway conditions (from inside France) call 0892 681 077

TOURIST OFFICE

Office de Tourisme, Donjon du Capitol, BP 0801, 31080 Toulouse cedex 6.
05 61 11 02 22 info@ot-toulouse.fr www.ot-toulouse.fr

HOTELS

Crowne Plaza, 7 place du Capitole, 31000 Toulouse.
162 rooms, from €110 s/d/t to €305. 05 61 61 19 19
hicptoulouse@alliance-hospitality.com www.ichotelsgroup.com

Holiday Inn, 13 place Wilson, 31000 Toulouse.
130 rooms, from €90 s/d/t to €160
05 61 10 70 70 hicapoul@guichard.fr www.ichotelsgroup.com

Novotel Centre, 5 Place Alfonse Jourdain, 31000 Toulouse.
135 rooms, from €80.00 s/d/t to €136 s/d/t.
05 61 21 74 74 H0906@accor-hotels.com www.accor-hotels.com

Hotel Garonne, 22 descant de la Halle aux Poissons, 31000 Toulouse.
14 rooms, from €150 s/d/t to €259.
05 34 31 94 80 www.hotelgaronne.com

Athenee, 13 rue Matabiau, 31000 Toulouse.
35 rooms, from €107 s/d/t to €117.
05 61 63 10 63 Hotel-athenee@wanadoo.fr www.athenee-hotel.com

TREVISO

Founded	1932
Stadium	Stadio Comunale di Monigio, Via Olimpia, 31100 Treviso
Capacity	9,000
Tel	04 22 32 42 38
Web	www.benettonrugby.it
Colours	Green and White hoops
Coach	Craig Green
Club captain	Alessandro Troncon

FIXTURES

Consult press for changes and for kick-off times.

Friday 21st October 2005 v Ulster	AWAY	19.30
Saturday 29th October 2005 v Saracens	HOME	14.00
Sunday 11th December 2005 v Biarritz	AWAY	
16/17/18 December 2005 v Biarritz	HOME	
13/14/15 January 2006 v Saracens	AWAY	
20/21/22 January 2006 v Ulster	HOME	

The winner of each group qualifies for the quarter finals along with the two best second placed teams. Each qualifying club will be seeded according to results of its pool matches. The four top seeds will play their quarter final match at home.

Quarter Finals	Saturday 1st April and Sunday 2nd April, 2006
Semi Finals	Saturday 22nd April and Sunday 23rd April, 2006.
Final	Saturday 20th May 2006 at the Millennium Stadium, Cardiff

Tickets are now on sale from www.ticketmaster.co.uk at £15, £25, £35 and £45

ERC RECORD

Participations 8	Matches 42	Won 14	Lost 28	Drawn 0

TRAVEL

AIR

To Venice - Marco Polo: There are direct flights from GB and Ireland.

Easyjet	Bristol, London Gatwick
British Airways	London Gatwick
Aer Lingus	Dublin

There are direct flights from France with Air France from Paris CDG, Lyon.

Ryanair fly to Venice-treviso from Liverpool, London Luton, London Stansted and Paris-Beauvais.

RAIL

Trains run to the Treviso Centrale station which is well served by the Venezia-Mestre mainline station in Venice.

ROAD

Treviso is 30km due north of Venice and 265km west of Milan. From these two cities you will approach Treviso on the A27 motorway. On leaving the autostrada at Treviso, take the via Adige - SR53 for 2.5 km, then the Tangenziale for 80 m. Turn right into the via Noalese - SR515 and continue for 1.8 km. Turn left into Piazzale Pistoia for 100 m then continue on via Feltrina for 1.6 km. Turn right into viale Olimpia for 200 m to the stadium.

TOURIST OFFICE

Ufficio I.A.T., Piazza Monte di Pietà 8, 31100 Treviso
04 22 54 76 32 iat.treviso@provincia.treviso.it www.turismo.provincia.turismo.it

HOTELS

Ca del Galletto, Via Santa Bona Vecchia 30, Treviso.
65 rooms, from €100.
0422 432550 info@hotelcadelgalletto.it www.hotelcadelgalletto.it

Al Fogher, Viale della Repubblica 10, Treviso.
54 rooms, from €95.
0422 432950 htl@alfogher.com www.alfogher.com

Scala, Viale Felissent angolo Cal di Breda 1, Treviso.
20 rooms, from €65.
0422 307600 hscala@hotelscala.com

Al Giardino, Via Sant'Antonino 300, Treviso.
43 rooms, from €55.
0422 406406 Albgiard@tin.it

Il Cascinale, Via Torre d'Orlando, Treviso.
14 rooms, from €35.
0422 402203 info@agriturismoilcascinale.it www.agriturismoilcascinale.it

ULSTER

Founded	1879
Stadium	Ravenhill
Address	Ravenhill Park, Belfast, BT6 0DG
Capacity	12,000
Website	www.ulsterrugby.com
E-mail	reception@ulsterrugby.com
Telephone for tickets	028 9064 9141
Email for tickets	tickets@ulsterrugby.com
Internet tickets	www.ulsterrugbytickets.com
Club shop	Ulster Rugby, 85 Ravenhill Park, Belfast, BT6 0DG
Tel	028 9049 3222
Web	www.ulsterrugbystore.com
Colours	White shirts and shorts with red trim
Coaches	Mark McCall
Club captain	Andy Ward

FIXTURES

Consult press for changes and for kick-off times.

Friday 21st October 2005 v Treviso	HOME	19.30
Saturday 29th October 2005 v Biarritz	AWAY	16.00
Friday 09th December 2005 v Saracens	HOME	19.30
16/17/18 December 2005 v Saracens	AWAY	
13/14/15 January 2006 v Biarritz	HOME	
20/21/22 January 2006 v Treviso	AWAY	

Ulster (cont)

ERC RECORD

Participations 10	Matches 57	Won 24	Lost 31	Drawn 2

REACHING THE CITY

AIR

Belfast is served by an international airport, just two miles from, the city centre.
028 9093 9093 www.belfastcityairport.com

Direct flights to Belfast from GB and Ireland

Aer Arann	Cork.
British Airways	Manchester.
Bmi	London Heathrow.
Flybe	Aberdeen, Birmingham, Bristol, Edinburgh, Exeter, Glasgow, Jersey, Leeds/Bradford, Liverpool, London Gatwick, Newcastle, Norwich, Southampton
A2bairways	Blackpool

Directions from the airport to the city centre: Turn right from the airport on to the Sydenham-by-pass. Follow the signs to the City Centre.

SEA

Stena Line operate crossings from Stranraer to Belfast Port and from Fleetwood to Larne, while P&O offer services from Cairnryan and Troon. There are also regular crossings from Holyhead to Dublin.

RAIL

The closest train station to Ravenhill is Belfast Central Station.
028 9066 6630
www.translink.co.uk

Directions from the station to the ground: Turn right from Central Station on to East Bridge Street. Turn right at the main junction on to Ravenhill Road. Drive for approx half a mile and turn right onto Ardenlee Avenue. Turn right onto Shelbourne Road. Turn right at the end of Shelbourne onto Onslow Parade and Ravenhill is located at the top of the road on the right hand corner.

ROAD

Head out of the city centre on the Albertridge Road and when you reach the Woodstock Link take the second road on right (Woodstock Road). Travel approx 2 miles and turn right onto Onslow Parade just before you approach the roundabout. Ravenhill is located at the top of Onslow Parade on the left hand side.

Local taxi services

Value Cabs	028 9080 9080
Fon-A-Cab	028 9033 3333

TOURIST OFFICE

Belfast & Northern Ireland Welcome Centre, 47 Donegall Place, Belfast.
028 9024 6609 info@belfastvisitor.com www.belfastvisitor.com

HOTELS

Hastings Europa Hotel, Great Victoria Street, Belfast, BT2 7AP.
240 rooms, from £85s, £115 d/t. Rack £120 s, £150 d/t.
028 9027 1066 sales@eur.hastingshotels.com www.hastingshotels.com

Ramada Belfast, Shaws Bridge, Belfast, BT8 7XA.
118 rooms, from £110 s/d/t.
028 9092 3500 mail@ramadabelfast.com www.ramadabelfast.com

Ten Square, 10 Donegall Square South, Belfast, BT1 5JD.
23 rooms, from £129 s/d/t to £240 rack.
028 9024 1001 reservations@tensquare.co.uk www.tensquare.co.uk

Jurys Inn Belfast, Fisherwick Place, Great Victoria Street, Belfast, BT2 7AP.
190 rooms £75 s/d/t.
028 9053 3500 jurysinnbelfast@jurysdoyle.com www.jurysdoyle.com

Express by Holiday Inn, 106A University St, Belfast, BT7 1HP.
114 rooms, from £65 to £75 s/d/t.
028 9031 1909 express@holidayinn/ireland.com www.exhi-belfast.com

LONDON WASPS

Founded	1867
Stadium	Causeway Stadium
Address	Twyford Avenue Spports Ground, London, W3 9QA
Capacity	10,200
Tel	01494 769471
Website	www.wasps.co.uk
Telephone for tickets	0870 414 15 15
Internet tickets	www.wasps.co.uk
Club shop	www.wasps.co.uk/main_shop.ink
Tel	01494 472 100 or 01494 450 957
Colours	Black shirt with gold trim, black shorts
Coaches	Shaun Edwards, Craig Dowd, Leon Holden
Club captain	Lawrence Dallaglio

FIXTURES

Consult press for changes and for kick-off times.

Sunday 23rd October 2005 v Edinburgh	AWAY	13.00
Sunday 30th October 2005 v Toulouse	HOME	15.00
Sunday 11th December 2005 v Llanelli Scarlets	AWAY	13.00
16/17/18 December 2005 v Llanelli Scarlets	HOME	
13/14/15 January 2006 v Toulouse	AWAY	
20/21/22 January 2006 v Edinburgh	HOME	

ERC RECORD

Participations 7	Matches 45	Won 29	Lost 16 Drawn 0

REACHING THE TOWN

BY AIR

Please see the appropriate section in the chapter on London.

BY RAIL

High Wycombe is the closest railway station to the Causeway Stadium. Try these websites for more information
www.chilternrailways.co.uk
www.nationalrail.co.uk

London Wasps (cont)

Directions from the station to the ground:

Walk - approx 2.5 miles [4.5km] from bus station - Temple St. / Desborough Rd. / Desborough St. / Abercombie Av. / Dashwood Av. / Mill End Rd. / Lane End Rd. / Hillbottom Rd / Causeway Stadium.

Local Taxi Services:

Neales Taxis and Minibuses	01494 522 555 01494 463 399
Crown Taxis	01494 446 644
High Street Taxi	01494 461 911
Eagle	01494 444 414

ROAD

Navigate your way on to the A40 A40 Oxford Road/West Wycombe Road - 3Km - turn left A4010 Chapel Lane - 1Km junction ["Hourglass" pub/garage] - turn right Lane End Road - 0.5Km roundabout - turn right Hillbottom Road + Causeway Stadium. For instructions online try www.viamichelin.com.

BUS [WEEKDAYS]

Walk to Bus station [10-15mins] Bus 315/339 to "Hourglass" pub.
then walk [10-15min]-Lane End Road - Hillbottom Road - Causeway Stadium
Bus [matchdays] free shuttle buses rail/bus station to stadium from 2 hrs before KO.

TOURIST OFFICE

High Wycombe Tourist Information Centre, Pauls Row, HP11 2HQ
01494 421892 tourism_enquiries@wycombe.gov.uk

HOTELS HIGH WYCOMBE

Holiday Inn High Wycombe, Handycross, Bucks HP11 1TL. Junction 4 M40, 1 mile by A404.
113 rooms, from £45 pp per night. Rack £160 s/d/t.
0870 4009042 Reservations-highwycombe@ichotelsgroup.com
www.ichotelsgroup.com

Premier Travel Inn, Thanstead Farm, London Rd, Loudwater, Nr High Wycombe, Bucks HP10 9YL.
3 miles south east of the town along the A40.
81 rooms, from £49.95 s/d/t.
08701 977 135 www.premiertravelinn.com

Crowne Plaza Marlow, Fieldhouse Lane, Marlow, Bucks SL7 1GJ.
4 miles from High Wycombe along A404.
154 rooms, from £80 s, £100 d/t.
0870 444 8940 enquiries@crowneplazamarlow.co.uk
www.windsor.marlow.crowneplaza.com

Compleat Angler, Marlow Bridge, Bisham Rd, Bucks, SL7 1RG.
4 miles from High Wycombe along A404.
61 rooms, from £133 s, £230 d/t.
0870 400 8100 General.compleatangler@macdonald-hotels.co.uk
www.compleatangler-hotel.co.uk

Holly Tree House, Burford Close, Marlow Bottom, Bucks SL7 3NE.
9 rooms, from £69.50 s, £84 d/t.
01628 891110 hollytreeaccommodation@yahoo.co.uk

The winner of each group qualifies for the quarter finals along with the two best second placed teams. Each qualifying club will be seeded according to results of its pool matches. The four top seeds will play their quarter final match at home.

Quarter Finals	Saturday 1st April and Sunday 2nd April, 2006
Semi Finals	Saturday 22nd April and Sunday 23rd April, 2006.
Final	Saturday 20th May 2006 at the Millennium Stadium, Cardiff

Tickets are now on sale from www.ticketmaster.co.uk at £15, £25, £35 and £45

RBS Six Nations Championship 2006

Sat 4 Feb	13.30	Ireland	v	Italy	Lansdowne Road, Dublin
Sat 4 Feb	15.30	England	v	Wales	Twickenham, London
Sun 5 Feb	15.00	Scotland	v	France	Murrayfield, Edinburgh
Sat 11 Feb	14.30	France	v	Ireland	Stade de France, Paris
Sat 11 Feb	17.00	Italy	v	England	Stadio Flaminio, Rome
Sun 12 Feb	15.00	Wales	v	Scotland	Millennium Stadium, Cardiff
Sat 25 Feb	15.00	France	v	Italy	Stade de France, Paris
Sat 25 Feb	17.30	Scotland	v	England	Murrayfield, Scotland
Sun 26 Feb	15.00	Ireland	v	Wales	Lansdowne Road, Dublin
Sat 11 Mar	13.30	Wales	v	Italy	Millennium Stadium, Cardiff
Sat 11 Mar	15.30	Ireland	v	Scotland	Lansdowne Road, Dublin
Sun 12 Mar	16.00	France	v	England	Stade de France, Paris
Sat 18 Mar	14.30	Italy	v	Scotland	Stadio Flaminio, Rome
Sat 18 Mar	15.30	Wales	v	France	Millennium Stadium, Cardiff
Sat 18 Mar	17.30	England	v	Ireland	Twickenham, London

Rugby World Cup 2007

GROUP A	GROUP B
England	Australia
South Africa	Wales
Samoa (1st Qualifier – Oceania)	Fiji (2nd Qualifier – Oceania)
3rd Qualifier – Americas	2nd Qualifier – Americas
2nd Qualifier – Play Offs	1st Qualifier – Asia

GROUP C	GROUP D
New Zealand	France
Scotland	Ireland
1st Qualifier – Europe	1st Qualifier – Americas
2nd Qualifier – Europe	3rd Qualifier – Europe
1st Qualifier – Play Offs	1st Qualifier - Africa

DATE	GAME	VENUE	
Fri 7th Sep	France v Americas 1	Stade de France, St.Denis	D
Sat 8th Sep	England v Americas 3	Stade Félix-Bollaert, Lens	A
Sat 8th Sep	Australia v Asia	Stade Gerland, Lyon	B
Sat 8th Sep	New Zealand v Europe 1	Stade Vélodrome, Marseille	C
Sun 9th Sep	Ireland v Africa	Stade Lescure, Bordeaux	D
Sun 9th Sep	Wales v Americas 2	Stade de la Beaujoire, Nantes	B
Sun 9th Sep	South Africa v Samoa	Parc des Princes, Paris	A
Sun 9th Sep	Scotland v Qualifier 1	Stade Geoffroy-Guichard, St.Etienne	C
Tue 11th Sep	Americas 1 v Europe 3	Stade Gerland, Lyon	D
Wed 12th Sep	Europe 1 v Europe 2	Stade Vélodrome, Marseille	C
Wed 12th Sep	America 3 v Qualifier 2	Stade de la Mosson, Montpellier	A
Wed 12th Sep	Asia v Fiji	Stadium, Toulouse	B
Fri 14th Sep	England v South Africa	Stade de France, St.Denis	A

Fixtures: Rugby World Cup (cont)

DATE	GAME	VENUE	
Sat 15th Sep	Ireland v Europe 3	Stade Lescure, Bordeaux	D
Sat 15th Sep	Wales v Australia	Millennium Stadium, Cardiff	B
Sat 15th Sep	New Zealand v Qualifier 1	Stade Gerland, Lyon	C
Sun 16th Sep	Fiji v Americas 2	Millennium Stadium, Cardiff	B
Sun 16th Sep	Samoa v Qualifier 2	Stade de la Mosson, Montpellier	A
Sun 16th Sep	France v Africa	Stadium, Toulouse	D
Tue 18th Sep	Scotland v Europe 2	Murrayfield, Edinburgh	C
Wed 19th Sep	Europe 1 v Qualifier 1	Parc des Princes, Paris	C
Thu 20th Sep	Wales v Asia	Millennium Stadium, Cardiff	B
Fri 21st Sep	France v Ireland	Stade de France, St.Denis	D
Sat 22nd Sep	South Africa v Qualifier 2	Stade Félix-Bollaert, Lens	A
Sat 22nd Sep	Americas 1 v Africa	Stade Vélodrome, Marseille	D
Sat 22nd Sep	England v Samoa	Stade de la Beaujoire, Nantes	A
Sun 23rd Sep	Scotland v New Zealand	Murrayfield, Edinburgh	C
Sun 23rd Sep	Australia v Fiji	Stade de la Mosson, Montpellier	B
Tue 25th Sep	Americas 2 v Asia	Stade Lescure, Bordeaux	B
Tue 25th Sep	Europe 2 v Qualifier 1	Stadium, Toulouse	C
Wed 26th Sep	Europe 3 v Africa	Stade Félix-Bollaert, Lens	D
Wed 26th Sep	Samoa v Americas 3	Geoffroy-Guichard, St.Etienne	A
Fri 28th Sep	England v Qualifier 2	Parc des Princes, Paris	A
Sat 29th Sep	Australia v Americas 2	Stade Lescure, Bordeaux	B
Sat 29th Sep	Wales v Fiji	Stade de la Beaujoire, Nantes	B
Sat 29th Sep	Scotland v Europe 1	Geoffroy Guichard, St.Etienne	C
Sat 29th Sep	New Zealand v Europe 2	Stadium, Toulouse	C
Sun 30th Sep	France v Europe 3	Stade Vélodrome, Marseille	D
Sun 30th Sep	South Africa v Americas 3	Stade de la Mosson, Montpellier	A
Sun 30th Sep	Ireland v Americas 1	Parc des Princes, Paris	D

QUARTER FINALS

Sat 6th Oct	QF1	Winner – Pool B v Runner-up - Pool A	Stade Vélodrome, Marseille
Sat 6th Oct	QF2	Winner – Pool C v Runner-up - Pool D	Millennium Stadium, Cardiff
Sun 7th Oct	QF 3	Winner – Pool A v Runner-up - Pool B	Stade Vélodrome, Marseille
Sun 7th Oct	QF 4	Winner – Pool D v Runner-up - Pool C	Stade de France, St.Denis

SEMI-FINALS

Sat 13th Oct	Winner – QF1 v Winner QF2	Stade de France, St.Denis
Sun 14th Oct	Winner – QF3 v Winner QF4	Stade de France, St.Denis
Fri 19th Oct	3rd place play-off	Parc des Princes, Paris

FINAL

Sat 20th Oct	Stade de France, St.Denis

Heineken Cup

POOL 1: Munster, Castres Olympique, Sale Sharks, Newport-Gwent Dragons
POOL 2: Calvisano, Perpignan, Leeds Tykes, Cardiff Blues
POOL 3: Ospreys, Stade Francais Paris, Leicester Tigers, Clermont Auvergne
POOL 4: Biarritz Olympique Pays-Basque, Saracens, Ulster Rugby , Benetton Treviso
POOL 5: Glasgow, Bourgoin, Bath Rugby, Leinster
POOL 6: London Wasps, Toulouse, Llanelli Scarlets, Edinburgh Rugby

The winner of each group qualifies for the quarter finals along with the two best second placed teams. Each qualifying club will be seeded according to results of its pool matches. The four top seeds will play their quarter final match at home.

ROUND 1

Fri 21 Oct	Sale	v	Munster	1
Sat 22Oct	Castres	v	Newport	1
Sat 22 Oct	Cardiff	v	Leeds	2
Sat 22 Oct	Calvisano	v	Perpignan	2
Sun 23 Oct	Neath-Swansea	v	Stade Français	3
Sat 22 Oct	Leicester	v	Clermont	3
Fri 21 Oct	Ulster	v	Treviso	4
Sun 23 Oct	Saracens	v	Biarritz	4
Fri 21 Oct	Bourgoin	v	Glasgow	5
Sat 22 Oct	Leinster	v	Bath	5
Sat 22 Oct	Toulouse	v	Llanelli	6
Sun 23 Oct	Edinburgh	v	Wasps	6

ROUND 2

Sat 29 Oct	Munster	v	Castres	1
Fri 28 Oct	Newport	v	Sale	1
Fri 28 Oct	Leeds	v	Calvisano	2
Fri 28 Oct	Perpignan	v	Cardiff	2
Sat 29 Oct	Stade Français	v	Leicester	3
Sun 30 Oct	Clermont	v	Neath-Swansea	3
Sat 29 Oct	Treviso	v	Saracens	4
Sat 29 Oct	Biarritz	v	Ulster	4
Sun 30 Oct	Glasgow	v	Leinster	5
Sat 29 Oct	Bath	v	Bourgoin	5
Sat 29 Oct	Llanelli	v	Edinburgh	6
Sun 30 Oct	Wasps	v	Toulouse	6

ROUND 3

Fri 9 Dec	Castres	v	Sale	1
Sat 10 Dec	Newport	v	Munster	1
Sat 10 Dec	Calvisano	v	Cardiff	2
Sun 11 Dec	Leeds	v	Perpignan	2
Sun 11 Dec	Leicester	v	Neath-Swansea	3
Sat 10 Dec	Clermont	v	Stade Français	3
Fri 9 Dec	Ulster	v	Saracens	4
Sun 11 Dec	Biarritz	v	Treviso	4
Sat 10 Dec	Leinster	v	Bourgoin	5
Sat 10 Dec	Bath	v	Glasgow	5

Fixtures: Heineken Cup (cont)

Sat 10 Dec	Edinburgh	v	Toulouse	6
Sun 11 Dec	Llanelli	v	Wasps	6

ROUND 4

16/17/18 Dec	Sale	v	Castres	1
16/17/18 Dec	Munster	v	Newport	1
16/17/18 Dec	Cardiff	v	Calvisano	2
16/17/18 Dec	Perpignan	v	Leeds	2
16/17/18 Dec	Neath-Swansea	v	Leicester	3
16/17/18 Dec	Stade Français	v	Clermont	3
16/17/18 Dec	Saracens	v	Ulster	4
16/17/18 Dec	Treviso	v	Biarritz	4
16/17/18 Dec	Bourgoin	v	Leinster	5
16/17/18 Dec	Glasgow	v	Bath	5
16/17/18 Dec	Toulouse	v	Edinburgh	6
16/17/18 Dec	Wasps	v	Llanelli	6

2006

ROUND 5

13/14/15 Jan	Castres	v	Munster	1
13/14/15 Jan	Sale	v	Newport	1
13/14/15 Jan	Calvisano	v	Leeds	2
13/14/15 Jan	Cardiff	v	Perpignan	2
13/14/15 Jan	Leicester	v	Stade Français	3
13/14/15 Jan	Neath-Swansea	v	Clermont	3
13/14/15 Jan	Saracens	v	Trevise	4
13/14/15 Jan	Ulster	v	Biarritz	4
13/14/15 Jan	Leinster	v	Glasgow	5
13/14/15 Jan	Bourgoin	v	Bath	5
13/14/15 Jan	Edinburgh	v	Llanelli	6
13/14/15 Jan	Toulouse	v	Wasps	6

ROUND 6

20/21/22 Jan	Munster	v	Sale	1
20/21/22 Jan	Newport	v	Castres	1
20/21/22 Jan	Leeds	v	Cardiff	2
20/21/22 Jan	Perpignan	v	Calvisano	2
20/21/22 Jan	Stade Français	v	Neath-Swansea	3
20/21/22 Jan	Clermont	v	Leicester	3
20/21/22 Jan	Treviso	v	Ulster	4
20/21/22 Jan	Biarritz	v	Saracens	4
20/21/22 Jan	Glasgow	v	Bourgoin	5
20/21/22 Jan	Bath	v	Leinster	5
20/21/22 Jan	Llanelli	v	Toulouse	6
20/21/22 Jan	Wasps	v	Edinburgh	6

QUARTER FINALS

Sat 1st April	Sun 2nd April

SEMI FINALS

Sat 22nd April	Sun 23rd April

FINAL

Sat 20th May 2006	Millennium Stadium, Cardiff

Heineken Qualifiers & Websites

FRANCE	GROUP	WEBSITE
Castres Olympique	1	www.castres-olympiques.fr
Perpignan	2	www.usap.fr
Stade Français	3	www.stade.fr
Clermont Auvergne	3	www.asm-rugby.fr
Biarritz	4	www.bo-pb.com
Bourgoin	5	www.csbj-rugby.fr
Stade Toulousain	6	www.stade-toulousain.fr

IRELAND	GROUP	WEBSITE
Munster	1	www.munsterrugby.ie
Ulster	4	www.leinsterrugby.ie
Leinster	5	www.ulsterrugby.ie

ENGLAND	GROUP	WEBSITE
Sale Sharks	1	www.salesharks.com
Leeds	2	www.leedsrugby.com
Leicester	3	www.leicestertigers.com
Saracens	4	www.saracens.com
Bath	5	www.bathrugby.com
Wasps	6	www.wasps.co.uk

WALES	GROUP	WEBSITE
Newport-Gwent Dragons	1	www.newportgwentdragons.com
Cardiff Blues	2	www.cardiffblues.com
Neath-Swansea Ospreys	3	www.ospreysrugby.com
Llanelli Scarlets	6	www.scarlets.co.uk

SCOTLAND	GROUP	WEBSITE
Glasgow	5	www.glasgow.rugby.com
Edinburgh Rugby	6	www.edinburghrugby.com

ITALY	GROUP	WEBSITE
Calvisano	2	www.calvisanorugby.it
Benetton Treviso	4	www.benettonrugby.it

European Challenge 2005 - 2006

GROUP DRAW

1. Narbonne, Northampton Saints, Bristol Rugby, Viadana
2. Agen, Pau, London Irish, Parma
3. Bayonne, Toulon, Gloucester, Bucharest
4. Brive, Newcastle Falcons, Border Reivers, L'Aquila
5. Montpellier, Worcester Warriors, Connaught, Catana

FORMAT

Home and Away group matches (same weekends as the Heineken Cup).
Winners of the five groups qualify for the quarter-finals along with the three best second placed teams.
Quarter-finals and Semi-Finals decided over one match and played on the ground of the designated team.
Final to be played on a neutral ground, 20th or 21st May 2006.

ROUND 1

21/22/23 Oct	Narbonne	v	Bristol Rugby	1
21/22/23 Oct	Northampton Saints	v	Viadana	1
21/22/23 Oct	Overmach Parma	v	SU Agen	2
21/22/23 Oct	Section Paloise	v	London Irish	2
21/22/23 Oct	Bayonne	v	Gloucester Rugby	3
21/22/23 Oct	Bucuresti	v	Toulon	3
21/22/23 Oct	L'Aquila	v	The Scottish Borders	4
21/22/23 Oct	Newcastle Falcons	v	Brive	
21/22/23 Oct	Connacht	v	Catania	5
21/22/23 Oct	Worcester Warriors	v	Montpellier	5

ROUND 2

28/29/30 Oct	Bristol Rugby	v	Northampton Saints	1
28/29/30 Oct	Viadana	v	Narbonne	1
28/29/30 Oct	London Irish	v	Overmach Parma	2
28/29/30 Oct	SU Agen	v	Section Paloise	2
28/29/30 Oct	Gloucester Rugby	v	Bucuresti	3
28/29/30 Oct	Toulon	v	Bayonne	3
28/29/30 Oct	Brive	v	L'Aquila	4
28/29/30 Oct	The Scottish Borders	v	Newcastle Falcons	4
28/29/30 Oct	Catania	v	Worcester Warriors	5
28/29/30 Oct	Montpellier	v	Connacht	5

ROUND 3

9/10/11 Dec	Northampton Saints	v	Narbonne	1
9/10/11 Dec	Viadana	v	Bristol Rugby	1
9/10/11 Dec	London Irish	v	SU Agen	2
9/10/11 Dec	Section Paloise	v	Overmach Parma	2
9/10/11 Dec	Bucuresti	v	Bayonne	3
9/10/11 Dec	Toulon	v	Gloucester Rugby	3
9/10/11 Dec	L'Aquila	v	Newcastle Falcons	4
9/10/11 Dec	The Scottish Borders	v	Brive	4
9/10/11 Dec	Montpellier	v	Catania	5
9/10/11 Dec	Worcester Warriors	v	Connacht	5

ROUND 4

16/17/18 Dec	Bristol Rugby	v	Viadana	1
16/17/18 Dec	Narbonne	v	Northampton Saints	1
16/17/18 Dec	Overmach Parma	v	Section Paloise	2
16/17/18 Dec	SU Agen	v	London Irish	2
16/17/18 Dec	Bayonne	v	Bucuresti	3
16/17/18 Dec	Gloucester Rugby	v	Toulon	3
16/17/18 Dec	Brive	v	The Scottish Borders	4
16/17/18 Dec	Newcastle Falcons	v	L'Aquila	4
16/17/18 Dec	Catania	v	Montpellier	5
16/17/18 Dec	Connacht	v	Worcester Warriors	5

ROUND 5

13/14/15 Jan	Narbonne	v	Viadana	1
13/14/15 Jan	Northampton Saints	v	Bristol Rugby	1
13/14/15 Jan	Overmach Parma	v	London Irish	2
13/14/15 Jan	Section Paloise	v	SU Agen	2
13/14/15 Jan	Bayonne	v	Toulon	3
13/14/15 Jan	Bucuresti	v	Gloucester Rugby	3
13/14/15 Jan	L'Aquila	v	Brive	4
13/14/15 Jan	Newcastle Falcons	v	The Scottish Borders	4
13/14/15 Jan	Connacht	v	Montpellier	5
13/14/15 Jan	Worcester Warriors	v	Catania	5

ROUND 6

20/21/22 Jan	Bristol Rugby	v	Narbonne	1
20/21/22 Jan	Viadana	v	Northampton Saints	1
20/21/22 Jan	London Irish	v	Section Paloise	2
20/21/22 Jan	SU Agen	v	Overmach Parma	2
20/21/22 Jan	Gloucester Rugby	v	Bayonne	3
20/21/22 Jan	Toulon	v	Bucuresti	3
20/21/22 Jan	Brive	v	Newcastle Falcons	4
20/21/22 Jan	The Scottish Borders	v	L'Aquila	4
20/21/22 Jan	Catania	v	Connacht	5
20/21/22 Jan	Montpellier	v	Worcester Warriors	5

QUARTER FINALS	**01/02 APRIL**
SEMI FINALS	**22/23 APRIL**
FINAL	**20 MAY**

Guinness Premiership

After the 22 rounds of the Premiership, there will two Premiership Semi-Finals between the teams which finish first, second third and fourth in the table. The winners of these matches will play the Premiership Grand Final, at Twickenham on Sat May 27th.

The four next highest placed clubs that have not already qualified for the European Cup for the 2006-2007 season will qualify for the Wild Card Semi-Finals. The highest placed club will play its semi-final at home against the fourth highest placed club. The second highest placed club will play its semi-final at home against the third highest placed club. The winners of these matches will meet in the Wild-Card Final at Twickenham on Sat May 27th.

ROUND 1

DATE		HOME		AWAY	VENUE
Fri 2 Sep	20:00	Sale	v	Newcastle	Edgeley Park
Sat 3 Sep	14:00	Wasps	v	Saracens	Twickenham
Sat 3 Sep	15:00	Leicester	v	Northampton	Welford Road
Sat 3 Sep	16:20	Leeds	v	London Irish	Twickenham
Sun 4 Sep	13:00	Bristol	v	Bath	Memorial Stadium
Sun 4 Sep	15:00	Worcester	v	Gloucester	Sixways

ROUND 2

DATE		HOME		AWAY	VENUE
Sat 10 Sep	14.15	Bath	v	Northampton	The Rec
Sat 10 Sep	14.45	Wasps	v	Leicester	Causeway
Sat 10 Sep	15.00	Gloucester	v	Sale	Kingsholm
Sat 11 Sep	14.30	Newcastle	v	Bristol	Kingston Park
Sat 11 Sep	15.00	London Irish	v	Worcester	Madejski
Sat 11 Sep	15.00	Saracens	v	Leeds	Vicarage Road

ROUND 3

DATE		HOME		AWAY	VENUE
Fri 16 Sep	20.00	Sale	v	London Irish	Edgeley Park
Sat 17 Sep	14.00	Worcester	v	Saracens	Sixways
Sat 17 Sep	14.45	Northampton	v	Newcastle	Franklin's Gardens
Sat 17 Sep	15.00	Leicester	v	Bath	Welford Road
Sun 18 Sep	14.30	Leeds	v	Wasps	Headingley
Sun 18 Sep	15.00	Bristol	v	Gloucester	Memorial Stadium

ROUND 4

DATE		HOME		AWAY	VENUE
Sat 24 Sep	14.45	Gloucester	v	Northampton	Kingsholm
Sat 24 Sep	15.00	London Irish	v	Bristol	Madejski
Sat 25 Sep	14.30	Leeds	v	Leicester	Headingley
Sun 25 Sep	14.30	Newcastle	v	Bath	Kingston Park
Sun 25 Sep	15.00	Wasps	v	Worcester	Causeway
Sun 25 Sep	15.00	Saracens	v	Sale	Vicarage Road

ROUND 5

DATE		HOME		AWAY	VENUE
Fri 14 Oct	19.45	Leicester	v	Newcastle	Welford Road
Fri 14 Oct	20.00	Sale	v	Wasps	Edgeley Park
Fri 14 Oct	20.00	Worcester	v	Leeds	Sixways
Sat 15 Oct	14.45	Bath	v	Gloucester	The Rec
Sat 15 Oct	15.00	Northampton	v	London Irish	Franklin's Gardens
Sun 16 Oct	15.00	Bristol	v	Saracens	Memorial Stadium

FIXTURES

ROUND 6

DATE		HOME		AWAY	VENUE
Fri 4 Nov	20.00	Wasps	v	Bristol	Causeway
Sat 5 Nov	14.45	Worcester	v	Leicester	Sixways
Sat 5 Nov	14.45	Leeds	v	Sale	Headingley
Sat 5 Nov	15.00	Gloucester	v	Newcastle	Kingsholm
Sat 5 Nov	15.00	London Irish	v	Bath	Madejski
Sat 5 Nov	15.00	Saracens	v	Northampton	Vicarage Road

ROUND 7

Fri 11 Nov	19.45	Newcastle	v	London Irish	Kingston Park
Fri 11 Nov	20.00	Sale	v	Worcester	Edgeley Park
Sat 12 Nov	12.30	Northampton	v	Wasps	Franklin's Gardens
Sat 12 Nov	15.00	Leicester	v	Gloucester	Welford Road
Sun 13 Nov	14.15	Bath	v	Saracens	The Rec
Sun 13 Nov	15.00	Bristol	v	Leeds	Memorial Stadium

ROUND 8

Fri 18 Nov	20.00	Sale	v	Leicester	Edgeley Park
Fri 18 Nov	20.00	Worcester	v	Bristol	Sixways
Sun 20 Nov	14.30	Leeds	v	Northampton	Headingley
Sun 20 Nov	15.00	London Irish	v	Gloucester	Madejski
Sun 20 Nov	15.00	Wasps	v	Bath	Causeway
Sun 20 Nov	15.00	Saracens	v	Newcastle	Vicarage Road

ROUND 9

Fri 25 Nov	19.45	Bath	v	Leeds	The Rec
Sat 26 Nov	12.30	Gloucester	v	Saracens	Kingsholm
Sat 26 Nov	12.30	Northampton	v	Worcester	Franklin's Gardens
Sat 26 Nov	14.45	Leicester	v	London Irish	Welford Road
Sun 27 Nov	14.30	Newcastle	v	Wasps	Kingston Park
Sun 27 Nov	15.00	Bristol	v	Sale	Memorial Stadium

ROUND 10

Mon 26 Dec	14.00	Worcester	v	Bath	Sixways
Mon 26 Dec	15.00	Wasps	v	Gloucester	Causeway
Mon 26 Dec	15.00	Sale	v	Northampton	Edgeley Park
Tues 27 Dec	14.30	Leeds	v	Newcastle	Headingley
Tues 27 Dec	15.00	Bristol	v	Leicester	Memorial Stadium
Tues 27 Dec	15.00	Saracens	v	London Irish	Vicarage Road

ROUND 11 - INTO 2006

Sat 31 Dec	14.45	London Irish	v	Wasps	Madejski
Sat 31 Dec	15.00	Gloucester	v	Leeds	Kingsholm
Sun 1 Jan	TBC	Newcastle	v	Worcester	Kingston Park
Sun 1 Jan	15.00	Northampton	v	Bristol	Franklin's Gardens
Sun 1 Jan	15.00	Bath	v	Sale	The Rec
Mon 2 Jan	14.15	Leicester	v	Saracens	Welford Road

Fixtures: Guinness Premiership (cont)

ROUND 12

Sat 7 Jan	14.00	Worcester	v	Northampton	Sixways
Sun 8 Jan	14.30	Leeds	v	Bath	Headingley
Sun 8 Jan	15.00	London Irish	v	Leicester	Madejski
Sun 8 Jan	15.00	Wasps	v	Newcastle	Causeway
Sun 8 Jan	15.00	Sale	v	Bristol	Edgeley Park
Sun 8 Jan	15.00	Saracens	v	Gloucester	Vicarage Road

ROUND 13

27/28 Jan	TBC	Newcastle	v	Saracens	Kingston Park
Sat 28 Jan	14.15	Bath	v	Wasps	The Rec
Sat 28 Jan	15.00	Bristol	v	Worcester	Memorial Stadium
Sat 28 Jan	15.00	Gloucester	v	London Irish	Kingsholm
Sat 28 Jan	15.00	Leicester	v	Sale	Welford Road
Sat 28 Jan	15.00	Northampton	v	Leeds	Franklin's Gardens

ROUND 14

Fri 10 Feb	20.00	Leeds	v	Bristol	Headingley
Sat 11 Feb	14.00	Gloucester	v	Leicester	Kingsholm
Sat 11 Feb	14.00	Worcester	v	Sale	Sixways
Sun 12 Feb	15.00	London Irish	v	Newcastle	Madejski
Sun 12 Feb	15.00	Wasps	v	Northampton	Causeway
Sun 12 Feb	15.00	Saracens	v	Bath	Vicarage Road

ROUND 15

Fri 17 Feb	20.00	Sale	v	Leeds	Edgeley Park
Sat 18 Feb	14.15	Bath	v	London Irish	The Rec
Sat 18 Feb	15.00	Leicester	v	Worcester	Welford Road
Sat 18 Feb	15.00	Northampton	v	Saracens	Franklin's Gardens
Sun 19 Feb	14.30	Newcastle	v	Gloucester	Kingston Park
Sun 19 Feb	15.00	Bristol	v	Wasps	Memorial Stadium

ROUND 16

Fri 24 Feb	20.00	Leeds	v	Worcester	Headingley
Sat 25 Feb	15.00	Gloucester	v	Bath	Kingsholm
Sat 26 Feb	13.00	London Irish	v	Northampton	Madejski
Sat 26 Feb	14.30	Newcastle	v	Leicester	Kingston Park
Sat 26 Feb	15.00	Wasps	v	Sale	Causeway
Sat 26 Feb	15.00	Saracens	v	Bristol	Vicarage Road

ROUND 17

Fri 10 Mar	20.00	Sale	v	Saracens	Edgeley Park
Fri 10 Mar	20.00	Worcester	v	Wasps	Sixways
Sat 11 Mar	14.15	Bath	v	Newcastle	The Rec
Sat 11 Mar	15.00	Leicester	v	Leeds	Welford Road
Sat 11 Mar	15.00	Northampton	v	Gloucester	Franklin's Gardens
Sat 12 Mar	13.00	Bristol	v	London Irish	Memorial Stadium

ROUND 18

Sat 25 Mar	14.15	Bath	v	Leicester	The Rec
Sat 25 Mar	15.00	Gloucester	v	Bristol	Kingsholm
Sat 25 Mar	15.00	London Irish	v	Sale	Madejski
Sun 26 Mar	14.30	Newcastle	v	Northampton	Kingston Park
Sun 26 Mar	15.00	Wasps	v	Leeds	Causeway
Sun 26 Mar	15.00	Saracens	v	Worcester	Vicarage Road

ROUND 19

Fri 7 Apr	20.00	Sale	v	Gloucester	Edgeley Park
Sat 8 Apr	14.00	Worcester	v	London Irish	Sixways
Sat 8 Apr	15.00	Leicester	v	Wasps	Welford Road
Sat 8 Apr	15.00	Northampton	v	Bath	Franklin's Gardens
Sun 9 Apr	14.30	Leeds	v	Saracens	Headingley
Sun 9 Apr	15.00	Bristol	v	Newcastle	Memorial Stadium

ROUND 20

Sat 15 Apr	14.15	Bath	v	Bristol	The Rec
Sat 15 Apr	15.00	Gloucester	v	Worcester	Kingsholm
Sat 15 Apr	15.00	London Irish	v	Leeds	Madejski
Sat 15 Apr	15.00	Northampton	v	Leicester	Franklin's Gardens
Sun 16 Apr	14.30	Newcastle	v	Sale	Kingston Park
Sun 16 Apr	15.00	Saracens	v	Wasps	Vicarage Road

ROUND 21

28/29 Apr	TBC	Saracens	v	Leicester	Vicarage Road
Fri 28 Apr	20.00	Sale	v	Bath	Edgeley Park
Sat 29 Apr	14.00	Worcester	v	Newcastle	Sixways
Sat 29 Apr	14.30	Leeds	v	Gloucester	Headingley
Sat 29 Apr	15.00	Bristol	v	Northampton	Memorial Stadium
Sat 29 Apr	15.00	Wasps	v	London Irish	Causeway

ROUND 22

Sat 6 May	15.00	Bath	v	Worcester	The Rec
Sat 6 May	15.00	Gloucester	v	Wasps	Kingsholm
Sat 6 May	15.00	Leicester	v	Bristol	Welford Road
Sat 6 May	15.00	London Irish	v	Saracens	Madejski
Sat 6 May	15.00	Newcastle	v	Leeds	Kingston Park
Sat 6 May	15.00	Northampton	v	Sale	Franklin's Gardens

SEMI-FINALS

12/13/14 May	TBC	Wildcard Semi-Final 1	TBC
12/13/14 May	TBC	Wildcard Semi-Final 2	TBC
12/13/14 May	TBC	Premiership Semi-Finals	TBC

FINALS

27 May	TBC	Wildcard Final	Twickenham
27 May	TBC	Premiership Final	Twickenham

Celtic League

DATE		HOME		AWAY	VENUE
Fri 2 Sep	19:10	Llanelli Scarlets	v	Edinburgh Rugby	Stradey Park
Fri 2 Sep	19:10	Munster	v	The Scottish Borders	Thomond Park
Fri 2 Sep	19:30	Glasgow Rugby	v	Dragons	Hughenden
Sat 3 Sep	14:30	Connacht	v	Cardiff Blues	Sportsground
Sun 4 Sep	17:10	Ospreys	v	Leinster	Morfa Stadium
9/10/11 Sep	TBC	Leinster	v	Glasgow Rugby	Donnybrook
Fri 9 Sep	19:10	Cardiff Blues	v	Ulster	ArmsPark
Sat 10 Sep	16:00	Edinburgh Rugby	v	Connacht	Murrayfield
Sat 10 Sep	18:00	Munster	v	Ospreys	Musgrave Park
Sun 11 Sep	16:00	The Scottish Borders	v	Llanelli Scarlets	Netherdale
Tue 13 Sep	19:35	Ospreys	v	Dragons	Morfa Stadium
Wed 14 Sep	19:10	Cardiff Blues	v	Llanelli Scarlets	Arms Park
Fri 16 Sep	19:10	Leinster	v	Dragons	Donnybrook
Fri 16 Sep	19:30	Ulster	v	Edinburgh Rugby	RaFrihill
Sat 17 Sep	17:30	Llanelli Scarlets	v	Connacht	Racecourse Ground
Sat 17 Sep	19:30	Glasgow Rugby	v	Munster	Hughenden
Sun 18 Sep	16:00	The Scottish Borders	v	Ospreys	Netherdale
Fri 23 Sep	19:10	Munster	v	Llanelli Scarlets	Thomond Park
Sat 24 Sep	14:30	Connacht	v	The Scottish Borders	Sportsground
Sat 24 Sep	17:30	Dragons	v	Ulster	Rodney Parade
Sat 24 Sep	19:30	Glasgow Rugby	v	Cardiff Blues	Hughenden
Sun 25 Sep	15:00	Edinburgh Rugby	v	Ospreys	Murrayfield
Sat 1 Oct	14:00	Connacht	v	Munster	Sportsground
Sat 1 Oct	17:30	Leinster	v	Ulster	Donnybrook
Sun 2 Oct	15:00	Edinburgh Rugby	v	Glasgow Rugby	Murrayfield
Fri 7 Oct	19:10	Ulster	v	Connacht	RaFrihill
Sun 9 Oct	15:00	Munster	v	Leinster	Musgrave Park
Sun 9 Oct	16:00	The Scottish Borders	v	Edinburgh Rugby	Netherdale
Fri 14 Oct	19:10	Ospreys	v	Connacht	Morfa Stadium
Fri 14 Oct	19:30	Edinburgh Rugby	v	Dragons	Murrayfield
Sat 15 Oct	17:30	Leinster	v	Cardiff Blues	Donnybrook
Sat 15 Oct	19:30	The Scottish Borders	v	Ulster	Netherdale
Sun 16 Oct	16:10	Llanelli Scarlets	v	Glasgow Rugby	Stradey Park
4/5/6 Nov	TBC	Cardiff Blues	v	Munster	Arms Park
4/5/6 Nov	TBC	Leinster	v	EdinburghRugby	Donnybrook
Fri 4 Nov	19:10	Ulster	v	Ospreys	RaFrihill
Fri 4 Nov	19:30	Glasgow Rugby	v	Connacht	Hughenden
Sun 6 Nov	16:10	Dragons	v	The Scottish Borders	Rodney Parade

DATE		HOME		AWAY	VENUE
Sat 3 Dec	14:00	Connacht	v	Leinster	Sportsground
Sat 3 Dec	19:10	Munster	v	Ulster	Musgrave Park
Sun 4 Dec	15:00	Glasgow Rugby	v	Edinburgh Rugby	Hughenden
Thu 22 Dec	19:10	Munster	v	Connacht	Musgrave Park
Thu 22 Dec	19:35	Ospreys	v	Cardiff Blues	Morfa Stadium
Fri 23 Dec	19:10	Dragons	v	Llanelli Scarlets	Rodney Parade
Fri 23 Dec	19:30	Ulster	v	Leinster	RaFrihill
Mon 26 Dec	15:00	Edinburgh Rugby	v	The Scottish Borders	Murrayfield
Tue 27 Dec	16:10	Cardiff Blues	v	Dragons	Arms Park
Wed 28 Dec	14:30	Llanelli Scarlets	v	Ospreys	Stradey Park
Sat 31 Dec	14:00	Connacht	v	Ulster	Sportsground
Sat 31 Dec	17:30	Leinster	v	Munster	Donnybrook

2006

DATE		HOME		AWAY	VENUE
Sun 1 Jan	15:10	Dragons	v	Ospreys	Rodney Parade
Sun 1 Jan	16:00	The Scottish Borders	v	Glasgow Rugby	Netherdale
Mon 2 Jan	16:10	Llanelli Scarlets	v	Cardiff Blues	Stradey Park
6/7/8 Jan	TBC	Dragons	v	Connacht	Rodney Parade
6/7/8 Jan	TBC	Llanelli Scarlets	v	Leinster	Stradey Park
Fri 6 Jan	19:30	Ulster	v	Glasgow Rugby	RaFrihill
Sat 7 Jan	19:30	Edinburgh Rugby	v	Munster	Murrayfield
Sun 8 Jan	16:00	The Scottish Borders	v	Cardiff Blues	Netherdale
27/28/29 Jan	TBC	Cardiff Blues	v	Edinburgh Rugby	Arms Park
27/28/29 Jan	TBC	Leinster	v	The Scottish Borders	Donnybrook
27/28/29 Jan	TBC	Munster	v	Dragons	Musgrave Park
Fri 27 Jan	19:30	Ulster	v	Llanelli Scarlets	RaFrihill
Sun 29 Jan	15:00	Glasgow Rugby	v	Ospreys	Hughenden
17/18/19 Feb	TBC	Connacht	v	Llanelli Scarlets	Sportsground
17/18/19 Feb	TBC	Dragons	v	Leinster	Rodney Parade
17/18/19 Feb	TBC	Munster	v	Glasgow Rugby	Thomond Park
17/18/19 Feb	TBC	Ospreys	v	The Scottish Borders	Morfa Stadium
Sat 18 Feb	19:30	Edinburgh Rugby	v	Ulster	Murrayfield
3/4/5 Mar	TBC	Cardiff Blues	v	Ospreys	ArmsPark
3/4/5 Mar	TBC	Leinster	v	Connacht	Donnybrook
3/4/5 Mar	TBC	Llanelli Scarlets	v	Dragons	Stradey Park
Fri3 Mar	19:30	Ulster	v	Munster	RaFrihill
Sun5 Mar	15:00	Glasgow Rugby	v	The Scottish Borders	Hughenden
24/25/26 Mar	TBC	Cardiff Blues	v	Glasgow Rugby	Arms Park
24/25/26 Mar	TBC	Llanelli Scarlets	v	Munster	Stradey Park
24/25/26 Mar	TBC	Ospreys	v	Edinburgh Rugby	Morfa Stadium
Fri 24 Mar	19:30	The Scottish Borders	v	Connacht	Netherdale
Fri 24 Mar	19:30	Ulster	v	Dragons	RaFrihill

Fixtures: Celtic League (cont)

DATE		HOME		AWAY	VENUE
7/8/9 Apr	TBC	Dragons	v	Munster	Rodney Parade
7/8/9 Apr	TBC	Llanelli Scarlets	v	Ulster	Racecourse Ground
7/8/9 Apr	TBC	Ospreys	v	Glasgow Rugby	Morfa Stadium
Sat 8 Apr	19:30	Edinburgh Rugby	v	Cardiff Blues	Murrayfield
Sun 9 Apr	16:00	The Scottish Borders	v	Leinster	Netherdale
14/15/16 Apr	TBC	Cardiff Blues	v	The Scottish Borders	Arms Park
14/15/16 Apr	TBC	Connacht	v	Dragons	Sportsground
14/15/16 Apr	TBC	Leinster	v	Llanelli Scarlets	Donnybrook
14/15/16 Apr	TBC	Munster	v	Edinburgh Rugby	Thomond Park
Fri 14 Apr	19:30	Glasgow Rugby	v	Ulster	Hughenden
18/19 Apr	TBC	Dragons	v	CardiffBlues	Rodney Parade
18/19 Apr	TBC	Ospreys	v	Llanelli Scarlets	Morfa Stadium
28/29/30 Apr	TBC	Cardiff Blues	v	Connacht	Arms Park
28/29/30 Apr	TBC	Dragons	v	Glasgow Rugby	Rodney Parade
28/29/30 Apr	TBC	Leinster	v	Ospreys	Donnybrook
Fri 28 Apr	19:30	Edinburgh Rugby	v	Llanelli Scarlets	Murrayfield
Sun 30 Apr	16:00	The Scottish Borders	v	Munster	Netherdale
5/6/7 May	TBC	Connacht	v	Edinburgh Rugby	Sportsground
5/6/7 May	TBC	Llanelli Scarlets	v	The Scottish Borders	Stradey Park
5/6/7 May	TBC	Ospreys	v	Munster	Morfa Stadium
Fri 5 May	19:30	Glasgow Rugby	v	Leinster	Hughenden
Fri 5 May	19:30	Ulster	v	Cardiff Blues	RaFrihill
12/13/14 May	TBC	Cardiff Blues	v	Leinster	Arms Park
12/13/14 May	TBC	Connacht	v	Ospreys	Sportsground
12/13/14 May	TBC	Dragons	v	Edinburgh Rugby	Rodney Parade
Fri 12 May	19:30	Ulster	v	The Scottish Borders	RaFrihill
Sun 14 May	15:00	Glasgow Rugby	v	Llanelli Scarlets	Hughenden
26/27/28 May	TBC	Connacht	v	Glasgow Rugby	Sportsground
26/27/28 May	TBC	Munster	v	Cardiff Blues	Thomond Park
26/27/28 May	TBC	Ospreys	v	Ulster	Morfa Stadium
Fri 26 May	19:30	Edinburgh Rugby	v	Leinster	Murrayfield
Sun 28 May	16:00	The Scottish Borders	v	Dragons	Netherdale

Powergen Anglo-Welsh Cup

The four Pool winners in the new competition will move forward into the Semi-Finals in the new year.

POWERGEN CUP

POOL A: Bath Rugby, Neath-Swansea Ospreys, Gloucester, Bristol Rugby
POOL B: London Irish, London Wasps, Cardiff Blues, Saracens
POOL C: Leeds Tykes, Newcastle Falcons, Llanelli Scarlets, Sale Sharks
POOL D: Newport-Gwent Dragons, Leicester Tigers, Worcester Warriors, Northampton Saints

ROUND 1

Sep 30 / Oct 1 / 2	Bath Rugby	v	Bristol Rugby	A
Sep 30 / Oct 1 / 2	Gloucester	v	Neath-Swansea Ospreys	A
Sep 30 / Oct 1 / 2	London Irish	v	London Wasps	B
Sep 30 / Oct 1 / 2	Cardiff Blues	v	Saracens	B
Sep 30 / Oct 1 / 2	Leeds Tykes	v	Llanelli Scarlets	C
Sep 30 / Oct 1 / 2	Newcastle Falcons	v	Sale Sharks	C
Sep 30 / Oct 1 / 2	Newport-Gwent Dragons	v	Leicester Tigers	D
Sep 30 / Oct 1 / 2	Worcester Warriors	v	Northampton Saints	D

ROUND 2

Oct 7 / 8/ 9	Neath-Swansea Ospreys	v	Bath Rugby	A
Oct 7 / 8/ 9	Bristol Rugby	v	Gloucester	A
Oct 7 / 8/ 9	Saracens	v	London Irish	B
Oct 7 / 8/ 9	London Wasps	v	Cardiff Blues	B
Oct 7 / 8/ 9	Sale Sharks	v	Leeds Tykes	C
Oct 7 / 8/ 9	Llanelli Scarlets	v	Newcastle Falcons	C
Oct 7 / 8/ 9	Northampton Saints	v	Newport-Gwent Dragons	D
Oct 7 / 8/ 9	Leicester Tigers	v	Worcester Warriors	D

ROUND 3

Dec 1 / 2/ 3	Bath Rugby	v	Gloucester	A
Dec 1 / 2/ 3	Bristol Rugby	v	Neath-Swansea Ospreys	A
Dec 1 / 2/ 3	London Irish	v	Cardiff Blues	B
Dec 1 / 2/ 3	London Wasps	v	Saracens	B
Dec 1 / 2/ 3	Leeds Tykes	v	Newcastle Falcons	C
Dec 1 / 2/ 3	Llanellli Scarlets	v	Sale Sharks	C
Dec 1 / 2/ 3	Newport-Gwent Dragons	v	Worcester Warriors	D
Dec 1 / 2/ 3	Leicester Tigers	v	Northampton Saints	D

SEMI FINALS	**MARCH 4/5**
POWERGEN CUP FINAL	**APRIL 8/9**

Top I4 Fixtures

ROUND 1

DATE		HOME		AWAY	VENUE
Fri 19 Aug	20.45	Toulon	v	Biarritz	Mayol
Sat 20 Aug	17.30	Narbonne	v	Stade Français	Parc des Sports et de l'Amitié
Sat 20 Aug	18.30	Brive	v	Bourgoin	Parc Municipal des Sports
Sat 20 Aug	18.30	Pau	v	Clermont	Du Hameau
Sat 20 Aug	18.30	Montpellier	v	Castres	Sabathé
Sat 20 Aug	18.30	Perpignan	v	Agen	Aimé Giral
Sat 20 Aug	21.00	Bayonne	v	Toulouse	Jean Dauger

ROUND 2

Fri 26 Aug	20.45	Biarritz	v	Perpignan	Parc des Sports d'Aguiléra
Sat 27 Aug	17.30	Stade Français	v	Toulon	Jean Bouin
Sat 27 Aug	18.30	Bourgoin	v	Bayonne	Pierre-Rajon
Sat 27 Aug	18.30	Clermont	v	Montpellier	Parc des sports Marcel-Michelin
Sat 27 Aug	18.30	Castres	v	Narbonne	Pierre-Antoine
Sat 27 Aug	18.30	Agen	v	Brive	Armandie
Sat 27 Aug	21.00	Toulouse	v	Pau	Ernest-Wallon

ROUND 3

Fri 2 Sep	20.30	Agen	v	Biarritz	Armandie
Sat 3 Sep	17.30	Pau	v	Bourgoin	Du Hameau
Sat 3 Sep	18.30	Brive	v	Bayonne	Parc municipal des Sports
Sat 3 Sep	18.30	Montpellier	v	Toulouse	Sabathé
Sat 3 Sep	18.30	Narbonne	v	Clermont	Parc des Sports et de l'Amitié
Sat 3 Sep	18.30	Toulon	v	Castres	Mayol
Sun 4 Sep	20.45	Perpignan	v	Stade Français	Aimé Giral

ROUND 4

Fri 9 Sep	20.30	Stade Français	v	Agen	Jean Bouin
Sat 10 Sep	15.00	Toulouse	v	Narbonne	Ernest-Wallon
Sat 10 Sep	17.30	Castres	v	Perpignan	Pierre-Antoine
Sat 10 Sep	18.30	Bourgoin	v	Montpellier	Pierre-Rajon
Sat 10 Sep	18.30	Clermont	v	Toulon	Parc des sports Marcel-Michelin
Sat 10 Sep	18.30	Bayonne	v	Pau	Jean Dauger
Sat 10 Sep	18.30	Biarritz	v	Brive	Parc des Sports d'Aguiléra

ROUND 5

16 / 17 Sep	Narbonne	v	Bourgoin	Parc des Sports et de l'Amitié
16 / 17 Sep	Toulon	v	Toulouse	Mayol
16 / 17 Sep	Perpignan	v	Clermont	Aimé Giral
16 / 17 Sep	Agen	v	Castres	Armandie
16 / 17 Sep	Biarritz	v	Stade Français	Parc des Sports d'Aguiléra
16 / 17 Sep	Montpellier	v	Bayonne	Sabathé
16 / 17 Sep	Brive	v	Pau Parc	Municipal des Sports

ROUND 6

DATE	HOME		AWAY	VENUE
23 / 24 Sep	Bourgoin	v	Toulon	Pierre-Rajon
23 / 24 Sep	Toulouse	v	Perpignan	Ernest-Wallon
23 / 24 Sep	Clermont	v	Agen	Parc des sports Marcel-Michelin
23 / 24 Sep	Castres	v	Biarritz	Pierre-Antoine
23 / 24 Sep	Bayonne	v	Narbonne	Jean Dauger
23 / 24 Sep	Pau	v	Montpellier	Du Hameau
23 / 24 Sep	Stade Français	v	Brive	Jean Bouin

ROUND 7

30 Sep / 1 Oct	Perpignan	v	Bourgoin	Aimé Giral
30 Sep / 1 Oct	Agen	v	Toulouse	Armandie
30 Sep / 1 Oct	Biarritz	v	Clermont	Parc des Sports d'Aguiléra
30 Sep / 1 Oct	Stade Français	v	Castres	Jean Bouin
30 Sep / 1 Oct	Toulon	v	Bayonne	Mayol
30 Sep / 1 Oct	Narbonne	v	Pau	Parc des Sports et de l'Amitié
30 Sep / 1 Oct	Brive	v	Montpellier	Parc Municipal des Sports

ROUND 8

07 / 09 oct	Bourgoin	v	Agen	Pierre-Rajon
07 / 09 oct	Castres	v	Brive	Pierre-Antoine
07 / 09 oct	Clermont	v	Stade Français	Parc des sports Marcel-Michelin
07 / 09 oct	Bayonne	v	Perpignan	Jean Dauger
07 / 09 oct	Pau	v	Toulon	Du Hameau
07 / 09 oct	Montpellier	v	Narbonne	Sabathé
Sun 9 oct	Toulouse	v	Biarritz	Ernest-Wallon

ROUND 9

14 / 15 oct	Biarritz	v	Bourgoin	Parc des Sports d'Aguiléra
14 / 15 oct	Stade Français	v	Toulouse	Jean Bouin
14 / 15 oct	Castres	v	Clermont	Pierre-Antoine
14 / 15 oct	Agen	v	Bayonne	Armandie
14 / 15 oct	Perpignan	v	Pau	Aimé Giral
14 / 15 oct	Toulon	v	Montpellier	Mayol
14 / 15 oct	Brive	v	Narbonne	Parc Municipal des Sports

ROUND 10

11 / 12 Nov	Bourgoin	v	Stade Français	Pierre-Rajon
11 / 12 Nov	Toulouse	v	Castres	Ernest-Wallon
11 / 12 Nov	Bayonne	v	Biarritz	Jean Dauger
11 / 12 Nov	Pau	v	Agen	Du Hameau
11 / 12 Nov	Montpellier	v	Perpignan	Sabathé
11 / 12 Nov	Narbonne	v	Toulon	Parc des Sports et de l'Amitié
11 / 12 Nov	Clermont	v	Brive	Parc des sports Marcel-Michelin

Fixtures: Top 14 (cont)

ROUND 11

DATE	HOME		AWAY	VENUE
18 / 19 Nov	Castres	v	Bourgoin	Pierre-Antoine
18 / 19 Nov	Clermont	v	Toulouse	Parc des sports Marcel-Michelin
18 / 19 Nov	Stade Français	v	Bayonne	Jean Bouin
18 / 19 Nov	Biarritz	v	Pau	Parc des Sports d'Aguiléra
18 / 19 Nov	Agen	v	Montpellier	Armandie
18 / 19 Nov	Perpignan	v	Narbonne	Aimé Giral
18 / 19 Nov	Brive	v	Toulon	Parc Municipal des Sports

ROUND 12

2 / 3 Dec	Bourgoin	v	Clermont	Pierre-Rajon
2 / 3 Dec	Bayonne	v	Castres	Jean Dauger
2 / 3 Dec	Pau	v	Stade Français	Du Hameau
2 / 3 Dec	Montpellier	v	Biarritz	Sabathé
2 / 3 Dec	Narbonne	v	Agen	Parc des Sports et de l'Amitié
2 / 3 Dec	Toulon	v	Perpignan	Mayol
2 / 3 Dec	Brive	v	Toulouse	Parc Municipal des Sports

ROUND 13

23 Dec	Toulouse	v	Bourgoin	Ernest-Wallon
23 Dec	Clermont	v	Bayonne	Parc des sports Marcel-Michelin
23 Dec	Castres	v	Pau	Pierre-Antoine
23 Dec	Stade Français	v	Montpellier	Jean Bouin
23 Dec	Biarritz	v	Narbonne	Parc des Sports d'Aguiléra
23 Dec	Agen	v	Toulon	Armandie
23 Dec	Perpignan	v	Brive	Aimé Giral

2006

ROUND 14

6 / 8 Jan	Bourgoin	v	Brive	Pierre-Rajon
6 / 8 Jan	Toulouse	v	Bayonne	Ernest-Wallon
6 / 8 Jan	Clermont	v	Pau	Parc des sports Marcel-Michelin
6 / 8 Jan	Castres	v	Montpellier	Pierre-Antoine
6 / 8 Jan	Stade Français	v	Narbonne	Jean Bouin
6 / 8 Jan	Biarritz	v	Toulon	Parc des Sports d'Aguiléra
6 / 8 Jan	Agen	v	Perpignan	Armandie

ROUND 15

27 / 28 Jan	Bayonne	v	Bourgoin	Jean Dauger
27 / 28 Jan	Pau	v	Toulouse	Du Hameau
27 / 28 Jan	Montpellier	v	Clermont	Sabathé
27 / 28 Jan	Narbonne	v	Castres	Parc des Sports et de l'Amitié
27 / 28 Jan	Toulon	v	Stade Français	Mayol
27 / 28 Jan	Perpignan	v	Biarritz	Aimé Giral
27 / 28 Jan	Brive	v	Agen	Parc Municipal des Sports

ROUND 16

DATE	HOME		AWAY	VENUE
3 / 4 Feb	Bourgoin	v	Pau	Pierre-Rajon
3 / 4 Feb	Toulouse	v	Montpellier	Ernest-Wallon
3 / 4 Feb	Clermont	v	Narbonne	Parc des sports Marcel-Michelin
3 / 4 Feb	Castres	v	Toulon	Pierre-Antoine
3 / 4 Feb	Stade Français	v	Perpignan	Jean Bouin
3 / 4 Feb	Biarritz	v	Agen	Parc des Sports d'Aguiléra
3 / 4 Feb	Bayonne	v	Brive	Jean Dauger

ROUND17

17 / 18 Feb	Montpellier	v	Bourgoin	Sabathé
17 / 18 Feb	Narbonne	v	Toulouse	Parc des Sports et de l'Amitié
17 / 18 Feb	Toulon	v	Clermont	Mayol
17 / 18 Feb	Perpignan	v	Castres	Aimé Giral
17 / 18 Feb	Agen	v	Stade Français	Armandie
17 / 18 Feb	Pau	v	Bayonne	Du Hameau
17 / 18 Feb	Brive	v	Biarritz	Parc Municipal des Sports

ROUND 18

3 / 4 Mar	Bourgoin	v	Narbonne	Pierre-Rajon
3 / 4 Mar	Toulouse	v	Toulon	Ernest-Wallon
3 / 4 Mar	Clermont	v	Perpignan	Parc des sports Marcel-Michelin
3 / 4 Mar	Castres	v	Agen	Pierre-Antoine
3 / 4 Mar	Stade Français	v	Biarritz	Jean Bouin
3 / 4 Mar	Bayonne	v	Montpellier	Jean Dauger
3 / 4 Mar	Pau	v	Brive	Du Hameau

ROUND 19

17 / 18 Mar	Toulon	v	Bourgoin	Mayol
17 / 18 Mar	Perpignan	v	Toulouse	Aimé Giral
17 / 18 Mar	Agen	v	Clermont	Armandie
17 / 18 Mar	Biarritz	v	Castres	Parc des Sports d'Aguiléra
17 / 18 Mar	Narbonne	v	Bayonne	Parc des Sports et de l'Amitié
17 / 18 Mar	Montpellier	v	Pau	Sabathé
17 / 18 Mar	Brive	v	Stade Français	Parc Municipal des Sports

ROUND 20

24 / 25 Mar	Bourgoin	v	Perpignan	Pierre-Rajon
24 / 25 Mar	Toulouse	v	Agen	Ernest-Wallon
24 / 25 Mar	Clermont	v	Biarritz	Parc des sports Marcel-Michelin
24 / 25 Mar	Castres	v	Stade Français	Pierre-Antoine
24 / 25 Mar	Bayonne	v	Toulon	Jean Dauger
24 / 25 Mar	Pau	v	Narbonne	Du Hameau
24 / 25 Mar	Montpellier	v	Brive	Sabathé

Fixtures: Top 14 (cont)

ROUND 21

DATE	HOME		AWAY	VENUE
7 / 8 Apr	Agen	v	Bourgoin	Armandie
7 / 8 Apr	Biarritz	v	Toulouse	Parc des Sports d'Aguiléra
7 / 8 Apr	Stade Français	v	Clermont	Jean Bouin
7 / 8 Apr	Perpignan	v	Bayonne	Aimé Giral
7 / 8 Apr	Toulon	v	Pau	Mayol
7 / 8 Apr	Narbonne	v	Montpellier	Parc des Sports et de l'Amitié
7 / 8 Apr	Brive	v	Castres	Parc Municipal des Sports

ROUND 22

DATE	HOME		AWAY	VENUE
14 / 15 Apr	Bourgoin	v	Biarritz	Pierre-Rajon
14 / 15 Apr	Toulouse	v	Stade Français	Ernest-Wallon
14 / 15 Apr	Clermont	v	Castres	Parc des sports Marcel-Michelin
14 / 15 Apr	Bayonne	v	Agen	Jean Dauger
14 / 15 Apr	Pau	v	Perpignan	Du Hameau
14 / 15 Apr	Montpellier	v	Toulon	Sabathé
14 / 15 Apr	Narbonne	v	Brive	Parc des Sports et de l'Amitié

ROUND 23

DATE	HOME		AWAY	VENUE
28 / 29 Apr	Stade Français	v	Bourgoin	Jean Bouin
28 / 29 Apr	Castres	v	Toulouse	Pierre-Antoine
28 / 29 Apr	Biarritz	v	Bayonne	Parc des Sports d'Aguiléra
28 / 29 Apr	Agen	v	Pau	Armandie
28 / 29 Apr	Perpignan	v	Montpellier	Aimé Giral
28 / 29 Apr	Toulon	v	Narbonne	Mayol
28 / 29 Apr	Brive	v	Clermont	Parc Municipal des Sports

ROUND 24

DATE	HOME		AWAY	VENUE
5 / 6 May	Bourgoin	v	Castres	Pierre-Rajon
5 / 6 May	Toulouse	v	Clermont	Ernest-Wallon
5 / 6 May	Bayonne	v	Stade Français	Jean Dauger
5 / 6 May	Pau	v	Biarritz	Du Hameau
5 / 6 May	Montpellier	v	Agen	Sabathé
5 / 6 May	Narbonne	v	Perpignan	Parc des Sports et de l'Amitié
5 / 6 May	Toulon	v	Brive	Mayol

ROUND 25

DATE	HOME		AWAY	VENUE
12 / 13 May	Clermont	v	Bourgoin	Parc des sports Marcel-Michelin
12 / 13 May	Castres	v	Bayonne	Pierre-Antoine
12 / 13 May	Stade Français	v	Pau	Jean Bouin
12 / 13 May	Biarritz	v	Montpellier	Parc des Sports d'Aguiléra
12 / 13 May	Agen	v	Narbonne	Armandie
12 / 13 May	Perpignan	v	Toulon	Aimé Giral
12 / 13 May	Toulouse	v	Brive	Ernest-Wallon

ROUND 26

DATE	HOME		AWAY	VENUE
27 May	Bourgoin	v	Toulouse	Pierre-Rajon
27 May	Bayonne	v	Clermont	Jean Dauger
27 May	Pau	v	Castres	Du Hameau
27 May	Montpellier	v	Stade Français	Sabathé
27 May	Narbonne	v	Biarritz	Parc des Sports et de l'Amitié
27 May	Toulon	v	Agen	Mayol
27 May	Brive	v	Perpignan	Parc Municipal des Sports

The Semi-Finals will be played between the first four clubs in the Championship after the 26th round of matches. The team which finishes first after the 26th round will play the team which finishes third and the team finishing second will play the team finishing fourth in a semi-final.

SEMI-FINALS	2 /3 / 4 JUNE

FINAL	10 JUNE	STADE DE FRANCE

Super 10 Fixtures 2005 – 2006

ROUND 1

DATE	HOME		AWAY
Sat 3 Sep	Carrera Petrarca Padova	v	Benetton Treviso
Sat 3 Sep	Ghial Calvisano	v	SKG Gran Parma
Sat 3 Sep	Overmach Parma	v	Adriatic LNG Rovigo
Sat 3 Sep	Frieziamestre	v	Amatori Catania
Sat 3 Sep	Arix Viadana	v	Conad L'Aquila

ROUND 2

Sat 10 Sep	SKG Gran Parma	v	Arix Viadana
Sat 10 Sep	Carrera Petrarca Padova	v	Ghial Calvisano
Sat 10 Sep	Amatori Catania	v	Adriatic LNG Rovigo
Sat 10 Sep	Conad L'Aquila	v	Overmach Parma
Sat 10 Sep	Benetton Treviso	v	Frieziamestre

ROUND 3

Sat 17 Sep	Arix Viadana	v	Ghial Calvisano
Sat 17 Sep	Frieziamestre	v	Conad L'Aquila
Sat 17 Sep	Amatori Catania	v	SKG Gran Parma
Sat 17 Sep	Overmach Parma	v	Carrera Petrarca Padova
Sat 17 Sep	Adriatic LNG Rovigo	v	Benetton Treviso

ROUND 4

Wed 21 Sep	Benetton Treviso	v	Arix Viadana
Wed 21 Sep	Carrera Petrarca Padova	v	Frieziamestre
Wed 21 Sep	Ghial Calvisano	v	Adriatic LNG Rovigo
Wed 21 Sep	SKG Gran Parma	v	Overmach Parma
Wed 21 Sep	Conad L'Aquila	v	Amatori Catania

Fixtures: Super 10 (cont)

ROUND 5

DATE	HOME		AWAY
Sun 25 Sep	Overmach Parma	v	Benetton Treviso
Sun 25 Sep	Amatori Catania	v	Ghial Calvisano
Sun 25 Sep	Arix Viadana	v	Carrera Petrarca Padova
Sun 25 Sep	Frieziamestre	v	SKG Gran Parma
Sun 25 Sep	Adriatic LNG Rovigo	v	Conad L'Aquila

ROUND 6

DATE	HOME		AWAY
Sat 1 Oct	Arix Viadana	v	Adriatic LNG Rovigo
Sat 1 Oct	Carrera Petrarca Padova	v	SKG Gran Parma
Sat 1 Oct	Ghial Calvisano	v	Frieziamestre
Sat 1 Oct	Overmach Parma	v	Amatori Catania
Sat 1 Oct	Benetton Treviso	v	Conad L'Aquila

ROUND 7

DATE	HOME		AWAY
Sat 8 Oct	Conad L'Aquila	v	Ghial Calvisano
Sat 8 Oct	SKG Gran Parma	v	Benetton Treviso
Sat 8 Oct	Adriatic LNG Rovigo	v	Carrera Petrarca Padova
Sat 8 Oct	Amatori Catania	v	Arix Viadana
Sat 8 Oct	Frieziamestre	v	Overmach Parma

ROUND 8

DATE	HOME		AWAY
Sat 15 Oct	Arix Viadana	v	Frieziamestre
Sat 15 Oct	Carrera Petrarca Padova	v	Conad L'Aquila
Sat 15 Oct	Ghial Calvisano	v	Overmach Parma
Sat 15 Oct	SKG Gran Parma	v	Adriatic LNG Rovigo
Sat 15 Oct	Benetton Treviso	v	Amatori Catania

ROUND 9

DATE	HOME		AWAY
Sat 5 Nov	Conad L'Aquila	v	SKG Gran Parma
Sat 5 Nov	Overmach Parma	v	Arix Viadana
Sat 5 Nov	Amatori Catania	v	Carrera Petrarca Padova
Sat 5 Nov	Ghial Calvisano	v	Benetton Treviso
Sat 5 Nov	Frieziamestre	v	Adriatic LNG Rovigo

ROUND 10

DATE	HOME		AWAY
Sat 3 Dec	Adriatic LNG Rovigo	v	Overmach Parma
Sat 3 Dec	SKG Gran Parma	v	Ghial Calvisano
Sat 3 Dec	Benetton Treviso	v	Carrera Petrarca Padova
Sat 3 Dec	Conad L'Aquila	v	Arix Viadana
Sat 3 Dec	Amatori Catania	v	Frieziamestre

2006

ROUND 11

DATE	HOME		AWAY
Sat 7 Jan	Frieziamestre	v	Benetton Treviso
Sat 7 Jan	Overmach Parma	v	Conad L'Aquila
Sat 7 Jan	Adriatic LNG Rovigo	v	Amatori Catania
Sat 7 Jan	Ghial Calvisano	v	Carrera Petrarca Padova
Sat 7 Jan	Arix Viadana	v	SKG Gran Parma

ROUND 12

DATE	HOME		AWAY
Sat 25 Mar	Conad L'Aquila	v	Frieziamestre
Sat 25 Mar	Ghial Calvisano	v	Arix Viadana
Sat 25 Mar	Carrera Petrarca Padovav	v	Overmach Parma
Sat 25 Mar	SKG Gran Parma	v	Amatori Catania
Sat 25 Mar	Benetton Treviso	v	Adriatic LNG Rovigo

ROUND 13

DATE	HOME		AWAY
Sat 1 Apr	Amatori Catania	v	Conad L'Aquila
Sat 1 Apr	Overmach Parma	v	SKG Gran Parma
Sat 1 Apr	Adriatic LNG Rovigo	v	Ghial Calvisano
Sat 1 Apr	Frieziamestre	v	Carrera Petrarca Padova
Sat 1 Apr	Arix Viadana	v	Benetton Treviso

ROUND 14

DATE	HOME		AWAY
Sat 8 Apr	SKG Gran Parma	v	Frieziamestre
Sat 8 Apr	Carrera Petrarca Padova	v	Arix Viadana
Sat 8 Apr	Ghial Calvisano	v	Amatori Catania
Sat 8 Apr	Benetton Treviso	v	Overmach Parma
Sat 8 Apr	Conad L'Aquila	v	Adriatic LNG Rovigo

ROUND 15

DATE	HOME		AWAY
Sat 15 Apr	Conad L'Aquila	v	Benetton Treviso
Sat 15 Apr	Amatori Catania	v	Overmach Parma
Sat 15 Apr	Frieziamestre	v	Ghial Calvisano
Sat 15 Apr	SKG Gran Parma	v	Carrera Petrarca Padova
Sat 15 Apr	Adriatic LNG Rovigo	v	Arix Viadana

ROUND 16

DATE	HOME		AWAY
Sat 22 Apr	Ghial Calvisano	v	Conad L'Aquila
Sat 22 Apr	Carrera Petrarca Padova	v	Adriatic LNG Rovigo
Sat 22 Apr	Benetton Treviso	v	SKG Gran Parma
Sat 22 Apr	Overmach Parma	v	Frieziamestre
Sat 22 Apr	Arix Viadana	v	Amatori Catania

ROUND 17

DATE	HOME		AWAY
Sat 29 Apr	Amatori Catania	v	Benetton Treviso
Sat 29 Apr	Adriatic LNG Rovigo	v	SKG Gran Parma
Sat 29 Apr	Overmach Parma	v	Ghial Calvisano
Sat 29 Apr	Conad L'Aquila	v	Carrera Petrarca Padova
Sat 29 Apr	Frieziamestre	v	Arix Viadana

ROUND 18

DATE	HOME		AWAY
Sat 6 May	SKG Gran Parma	v	Conad L'Aquila
Sat 6 May	Arix Viadana	v	Overmach Parma
Sat 6 May	Carrera Petrarca Padova	v	Amatori Catania
Sat 6 May	Benetton Treviso	v	Ghial Calvisano
Sat 6 May	Adriatic LNG Rovigo	v	Veneziamestre

ACKNOWLEDGEMENTS

A big thanks to photographer Mike Wilkinson, of the Sunday Times, and Dave Gibson, who has just set up a brilliant picture agency in Scotland. Also to the Karen Earl PR agency (Roberto Coladangelo and Fiona Foster in particular). They represent RBS and kindly let us use their pictures; and to all those who furnished us with help and support whilst putting this directory together. Thanks also to Matthew Blake for his expert knowledge of what goes on after midnight, and also to Walter Ellis, a brilliant New York based feature writer who spends his summers in France.

Michelin guides, green and red, were invaluable sources of information. They are encyclopaedic and exhaustively constructed, but you would need to buy several volumes to get what you need for the 6 Nations. The Good Food Guide (Which) is first class on British restaurants. Their new guides come out every October. The Campaign for Real Ale's Good Beer Guide was also very useful. I owe them a debt of gratitude for other Baytree Press guides. Gault & Millaud are excellent on France.

The tourist boards in Rome, Paris, Cardiff, Edinburgh, London and Dublin were also exceptionally supportive, allowing us – amongst other things – to use their materials in preparing our mapping. Their websites were also very good.

The List, Time Out, Blue Guides and a whole host of pocket books were digested as we tramped the streets, lurching from tavern to restaurant, hotel to nightclub. Also, thanks to the entire Cummins family in Dublin and Julieann Relihan for some fine shopping tips.

Mark Porter

PICTURE CREDITS

ENGLAND
Landmarks and panoramics: © VisitLondon and Mark Porter
Rugby action: © Dave Gibson/Photosport & PA/Empics

FRANCE
Landmarks and panoramics: © Paris Tourist Office – photographers: Stéphane Querbes, Catherine Balet, Angélique Clément, David Lefranc, Claire Pignol, Henri Garat & Arnaud Terrier.
Rugby action: © Dave Gibson & PA/Empics

IRELAND
Landmarks and panoramics: © Failte Ireland
Rugby action: © Mike Wilkinson

ITALY
Landmarks and panoramics: © Rome Tourist Board
Rugby action: © Dave Gibson/Fotosport & PA/Empics

SCOTLAND
Landmarks and panoramics: © Scottish Viepoint
Rugby action: © Dave Gibson/Fotosport

WALES
Landmarks and panoramics: © Wales Tourist Board
Rugby action: © Dave Gibson/Fotosport & Mike Wilkinson

COVER PICTURE
© Dave Gibson/Fotosport

OLD CHINA HAND

8 Tysoe St
Clerkenwell
EC1 4RQ

020 7278 7630

Between Sadler's Wells and Exmouth Market

www.oldchinahand.co.uk

- open most nights until 2am
- cask conditioned ales from small breweries, with O'Hanlon's beers back on board
- over 50 bottled beers & ciders from all over the globe, plus extensive wine list
- Chinese dishes specially prepared by our dim sum chef
- dim sum menu ideal for large parties, meetings or conferences
- upstairs dining room seats 30
- rent the entire pub for private parties of more than 80
- live jazz Wednesday and Saturday nights
- two plasma screens to show all sports on request (especially rugby)

Beauclerc
Investment Properties
Riding Mill, Northumberland

We invite you to seek/view/buy or rent any of our properties in Portugal/Algarve/UK and many other locations throughout the world.

Marsden House (New block)/Bolton
Luxury Penthouse Flat for Sale or Rent.

Feidlim MacLoughlin	*Ben MacLoughlin*	*Isi Brekon*
0777 6218118	0781 0897418	0774 8846983

Want to be at Twickenham?

Join the England Rugby Supporters Club to enter the ERSC international ticket ballots

Set up to offer England Rugby fans a new route to tickets for international matches at Twickenham, the ERSC has an allocation of tickets per match which members are invited to apply for through a ballot. The club also offers:

- **Discounts on tickets for other matches**
- **10% discount at The Rugby Store**
- **Free subscription to England Rugby magazine**
- **Crowd beating members' only bar**

Join today!

Visit: **www.rfu.com/ersc**
Hotline: **0870 240 1642**
Info: **englandsupporters@rfu.com**
Please quote ref: 6NG